The 1st Joint Workshop on Large Language Models and Structure Modeling (XLLM 2025)

Vienna, Austria
1 August 2025

ISBN: 979-8-3313-2423-0

Printed from e-media with permission by:

Curran Associates, Inc.
57 Morehouse Lane
Red Hook, NY 12571

CURRAN ASSOCIATES INC.
proceedings
.com

Some format issues inherent in the e-media version may also appear in this print version.

Printed with permission by Curran Associates, Inc. (2025)

Association for Computational Linguistics
209 N. Eighth Street
Stroudsburg, Pennsylvania 18360

Phone: 1-570-476-8006
Fax: 1-570-476-0860

acl@aclweb.org

Additional copies of this publication are available from:

Curran Associates, Inc.
57 Morehouse Lane
Red Hook, NY 12571 USA
Phone: 845-758-0400
Fax: 845-758-2633
Email: curran@proceedings.com
Web: www.proceedings.com

XLLM 2025

The 1st Joint Workshop on Large Language Models and Structure Modeling

Proceedings of the Workshop

August 1, 2025

Introduction

Language structure modeling has long been a crucial subfield of natural language processing (NLP) that entails understanding the underlying semantic or syntactic structure of language and texts. Language structures can broadly range from low-level morphological/syntactic types (e.g., dependency structures and phrasal constituent structures) to high-level discourse/semantic structures (e.g., semantic parsing, semantic role labeling, abstract meaning representation), and can even extend to more NLP applications, multi-lingual and multi-modal scenarios in a broader sense, such as information extraction and structured sentiment analysis, etc. In previous days, modeling, inferring, and learning about linguistic structures constituted an indispensable component in many NLP systems and were the key focus of a large proportion of NLP research. The methodologies and paradigms concerning language structure modeling have always changed dramatically since each deep learning revolution started around a decade ago. In the last two to three years, Large Language Models (LLMs) have emerged, demonstrating unprecedented language understanding and generalization capabilities in effectively addressing a wide range of tasks. This raises a critical question: Is NLP structure modeling still worth exploring in the LLM era? Do the methods and tasks before LLMs still hold value?

On the one hand, we wonder whether previous NLP structure modeling tasks, such as those concerning morphological/syntactic/semantic/discourse structures and high-level structure-aware applications, can achieve even stronger task performance with the powerful capabilities of LLMs. On the other hand, we are also considering whether it is still necessary to model the underlying structures of language, given that large-scale pretraining on the surface form alone can endow LLMs with extraordinarily powerful language capabilities. In particular, can language structure modeling be beneficial for improving or understanding LLMs? Thus, this 1st Joint Workshop on Large Language Models and Structure Modeling (XLLM 2025) at ACL 2025 aims to encourage discussions and highlight methods for language structure modeling in the era of LLMs. We will explore two main directions: LLM for Structure Modeling (LLM4X) and Structure Modeling for LLM (X4LLM).

In the interest of having a broad conversation, inclusive of different disciplinary norms, we invited submissions of different kinds. Authors were able to choose between: (1) archival papers which will be published in the XLLM proceedings as well as presented during the workshop, and (2) non-archival papers which are not published in the proceedings but are given a presentation slot during the workshop. Archival papers may be long (up to 9 pages) or short (up to 5 pages), and went through mutually anonymous peer review by our program committee members or were already reviewed through ACL Rolling Review (ARR). Non-archival papers include extended abstracts which were also subjected to mutually anonymous peer review by our program committee. In addition to paper contributions, we are organizing open challenges on structure-related NLP tasks, including:
- Task-I: Dialogue-Level Dependency Parsing (DiaDP)
- Task-II: Speech Event Extraction (SpeechEE)
- Task-III: LLM for Structural Reasoning (LLM-SR)
- Task-IV: Document-level Information Extraction (DocIE)

For top-5 teams, we invite them to write technical papers that are also included into XLLM proceedings, where the champion team will give oral presentation.

After the hard process of reviewing all submissions, the program committee chose i) 21 archival regular papers, including 6 oral and 25 poster presentations, ii) 11 archival challenge papers, including 4 oral and 7 poster presentations, and iii) 12 non-archival papers. Among all the submissions, we received 4 submissions through ARR. The program committee is excited about the quality of the accepted papers and expects lively discussion and exchange at the conference. For all the winning participants of our open challenges, we issued certificates for their performance, and for parts of the tasks, we also awarded cash prizes.

The XLLM workshop invited 4 keynote speakers: Kyunghyun Cho, Elsa Olivetti, Marinka Zitnik, Huan Sun, and Lei Li. Additionally, a poster session, invited oral talks, and a panel discussion on future research directions will be held.

As a final note, we would like to thank the authors, invited speakers, committee members, and our scientific advisory board for helping make this workshop happen. We also wish to express our sincere gratitude to ACL for hosting our conference and for arranging the logistics and infrastructure that allow us to hold XLLM 2024 as a hybrid conference. Welcome to XLLM 2024, welcome to Vienna, Austria!

- Organizing Committee of XLLM

Organizing Committee

General Chairs

Hao Fei, National University of Singapore
Kewei Tu, ShanghaiTech University

Program Chairs

Zixia Jia, BigAI
Yuhui Zhang, Stanford University

Publication Chair

Xiang Hu, Ant Research

Shared Task Chairs

Hao Fei, National University of Singapore
Zixia Jia, BigAI
Bing Wang, Harbin Institute of Technology (Shenzhen)
Meishan Zhang, Harbin Institute of Technology (Shenzhen)
Zilong Zheng, BigAI

Website Chair

Hao Fei, National University of Singapore

Advisery Committee

Yixin Cao, Fudan University
Wenjuan Han, Beijing Jiaotong University
Wei Lu, Singapore University of Technology and Design
Lilja Øvrelid, University of Oslo
N. Siddharth, University of Edinburgh
Nianwen Xue, Brandeis University
Yue Zhang, Westlake University

Invited Keynote Speakers

Mark Johnson, Macquarie University
Jan Hajič, Charles University
Heng Ji, University of Illinois Urbana-Champaign
Nianwen Xue, Brandeis University

Program Committee

Area Chairs

Shengqiong Wu, National University of Singapore
Bobo Li, National University of Singapore

Program Committee

David Chiang, University of Notre Dame
Xuanjing Huang, Fudan University
Milos Stanojevic, University College London
Jennifer Hu, Harvard University
Lei Li, Carnegie Mellon University
Joakim Nivre, Uppsala University
Marianna Apidianaki, University of Pennsylvania
Zhiyuan Liu, Tsinghua University
Qian Liu, University of Auckland
Djamé Seddah, University Paris-Sorbonne
Songlin Yang, Massachusetts Institute of Technology
Jayeol Chun, Brandeis University
Lizi Liao, Singapore Management University
Natha Schneider, Georgetown University
Zuchao Li, Wuhan University
Attapol Rutherford, Chulalongkorn University
Xinya Du, University of Texas at Dallas
Freda Shi, University of Waterloo
Jeff Flanigan, University of California, Santa Cruz
Hongyu Lin, Chinese Academy of Sciences
Jinlan Fu, National University of Singapore
Liangming Pan, University of Arizona
Matthias Lindemann, University of Edinburgh
Zhuosheng Zhang, Shanghai Jiao Tong University
Mattia Opper, University of Edinburgh
Yanpeng Zhao, Beijing Institute for General Artificial Intelligence
Shira Wein, Amherst College
Kai He, National University of Singapore
Wenyue Hua, University of California, Santa Barbara
Anjiang Wei, Stanford University
Ryo Yoshida, University of Tokyo
Lei Li, University of Hong Kong
Julia Bonn, University of Colorado at Boulder
Chao Lou, ShanghaiTech University
Haoyi Wu, ShanghaiTech University
Yu Zhang, Soochow University
Jishnu Ray Chowdhury, University of Illinois Chicago

Table of Contents

Program

Friday, August 1, 2025

09:00 - 08:50	*Opening Remarks*
10:30 - 09:00	*Keynote Session-1*
11:00 - 10:30	*Coffee break*
12:00 - 11:00	*Oral Session-1*
12:30 - 12:00	*Poster Session-1*
14:00 - 12:30	*Lunch Break*
15:30 - 14:00	*Keynote Session-2*
16:00 - 15:30	*Coffee break*
16:45 - 16:00	*Oral Session-2*
17:00 - 16:45	*Closing Remarks*
17:30 - 17:00	*Poster Session-2*

Fine-Tuning Large Language Models for Relation Extraction within a Retrieval-Augmented Generation Framework

Sefika Efeoglu[1] **Adrian Paschke**[1,2]
[1]Freie Universitaet Berlin, Takustraße 9, 14195 Berlin
[2]Data Analytic Center (DANA), Fraunhofer Institute FOKUS, Berlin, Germany
sefika.efeoglu@fu-berlin.de, adrian.paschke@fu-berlin.de

Abstract

Information Extraction (IE) plays a pivotal role in transforming unstructured data into structured formats, such as Knowledge Graphs. One of the main tasks within IE is Relation Extraction (RE), which identifies relations between entities in text data. This process enriches the semantic understanding of documents, enabling more precise information retrieval and query answering. Recent works leveraging pre-trained language models have demonstrated significant performance improvements in RE. In the current era of Large Language Models (LLMs), fine-tuning these LLMs can mitigate the limitations of zero-shot RE methods, particularly in overcoming the domain adaptation challenges inherent in RE. This work explores not only the effectiveness of fine-tuned LLMs but also their integration into a Retrieval-Augmented Generation (RAG)-based RE approach to address domain adaptation challenges when general-purpose LLMs serve as generators within the RAG framework. Empirical evaluations on the TACRED, TACRED-Revisited (TACREV), and Re-TACRED datasets reveal substantial performance improvements with fine-tuned LLMs, such as Llama2-7B, Mistral-7B, and Flan-T5 Large and surpass previous methods on these datasets.

1 Introduction

Information Extraction (IE) converts unstructured data into structured formats, such as Knowledge Graphs (KGs). A key IE task is Relation Extraction (RE), which identifies relationships between entities in text at sentence (See Figure 1) or document levels (Grishman, 2015). RE methods include supervised, unsupervised, and rule-based approaches (Aydar et al., 2020; Pawar et al., 2017). Supervised RE methods generally yield strong performance but require extensive labeled data. However, recent studies show that RE methods using pre-trained language models (PLMs) can surpass traditional supervised approaches (Zhou and Chen, 2022; Li et al., 2022; Wang et al., 2022). In the era of Large Language Models (LLMs), Retrieval-Augmented Generation (RAG) (Gao et al., 2023; Lewis et al., 2020) using zero-shot prompting settings, in-context learning (Pan et al., 2024), or simple vanilla prompting (Kai Zhang, 2023), have been utilized for RE without the need for additional model training.

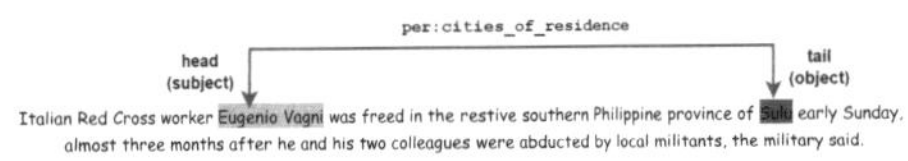

Figure 1: Representation of a relation, per:cities_of_residence, between head and tail entities in a sentence from the TACRED dataset.

The RAG-based prompting approach performs well when entity relations are easily derived from sentence tokens but struggles when relation types are not introduced into LLMs (Efeoglu and Paschke, 2024). General-purpose LLMs, like Mistral (Jiang et al., 2023), Llama2 (Touvron et al., 2023), and Flan-T5 (Chung et al., 2022), also show shortcomings in RE tasks due to insufficient domain-specific relation knowledge (Efeoglu and Paschke, 2024; Kai Zhang, 2023; Xiong et al., 2023). Incorporating these relation types into LLMs could enhance RE through zero-shot prompting (Efeoglu and Paschke, 2024). To tackle this issue, we fine-tune language models on small sets of RE prompt datasets to enhance their ability to identify relations between entities at the sentence level. To evaluate the performance of fine-tuned LLMs, we conduct experiments using Llama2-7B [1] (Touvron et al., 2023), Mistral-7B-Instruct-v0.2 [2] (Jiang

[1]https://huggingface.co/meta-llama/Llama-2-7b-chat-hf, accessed on 14.05.2025

[2]https://huggingface.co/mistralai/Mistral-7B-Instruct-v0.2, accessed on 14.05.2025

Proceedings of the 1st Joint Workshop on Large Language Models and Structure Modeling (XLLM 2025), pages 1–7
August 1, 2025

et al., 2023), and Flan T5 Large (Chung et al., 2022) across three RE benchmark datasets: TACRED (Zhang et al., 2017), TACRED-Revisited (TACREV)(Alt et al., 2020) and Re-TACRED (Stoica et al., 2021). In this work, fine-tuning is used to overcome the limitations of zero-shot LLM prompting settings, such as RAG4RE (Efeoglu and Paschke, 2024), in identifying relations between entities across TACRED and its variants. The contributions of our approach are as follows:

- Fine-tuning greatly improved LLM performance, with Flan-T5 Large outperforming larger models like Mistral-7B-Instruct-v0.2 and Llama2-7B on TACRED and its variants.
- Our fine-tuned LLMs, evaluated within RAG4RE, showed strong results on these datasets.
- This study is the first to fine-tune LLMs for the RE task and to systematically compare smaller and larger models like Mistral-7B-Instruct-v0.2 and Llama2-7B by parameter count.

The rest of this paper first summarizes RE approaches using the language models in Section 2 and then introduces our proposed approach [3] in Section 3. Afterwards, the experimental setup and results are presented in Section 4 and discussed in Section 5. Lastly, all concluding remarks and future works are summarized in Section 6.

2 Related Works

Relation Extraction (RE), as a core task of Information Extraction (IE), plays a significant role in natural language processing. RE aims to identify or classify the relations between (head and tail) entities in a given text. In this work, we primarily focus on sentence-level RE approaches.

RE can be achieved through various methods: supervised, unsupervised, distant supervision, weak supervision, and rule-based (Pawar et al., 2017). Supervised methods require costly, annotated data (Pawar et al., 2017); distant supervision reduces data needs but risks noise (Aydar et al., 2020); weak supervision may lead to semantic drift (Agichtein and Gravano, 2000); and rule-based methods are limited by predefined rules (Pawar et al., 2017). In addition to the fundamental approaches, leading RE methods with fine-tuned LLMs include Cohen et al.'s span prediction for broader entity relations (Cohen et al., 2020), DeepStruct's structural enhancements, Zhou et al.'s entity-aware self-attention (Zhou and Chen, 2022), and Li et al.'s label graph for top-K prediction analysis (Li et al., 2022). Furthermore, Zhang et al. (Kai Zhang, 2023) used multiple-choice prompts, improving RE predictions with added context, though it does not surpass prior rule-based methods. Chen et al. (Chen et al., 2024) introduced context-aware prompt tuning, while RAG4RE (Efeoglu and Paschke, 2024) utilized retrieval-augmented prompting, all tested on TACRED and similar benchmarks.

In this work, we aim to fine-tune LLMs on RE prompt datasets to improve domain adaptation and evaluate their performance on benchmark datasets.

3 Methodology

This work addresses the challenge of sentence-level RE using general-purpose LLMs with zero-shot prompting. General-purpose LLMs struggle with domain-specific relation types, so we fine-tune them on a small RE prompt dataset to improve their ability to identify entity relations. We detail the fine-tuning process in Section 3.1 and describe the integration of fine-tuned LLMs into the RAG4RE approach in Section 3.2.

3.1 Fine-tuning Models on Prompt Datasets

We fine-tune both encoder-decoder models (such as Flan-T5) and decoder-only models, e.g., Llama2-7B and Mistral-7B, on RE prompt datasets using the Supervised Fine-Tuning Trainer (SFT) [4]. This fine-tuning process facilitates domain adaptation for general-purpose LLMs. The SFT approach, which requires labeled training data, is straightforward to implement and train. Additionally, we utilize the Low-Rank Adaptation for quantized language models (QLoRA) method (Dettmers et al., 2023) to fine-tune LLMs. QLoRA optimizes model parameters for text generation while minimizing memory usage on GPUs, which is crucial in scenarios with limited GPU memory.

3.1.1 Prompt Dataset Generation.

The RE prompt dataset is constructed following the template outlined in a previous study by (Efeoglu

[3] The source code: `https://github.com/sefeoglu/fine-tuned-llm-relation-extraction`

[4] SFT: `https://huggingface.co/docs/trl/sft_trainer`

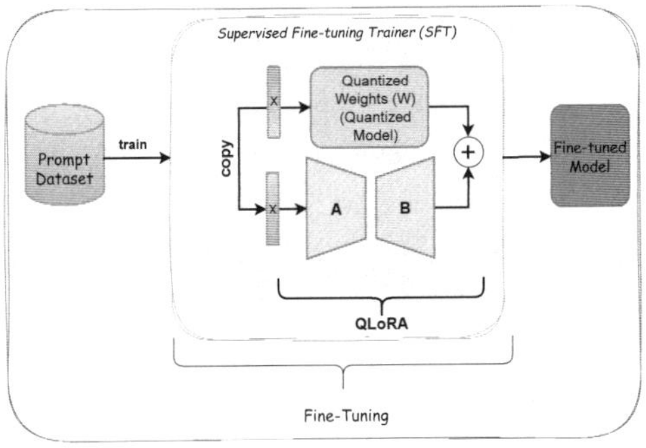

Figure 2: Fine-tuning a pre-trained model on a prompt dataset alongside the QLoRA adapter and SFT.

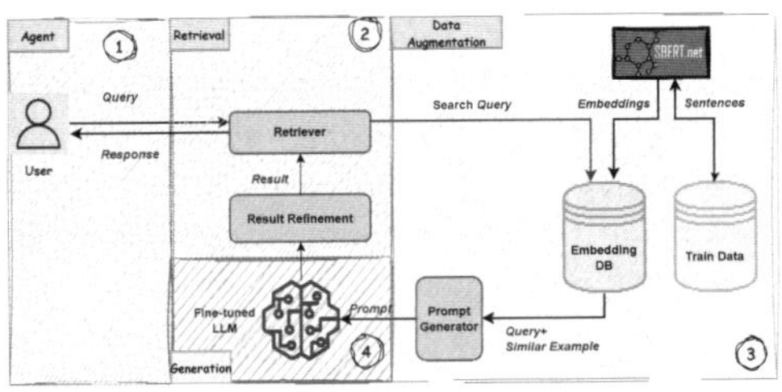

Figure 3: RAG with fine-tuned Large Language Models.

and Paschke, 2024). This dataset originates from a supervised dataset within a single domain and utilizes a specialized template for fine-tuning, as illustrated in Figure 4.

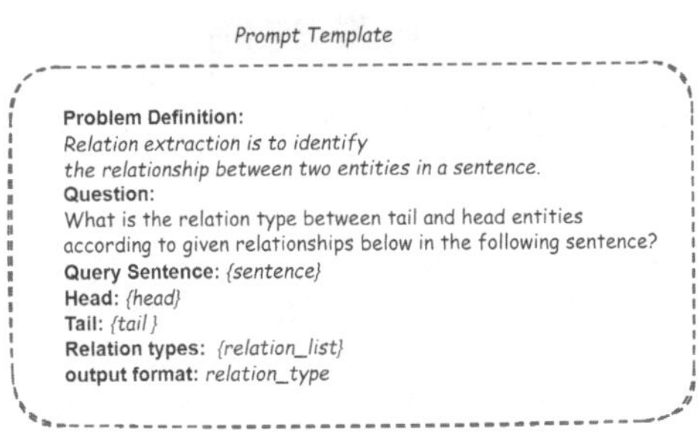

Figure 4: A prompt template for fine-tuning a Large Language Model.

3.1.2 Parameter Efficient Fine-Tuning.

We utilize QLoRA, a parameter-efficient fine-tuning method that begins by applying quantization to a pre-trained language model. This technique reduces the model's high-precision floating-point representation to a lower precision, thus decreasing memory usage. In particular, we use the "4-bit NormalFloat (NF4)" format, which is optimized for normally distributed data and has been shown to outperform traditional 4-bit integers and floats (Dettmers et al., 2023). Following quantization, LoRA is applied to specific model modules. Fine-tuning is subsequently conducted using the SFT on a single-domain, task-specific prompt dataset. The entire process is illustrated in Figure 2.

3.2 Retrieval-Augmented Generation with Fine-Tuned Models

The Retrieval-Augmented Generation-based Relation Extraction (RAG4RE) approach, introduced by (Efeoglu and Paschke, 2024), comprises three modules: i.) Retrieval, ii.) Data Augmentation, and iii.) Generation. In our implementation, we integrate fine-tuned LLMs, trained on RE prompt datasets, into the generation module of the RAG4RE approach (Efeoglu and Paschke, 2024) to address the task of identifying relations between entities in sentences, as illustrated in Figure 3. Specifically, the LLM used in the generation module of RAG4RE is replaced with our fine-tuned LLMs, while all other components of RAG4RE remain unchanged.

4 Evaluation

We evaluate our approach using three benchmark datasets and language models. In Section 4.1, we detail the datasets, metrics, and experimental settings, including the fine-tuning of language models and the use of Retrieval-Augmented Generation with these fine-tuned models. Then, we present and analyze the experimental results, comparing them with those of previous high-performing RE methods in Section 4.2.

4.1 Experimental Setup

Through this section, we initially introduce the datasets utilized for evaluation, followed by a detailed settings used on the fine-tuning and the RAG4RE framework (Efeoglu and Paschke, 2024) leveraging our fine-tuned language model within its generation module.

Datasets. We utilize three RE benchmark datasets: TACRED (Zhang et al., 2017), TACREV (Alt et al., 2020), and Re-TACRED (Stoica et al., 2021) as detailed in Table 1. The prompt datasets are generated from the validation partitions of the benchmark datasets. The training datasets are utilized in the Embedding Database (DB) of RAG4RE (Efeoglu and Paschke, 2024), while the test splits are used for evaluation. We ensure a strict separation between the training and test splits across all benchmark datasets.

Table 1: The table gives the number of sentences in the test, train, and prompt datasets, as well as the number of relations per benchmark dataset.

Split	TACRED	TACREV	Re-TACRED
Train	68124	68124	58465
Test	15509	15509	13418
Validation	22631	22631	19584
Prompt Dataset (Generated from Validation)	22631	22631	19584
# of Relations	42	42	40

4.1.1 Metrics

The benchmark datasets used—TACRED and its variants—are imbalanced, with a high proportion of "no_relation" labels (Alt et al., 2020; Stoica et al., 2021), necessitating the use of micro metrics. For instance, in the TACRED test split, 12,184 out of 15,509 relations are labeled as "no_relation". We evaluate our experiments using the micro F1-score, precision, and recall across all three benchmark datasets.

4.1.2 Settings for Models

We employed the fine-tuning approach from Section 3.1, using a single GPU with 48 GB of memory and the parameters detailed below. Building on prior studies in RE with language models (Efeoglu and Paschke, 2024; Kai Zhang, 2023), we utilized the following LLMs:

- Flan T5 Large: An encoder-decoder model (Chung et al., 2022; Pan et al., 2024) with 770M parameters. LoRA parameters: alpha=32, dropout=0.01, r=4. Hyperparameters: learning rate=5e-5, batch size=8, one epoch.

- Mistral-7B (Jiang et al., 2023; Pan et al., 2024) and Llama2-7B (Pan et al., 2024; Touvron et al., 2023): Decoder-only models with 7B parameters, used in (Efeoglu and Paschke, 2024). We used Mistral-7B-Instruct-v0.2 [5]. LoRA parameters: alpha=16, dropout=0.1, r=64. Hyperparameters: learning rate=2e-4, batch size=4, one epoch, weight decay=0.001.

[5]https://huggingface.co/mistralai/Mistral-7B-Instruct-v0.2

4.1.3 Settings for RAG4RE

Due to limited GPU resources, we were unable to fine-tune the Flan-T5 XL model used in the original RAG4RE (Efeoglu and Paschke, 2024). Therefore, all experimental settings are replicated from RAG4RE with Flan-T5 Large. We strictly adhere to the experimental setups established in RAG4RE for our study.

4.2 Results

We evaluated language models fine-tuned on prompt datasets detailed at Table 1 in Section 4.1. Furthermore, we integrated these fine-tuned language models into the RAG4RE (Efeoglu and Paschke, 2024). It is worth noting that due to constraints in GPU resources, we opted to utilize Flan-T5 Large instead of Flan-T5 XL or XXL for fine-tuning. Hence, we chose Flan-T5 Large and meticulously replicated the RAG4RE experiments within the confines of our work. In this section, we first introduce the results of our fine-tuned models and then the results of RAG4RE approach using our fine-tuned models.

With regard to evaluation of fine-tuned LLMs alongside LoRA on four different datasets, fine-tuned Mistral-7B models accomplish outstanding performance at Table 2. Notably, these fine-tuned Mistral-7B models achieve remarkable F1 scores of 89.64%, 94.61%, and 90.09% on TACRED, TACREV, and Re-TACRED, respectively (see Table 2). The Llama2-7B models fine-tuned on TACRED and TACREV follow the fine-tuned Mistral-7B models with micro-F1 scores of 88.20% and 93.75%. Unfortunately, the fine-tuned Llama2-7B models could not exhibit the same performance on Re-TACRED at Table 2. The fine-tuned Flan-T5 Large model takes second place with a F1 score of 86.94% on Re-TACRED dataset (see Table 2). Moreover, fine-tuning LLMs outperformed simple query prompting and the previously introduced RAG4RE method (Efeoglu and Paschke, 2024). Additionally, we integrated these fine-tuned LLMs into the RAG4RE approach (Efeoglu and Paschke, 2024) in order to explore their potential in addressing the limitations of general-purpose LLMs.

Remarkably, the integration of fine-tuned models into RAG4RE yielded significant improvements across all three datasets, including TACRED, TACREV and Re-TACRED, particularly when leveraging Flan-T5 Large at Table 2. While we observed enhancements in RAG4RE's perfor-

Table 2: Experimental results on three benchmark datasets using different large language models (LLMs) and methods.

		TACRED			TACREV			Re-TACRED		
LLM	**Method**	**P (%)**	**R (%)**	**F1 (%)**	**P (%)**	**R (%)**	**F1 (%)**	**P (%)**	**R (%)**	**F1 (%)**
T5 Large	Simple Query	95.10	03.18	06.16	96.72	06.90	12.89	90.91	00.26	00.51
	RAG4RE	85.99	34.50	49.20	91.28	08.20	15.04	80.77	00.27	00.53
	Fine-tuning (QLoRA)	86.74	86.76	86.74	89.93	90.13	90.03	86.27	87.62	86.94
	RAG4RE + Fine-tuning	89.93	94.17	**92.00**	95.02	93.66	94.34	92.31	93.73	**93.01**
LLaMA2-7B	Simple Query (Efeoglu and Paschke, 2024)	84.97	01.21	02.38	74.64	00.44	00.87	80.20	00.94	01.86
	RAG4RE (Efeoglu and Paschke, 2024)	81.23	55.01	65.59	84.89	54.57	66.43	55.93	03.46	06.52
	Fine-tuning (QLoRA)	88.07	88.34	88.20	90.07	97.73	93.75	87.54	44.58	59.08
	RAG4RE + Fine-tuning	80.29	89.18	84.50	84.10	97.26	90.22	83.53	68.16	75.07
Mistral-7B	Simple Query (Efeoglu and Paschke, 2024)	94.67	11.96	21.23	92.34	05.15	09.75	64.64	05.48	10.11
	RAG4RE (Efeoglu and Paschke, 2024)	87.81	30.10	44.83	93.23	22.59	36.36	60.19	30.08	40.11
	Fine-tuning (QLoRA)	94.73	85.06	89.64	95.79	93.48	**94.61**	92.40	87.83	90.09
	RAG4RE + Fine-tuning	86.57	82.88	84.68	97.58	79.33	87.50	90.86	85.95	88.33

mance, as detailed in (Efeoglu and Paschke, 2024), with the integration of fine-tuned Llama-7B on Re-TACRED, it is noteworthy that this improvement was not observed on TACRED and TACREV. Regrettably, the results indicate that the use of Mistral-7B as the fined-tuned LLM did not yield improvements in the results of RE. The reason why the performance of the RAG4RE approach could not be improved when fine-tuned decoder-only models are used as a generator in its architecture (see Figure 3) might be related to catastrophic forgetting. Previous work fine-tuning language models on a single task is also dealing with the same forgetting problem (Feng et al., 2024).

As a result, the fine-tuned Flan-T5 Large models consistently achieved the highest F1 scores among all the experiments conducted in this work, particularly when integrated into the RAG4RE framework proposed in (Efeoglu and Paschke, 2024). However, fine-tuned Mistral is slightly better than RAG4RE using fine-tuned Flan-T5 Large on TACREV. In addition to the findings of the experiments using Flan-T5 Large, both fine-tuning language models on the dataset and integrating these fine-tuned models into RAG4RE outperformed zero-shot prompting approaches, such as simple queries and RAG4RE (Efeoglu and Paschke, 2024) (see Table 2).

5 Discussion

Our findings demonstrate significant improvements over the original RAG4RE (Efeoglu and Paschke, 2024) results on the TACRED, TACREV, and Re-TACRED datasets, as shown in Table 3, when fine-tuned Flan-T5 Large models are integrated into the RAG4RE approach. Fine-tuning language models, particularly in the context of domain adaptation, led to substantial performance enhancements for both general-purpose LLMs and RAG4RE (Efeoglu and Paschke, 2024) (see Table 3). The F1 scores of RAG4RE combined with fine-tuned LLMs surpassed those of previous approaches across all three datasets, as illustrated in Table 3. Similarly, the F1 scores of the fine-tuned LLMs exceeded those of prior approaches that employed both zero-shot prompting and pre-trained language models (PLMs) (see Table 3). The best-performing results in our experiments, reported in Table 3, surpassed those of approaches using both zero-shot prompting and PLMs on the TACRED, TACREV, and Re-TACRED datasets, achieving F1 scores of 92.00%, 94.61%, and 93.01%, respectively. Furthermore, our RAG4RE+Fine-tuning approach also outperformed the original RAG4RE utilizing general-purpose LLMs. Therefore, our fine-tuned LLMs achieved outstanding results on the TACRED, TACREV, and Re-TACRED datasets when integrated into the RAG4RE framework (Efeoglu and Paschke, 2024).

6 Conclusion

We address domain adaptation challenges in zero-shot relation extraction (RE) with general-purpose LLMs by fine-tuning Flan-T5 Large, Mistral-7B-Instruct-v0.2, and Llama2-7B on TACRED, TACREV, and Re-TACRED datasets. Our fine-tuned models outperformed previous methods, including RAG4RE (Efeoglu and Paschke, 2024). Integrating these fine-tuned LLMs into RAG4RE significantly enhanced its performance, especially with Flan-T5 Large. However, Llama2-7B and Mistral-7B showed inconsistent F1 scores, likely due to single-task fine-tuning issues. Future work will explore multi-task fine-tuning for RE and entity recognition to mitigate catastrophic forgetting (Feng et al., 2024; Liu et al., 2023; Yang et al., 2024).

Table 3: A comparison of our best-performing results with those of prior works in terms of F1-score.

Method Type	Method	TACRED	TACREV	Re-TACRED
PLM-based	DeepStruct (Wang et al., 2022)	76.8%	-	-
	EXOBRAIN (Zhou and Chen, 2022)	75.0%	-	91.4%
	KLG (Li et al., 2022)	-	84.1%	-
	SP (Cohen et al., 2020)	74.8%	-	
	GAP (Chen et al., 2024)	72.7%	82.7%	91.4%
Zero-Shot prompting	LLMQA4RE (Kai Zhang, 2023)	52.2%	53.4%	66.5%
	RationaleCL (Xiong et al., 2023)	80.8%	-	-
	RAG4RE (Efeoglu and Paschke, 2024)	86.6%	88.3%	73.3%
	RAG4RE+Fine-tuning (Ours)	**92.00%**	94.34%	**93.01%**
	Fine-tuning (Ours)	89.64%	**94.61%**	90.09%

Limitations

This approach requires an embedding database within the data augmentation module of the RAG and retrieves the most similar sentence for use in the RAG module. The most similar sentence with the sentence in the query might have low similarity score. The pre-trained language models may already be familiar with these datasets, as noted in (Efeoglu and Paschke, 2024), since they might be trained on these benchmark datasets.

References

Eugene Agichtein and Luis Gravano. 2000. Snowball: Extracting relations from large plain-text collections. In *Proceedings of the Fifth ACM Conference on Digital Libraries*, DL '00, page 85–94, New York, NY, USA. Association for Computing Machinery.

Christoph Alt, Aleksandra Gabryszak, and Leonhard Hennig. 2020. TACRED revisited: A thorough evaluation of the TACRED relation extraction task. In *Proceedings of the 58th Annual Meeting of the Association for Computational Linguistics*, pages 1558–1569, Online. Association for Computational Linguistics.

Mehmet Aydar, Ozge Bozal, and Furkan Ozbay. 2020. Neural relation extraction: a survey. *arXiv preprint*.

Zhenbin Chen, Zhixin Li, Yufei Zeng, Canlong Zhang, and Huifang Ma. 2024. Gap: A novel generative context-aware prompt-tuning method for relation extraction. *Expert Systems with Applications*, 248:123478.

Hyung Won Chung, Le Hou, Shayne Longpre, Barret Zoph, Yi Tay, William Fedus, Eric Li, Xuezhi Wang, Mostafa Dehghani, Siddhartha Brahma, Albert Webson, Shixiang Shane Gu, Zhuyun Dai, Mirac Suzgun, Xinyun Chen, Aakanksha Chowdhery, Sharan Narang, Gaurav Mishra, Adams Yu, and 12 others. 2022. Scaling instruction-finetuned language models. *arXiv preprint*.

Amir DN Cohen, Shachar Rosenman, and Yoav Goldberg. 2020. Relation classification as two-way span-prediction. *arXiv preprint arXiv:2010.04829*.

Tim Dettmers, Artidoro Pagnoni, Ari Holtzman, and Luke Zettlemoyer. 2023. Qlora: Efficient finetuning of quantized llms. *Preprint*, arXiv:2305.14314.

Sefika Efeoglu and Adrian Paschke. 2024. Retrieval-augmented generation-based relation extraction. *Preprint*, arXiv:2404.13397.

Wenfeng Feng, Chuzhan Hao, Yuewei Zhang, Yu Han, and Hao Wang. 2024. Mixture-of-loras: An efficient multitask tuning for large language models. *Preprint*, arXiv:2403.03432.

Yunfan Gao, Yun Xiong, Xinyu Gao, Kangxiang Jia, Jinliu Pan, Yuxi Bi, Yi Dai, Jiawei Sun, and Haofen Wang. 2023. Retrieval-augmented generation for large language models: A survey. *arXiv preprint arXiv:2312.10997*.

Ralph Grishman. 2015. Information extraction. *IEEE Expert*, 30(5):8–15.

Albert Q Jiang, Alexandre Sablayrolles, Arthur Mensch, Chris Bamford, Devendra Singh Chaplot, Diego de las Casas, Florian Bressand, Gianna Lengyel, Guillaume Lample, Lucile Saulnier, and 1 others. 2023. Mistral 7b. *arXiv preprint arXiv:2310.06825*.

Yu Su Kai Zhang, Bernal Jiménez Gutiérrez. 2023. Aligning instruction tasks unlocks large language models as zero-shot relation extractors. In *Findings of ACL*.

Patrick Lewis, Ethan Perez, Aleksandra Piktus, Fabio Petroni, Vladimir Karpukhin, Naman Goyal, Heinrich Küttler, Mike Lewis, Wen-tau Yih, Tim Rocktäschel, Sebastian Riedel, and Douwe Kiela. 2020. Retrieval-augmented generation for knowledge-intensive nlp tasks. In *Proceedings of the 34th International Conference on Neural Information Processing Systems*, NIPS'20, Red Hook, NY, USA. Curran Associates Inc.

Bo Li, Wei Ye, Jinglei Zhang, and Shikun Zhang. 2022. Reviewing labels: Label graph network with top-k prediction set for relation extraction. *Preprint*, arXiv:2212.14270.

Bingchang Liu, Chaoyu Chen, Cong Liao, Zi Gong, Huan Wang, Zhichao Lei, Ming Liang, Dajun Chen, Min Shen, Hailian Zhou, Hang Yu, and Jianguo Li.

2023. Mftcoder: Boosting code llms with multitask fine-tuning. *Preprint*, arXiv:2311.02303.

Shirui Pan, Linhao Luo, Yufei Wang, Chen Chen, Jiapu Wang, and Xindong Wu. 2024. Unifying large language models and knowledge graphs: A roadmap. *IEEE Transactions on Knowledge and Data Engineering*.

Sachin Pawar, Girish K. Palshikar, and Pushpak Bhattacharyya. 2017. Relation extraction : A survey. *arXiv preprint*.

George Stoica, Emmanouil Antonios Platanios, and Barnabas Poczos. 2021. Re-tacred: Addressing shortcomings of the tacred dataset. *Proceedings of the AAAI Conference on Artificial Intelligence*, 35(15):13843–13850.

Hugo Touvron, Louis Martin, Kevin R. Stone, Peter Albert, Amjad Almahairi, Yasmine Babaei, Nikolay Bashlykov, Soumya Batra, Prajjwal Bhargava, Shruti Bhosale, Daniel M. Bikel, Lukas Blecher, Cristian Cantón Ferrer, Moya Chen, Guillem Cucurull, David Esiobu, Jude Fernandes, Jeremy Fu, Wenyin Fu, and 49 others. 2023. Llama 2: Open foundation and fine-tuned chat models. *ArXiv*, abs/2307.09288.

Chenguang Wang, Xiao Liu, Zui Chen, Haoyun Hong, Jie Tang, and Dawn Song. 2022. DeepStruct: Pretraining of language models for structure prediction. In *Findings of the Association for Computational Linguistics: ACL 2022*, pages 803–823, Dublin, Ireland. Association for Computational Linguistics.

Weimin Xiong, Yifan Song, Peiyi Wang, and Sujian Li. 2023. Rationale-enhanced language models are better continual relation learners. In *Proceedings of the 2023 Conference on Empirical Methods in Natural Language Processing*, pages 15489–15497, Singapore. Association for Computational Linguistics.

Haoran Yang, Yumeng Zhang, Jiaqi Xu, Hongyuan Lu, Pheng Ann Heng, and Wai Lam. 2024. Unveiling the generalization power of fine-tuned large language models. *Preprint*, arXiv:2403.09162.

Yuhao Zhang, Victor Zhong, Danqi Chen, Gabor Angeli, and Christopher D. Manning. 2017. Position-aware attention and supervised data improve slot filling. In *Proceedings of the 2017 Conference on Empirical Methods in Natural Language Processing*, pages 35–45, Copenhagen, Denmark. Association for Computational Linguistics.

Wenxuan Zhou and Muhao Chen. 2022. An improved baseline for sentence-level relation extraction. In *Proceedings of the 2nd Conference of the Asia-Pacific Chapter of the Association for Computational Linguistics and the 12th International Joint Conference on Natural Language Processing (Volume 2: Short Papers)*, pages 161–168, Online only. Association for Computational Linguistics.

Benchmarking Table Extraction: Multimodal LLMs vs Traditional OCR

[1,2]Guilherme G.M. Nunes, [1]Vitor Rolla, [1]Duarte Pereira, [1]Vasco Alves, [1]André Carreiro, [2]Márcia Lourenço Baptista
[1]Fraunhofer AICOS, Portugal
[2]Information Management School (IMS)
Universidade Nova de Lisboa, Portugal
{guilherme.nunes, vitor.rolla}@fraunhofer.pt

Abstract

This paper compares two approaches for table extraction from images: deep learning computer vision and Multimodal Large Language Models (MLLMs). Computer vision models for table extraction, such as the Table Transformer model (TATR), have enhanced the extraction of complex table structural layouts by leveraging deep learning for precise structural recognition combined with traditional Optical Character Recognition (OCR). Conversely, MLLMs, which process both text and image inputs, present a novel approach by potentially bypassing the limitations of TATR plus OCR methods altogether. Models such as GPT-4o, Phi-3 Vision, and Granite Vision 3.2 demonstrate the potential of MLLMs to analyze and interpret table images directly, offering enhanced accuracy and robust extraction capabilities. A state-of-the-art metric like Grid Table Similarity (GriTS) evaluated these methodologies, providing nuanced insights into structural and text content effectiveness. Utilizing the PubTables-1M dataset, a comprehensive and widely used benchmark in the field, this study highlights the strengths and limitations of each approach, setting the stage for future innovations in table extraction technologies. Results show that deep learning computer vision techniques still have a slight edge when extracting table structural layout, but in terms of text cell content, MLLMs are far better.

1 Introduction

With the increasing volume of digital documents, such as records, manuals, and scientific papers, processing and transforming them into representations that allow proper extraction of information has become highly challenging (Staar et al., 2018). Many of these documents contain tables, as they help represent data in an organized, readable, and straightforward manner. However, automatically identifying and extracting structural layout and content information becomes more complex, which can be crucial in scientific and business applications (Chen et al., 2023; Burdick et al., 2020).

This work explores and compares two strategies for extracting tables contained in images in a structured manner: (a) a deep learning computer vision model, Table Transformer (TATR), combined with Optical Character Recognition (OCR) and (b) the novel Multimodal Large Language Models (MLLMs). These approaches were evaluated using metrics that capture how well they extract the tables' structural and text content.

The remainder of this paper is structured as follows. Section 2 provides an overview of existing and related work. Section 3 outlines the followed methodology and experiment details and Section 4 discusses the obtained results. Finally, conclusions and limitations are drawn in Sections 5 and 6.

2 Related Work

This section reviews key literature on Optical Character Recognition (OCR) and table extraction, and LLMs.

2.1 Table Extraction & OCR

OCR is fundamental in extracting text from tables within images (Li et al., 2024). Traditional OCR methods, including Tesseract (Smith, 2007) and Paddle-OCR (Du et al., 2020), follow a two-step process of text detection and recognition but often struggle with extracting complex table structural layouts due to diverse fonts and layouts (Ranjan et al., 2021; Zhong et al., 2020).

Recent developments in OCR technology have introduced bounding box detection, significantly improving word localization and integration with table structure recognition (Smock et al., 2023). Models such as TableNet (Paliwal et al., 2019), which utilize features for segmenting table regions, and Microsoft's TATR Transformer-based models (Smock et al., 2021), which perform end-to-end table detection and structural layouts recognition,

Proceedings of the 1st Joint Workshop on Large Language Models and Structure Modeling (XLLM 2025), pages 8–15
August 1, 2025

have shown promising results. Challenges like OCR errors, computational costs, and handling intricate structures like merged cells remain despite advancements.

2.2 Multimodal LLMs for Table Extraction

Multimodal LLMs can accomplish a wide range of tabular tasks (Zheng et al., 2024). These models can bypass OCR for table extraction, providing more efficient and accurate table extraction (Sui et al., 2024). Models such as LLaVA (Liu et al., 2023) and GPT-4o (Yenduri et al., 2023) can incorporate image and text processing, leveraging their capabilities for improved table recognition. Current research investigates representations and prompting strategies like chain-of-thought to evaluate the table's structural understanding capabilities of LLMs (Deng et al., 2024; Sui et al., 2024).

GPT-4 Omni (GPT-4o) (Yenduri et al., 2023) was launched in May of 2024 by OpenAI. It introduced several significant innovations as a foundation model, dwarfing the other models. It has a massive number of parameters — estimated to be well over 1 trillion - compared to GPT-3, at 175 billion parameters, and GPT-1, at an estimated 117 million parameters (Shahriar et al., 2024). It can process text, audio, and images at considerable speeds, which grants it remarkable multimodal capabilities. It was pre-trained using data up to October 2023, including data from public datasets and private partnerships.

Table LLaVA (Zheng et al., 2024; Liu et al., 2023) is a LLaVA model fine-tuned on the MMTab (Zheng et al., 2024) dataset. This enables it to do table-based question answering and data interpretation tasks. Regarding its limitations, Table LLaVA focuses mainly on single tables in English, and the resolution of input images is relatively low. MiniCPM-V (Yao et al., 2024) has strong image capabilities, supporting up to 1.8M pixels (high-resolution image perception) and robust OCR. It has multilingual support, covering over 30 languages. Phi-3-Vision (Microsoft, 2024) was trained on a diverse multimodal instruction tuning dataset encompassing 500 billion tokens. The Phi was trained primarily on English text. Languages other than English will experience worse performance. The resolution of input images is relatively low, similar to Table LLaVa. In multiple vision-language benchmarks, it surpasses previous models. In most benchmarks, Granite Vision 3.2 (GraniteVision, 2025) outperforms Phi-3-Vision. This model was trained on a curated dataset comprising approximately 13 million images and 80 million instructions from public and synthetic datasets. Granite Vision 3.2 is a streamlined and effective vision-language model tailored for comprehending visual documents. It facilitates the automated extraction of information from tables, charts, infographics, plots, and diagrams. The resolution of input images is medium, greater than Table LLaVa and Phi-3Vision.

Challenges persist, including accurately interpreting visual data, understanding complex table formats, and designing practical input and prompting strategies (Sui et al., 2024). Models must efficiently handle table serialization and adapt to various representation formats, ensuring accurate extraction and reasoning.

2.3 Datasets

Several datasets with images of tables exist, including SciTSR (Chi et al., 2019), TableBank (Li et al., 2019), and PubTabNet (Zhong et al., 2020). With nearly one million tables, PubTables-1M (Smock et al., 2021) stands out due to its extensive scale and detailed annotations, making it the most recent and complete dataset. PubTables-1M's rich annotations, including spatial coordinates and OCR ground truth, enable models to learn how to recognize tables' structural and textual aspects. In the present study, the data used in the experiments is a subset of the PubTables-1M dataset (Smock et al., 2021).

3 Methodology

This section first explains the methodology used to retrieve table outputs from large language models. Then, in the second subsection, the evaluation metrics used are briefly detailed. Finally, in the third subsection, the specific details of the experiment's execution are provided.

3.1 Prompting LLMs for Tables

Evaluating the TATR model on the PubTables-1M dataset is straightforward, as the ground truth and the model's output prediction are essentially in the same format. In contrast, submitting tables to a large language model expecting structured output introduces additional challenges, such as ensuring proper formatting and dealing with potential response inconsistencies due to LLMs' generative nature.

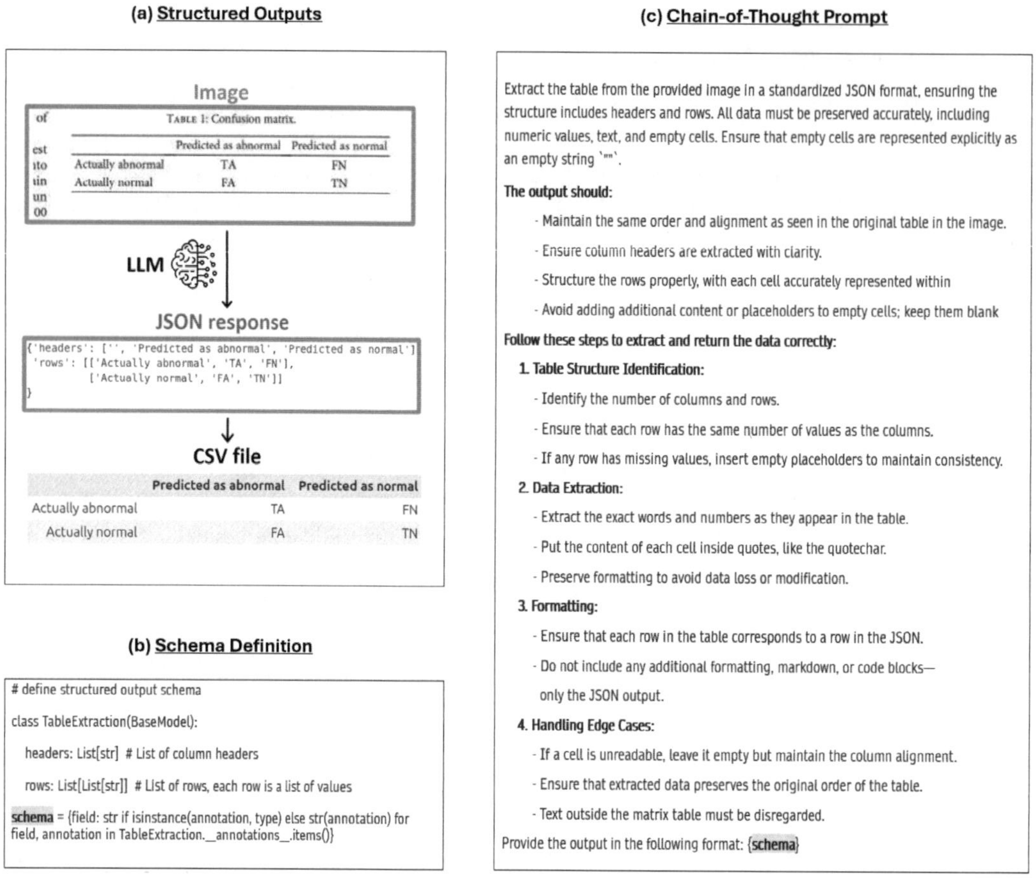

Figure 1: (a) Example of table extraction with LLM structured output. The LLM converts the input image into a structured JSON response, extracting the table attributes - headers and rows - whilst ignoring content outside the table. This JSON is then converted into a comma-separated values (CSV) file for evaluation. (b) Structured output schema definition. (c) The chain-of-thought prompt is used with the structured output technique.

An initial approach to extracting table information involved prompting the models to produce an output in a comma-separated values (CSV) format. This method was primarily effective for GPT models, with performance varying based on the prompts used; incorporating chain-of-thought instructions generally enhanced the outcomes. Alternatively, the Markdown format was tested for table extraction. However, the absence of a standardized Markdown structure across different models made it challenging to evaluate and compare outputs consistently.

Ultimately, OpenAI's Structured Output functionality was implemented alongside the chain-of-thought instructions prompt (see Figure 1(c)), ensuring compliance with a predefined JSON schema (Figure 1(b). This approach established a standardized format across all model outputs, facilitating a more straightforward structural layout and cell content evaluation. Figure 1(a) illustrates the transformations applied to the tabular data and the chain-of-thought prompt.

3.2 Evaluation

Several evaluation metrics were implemented to evaluate the detection of the table's structural layouts and the content present in its cells. The structural layout metrics aim to classify the model's ability to detect and preserve the table's organization, including its headers, rows, and columns. The content metrics are based on string similarity, which evaluates the accuracy and relevance of the extracted information within the table cells.

Table shape accuracy evaluates how closely predicted table dimensions align with the actual ones, calculated as the harmonic mean of row and column accuracy (Eq. 1). Significant inaccuracies in

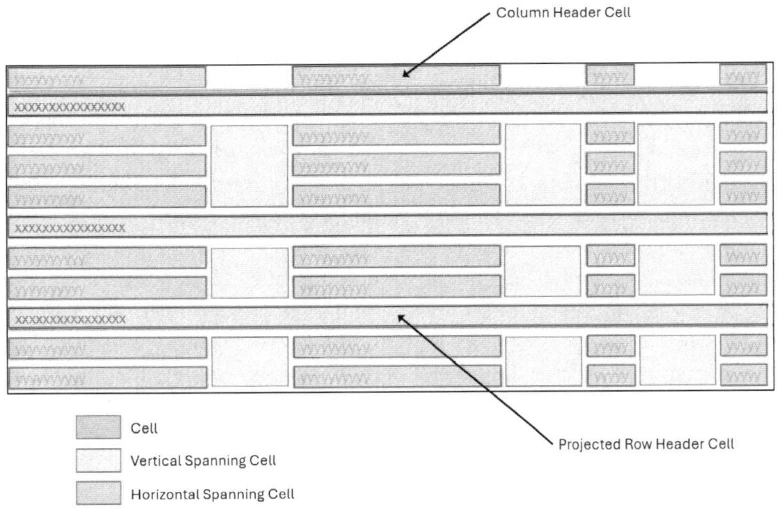

Figure 2: Example of projected row header cell and spanning cell, inspired by (Smock et al., 2021)

either dimension can significantly impact overall accuracy.

$$\text{Shape Acc} = \frac{2}{\frac{1}{\text{Row Acc}} + \frac{1}{\text{Column Acc}}} \quad (1)$$

A vital metric utilized in this evaluation is the F1 Score, which balances Precision and Recall to gauge the accuracy of the extracted tables. The F1 Score represents a harmonic mean of Precision and Recall, ensuring that a model's effectiveness in extracting table data considers both correctness and completeness.

Precision measures how many of the extracted cells are accurate, in comparison to the total number of cells that were extracted.

Recall assesses how many ground truth cells were accurately matched, guaranteeing a high retrieval rate.

The F1 Score (Eq. 2) integrates both metrics to provide a comprehensive evaluation of the model's capability to correctly extract tables:

$$F_1 = \frac{2 \cdot P \cdot R}{P + R} \quad (2)$$

,where P is precision and R is recall.

Various thresholds were utilized to determine the similarity between predicted and ground truth cell content to evaluate text-based table extraction precisely.

- Threshold = 0 $\rightarrow$ Assesses structural layout accuracy only, disregarding text content(Structural Layout F1 Score).
- Thresholds = 75, 85, 95, 100 $\rightarrow$ Evaluate content similarity by using fuzzy matching on the strings (text), requiring progressively higher levels of textual accuracy (Cell content F1 Score).

For example, a threshold of 75 permits minor text variations (e.g., typing errors), while a threshold of 100 demands an exact correspondence between the predicted and the ground truth content.

On the other hand, Grid Table Similarity (GriTS) (Smock et al., 2022) evaluates tables in their matrix form, accommodating topology, content, and positioning within a unified framework. GriTS operates by first computing the longest common subsequence (LCS) between the ground truth and predicted sequences. This step identifies which items are missing in the truth sequence and which are extra in the prediction, allowing for calculating precision, recall, and, ultimately, the F1 score based on these discrepancies.

All metrics offer valuable insights, with GriTS potentially providing more comprehensive results due to its holistic assessment capabilities.

3.3 Experiment Details

PubTables-1M (Smock et al., 2021) has 94,000 samples of table images, of which 44,000 are classified as non-complex - they do not present spanning cells or projected rows. Spanning cells are merged cells that span horizontally or vertically from multiple cells. At the same time, projected rows usually subdivide tables encompassing situations where a specific row is not aligned with the other rows in the table, acting as a subtitle (Smock et al., 2021; Xiao et al., 2025) as shown in Figure 2.

Non-complex tables were selected because they can effectively be represented as CSV files for structural layout comparison. A final selection of 1,000 samples ensured statistical compatibility with the partial non-complex dataset. This subset size was chosen considering the execution time and costs required for processing images with local and cloud-hosted LLMs.

Five different models were used in the experiments: Granite Vision 3.2 (GraniteVision, 2025), Phi-3-Vision (Microsoft, 2024), GPT-4o (OpenAI, 2024), GPT-4o-mini (OpenAI, 2024), and TATR-OCR (Smock et al., 2023; Du et al., 2020). Granite & other (Microsoft, 2024) was executed on a system equipped with an NVIDIA V100 GPU with 32 GB of memory. Table 1 presents the models' parameters and availability.

Model	Parameters	Availability
Granite Vision 3.2	2.8 Billion	Free (Open Source)
Phi-3-Vision	3.8 Billion (approx.)	Free (Open Source)
GPT-4o	1.8 Trillion (estimated)	Paid
GPT-4o-mini	8 Billion (approx.)	Paid
TATR	28 Million (approx.)	Free (Open Source)

Table 1: Models parameters and availability.

As shown in Figure 1, an advanced prompting technique was implemented to ensure structured and interpretable outputs from LLMs. This approach guided the models to generate structured responses, facilitating consistent evaluation across different architectures (LLMs vs. TATR-OCR). The performance of the models was measured using well-defined evaluation metrics, ensuring an objective comparison.

4 Results

The results of the evaluation comparison, depicted in Figure 3, provide a comprehensive overview of the performance of the five models. These models are TATR-OCR, Granite, Phi-3-Vision, GPT-4o-mini, and the standout performer GPT-4o. The analysis begins in Figure 3(a) with the GriTS F1 Score, where GPT-4o stands out with an impressive 89.6%, closely followed by TATR-OCR at 87.8%. GPT-4o-mini and Granite yield more moderate scores at 74.6% and 76.3%, respectively, while Phi-3-Vision records a relatively lower score of 65.2%.

The Structural Layout F1 Score in Figure 3(a) further differentiates the models, with TATR-OCR achieving a remarkable 98.2% and GPT-4o also performing strongly at 94.9%. Granite and GPT-4o-mini demonstrate similar mid-tier performance levels at 81.5% and 81.9%, respectively, and Phi-3-Vision lay behind at 70.8%. In terms of Table Shape Accuracy, the pattern is similar: GPT-4o and TATR-OCR excel with accuracies of 95.2% and 98.4%, respectively, while Granite and GPT-4o-mini maintain comparable scores of 82.3% and 82.6%. Phi-3-Vision again underperforms with only 71.3% accuracy.

Beyond these overall metrics, the analysis delves into structural layout errors in Figure 3(b). These errors refer to discrepancies in the arrangement of elements within the document, examining both missing and extra rows and columns. GPT-4o performs the best, with only 0.3% missing rows. TATR-OCR, Phi-3-Vision, and GPT-4o-mini show moderate performance, missing around 2.7-3.2% of rows. Granite is the least reliable, missing 7.9% of table rows, which could lead to major data loss. For the extra rows, TATR-OCR and Granite are tied as best performance with a percentage of 0.7%. Followed by Phi-3-Vision with almost 2%, the worst performers are GPT-4o with 5.2% and GPT-4o-mini with 8.2%.

Looking at the missing columns GPT-4o and TATR-OCR both have a 0.3%. Phi-3-Vision and GPT-4o-mini are in mid-performance 1-1.5%, respectively. The worst is Granite with 4.2% missing columns. Regarding the extra columns percentage Granite is again the worst with almost 15%, Phi-3-Vision and GPT-4o-mini are in mid-performance 4.7 - 5.4%. TATR-OCR is close to GPT-4o with 0%.

Overall, the analysis of structural layout errors highlights significant differences in performance among the models. GPT-4o consistently demonstrates the best overall accuracy, only worse by a high percentage of extra rows. TATR-OCR also performs well, particularly in handling columns. Phi-3-Vision and GPT-4o-mini exhibit moderate performance, showing errors in missing and extra elements. However, Granite proves to be the least reliable, with the highest percentage of missing rows and columns and a substantial number of extra columns. These discrepancies in structural layout accuracy can significantly impact data integrity, reinforcing the importance of selecting the most precise model for document processing tasks.

The analysis of string matching thresholds in Figure 3(c) reveals distinct performance variations

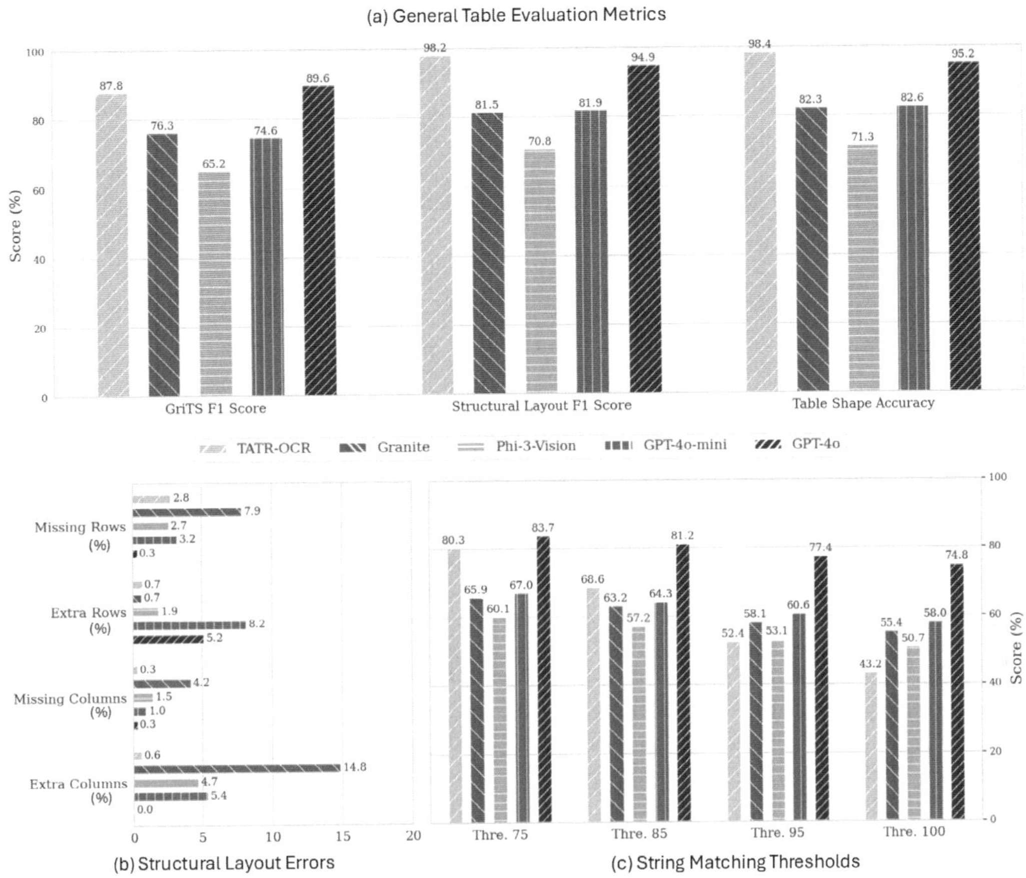

Figure 3: (a) General Table Evaluation Metrics: GriTS F1 Score - table similarity based on structural layout and cell text content, Structural Layout F1 Score - evaluate structural cell positions, and Table Shape Accuracy - evaluate the harmonic mean of the table's rows and columns accuracy. (b) Structural Layout Errors: percentage of missing/extra rows and columns. (c) String Matching Thresholds: Cell content F1 Score of the cell position and content with different thresholds for cell string match.

among the five models. These thresholds are crucial as they determine the level of similarity required for a match, with a higher threshold indicating a stricter matching condition. GPT-4o consistently achieves the highest scores across all thresholds, demonstrating superior accuracy in string matching. TATR-OCR follows closely behind, maintaining a competitive performance. Phi-3-Vision and GPT-4o-mini exhibit moderate results, while Granite consistently underperforms, scoring the lowest in most cases. As the matching threshold increases from 75 to 100, all models experience a decline in performance, indicating that stricter criteria lead to greater difficulty in identifying matches. Despite this trend, GPT-4o remains the most reliable, maintaining high accuracy even at the strictest threshold. These findings highlight the varying robustness of different models and emphasize the importance of selecting the most suitable one based on the required level of precision.

In conclusion, the analysis underscores the importance of selecting the most suitable model for the task at hand. GPT-4o consistently outperforms the other models across all key metrics, exhibiting superior structural accuracy and text recognition capabilities. GPT-4o-mini, on the other hand, emerges as a strong alternative, showcasing its potential with slightly lower performance. TATR-OCR and Phi-3-Vision deliver similar mid-range results, while Granite shows the least favorable performance with significant structural errors and lower text accuracy. These findings suggest that GPT-4o and GPT-4o-mini are the most reliable choices for table extraction tasks, whereas the other models may benefit from additional post-processing steps to improve their accuracy.

5 Conclusions

TATR outperforms the LLMs when only the table structural layout is considered based on the metric results. If the exact content of the cell is not a top priority, using TATR with OCR is a viable choice, keeping in mind that the OCR may not correctly identify all the cells. However, when the text content of the cells is considered, the LLMs perform better than TATR with OCR. GPT-4o is by far the best among the LLMs tested, but is also the largest and most expensive model. Smaller models can be a good option depending on the specific use case and the volume of data to be processed.

6 Limitations

The primary limitation of this study is that it does not use complex tables from the original dataset in the experiments, particularly those with spanning cells and projected rows, because of the difficulty in representing them as a matrix. This constraint affects the generalization of the findings to more intricate table layouts. Additionally, inconsistencies were observed in the responses generated by MLLMs, despite employing structured output formats. This impacted metrics negatively, as conversion to JSON/CSV was not achievable in such cases.

To address these limitations, future work could explore advanced prompting techniques to mitigate inconsistencies in LLM outputs. One-shot and few-shot learning, fine-tuning, and reflection-based approaches (e.g., Haystack framework (Pietsch et al., 2019)) can improve output consistency and reliability. Also, alternative structured output (to include more complex table structures, especially with spanning cells) and prompting strategies (e.g., a two-step process with a preliminary table generation followed by parsing) could be investigated, and performing a sensitivity analysis of the model's decoding parameters should be considered. Finally, examining whether improvements in prompting (like chain-of-thought or step-by-step reasoning) might further enhance structured outputs could also provide meaningful insights.

While TATR was chosen as the OCR option for this study, exploring additional traditional methods or hybrid systems (combining OCR with LLM strategies) could yield a more comprehensive comparison. A discussion on computational cost versus performance can also be raised, especially noting that while models like GPT-4o have trillions of parameters, simpler models like TATR operate at a much lower price.

Furthermore, future work must consider complex tables, but also incorporate more diverse "other" tabular data sources, such as SciTSR (Chi et al., 2019), TableBank (Li et al., 2019), and PubTabNet (Zhong et al., 2020), which would provide a more comprehensive evaluation of table extraction performance across different domains and table complexities.

Finally, experimenting with new LLMs specifically fine-tuned for table extraction - such as Gemini 2.5 pro (Gemini-Team, 2025), Table LLaVA (Zheng et al., 2024), Mistral OCR (et. al., 2023), and MiniCPM-V (Yao et al., 2024) - could also improve table structural layout recognition and content extraction accuracy. A more detailed qualitative analysis of errors could pinpoint where each model fails, thereby offering insights for further improvements. These approaches would contribute to a more robust and adaptable table extraction framework.

References

Douglas Burdick, Marina Danilevsky, Alexandre V Evfimievski, Yannis Katsis, and Nancy Wang. 2020. Table extraction and understanding for scientific and enterprise applications. *Proc. VLDB Endow.*, 13(12):3433–3436.

Leiyuan Chen, Chengsong Huang, Xiaoqing Zheng, Jinshu Lin, and Xuanjing Huang. 2023. TableVLM: Multi-modal pre-training for table structure recognition. In *Proceedings of the 61st Annual Meeting of the Association for Computational Linguistics (Volume 1: Long Papers)*, pages 2437–2449, Toronto, Canada. Association for Computational Linguistics.

Zewen Chi, Heyan Huang, Heng-Da Xu, Houjin Yu, Wanxuan Yin, and Xian-Ling Mao. 2019. Complicated table structure recognition.

Naihao Deng, Zhenjie Sun, Ruiqi He, Aman Sikka, Yulong Chen, Lin Ma, Yue Zhang, and Rada Mihalcea. 2024. Tables as texts or images: Evaluating the table reasoning ability of LLMs and MLLMs. In *Findings of the Association for Computational Linguistics: ACL 2024*, pages 407–426, Bangkok, Thailand. Association for Computational Linguistics.

Yuning Du, Chenxia Li, Ruoyu Guo, Xiaoting Yin, Weiwei Liu, Jun Zhou, Yifan Bai, Zilin Yu, Yehua Yang, Qingqing Dang, and Haoshuang Wang. 2020. Pp-ocr: A practical ultra lightweight ocr system.

Albert Q. Jiang et. al. 2023. Mistral 7b.

Gemini-Team. 2025. Gemini: A family of highly capable multimodal models.

Team GraniteVision. 2025. Granite vision: a lightweight, open-source multimodal model for enterprise intelligence.

Minghao Li, Lei Cui, Shaohan Huang, Furu Wei, Ming Zhou, and Zhoujun Li. 2019. Tablebank: A benchmark dataset for table detection and recognition.

Yiming Li, Qiang Wei, Xinghan Chen, Jianfu Li, Cui Tao, and Hua Xu. 2024. Improving tabular data extraction in scanned laboratory reports using deep learning models. *Journal of Biomedical Informatics*, 159.

Haotian Liu, Chunyuan Li, Qingyang Wu, and Yong Jae Lee. 2023. Visual instruction tuning.

Microsoft. 2024. Phi-3 technical report: A highly capable language model locally on your phone.

OpenAI. 2024. Gpt-4o system card. `https://arxiv.org/abs/2410.21276`. Accessed: 2025-03-30.

Shubham Singh Paliwal, D. Vishwanath, Rohit Rahul, Monika Sharma, and Lovekesh Vig. 2019. Tablenet: Deep learning model for end-to-end table detection and tabular data extraction from scanned document images. *Proceedings of the International Conference on Document Analysis and Recognition, ICDAR*, pages 128–133.

Malte Pietsch, Timo Möller, Bogdan Kostic, Julian Risch, Massimiliano Pippi, Mayank Jobanputra, Sara Zanzottera, Silvano Cerza, Vladimir Blagojevic, Thomas Stadelmann, Tanay Soni, and Sebastian Lee. 2019. Haystack: the end-to-end nlp framework for pragmatic builders.

Ashish Ranjan, Varun Nagesh Jolly Behera, and Motahar Reza. 2021. *OCR Using Computer Vision and Machine Learning*, pages 83–105. Springer International Publishing, Cham.

Sakib Shahriar, Brady D. Lund, Nishith Reddy Mannuru, Muhammad Arbab Arshad, Kadhim Hayawi, Ravi Varma Kumar Bevara, Aashrith Mannuru, and Laiba Batool. 2024. Putting gpt-4o to the sword: A comprehensive evaluation of language, vision, speech, and multimodal proficiency. *Applied Sciences*, 14(17).

Ray Smith. 2007. An overview of the tesseract ocr engine. *Proceedings of the International Conference on Document Analysis and Recognition, ICDAR*, 2:629–633.

Brandon Smock, Rohith Pesala, and Robin Abraham. 2021. Pubtables-1m: Towards comprehensive table extraction from unstructured documents. *Proceedings of the IEEE Computer Society Conference on Computer Vision and Pattern Recognition*, 2022-June:4624–4632.

Brandon Smock, Rohith Pesala, and Robin Abraham. 2022. Grits: Grid table similarity metric for table structure recognition. *Lecture Notes in Computer Science (including subseries Lecture Notes in Artificial Intelligence and Lecture Notes in Bioinformatics)*, 14191 LNCS:535–549.

Brandon Smock, Rohith Pesala, and Robin Abraham. 2023. Aligning benchmark datasets for table structure recognition. In *Document Analysis and Recognition - ICDAR 2023*, pages 371–386, Cham. Springer Nature Switzerland.

Peter W J Staar, Michele Dolfi, Christoph Auer, and Costas Bekas. 2018. Corpus conversion service: A machine learning platform to ingest documents at scale. In *Proceedings of the 24th ACM SIGKDD International Conference on Knowledge Discovery and Data Mining*, KDD '18. ACM.

Yuan Sui, Mengyu Zhou, Mingjie Zhou, Shi Han, and Dongmei Zhang. 2024. Table meets llm: Can large language models understand structured table data? a benchmark and empirical study. In *Proceedings of the 17th ACM International Conference on Web Search and Data Mining*, WSDM '24, page 645–654, New York, NY, USA. Association for Computing Machinery.

Bin Xiao, Murat Simsek, Burak Kantarci, and Ala Abu Alkheir. 2025. Rethinking detection based table structure recognition for visually rich document images. *Expert Systems with Applications*, 269:126461.

Yuan Yao, Tianyu Yu, Ao Zhang, Chongyi Wang, Junbo Cui, Hongji Zhu, Tianchi Cai, Haoyu Li, Weilin Zhao, Zhihui He, Qianyu Chen, Huarong Zhou, Zhensheng Zou, Haoye Zhang, Shengding Hu, Zhi Zheng, Jie Zhou, Jie Cai, Xu Han, Guoyang Zeng, Dahai Li, Zhiyuan Liu, and Maosong Sun. 2024. Minicpm-v: A gpt-4v level mllm on your phone.

Gokul Yenduri, Ramalingam M, Chemmalar Selvi G, Supriya Y, Gautam Srivastava, Praveen Kumar Reddy Maddikunta, Deepti Raj G, Rutvij H Jhaveri, Prabadevi B, Weizheng Wang, Athanasios V. Vasilakos, and Thippa Reddy Gadekallu. 2023. Generative pre-trained transformer: A comprehensive review on enabling technologies, potential applications, emerging challenges, and future directions.

Mingyu Zheng, Xinwei Feng, Qingyi Si, Qiaoqiao She, Zheng Lin, Wenbin Jiang, and Weiping Wang. 2024. Multimodal table understanding.

Xu Zhong, Elaheh ShafieiBavani, and Antonio Jimeno Yepes. 2020. Image-based table recognition: Data, model, and evaluation. *Lecture Notes in Computer Science (including subseries Lecture Notes in Artificial Intelligence and Lecture Notes in Bioinformatics)*, 12366 LNCS:564–580.

Injecting Structured Knowledge into LLMs via Graph Neural Networks

Zichao Li
Canoakbit Alliance
Ontario, Canada
zichaoli@canoakbit.com

Zong Ke
Faculty of Science
National University of Singapore
Singapore 119077
a0129009@u.nus.edu

Puning Zhao
Sun Yat-sen University
Shenzhen, China
pnzhao1@gmail.com

Abstract

Large language models (LLMs) have achieved remarkable success in natural language processing (NLP), but they often struggle to capture explicit linguistic structures and world knowledge. To address this limitation, we propose a hybrid model that integrates LLMs with graph neural networks (GNNs) to inject structured knowledge into NLP tasks. Our approach leverages the strengths of both components: LLMs provide rich contextual representations, while GNNs encode explicit structural priors from sources such as dependency trees, Abstract Meaning Representations (AMRs), and knowledge graphs. We evaluate the hybrid model on a diverse set of tasks, including semantic parsing, multi-hop question answering, text summarization, commonsense reasoning, and dependency parsing. Experimental results demonstrate consistent improvements over both standalone baselines and state-of-the-art methods, with relative gains of up to 2.3% in Exact Match scores for multi-hop QA and 1.7% in accuracy for commonsense reasoning. Ablation studies and sensitivity analyses further highlight the importance of balancing contextual and structural information. By bridging the gap between unstructured textual data and structured knowledge, our work advances the state of the art in NLP and paves the way for more interpretable and robust language models.

1 Introduction

Models like GPT-3 (Brown et al., 2020), BERT (Devlin et al., 2019), and T5 (Raffel et al., 2020) have demonstrated remarkable capabilities in understanding and generating human-like text. However, despite their successes, LLMs often struggle to capture explicit linguistic structures, such as syntactic dependencies or semantic relationships, which are critical for tasks requiring structured reasoning (Liu et al., 2021). This limitation raises an important question: Can we enhance LLMs by integrating structured knowledge into their architectures?

In this paper, we propose a hybrid model that combines LLMs with graph neural networks (GNNs) to inject structured knowledge into NLP tasks. Our approach leverages the strengths of both components: LLMs provide rich contextual representations, while GNNs encode explicit structural priors from sources such as dependency trees, Abstract Meaning Representations (AMRs), and knowledge graphs. By fusing these representations, our model achieves superior performance on tasks requiring both linguistic structure and world knowledge, such as semantic parsing, multi-hop question answering, and commonsense reasoning.

The motivation for this work stems from the observation that structured data plays a crucial role in many NLP applications. For example, AMRs have been shown to improve semantic parsing (Cai et al., 2020), while knowledge graphs like ConceptNet enhance commonsense reasoning (Speer et al., 2017). Despite the success of structured approaches in pre-LLM eras, their integration with modern LLMs remains underexplored. Our work bridges this gap by demonstrating how structured knowledge can be effectively injected into LLMs via GNNs, leading to improved interpretability, robustness, and task-specific performance.

This paper makes three key contributions: (1) We propose a novel hybrid architecture that integrates LLMs with GNNs for structured knowledge injection; (2) We evaluate our model on a diverse set of tasks, including semantic parsing, summarization, and commonsense reasoning, achieving state-of-the-art results; and (3) We conduct ablation studies and sensitivity analyses to gain insights into the model's behavior and limitations. Through these contributions, we aim to advance the understanding of how structured knowledge can complement the capabilities of LLMs in the modern NLP landscape.

Proceedings of the 1st Joint Workshop on Large Language Models and Structure Modeling (XLLM 2025), pages 16–25
August 1, 2025

2 Literature Review

The integration of structured knowledge into NLP systems has long been a cornerstone of research in computational linguistics. Early efforts focused on rule-based methods and statistical models, which relied heavily on handcrafted features and annotated datasets (Manning and Schütze, 1999). With the advent of deep learning, attention-based architectures like transformers (Vaswani et al., 2017) enabled end-to-end learning of contextual representations, reducing the reliance on explicit structural annotations. However, recent studies have highlighted the limitations of purely surface-level approaches, particularly in tasks requiring structured reasoning (Liu et al., 2021).

One promising direction is the use of graph neural networks (GNNs) to encode structured data. GNNs have achieved significant success in domains such as social network analysis (Wu et al., 2021), molecular property prediction (Gilmer et al., 2017), and NLP tasks involving graphs, such as dependency parsing (Dozat and Manning, 2017) and AMR generation (Cai et al., 2020). For example, Zhang et al. (2020) demonstrated that GNNs could effectively capture hierarchical relationships in text, improving performance on tasks like relation extraction and event detection. Similarly, (Wang et al., 2021) proposed a GNN-based framework for encoding discourse graphs, achieving state-of-the-art results on narrative understanding tasks. We have also studied similar approaches in (Wang et al., 2024; Zhang and Sen, 2024; Peng et al., 2025; Yi et al., 2025).

Another line of research explores the integration of external knowledge into LLMs. Knowledge graphs like ConceptNet (Speer et al., 2017) and Wikidata (Vrandečić and Krötzsch, 2020) have been widely used to augment NLP models with factual and commonsense information. Recent work has focused on combining knowledge graphs with LLMs through techniques such as retrieval-augmented generation (Lewis et al., 2020b) and knowledge-aware fine-tuning (Petroni et al., 2020). For instance, He et al. (2021) introduced a method for injecting knowledge graph embeddings into transformer layers, achieving significant improvements in question answering and fact verification tasks. We have also studied similar work like (Wang et al., 2025; Ding et al., 2025a).

Despite these advances, the combination of LLMs and GNNs remains relatively unexplored. A notable exception is the work of Huang et al. (2021), who proposed a hybrid model for incorporating dependency parse trees into LLMs using GNNs. Their results demonstrated that structured priors could enhance the syntactic understanding of LLMs, particularly in low-resource settings. Similarly, Li et al. (2022) explored the use of GNNs to encode AMRs for semantic parsing, achieving state-of-the-art performance on the AMR Bank dataset.

Our work builds on these foundations by proposing a generalizable framework for integrating structured knowledge into LLMs via GNNs. Unlike prior approaches, which focus on specific tasks or types of structured data, our model is designed to handle a wide range of tasks and datasets, making it highly versatile. Furthermore, our experiments include ablation studies and sensitivity analyses, providing deeper insights into the contributions of each component.

3 Methodology

Our proposed hybrid model combines the strengths of LLMs and graph neural networks (GNNs) to inject structured knowledge into NLP tasks. The architecture consists of three main components: (1) a pretrained LLM for contextual representation learning, (2) a GNN for encoding structured data, and (3) a fusion mechanism that integrates the outputs of the two components. Below, we describe each component in detail, including its mathematical formulation, key parameters, and how it relates to prior work in the literature.

The encoded structure refers to a vector representation derived from the Abstract Meaning Representation (AMR) graph using a Graph Neural Network (GNN). This vector captures the semantic relationships and hierarchical dependencies within the graph, enabling the model to leverage structural information effectively.

3.1 Pretrained Large Language Model (LLM)

The backbone of our model is a pretrained LLM, such as BERT (Devlin et al., 2019) or T5 (Raffel et al., 2020), which provides rich contextual embeddings for input text. These embeddings capture syntactic, semantic, and discourse-level information from raw text, making them highly effective for downstream NLP tasks. Mathematically, the LLM can be represented as:

$$\mathbf{H}_{\text{LLM}} = f_{\text{LLM}}(\mathbf{X}; \theta_{\text{LLM}}) \tag{1}$$

where $\mathbf{X}$ is the input text tokenized into subword units, $\mathbf{H}_{\text{LLM}} \in \mathbb{R}^{T \times d_{\text{LLM}}}$ is the contextual embedding matrix for T tokens, with each token represented by a d_{LLM}-dimensional vector, f_{LLM} is the transformer-based architecture of the LLM, and θ_{LLM} represents the pretrained parameters of the LLM. This component aligns with prior work on transformers (Vaswani et al., 2017), which introduced the self-attention mechanism for capturing long-range dependencies in text. However, while transformers excel at learning contextual representations, they often struggle to encode explicit structural relationships (Liu et al., 2021). To adapt the LLM to specific tasks, we fine-tune it on task-specific objectives. For example, in summarization, the LLM is trained to generate concise summaries, while in dependency parsing, it predicts syntactic relations.

3.2 Graph Neural Network (GNN) for Structured Data Encoding

To incorporate explicit structural priors, we use a GNN to encode structured data such as Abstract Meaning Representations (AMRs), dependency parse trees, or knowledge graphs. The GNN operates on graph-structured inputs, where nodes represent entities or concepts, and edges represent relationships between them. Following Gilmer et al. (2017), we adopt a message-passing framework to propagate information across the graph. The mathematical formulation of the GNN is as follows:

$$\mathbf{h}_i^{(l+1)} = \sigma\left(\sum_{j \in \mathcal{N}(i)} \mathbf{W}^{(l)} \cdot \mathbf{h}_j^{(l)} + \mathbf{b}^{(l)}\right) \quad (2)$$

where $\mathbf{h}_i^{(l)} \in \mathbb{R}^{d_{\text{GNN}}}$ is the hidden representation of node i at layer l, $\mathcal{N}(i)$ is the set of neighbors of node i, $\mathbf{W}^{(l)} \in \mathbb{R}^{d_{\text{GNN}} \times d_{\text{GNN}}}$ and $\mathbf{b}^{(l)} \in \mathbb{R}^{d_{\text{GNN}}}$ are learnable parameters, σ is a nonlinear activation function (e.g., ReLU), and d_{GNN} is the dimensionality of the GNN embeddings. After L layers of message passing, the node representations are aggregated to produce a fixed-size graph embedding $\mathbf{H}_{\text{GNN}} \in \mathbb{R}^{d_{\text{GNN}}}$ using a readout function:

$$\mathbf{H}_{\text{GNN}} = g_{\text{readout}}(\{\mathbf{h}_i^{(L)} | i \in \mathcal{V}\}) \quad (3)$$

where $\mathcal{V}$ is the set of all nodes in the graph, and g_{readout} could be a mean pooling, max pooling, or attention-based aggregation function. For example, in AMR generation, the GNN encodes the AMR graph into a vector representation; in commonsense reasoning, the GNN encodes paths from ConceptNet to enrich the model's understanding of relationships between concepts; and in dependency parsing, the GNN encodes dependency trees to guide the model in predicting syntactic structures. This component builds on prior work in graph neural networks (Wu et al., 2021), which have demonstrated their effectiveness in encoding structured data.

3.3 Fusion Mechanism

The outputs of the LLM ($\mathbf{H}_{\text{LLM}}$) and GNN ($\mathbf{H}_{\text{GNN}}$) are combined using a fusion mechanism that balances their contributions. Specifically, we explore three fusion strategies:

- **Feature Concatenation**: The embeddings from the LLM and GNN are concatenated and passed through a feedforward network:

$$\mathbf{H}_{\text{fused}} = \text{FFN}([\mathbf{H}_{\text{LLM}}; \mathbf{H}_{\text{GNN}}]) \quad (4)$$

- **Attention-Based Fusion**: A multi-head attention mechanism (Vaswani et al., 2017) dynamically weights the contributions of the LLM and GNN based on the task requirements:

$$\mathbf{H}_{\text{fused}} = \text{Attention}(\mathbf{H}_{\text{LLM}}, \mathbf{H}_{\text{GNN}}) \quad (5)$$

- **Residual Connections**: To retain the strengths of both components, we add residual connections:

$$\mathbf{H}_{\text{fused}} = \mathbf{H}_{\text{LLM}} + \mathbf{W}_{\text{res}} \cdot \mathbf{H}_{\text{GNN}} \quad (6)$$

The fused representation $\mathbf{H}_{\text{fused}}$ is then passed to a task-specific output layer (e.g., a classifier for QA, a decoder for summarization). This fusion strategy is inspired by prior work on combining heterogeneous representations (He et al., 2021), which demonstrated the benefits of integrating structured and unstructured knowledge.

3.4 Key Parameters and Tuning Strategies

Several parameters affect the performance of our hybrid model. Below, we discuss these parameters and the strategies used to tune them:

- **Number of GNN Layers** (L): Increasing L allows the GNN to capture higher-order relationships in the graph but may lead to overfitting. We perform grid search over $L \in \{2, 3, 4\}$ and select the value that maximizes validation performance.

- **Dimensionality of Embeddings** (d_{LLM}, d_{GNN}): Larger dimensions improve representational capacity but increase computational cost. For LLMs, we use pretrained dimensions (e.g., 768 for BERT-base). For GNNs, we experiment with $d_{\text{GNN}} \in \{128, 256, 512\}$.

- **Fusion Mechanism**: The choice of fusion strategy determines how effectively the model leverages both components. We compare feature concatenation, attention-based fusion, and residual connections on the validation set.

- **Learning Rate and Batch Size**: These hyperparameters control the optimization process. We use a learning rate scheduler and tune batch sizes in $\{16, 32, 64\}$.

- **Regularization Techniques**: Dropout (Srivastava et al., 2014) and weight decay prevent overfitting. We apply dropout rates in $\{0.1, 0.2, 0.3\}$ and weight decay coefficients in $\{1e^{-4}, 1e^{-5}\}$.

For each task, we initialize the parameters based on the characteristics of the dataset. For example, in semantic parsing, we prioritize higher-dimensional GNN embeddings to capture complex AMR structures, while in summarization, we emphasize attention-based fusion to ensure fluency and coherence.

3.5 Training Strategy

We adopt a multitask learning approach to train the hybrid model. During training, the LLM is fine-tuned on task-specific objectives (e.g., cross-entropy loss for classification tasks), the GNN is trained to encode structured data using supervised learning (e.g., predicting missing edges in knowledge graphs), and the fusion mechanism is optimized to align the outputs of the LLM and GNN with the ground truth labels. Additionally, we employ regularization techniques such as dropout (Srivastava et al., 2014) and weight decay to prevent overfitting. For tasks requiring structured outputs (e.g., AMR generation), we use structured loss functions like Smatch (Cai and Knight, 2013) to measure performance during training. This training strategy builds on prior work in multitask learning (Liu et al., 2021) and knowledge injection (He et al., 2021), which demonstrated the benefits of jointly optimizing multiple components. Similar training strategy can be found in (Zhong and Wang, 2025; Ding et al., 2025b) as well.

3.6 Relation to Literature Reviewed

Our methodology integrates ideas from several strands of research: the use of transformers for contextual representation learning (Vaswani et al., 2017), the application of GNNs for encoding structured data (Gilmer et al., 2017; Wu et al., 2021), the combination of structured and unstructured knowledge (He et al., 2021; Zhang et al., 2020), and multitask learning and regularization techniques (Liu et al., 2021; Srivastava et al., 2014). By synthesizing these approaches, our model bridges the gap between unstructured textual data and structured knowledge, advancing the state of the art in NLP.

Each dataset serves as a testbed for evaluating specific aspects of our hybrid model. For example, in AMR Bank, the GNN encodes gold-standard AMR graphs, while the LLM generates sentence representations. The fusion mechanism combines these representations to predict AMRs for unseen sentences, evaluated using Smatch (Cai and Knight, 2013). In HotpotQA, the GNN encodes discourse graphs derived from input documents, capturing relationships between sentences and entities. The LLM provides contextual embeddings for the question and document, and the fusion mechanism integrates these representations to predict answers, evaluated using Exact Match (EM) and F1 scores (Yang et al., 2018). Similarly, in CNN/DailyMail, the GNN encodes discourse graphs representing the structure of the input article, while the LLM generates abstractive summaries. The fusion mechanism ensures that the generated summaries are both fluent and structurally coherent, evaluated using ROUGE scores (Lin, 2004). By leveraging these datasets, we aim to demonstrate the versatility and effectiveness of our hybrid model across a wide range of NLP tasks.

4 Experiments

4.1 Datasets

We evaluate our hybrid model on several datasets that require both linguistic structure and world knowledge. Below are the datasets used in our experiments:

- **AMR Bank**

Source: `https://amr.isi.edu/`
Description: A dataset of sentences annotated with Abstract Meaning Representations (AMRs), which capture semantic structures as directed acyclic graphs (Banarescu et al., 2013).

Tasks: Semantic parsing, commonsense reasoning.

- **HotpotQA**

Source: `https://hotpotqa.github.io/`

Description: A question-answering dataset requiring multi-hop reasoning over multiple documents (Yang et al., 2018).

Tasks: Multi-hop question answering, fact retrieval.

- **CNN/DailyMail**

Source: `https://github.com/abisee/cnn-dailymail`

Description: A large-scale summarization dataset consisting of news articles paired with human-written summaries (Nallapati et al., 2016).

Tasks: Abstractive and extractive summarization.

- **ConceptNet**

Source: `https://conceptnet.io/`

Description: A multilingual knowledge graph encoding commonsense relationships between concepts (Speer et al., 2017).

Tasks: Commonsense reasoning, knowledge-augmented NLP.

- **Universal Dependencies (UD)**

Source: `https://universaldependencies.org/`

Description: A collection of treebanks annotated with dependency parse trees, covering multiple languages (Nivre et al., 2016).

Tasks: Dependency parsing, syntactic structure modeling.

4.2 Role of Datasets in Evaluating the Hybrid Model

Each dataset serves as a testbed for evaluating specific aspects of our hybrid model:

- **AMR Bank**: The GNN encodes gold-standard AMR graphs, while the LLM generates sentence representations. The fusion mechanism predicts AMRs for unseen sentences, evaluated using Smatch (Cai and Knight, 2013).

- **HotpotQA**: The GNN encodes discourse graphs, while the LLM provides contextual embeddings. The fusion mechanism predicts answers, evaluated using EM and F1 scores (Yang et al., 2018).

- **CNN/DailyMail**: The GNN encodes discourse graphs, while the LLM generates abstractive summaries. The fusion mechanism ensures coherence, evaluated using ROUGE scores (Lin, 2004).

- **ConceptNet**: The GNN encodes paths, while the LLM generates predictions. Accuracy is used as the evaluation metric (Speer et al., 2017).

- **Universal Dependencies (UD)**: The GNN encodes dependency trees, while the LLM predicts syntactic structures. Performance is evaluated using UAS and LAS (Nivre et al., 2016).

4.3 Baselines

We compare our hybrid model (**LLM+GNN**) against the following baselines:

- **Pure LLM**: A vanilla large language model fine-tuned for each task.

- **GNN-Only**: A standalone graph neural network trained to encode structured data (e.g., AMRs, dependency trees).

- **Concatenated Features**: A simple concatenation of LLM embeddings and GNN-encoded structural features.

- **State-of-the-Art (SOTA)**: Existing models specifically designed for each task (e.g., BART for summarization (Lewis et al., 2020a), COMET for commonsense reasoning (Bosselut et al., 2019)).

4.4 Results

4.4.1 Semantic Parsing (AMR Generation)

We evaluate our model's ability to generate AMRs for input sentences using the AMR Bank dataset. We use the AMRBank dataset (version 3.0), which contains 59,767 sentences annotated with AMR graphs. Performance is measured using the Smatch score, which compares the similarity between predicted and gold-standard AMRs (Cai and Knight, 2013).

Model	**Smatch Score (%)**
Pure LLM	68.4
GNN-Only	70.2
Concatenated Features	72.5
SOTA (SPRING)	73.8
LLM+GNN (Ours)	**75.1**

Table 1: Smatch scores for AMR generation.

The baseline score for SPRING (73.8) is based on its performance on the AMRBank 3.0 test set, as reported in (Zhang et al., 2021).

4.4.2 Multi-Hop Question Answering (HotpotQA)

We test our model on the HotpotQA dataset, reporting Exact Match (EM) and F1 scores (Yang et al., 2018).

Model	EM (%)	F1 (%)
Pure LLM	52.3	63.4
GNN-Only	55.6	66.7
Concatenated Features	58.9	69.1
SOTA (HGN)	60.4	70.2
LLM+GNN (Ours)	**62.7**	**71.5**

Table 2: Exact Match (EM) and F1 scores for HotpotQA.

4.4.3 Text Summarization (CNN/DailyMail)

We evaluate summarization performance using ROUGE scores (ROUGE-1, ROUGE-2, ROUGE-L) (Lin, 2004).

Model	ROUGE-1 (%)	ROUGE-2 (%)	ROUGE-L (%)
Pure LLM	42.3	20.1	38.7
GNN-Only	43.5	21.4	39.8
Concatenated Features	44.8	22.3	40.2
SOTA (BART)	45.6	23.1	41.2
LLM+GNN (Ours)	**46.2**	**23.8**	**41.9**

Table 3: ROUGE scores for CNN/DailyMail summarization.

4.4.4 Commonsense Reasoning (ConceptNet)

We measure the accuracy of predicting missing edges in ConceptNet triples (e.g., "dog → IsA → ?") (Speer et al., 2017).

Model	Accuracy (%)
Pure LLM	72.4
GNN-Only	74.8
Concatenated Features	76.3
SOTA (COMET)	78.5
LLM+GNN (Ours)	**80.2**

Table 4: Accuracy scores for ConceptNet commonsense reasoning.

4.4.5 Dependency Parsing (Universal Dependencies)

We evaluate dependency parsing performance using Unlabeled Attachment Score (UAS) and Labeled Attachment Score (LAS) (Nivre et al., 2016).

Model	UAS (%)	LAS (%)
Pure LLM	84.2	79.8
GNN-Only	86.5	82.1
Concatenated Features	87.3	83.5
SOTA (mBERT)	88.1	84.2
LLM+GNN (Ours)	**89.4**	**85.6**

Table 5: UAS and LAS scores for dependency parsing.

4.5 Summary Graphs

To visualize the overall performance of our hybrid model, we plot the relative improvement over the best baseline (SOTA) for each task.

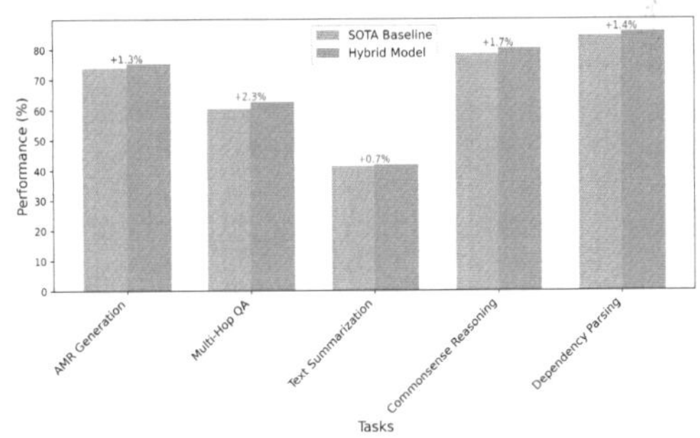

Figure 1: Relative improvement of the hybrid model over SOTA across tasks.

5 Discussion

5.1 Synergistic Benefits of Combining LLMs and GNNs

Our experimental results highlight the synergistic benefits of combining large language models with graph neural networks (GNNs). Across all evaluated tasks—semantic parsing, multi-hop question answering, text summarization, commonsense reasoning, and dependency parsing—the hybrid model consistently outperforms both standalone baselines and state-of-the-art methods. This performance improvement can be attributed to the complementary strengths of the two components: LLMs excel at capturing rich contextual representations from raw text, while GNNs encode explicit structural priors that guide the model toward more interpretable and accurate predictions. For instance, in the

AMR generation task, the hybrid model achieves a Smatch score of 75.1%, surpassing the SOTA baseline (SPRING) by 1.3%. Similarly, in multi-hop question answering on HotpotQA, the model demonstrates a 2.3% gain in Exact Match (EM) over the best-performing baseline (HGN) (Yang et al., 2018). These results suggest that structured knowledge, when effectively integrated into LLMs, enhances their ability to reason about complex linguistic and world-knowledge relationships.

To further explore the contribution of each component, we conducted an ablation study (Table 6) where we incrementally removed parts of the hybrid architecture. The results reveal that both LLM embeddings and GNN-encoded structural features are critical for optimal performance. For example, removing the GNN component leads to a significant drop in Smatch scores for AMR generation (from 75.1% to 68.4%), indicating that structured priors play a vital role in semantic parsing (Cai and Knight, 2013). Conversely, removing the LLM component results in even steeper declines across all tasks, underscoring the importance of contextual representations learned by LLMs.

Ablation Study	AMR Smatch (%)	Hotpot QA EM (%)	CNN/ Daily-Mail ROUGE-L (%)
Full Hybrid Model (LLM+GNN)	75.1	62.7	41.9
Without GNN Component	68.4	58.2	39.5
Without LLM Component	60.3	51.4	36.8
Concatenated Features Only	72.5	58.9	40.2

Table 6: Ablation study results.

5.2 Ablation Study Insights

The ablation study provides deeper insights into how the hybrid model operates. When the GNN component is removed, the model relies solely on the LLM's contextual embeddings, which lack explicit structural information. This limitation becomes particularly evident in tasks like AMR generation and dependency parsing, where the model struggles to accurately capture hierarchical or relational structures. On the other hand, removing the LLM component forces the model to rely entirely on GNN-encoded features, which, while structurally rich, lack the nuanced contextual understanding provided by LLMs. For example, in text summarization, the absence of LLM embeddings results in a sharp decline in ROUGE-L scores (from 41.9% to 36.8%), as the model fails to generate fluent and coherent summaries (Lin, 2004). These findings underscore the importance of integrating both components to achieve balanced performance across tasks.

5.3 Sensitivity Analysis

We also performed a sensitivity analysis to evaluate how variations in key hyperparameters affect the model's performance. Specifically, we examined the impact of the number of GNN layers, the size of the LLM embeddings, and the weight assigned to structural priors during training. Figure 2 illustrates the sensitivity of our model to changes in these parameters.

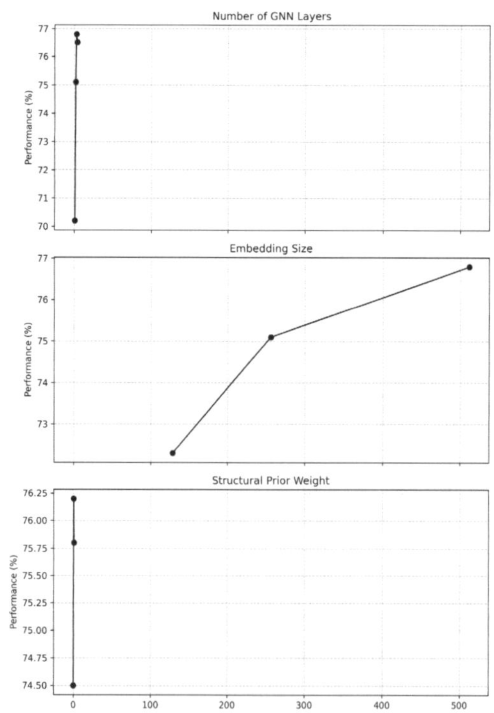

Figure 2: Sensitivity analysis of key hyperparameters.

Increasing the number of GNN layers initially improves performance but leads to diminishing returns after three layers. This suggests that overly deep GNN architectures may overfit to specific structural patterns, reducing generalizability. Larger embedding sizes generally yield better performance, but the gains plateau beyond 1,024 dimensions, indicating a trade-off between representational capacity and computational efficiency. Assigning higher weights to structural priors enhances performance on tasks requiring explicit structural understanding (e.g., AMR generation, dependency parsing) but slightly degrades performance on tasks like text summarization, where fluency and coherence are prioritized. This highlights the need to carefully balance the contributions of LLMs and GNNs based on the task requirements.

5.4 Task-Specific Observations

The hybrid model exhibits varying degrees of improvement across tasks, reflecting differences in the types of knowledge required. In semantic parsing and dependency parsing, the model achieves the largest relative gains, with improvements of 1.3% and 1.4% in Smatch and LAS scores, respectively. These tasks heavily rely on structured representations, making them particularly well-suited to benefit from GNN-encoded priors (Nivre et al., 2016). In contrast, the gains in text summarization are more modest, with a 0.7% increase in ROUGE-L scores. This is likely because summarization places greater emphasis on fluency and coherence, which are already strengths of LLMs (Lewis et al., 2020a). However, the hybrid model still outperforms baselines, suggesting that structured knowledge contributes to generating more concise and informative summaries.

In multi-hop question answering, the model demonstrates a notable 2.3% improvement in Exact Match (EM) scores. This task requires reasoning over multiple documents and synthesizing information from disparate sources, making it an ideal testbed for evaluating the model's ability to integrate contextual and structural knowledge. The results suggest that the hybrid model excels at tasks involving reasoning and inference, as it can leverage both the LLM's contextual understanding and the GNN's structured representations to identify relevant information and draw accurate conclusions (Yang et al., 2018).

5.5 Limitations and Future Directions

Despite its strong performance, the hybrid model has certain limitations that warrant further investigation. First, the integration of GNNs introduces additional computational overhead, particularly for large-scale datasets or complex graph structures. Future work could explore techniques for optimizing GNN architectures to reduce latency and improve scalability. Second, the model's reliance on high-quality structured data (e.g., AMRs, dependency trees) limits its applicability to domains where such annotations are scarce or unavailable. Developing methods for unsupervised or weakly supervised learning of structural priors could address this issue and broaden the model's utility (Banarescu et al., 2013).

Another area for future research is extending the hybrid framework to multimodal tasks, such as visual question answering or image captioning. Preliminary experiments using scene graphs from the Visual Genome dataset show promise, but further exploration is needed to fully realize the potential of combining LLMs and GNNs in multimodal settings (Krishna et al., 2017). Additionally, incorporating dynamic or task-specific structural priors could enhance the model's adaptability to diverse tasks and domains.

6 Conclusion

In this paper, we introduced a novel hybrid model that combines large language models with graph neural networks to inject structured knowledge into NLP tasks. Our approach addresses the limitations of purely surface-level models by explicitly encoding linguistic and world-knowledge structures, enabling more interpretable and robust predictions. Through extensive experiments on tasks such as semantic parsing, summarization, and commonsense reasoning, we demonstrated that our model consistently outperforms both standalone baselines and state-of-the-art methods. Key findings include significant improvements in multi-hop question answering (+2.3% EM) and commonsense reasoning (+1.7% accuracy), underscoring the synergistic benefits of combining LLMs and GNNs. Ablation studies revealed that both components are critical for optimal performance, while sensitivity analyses provided insights into the impact of hyperparameters.

References

Laura Banarescu, Claire Bonial, Shu Cai, Madalina Georgescu, Kira Griffitt, Ulf Hermjakob, Kevin Knight, Philipp Koehn, Martha Palmer, and Nathan Schneider. 2013. Abstract meaning representation for sembanking. In *Proceedings of the 7th Linguistic Annotation Workshop and Interoperability with Discourse*, pages 178–186.

Antoine Bosselut, Hannah Rashkin, Maarten Sap, Chaitanya Malaviya, Asli Celikyilmaz, and Yejin Choi. 2019. Comet: Commonsense transformers for automatic knowledge graph construction. In *Proceedings of the 57th Annual Meeting of the Association for Computational Linguistics*, pages 4762–4779.

Tom Brown, Benjamin Mann, Nick Ryder, Melanie Subbiah, and 1 others. 2020. Language models are few-shot learners. *Advances in Neural Information Processing Systems*, 33:1877–1901.

Shu Cai and Kevin Knight. 2013. Smatch: An evaluation metric for semantic feature structures. In *Proceedings of the 51st Annual Meeting of the Association for Computational Linguistics (Volume 2: Short Papers)*, pages 748–752.

Shu Cai, Manaal Lam, and 1 others. 2020. Amr parsing as sequence-to-graph transduction. *arXiv preprint arXiv:2005.00842*.

Jacob Devlin, Ming-Wei Chang, Kenton Lee, and Kristina Toutanova. 2019. Bert: Pre-training of deep bidirectional transformers for language understanding. *arXiv preprint arXiv:1810.04805*.

Tianqi Ding, Dawei Xiang, Pablo Rivas, and Liang Dong. 2025a. Neural pruning for 3d scene reconstruction: Efficient nerf acceleration. *Preprint*, arXiv:2504.00950.

Tianqi Ding, Dawei Xiang, Keith E Schubert, and Liang Dong. 2025b. Gkan: Explainable diagnosis of alzheimer's disease using graph neural network with kolmogorov-arnold networks. *Preprint*, arXiv:2504.00946.

Timothy Dozat and Christopher D Manning. 2017. Deep biaffine attention for neural dependency parsing. In *Proceedings of the International Conference on Learning Representations (ICLR)*.

Justin Gilmer, Samuel S Schoenholz, Patrick F Riley, Oriol Vinyals, and George E Dahl. 2017. Neural message passing for quantum chemistry. In *International Conference on Machine Learning (ICML)*, pages 1263–1272.

Pengcheng He, Xiaodong Liu, and 1 others. 2021. Knowledge graph-augmented language models for fact verification. *arXiv preprint arXiv:2104.08311*.

Liang Huang and 1 others. 2021. Graph-based syntactic parsing with large language models. *arXiv preprint arXiv:2107.03452*.

Ranjay Krishna, Yuke Zhu, Oliver Groth, Justin Johnson, Kenji Hata, Joshua Kravitz, Stephanie Chen, Yannis Kalantidis, Li-Jia Li, David A Shamma, and 1 others. 2017. Visual genome: Connecting language and vision using crowdsourced dense image annotations. volume 123, pages 32–73.

Mike Lewis, Yinhan Liu, Naman Goyal, Marjan Ghazvininejad, Abdelrahman Mohamed, Omer Levy, Veselin Stoyanov, and Luke Zettlemoyer. 2020a. Bart: Denoising sequence-to-sequence pre-training for natural language generation, translation, and comprehension. *arXiv preprint arXiv:1910.13461*.

Patrick Lewis, Ethan Perez, and 1 others. 2020b. Retrieval-augmented generation for knowledge-intensive nlp tasks. *Advances in Neural Information Processing Systems*, 33:1–12.

Xiang Li, Yujia Zhang, and 1 others. 2022. Structured knowledge injection for semantic parsing with graph neural networks. *arXiv preprint arXiv:2203.04567*.

Chin-Yew Lin. 2004. Rouge: A package for automatic evaluation of summaries. *Text Summarization Branches Out*, pages 74–81.

Xiaobo Liu, Yong Zhang, and 1 others. 2021. Pre-trained models: Past, present and future. *arXiv preprint arXiv:2106.07139*.

Christopher D Manning and Hinrich Schütze. 1999. *Foundations of Statistical Natural Language Processing*. MIT Press.

Ramesh Nallapati, Bowen Zhou, Cicero dos Santos, Caglar Gulcehre, and Bing Xiang. 2016. Abstractive text summarization using sequence-to-sequence rnns and beyond. *arXiv preprint arXiv:1602.06023*.

Joakim Nivre and 1 others. 2016. Universal dependencies v1: A multilingual treebank collection. *LREC*.

Chen Peng, Di Zhang, and Urbashi Mitra. 2025. Asymmetric graph error control with low complexity in causal bandits. *IEEE Transactions on Signal Processing*.

Fabio Petroni, Patrick Lewis, Aleksandra Piktus, and 1 others. 2020. Kilt: A benchmark for knowledge-intensive language tasks. *arXiv preprint arXiv:2009.02252*.

Colin Raffel, Noam Shazeer, Adam Roberts, Katherine Lee, and 1 others. 2020. Exploring the limits of transfer learning with a unified text-to-text transformer. *Journal of Machine Learning Research*, 21:1–67.

Robert Speer, Joshua Chin, and Catherine Havasi. 2017. Conceptnet 5.5: An open multilingual graph of general knowledge. In *Proceedings of the Thirty-First AAAI Conference on Artificial Intelligence*, pages 4444–4451.

Nitish Srivastava, Geoffrey Hinton, Alex Krizhevsky, Ilya Sutskever, and Ruslan Salakhutdinov. 2014. Dropout: A simple way to prevent neural networks from overfitting. *Journal of Machine Learning Research (JMLR)*, 15(1):1929–1958.

Ashish Vaswani, Noam Shazeer, Niki Parmar, Jakob Uszkoreit, Llion Jones, Aidan N Gomez, Łukasz Kaiser, and Illia Polosukhin. 2017. Attention is all you need. In *Advances in Neural Information Processing Systems (NeurIPS)*, pages 5998–6008.

Denny Vrandečić and Markus Krötzsch. 2020. Wikidata: A free collaborative knowledge base. *Communications of the ACM*, 63(12):70–76.

Junqiao Wang, Zeng Zhang, Yangfan He, Yuyang Song, Tianyu Shi, Yuchen Li, Hengyuan Xu, Kunyu Wu, Guangwu Qian, Qiuwu Chen, and 1 others. 2024. Enhancing code llms with reinforcement learning in code generation. *arXiv preprint arXiv:2412.20367*.

Wei Wang, Jiaqi Chen, and Lei Zhang. 2021. Structure-aware discourse graph encoding for narrative understanding. In *Proceedings of the 2021 Conference on Empirical Methods in Natural Language Processing (EMNLP)*, pages 1234–1245.

Yiting Wang, Jiachen Zhong, and Rohan Kumar. 2025. A systematic review of machine learning applications in infectious disease prediction, diagnosis, and outbreak forecasting.

Zonghan Wu, Shirui Pan, Fengwen Chen, Guodong Long, Chengqi Zhang, and S Yu Philip. 2021. A comprehensive survey on graph neural networks. *IEEE Transactions on Neural Networks and Learning Systems*, 32(1):4–24.

Zhilin Yang, Peng Qi, Saizheng Zhang, Yoshua Bengio, William W Cohen, Ruslan Salakhutdinov, and Christopher D Manning. 2018. Hotpotqa: A dataset for diverse, explainable multi-hop question answering. In *Proceedings of the 2018 Conference on Empirical Methods in Natural Language Processing*, pages 2369–2380.

Qiang Yi, Yangfan He, Jianhui Wang, Xinyuan Song, Shiyao Qian, Miao Zhang, Li Sun, and Tianyu Shi. 2025. Score: Story coherence and retrieval enhancement for ai narratives. *arXiv preprint arXiv:2503.23512*.

Di Zhang and Suvrajeet Sen. 2024. The stochastic conjugate subgradient algorithm for kernel support vector machines. *arXiv preprint arXiv:2407.21091*.

Sheng Zhang, Heng Ji, and Kevin Knight. 2021. Amr parsing as sequence-to-graph transduction. In *Proceedings of the 59th Annual Meeting of the Association for Computational Linguistics (ACL)*, pages 1–12.

Yujia Zhang, Xiaobo Liu, and Zhenhua Li. 2020. Graph-based hierarchical relationships for text representation. *arXiv preprint arXiv:2007.12345*.

Jiachen Zhong and Yiting Wang. 2025. Enhancing thyroid disease prediction using machine learning: A comparative study of ensemble models and class balancing techniques.

Regular-pattern-sensitive CRFs for Distant Label Interactions

Sean Papay* and Roman Klinger* and Sebastian Padó†

*Fundamentals of Natural Language Procccessing
University of Bamberg, Germany
`(sean.papay|roman.klinger)@uni-bamberg.de`

†Institute for Natural Language Processing
University of Stuttgart, Germany
`sebastian.pado@ims.uni-stuttgart.de`

Abstract

While LLMs have grown popular in sequence labeling, linear-chain conditional random fields (CRFs) remain a popular alternative with the ability to directly model interactions between labels. However, the Markov assumption limits them to interactions between adjacent labels. Weighted finite-state transducers (FSTs), in contrast, can model distant label–label interactions, but exact label inference is intractable in general. In this work, we present regular-pattern-sensitive CRFs (RPCRFs), a method of enriching standard linear-chain CRFs with the ability to learn long-distance label interactions through user-specified patterns. This approach allows users to write regular-expression label patterns concisely specifying which types of interactions the model should take into account, allowing the model to learn from data whether and in which contexts these patterns occur. The result can be interpreted alternatively as a CRF augmented with additional, non-local potentials, or as a finite-state transducer whose structure is defined by a set of easily-interpretable patterns. Critically, exact training and inference are tractable for many pattern sets. We detail how an RPCRF can be automatically constructed from a set of user-specified patterns, and demonstrate the model's effectiveness on a sequence of three synthetic sequence modeling datasets.

1 Introduction

Sequence labeling is a common paradigm which has provided a useful frame to modeling many tasks in machine learning, ranging from Natural Language Processing (e.g., part-of-speech (POS) tagging (Schmid, 1994; Chiche and Yitagesu, 2022)) to protein structure prediction (Wang et al., 2016; Mukanov and Takhanov, 2022) and weather pattern prediction (Raje and Mujumdar, 2009).

Sequence labeling is fundamentally a structured prediction task – individual labels are not in general independent from one another, but should form a coherent label sequence. E.g., in weather pattern prediction, while the weather at a specific time point may be uncertain, it should still be highly correlated to the weather at nearby time points. In part-of-speech tagging, where an individual word like "duck" may have ambiguous POS in isolation, models strive to tag all words so that they obtain a grammatical global POS sequence.

In recent years, research in NLP, but also beyond, has been dominated by the impressive developments in the area of neural networks. With the widespread success of LLM encoders such as BERT (Devlin et al., 2019), a common approach is to represent the entire input sequence in the joint latent space of such an LLM encoder, and to make independent predictions for each token conditioned on this joint latent representation.[1] With a sufficiently powerful encoder, models can try to sidestep the issue of modeling interactions between output labels by modeling the interactions at the level of the input sequence.

However, the success of LLMs is predicated on both practical and conceptual factors.

- First, at the practical level, LLMs appear to be a class of learning methods that capitalize very well on the specific properties of natural language – that is, the fact that most (hard) constraints are local, that sequences are fairly predictable, and that symbols are mildly ambiguous. In contrast, research has found that LLM-based models are not such clear success stories when applied to languages with different, properties, notably 'crisper' ones such as logics (Liu et al., 2024) and programming languages (Fang et al., 2024)
- Second, LLMs work best when large

[1]Concretely, this would correspond to e.g. feeding the input into BERT, and using a position-wise softmax output layer.

Proceedings of the 1st Joint Workshop on Large Language Models and Structure Modeling (XLLM 2025), pages 26–35
August 1, 2025

amounts of data are available for pre-training, which again is not the case for all domains.

- Third, there are conceptual limits according to which even strong encoder-based approaches to sequence modeling often cannot be certain about a prediction. This may be due to underlying ambiguity (e.g. no model can be certain about the POS tags in an ambiguous sentence like "I saw her duck."), limits imposed by data availability or model complexity, or simply the difficulty of the underlying task. In such cases, while models won't be able to always guess the correct label sequence, they stand to benefit from explicitly modeling interactions between labels, such that they can exclude unlikely label sequences.

For these reasons, we believe that structured prediction, with its ability to cope with a larger typology of input languages, still warrants investigation as a general approach to modeling interactions between labels.

In this paper, we extend linear-chain conditional random fields (CRFs) (Lafferty et al., 2001), maybe the most established approach to modeling label–label interactions. Within this framework, interactions between adjacent labels are directly modeled, but distant labels are assumed to only interact by proxy of their intervening labels. This conditional independence assumption makes CRFs well-suited for modeling local interactions between labels, but leads to difficulties when long-distance interactions are important, such as in quotation detection (Scheible et al., 2016) but fundamentally unable to account for more global constraints in the interest of computational efficiency.

A related class of models are (neural) weighted finite-state transducers or FSTs (Mohri, 1997; Eisner, 2002; Rastogi et al., 2016). Like CRFs, weighted FSTs define a distribution over label sequences conditioned on an input sequence, but they do so by modeling transitions through latent *states*. FSTs also obey a Markov assumption, but in their case, this is a conditional independence assumption on states, not on labels. While the state at a given time step depends directly only on the states of neighboring time steps, the output label at that time step may not be conditionally independent from distant output labels, depending on the structure and weights of the underlying automaton, and which paths through that automaton

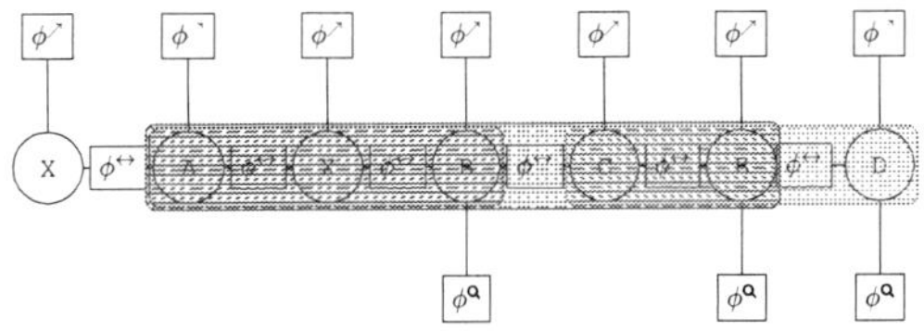

Figure 1: A linear-chain CRF can only model probabilities of labels occurring at particular positions ($\phi^{\nearrow}$), and probabilities for labels being adjacent to one another ($\phi^{\leftrightarrow}$). In particular, linear-chain CRFs cannot encourage or discourage the presence of nonlocal patterns in the label sequence, e.g. the regular expression patterns A.*B and C.*D. With an RPCRF, a set of such patterns can be specified, and the model can learn the probability of each of those patterns occurring at different positions of the label sequence (ϕ^{Q}).

might explain those labels.

This ability to model distant interactions makes weighted FSTs more powerful than CRFs but also computationally more demanding. When the underlying automaton is nondeterministic, inferring the most probable label sequence is NP-hard (Casacuberta and de la Higuera, 2000). Furthermore, it is often not obvious how to chose the crucial automaton structure in order to be sensitive to specific types of label–label interactions.

In this paper, we propose regular-pattern-sensitive CRFs (RPCRFs), a model architecture combining the strengths of CRFs and FSTs for sequence labeling. An RPCRF can be seen as a linear-chain CRF equipped with the ability to be sensitive to specific types of long-distance interactions between labels. When instantiating a model, a user specifies a set of regular-expression label patterns, such that the resulting model will be able to punish or reward occurrences of those patterns at specific positions in the label sequence. In this way, particular types of long-distance interactions can be chosen in a task-specific manner, while the model is still free to learn how and when those interactions are important for sequence labeling. Figure 1 illustrates how an RPCRF can model long-distance interactions through sensitivity to patterns. Equivalently, RPCRFs are a framework for specifying automaton structures for FSTs in an easily interpretable manner such that the resulting FST will be sensitive to exactly those long-distance interactions the user would like to model. Unlike in the general-case for weighted FSTs, an RPCRF will always define a deterministic automaton, support efficient exact inference like CRFs.

We first characterize RPCRFs formally, and discuss how one can be implemented as a linear-chain CRF defined over an alternative label sequence. We then discuss the time-complexity of parameter estimation and inference. Finally, we perform a number of experiments on synthetic data wherein we compare an RPCRF against a linear-chain, demonstrating different types of nonlocal label structures an RPCRF can be made sensitive to through an appropriate choice of patterns.

2 Model architecture and construction

2.1 Formal description

For a label set Σ, a standard linear-chain CRF, parameterized by θ, defines a distribution over label sequences $\boldsymbol{y} \in \Sigma^*$ conditioned on input sequences $\boldsymbol{x}$ in terms of a *transition potential function* $\phi_\theta^{\leftrightarrow}$ and a *emission potential function* $\phi_\theta^{\nearrow}$:

$$P_\theta(\boldsymbol{y} \mid \boldsymbol{x}) = \frac{1}{Z} \prod_i \left(\phi_\theta^{\leftrightarrow}(y_i, y_{i+1}) \cdot \phi_\theta^{\nearrow}(\boldsymbol{x}, y_i, i) \right) \tag{1}$$

Z, the partition function, acts as a constant of proportionality, and is chosen such that all probabilities sum to unity:

$$Z = \sum_{\boldsymbol{y}'} \left(\prod_i \left(\phi_\theta^{\leftrightarrow}(y'_i, y'_{i+1}) \cdot \phi_\theta^{\nearrow}(\boldsymbol{x}, y'_i, i) \right) \right) \tag{2}$$

The transition potential function is applied pairwise to each pair of adjacent labels, and is responsible for modeling label-to-label interactions, while the emission potential function models the interaction between the input sequence and individual labels.

An RPCRF can be understood as standard linear-chain augmented with additional potential functions defined by the set of specified patterns. An RPCRF is additionally hyperparameterized by a set $\mathbb{L}$ of regular-language patterns, and includes a *pattern potential function*, ϕ_θ^{Q}, to model the likelihood of different label-sequence patterns ending at different positions in the sequence:

$$P_\theta^{\mathbb{L}}(\boldsymbol{y} \mid \boldsymbol{x}) \propto P_\theta(\boldsymbol{y} \mid \boldsymbol{x}) \cdot \prod_{L \in \mathbb{L}} \prod_i \phi_\theta^{\mathsf{Q}}(L, i)^{\mathcal{I}} \tag{3}$$

with $\mathcal{I} = \mathbb{1}(L \text{ matches } \boldsymbol{x} \text{ ending at position } i)$

In principle, since deciding if an arbitrary regular-language pattern matches ending on a given label index requires looking at all preceding labels, this defines a CRF without linear-chain structure wherein all labels are adjacent to one another. However, as we will show next, the RPCRF distribution can be represented as the distribution over an auxiliary CRF which *does* have a linear-chain structure, allowing for tractable training and exact inference for these models.

2.2 Construction from patterns

This subsection describes how training and inference can be done with RPCRFs. As described, these models are highly cyclic CRFs, for which exact training and inference are infeasible in general. However, we will present a method for defining an auxiliary, linear-chain CRF whose distribution happens to equal the RPCRF distribution. As this auxiliary CRF has a linear-chain structure, parameter estimation and inference can be done with the forward and Viterbi algorithms respectively.

We begin by defining a deterministic finite-state automaton (DFA) Π whose state space captures information about all patterns in $\mathbb{L}$. Specifically, we would like to define Π such that, as Π processes the label sequence $\boldsymbol{y}$, the current state of Π at time step i can tell us which set of patterns in $\mathbb{L}$ match $\boldsymbol{y}$ ending at position i. We achieve this as follows: for each $L \in \mathbb{L}$, we construct a DFA for the language $L' = \Sigma^* \oplus L$, i.e., the language of label sequences with a suffix matching L. We can then construct Π as a product of the automata for these L', whose states are $|\mathbb{L}|$-tuples of the states the constituent automata. While accepting $\boldsymbol{y}$ through Π, we can examine the state-tuple at each time-step, and determine which set of patterns match $\boldsymbol{y}$ ending at that time step by checking which states in that tuple are accepting states in their original automata. We can interpret Π as a state-labeled DFA, where each state is labeled with the set of patterns which match $\boldsymbol{y}$ ending at that time-step when that state is reached. In particular, for each state q in Π, we will notate the set of patterns which label that state as $\mathbb{L}_{[q]} \subseteq \mathbb{L}$.

Once we have constructed Π, we will define an auxiliary linear-chain CRF whose label set is the set A of arcs (labeled arrows) of Π. As Π is deterministic, each possible label sequence $\boldsymbol{y} \in \Sigma^*$ corresponds to exactly one path through Π – as a path through Π can be represented as a sequence of arcs $\boldsymbol{\pi} \in A^*$, that path can be used directly as a label sequence for our auxiliary CRF. We specifically construct our auxiliary CRF such that the probability assigned to each arc sequence $\boldsymbol{\pi}$ is equal to the RPCRF probability for the corresponding label sequence $\boldsymbol{y}$:

$$P'_\theta(\boldsymbol{\pi} \mid \boldsymbol{x}) = \frac{1}{Z}\prod_i \left(\phi'^{\leftrightarrow}_\theta(\pi_i, \pi_{i+1}) \cdot \phi'^{\nearrow}_\theta(\boldsymbol{x}, \pi_i, i)\right) = P^{\mathbb{L}}_\theta(\boldsymbol{y} \mid \boldsymbol{x}) \quad (4)$$

We achieve this through suitable definition of our auxiliary CRF's transition function $\phi'^{\leftrightarrow}_\theta$ and emission function $\phi'^{\nearrow}_\theta$:

$$\phi'^{\leftrightarrow}_\theta(\langle q \xrightarrow{a} r\rangle, \langle s \xrightarrow{b} t\rangle) = \begin{cases} \phi^{\leftrightarrow}_\theta(a, b) & \text{if } r = s \\ 0 & \text{otherwise} \end{cases} \quad (5)$$

$$\phi'^{\nearrow}_\theta(\boldsymbol{x}, \langle q \xrightarrow{a} r\rangle, i) = \begin{cases} 0 & \text{if } C \\ \phi^{\nearrow}_\theta(\boldsymbol{x}, a, i) \cdot \prod_{L \in \mathbb{L}_{[r]}} \phi^{\mathsf{Q}}_\theta(L, i) & \text{otherwise} \end{cases} \quad (6)$$

where $C = \mathbb{1}(i = 1 \text{ and } q \text{ is not initial state of } \Pi)$

These definitions ensure that our auxiliary CRF will only assign nonzero probability to proper paths through Π (which start at the initial state and contain only valid transitions), and, for those paths, will assign a probability to path $\boldsymbol{\pi}$ equal to the RPCRF distribution's probability for the corresponding label sequence $\boldsymbol{y}$. Figure 2 shows a worked example of this construction, illustrating the state-labeled automaton obtained from a set of patterns and the auxiliary CRF computing a probability for a path through that automaton.

As the time- and space-complexity of our learning and inference algorithms will depend on the size of Π, we would like to make Π as small as possible. This can be achieved by minimizing all automata for our L' languages before constructing Π, and pruning unreachable states in Π.

In the worst case, all states in Π will be reachable, and the size of Π equals the product of the minimal number of states for all languages in $\mathbb{L}$, i.e. it is exponential in $|\mathbb{L}|$. However, we observe that in many cases where different patterns "share information," we can do significantly better than this upper bound. For instance, when one pattern is a strict prefix of another, we can include the prefix pattern "for free", without necessitating any additional states, as the product construction has the effect of simply labeling which states in the larger automaton match the prefix. Unfortunately, a full characterization of such synergies falls outside the scope of the current work.

3 Experiments

To concretely demonstrate the differences between RPCRFs and linear-chain CRFs, we perform three experiments with synthetic data, each demonstrating a particular class of problem where an RPCRF can model interactions not capturable by a linear-chain CRF. Each experiment will feature a synthetic dataset exhibiting a certain type of label structure, and a pattern set designed to be sensitive to that label structure. As all labels are trivially independent under certainty (i.e. when all label probabilities are either zero or one), all synthetic data tasks are fundamentally underspecified, such that models will always need to "guess" the right answer from some space of possibilities. Thus, for each experiment, in addition to reporting model performance, we will report the highest level of performance possible by a hypothetical model employing an optimal strategy.

For all synthetic data experiments, we will use digits as input symbols, and letters and underscores as output labels, with the specific meanings of these symbols varying by experiment. For all experiments, the emission and pattern potential functions are represented with a biLSTM neural network (Hochreiter and Schmidhuber, 1997), and the transition function is represented as a parameter matrix. All parameters are jointly optimized until convergence using the Adam optimizer (Kingma and Ba, 2015).

We evaluate all tasks via exact-match accuracy. That means that we count a model as correct only when it predicts the label sequence exactly correct, and we don't assign partial credit. This turns out to be quite important, as many less-strict evaluation methods are explicitly insensitive to the global structures we are trying to capture. For instance, when evaluating by token-wise accuracy, models are not rewarded for producing globally plausible label sequences, only for ensuring that each individual label is likely in isolation, something that linear-chain CRFs are already capable of.

3.1 Experiment 1: Cardinality patterns

A common source of label interdependencies in sequence labeling is given by global constraints on how often a particular label occurs. Under such constraints, each label can directly depend on each

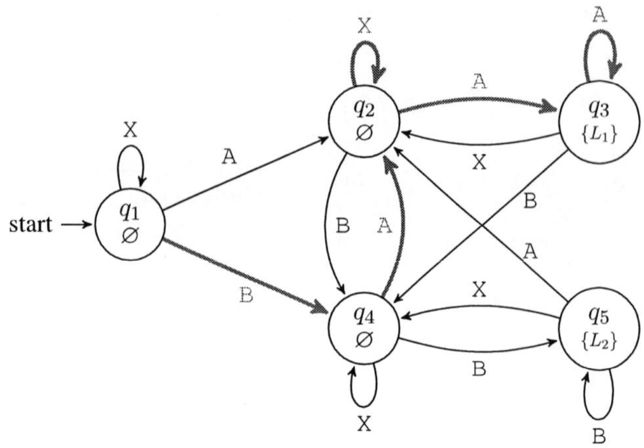

(a) A DFA for for Π. The path through this automaton for the string BAXAA is marked.

$$A = \{\langle q_1 \xrightarrow{X} q_1\rangle, \langle q_1 \xrightarrow{A} q_2\rangle, \langle q_1 \xrightarrow{B} q_4\rangle, \langle q_2 \xrightarrow{X} q_2\rangle, \langle q_2 \xrightarrow{A} q_3\rangle, \langle q_2 \xrightarrow{B} q_4\rangle, \langle q_3 \xrightarrow{X} q_2\rangle,$$
$$\langle q_3 \xrightarrow{A} q_3\rangle, \langle q_3 \xrightarrow{B} q_4\rangle, \langle q_4 \xrightarrow{A} q_2\rangle, \langle q_4 \xrightarrow{X} q_4\rangle, \langle q_4 \xrightarrow{B} q_5\rangle, \langle q_4 \xrightarrow{A} q_2\rangle, \langle q_4 \xrightarrow{X} q_3\rangle, \langle q_4 \xrightarrow{B} q_4\rangle\}$$

(b) A, the set of arcs in Π, which will be used as the label set for the auxiliary CRF.

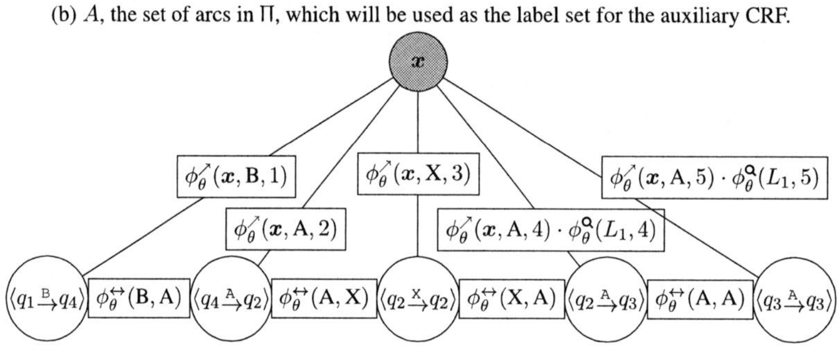

(c) The auxiliary CRF calculating the probability for the arc sequence corresponding to $\boldsymbol{y}$'s path through Π. Since q_3 corresponds to an accepting state for L_1, the emission function incorporates the pattern potential for L_1 at time steps which end on q_3. The resulting probability equals the RPCRF probability for the string $\boldsymbol{y}$.

Figure 2: A worked example for the label string $\boldsymbol{y}$ = BAXAA of an RPCRF with two patterns: L_1 = AX*A and L_2 = BX*B. (a) shows Π, the state-labeled automaton we obtain from these two languages, (b) shows the set of arcs in Π, which will be tags for our auxiliary CRF, and (c) demonstrates how we use our auxiliary CRF to calculate a probability for $\boldsymbol{y}$.

other label. For example, if we know that a particular label must occur exactly once in a sequence, assigning that label to any particular position affects the marginal distribution of every other position. These constraints may be soft, though – for example, in the classification of daily activities from a smartwatch data sequence, users typically go running once a day, but might run twice, or not at all (Kwon and Choi, 2018).

In order to investigate an RPCRF's ability to model such cardinality constraints, we construct a synthetic dataset of $(\boldsymbol{x}, \boldsymbol{y})$ pairs. For each pair, $\boldsymbol{x}$ consists of a single non-zero digit k, followed by nine zeros. The first label of $\boldsymbol{y}$ is always _, and, of the remaining nine labels, exactly k are A, with all others being _. We chose the value of k uniformly randomly, and then uniformly randomly select which k positions should be labeled as A.

Table 1: Example for Experiment 1 (cardinality patterns). The first token of each input specifies the number of As in the output.

$\boldsymbol{x}$	3000000000	9000000000	1000000000
$\boldsymbol{y}$	__A_AA____	_AAAAAAAAA	______A___

As patterns, we use a set of nine regular lan-

Table 2: Results for Experiment 1 (EM acc. = Exact-match accuracy; Opt. str. = optimal strategy).

Model	EM acc. (%)	% Opt. str.
Optimal strategy	14.64	–
LSTM+CRF	11.27	76.98
LSTM+RPCRF	14.61	99.80

guages $\mathbb{L} = \{L_1, \cdots, L_9\}$:

$$L_k = \texttt{\^{}}(\_^*\texttt{a})^k\_^*\texttt{\$} \tag{7}$$

Each L_k matches label sequences with exactly k occurrences of A. As pattern can match only a complete label sequence, and as the languages are disjoint, only one pattern can match any given label sequence. An RPCRF should be able to learn from the first token of the input sequence which pattern should apply to the label sequence, and assign only that pattern a high weight with its pattern potential function, resulting in the model always predicting the correct number of As. Conversely, while a CRF can learn that the A label should be more or less likely depending on the value of k, it has no mechanism for enforcing a specific number of A labels (except in the case for $k = 9$, wherein the output is deterministic).

Table 1 gives examples of some datapoints for this experiment. Table 2 summarizes the performance of RPCRF and linear-chain CRFs on this task. We see that an RPCRF is able to achieve near-optimal accuracy. On the other hand, the linear-chain CRF, unable to directly enforce cardinality constraints, can only achieve approximately 77% of the optimal strategy's accuracy.

3.2 Experiment 2: Agreement patterns

Commonly for sequence labeling tasks, the presence of one type of label in a sequence might be highly informative about the presence or absence of other labels at distant positions in the sequence. For instance, when using sequence labeling to label named entities in text, an entity of type EVENT may be likely to occur in the same document as an entity of type DATE, while there may be no such affinity between entities of types LAW and WORK_OF_ART. In the extreme case, certain labels might be guaranteed to co-occur in a document, or alternatively forbidden from doing so.

To investigate an RPCRF's ability to learn such interactions, we construct a synthetic sequence-labeling dataset which exhibits strong agreement

Table 3: Example for Experiment 2 (agreement patterns): model must learn which pairs of non-zero output labels correspond (A/B, C/D, E/F).

x	0010000100	0011000000	0001000001
y	__A____B__	__DC______	___F_____E

interactions between distant labels. In each $(\boldsymbol{x}, \boldsymbol{y})$ pair, $\boldsymbol{x}$ is a length-ten sequence containing eight zeros and exactly two ones, which represent entities to be labeled. The corresponding $\boldsymbol{y}$ assigns a _ label to all zeros, and a letter from A to F to the two ones. Importantly, these letter labels are selected such that A must co-occur with a B, C with a D, and E with an F. Table 3 provides some example $(\boldsymbol{x}, \boldsymbol{y})$-pairs for this experiment.

We assume a setting where model users know that *some* co-occurrence constraints exist, but do not know the particular letters which can or cannot co-occur. Thus, as patterns, we use a set of $\binom{6}{2} = 15$ languages, with each language matching a label sequence containing two distinct labels exactly once:

$$\mathbb{L} = \Big\{ \texttt{\^{}}\_^* (\alpha\_^*\beta \mid \beta\_^*\alpha)\_^*\texttt{\$} : \{\alpha, \beta\} \subseteq \{\texttt{A}, \texttt{B}, \texttt{C}, \texttt{D}, \texttt{E}, \texttt{F}\}, \alpha \neq \beta \Big\} \tag{8}$$

Our model is thus responsible for learning which label pairs agree and disagree with one another.

Table 4 shows the results on this experiment for an RPCRF and for a linear-chain CRF baseline. As before, our RPCRF-based model achieves nearly optimal performance, while the linear-chain CRF, unable to learn the relationships between distant labels, lags significantly behind. Interestingly, the linear-chain CRF is able to model agreement in *some* cases – namely when the two entities happen to be directly adjacent Due to this, it performs better than the $\frac{1}{36}$ odds we would expect from having it label the two entities independently, but fails in cases where the entities are distant from one another.

3.3 Experiment 3: Battleship

While this paper has thus-far focused largely on CRFs with a linear-chain structure, CRFs are also commonly used for 2-dimensional data in tasks such as image segmentation (Chen et al., 2017). In such a setting, instead of labeling elements of a sequence, individual pixels or grid cells are labeled. Crucially, such a setting usually envisions

Table 4: Results for Experiment 2 on agreement patterns (EM acc. = Exact-match accuracy; Opt. str. = optimal strategy).

Model	EM acc. (%)	% Opt. str.
Optimal strategy	16.67	–
LSTM+CRF	6.97	41.81
LSTM+RPCRF	16.60	99.58

each pixel as directly adjacent to all four of its orthogonal neighbors, leading to a highly cyclic graph structure not amenable to tractable exact inference (Murphy et al., 1999).

With appropriate encoding and patterns, RPCRFs can also be used for labeling such 2-dimensional data. Any 2-dimensional grid can be serialized row-by-row into a linear sequence. Cells which neighbored horizontally in the original grid are still neighbors in the sequence, while vertical neighbors are now separated by from one another by a constant distance equal to the grid width. By writing patterns that are specifically sensitive to labels separated by exactly this distance, we can enable an RPCRF to model interactions between vertically adjacent cells in our original grid.

We demonstrate this concretely with a synthetic task on a 5×5 grid. Somewhere on this grid, a 4×1 battleship is hiding, positioned and oriented randomly. The input sequence $\boldsymbol{x}$ comprises all zeros, except for a single one, at some randomly-chosen cell of the battleship. In the label sequence $\boldsymbol{y}$, each cell occupied by the battleship is labeled A, while all other cells are labeled _. The model's task is thus to guess the position and location of the battleship, given only a single "hit."

Table 5 illustrates some input-output pairs. We use a single pattern, sensitive to two As separated by four _s (i.e., vertically adjacent in the grid):

$$\mathbb{L} = \{\texttt{A\_\_\_\_A}\} \tag{9}$$

This allows RPCRF to be sensitive to vertically adjacent pairs of As in the label sequence (at least when all intervening labels are instances of _).

Table 6 reports the performance of our two models. In this case, the RPCRF-based model does not achieve the performance of the optimal strategy here. This is due to a limitation in the pattern used: while the model can use its pattern to ensure the predicted As are adjacent, it has no mechanism for ensuring that it predicts the correct *number* of As. Nonetheless, even though the provided pattern set cannot capture all structural properties of the label sequences, we still see significant improvements over a linear-chain CRF.

4 Related Work

Our proposed approach is one of many ways for extending a linear-chain CRF in a manner that selectively circumvents the Markov assumption of default CRFs. Here we will briefly discuss some alternate formalisms for defining and working with such 'higher-order' CRFs.

Pattern-based CRFs. A conceptually similar approach to our current proposal are pattern-based CRFs (Ye et al., 2009; Takhanov and Kolmogorov, 2013). As with our regular-pattern-sensitive CRFs, pattern-based CRFs allow practitioners to specify a set of label patterns, allowing the CRF to learn long-distance dependencies by either encouraging or discouraging the presence of these patterns at particular locations of the label sequence. However, the patterns in pattern-based CRFs are limited to exact string matches, while our RPCRFs allow for arbitrary regular-expression patterns. Critically, a pattern-based CRF can only model dependencies as distant as its longest search pattern, while RPCRFs can easily be designed to learn dependencies over arbitrary distances, as our Experiment 1 demonstrated.

Semi-Markov CRFs. Another approach commonly used for allowing CRFs to learn non-local label interactions are semi-Markov CRFs (Sarawagi and Cohen, 2004). Under this formalism, rather than labeling each individual token, a semi-Markov CRF outputs a segmentation of the input, labeling each segment. While segment labels must follow the Markov assumption (each segment's label depends directly only on its neighboring segments), the model's behavior *within* each segment may be non-Markovian. Such models offer an efficient approach to modeling certain types of nonlocal interactions, but these interactions are limited to occurring within the same segment, again in contrast to our model.

Skip-chain CRFs. A skip-chain CRFs (Sutton and McCallum, 2007) is an otherwise linear-chain CRF augmented with *skip-connections*, a number of connections directly connecting otherwise distant labels in the sequence. The exact structure

Table 5: Example for Experiment 3 (battleship). Each input marks a single cell of the battleship, while the output marks all of its cells. Inputs/outputs are shown as 5×5 grids here but are treated as length-25 sequences by models.

	0	0	0	0	0	0	0	0	0	0	0	0	0	0	0
	0	0	0	0	0	0	0	0	0	0	0	0	0	0	0
x	0	0	0	1	0	1	0	0	0	0	1	0	0	0	0
	0	0	0	0	0	0	0	0	0	0	0	0	0	0	0
	0	0	0	0	0	0	0	0	0	0	0	0	0	0	0
	_	_	_	A	_	_	_	_	_	_	_	_	_	_	_
	_	_	_	A	_	_	_	_	_	_	A	_	_	_	_
y	_	_	_	A	_	A	A	A	A	_	A	_	_	_	_
	_	_	_	A	_	_	_	_	_	_	A	_	_	_	_
	_	_	_	_	_	_	_	_	_	_	A	_	_	_	_

Table 6: Results for Experiment 3, Battleship (EM acc. = Exact-match accuracy; Opt. str. = optimal strategy).

Model	EM acc. (%)	% Opt. str.
Optimal strategy	31.25	–
LSTM+CRF	2.50	8.00
LSTM+RPCRF	12.49	39.98

of these skip connections can be specified according to the task, and may even be specified conditioned on the input sequence. This provides a conceptually straightforward way to enable linear-chain CRFs to model long-distance dependencies. While skip connections can be selected to account for many possible types of long-distance interactions, the resulting graphs are highly cyclic, and often require approximate techniques for parameter estimation and inference. Nonetheless, with certain connection structures, tricks are possible to allow for exact training and inference on skip-chain CRFs (Galley, 2006).

Regular-constrained CRFs. Regular-constrained CRFs (Papay et al., 2022) enforce that a model's output sequence *must* match some user-specified regular expression. While this enables linear-chain CRFs to respect non-local label interactions, our proposal allows a CRF to learn the likelihood of regular expressions matching at different positions in the label sequence. Thus, a regular-constrained CRF can be understood as a special case of a RPCRF with a single pattern (the complement of the user-specified language) given a constant potential of zero. While regular-constrained CRFs are limited to enforcing constraints known a priori, our regular-pattern-sensitive CRFs can *learn* when different label patterns are likely or unlikely.

5 Conclusions

This paper introduced regular-pattern-sensitive CRFs, a method for enriching linear-chain CRFs with the ability to learn long-distance interactions which occur within user-specified regular-expression patterns. By representing all patterns in a single state-labeled DFA, and using an auxiliary CRF to represent a distribution over paths through this DFA, we can selectively extend CRFs with non-local features while preserving efficient parameter learning and inference.

Regular patterns are often sufficient to model the relevant structures in the domain, as Experiment 2 illustrates. More complex structures can often be rewritten with regular patterns by assuming a maximum input length (cf. (Mohri and Nederhof, 2001) and Experiment 1). Even when regular-language patterns cannot fully capture the dependency structure of the labels, and imperfect approximation can still yield a substantial improvement, as we found in Experiment 3.

Regular patterns offer a flexible and powerful tool for incorporating domain knowledge into sequence classification models that combine the knowledge-based and data-driven paradigms in a promising fashion. Sequence labeling models can be made to account for specific tasks' output structures by simply specifying regular-expression patterns, without the need to explicitly construct an FST or otherwise adapt the model architecture.

A promising direction for future work lies in the combination of RPCRFs with LLM encoders. The strengths of these two paradigms could prove complementary, and LLMs with RPCRF output layers may make good models for structured prediction tasks such as relation extraction or semantic role labeling, where it is necessary to model both linguistic interactions in the input as well as structural interactions in the output.

Limitations

While training and inference time for RPCRFs are quadratic in the number of arcs in the underlying automaton, this number is worst-case exponential in the number of patterns, limiting our model's use with some large sets of patterns. While some combinations of patterns synergize and yield small automata, we do not have a formal characterization of which combinations of patterns lead to tractable models.

References

Francisco Casacuberta and Colin de la Higuera. 2000. Computational complexity of problems on probabilistic grammars and transducers. In *Grammatical Inference: Algorithms and Applications*, pages 15–24, Berlin, Heidelberg. Springer Berlin Heidelberg.

Liang-Chieh Chen, George Papandreou, Iasonas Kokkinos, Kevin Murphy, and Alan L Yuille. 2017. Deeplab: Semantic image segmentation with deep convolutional nets, atrous convolution, and fully connected crfs. *IEEE transactions on pattern analysis and machine intelligence*, 40(4):834–848.

Alebachew Chiche and Betselot Yitagesu. 2022. Part of speech tagging: a systematic review of deep learning and machine learning approaches. *Journal of Big Data*, 9(1):10.

Jacob Devlin, Ming-Wei Chang, Kenton Lee, and Kristina Toutanova. 2019. BERT: Pre-training of deep bidirectional transformers for language understanding. In *Proceedings of the 2019 Conference of the North American Chapter of the Association for Computational Linguistics: Human Language Technologies, Volume 1 (Long and Short Papers)*, pages 4171–4186, Minneapolis, Minnesota. Association for Computational Linguistics.

Jason Eisner. 2002. Parameter estimation for probabilistic finite-state transducers. In *Proceedings of the 40th Annual Meeting of the Association for Computational Linguistics*, pages 1–8, Philadelphia, Pennsylvania, USA. Association for Computational Linguistics.

Chongzhou Fang, Ning Miao, Shaurya Srivastav, Jialin Liu, Ruoyu Zhang, Ruijie Fang, Asmita, Ryan Tsang, Najmeh Nazari, Han Wang, and Houman Homayoun. 2024. Large language models for code analysis: do llms really do their job? In *Proceedings of the 33rd USENIX Conference on Security Symposium*, SEC '24, USA. USENIX Association.

Michel Galley. 2006. A skip-chain conditional random field for ranking meeting utterances by importance. In *Proceedings of the 2006 Conference on Empirical Methods in Natural Language Processing*, pages 364–372, Sydney, Australia. Association for Computational Linguistics.

Sepp Hochreiter and Jürgen Schmidhuber. 1997. Long short-term memory. *Neural computation*, 9(8):1735–1780.

Diederik P. Kingma and Jimmy Ba. 2015. Adam: A method for stochastic optimization. In *Proceedings of the International Conference on Learning Representations*, San Diego, CA.

Min-Cheol Kwon and Sunwoong Choi. 2018. Recognition of daily human activity using an artificial neural network and smartwatch. *Wireless Communications and Mobile Computing*.

John D. Lafferty, Andrew McCallum, and Fernando C. N. Pereira. 2001. Conditional Random Fields: Probabilistic Models for Segmenting and Labeling Sequence Data. In *Proceedings of the Eighteenth International Conference on Machine Learning*, pages 282–289.

Jinxin Liu, Shulin Cao, Jiaxin Shi, Tingjian Zhang, Lunyiu Nie, Linmei Hu, Lei Hou, and Juanzi Li. 2024. How proficient are large language models in formal languages? an in-depth insight for knowledge base question answering. In *Findings of the Association for Computational Linguistics: ACL 2024*, pages 792–815, Bangkok, Thailand. Association for Computational Linguistics.

Mehryar Mohri. 1997. Finite-state transducers in language and speech processing. *Computational Linguistics*, 23(2):269–311.

Mehryar Mohri and Mark-Jan Nederhof. 2001. Regular approximation of context-free grammars through transformation. In *Robustness in language and speech technology*, pages 153–163. Springer.

Zhalgas Mukanov and Rustem Takhanov. 2022. Learning the pattern-based CRF for prediction of a protein local structure. *Informatica*, 46(6).

Kevin P. Murphy, Yair Weiss, and Michael I. Jordan. 1999. Loopy belief propagation for approximate inference: An empirical study. In *Proceedings of the Fifteenth Conference on Uncertainty in Artificial Intelligence*, page 467–475, Stockholm, Sweden. Morgan Kaufmann Publishers Inc.

Sean Papay, Roman Klinger, and Sebastian Pado. 2022. Constraining linear-chain CRFs to regular languages. In *International Conference on Learning Representations*.

Deepashree Raje and P. P. Mujumdar. 2009. A conditional random field–based downscaling method for assessment of climate change impact on multisite daily precipitation in the mahanadi basin. *Water Resources Research*, 45(10).

Pushpendre Rastogi, Ryan Cotterell, and Jason Eisner. 2016. Weighting finite-state transductions with neural context. In *Proceedings of the 2016 Conference of the North American Chapter of the Association for Computational Linguistics: Human Language*

Technologies, pages 623–633, San Diego, California. Association for Computational Linguistics.

Sunita Sarawagi and William W Cohen. 2004. Semi-markov conditional random fields for information extraction. In *Advances in Neural Information Processing Systems*, volume 17. MIT Press.

Christian Scheible, Roman Klinger, and Sebastian Padó. 2016. Model architectures for quotation detection. In *Proceedings of the 54th Annual Meeting of the Association for Computational Linguistics (Volume 1: Long Papers)*, pages 1736–1745, Berlin, Germany. Association for Computational Linguistics.

Helmut Schmid. 1994. Part-of-speech tagging with neural networks. In *Proceedings of the 15th International Conference on Computational Linguistics*, Kyoto, Japan.

Charles Sutton and Andrew McCallum. 2007. An introduction to conditional random fields for relational learning.

Rustem Takhanov and Vladimir Kolmogorov. 2013. Inference algorithms for pattern-based crfs on sequence data. In *Proceedings of the International Conference on Machine Learning*, pages 145–153.

Sheng Wang, Jian Peng, Jianzhu Ma, and Jinbo Xu. 2016. Protein secondary structure prediction using deep convolutional neural fields. *Scientific reports*, 6(1):1–11.

Nan Ye, Wee Lee, Hai Chieu, and Dan Wu. 2009. Conditional random fields with high-order features for sequence labeling. In *Proceedings of Advances in Neural Information Processing Systems*. Curran Associates, Inc.

From Syntax to Semantics: Evaluating the Impact of Linguistic Structures on LLM-Based Information Extraction

Anushka Swarup[1], Avanti Bhandarkar[1], Ronald Wilson[1], Tianyu Pan[1], Damon L. Woodard[1]

[1]Florida Institute for National Security, University of Florida, Gainesville FL 32611, USA.
Correspondence: aswarup@ufl.edu

Abstract

Large Language Models (LLMs) have brought significant breakthroughs across all areas of Natural Language Processing (NLP), including Information Extraction (IE). However, knowledge gaps remain regarding their effectiveness in extracting entity-relation triplets, i.e. Joint Relation Extraction (JRE). JRE has been a key operation in creating knowledge bases that can be used to enhance Retrieval Augmented Generation (RAG) systems. Prior work highlights low-quality triplets generated by LLMs. Thus, this work investigates the impact of incorporating linguistic structures, such as constituency and dependency trees and semantic role labeling, to enhance the quality of the extracted triplets. The findings suggest that incorporating specific structural information enhances the uniqueness and topical relevance of the triplets, particularly in scenarios where multiple relationships are present[1].

1 Introduction

IE is a crucial NLP task that extracts structured knowledge from unstructured data. Named Entity Recognition (NER) and Relation Extraction (RE) are two essential sub-processes that facilitate IE. They play an integral role in the population of knowledge bases (KBs), where entities serve as nodes and relationships as connecting links. Most recently, NER and RE have been employed to create knowledge graphs for GraphRAG applications (Edge et al., 2024; Han et al., 2024). A popular paradigm, JRE, unifies NER and RE by identifying entities and relationships in a single task from the text sample. JRE garnered significant attention from the NLP community before LLMs emerged. However, research on this topic has become scarce with the advent of LLMs, leaving a gap in understanding their impact on JRE.

The limited studies exploring LLMs for JRE have highlighted issues such as redundancy in extracted triplets and low topical similarity to the target sentence (Swarup et al., 2025). These issues are further exacerbated when there is a possibility of multiple relationships. These problems, coupled with the challenges in evaluation caused by the open-ended nature of the LLMs (Wadhwa et al., 2023), have limited their usage for this task. However, LLMs possess vast knowledge and strong instruction-following capabilities, suggesting their potential to serve as effective joint extractors.

Linguistic structures have been employed as an aid for IE systems through the advancements in NLP. On the one hand, dependency trees (DT) have imparted fine-grained knowledge about the connections between the words in a sentence to neural networks (Tian et al., 2021; Miwa and Bansal, 2016; Chen et al., 2021). On the other hand, Semantic Role Labeling (SRL) has shown close connections with OpenIE triplets (Christensen et al., 2011, 2010). Additionally, constituency trees (CT) have provided a structured representation of input text to the models (Jiang and Diesner, 2019).

This work investigates the potential of using linguistic structures CT, DT, and SRL as additional knowledge to the LLMs to enhance their performance on sentence-level JRE. The goal is to improve their fine-grained semantic understanding from the comparatively shorter context present at the sentence level. Our findings indicate that structural information improves the quality of extracted triplets, especially with smaller models. Additionally, these linguistic structures help LLMs better handle text with multiple relationships, ensuring more accurate and contextually relevant triplets.

2 Methodology

Problem Statement: Given a sentence S and an LLM-based joint relation extractor M, the objec-

[1]Code: `https://github.com/anushkasw/StructLLM`

Proceedings of the 1st Joint Workshop on Large Language Models and Structure Modeling (XLLM 2025), pages 36–48
August 1, 2025 ©2025 Association for Computational Linguistics

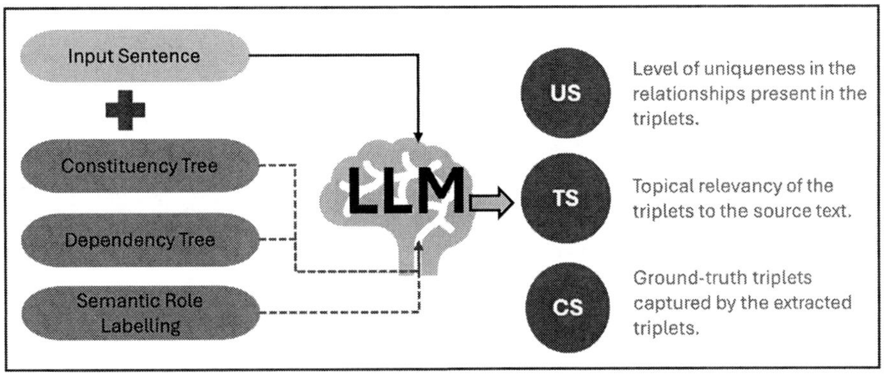

Figure 1: Pipeline to study the influence of linguistic structures on LLMs for JRE.

tive of M is to extract a set of entity-relation triplets of the form $(e1, r, e2)$, where $e1$ and $e2$ are entities, and r represents the relationship between them. Note that information about the entities is not provided apriori. Target relationships may be constrained to a predefined set if required.

2.1 Prompt Engineering

This study investigates the capabilities of LLMs in jointly extracting entities from sentences. A multi-task approach where the prompt instructs the LLMs first to extract all entities from the input sentence and then extract all possible entity and relation triplets was used. This prompting style was used to maximize the LLMs' triplet predictions.

Existing literature shows no significant gain with In-context learning-based (ICL) few-shot strategies for JRE (Li et al., 2023; Swarup et al., 2025). Thus, this work employs zero-shot prompting with two variations. First, when the knowledge of the dataset's relation space is verbalized in the prompt (**rel++**), and second, in an open setting where no such knowledge is provided (**open**). Examples of all prompt types are in Appendix A.3

2.2 Linguistic Structures

Three widely used linguistic structures were selected for this study based on the type of knowledge they provide. First, CTs were incorporated into the LLMs' prompts to assess the impact of syntactic information on JRE. Second, DTs were used to encode both semantic and syntactic relationships, offering valuable insights into word dependencies, even across distant words. Finally, SRL was included due to its strong alignment with the JRE objective, where arguments and verbs can capture the roles of entities and relationships.

2.3 Experimental Setup

Figure 1 depicts the pipeline for this work. This study employs five LLMs as joint relation extractors: OpenChat-3.5 (7B), Meta-Llama-3.1-8B-Instruct (8B), Mistral-Nemo-Instruct-2407 (12B), Gemma-2-9B-IT (9B), and GPT-4o. These models were selected to ensure representation from major LLM families. Multiple parsers were utilized to extract the structural information. Specifically, AllenNLP[2] was used to obtain all three linguistic structures discussed above. Stanza (Qi et al., 2020) was employed to extract CT and DT. As SRL is not supported by stanza, DeepSRL (He et al., 2017) was used as an alternate extractor.

Next, NYT10 (Riedel et al., 2010), TACRED (Zhang et al., 2017), and CrossRE (Bassignana and Plank, 2022) datasets were chosen for this study. Most of these datasets have proven to be challenging for past models. Additionally, the composition of the datasets shows that they have a high percentage of samples consisting of multiple relations, which is a challenging use case. Details regarding the pre-processing steps and statistics of the datasets can be found in Appendix A.1.2.

Subsequently, four experiments were conducted with the configurations: instruction only (**baseline**), instruction+CT (**base+ct**), instruction+DT (**base+dt**), and instruction+SRL (**base+srl**). As the names suggest, these experiments are based on the type of structural information added to the baseline prompt.

Multiple strategies were employed to evaluate the performance of the LLMs for JRE. This work employs traditional metrics (precision, recall, and F1-score) and soft metrics introduced in the Gen-

[2]https://docs.allennlp.org/models/main/

RES benchmark (Jiang et al., 2024). Specifically Uniqueness Score (*US*), Topical Similarity (*TS*), and Completeness Score (*CS*). More implementation details can be found in the source paper and Appendix A.1.4. Finally, the goal of this study was to investigate the performance variations with the *base+dt*, *base+ct* and *base+srl* experiments as compared to the baseline experiments. The Mann–Whitney U test was employed for this purpose to test the statistical significance of the observations ($p\_value < 0.05$).

3 Results

This study investigates the influence of linguistic structures on LLM-based JRE models. As discussed above, both traditional and soft metrics were used to quantify the influence of these elements. Table 2 in the Appendix shows the LLM performances using traditional metrics. The negligible scores attained by the LLMs highlight the impracticality of using these metrics for evaluation. The open-ended nature of the LLM output makes exact matching with ground truth labels almost impossible to perform. Thus, the rest of the study employs soft metrics to assess the quality of the triplets.

Figure 2 depicts the performance of the selected LLMs across datasets and prompting strategies. It can be observed that adding structural information helped enhance the quality of triplets, specifically increasing their uniqueness and topical similarity. However, it had a detrimental effect on the completeness with respect to the ground truths. Fine-grained dataset-specific scores can be found in the Appendix in Table 3.

Structure reduces redundancy in triplets. The findings show that incorporating structural elements such as DT leads to enhancements in triplet extraction across LLMs such as OpenChat, Gemma, and Mistral, as evidenced by the increase in average *US* scores. DT captures crucial syntactical relationships even between distant words in a sentence. This structural information likely enhances the LLMs' comprehension of the text, preventing them from extracting similar relationships. Furthermore, this effect was particularly pronounced for CrossRE, a dataset containing samples from multiple domains, where statistically significant *US* gains were observed.

Structure enhances topical similarity. Incorporating SRL information resulted in more topically relevant triplets across most LLM-dataset combinations, as reflected by the increase in average *TS* scores. Statistically significant gains were observed for Openchat, Llama, Gemma and Mistral across datasets. This suggests that SRL helps LLMs focus more effectively on the language used in the text. SRL outputs closely align with the triplet structure, where arguments often correspond to entities and verbs to relationships. It is likely that LLMs recognize this alignment and leverage SRL to extract triplets. Since SRL outputs are inherently constrained to the sentence context, the LLM's predictions also become more contextually grounded, thereby improving topical relevance.

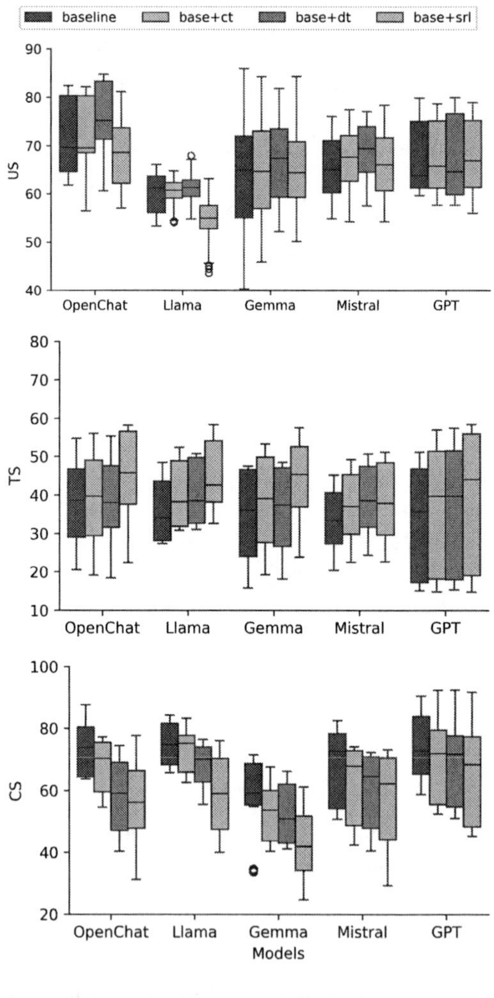

Figure 2: US, TS, CS scores for different LLM-based JRE models across datasets, seeds, and prompting strategies. The x-axis is organized from the LLMs with the fewest parameters to the most parameters. Note that the y-axis range has been adjusted to enhance the visibility of metric variations.

Structure deviates triplets from the ground-truth. The results indicate a linear reduction in *CS* as more advanced structures were incorporated. *CS* measures the comprehensiveness of extracted triplets relative to the ground truth. The observed decline from the *baseline* to *base+srl* suggests that as LLMs integrate more advanced linguistic structures—imparting higher-order and semantic knowledge—their alignment with ground-truth triplets decreases. Previous research has highlighted the limitations of ground truth triplets in most state-of-the-art datasets, suggesting that these triplets are often highly specific and limiting. With the addition of richer semantic information, LLMs tend to generate generalized yet semantically accurate predictions, which may contribute to the decline in *CS*. Additionally, the drop in completeness may also be a byproduct of redundancy reduction. Rather than failing to extract essential information, the model might be filtering out less meaningful triplets.

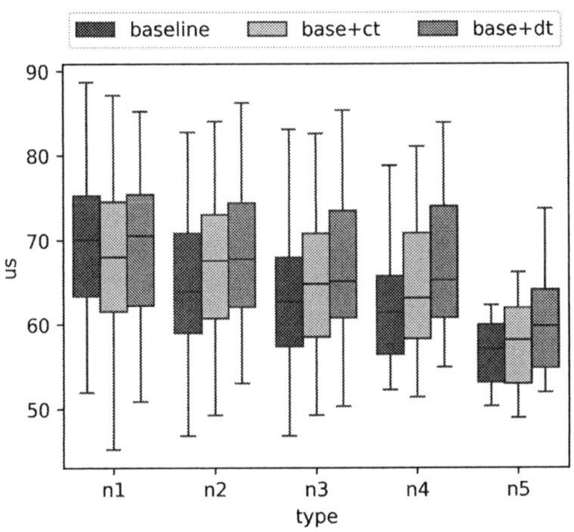

Figure 3: Addition of CT and DT structures prevents uniqueness reduction as the number of relations increases compared to the "baseline" experiments for most categories. Performances are shown across datasets, models, seeds, and prompt types. Note that the y-axis range has been adjusted to enhance the visibility of metric variations.

4 Discussion

The results highlight the redundancy reduction in the extracted triplets, specifically when dependency-based structural information was added to the LLM's prompt. Previous research has highlighted that triplet redundancy increases when the source text contains multiple relationships. To analyze this effect, the *US* scores were examined across sentence categories with varying numbers of ground truth relations. The methodology for this experiment can be found in the Appendix in section A.1.5. Figure 3 indicates that linguistic structures help maintain the uniqueness of extracted triplets compared to baseline LLMs. While the *US* score for *baseline* experiments decreases as the number of relations increases, the *US* scores for LLMs with structural information remain relatively consistent. Additionally, statistically significant gain was observed between the "baseline" and "base+dt" experiments in the *n2-n5* categories. Thus, it can be inferred that linguistic structures help LLMs differentiate between distinct relationships, thereby helping them extract only the most relevant triplets. Some examples of how LLMs can filter out similar meaning triplets by enhancing their semantic reasoning capabilities can be found in Appendix A.2.2.

4.1 Related Works

4.1.1 LLMs for JRE

In recent years, many studies have investigated using LLMs for various IE tasks. Most such studies have focused on the applications of Named Entity Recognition (NRE) (Xie et al., 2023; Kim et al., 2024) and Relation Classification (RC) (Wan et al., 2023; Xu et al., 2023). Very few studies have been conducted for the JRE objective, likely due to the difficulties in evaluation. These studies investigate the potential of using LLMs as zero-shot and few-shot extractors by experimenting with various ICL and prompting strategies (Li et al., 2023; Wadhwa et al., 2023; Swarup et al., 2025). Recently, the GenRES benchmark (Jiang et al., 2024) was proposed to qualitatively evaluate LLM-based JRE extractors.

4.1.2 Structural Modeling for IE

Linguistic structures have been widely used to aid language models for extracting entities and relationships. CTs have been used to provide structured information about the associated text by detailing syntactical knowledge about various grammatical components (Jiang and Diesner, 2019). DTs further enhance this knowledge by highlighting the relationships between words in the sentence, making them a widespread technique in the RC literature (Tian et al., 2021; Miwa and Bansal, 2016; Chen et al., 2021). Finally, SRL has been known to provide semantic understanding of the sentence. They have been employed as a tool in OpenIE systems to extract entities and relations from the text in an unsupervised setting (Christensen et al., 2011, 2010; Barnickel et al., 2009).

5 Conclusion

This study investigates how incorporating linguistic structures influences LLMs' entity and relation extraction capabilities. The results highlight the improved quality of extracted triplets when structural information is incorporated into the LLMs' prompts. This enhancement in quality was achieved through the reduction of redundant triplets (especially in the presence of multiple relationships) and increased similarity to the source text—both critical in real-world applications. For instance, in a KB construction task from finance data where multiple relationships are common, redundant triplets can create unnecessary paths, reducing the efficiency of the KB. In contrast, topical relevance is critical when extracting knowledge from user-facing systems such as chatbots, making extracting the most relevant entities and relationships essential.

Further, the study highlights a potential drawback: the inclusion of structural information for quality enhancement comes at the cost of misalignment from the ground truth labels, which are oftentimes very restrictive. This finding suggests a trade-off between completeness and uniqueness, which should be carefully considered based on the application's requirements. Finally, there is a need to re-evaluate SOTA datasets in IE, as many contain highly specific and constrained labels. Developing datasets with more generalized label spaces would provide a more comprehensive evaluation framework for IE systems in the LLM era.

Limitations

This study highlights the influence of linguistic structures on LLM performance in JRE, using well-established tools to extract these structures. However, linguistic structure extraction can come with inherent noise, as noted in prior research. However, investigating noise reduction strategies, such as pruning the branches of the trees, was not part of the scope of this paper. This avenue can be explored as future work.

Additionally, we acknowledge that the introduction of the structural elements can introduce noise in the extracted triplets. Thus, an assessment of the factuality of the triplets is imperative. However, existing factualness metrics, including the one present in the GenRES benchmark relies on triplet-level LLM evaluation, which preliminary experiments showed as unreliable and difficult to scale. Despite these challenges, we recognize the importance of this dimensions and aim to find ways to incorporate these metrics in future work.

References

Thorsten Barnickel, Jason Weston, Ronan Collobert, Hans-Werner Mewes, and Volker Stümpflen. 2009. Large scale application of neural network based semantic role labeling for automated relation extraction from biomedical texts. *PloS one*, 4(7):e6393.

Elisa Bassignana and Barbara Plank. 2022. What do you mean by relation extraction? a survey on datasets and study on scientific relation classification. In *Proceedings of the 60th Annual Meeting of the Association for Computational Linguistics: Student Research Workshop*, pages 67–83, Dublin, Ireland. Association for Computational Linguistics.

Guimin Chen, Yuanhe Tian, Yan Song, and Xiang Wan. 2021. Relation extraction with type-aware map memories of word dependencies. In *Findings of the Association for Computational Linguistics: ACL-IJCNLP 2021*, pages 2501–2512, Online. Association for Computational Linguistics.

Janara Christensen, Mausam, Stephen Soderland, and Oren Etzioni. 2011. An analysis of open information extraction based on semantic role labeling. In *Proceedings of the sixth international conference on Knowledge capture*, pages 113–120.

Janara Christensen, Stephen Soderland, Oren Etzioni, et al. 2010. Semantic role labeling for open information extraction. In *Proceedings of the NAACL HLT 2010 first international workshop on formalisms and methodology for learning by reading*, pages 52–60.

Timothy Dozat and Christopher D Manning. 2016. Deep biaffine attention for neural dependency parsing. *arXiv preprint arXiv:1611.01734*.

Darren Edge, Ha Trinh, Newman Cheng, Joshua Bradley, Alex Chao, Apurva Mody, Steven Truitt, Dasha Metropolitansky, Robert Osazuwa Ness, and Jonathan Larson. 2024. From local to global: A graph rag approach to query-focused summarization. *arXiv preprint arXiv:2404.16130*.

Haoyu Han, Yu Wang, Harry Shomer, Kai Guo, Jiayuan Ding, Yongjia Lei, Mahantesh Halappanavar, Ryan A Rossi, Subhabrata Mukherjee, Xianfeng Tang, et al. 2024. Retrieval-augmented generation with graphs (graphrag). *arXiv preprint arXiv:2501.00309*.

Luheng He, Kenton Lee, Mike Lewis, and Luke Zettlemoyer. 2017. Deep semantic role labeling: What works and what's next. In *Proceedings of the 55th*

Annual Meeting of the Association for Computational Linguistics (Volume 1: Long Papers), pages 473–483, Vancouver, Canada. Association for Computational Linguistics.

Ming Jiang and Jana Diesner. 2019. A constituency parsing tree based method for relation extraction from abstracts of scholarly publications. In *Proceedings of the Thirteenth Workshop on Graph-Based Methods for Natural Language Processing (TextGraphs-13)*, pages 186–191, Hong Kong. Association for Computational Linguistics.

Pengcheng Jiang, Jiacheng Lin, Zifeng Wang, Jimeng Sun, and Jiawei Han. 2024. GenRES: Rethinking evaluation for generative relation extraction in the era of large language models. In *Proceedings of the 2024 Conference of the North American Chapter of the Association for Computational Linguistics: Human Language Technologies (Volume 1: Long Papers)*, pages 2820–2837, Mexico City, Mexico. Association for Computational Linguistics.

Hongjin Kim, Jai-Eun Kim, and Harksoo Kim. 2024. Exploring nested named entity recognition with large language models: Methods, challenges, and insights. In *Proceedings of the 2024 Conference on Empirical Methods in Natural Language Processing*, pages 8653–8670, Miami, Florida, USA. Association for Computational Linguistics.

Bo Li, Gexiang Fang, Yang Yang, Quansen Wang, Wei Ye, Wen Zhao, and Shikun Zhang. 2023. Evaluating chatgpt's information extraction capabilities: An assessment of performance, explainability, calibration, and faithfulness. *arXiv preprint arXiv:2304.11633*.

Jiangming Liu and Yue Zhang. 2017. In-order transition-based constituent parsing. *Transactions of the Association for Computational Linguistics*, 5:413–424.

Makoto Miwa and Mohit Bansal. 2016. End-to-end relation extraction using LSTMs on sequences and tree structures. In *Proceedings of the 54th Annual Meeting of the Association for Computational Linguistics (Volume 1: Long Papers)*, pages 1105–1116, Berlin, Germany. Association for Computational Linguistics.

Peng Qi, Timothy Dozat, Yuhao Zhang, and Christopher D Manning. 2019. Universal dependency parsing from scratch. *arXiv preprint arXiv:1901.10457*.

Peng Qi, Yuhao Zhang, Yuhui Zhang, Jason Bolton, and Christopher D Manning. 2020. Stanza: A python natural language processing toolkit for many human languages. *arXiv preprint arXiv:2003.07082*.

Sebastian Riedel, Limin Yao, and Andrew McCallum. 2010. Modeling relations and their mentions without labeled text. In *Machine Learning and Knowledge Discovery in Databases*, pages 148–163, Berlin, Germany. Springer Berlin Heidelberg.

Peng Shi and Jimmy Lin. 2019. Simple bert models for relation extraction and semantic role labeling. *arXiv preprint arXiv:1904.05255*.

Mitchell Stern, Jacob Andreas, and Dan Klein. 2017. A minimal span-based neural constituency parser. In *Proceedings of the 55th Annual Meeting of the Association for Computational Linguistics (Volume 1: Long Papers)*, pages 818–827, Vancouver, Canada. Association for Computational Linguistics.

Anushka Swarup, Tianyu Pan, Ronald Wilson, Avanti Bhandarkar, and Damon Woodard. 2025. LLM4RE: A data-centric feasibility study for relation extraction. In *Proceedings of the 31st International Conference on Computational Linguistics*, pages 6670–6691, Abu Dhabi, UAE. Association for Computational Linguistics.

Ryuichi Takanobu, Tianyang Zhang, Jiexi Liu, and Minlie Huang. 2019. A hierarchical framework for relation extraction with reinforcement learning. In *Proceedings of the Thirty-Third AAAI Conference on Artificial Intelligence and Thirty-First Innovative Applications of Artificial Intelligence Conference and Ninth AAAI Symposium on Educational Advances in Artificial Intelligence*, AAAI'19/IAAI'19/EAAI'19. AAAI Press.

Yuanhe Tian, Guimin Chen, Yan Song, and Xiang Wan. 2021. Dependency-driven relation extraction with attentive graph convolutional networks. In *Proceedings of the 59th Annual Meeting of the Association for Computational Linguistics and the 11th International Joint Conference on Natural Language Processing (Volume 1: Long Papers)*, pages 4458–4471.

Somin Wadhwa, Silvio Amir, and Byron C Wallace. 2023. Revisiting relation extraction in the era of large language models. In *Proceedings of the conference. Association for Computational Linguistics. Meeting*, volume 2023, page 15566.

Zhen Wan, Fei Cheng, Zhuoyuan Mao, Qianying Liu, Haiyue Song, Jiwei Li, and Sadao Kurohashi. 2023. GPT-RE: In-context learning for relation extraction using large language models. In *Proceedings of the 2023 Conference on Empirical Methods in Natural Language Processing*, pages 3534–3547, Singapore. Association for Computational Linguistics.

Tingyu Xie, Qi Li, Jian Zhang, Yan Zhang, Zuozhu Liu, and Hongwei Wang. 2023. Empirical study of zero-shot NER with ChatGPT. In *Proceedings of the 2023 Conference on Empirical Methods in Natural Language Processing*, pages 7935–7956, Singapore. Association for Computational Linguistics.

Xin Xu, Yuqi Zhu, Xiaohan Wang, and Ningyu Zhang. 2023. How to unleash the power of large language models for few-shot relation extraction? In *Proceedings of The Fourth Workshop on Simple and Efficient Natural Language Processing (SustaiNLP)*, pages 190–200, Toronto, Canada (Hybrid). Association for Computational Linguistics.

Yuhao Zhang, Victor Zhong, Danqi Chen, Gabor Angeli, and Christopher D. Manning. 2017. Position-aware attention and supervised data improve slot filling. In

Proceedings of the 2017 Conference on Empirical Methods in Natural Language Processing (EMNLP 2017), pages 35–45.

A Appendix

A.1 Implementation Details

This section discusses additional details regarding the experimental methodology used for this study.

A.1.1 Model Configurations

Table depicts the detailed model configuration along with the parameters used for this study.

A.1.2 Dataset Details

NYT10, TACRED, and CrossRE datasets were chosen for this study. Since these datasets were created with the RC objective in mind, they had to be converted into a format compatible with JRE. For this, duplicate samples were grouped, and entity and relation triplets were created from the ground truth data provided. Table 1 depicts the test data statistics of the datasets. It can be observed that the grouping facilitated the possibility of multiple triplets associated with the text samples. Finally, according to the trend in the literature, the original test sets were sampled using three random seeds (13, 42, and 100) to lower the cost of LLM processing and provide variability in the experiments. Some additional preprocessing details for the datasets are as follows:

- **NYT10.** The preprocessed version of the dataset (Takanobu et al., 2019) was used for this study.
- **TACRED.** The dataset contains no_relation relationships in the ground truth triplet. It is impractical and redundant for the JRE objective to make the LLM extract triplets where the entities do not have a relationship. Thus, all triplets with the no_relation label were removed at the preprocessing stage.
- **CrossRE.** This dataset was used as-is.

Table 1: Dataset Statistics

Datasets	#n[1]	#r[2]	n1	n2	n3	n4	>n5
CrossRE	913	17	139	134	104	131	405
NYT10	2003	29	1478	307	89	114	15
TACRED	1154	41	841	201	62	25	25

[1] Number of samples [2] Number of relations in the dataset

A.1.3 Parsers

Figure 4 shows how the linguistic structures are incorporated in the LLM's prompt. More details about the parsers used to extract linguistic structures for this study are as follows:

- **AllenNLP.** This study employs a biaffine dependency parser[3] (Dozat and Manning, 2016), constituency parser[4] based on elmo-embeddings (Stern et al., 2017) and BERT-based SRL parser[5] (Shi and Lin, 2019).
- **Stanza[6] (Qi et al., 2020).** This study employs the shift-reduce constituency parser (Liu and Zhang, 2017) and a deep biaffine graph-based dependency parser (Qi et al., 2019).
- **DeepSRL[7] (He et al., 2017).** This study employs an ensemble of deep BiLSTM architecture for SRL.

A.1.4 Evaluation Metrics

As discussed above, TS, CS, and US were used to assess the quality of the extracted JRE triplets. The original methodology (Jiang et al., 2024) was followed to calculate the metrics. Here are some additional details:

- **TS.** This metric was used to quantify the topical similarity of the extracted triplets to the source text. For this, LDA topic modeling was done to extract 150 topics from the test sets of each dataset.
- **US.** This metric was used to calculate the level of uniqueness among the triplets extracted for each test sample. It was calculated by performing similarity matching on the embeddings of the extracted triplets from one another. The triplet embeddings were calculated using OpenAI's *"text-embedding-ada-002"*, and the similarity threshold was set to 0.95.

[3] https://storage.googleapis.com/allennlp-public-models/biaffine-dependency-parser-ptb-2020.04.06.tar.gz

[4] https://storage.googleapis.com/allennlp-public-models/elmo-constituency-parser-2020.02.10.tar.gz

[5] https://storage.googleapis.com/allennlp-public-models/structured-prediction-srl-bert.2020.12.15.tar.gz

[6] https://stanfordnlp.github.io/stanza/index.html

[7] https://github.com/luheng/deep_srl/tree/master?tab=readme-ov-file

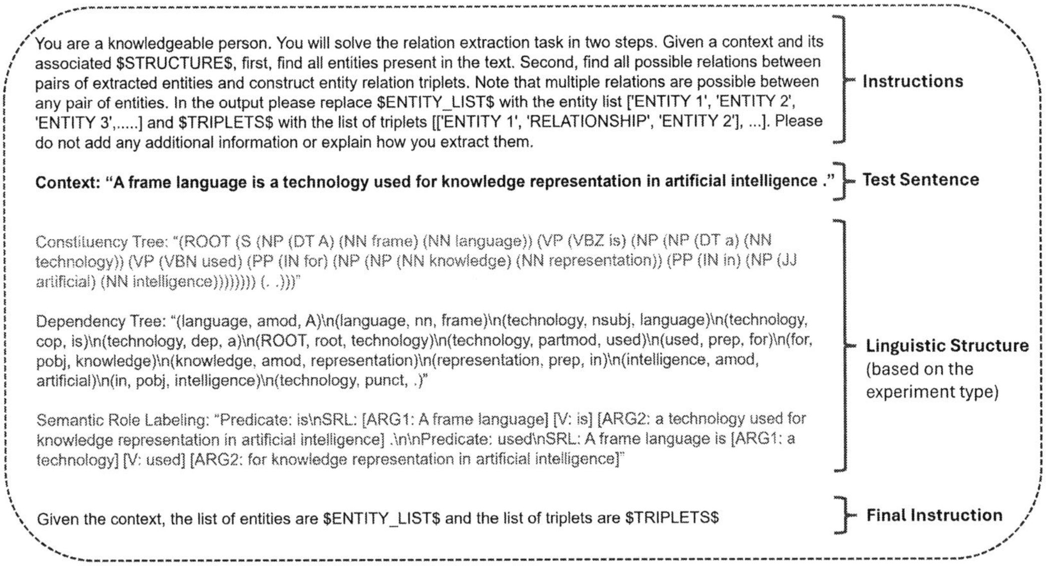

Figure 4: Example of integration of linguistic structures in LLM's prompt.

- **CS.** This metric measures the ground truth triplets covered in the LLMs extraction. It was calculated by performing similarity matching on the extracted triplet embeddings with those of the ground-truth triplets using OpenAI's *"text-embedding-ada-002"* and a similarity threshold of 0.95.

A.1.5 Multiple Relations

To analyze the influence of linguistic structures on samples with multiple relations (discussed in Section 4), we categorized the dataset samples into five groups: n1 (single ground truth relation), n2 (two relations), n3 (three relations), n4 (four relations), and n5 (five or more relations). Table A.1.2 presents the statistics for these categories. Notably, NYT10 contains an insignificant number of samples in the n5 category, while TACRED has very few in both n4 and n5. Consequently, these categories were omitted from calculations for the respective datasets. Additionally, due to the high variability of samples within each category across datasets, we performed 5000 bootstrap experiments by sampling 80, 60, and 100 samples per category for NYT10, TACRED, and CrossRE, respectively, while calculating the metric scores.

A.2 Additional Results

This section showcases results at the dataset and parser-level to provide additional insights.

A.2.1 Dataset-specific Performances

Table 2 depicts dataset-level performances of the LLMs across the four experiments using traditional metrics - precision (P), recall (recall), and F1-score (F1). As mentioned in the main paper, all LLMs attain negligible scores, with GPT as the highest performer. These performances are not a good representation of the LLM extractions. Thus, soft metrics were chosen as the mode of analysis in this study.

Table 3 presents the dataset-level performance of the LLMs across US, TS, and CS dimensions. Overall, the influence of linguistic structures was best observed on the CrossRE dataset. This dataset contains challenging samples from multiple domains such as science, literature, politics, etc., suggesting that linguistic structures can aid in cross-domain understanding of language by LLMs. For the LLMs, smaller models such as OpenChat were most influenced by linguistic knowledge, and the largest model, i.e., GPT, was the least influenced. As the size increases, more and more knowledge is stored in the model's parameters. It is possible that larger models don't require additional assistance as they already contain sufficient knowledge.

A.2.2 Quality Enhancement

Some examples of quality enhancement using linguistic structures are discussed in this section. Table 4 shows two examples where the addition of DT helped reduce the redundancy of the triplets. In the

Table 2: Traditional metric-based evaluation of LLMs for the chosen datasets.

LLM	EXP	NYT10			TACRED			CrossRE		
		P	**R**	**F1**	**P**	**R**	**F1**	**P**	**R**	**F1**
GPT	baseline	11.86	16.48	12.67	10.47	14.42	11.19	3.63	4.57	3.78
	base+ct	11.02	15.93	11.98	9.79	14.13	10.63	2.65	3.78	2.87
	base+dep	10.34	15.76	11.42	8.82	13.13	9.66	2.63	3.42	2.78
	base+srl	9.66	14.24	10.57	7.64	11.83	8.55	2.64	3.40	2.78
Gemma	baseline	4.67	6.67	5.01	2.64	3.41	2.67	2.39	2.69	2.35
	base+ct	2.79	4.68	3.12	2.11	3.43	2.29	1.55	2.01	1.60
	base+dep	2.42	3.97	2.69	2.12	3.04	2.23	1.08	1.55	1.13
	base+srl	2.48	4.30	2.85	1.82	2.51	1.91	0.73	0.93	0.73
Llama	baseline	0.64	2.59	0.93	0.10	0.29	0.12	1.12	2.50	1.46
	base+ct	0.49	2.43	0.75	0.10	0.39	0.13	0.73	2.00	0.99
	base+dep	0.34	1.82	0.52	0.06	0.30	0.09	0.50	1.34	0.67
	base+srl	0.38	2.03	0.60	0.03	0.10	0.04	0.60	1.73	0.83
Mistral	baseline	3.24	8.27	4.11	2.24	5.21	2.79	1.97	2.56	2.06
	base+ct	2.30	5.76	2.91	1.98	4.97	2.51	1.96	2.47	2.04
	base+dep	2.22	5.81	2.76	1.48	3.80	1.87	1.45	2.04	1.57
	base+srl	2.41	6.21	3.02	1.77	4.17	2.18	1.51	2.11	1.62
OpenChat	baseline	1.82	6.30	2.50	0.57	2.54	0.86	1.72	2.46	1.89
	base+ct	1.45	5.54	2.07	0.59	2.79	0.92	0.96	1.72	1.14
	base+dep	1.13	4.71	1.67	0.47	2.26	0.74	0.60	0.87	0.65
	base+srl	1.11	4.56	1.63	0.37	1.58	0.57	0.73	1.06	0.79

first case, the addition of the DT helped the LLM extract a diverse set of triplets, which depicted varied relationships. On the other hand, the LLMs without DT could only extract relations of the type *"performed"*. Similarly, in the second example, the standalone LLM can extract relationships only with the entity *"John Mccain"*. However, adding DT helps the LLM extract unique relations such as *"conference calls, participants, bloggers"*, which requires advanced language understanding for extraction. Note that there are cases of erroneous triplets for all experiments, which should be tackled by future work.

Next, Table 5 presents two examples illustrating the topical improvements achieved by incorporating SRL information. These gains can be attributed to the contextual focus that the LLMs attain when structural information is provided. In both examples, the SRL information helps the LLM pay attention to the core topic of each sentence, i.e., the tour and the oil trade, respectively. Without the added structural information, the LLMs tend to focus on general relations, which are more fact-oriented.

A.3 Prompts

Refer to Figures 5-8 for the prompts used for this study.

Table 3: TS, CS, US scores for different LLM-based JRE models for the chosen datasets. * indicates experiments with statistically significant gain as compared to the baseline experiments ($p\_value < 0.05$).

Model	Dataset	Exp	TS	CS	US
OpenChat	NYT10	baseline	32.81	75.57	71
		base+dt	31.74	57.55	72.99
		base+srl	36.94	56.1	68.82
		base+ct	32.47	65.67	68.65
	TACRED	baseline	41.57	69.93	76.12
		base+dt	41.65	58.18	78.52
		base+srl	47.93	53.95	73.64
		base+ct	41.86	67.4	76.05
	CrossRE	baseline	39.29	76.37	64.71
		base+dt	41.11	59.25	75.11*
		base+srl	49.62	61.09	61.69
		base+ct	41.1	70.97	69.24*
Llama	NYT10	baseline	32.94	75.02	61.3
		base+dt	38.2	64.83	62.03
		base+srl	39.04	48.16	51.75
		base+ct	38.14	70.44	61.39
	TACRED	baseline	39	69.68	64.4
		base+dt	41.51	68.98	62.25
		base+srl	47.64	54.52	58.01
		base+ct	41.49	71.04	62.12
	CrossRE	baseline	35.88	80	55
		base+dt	41.11	70.54	59.38*
		base+srl	47.51	66.51	50.38
		base+ct	40.13	78.07	57.21

(continued on next page)

Model	Dataset	Exp	TS	CS	US
Gemma	NYT10	baseline	28.46	57.74	66.38
		base+dt	29.6	52.73	68.76
		base+srl	36.47	42.47	68.54
		base+ct	31.23	51.22	67.68
	TACRED	baseline	35.52	45.37	64.82
		base+dt	36.72	43.65	68.7
		base+srl	45.21	35.47	70.09
		base+ct	39.52	45.31	66.96
	CrossRE	baseline	39.18	69.83	60.36
		base+dt	41	60.9	62.36
		base+srl	49.99*	51.7	57.1
		base+ct	42.77	62.28	59.82
Mistral	NYT10	baseline	28.58	66.39	66.65
		base+dt	33.85	56.48	70.22
		base+srl	31.99	52.82	67.76
		base+ct	32.2	57.79	68.57
	TACRED	baseline	36.21	66.04	72.22
		base+dt	41.02	58.68	74.51
		base+srl	39.25	57.03	72.55
		base+ct	39.21	60.45	73.62
	CrossRE	baseline	35.62	72.96	57.67
		base+dt	40.9	65.35	61.67*
		base+srl	43.03	62.19	58.27
		base+ct	38.95	68.37	58.74
GPT	NYT10	baseline	28.64	77.84	69.11
		base+dt	31.37	72.49	67.83
		base+srl	32.05	69.15	68.11
		base+ct	30.68	72.64	67.94
	TACRED	baseline	34.01	64.4	70.32
		base+dt	36.81	66.42	73.07
		base+srl	38.23	62.55	73.18
		base+ct	36.67	66.62	72.39
	CrossRE	baseline	38.32	79.89	62.07
		base+dt	42.79	71.74	61.22
		base+srl	47.7	68.21	61.9
		base+ct	42.35	73.86	62.11

Table 4: Examples of US enhancement with DT. Only a small set of triples are shown for each prediction.

Sentence	EXP	Model/ Prompt	US	Predicted Triplets
In 2006, along with Sonu Nigam, Sunidhi Chauhan and Shiamak Davar, Ghoshal performed the theme song of 2010 Commonwealth Games at its closing ceremony, as an invitation to everyone to the following Commonwealth Games in Delhi.	baseline	Llama/ rel++	0.16	(ghoshal, performed, 2010 commonwealth games), (ghoshal, performed, commonwealth games in delhi), (ghoshal, performed, everyone), (ghoshal, performed, following commonwealth games), (sonu nigam, performed, 2010 commonwealth games), (sonu nigam, performed, theme song of 2010 commonwealth games)
	base+dt	Llama/ rel++	0.91	(sonu nigam, related to, sunidhi chauhan), (sonu nigam, related to, shiamak davar), (ghoshal, performed, the theme song), (ghoshal, performed, 2010 commonwealth games), (2010 commonwealth games, located in, delhi), (everyone, invited to, the following commonwealth games)
several times this week – while wrapping up a town hall meeting in des moines , or a conference call with bloggers from sioux city , iowa – senator john mccain and his listeners were told that there was time for just one more question.	baseline	Gemma/ open	0.33	(john mccain, is from, iowa), (john mccain, held a meeting in, des moines), (john mccain, had a call with, bloggers from sioux city)
	base+dt	Gemma/ open	0.96	(town hall meeting, location, des moines), (town hall meeting, part of, conference call), (conference call, participants, bloggers), (bloggers, location, sioux city), (time, limited to, one question)

Table 5: Examples of TS enhancement with SRL. Only a small set of triples are shown for each prediction.

Sentence	EXP	Model/ Prompt	TS	Predicted Triplets
A third UK tour for 2017 / 2018 opened at the Curve in Leicester, and also toured to the Birmingham Hippodrome, the Bord Gáis Energy Theatre in Dublin, the Wales Millennium Centre in Cardiff , the Edinburgh Festival Theatre , the Mayflower Theatre in Southampton and the Palace Theatre in Manchester.	baseline	Llama/ open	0.00	(uk, located_in, leicester),(uk, located_in, birmingham hippodrome), (bord gáis energy theatre, located_in, dublin)
	base+srl	Llama/ open	0.88	(a third uk tour for 2017 / 2018, opened at, the curve), (a third uk tour for 2017 / 2018, opened in, leicester), (a third uk tour for 2017 / 2018, toured to, the birmingham hippodrome), (a third uk tour for 2017 / 2018, toured to, the bord gáis energy theatre), (a third uk tour for 2017 / 2018, toured to, dublin)
feud leads to oil cutoff – supplies of russian crude oil headed to european markets came to a halt overnight, in the latest manifestation of rapidly deteriorating relations between russia and belarus.	baseline	Mistral/ rel++	0.00	(russia, person and nationality, belarus), (russia, country and administrative divisions, belarus), (russia, country and capital, moscow)
	base+srl	Mistral/ rel++	0.98	(feud, leads_to, oil cutoff), (russia, produces, crude oil), (russia, exports_to, european markets)

You are a knowledgeable person. You will solve the relation extraction task in two steps. Given a context, first, find all entities present in the text. Second, find all possible relations between pairs of extracted entities and construct entity relation triplets. Note that multiple relations are possible between any pair of entities. In the output please replace $ENTITY_LIST$ with the entity list ['ENTITY 1', 'ENTITY 2', 'ENTITY 3',.....] and $TRIPLETS$ with the list of triplets [['ENTITY 1', 'RELATIONSHIP', 'ENTITY 2'], ...]. Please do not add any additional information or explain how you extract them.

Context: $TEXT$
Given the context, the list of entities are $ENTITY_LIST$ and the list of triplets are $TRIPLETS$

Figure 5: Prompt used for "baseline" experiments in the "open" setting.

You are a knowledgeable person. You will solve the relation extraction task in two steps. Given a context, first, find all entities present in the text. Second, find all possible relations between pairs of extracted entities and construct entity relation triplets. Note that multiple relations are possible between any pair of entities. In the output please replace $ENTITY_LIST$ with the entity list ['ENTITY 1', 'ENTITY 2', 'ENTITY 3',.....] and $TRIPLETS$ with the list of triplets [['ENTITY 1', 'RELATIONSHIP', 'ENTITY 2'], ...]. Please do not add any additional information or explain how you extract them.

Possible Relation Types: $RELATION_SET$

Context: $TEXT$
Given the context, the list of entities are $ENTITY_LIST$ and the list of triplets are $TRIPLETS$

Figure 6: Prompt used for "baseline" experiments in the "rel++" setting.

You are a knowledgeable person. You will solve the relation extraction task in two steps. Given a context and its associated $STRUCTURE$, first, find all entities present in the text. Second, find all possible relations between pairs of extracted entities and construct entity relation triplets. Note that multiple relations are possible between any pair of entities. In the output please replace $ENTITY_LIST$ with the entity list ['ENTITY 1', 'ENTITY 2', 'ENTITY 3',.....] and $TRIPLETS$ with the list of triplets [['ENTITY 1', 'RELATIONSHIP', 'ENTITY 2'], ...]. Please do not add any additional information or explain how you extract them.

Context: $TEXT$
$STRUCTURE$: $STRING$
Given the context, the list of entities are $ENTITY_LIST$ and the list of triplets are $TRIPLETS$

Figure 7: Prompt used for "base+structure" experiments in the "open" setting.

You are a knowledgeable person. You will solve the relation extraction task in two steps. Given a context and its associated $STRUCTURE$, first, find all entities present in the text. Second, find all possible relations between pairs of extracted entities and construct entity relation triplets. Note that multiple relations are possible between any pair of entities. In the output please replace $ENTITY_LIST$ with the entity list ['ENTITY 1', 'ENTITY 2', 'ENTITY 3',.....] and $TRIPLETS$ with the list of triplets [['ENTITY 1', 'RELATIONSHIP', 'ENTITY 2'], ...]. Please do not add any additional information or explain how you extract them.

Possible Relation Types: $RELATION_SET$

Context: $TEXT$
$STRUCTURE$: $STRING$
Given the context, the list of entities are $ENTITY_LIST$ and the list of triplets are $TRIPLETS$

Figure 8: Prompt used for "base+structure" experiments in the "rel++" setting.

Detecting Referring Expressions in Visually Grounded Dialogue with Autoregressive Language Models

Bram Willemsen and Gabriel Skantze
Division of Speech, Music and Hearing
KTH Royal Institute of Technology
Stockholm, Sweden
{bramw,skantze}@kth.se

Abstract

In this paper, we explore the use of a text-only, autoregressive language modeling approach for the extraction of referring expressions from visually grounded dialogue. More specifically, the aim is to investigate the extent to which the linguistic context alone can inform the detection of mentions that have a (visually perceivable) referent in the visual context of the conversation. To this end, we adapt a pretrained large language model (LLM) to perform a relatively course-grained annotation of mention spans in unfolding conversations by demarcating mention span boundaries in text via next-token prediction. Our findings indicate that even when using a moderately sized LLM, relatively small datasets, and parameter-efficient fine-tuning, a text-only approach can be effective, highlighting the relative importance of the linguistic context for this task. Nevertheless, we argue that the task represents an inherently multimodal problem and discuss limitations fundamental to unimodal approaches.

1 Introduction

In conversation, speakers often make reference to objects, events, or concepts. Words and phrases that are used with referential intent are known as *referring expressions* (REs). Effective communication hinges on the ability of the participants in the conversation to recognize these expressions and to determine what it is that they refer to, i.e., their *referents*. Within the context of a discourse, identification of an intended referent for a given RE may necessitate coreference resolution, i.e., the process of linking expressions that have the same referent. To illustrate this need, consider the following hypothetical exchange, with coreferring expressions underlined:

(1) **A**: Have you seen Schrödinger's cat?
(2) **B**: Yeah, here it is.
(3) **A**: It is looking a bit worse for wear.

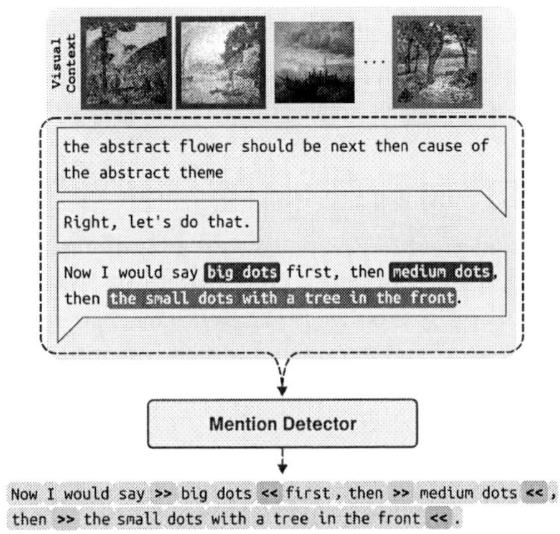

Figure 1: Visualization of the proposed mention detection method. The **Mention Detector** takes as input the most recent dialogue message, preceded by the available dialogue history, and autoregressively outputs an annotated reproduction of the last message while inserting mention span boundary tokens (the start and end of mention spans are represented by >> and <<, respectively) where appropriate. Excerpt shown is from a dialogue collected by Willemsen et al. (2022). Highlighted mentions in original dialogue and visual context with highlighted referent images are shown solely for illustrative purposes: the former is not available to the model at inference time, the latter neither at inference nor at training time.

Without access to the discourse context, "*it*" and "*It*" have indeterminate referents. By having knowledge of the prior contributions to the conversation, it is clear that both pronouns are anaphors with "*Schrödinger's cat*" as their antecedent.

The identification of REs, or *mentions*[1], in various types of discourse is a long-standing natural language processing (NLP) task commonly referred to as *mention detection* (MD). Simply put,

[1]We use *referring expression* and *mention* interchangeably throughout this paper.

Proceedings of the 1st Joint Workshop on Large Language Models and Structure Modeling (XLLM 2025), pages 49–60
August 1, 2025 ©2025 Association for Computational Linguistics

when a given discourse is represented as a text document, the goal of MD is to identify any and all spans of text that refer to some predetermined type of referent, such as named entities or events.

In this paper, we explore the problem of MD for conversation, specifically with a focus on the downstream purpose of reference resolution in visually grounded dialogue. That is, our aim is to identify the REs that have a (visually perceivable) referent in the visual context of the conversation. Of particular interest is the extent to which the linguistic context alone is able to inform predictions for what is arguably, inherently, a multimodal problem. In addition, we experiment with different context windows to investigate how dialogue history affects MD performance. The expectation is that providing access to additional linguistic context in the form of preceding messages will generally lead to increased performance. To illustrate by example, whether the use of "*that*" in the exclaimed utterance "*Take that!*" is referential or instead part of a non-referential interjection cannot be known without additional context.

In line with recent work on generative information extraction (see e.g., Zhang et al., 2025), we frame MD in visually grounded dialogue as an autoregressive language modeling problem. More specifically, we propose to train a model to generate annotated reproductions of utterances: for a given utterance, in the process of generating a copy of the original message content, the model is expected to insert span boundary tokens indicating the start and end of mention spans, when and where appropriate. An illustration of the proposed approach is shown in Figure 1. Our experiments involve the parameter-efficient fine-tuning (Dettmers et al., 2023) of a large language model (LLM) on annotated conversations from two different visually grounded dialogue datasets, namely A GAME OF SORTS (AGOS, Willemsen et al., 2022) and PHOTOBOOK (PB, Haber et al., 2019). For AGOS, we make use of the mention annotations from Willemsen et al. (2023). For PB, we adopt a similar annotation protocol to manually create the required mention annotations for a subset of the dataset.[2]

Results of our experiments with the 8B-parameter variant of LLAMA 3.1 (Grattafiori et al., 2024) are promising, suggesting that the linguistic context can be relatively revealing for our purpose. Note that our findings are in spite of the fact that our datasets are relatively small, our LLM is relatively moderately sized, and our fine-tuning is parameter-efficient. Nevertheless, we must contend with some limitations that are fundamental to unimodal approaches to multimodal problems, as well as the nature of the referential language in task-oriented dialogues. We provide additional discussion on these matters.

2 Background

MD has long been an essential component, or the central focus, of systems addressing various NLP tasks, such as named entity recognition (e.g., Lample et al., 2016; Devlin et al., 2019; Straková et al., 2019), event detection (e.g., Lai et al., 2020), and coreference resolution (e.g., Lee et al., 2013; Poesio et al., 2018). Earlier, rule-based approaches to MD were frequently built atop a dependency parse of a text, and would, over time, incorporate increasingly more powerful statistical models into the pipeline (e.g., Florian et al., 2010; Lee et al., 2013). The required sophistication of the approach generally depended on the downstream task. For coreference resolution, for example, simple heuristics leading to high recall would suffice if other parts of the system could compensate with higher precision (e.g., Lee et al., 2013). Interestingly, comparisons between different coreference resolution systems have often been conducted on the basis of gold, instead of predicted, mentions. This effectively side-steps MD in an effort to focus on isolating the system's downstream performance. However, there tend to be notable performance gaps between these idealized and the realistic scenarios. As Poesio et al. (2023) note, generally, the overall performance of a coreference resolution system has been contingent on the accuracy of the output from its MD component.

Following advances in neural language modeling, approaches to MD based on neural models (e.g., Lample et al., 2016; Poesio et al., 2018; Devlin et al., 2019; Straková et al., 2019; Lai et al., 2020; Yu et al., 2020) have gradually superseded the earlier methods. These increasingly more data-driven methods promised to do away with the need for extensive feature engineering. Particularly consequential has been the adoption of general purpose, pretrained language models based on the Transformer architecture (Vaswani et al., 2017), examples of which include the encoder-only BERT

[2]https://github.com/willemsenbram/mention-detection-vgd, doi:10.5281/zenodo.15500581

(Devlin et al., 2019) and the decoder-only GPT (Radford et al., 2018). BERT-based representations have been the backbone of numerous NLP systems, including those that deal with MD (e.g., Devlin et al., 2019; Straková et al., 2019; Yu et al., 2020).

Of particular interest here are the autoregressive LLMs at the heart of most work on generative information extraction (see e.g., Zhang et al., 2025). Various studies have shown that framing tasks involving structured predictions as autoregressive language modeling problems can be effective (e.g., Cao et al., 2021; Liu et al., 2022; Deußer et al., 2024). Given an unstructured text, the model is trained to return, via next-token prediction, a structured representation of the input. Although the feasibility of this approach has been shown for commonly used benchmarks that involve some form of MD (e.g., Kim et al., 2003; Tjong Kim Sang and De Meulder, 2003), to the best of our knowledge, it has yet to be applied to visually grounded dialogue. In this paper, we explore to what extent we can adapt a pretrained LLM via parameter-efficient fine-tuning (Hu et al., 2022; Dettmers et al., 2023) to the task of MD in visually grounded dialogue using this approach.

3 Method

3.1 Problem description

In general, the goal of MD is to identify all expressions in a document D that satisfy some prescribed definition of a *mention*. When D is a *visually grounded* dialogue, we define it as $D = (V, L)$, where V is the visual context and L the linguistic context of the conversation. A dialogue is considered visually grounded when L contains one or more references to V. That is, within the linguistic context, there exists one or more expressions that have a (visually perceivable) referent that is present in the visual context of the conversation.

3.2 Task definition

In this work, we consider MD in visually grounded dialogue to be the task of identifying all expressions in L for which there exists a referent in V. Here, we focus on visually grounded dialogues of which V is composed of a set of v independent images, $V = \{I_1, I_2, ..., I_v\}$. The linguistic context L can be represented as a sequence of n utterances[3], $L = (u_1, u_2, ..., u_n)$. In turn, each utterance u_i can be represented as a sequence of m_i tokens, $u_i = (t_{i1}, t_{i2}, ..., t_{im_i})$. We think of mentions in terms of spans. We can define a mention span as a contiguous subsequence of tokens from an utterance u_i, denoted as $(t_{ij}, ..., t_{ik}) \subseteq u_i$, where $1 \leq j \leq k \leq m_i$. Together, these tokens constitute an expression that (indirectly) refers to one or more of the images. Note that in contrast with other types of documents, dialogue is interactive and contributions to L are cumulative, happening over time. It is important to account for the incremental nature of conversation when addressing this task.

[3]We use *utterance* and *message* interchangeably throughout this paper.

3.3 Proposed approach

Core to our approach is the framing of MD in visually grounded dialogue as a next-token prediction task. Given the incremental nature of conversation, we process each dialogue at the utterance level, prepending to each utterance a token indicating the speaker. For a given utterance u_i, we train an autoregressive language model f to reproduce exactly the original content of u_i, but with span boundary tokens inserted if and where appropriate to indicate the start and end of mention spans.

Crucially, however, we propose to condition the generation of the target sequence u_i' not only on the current utterance u_i, but also on additional preceding linguistic context, i.e., the available dialogue history, as prior messages may inform predictions. When considering prior messages in the modeling process, we can define the generation of u_i' as $u_i' = f(u_i, H)$, where H is the dialogue history available to the model.[4] The available dialogue history H is defined as a contiguous subsequence of utterances from L, denoted as $H = (u_{i-h}, u_{i-h+1} ..., u_{i-1})$, where $0 \leq h \leq w$, where h is the number of prior messages available to the model and w is an optionally predefined maximum number of preceding messages to be considered. For a visualization of the proposed approach, see Figure 1.

4 Experiments

The language modeling experiments presented in this paper involve the fine-tuning of pretrained models on dialogues from two different, though

[4]We must note that for the experiments reported in this paper, we found that repeating utterance u_i in the input to the model had a positive impact on downstream performance; a slight deviation from the more general definition provided here. For an example of the formatting of training samples, see Appendix B.

closely related, visually grounded dialogue tasks, namely A GAME OF SORTS (AGOS, Willemsen et al., 2022) and PHOTOBOOK (PB, Haber et al., 2019). We first perform cross-validation to score MD performance on each dataset separately. We then assess cross-dataset transfer by training on one dataset and testing on the other. In addition, we investigate the effects of dialogue history on MD performance, i.e., whether the model benefits from having access to preceding messages when making its predictions, by experimenting with different context window sizes, i.e., providing access to different numbers of preceding messages. Finally, as points of comparison, we assess the MD performance of a baseline based on noun phrase (NP) extraction using constituency parsing, as well as that of an encoder-only LLM fine-tuned for sequence labeling.

4.1 Data

Both AGOS and PB are tasks designed around eliciting repeated references to various sets of real-world images—such as those found in the MS COCO (Lin et al., 2014) and Open Images (Kuznetsova et al., 2020) datasets—in conversational settings. Moreover, both tasks have a deliberate asymmetry in their visual contexts that participants have to overcome to successfully complete the task. This ensured that speakers would produce non-trivial REs that made reference to the images' visual content.

4.1.1 A Game Of Sorts (AGOS)

AGOS is a collaborative image ranking task. Two participants are shown a set of nine images which they are asked to rank, in descending order and one at a time, based on a given sorting criterion. The goal of the task is for the participants to, through conversation, arrive at a ranking which both deem satisfactory. Although both participants see the same set of images, they cannot see each other's perspective. The position of the images on their respective screens has been randomized, forcing the participants to refer to the images by referencing their visual content. To ensure repeated mentions of the same referents, the task is performed over multiple (four) rounds, and the same set of images is used each round.

The AGOS dataset consists of 15 dialogues. Each AGOS image set consists of nine images from the same of one of five image categories, namely cars, dogs, paintings, pastries, or phones. Three dialogues were collected per image category.

	AGOS	PB-GOLD
# Dialogues	15	50
# Messages (🗨)	1,800	3,335
# Mentions (🖋)	1,486	2,111
# Characters (**A**)	86,516	96,774
# Words (**AB**)	19,843	22,889
% 🗨 with 🖋	60.33%	61.02%
% 🗨 with > 1 🖋	17.94%	1.95%
# **A** in 🖋	27,574	61,771
% **A** in 🖋: **A** in 🗨	31.87%	63.83%
# **AB** in 🖋	5,708	12,880
% **AB** in 🖋: **AB** in 🗨	28.77%	56.27%
$\bar{X}$ **A** in 🗨	48.06 (43.57)	29.02 (24.83)
$\bar{X}$ **A** in 🖋	18.56 (15.76)	29.26 (23.35)
$\bar{X}$ **AB** in 🗨	11.02 (9.52)	6.86 (5.40)
$\bar{X}$ **AB** in 🖋	3.84 (3.20)	6.10 (4.86)

Table 1: Descriptive statistics for the AGOS and PB-GOLD datasets. *Note.* Explanation of symbols and abbreviations: 🗨 = Messages; 🖋 = Mentions; **A** = Characters; **AB** = Words; $\bar{X}$ = average (mean). Standard deviation between brackets. Scores and standard deviations are rounded to the nearest hundredth.

4.1.2 PhotoBook (PB)

PB is a collaborative image identification task. Two participants are shown partially dissimilar sets of six visually similar images; some of the images will be shown to both participants, while others are shown to only one of the participants. Each participant has three of their six images highlighted. The goal of the task is for the participants to, through conversation and without seeing each other's perspective, identify for these highlighted images whether or not they have them in common. To ensure repeated mentions of the same referents, the task is performed over multiple (five) rounds, and while the set of images shown to participants changes from round to round, the image sets are constructed in such a way that each image is shown multiple times to at least one of the participants.

The PB dataset consists of 2.5K dialogues. Each PB image set, as shown to each participant, consists of six images that prominently feature two objects, each object belonging to a different image category. These two image categories form the "image domain" of the conversation; each image shown throughout the interaction will feature at least one object from each category. For our experiments, we make use of the so-called PB-GOLD subset, as referenced in Takmaz et al. (2022), which

		AGOS				PB-GOLD			
		0	3	7	19	0	3	7	19
LLAMA	P	.896 (.03)	.922 (.02)	.919 (.02)	.923 (.03)	.933 (.02)	.936 (.03)	.940 (.02)	.943 (.02)
	R	.835 (.04)	.865 (.03)	.883 (.03)	.884 (.03)	.927 (.01)	.925 (.01)	.934 (.01)	.937 (.02)
	F_1	.863 (.02)	.892 (.01)	.900 (.01)	.902 (.01)	.930 (.01)	.930 (.02)	.937 (.02)	.940 (.02)
	J	.811 (.03)	.849 (.03)	.856 (.02)	.858 (.02)	.921 (.01)	.922 (.01)	.933 (.01)	.933 (.01)
M-BERT	P	.827 (.04)	.842 (.03)	.843 (.03)	.863 (.04)	.916 (.02)	.918 (.02)	.924 (.01)	.930 (.02)
	R	.812 (.05)	.835 (.03)	.837 (.04)	.853 (.01)	.909 (.01)	.912 (.01)	.908 (.01)	.917 (.02)
	F_1	.819 (.04)	.838 (.02)	.839 (.02)	.857 (.02)	.912 (.02)	.915 (.01)	.916 (.01)	.924 (.02)
	J	.786 (.04)	.815 (.02)	.814 (.02)	.825 (.01)	.909 (.01)	.914 (.01)	.913 (.01)	.920 (.01)

Table 2: Cross-validated mention detection performance of fine-tuned LLAMA 3.1 8B (LLAMA, top) and MODERNBERT-large (M-BERT, bottom) on AGOS and PB-GOLD for four different context windows, i.e., 0, 3, 7, and 19 preceding messages. *Note.* P = Precision; R = Recall; F_1 = F_1 score; J = Jaccard index. Scores are rounded to the nearest thousand, standard deviations to the nearest hundredth.

consists of 50 dialogues for which the authors have provided some annotations at the utterance level.

4.1.3 Mention annotations

In this work, we make use of the manually annotated mention spans from Willemsen et al. (2023). These spans indicate the linguistic expressions that have a (visually perceivable) referent in the visual context of the conversation. More specifically, these are either singletons or REs that are part of an identity relation with other mentions in the linguistic context that have one or more of the images as their referents. For the annotation of the mention spans, Willemsen et al. (2023) were aided by speakers' self-annotations, as participants were required to indicate whether or not a message was meant to include one or more references to one or more of the images. In the messages which contained such references, the longest, most specific spans with images as their referents were marked. The resulting annotations are relatively course-grained. We adopt this protocol for our annotation of the PB-GOLD dialogues. Although PB has no self-annotations, referential ambiguities can be resolved by scrutiny of the full dialogue context. We report descriptive statistics of both datasets in Table 1.

4.2 Model specifications

For each experiment involving the proposed autoregressive language modeling approach, we fine-tune LLAMA 3.1 8B (Grattafiori et al., 2024) using QLoRA (Dettmers et al., 2023) on a single 24GB NVIDIA GeForce RTX 3090. We calculate the loss only over tokens of the target message, masking the loss over tokens that are part of the preceding dialogue context. We make use of the model's existing vocabulary for any special tokens, such as those indicating span boundaries. Fine-tuned model output is generated using constrained decoding. That is, at every time step we dynamically restrict the vocabulary, where the allowed tokens include the next token from the input utterance and any valid special tokens. Hyperparameters are listed in Table 6 in Appendix A. For an example of the formatting of training samples for fine-tuning, see Appendix B. For additional implementation details, we refer the reader to our repository.[2]

4.2.1 Baselines

NP extraction using constituency parsing As mentions are predominantly NPs, we opt for a simple baseline model that automatically extracts NPs from the dialogues using the constituency parser from the Stanza toolkit (Qi et al., 2020). The backbone of this parser is ELECTRA-large (Clark et al., 2020) trained on a revised version of the third release of the Penn Treebank (Marcus et al., 1993). We extract the most expansive spans, but discard certain candidate phrases. For instance, as the dialogues involve text-based conversations in which the participants are not able to see each other, we can disregard various personal pronouns (e.g., "*I*", "*you*", "*me*") as these were not considered to be mentions here.

Sequence labeling with MODERNBERT It has been common practice to treat problems that center on the detection of spans in text, such as MD, as sequence labeling tasks (e.g., Lample et al., 2016). When given a sequence (of tokens), the objective is to assign each element a label such that span boundaries can be inferred. Tag sets are frequently based on the IOB format (Ramshaw and Marcus, 1995): the B tag indicates that an element begins a span, the I tag indicates that an element is inside of a span, and the O tag indicates that an element is outside of a span. For our purpose, we adopt the IOB tag set and fine-tune MODERNBERT-large (Warner et al., 2024) to predict for each token of a given utterance the correct label. As the name suggests, MODERNBERT is a more recent encoder-only LLM that improves upon the original BERT architecture. Similar to the LLAMA-based experiments, for the experiments that are meant to demonstrate the effects of dialogue history on downstream performance, we provide preceding messages as context, masking the loss over all labels except those of the target message. Each model is fine-tuned on a single 24GB NVIDIA GeForce RTX 3090. Hyperparameters are listed in Table 7 in Appendix A. For additional implementation details, we refer the reader to our repository.[2]

Note that in this formulation of the problem using the basic IOB format, it is not possible to accurately label nested mentions. However, there are very few cases of nesting in the datasets used for the experiments reported in this paper. Therefore, this shortcoming has negligible impact on the current evaluation of the approach.

4.3 Evaluation

Our first experiments involve cross-validation on both datasets. We evaluate using the same five-fold cross-validation protocol adopted by prior work on the AGOS dataset (Willemsen et al., 2023; Willemsen and Skantze, 2024), which partitions the dataset along its five image sets. We similarly perform five-fold cross-validation on the PB-GOLD dataset. However, as there is no predefined, deterministic split for PB-GOLD, we split the data randomly. Our second set of experiments concerns an investigation into cross-dataset transfer. This means that we fine-tune models on the entirety of AGOS and test on the entirety of PB-GOLD, and vice versa.

In addition, we test the effects of dialogue history on MD performance. For each of the aforementioned experiments, we fine-tune models for four different context windows, 0, 3, 7, and 19, meaning the models have access to no, three, seven, or 19 preceding messages, respectively.

4.3.1 Metrics

We measure mention detection performance in terms of precision, recall, F_1 score, and intersection over union of ground truth (gold spans) and predicted mention spans at the character level (i.e., Jaccard index).[5]

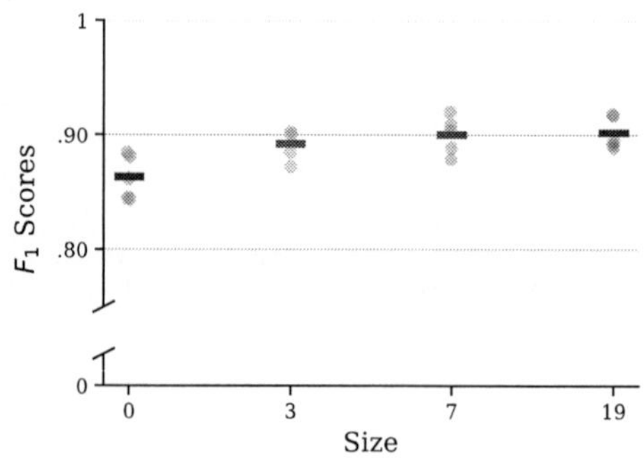

Figure 2: Mention detection performance of fine-tuned LLAMA 3.1 8B in terms of F_1 scores $[0, 1]$ as a function of the size of the context window, i.e., the maximum number of preceding messages considered from the available dialogue history. Shown are results of each fold (dots) and their average (bar) for four different context windows, i.e., 0, 3, 7, and 19.

We calculate precision, recall, and F_1 scores based on exact mention span matches. This means that a predicted mention is considered a true positive only if it matches a gold span exactly and is treated as a false positive otherwise. Conversely, a ground truth mention for which there is no exact matching prediction is considered a false negative.

We use a measure based on the Jaccard index to score the extent to which ground truth and predicted mention spans overlap, which permits the scoring of partial matches. For each message, we find the optimal assignment of predicted and ground truth spans based on the number of corresponding character indices. We calculate the Jaccard index for each pair of matched spans. In the event that no match exists—that is, there is no overlap between a ground truth mention and any of the predicted spans (false negative), or there exists no ground truth mention for a predicted span (false positive)—, the score for this particular span is 0.

All the aforementioned mention detection metrics are bound $[0, 1]$, with higher scores indicating better performance.

5 Results

Before reporting the results of our fine-tuning experiments, we first highlight some of the descriptive statistics reported in Table 1 to aid in understanding the composition of the data. As shown in Table 1, PB-GOLD contains over three times

[5]Character-level evaluation avoids tokenization issues when span boundary tokens are placed within words.

	🚗	🐕	🖌	🎂	📱	$\bar{X}$
P	.881	.954	.934	.912	.933	.923 (.03)
R	.897	.842	.902	.924	.855	.884 (.03)
F_1	.889	.894	.918	.918	.892	.902 (.01)
J	.853	.823	.881	.874	.857	.858 (.02)

Table 3: Cross-validated mention detection performance of fine-tuned LLAMA 3.1 8B on AGOS based on a context window of 19, i.e., a dialogue history consisting of 19 preceding messages. Results are shown for each fold as well as their average ($\bar{X}$). *Note.* P = Precision; R = Recall; F_1 = F_1 score; J = Jaccard index; Symbols represent folds: 🚗 = Cars; 🐕 = Dogs; 🖌 = Paintings; 🎂 = Pastries; 📱 = Phones. Standard deviation between brackets. Scores are rounded to the nearest thousand, standard deviations to the nearest hundredth.

more dialogues than AGOS. However, on average, the AGOS dialogues are considerably longer and have almost twice as many messages per dialogue. While the percentage of messages with mentions is comparable, AGOS has a much higher rate of messages that contain more than one mention than PB-GOLD. Nevertheless, mentions make up notably less of the overall content of the AGOS dialogues than of the PB-GOLD dialogues; the number of characters and words dedicated to mentions relative to the total number of characters and words in the messages is substantially lower for AGOS than for PB-GOLD. Finally, the average AGOS mention is shorter than the average PB-GOLD mention.

5.1 Cross-validation

Shown in Table 2 are the cross-validated results from fine-tuning and evaluating models on the AGOS and PB-GOLD datasets. For each context window, scores are reported as averages over all folds for each MD performance metric. In addition, the results reported in Table 3 are from fine-tuning and evaluating LLAMA on the AGOS dataset using the maximum context window size we considered for this work, i.e., a context window of size 19. In Table 3, scores are shown per fold in addition to their averages over all folds, for each MD performance metric. We found that, despite some variance between folds, scores resulting from fine-tuning LLAMA were relatively high overall. In comparison, the performance of MODERNBERT is relatively competitive, but it does lag behind that of LLAMA. The observed results suggest that the models were, on average, somewhat more performant on the PB-GOLD than they were on the AGOS data. Moreover, we observed that the models generally benefited from an increase in context window size; on average, we found that providing the models with a greater number of preceding messages increased MD performance, but noted that there were diminishing returns. The observed trend was somewhat more apparent for AGOS than for PB-GOLD. Figure 2 provides a visualization of this trend based on the F_1 scores for AGOS.

5.2 Cross-dataset transfer

Table 4 shows results from fine-tuning models on AGOS and testing on PB-GOLD (AGOS $\rightarrow$ PB-GOLD), and vice versa (PB-GOLD $\rightarrow$ AGOS). Although scores were shown to trail those of the cross-validation experiments, the observed MD performance was still indicative of a relatively high degree of successful transfer overall. Again, LLAMA's performance was shown to exceed that of MODERNBERT. A noteworthy observation was that AGOS $\rightarrow$ PB-GOLD consistently resulted in higher scores than PB-GOLD $\rightarrow$ AGOS on all MD performance metrics. Similarly to results from our cross-validation experiments, we observed that, on average, an increase in the size of the context window tended to result in improved performance. These findings suggest that providing the models with at least some preceding messages can already be beneficial.

5.3 Comparison with NP extraction

The results reported in Table 5 show the MD performance of a method based on constituency parsing for the automatic extraction of NPs. Although recall may seem relatively high considering that the focus of this baseline model was solely on NP extraction, it bears repeating that most mentions tend to be NPs, though they are not always presented in a straightforward, parsable manner or context. Perhaps unsurprisingly, especially when comparing against our proposed approach, this naive method for MD is relatively imprecise, as the false positive rate ends up being relatively high when predicting virtually all NPs to be referential in nature.

5.4 Error analysis

When examining the output generated by LLAMA, we found various errors to be consistent between the different context windows. Although the models appeared to be relatively robust against the noise in the input, certain mentions were partially, or entirely, missed, as a result of ungrammatical phrasing. For partial matches, we observed some

		AGOS → PB-GOLD				PB-GOLD → AGOS			
		0	3	7	19	0	3	7	19
LLAMA	P	.798	.859	.864	.886	.775	.803	.810	.820
	R	.806	.838	.858	.845	.687	.676	.713	.744
	F_1	.802	.848	.861	.865	.728	.734	.758	.780
	J	.777	.816	.834	.839	.668	.666	.694	.722
M-BERT	P	.725	.768	.778	.795	.707	.735	.774	.777
	R	.650	.694	.687	.735	.610	.641	.704	.723
	F_1	.685	.729	.730	.764	.655	.685	.737	.749
	J	.662	.704	.698	.737	.595	.616	.665	.688

Table 4: Mention detection performance of fine-tuned LLAMA 3.1 8B (LLAMA, top) and MODERNBERT-large (M-BERT, bottom) in cross-data transfer experiments for four different context windows, i.e., 0, 3, 7, and 19 preceding messages. **AGOS → PB-GOLD** indicates training on AGOS and testing on PB-GOLD; **PB-GOLD → AGOS** indicates training on PB-GOLD and testing on AGOS. *Note.* P = Precision; R = Recall; F_1 = F_1 score; J = Jaccard index. Scores are rounded to the nearest thousand, standard deviations to the nearest hundredth.

	AGOS	PB-GOLD
P	.411	.377
R	.764	.607
F_1	.535	.465
J	.453	.530

Table 5: Mention detection performance of the Stanza NP extraction baseline. *Note.* P = Precision; R = Recall; F_1 = F_1 score; J = Jaccard index. Standard deviation between brackets. Scores are rounded to the nearest thousand, standard deviations to the nearest hundredth.

recurring errors in relation to structural ambiguities, leading to the exclusion of relative clauses or prepositional phrases, and the splitting of single into multiple mentions or the merging of multiple mentions into a single span. Furthermore, we found instances of ambiguous pronoun usage to be relatively frequent among errors, such as in the phrases *"let's go for it"* and *"let's do it"*, in which the use of *"it"* is referential, but it is not recognized as such without additional context. Interestingly, providing access to preceding messages ends up resolving the inaccuracy for the former and not for the latter, even though these seem to be very similar cases on the surface. Conversely, we also observed cases where usage of (pro)nouns was incorrectly predicted to be referential. Again, some of these errors were resolved by providing the model access to the dialogue history.

6 Discussion

In this paper, we explored the potential of an approach to mention detection (MD) in visually grounded dialogue based on autoregressive language modeling. Results from our experiments on conversations from the visually grounded dialogue tasks A GAME OF SORTS (AGOS, Willemsen et al., 2022) and PHOTOBOOK (PB, Haber et al., 2019) were promising, showing that a text-only approach that involves the parameter-efficient fine-tuning of LLMs to generate annotated reproductions of utterances can be effective. Moreover, we showed that providing the models with additional context from the dialogue history—that is, any messages that preceded the utterance under consideration—generally benefits performance. Although these findings were largely consistent between the competing methods presented in this work, within our experimental setup the generative approach to information extraction using the fine-tuned, decoder-only LLAMA model was shown to consistently outperform the sequence labeling approach based on the fine-tuned, encoder-only MODERNBERT.

Results from our cross-validation experiments showed that the models, on average, achieved better performance on the PB-GOLD than on the AGOS dataset. The cross-dataset transfer experiments revealed a notable performance gap between the two datasets; fine-tuning on the AGOS data seemed to result in the models being better able to generalize beyond their specific conversational domain than when fine-tuning on the PB-GOLD data. These findings suggest that AGOS offers a more challenging testbed when it comes to MD, as it was explored in this work, than PB-GOLD. Given that the primary focus of the PB task is the correct identification of images, participants' language use is disproportionally reserved for referential purposes. This was made apparent through a quantified characterization of the PB-GOLD mentions, indicating that mentions made up nearly two-thirds of the linguistic content of the dialogues. In contrast, with image identification being a secondary objective, mentions make up just shy of one-third of the linguistic content of the AGOS dialogues. In addition, mentions in the PB-GOLD dialogues are considerably longer, on average, than those in the AGOS dialogues. When qualitatively examining the mentions from both datasets, it becomes clear that the incidence rate of mentions that resemble image caption-like descriptions is notably higher for PB-GOLD than for AGOS. By and large, our findings suggest that AGOS offers its referring language use in a richer linguistic context than PB-GOLD, which aids the models' ability to generalize.

That being said, it would be reasonable to assume that the incidence rate of mentions in these task-oriented dialogues from both datasets is high compared to that of organic, non-task-oriented conversations. Conversations can go long stretches of time without the mention of a visually perceivable referent. Our approach relies heavily on there being exploitable regularities in the linguistic context. The extent to which conversations with comparatively sparse mention occurrences, and that take place outside of task-oriented settings, still exhibit such actionable patterns is, as of yet, unclear. For both AGOS and PB-GOLD, the probability that a given linguistic expression (indirectly) points to a referent that is visually perceivable by at least one of the participants in the conversation is high, simply as a consequence of the situational context, as the images are the focal point of the conversations. Discerning, from the linguistic context alone, whether an RE has such a referent becomes far more challenging, if not impossible, when the configuration of the visual context of the conversation is less constrained, more dynamic, and cannot be anticipated ahead of time. In other words, we may still be able to extract mention candidates with a high degree of accuracy, but the number of false positives—by which we here mean any candidates that currently have no visually perceivable referents—is likely to be significantly higher; this outcome reminds of the high recall settings favored by aforementioned prior work on coreference resolution.

Inevitably, a general solution to the problem will require a cross-modal approach. Although we make no assumptions regarding the manner of encoding, the visual information must somehow be incorporated to validate whether candidate mentions indeed have a referent in the visual context; even when the linguistic context strongly implies the existence of such a referent, we simply cannot be certain without a review of the visual context. Moreover, we are likely to see that end-to-end approaches will increasingly be favored over modular systems when it comes to addressing downstream tasks that have historically relied on some form of MD, but for which MD is simply a means to an end. Nevertheless, we expect that MD as a task in and of itself will remain relevant for niche applications for the foreseeable future. For one, it may continue to serve as a benchmark for the information extraction capabilities of models under varying conditions. Perhaps more interestingly, however, are real-world applications, such as its use as an information extraction tool for corpus linguistics.

Limitations

In this work, the focus has been on detecting REs that have a (visually perceivable) referent in the visual context of a conversation. Only singletons and mentions in an identity relation were considered, contingent on their referent being one or more of the images in the visual context. It is worth noting that there are some consequential differences between the images used by AGOS and PB. Where the focus of each AGOS image was on (an iconic view of) one entity from some image category, PB images depicted more complex scenes, purposely featuring multiple entities from different image categories. Perhaps unsurprisingly, when the task involves identification within a visually grounded conversational context, we find that the more complex the scene, the more frequently we have to consider a bridging relationship between mentions as a surrogate for identity. This highlights a complication with respect to the annotation of this domain that becomes increasingly problematic: the noisier (or more complex) the language use, the more ambiguous the boundaries. We expect this to be even more evident in unrestricted, spoken dialogue.

Regarding our cross-validation experiments, results were based on a five-fold split of the datasets. The AGOS dataset has a preferred partitioning that ensures minimal data leakage between the training and test data. For PB-GOLD, however, we did not find a sensible, deterministic split, as even when image domains were seemingly mutually exclusive, in reality there were frequent intrusions from other image categories. For instance, *people*—

which happens to be one of the author-defined image categories—are present in the vast majority of the photographs, often as salient entities, and frequently referenced as a result. Although we do not believe this has affected our overall conclusions, the random splitting may have resulted in inflated scores in the PB-GOLD cross-validation experiments. In addition, the language used in the dialogues from both datasets is exclusively English, meaning the experiments reported in this paper do not provide explicit insight into the extent to which the approach generalizes to other languages.

Finally, we have evaluated the proposed approach with one LLM undergoing a parameter-efficient fine-tuning regimen. We have not investigated performance differences between full-parameter and parameter-efficient fine-tuning, nor have we tested the extent to which other generative LLMs are able to perform the task. In addition, more exhaustive hyperparameter tuning has the potential to improve results further. It is conceivable that more optimal hyperparameters exist that could narrow the observed performance gap between LLAMA and MODERNBERT on this task. However, it would mainly serve to underscore the general importance of the linguistic context and demonstrate the viability of either approach.

Acknowledgements

This work was partially supported by the Wallenberg AI, Autonomous Systems and Software Program (WASP) funded by the Knut and Alice Wallenberg Foundation. The authors would like to thank Dmytro Kalpakchi, Jim O'Regan, Travis Wiltshire, Chris Emmery, Martina Rossi, and the anonymous reviewers for their helpful comments.

References

Nicola De Cao, Gautier Izacard, Sebastian Riedel, and Fabio Petroni. 2021. Autoregressive Entity Retrieval. In *9th International Conference on Learning Representations, ICLR 2021, Virtual Event, Austria, May 3-7, 2021*.

Kevin Clark, Minh-Thang Luong, Quoc V. Le, and Christopher D. Manning. 2020. ELECTRA: Pre-training Text Encoders as Discriminators Rather Than Generators. In *8th International Conference on Learning Representations, ICLR 2020, Addis Ababa, Ethiopia, April 26-30, 2020*.

Tim Dettmers, Artidoro Pagnoni, Ari Holtzman, and Luke Zettlemoyer. 2023. QLoRA: Efficient Finetuning of Quantized LLMs. In *Advances in Neural Information Processing Systems*, volume 36, pages 10088–10115. Curran Associates, Inc.

Tobias Deußer, Lars Hillebrand, Christian Bauckhage, and Rafet Sifa. 2024. Informed Named Entity Recognition Decoding for Generative Language Models. In *2024 IEEE International Conference on Big Data (BigData)*, pages 6001–6010.

Jacob Devlin, Ming-Wei Chang, Kenton Lee, and Kristina Toutanova. 2019. BERT: Pre-training of Deep Bidirectional Transformers for Language Understanding. In *Proceedings of the 2019 Conference of the North American Chapter of the Association for Computational Linguistics: Human Language Technologies, Volume 1 (Long and Short Papers)*, pages 4171–4186, Minneapolis, Minnesota. Association for Computational Linguistics.

Radu Florian, John Pitrelli, Salim Roukos, and Imed Zitouni. 2010. Improving Mention Detection Robustness to Noisy Input. In *Proceedings of the 2010 Conference on Empirical Methods in Natural Language Processing*, pages 335–345, Cambridge, MA. Association for Computational Linguistics.

Aaron Grattafiori, Abhimanyu Dubey, Abhinav Jauhri, Abhinav Pandey, Abhishek Kadian, Ahmad Al-Dahle, Aiesha Letman, Akhil Mathur, Alan Schelten, Alex Vaughan, Amy Yang, Angela Fan, Anirudh Goyal, Anthony Hartshorn, Aobo Yang, Archi Mitra, Archie Sravankumar, Artem Korenev, Arthur Hinsvark, and 542 others. 2024. The Llama 3 Herd of Models. _eprint: 2407.21783.

Janosch Haber, Tim Baumgärtner, Ece Takmaz, Lieke Gelderloos, Elia Bruni, and Raquel Fernández. 2019. The PhotoBook Dataset: Building Common Ground through Visually-Grounded Dialogue. In *Proceedings of the 57th Annual Meeting of the Association for Computational Linguistics*, pages 1895–1910, Florence, Italy. Association for Computational Linguistics.

Edward J. Hu, Yelong Shen, Phillip Wallis, Zeyuan Allen-Zhu, Yuanzhi Li, Shean Wang, Lu Wang, and Weizhu Chen. 2022. LoRA: Low-Rank Adaptation of Large Language Models. In *The Tenth International Conference on Learning Representations, ICLR 2022, Virtual Event, April 25-29, 2022*.

Jin-Dong Kim, Tomoko Ohta, Yuka Tateisi, and Jun'ichi Tsujii. 2003. GENIA corpus - a semantically annotated corpus for bio-textmining. In *Proceedings of the Eleventh International Conference on Intelligent Systems for Molecular Biology*, pages 180–182, Brisbane, Australia.

Alina Kuznetsova, Hassan Rom, Neil Alldrin, Jasper Uijlings, Ivan Krasin, Jordi Pont-Tuset, Shahab Kamali, Stefan Popov, Matteo Malloci, Alexander Kolesnikov, Tom Duerig, and Vittorio Ferrari. 2020. The Open Images Dataset V4: Unified image classification, object detection, and visual relationship detection at scale. *International Journal of Computer Vision*, 128(7):1956–1981.

Viet Dac Lai, Tuan Ngo Nguyen, and Thien Huu Nguyen. 2020. Event Detection: Gate Diversity and Syntactic Importance Scores for Graph Convolution Neural Networks. In *Proceedings of the 2020 Conference on Empirical Methods in Natural Language Processing (EMNLP)*, pages 5405–5411, Online. Association for Computational Linguistics.

Guillaume Lample, Miguel Ballesteros, Sandeep Subramanian, Kazuya Kawakami, and Chris Dyer. 2016. Neural Architectures for Named Entity Recognition. In *Proceedings of the 2016 Conference of the North American Chapter of the Association for Computational Linguistics: Human Language Technologies*, pages 260–270, San Diego, California. Association for Computational Linguistics.

Heeyoung Lee, Angel Chang, Yves Peirsman, Nathanael Chambers, Mihai Surdeanu, and Dan Jurafsky. 2013. Deterministic Coreference Resolution Based on Entity-Centric, Precision-Ranked Rules. *Computational Linguistics*, 39(4):885–916.

Tsung-Yi Lin, Michael Maire, Serge Belongie, James Hays, Pietro Perona, Deva Ramanan, Piotr Dollár, and C. Lawrence Zitnick. 2014. Microsoft COCO: Common Objects in Context. In *Computer Vision – ECCV 2014*, pages 740–755, Cham. Springer International Publishing.

Tianyu Liu, Yuchen Eleanor Jiang, Nicholas Monath, Ryan Cotterell, and Mrinmaya Sachan. 2022. Autoregressive Structured Prediction with Language Models. In *Findings of the Association for Computational Linguistics: EMNLP 2022*, pages 993–1005, Abu Dhabi, United Arab Emirates. Association for Computational Linguistics.

Mitchell P. Marcus, Beatrice Santorini, and Mary Ann Marcinkiewicz. 1993. Building a Large Annotated Corpus of English: The Penn Treebank. *Computational Linguistics*, 19(2):313–330.

Massimo Poesio, Yulia Grishina, Varada Kolhatkar, Nafise Moosavi, Ina Roesiger, Adam Roussel, Fabian Simonjetz, Alexandra Uma, Olga Uryupina, Juntao Yu, and Heike Zinsmeister. 2018. Anaphora Resolution with the ARRAU Corpus. In *Proceedings of the First Workshop on Computational Models of Reference, Anaphora and Coreference*, pages 11–22, New Orleans, Louisiana. Association for Computational Linguistics.

Massimo Poesio, Juntao Yu, Silviu Paun, Abdulrahman Aloraini, Pengcheng Lu, Janosch Haber, and Derya Cokal. 2023. Computational Models of Anaphora. *Annual Review of Linguistics*, 9:561–587.

Peng Qi, Yuhao Zhang, Yuhui Zhang, Jason Bolton, and Christopher D. Manning. 2020. Stanza: A Python Natural Language Processing Toolkit for Many Human Languages. In *Proceedings of the 58th Annual Meeting of the Association for Computational Linguistics: System Demonstrations*, pages 101–108, Online. Association for Computational Linguistics.

Alec Radford, Karthik Narasimhan, Tim Salimans, and Ilya Sutskever. 2018. Improving language understanding by generative pre-training.

Lance Ramshaw and Mitch Marcus. 1995. Text Chunking using Transformation-Based Learning. In *Proceedings of the Third Workshop on Very Large Corpora*, pages 82–94.

Jana Straková, Milan Straka, and Jan Hajic. 2019. Neural Architectures for Nested NER through Linearization. In *Proceedings of the 57th Annual Meeting of the Association for Computational Linguistics*, pages 5326–5331, Florence, Italy. Association for Computational Linguistics.

Ece Takmaz, Sandro Pezzelle, and Raquel Fernández. 2022. Less Descriptive yet Discriminative: Quantifying the Properties of Multimodal Referring Utterances via CLIP. In *Proceedings of the Workshop on Cognitive Modeling and Computational Linguistics*, pages 36–42, Dublin, Ireland. Association for Computational Linguistics.

Erik F. Tjong Kim Sang and Fien De Meulder. 2003. Introduction to the CoNLL-2003 Shared Task: Language-Independent Named Entity Recognition. In *Proceedings of the Seventh Conference on Natural Language Learning at HLT-NAACL 2003*, pages 142–147.

Ashish Vaswani, Noam Shazeer, Niki Parmar, Jakob Uszkoreit, Llion Jones, Aidan N Gomez, Łukasz Kaiser, and Illia Polosukhin. 2017. Attention is All you Need. In *Advances in Neural Information Processing Systems*, volume 30. Curran Associates, Inc.

Benjamin Warner, Antoine Chaffin, Benjamin Clavié, Orion Weller, Oskar Hallström, Said Taghadouini, Alexis Gallagher, Raja Biswas, Faisal Ladhak, Tom Aarsen, Nathan Cooper, Griffin Adams, Jeremy Howard, and Iacopo Poli. 2024. Smarter, Better, Faster, Longer: A Modern Bidirectional Encoder for Fast, Memory Efficient, and Long Context Finetuning and Inference. _eprint: 2412.13663.

Bram Willemsen, Dmytro Kalpakchi, and Gabriel Skantze. 2022. Collecting Visually-Grounded Dialogue with A Game Of Sorts. In *Proceedings of the Thirteenth Language Resources and Evaluation Conference*, pages 2257–2268, Marseille, France. European Language Resources Association.

Bram Willemsen, Livia Qian, and Gabriel Skantze. 2023. Resolving References in Visually-Grounded Dialogue via Text Generation. In *Proceedings of the 24th Meeting of the Special Interest Group on Discourse and Dialogue*, pages 457–469, Prague, Czechia. Association for Computational Linguistics.

Bram Willemsen and Gabriel Skantze. 2024. Referring Expression Generation in Visually Grounded Dialogue with Discourse-aware Comprehension Guiding. In *Proceedings of the 17th International Natural Language Generation Conference*, pages 453–469, Tokyo, Japan. Association for Computational Linguistics.

Juntao Yu, Bernd Bohnet, and Massimo Poesio. 2020. Neural Mention Detection. In *Proceedings of the Twelfth Language Resources and Evaluation Conference*, pages 1–10, Marseille, France. European Language Resources Association.

Zikang Zhang, Wangjie You, Tianci Wu, Xinrui Wang, Juntao Li, and Min Zhang. 2025. A Survey of Generative Information Extraction. In *Proceedings of the 31st International Conference on Computational Linguistics*, pages 4840–4870, Abu Dhabi, UAE. Association for Computational Linguistics.

A Hyperparameters

As a starting point for hyperparameter optimization, we took note of hyperparameters reported in prior work (e.g., Hu et al., 2022; Dettmers et al., 2023; Warner et al., 2024), performing minimal tuning mostly within suggested ranges.

Epochs	2
Batch size	8
Learning rate (LR)	`1e-4`
LR scheduler type	`cosine`
Warmup ratio	0.1
LoRA r	16
LoRA α	16
LoRA dropout	0
LoRA target modules	`*_proj`, `lm_head`

Table 6: Hyperparameters for QLoRA fine-tuning of LLAMA 3.1 8B. We use default values if not otherwise specified.

Epochs	4
Batch size	8
Learning rate	8e-5
Gradient accumulation steps	8
Warmup ratio	0.1
Weight decay	8e-6

Table 7: Hyperparameters for fine-tuning of MODERN-BERT-large. We use default values if not otherwise specified.

B Training example

The following is an example of a training sample from the AGOS dataset—for a context window of size 3—that was used to fine-tune LLAMA 3.1:

> B: Clear, I think my second choice would be the light grey one, which looks like in old style.\nA: I agree, its bottom seems to be pretty high as well.\nB: yeap!\nB: then, for the third one, is the dark grey one okay?\n\nB: then, for the third one, is the dark grey one okay? -> B: then, for the third one, is >> the dark grey << one okay?

Messages in the linguistic context are separated by single newline characters (\n). Each message is prepended with a token indicating the speaker (either A or B). The message we want annotated is separated from the linguistic context by two newline characters (\n\n). This message is followed by an inference token (->). The inference token is then followed by the annotated message, with span boundary tokens indicating the start (>>) and end (<<) of the mention span.

Exploring Multilingual Probing in Large Language Models: A Cross-Language Analysis

Daoyang Li[1,2], Haiyan Zhao[2], Qingcheng Zeng[3], Mengnan Du[2]
[1]University of Southern California, [2]New Jersey Institute of Technology,
[3]Northwestern University
daoyangl@usc.edu, mengnan.du@njit.edu

Abstract

Probing techniques for large language models (LLMs) have primarily focused on English, overlooking the vast majority of other world's languages. In this paper, we extend these probing methods to a multilingual context, investigating how LLMs encode linguistic structures across diverse languages. We conduct experiments on several open-source LLM models, analyzing probing accuracy, trends across layers, and similarities between probing vectors for multiple languages. Our key findings reveal: (1) a consistent performance gap between high-resource and low-resource languages, with high-resource languages achieving significantly higher probing accuracy; (2) divergent layer-wise accuracy trends, where high-resource languages show substantial improvement in deeper layers similar to English; and (3) higher representational similarities among high-resource languages, with low-resource languages demonstrating lower similarities both among themselves and with high-resource languages. These results provide insights into how linguistic structures are represented differently across languages in LLMs and emphasize the need for improved structure modeling for low-resource languages.

1 Introduction

Large language models (LLMs), such as GPT-4 (Achiam et al., 2023), Claude 3.5 (Anthropic, 2024), Llama 3 (Dubey et al., 2024), have demonstrated remarkable progress across a wide range of natural language processing tasks. As these models continue to advance, there is a growing need to understand their internal mechanisms and how they represent linguistic structures. Probing techniques have emerged as a valuable tool for investigating how LLMs encode and process structural information, offering insights into their decision-making processes and the nature of their learned representations (Ferrando et al., 2024a; Zhao et al., 2024; Zou et al., 2023).

However, a significant gap exists in our understanding of how LLMs represent linguistic structures across different languages. While extensive probing research has been conducted on English language representations, there are approximately 7,000 languages spoken worldwide, many of which remain understudied in the context of LLMs. This lack of multilingual analysis limits our understanding of how LLMs encode structural information across diverse linguistic contexts, particularly for low-resource languages that are often underrepresented in model training data and evaluations.

To address this research gap, we propose a multilingual probing approach to investigate the structural representation capabilities of LLMs across a diverse set of 16 languages, including both high-resource and low-resource languages. Our study extends probing techniques from English to a multilingual context, examining how LLMs encode linguistic structures in factual knowledge and sentiment classification tasks across different languages. Our key findings reveal that: (1) high-resource languages consistently achieve higher probing accuracy compared to low-resource languages; (2) high-resource languages exhibit similar trends to English across model layers, with accuracy improving significantly in deeper layers, while low-resource languages show relatively stable or only slightly improving accuracy; and (3) there are high similarities between probing vectors of high-resource languages, whereas low-resource languages demonstrate lower similarities both among themselves and with high-resource languages.

2 Probing Method

2.1 LLM Internal Representation

We study decoder-only LLMs, where each layer of a model consists of both multi-head attention blocks (MHA) and feed-forward networks (FFNs). In this work, we utilize frozen pretrained language

Proceedings of the 1st Joint Workshop on Large Language Models and Structure Modeling (XLLM 2025), pages 61–70
August 1, 2025 ©2025 Association for Computational Linguistics

models. Layers are indexed with $\ell \in L$, where L denotes the set of all layers in a model. For each layer, the computation starts and ends with a residual stream. The MHA first reads from the residual stream and performs computation, then adds its output back to the residual stream. The updated vector in the residual stream is then passed through MLPs to generate the output of the layer:

$$h_i^{\ell+1} = h_i^\ell + \text{MLP}^\ell \left(h_i^\ell + \text{Att}^\ell \left(h_i^\ell \right) \right), \quad (1)$$

where h_i^ℓ represents the hidden state of the i-th token in the input sequence at layer ℓ. We focus on the output representation space of each layer, particularly the residual stream at the end of each layer. We use the representation of the last token to represent the entire input sequence, as it is generally believed to integrate information from all previous tokens. This representation is denoted as h^ℓ, which will be simplified to h in the following section.

2.2 Linear Classifier Probing

In our analysis, we employed linear classifier probing (Ju et al., 2024a; Jin et al., 2024) to explore internal representations across various layers of LLMs. We extracted hidden states from the residual stream of each layer using two types of inputs (i.e., positive and negative) and utilized these representations to train a logistic regression model. By evaluating the performance of trained classifier, we are able to assess how well the hidden states at different layers encoded information relevant to answering factual questions or handling sentiment classification tasks. This approach provides valuable insights into the nature of the representations learned within the model.

To perform the probing, we employed a linear classifier approach. We define $h \in R^{n \times d_{\text{model}}}$ as the set of hidden features extracted from the LLM, where n is the number of samples and d_{model} represents the dimensionality of the hidden layer. The internal representation of each sample in a specific layer is denoted by $h^{(i)} \in R^{1 \times d_{\text{model}}}$. We utilize binary classification, assigning labels $y^{(i)} \in \{0, 1\}$. The objective function for our logistic regression classifier, incorporating L2 regularization, is formulated as:

$$J(\theta) = -\frac{1}{n} \sum_{i=1}^{n} L(h^{(i)}, y^{(i)}; \theta) + \frac{\lambda}{2n} \|\theta\|_2^2, \quad (2)$$

where $L(.)$ represents the cross-entropy loss:

$$L = y^{(i)} \log(\sigma(\theta^T h^{(i)})) + (1 - y^{(i)}) \log(1 - \sigma(\theta^T h^{(i)})), \quad (3)$$

Model	Layer	Representation Dimension
Qwen-0.5B	24	1024
Qwen-1.8B	24	2048
Qwen-7B	32	4096
Gemma-2B	18	2048
Gemma-7B	28	3072

Table 1: Model and corresponding layers.

where θ denotes the model parameters, λ is the regularization coefficient, and $\sigma(\cdot)$ represents the sigmoid activation function. By evaluating the accuracy of this classifier on the test set, we can evaluate the LLM's performance and gain insights into its internal representations across different languages and layers.

3 Experiment

In this section, we conduct comprehensive probing experiments to investigate how language models process different languages. Our analysis focuses on two key aspects: comparing accuracy across different model layers and examining correlations between probing vectors of various languages. Through these experiments, we seek to answer three fundamental research questions (**RQ**s):

- **RQ1** - Do other languages achieve comparable probing accuracy to English?
- **RQ2** - Do other languages exhibit similar layer-wise behavioral patterns to English?
- **RQ3** - What are the similarities between probing vectors across different languages?

3.1 Experiment Settings

In this section, we introduce the overall experimental settings of this papers.

Models: We evaluated the performance and internal representations across various languages using two open-source LLM families: Qwen (Bai et al., 2023) and Gemma (Team et al., 2024). The Qwen-1.5 architecture comprises 24 layers for smaller variants (0.5B & 1.8B) and 32 layers for the larger variant (7B), while the Gemma architecture features 18 layers for the 2B model and 28 layers for the 7B model. The representation vector dimensions vary across models: 1024 for Qwen-0.5B, 2048 for both Qwen-1.8B and Gemma-2B, 3072 for Gemma-7B, and 4096 for Qwen-7B. Table 1 provides a comprehensive overview of the models and their corresponding layer configurations.

Datasets: In the following experiments, we utilized a truthful dataset: *Cities* (Marks and Tegmark,

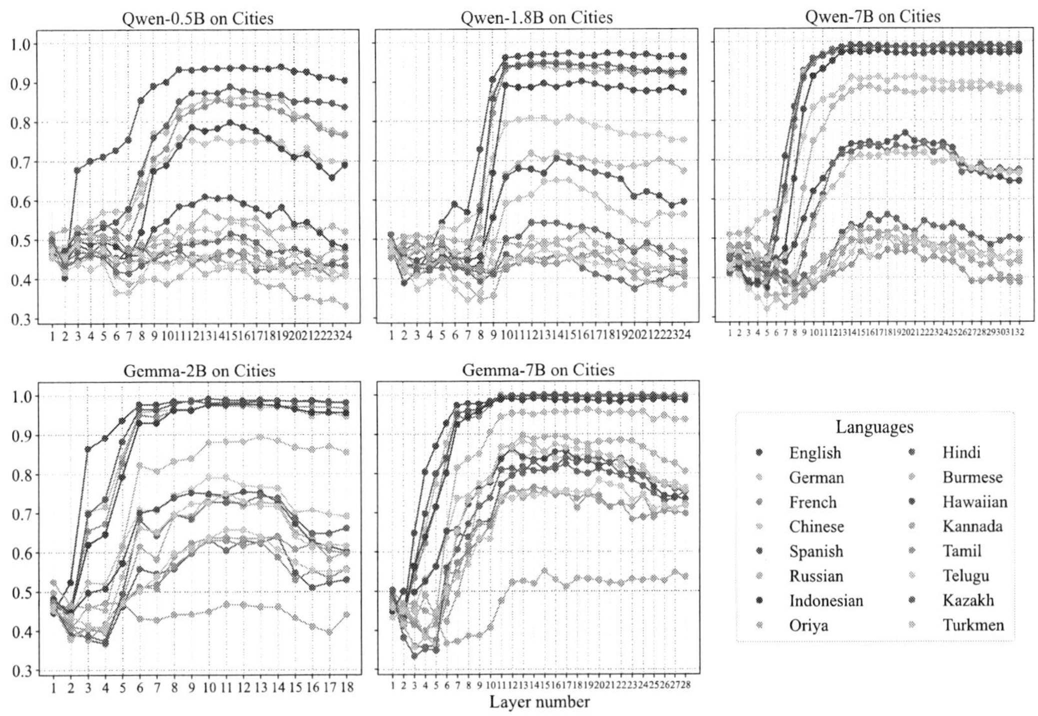

Figure 1: Layer-wise probing accuracy of 5 open-source LLMs across 16 languages.

2023), and a sentiment dataset: *Opinion* (Tatman, 2017). Cities contains 1496 samples, and Opinion contains 1000 samples.

- *Cities* (Marks and Tegmark, 2023): consists of statements about the location of cities from worldwide and their veracity labels (e.g., The city of Lyon is in France, which is true).
- *Opinion* (Tatman, 2017): consists of opinions of 20 famous hotels. It contains the hotel's name, opinion's polarity, and its source.

Our dataset encompasses 16 languages: English, German, French, Chinese, Spanish, Russian, Indonesian, Oriya, Hindi, Burmese, Hawaiian, Kannada, Tamil, Telugu, Kazakh, Turkmen. We categorized English, German, French, Chinese, Spanish, Russian, and Indonesian as high-resource languages, and rest of them as low-resource languages based on the volume of available digital content and linguistic resources. The original language of our two datasets are English, and we used Google Translate within deep-translator python library (Azam, 2024) to translate them into other 15 languages, as Google Translate supports translation between over 100 languages, and achieves high accuracy compared to other translation tools.

Implementation Details: To evaluate the performance of LLMs on each language, we use the template for the Cities dataset in English as "*Judge the statement is Positive or Negative. <Statement>*". The prompts of other languages utilize the same template translated by Google Translate. This allows us to prevent any context differences regarding the prompt design. We present the full set of prompt templates for all 16 languages in Figure 3 at the Appendix. We applied probing techniques to assess the information encoded within each layer of these models. For our probing analysis, we selected linear classifier probing for our experiments. Each dataset is divided into a training and a test set with an 8:2 ratio, and we adhered to the standard procedure for probing classifiers in LLMs, extracting feature representations from the final hidden states at each layer of the LLMs to serve as input to the probing classifier. The linear weight parameter θ of the logistic regression classifier is regarded as the probing vector for each language and layer.

3.2 Multilingual Accuracy

In this section, we explored (1) whether other languages besides English have the same probing accuracy as English and (2) whether they follow the

Table 2: Probing accuracy of various LLMs across different languages on the Cities dataset.

Model	High-Resource Languages							Low-Resource Languages									
	English	German	French	Chinese	Spanish	Russian	Indonesian	Oriya	Hindi	Burmese	Hawaiian	Kannada	Tamil	Telugu	Kazakh	Turkmen
Gemma-2B	0.98	0.95	0.97	0.69	0.98	0.87	0.95	0.44	0.53	0.60	0.60	0.60	0.56	0.56	0.66	0.62
Gemma-7B	0.99	0.99	0.99	0.76	0.99	0.93	0.99	0.54	0.76	0.81	0.74	0.72	0.70	0.72	0.75	0.76
Qwen-0.5B	0.90	0.77	0.76	0.70	0.84	0.52	0.69	0.47	0.41	0.33	0.48	0.43	0.45	0.42	0.43	0.41
Qwen-1.8B	0.96	0.92	0.92	0.75	0.93	0.67	0.87	0.47	0.41	0.37	0.60	0.42	0.40	0.43	0.44	0.56
Qwen-7B	0.99	0.98	0.98	0.88	0.98	0.88	0.97	0.45	0.50	0.44	0.65	0.40	0.39	0.46	0.67	0.67

same trend as English in different layers.

We present results on multilingual accuracy across our five evaluated models (Qwen-0.5B, Qwen-1.8B, Qwen-7B, Gemma-2B, Gemma-7B) on the cities and Opinion datasets. In Figure 1 and Table 2, we show the results of layer-wise probing accuracy on the Cities dataset. The results of Opinion dataset are included in Figure 4 in the Appendix. These results visualize how probing accuracy changes across model layers for all 16 languages. Based on these results, our analysis lead to two general observations as follows:

- *High-resource languages show higher accuracy, while low-resource languages have comparatively lower accuracy.* We conducted experiments using Cities and Opinion datasets, exploring the binary classification problem in 16 selected languages. Table 2 shows that in Cities dataset, high-resource languages such as French and German achieve at least 70% accuracy, even reaching over 90% accuracy for some models, while low-resource languages like Oriya and Hindi only achieve about 40% accuracy in the final layer.
- *High-resource languages follow similar trends to English, where accuracy significantly improves as the layers deepen. Low-resource languages maintain relatively stable probing accuracy or show only slight improvements.* Figure 1 shows that as model layers go deeper, English, French, and other high-resource languages could reach highest accuracy at the 11th layer. However, the probing accuracies of the low-resource languages have not improved significantly.

3.3 Similarity Correlation of Probing Vectors

In this section, we conducted similarity analysis on probing vectors θ across languages using two visualization approaches:

- **Correlation Heatmaps**: These visualize the pairwise similarities between probing vectors of all 16 languages. These highlight clustering patterns and resource-level disparities.
- **Layer-wise Similarity Plots**: They measure cosine similarity between each language's probing vector and English's across model layers, revealing representation dynamics.

For demonstration, Figure 2 shows results from the Qwen-1.8B model and Opinion dataset. In the Appendix, we extend this analysis to all five models (Qwen-0.5B, Qwen-1.8B, Qwen-7B, Gemma-2B, Gemma-7B) and both datasets (Opinion, Cities) through Figure 5 and Figure 6. Our analysis reveals the following three key patterns:

- The probing vectors of high-resource languages (English, German, French, Chinese, Spanish, Russian) demonstrate strong correlations with each other, as evidenced by the darker clusters in the heatmaps and consistently higher similarity curves in the trajectory plots. For instance, in the Qwen-1.8B Opinion task, German and French probing vectors maintain correlations above 0.6 with English across most layers. In contrast, low-resource languages show notably weaker correlations, both among themselves and with high-resource languages. This pattern is visible in the bright regions of the heatmaps for languages like Tamil, Telugu, and Oriya, with similarity scores typically remaining below 0.3 across all layers.
- The evolution of similarities across model layers reveals further insights into these representational differences. High-resource languages exhibit dynamic similarity patterns with English, often peaking in middle layers before slightly decreasing, while low-resource languages maintain relatively stable, low similarity levels throughout the model layers. These patterns persist across different model sizes and architectures in both the Qwen and Gemma families, and remain consistent across the Opinion and Cities datasets.

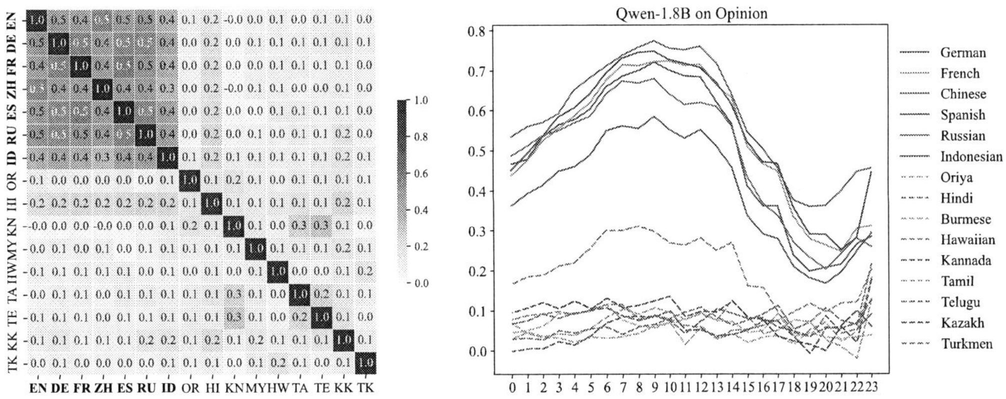

(a) Heatmap (b) Cosine similarity

Figure 2: (a) Heatmap of the similarities of probing vectors correlation across languages; (b) Cosine similarity of probing vectors with English. (Model: Qwen-1.8B, Dataset: Opinion).

4 Related Work

In this section, we review two lines of research that are most relevant to ours.

Multilingual Abilities of LLMs. The multilingual capabilities of LLMs have garnered increasing attention from researchers (Ali and Pyysalo, 2024; Jayakody and Dias, 2024). Recent studies have investigated the consistency of factual knowledge across different languages in multilingual pretrained language models (PLMs) (Fierro and Søgaard, 2022; Qi et al., 2023). Additionally, significant efforts have been directed towards enhancing the representation of low-resource languages (Abadji et al., 2022; Imani et al., 2023; Li et al., 2024). These investigations demonstrate that LLMs still possess considerable untapped potential in multilingual capabilities.

Probing Representations in LLMs. Probing is a popular method to investigate the internal representations for LLMs in recent days, which is widely used in LLM interpretability studies (Alain and Bengio, 2018; Taktasheva et al., 2021; Pimentel et al., 2020; Ferrando et al., 2024b; Wendler et al., 2024). Previous work demonstrate that different layers typically acquired different information (Jin et al., 2024; Ju et al., 2024b). Various works using probing technique to assess how they encode linguistic features (Liu et al., 2023; Marks and Tegmark, 2024).

Our study employs probing techniques to examine LLMs' performance and internal representations across different languages. The most closely related work is the Language Ranker (Li et al., 2024), which uses cosine similarity between a language's representation and English as a baseline. In contrast, our method utilizes linear classifier probing to evaluate performance across languages. This approach allows us to directly assess the model's ability to extract language-specific information, providing a more detailed view of LLMs' multilingual capabilities.

5 Conclusions and Future Work

In this work, our multilingual probing experiments on LLMs reveal significant disparities in performance and representational qualities across languages, suggesting potential limitations in how these models learn linguistic concepts. Specifically, high-resource languages consistently achieve higher probing accuracy and exhibit similar trends to English, with accuracy improving significantly in deeper layers. We also observe high similarities between probing vectors of high-resource languages, while low-resource languages demonstrate lower similarities both among themselves and with high-resource languages. These findings not only indicate the current limitations of LLMs in handling low-resource languages, but also suggest that these models may not be learning deeper linguistic concepts effectively across all languages.

In future, we plan to conduct research to address these gaps by developing more equitable and effective multilingual language models that can better capture universal linguistic concepts. Besides, we plan to extend this research to multimodal models that incorporate visual and textual information.

Limitations

In this work, we use machine translation to generate the prompt templates and question sentences from English to other languages, which may introduce noise. We only experiment with five open-source LLMs and two datasets. In the future, we would like to expand these findings with other datasets and models to confirm how well the LLMs' performance and representations generalize in these settings. Additionally, we just utilized linear classifier probing to do the experiments. We plan to explore more sophisticated probing methods beyond linear classifiers, which could offer deeper insights into the nature of linguistic representations within LLMs.

Acknowledgment

The work is in part supported by NSF #2310261. The views and conclusions in this paper are those of the authors and should not be interpreted as representing any funding agencies.

References

Julien Abadji, Pedro Ortiz Suarez, Laurent Romary, and Benoît Sagot. 2022. Towards a cleaner document-oriented multilingual crawled corpus. In *Proceedings of the Thirteenth Language Resources and Evaluation Conference*, pages 4344–4355, Marseille, France. European Language Resources Association.

Josh Achiam, Steven Adler, Sandhini Agarwal, Lama Ahmad, Ilge Akkaya, Florencia Leoni Aleman, Diogo Almeida, Janko Altenschmidt, Sam Altman, Shyamal Anadkat, et al. 2023. Gpt-4 technical report. *arXiv preprint arXiv:2303.08774*.

Guillaume Alain and Yoshua Bengio. 2018. Understanding intermediate layers using linear classifier probes. *Preprint*, arXiv:1610.01644.

Wazir Ali and Sampo Pyysalo. 2024. A survey of large language models for european languages. *Preprint*, arXiv:2408.15040.

Anthropic. 2024. Introducing claude 3.5 sonnet.

Safiul Azam. 2024. Deep translator. Accessed: 2024-09-03.

J. Bai, S. Bai, Y. Chu, Z. Cui, K. Dang, X. Deng, Y. Fan, W. Ge, Y. Han, F. Huang, B. Hui, L. Ji, M. Li, J. Lin, R. Lin, D. Liu, G. Liu, C. Lu, K. Lu, J. Ma, R. Men, X. Ren, X. Ren, C. Tan, S. Tan, J. Tu, P. Wang, S. Wang, W. Wang, S. Wu, B. Xu, J. Xu, A. Yang, H. Yang, J. Yang, S. Yang, Y. Yao, B. Yu, H. Yuan, Z. Yuan, J. Zhang, X. Zhang, Y. Zhang, Z. Zhang, C. Zhou, J. Zhou, X. Zhou, and T. Zhu. 2023. Qwen technical report. Technical report.

Abhimanyu Dubey, Abhinav Jauhri, Abhinav Pandey, Abhishek Kadian, Ahmad Al-Dahle, Aiesha Letman, Akhil Mathur, Alan Schelten, Amy Yang, Angela Fan, et al. 2024. The llama 3 herd of models. *arXiv preprint arXiv:2407.21783*.

Javier Ferrando, Gabriele Sarti, Arianna Bisazza, and Marta R Costa-jussà. 2024a. A primer on the inner workings of transformer-based language models. *arXiv preprint arXiv:2405.00208*.

Javier Ferrando, Gabriele Sarti, Arianna Bisazza, and Marta R. Costa-jussà. 2024b. A primer on the inner workings of transformer-based language models. *Preprint*, arXiv:2405.00208.

Constanza Fierro and Anders Søgaard. 2022. Factual consistency of multilingual pretrained language models. In *Findings of the Association for Computational Linguistics: ACL 2022*, pages 3046–3052.

Ayyoob Imani, Peiqin Lin, Amir Hossein Kargaran, Silvia Severini, Masoud Jalili Sabet, Nora Kassner, Chunlan Ma, Helmut Schmid, André Martins, François Yvon, and Hinrich Schütze. 2023. Glot500: Scaling multilingual corpora and language models to 500 languages. In *Proceedings of the 61st Annual Meeting of the Association for Computational Linguistics (Volume 1: Long Papers)*, pages 1082–1117, Toronto, Canada. Association for Computational Linguistics.

Ravindu Jayakody and Gihan Dias. 2024. Performance of recent large language models for a low-resourced language. *Preprint*, arXiv:2407.21330.

Mingyu Jin, Qinkai Yu, Jingyuan Huang, Qingcheng Zeng, Zhenting Wang, Wenyue Hua, Haiyan Zhao, Kai Mei, Yanda Meng, Kaize Ding, Fan Yang, Mengnan Du, and Yongfeng Zhang. 2024. Exploring concept depth: How large language models acquire knowledge at different layers? *Preprint*, arXiv:2404.07066.

T. Ju, W. Sun, W. Du, X. Yuan, Z. Ren, and G. Liu. 2024a. How large language models encode context knowledge? a layer-wise probing study. *arXiv preprint arXiv:2402.16061*.

Tianjie Ju, Weiwei Sun, Wei Du, Xinwei Yuan, Zhaochun Ren, and Gongshen Liu. 2024b. How large language models encode context knowledge? a layer-wise probing study. *Preprint*, arXiv:2402.16061.

Zihao Li, Yucheng Shi, Zirui Liu, Fan Yang, Ninghao Liu, and Mengnan Du. 2024. Quantifying multilingual performance of large language models across languages. *arXiv preprint arXiv:2404.11553*.

Kevin Liu, Stephen Casper, Dylan Hadfield-Menell, and Jacob Andreas. 2023. Cognitive dissonance: Why do language model outputs disagree with internal representations of truthfulness? *Preprint*, arXiv:2312.03729.

S. Marks and M. Tegmark. 2023. The geometry of truth: Emergent linear structure in large language model representations of true/false datasets. *arXiv preprint arXiv:2310.06824*.

Samuel Marks and Max Tegmark. 2024. The geometry of truth: Emergent linear structure in large language model representations of true/false datasets. *Preprint*, arXiv:2310.06824.

Tiago Pimentel, Josef Valvoda, Rowan Hall Maudslay, Ran Zmigrod, Adina Williams, and Ryan Cotterell. 2020. Information-theoretic probing for linguistic structure. *Preprint*, arXiv:2004.03061.

Jirui Qi, Raquel Fernández, and Arianna Bisazza. 2023. Cross-lingual consistency of factual knowledge in multilingual language models. In *The 2023 Conference on Empirical Methods in Natural Language Processing*.

Ekaterina Taktasheva, Vladislav Mikhailov, and Ekaterina Artemova. 2021. Shaking syntactic trees on the sesame street: Multilingual probing with controllable perturbations. In *Proceedings of the 1st Workshop on Multilingual Representation Learning*, pages 191–210, Punta Cana, Dominican Republic. Association for Computational Linguistics.

Rachael Tatman. 2017. Deceptive opinion spam corpus. Accessed: 2024-09-03.

G. Team, T. Mesnard, C. Hardin, R. Dadashi, S. Bhupatiraju, S. Pathak, L. Sifre, M. Rivière, M. S. Kale, J. Love, P. Tafti, L. Hussenot, A. Chowdhery, A. Roberts, A. Barua, A. Botev, A. Castro-Ros, A. Slone, A. Héliou, A. Tacchetti, A. Bulanova, A. Paterson, B. Tsai, B. Shahriari, C. L. Lan, C. A. Choquette-Choo, C. Crepy, D. Cer, D. Ippolito, D. Reid, E. Buchatskaya, E. Ni, E. Noland, G. Yan, G. Tucker, G.-C. Muraru, G. Rozhdestvenskiy, H. Michalewski, I. Tenney, I. Grishchenko, J. Austin, J. Keeling, J. Labanowski, J.-B. Lespiau, J. Stanway, J. Brennan, J. Chen, J. Ferret, J. Chiu, J. Mao-Jones, K. Lee, K. Yu, K. Millican, L. L. Sjoesund, L. Lee, L. Dixon, M. Reid, M. Mikuła, M. Wirth, M. Sharman, N. Chinaev, N. Thain, O. Bachem, O. Chang, O. Wahltinez, P. Bailey, P. Michel, P. Yotov, P. G. Sessa, R. Chaabouni, R. Comanescu, R. Jana, R. Anil, R. McIlroy, R. Liu, R. Mullins, S. L. Smith, S. Borgeaud, S. Girgin, S. Douglas, S. Pandya, S. Shakeri, S. De, T. Klimenko, T. Hennigan, V. Feinberg, W. Stokowiec, Y. hui Chen, Z. Ahmed, Z. Gong, T. Warkentin, L. Peran, M. Giang, C. Farabet, O. Vinyals, J. Dean, K. Kavukcuoglu, D. Hassabis, Z. Ghahramani, D. Eck, J. Barral, F. Pereira, E. Collins, A. Joulin, N. Fiedel, E. Senter, A. Andreev, and K. Kenealy. 2024. Gemma: Open models based on gemini research and technology. Technical report.

Chris Wendler, Veniamin Veselovsky, Giovanni Monea, and Robert West. 2024. Do llamas work in english? on the latent language of multilingual transformers. *arXiv preprint arXiv:2402.10588*.

Haiyan Zhao, Fan Yang, Himabindu Lakkaraju, and Mengnan Du. 2024. Opening the black box of large language models: Two views on holistic interpretability. *arXiv preprint arXiv:2402.10688*.

Andy Zou, Long Phan, Sarah Chen, James Campbell, Phillip Guo, Richard Ren, Alexander Pan, Xuwang Yin, Mantas Mazeika, Ann-Kathrin Dombrowski, et al. 2023. Representation engineering: A top-down approach to ai transparency. *arXiv preprint arXiv:2310.01405*.

Language	Prompt
English	Judge the statement is Positive or Negative.
German	Beurteilen Sie, ob die Aussage positiv oder negativ ist.
French	Jugez si l'énoncé est positif ou négatif.
Chinese	判断该陈述是正面的还是负面的。
Spanish	Juzgue si la afirmación es positiva o negativa.
Russian	Оцените, является ли утверждение положительным или отрицательным.
Indonesian	Tentukan apakah pernyataan tersebut positif atau negatif.
Oriya	ବିବେଚନା କରନ୍ତୁ ଯେ ବକ୍ତବ୍ୟଟି ସକାରାତ୍ମକ କି ନକାରାତ୍ମକ।
Hindi	निर्णय करें कि कथन सकारात्मक है या नकारात्मक।
Burmese	ထောက်ထားချက်သည်အနုမြူရောအနုတ်မြူရောဖြစ်သည်။
Hawaiian	E hoʻopaʻapaʻa inā he maikaʻi a i ʻole he maikaʻi ʻole ka ʻōlelo.
Kannada	ಹೇಳಿಕೆಯನ್ನು ಸಕಾರಾತ್ಮಕ ಅಥವಾ ಋಣಾತ್ಮಕ ಎಂದು ತೀರ್ಮಾನಿಸಿ.
Tmail	வாக்குமூலம் நேர்மையானதா அல்லது எதிர்மையானதா என்பதை மதிப்பீடு செய்யவும்.
Telugu	వాఖ్యానికి సానుకూలం లేదా ప్రతికూలం అని తీర్పు ఇవ్వండి.
Kazakh	Мәлімдеменің оң немесе теріс екенін анықтаңыз.
Turkmen	Beýannamanyň oňyn ýa-da otrisatelidigini kesgitläň.

Figure 3: Prompt templates of all languages used in experiments.

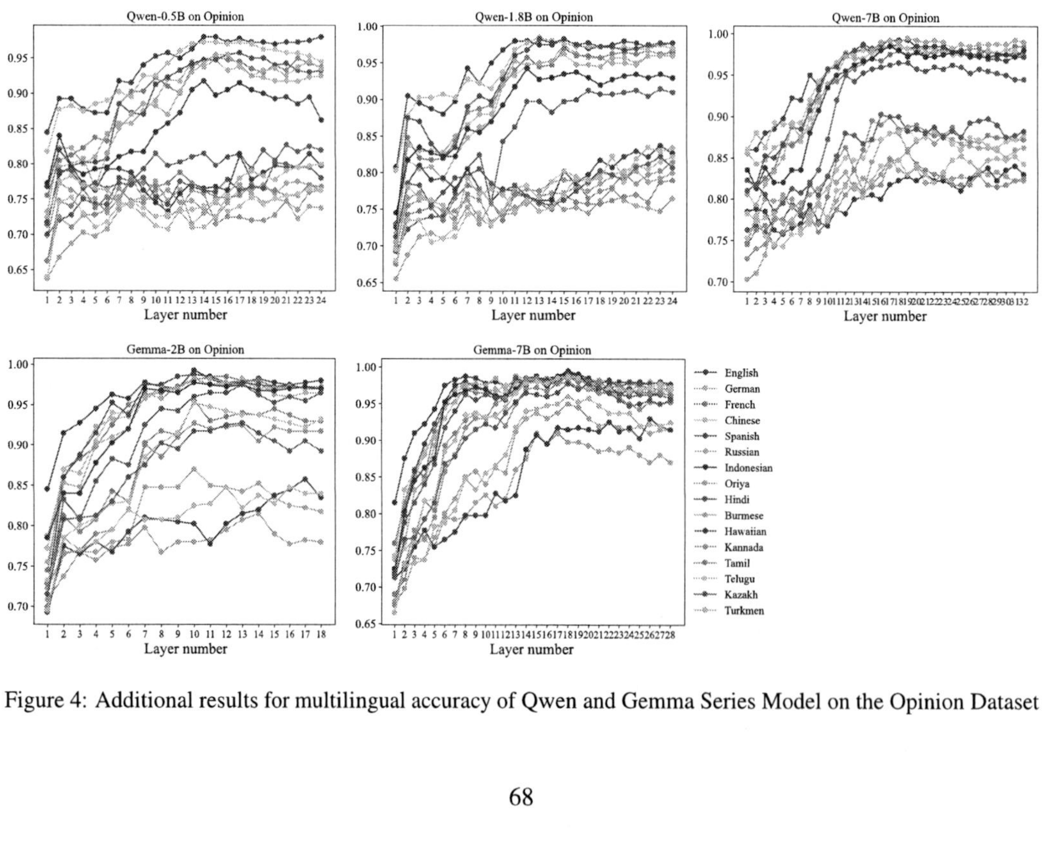

Figure 4: Additional results for multilingual accuracy of Qwen and Gemma Series Model on the Opinion Dataset

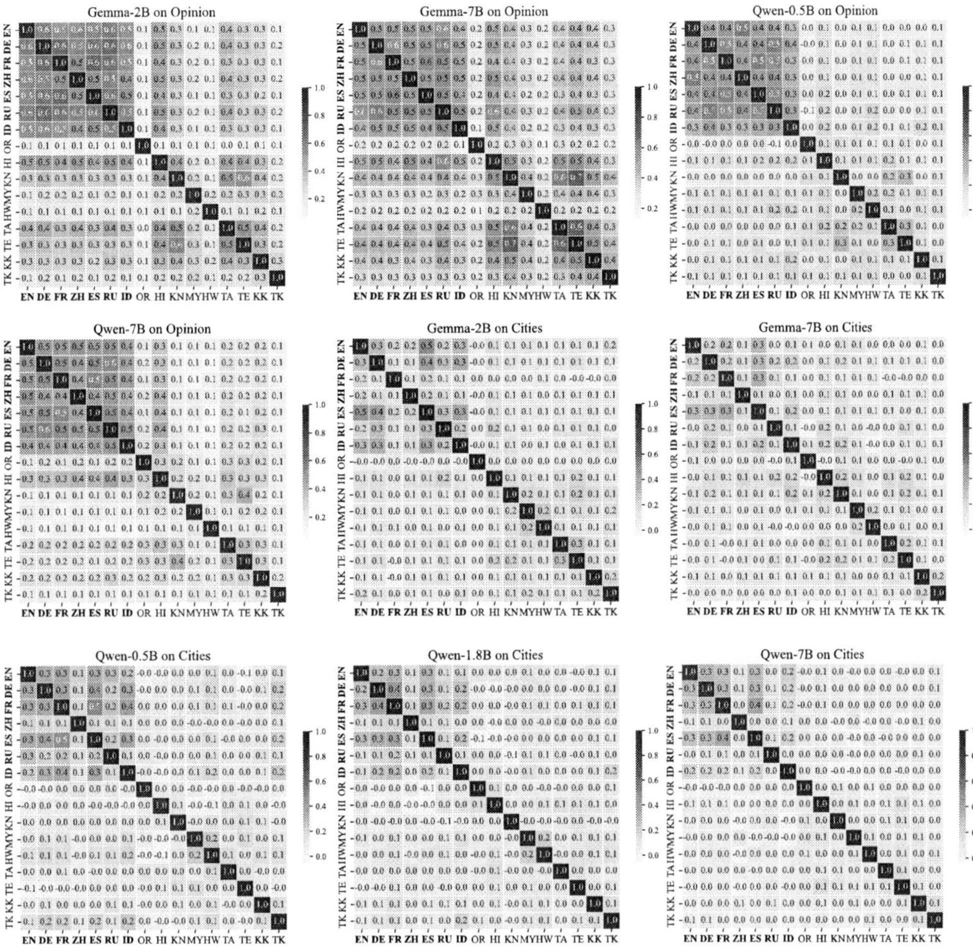

Figure 5: Heatmap of the similarities of probing vectors correlation across languages.

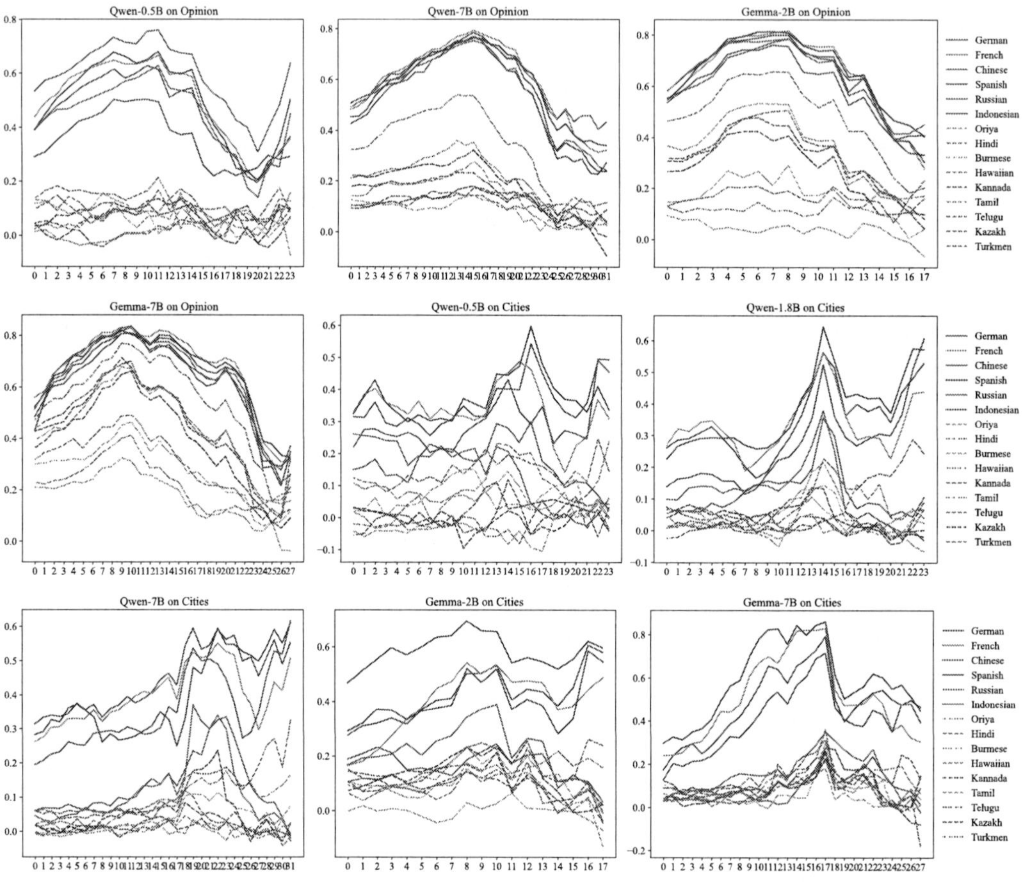

Figure 6: Cosine similarity of probing vectors with English across different language models (Qwen-0.5B, Qwen-7B, Gemma-2B, and Gemma-7B) and tasks (Opinion and Cities).

Self-Contrastive Loop of Thought Method for Text-to-SQL Based on Large Language Model

Fengrui Kang[1,2], **Mingxi Tan**[1], **Xianying Huang**[2,*], **Shiju Yang**[1]
[1]Xffuture, [2]Chongqing University of Technology
kenfree000@gmail.com, tanmingxi@xffuture.com,
hxy@cqut.edu.cn, yangshiju@xffuture.com
Correspondence: hxy@cqut.edu.cn

Abstract

Text-to-SQL is a task with excellent prospects and challenges, and it aims to convert natural language queries (NL) into corresponding structured query language (SQL) statements. The main challenge of this task is how to efficiently transform unstructured data and structured data. In recent years, the emergence of large language models (LLMs) has further promoted the development of this field. However, current LLM-based text-to-SQL methods rely on specific few-shot example construction, resulting in poor performance across domains. To solve this problem, we propose a text-to-SQL method of self-contrastive loop of thought structure. This method designs the LLM inference process as a loop structure based on the comparison of positive and negative examples. The model optimizes the generated results through continuous verification and error correction, greatly improving accuracy and reducing dependence on few-shot example construction. The experimental results on SPIDER and BIRD datasets show that this method can generate SQL with higher precision without relying on few-shot example construction.

1 Introduction

The goal of text-to-SQL is to generate SQL based on natural language. This technique can generate the corresponding SQL statements by verbal description. Due to its broad application prospect and challenge, this task has attracted wide attention(Bogin et al., 2019; Elgohary et al., 2020; Chen et al., 2021; Lin et al., 2020).

In the early stages, such research typically achieved text-to-SQL through rule-based designs and pre-trained models. Design methods improved the quality of SQL generation by reinforcing the alignment between text and database schemas, such as RAT-SQL (Wang et al., 2020), SDSQL(Hui et al., 2021), LGESQL(Cao et al., 2021), RESD-SQL(Li et al., 2023a). Additionally, some studies employed various pre-training strategies, such as TaBERT(Yin et al., 2020), GRAPPA(Yu et al., 2021), GAP(Zhao et al., 2022), and MIGA(Fu et al., 2023), these models enhanced ability to capture the complex relationship between natural language and SQL structures. Together, these efforts improve the performance of text-to-SQL.

With the development of LLM, recent studies have demonstrated the superior ability of LLM in complex tasks(Gao et al., 2023; Nan et al., 2023b; Imani et al., 2023). In the text-to-SQL field, the LLM-based approach exceeds previous work on multiple datasets without any fine-tuning or training(Gu et al., 2023; Pourreza et al., 2024; Nan et al., 2023a).

Based on the advanced performance of LLM, prompt-based methods have further promoted the progress of text-to-SQL. Typical work such as DIN-SQL(Pourreza and Rafiei, 2023), DAIL-SQL(Gao et al., 2024), TA-SQL(Qu et al., 2024)and MAC-SQL(Wang et al., 2023). These methods are based on the few-shot prompt method, combined with chain-of-thought technology to decompose the task to improve LLM performance.

Although the prompt-based method has made significant progress, it still has some problems. First, the performance depends on the quality of the few-shot examples, which can lead to LLM not achieving the potential performance. Second, most of this work uses a linear thinking workflow to guide LLM generation, which comprises the search space. Third, this work improves the ability to deal with complex problems through detailed decomposition tasks. However, it may introduce an additional risk of hallucination, which can adversely affect the results.

To solve the above problems, we propose a text-to-SQL method based on a self-contrastive loop

* Corresponding author

Proceedings of the 1st Joint Workshop on Large Language Models and Structure Modeling (XLLM 2025), pages 71–85
August 1, 2025 ©2025 Association for Computational Linguistics

of thought structure (SCL). The LLM generation process is constructed as a discriminant loop structure based on the contrast of positive and negative examples so that the model can improve the accuracy of the results in the continuous self-correction. This reduces the dependence on the construction of few-shot examples, and the generation relies only on the self-contrast between positive and negative examples. With this approach, the LLM can better focus on outputs similar to positive examples and exclude erroneous results similar to negative examples, reducing the inference burden of the LLM. On this basis, we summarize the contributions of this paper as follows.

- Designed a question-splitting strategy that enhances the utilization of question information via skeleton-based positive example retrieval and entity-schema linking. In addition, positive example retrieval replaces the few-shot construction, simplifying prompt design.

- Enhance the LLM's verification and selection abilities through result-guided execution and logical verification, integrated with a selection mechanism. This expands the search space for generation.

- A loop-of-thought structure is designed to guide the LLM through self-contrast between positive and negative examples, enhancing its ability to handle text-to-SQL tasks without relying on few-shot example construction.

2 Methodology

2.1 Overview

SCL-SQL is a self-contrastive framework for text-to-SQL. As shown in Figure 7. We first decouple the query into entity and skeleton parts to improve schema linking and example retrieval. Then, a loop-structured reasoning process guides the LLM to generate, execute, and verify SQL with both positive and negative examples. Finally, a voting-based mechanism selects the most reliable result.

2.2 Query Split

To fully utilize the information in the question, we propose a novel entity-skeleton splitting strategy that divides the question into entity and skeleton parts, which respectively guide schema linking and few-shot example construction.

2.2.1 Entity-guided Schema Linking

Schema linking identifies relevant schema elements (e.g., table names and columns), effectively reducing mismatches and minimizing hallucinations, as validated in prior studies (Gan et al., 2023; Yang et al., 2024). This work adopts an entity-guided approach by extracting keywords using YAKE (Campos et al., 2020), which divides the question into keyword (entity) and non-keyword (skeleton) parts, as shown in Equation 1.

$$\begin{aligned} T &= \{x_1, x_2, x_3, x_4, x_5, x_6, x_7, x_8, x_9, x_{10}\} \\ e &= \{x_2, x_4, x_7, x_8, x_9\}, \quad e \in T \\ s &= \{x_1, x_3, x_5, x_6, x_{10}\}, \quad s \in T \end{aligned} \tag{1}$$

Where T represents the original question, e represents the extracted entity, and s represents the question skeleton, where $e \cup s = T$.

The prompt for schema linking has three parts (entity e, full schema, question). The LLM matches all similar tables and corresponding columns during the linking process.

2.2.2 Skeleton-Guided Example Retrieval

An efficient dynamic retrieval method is introduced to replace manual few-shot example construction. Questions with similar intents (e.g., searching, counting, percentage calculation) exhibit similar structural patterns. By matching skeleton structures, representative positive examples can be retrieved to support model reasoning. The Jaccard coefficient is used to measure structural similarity between the current question and existing samples, as shown in Equation2.

$$Sim(s, D) = \frac{|s \cap D|}{|s \cup D|} \tag{2}$$

Where D represents existing data, s represents the question skeleton, the score calculated by each row of data is finally sorted from high to low, and the corresponding number of pieces is returned as positive examples by setting the initial positive number P_0. The advantage of this method is that it can ensure the efficiency of retrieval while performing accurate retrieval.

Retrieved positive examples are formatted as Question-SQL (QS) pairs, with the prefix `[valid]` added to each pair to indicate 'positive' identification in the prompt.

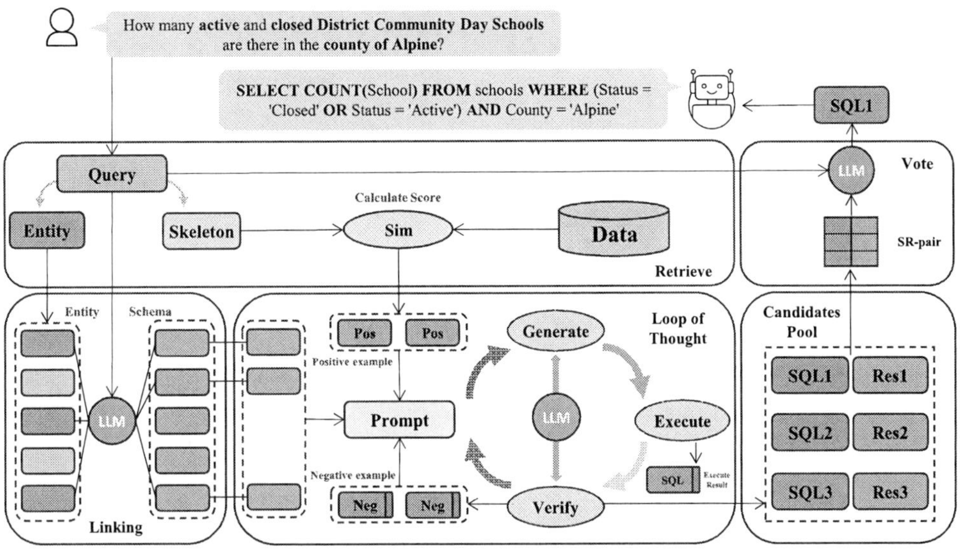

Figure 1: SCL-SQL structure illustration. The 'Pos' mark represents the positive sample, the 'Neg' mark represents the negative sample, and SQL and Res represent the generated SQL and the execution result. The numbers behind them indicate the number of loops in which they are generated.

2.3 Loop of Thought

We propose a loop-structured LLM reasoning process to address complex text-to-SQL problems. The loop consists of four stages: (1) Prompting, (2) Generation, (3) Execution, (4) Verification. The goal of these four stages is to enable the LLM to engage in iterative reasoning by comparing positive and negative examples. The specific process is illustrated as follows.

(1) Prompting: A prompt is constructed by integrating the original question, the linked database schema, positive examples retrieved via skeleton-guided example retrieval, and negative examples from the verification stage, aiming to guide the LLMâĂŹs SQL generation.

(2) Generation: The constructed prompt is fed into the LLM to generate candidate SQL statements.

(3) Execution: The generated SQL statements are executed, and both the SQL and their execution results are passed to the verification stage.

(4) Verification: A self-contrastive mechanism is applied, where the LLM evaluates whether the SQL and its result are logically correct. The verification outcome is represented as a binary pseudo-probability, with 0 indicating failure and 1 indicating success.

The most critical step in the loop of thought is result verification. However, (Huang et al., 2024) showed that directly relying on LLM for result verification and correction may lead to performance degradation. In the text-to-SQL task, the key evaluation criterion is whether the SQL retrieves the expected results. To address this, we design a result-guided verification mechanism, focusing on two aspects:

(1) Execution verification: Whether the SQL executes successfully and whether the result is empty.

(2) Logical verification: Whether the result logically matches the query intent. For instance, when querying the most sold car, the expected result should include the car's name. If irrelevant or multiple results are returned, the SQL is considered logically invalid.

If the verification passes, the SQL-Result (SR) pair is added to a candidate pool. If the pool contains only one entry, it is selected as the final output. If the verification fails, the SR pair is treated as a negative example and used in the next round of prompt construction. It is structured as a triplet SQL, result, cause, with a prefix label [invalid]. As shown in Figure 2.

In the whole process of the loop of thought, negative examples are not only used to correct errors but also an important tool to guide the LLM to optimize the thought of generation in the loop. By emphasizing negative examples, avoid repeating errors. The process is repeated until the verification passes or a maximum loop times L is reached. In this process, to reduce the influence of positive examples on modification, a positive decay mechanism is designed here. The number of positive examples will decrease with the increase in the number of negative examples, and their relationship is shown in Equation 3.

$$P = P_0 - \alpha \cdot N, \alpha \in \mathbb{Z} \tag{3}$$

Where P_0 represents the initial number of positive examples, P represents the current number of positive examples, N represents the number of negative examples, α is the correlation coefficient of positive and negative examples, and must be an integer. This mechanism aims to prevent the adverse effects of positive examples on modifications at a later stage.

Through this design, it is not necessary to make specific few-shot examples. The generation process can be manipulated by positive and negative examples. In loop execution, the LLM can quickly provide results for simple questions, while the LLM can call the loop to think repeatedly and provide more diverse responses for complex questions.

2.4 Candidates Selection

Despite loop-based refinement, LLM may still misjudge results. To mitigate this, each SR pair is stored in a candidate pool. When multiple candidates exist, a voting mechanism is employed to determine the final selection. The LLM evaluates each SR pair based on the user query and provides votes accordingly. Compared to directly correcting erroneous SQLs, selecting the best one through voting among existing candidates is more efficient and reliable. The effectiveness of this strategy is further analyzed in Section 4.3.

[valid]
Question: Please list the phone numbers of the schools with the top 3 SAT excellence rate.
SQL: SELECT phone_number FROM schools ORDER BY sat_excellence_rate DESC LIMIT 3;
[valid]
Question: List the names of the top 10 products with the highest customer ratings, but only
if they have more than 100 reviews.
SQL: SELECT product_name FROM products WHERE review_count > 100 ORDER BY customer_rating DESC LIMIT 10;

[invalid]
SQL:
SELECT employee_email FROM employees ORDER BY annual_salary DESC LIMIT 5;
Result:
OperationalError: no such column: employee_email
Reason:
employee_email does not exist in the table, which is obviously the incorrect column
[invalid]
SQL:
SELECT email, annual_salary FROM employees ORDER BY annual_salary DESC LIMIT 5;
Result:
[('john.doe@example.com', 150000), ('jane.smith@example.com', 145000).....
Reason:
The question only asks to return the mailbox, and the salary is returned inside, which obviously does not meet the requirements of the question

Figure 2: Positive and negative examples. Green [valid] indicates a positive example label, and red [invalid] indicates a negative example label.

3 Experiments

3.1 Setup

For the positive instance retrieval number P_0, we set it to 3, the maximum loop number L of the thinking loop to 3, and the correlation coefficient of positive and negative cases to 1. The temperature of LLM is set to 0.1.

3.2 Dataset

[1] SPIDER(Yu et al., 2018)[1]: A large-scale, complex cross-domain text-to-SQL dataset containing over 10,000 questions and nearly 6,000 unique SQL queries covering 200 databases and 138 different domains.

[2] BIRD(Li et al., 2023c)[2]: The most challenging large-scale cross-domain text-to-SQL benchmark. Contains 12,751 pairs of data and 95 databases covering 37 fields.

[1]https://yale-lily.github.io/spider
[2]https://bird-bench.github.io/

3.3 Baseline

To ensure a fair comparison, few-shot learning methods with validated results are selected as baseline models, such as DIN-SQL(Pourreza and Rafiei, 2023), DAIL-SQL(Gao et al., 2024), TA-SQL(Qu et al., 2024), MAC-SQL(Wang et al., 2023). The second category evaluates the improvement of LLMs using the proposed SCL method, with GPT-3.5, GPT-4, and GPT-4o as base models.

3.4 Evaluation Metrics

To facilitate comparison with other similar types of work, the evaluation process mainly includes the following two indicators: (1)EX: Represents the execution accuracy of the generated SQL by calculating how close the SQL is to the real SQL execution result. (2)VES: Used to calculate the efficiency of generating valid SQL. SQL efficiency considerations are added to accuracy.

3.5 Result

As shown in Table 1, SCL-SQL outperforms existing methods on SPIDER and BIRD, especially on the complex BIRD dataset. It achieves higher EX and VES scores, improving robustness and semantic accuracy. The gap between GPT-4 and GPT-4o further demonstrates the method's scalability. Our method generates executable and accurate SQL, highlighting its effectiveness and generalizability.

As shown in Table 2, SCL-SQL consistently enhances the performance of all evaluated LLMs. Notably, the improvements extend beyond simple queries, with significant gains on moderate and challenging samples. This demonstrates that SCL-SQL not only improves overall accuracy but also strengthens complex reasoning and schema understanding. Moreover, while stronger models already perform well, SCL-SQL further boosts their effectiveness, showing strong compatibility and generalizability across different model capacities.

3.6 Ablation Study

We conducted ablation experiments for the method proposed in the paper to verify the effectiveness of the proposed method. The ablation experimental results and analysis of different methods are shown in Table 3.

It can be seen that each module brings incremental improvements, but together they produce a synergistic effect. Positive examples enhance guidance, negative examples improve discrimination, and the thought loop significantly boosts iterative correction. Each module contributes from a different perspective, jointly achieving the best performance.

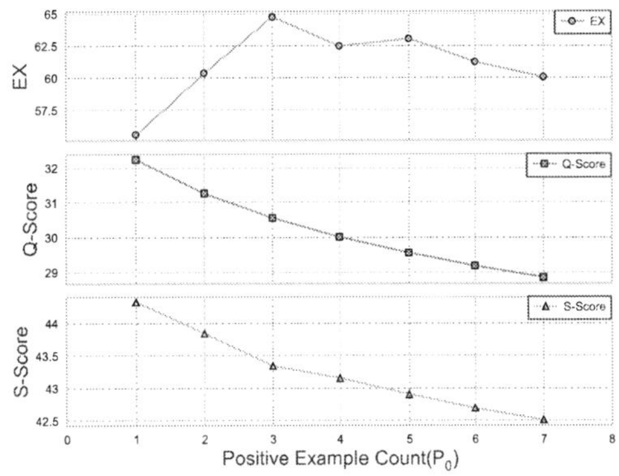

Figure 3: The effect of the number of positive examples, where EX represents the execution accuracy, and Q-Score represents the Jaccard score of the question versus the question in the positive example. S-Score indicates the Jaccard score of the ground truth SQL and the SQL in the positive example.

4 Analysis

To show the details of SCL-SQL, we conducted a detailed analysis of the parts of SCL-SQL, including hyper-parameter experiments and result analysis, where all analysis is based on the BIRD development set, and defaults are used for parameters not mentioned.

4.1 Effect of Number of Positive Examples

To verify the influence of positive examples on the result, we set a different number of initial positive examples (positive decay is off), and the result is shown in Figure 3.

It can be seen that the best results can be achieved when the initial positive example P_0 is set to 3. Beyond 3, there is a decrease in the generation accuracy due to the smaller Jaccard score of the retrieved sample. The performance drop beyond 3 positive examples is mainly due to the reduced relevance of additional positive examples. As more positive examples are added, their similarity to the current query decreases, introducing noise that misleads the model and lowers generation accuracy.

Method	SPIDER		BIRD			
	Dev	TEST	Dev		Test	
	EX(%)	EX(%)	EX(%)	VES(%)	EX(%)	VES(%)
DIN-SQL + GPT-4	82.80	85.30	50.72	58.79	55.90	59.44
DAIL-SQL + GPT-4	84.40	86.60	54.76	56.08	57.41	61.95
TA-SQL + GPT-4	85.00	–	56.19	–	59.14	–
MAC-SQL + GPT4	86.75	82.80	57.56	58.76	59.59	67.68
Ours(GPT-4)	87.04	86.35	62.25	65.62	–	–
Ours(GPT-4o)	**87.13**	**87.37**	**64.73**	**66.48**	**65.23**	**70.75**

Table 1: Result on SPIDER and BIRD, "–" indicates that the result is not provided

Method	Sim(%)	Mod(%)	Chall(%)	Total(%)
GPT-3.5	47.56	22.36	18.05	37.15
GPT-3.5 + SCL	57.08 (+9.52)	31.82 (+9.46)	20.83 (+2.78)	46.02 (+8.87)
GPT-4	54.27	34.62	31.94	46.21
GPT-4 + SCL	64.00 (+9.73)	63.44 (+28.82)	47.22 (+15.28)	62.25 (+16.04)
GPT-4o	58.59	43.53	40.68	52.99
GPT-4o + SCL	70.05 (+11.46)	59.05 (+15.52)	48.97 (+8.29)	64.73 (+11.74)

Table 2: Execution accuracy across different LLMs. 'Sim', 'Mod', and 'Chall' denote simple, moderate, and challenging subset samples. Numbers in parentheses indicate the relative improvement brought by SCL.

BIRD	EX(%)
SCL-SQL	**64.73**
w/o schema linking	62.58
w/o question split	63.23
w/o thought loop	58.34
w/o positive	60.16
w/o negative	59.32
w/o positive decay	62.23
w/o vote	61.47

Table 3: Result of ablation study. Where, w/o question split means that the question is no longer split, and the complete question is directly sent to the LLM. w/o thought loop indicates that the loop is closed and the method is executed linearly. w/o positive and w/o negative indicates that the positive example and negative example are not set respectively. w/o positive decay disables positive decay. w/o vote disables the voting mechanism and takes the last loop result as output.

4.2 Effect of Times of Loop

We set different values of L to examine the impact of loop execution times on overall performance and subset results (Sim, Mod, Chall), as shown in Figure 4.

Accuracy increases from $L = 1$ to $L = 3$, indicating that moderate iterations enhance the model's self-correction ability and decision quality. However, performance declines when $L > 3$, likely due to increased candidate pool complexity and noise interference.

Subset analysis reveals that performance on the simple subset remains relatively stable, while the moderate subset shows moderate improvements. The most significant gain is observed in the challenging subset, where accuracy peaks at $L = 3$. Beyond this point, performance decreases, suggesting that excessive iterations may introduce misleading information and hinder final judgment.

4.3 Selection Accuracy

Since the selected result from the candidate pool is not always correct, we further evaluated the accuracy of the selection mechanism. Specifically, we analyzed the loop execution behavior at $L = 3$, as shown in Figure 5, where "n-Loop" denotes samples that exit the loop at the n-th iteration. Figure 6 presents the statistics of selection errors (C-Error) at different loop stages.

It can be seen that selection errors (C-Error) account for only 3.1% of the total errors, indicating that the selection mechanism introduces relatively minor inaccuracies. Nevertheless, the loop mechanism still leads to a net performance gain, as the overall accuracy improves significantly from 58.34% to 64.73%. This demonstrates that although some selection errors occur, the overall effect of loop-based refinement remains positive.

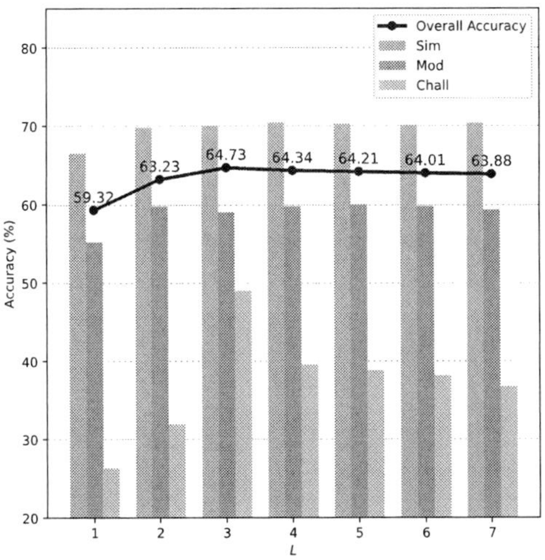

Figure 4: Result on the different number of loop cycles. The line represents the overall accuracy, and the blue, red, and green bars indicate the accuracy on the 'Sim', 'Mod', and 'Chall' subsets at different difficulty levels.

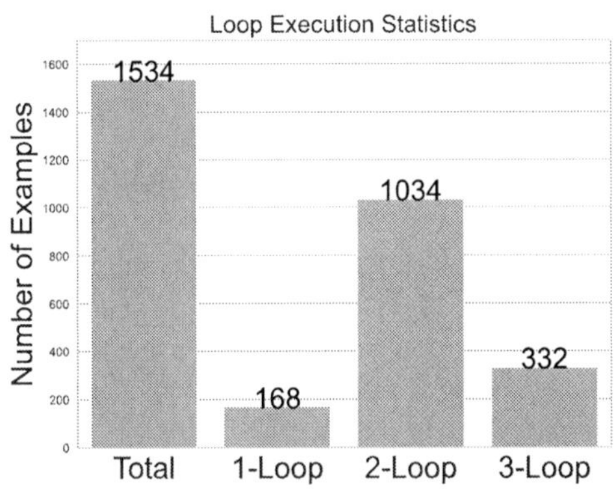

Figure 5: Loop execution statistics.

5 Related Work

5.1 Text-to-SQL

5.1.1 Design Method

The method based on the design method focuses on enhancing the relationship between text and database schema to improve the quality of SQL generation.

RAT-SQL(Wang et al., 2020) improved the schema encoding and feature representation in the encoder through the relational awareness self-attention mechanism and improved the generation accuracy. In addition, (Hui et al., 2021) proposes a multi-task text-to-SQL model (SDSQL) guided by schema dependency to capture the question interaction with the database schema without having to perform booting, significantly reducing inference time. LGESQL(Cao et al., 2021) enhances line graph coding and improves the parsing performance of heterogeneous graphs. S^2SQL(Hui et al., 2022) uses syntax-dependent information to strengthen the connection between the question and the database. Proton(Wang et al., 2022) extracted the relational structure from PLMs through the Poincare distance detection process to optimize the schema linking. RESDSQL(Li et al., 2023a) relieves the burden of schema linking in SQL parsing by decoupling schema linking from skeleton parsing.

5.1.2 Pre-training Method

Most existing Text-to-SQL pre-training methods use a single Transformer or Transformer-based encoder-decoder framework to capture task characteristics through different pre-training targets.

For example, TaBERT(Yin et al., 2020) performs well by combining natural language and tabular data representation. Similarly, GRAPPA(Yu et al., 2021) constructs and synthesizes data with SCFG and combines mask language model (MLM) pre-training to improve the table semantic parsing ability. Further, GAP(Zhao et al., 2022) enhanced the parsing ability through the joint learning of natural language and schematic representation. MIGA(Fu et al., 2023) designed four pre-training tasks based on T5(Raffel et al., 2020) to implement text-to-SQL. Similarly, GRAPHIX-T5(Li et al., 2023b) is enhanced by a graphic awareness layer. Codes(Li et al., 2024) employs incremental pre-training and data enhancement techniques to deal with schema linking and domain adaptation. Each method improves the performance of text-to-SQL parsing with different strategies.

5.1.3 Prompt-based Method

(Rajkumar et al., 2022; Liu et al., 2023) prove the advanced performance of various LLM on text-to-SQL. Then, around how to improve the performance of LLM in text-to-SQL, DIN-SQL(Pourreza and Rafiei, 2023) attempts to decompose complex text-to-SQL tasks into smaller subtasks to improve the performance of LLM in inference. DAIL-SQL(Gao et al., 2024) is a text-to-SQL solution that optimizes large language model prompts engineering, encodes SQL statements with structured knowledge, and reduces the impact of cross-domain knowledge to improve token efficiency. To eliminate the hallucination problem in LLM

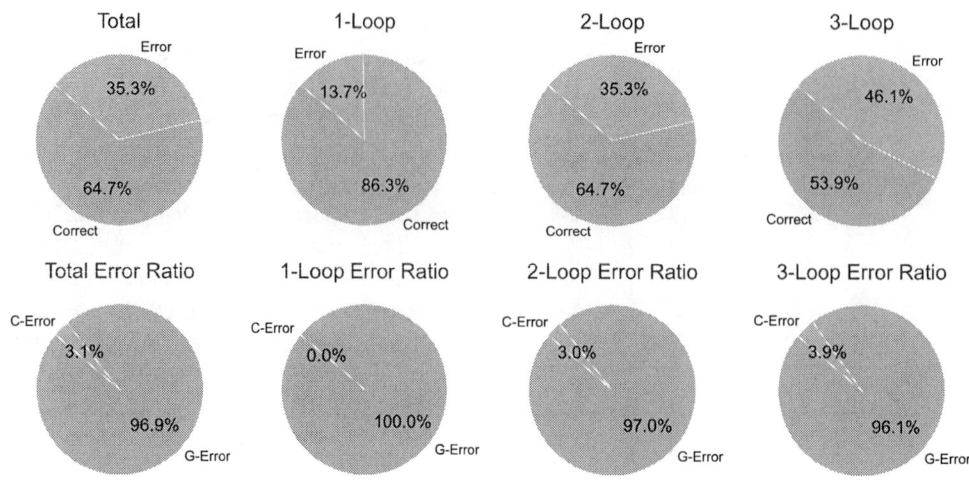

Figure 6: Error statistics. C-Error indicates an error caused by selection, and G-Error indicates an error caused by generation.

generation, TA-SQL(Qu et al., 2024) adjusted the model's processing methods for unfamiliar tasks by comparing them with previously trained tasks, reducing the model's dependence on the generalization ability to generate responses from scratch, thus significantly reducing the incidence of hallucination. MAC-SQL(Wang et al., 2023) further exploits the inference ability of LLM through serial collaboration of multiple agents.

5.2 Prompt Engineering

Although LLM have a strong understanding and inference ability, they still have difficulties in complex logical tasks such as mathematical operations and structured output. To this end, the research focus has shifted to solving problems step by step by prompt engineering guide LLM.

In this type of work, the chain of thought (CoT)(Wei et al., 2022) enhances complex reasoning ability through intermediate reasoning steps. The tree of thought (ToT)(Yao et al., 2023a) forms a tree-like structure through multiple reasoning paths to expand the search space. A mind map (GoT)(Besta et al., 2024) forms a network of crossing paths to generate more flexible solutions. ReAct(Yao et al., 2023b) proposes a general paradigm that combines reasoning and action with LLM. Prompt-based text-to-SQL methods often combine such prompt engineering to harness the potential of LLM.

6 Conclusion

We proposed a text-to-SQL method based on a self-contrastive loop of thought to solve the problem of LLM' dependence on few-shot example construction in text-to-SQL tasks. By designing the generation process as a discriminant loop structure based on a comparison of positive and negative examples, we significantly improved the accuracy and generalization of LLM and reduced the dependence on small samples. Experimental results show that the proposed method performs well on multiple data sets, and the generated SQL queries have higher accuracy. The contribution of this paper also includes the design of a question split strategy, execution, logical verification mechanism, and introduction of the "loop" structure to optimize the self-verification and error-correcting ability of LLM in text-to-SQL tasks.

7 Limitation

There are still limitations in the SCL-SQL method. The first is that it solves the problem of constructing few-shot examples in the generation process, but prompts of some complexity are still necessary. The second point is that the effect depends on the number and quality of the dataset. If the data set is too small or there are not enough similar examples, then the effect of this method will be greatly limited.

References

Maciej Besta, Nils Blach, Ales Kubicek, Robert Gerstenberger, Michal Podstawski, Lukas Gianinazzi, Joanna Gajda, Tomasz Lehmann, Hubert Niewiadomski, Piotr Nyczyk, and Torsten Hoefler. 2024. Graph of thoughts: Solving elaborate problems with large language models. In *Thirty-Eighth AAAI Conference on Artificial Intelligence, AAAI 2024, Thirty-Sixth Conference on Innovative Applications of Artificial Intelligence, IAAI 2024, Fourteenth Symposium on Educational Advances in Artificial Intelligence, EAAI 2014, February 20-27, 2024, Vancouver, Canada*, pages 17682–17690. AAAI Press.

Ben Bogin, Jonathan Berant, and Matt Gardner. 2019. Representing schema structure with graph neural networks for text-to-sql parsing. In *Proceedings of the 57th Conference of the Association for Computational Linguistics, ACL 2019, Florence, Italy, July 28- August 2, 2019, Volume 1: Long Papers*, pages 4560–4565. Association for Computational Linguistics.

Ricardo Campos, VÃ■tor Mangaravite, Arian Pasquali, AlÃ■pio Jorge, CÃl'lia Nunes, and Adam Jatowt. 2020. Yake! keyword extraction from single documents using multiple local features. *Information Sciences*, 509:257–289.

Ruisheng Cao, Lu Chen, Zhi Chen, Yanbin Zhao, Su Zhu, and Kai Yu. 2021. LGESQL: line graph enhanced text-to-sql model with mixed local and non-local relations. In *Proceedings of the 59th Annual Meeting of the Association for Computational Linguistics and the 11th International Joint Conference on Natural Language Processing, ACL/IJCNLP 2021, (Volume 1: Long Papers), Virtual Event, August 1-6, 2021*, pages 2541–2555. Association for Computational Linguistics.

Zhi Chen, Lu Chen, Hanqi Li, Ruisheng Cao, Da Ma, Mengyue Wu, and Kai Yu. 2021. Decoupled dialogue modeling and semantic parsing for multi-turn text-to-sql. *CoRR*, abs/2106.02282.

Ahmed Elgohary, Saghar Hosseini, and Ahmed Hassan Awadallah. 2020. Speak to your parser: Interactive text-to-sql with natural language feedback. In *Proceedings of the 58th Annual Meeting of the Association for Computational Linguistics, ACL 2020, Online, July 5-10, 2020*, pages 2065–2077. Association for Computational Linguistics.

Yingwen Fu, Wenjie Ou, Zhou Yu, and Yue Lin. 2023. MIGA: A unified multi-task generation framework for conversational text-to-sql. In *Thirty-Seventh AAAI Conference on Artificial Intelligence, AAAI 2023, Thirty-Fifth Conference on Innovative Applications of Artificial Intelligence, IAAI 2023, Thirteenth Symposium on Educational Advances in Artificial Intelligence, EAAI 2023, Washington, DC, USA, February 7-14, 2023*, pages 12790–12798. AAAI Press.

Yujian Gan, Xinyun Chen, and Matthew Purver. 2023. Re-appraising the schema linking for text-to-SQL. In *Findings of the Association for Computational Linguistics: ACL 2023*, pages 835–852, Toronto, Canada. Association for Computational Linguistics.

Dawei Gao, Haibin Wang, Yaliang Li, Xiuyu Sun, Yichen Qian, Bolin Ding, and Jingren Zhou. 2024. Text-to-sql empowered by large language models: A benchmark evaluation. *Proc. VLDB Endow.*, 17(5):1132–1145.

Luyu Gao, Aman Madaan, Shuyan Zhou, Uri Alon, Pengfei Liu, Yiming Yang, Jamie Callan, and Graham Neubig. 2023. PAL: program-aided language models. In *International Conference on Machine Learning, ICML 2023, 23-29 July 2023, Honolulu, Hawaii, USA*, volume 202 of *Proceedings of Machine Learning Research*, pages 10764–10799. PMLR.

Zihui Gu, Ju Fan, Nan Tang, Songyue Zhang, Yuxin Zhang, Zui Chen, Lei Cao, Guoliang Li, Sam Madden, and Xiaoyong Du. 2023. Interleaving pre-trained language models and large language models for zero-shot NL2SQL generation. *CoRR*, abs/2306.08891.

Jie Huang, Xinyun Chen, Swaroop Mishra, Huaixiu Steven Zheng, Adams Wei Yu, Xinying Song, and Denny Zhou. 2024. Large language models cannot self-correct reasoning yet. In *The Twelfth International Conference on Learning Representations, ICLR 2024, Vienna, Austria, May 7-11, 2024*. OpenReview.net.

Binyuan Hui, Ruiying Geng, Lihan Wang, Bowen Qin, Bowen Li, Jian Sun, and Yongbin Li. 2022. S^2sql: Injecting syntax to question-schema interaction graph encoder for text-to-sql parsers. *CoRR*, abs/2203.06958.

Binyuan Hui, Xiang Shi, Ruiying Geng, Binhua Li, Yongbin Li, Jian Sun, and Xiaodan Zhu. 2021. Improving text-to-sql with schema dependency learning. *CoRR*, abs/2103.04399.

Shima Imani, Liang Du, and Harsh Shrivastava. 2023. Mathprompter: Mathematical reasoning using large language models. In *Proceedings of the The 61st Annual Meeting of the Association for Computational Linguistics: Industry Track, ACL 2023, Toronto, Canada, July 9-14, 2023*, pages 37–42. Association for Computational Linguistics.

Haoyang Li, Jing Zhang, Cuiping Li, and Hong Chen. 2023a. RESDSQL: decoupling schema linking and skeleton parsing for text-to-sql. In *Thirty-Seventh AAAI Conference on Artificial Intelligence, AAAI 2023, Thirty-Fifth Conference on Innovative Applications of Artificial Intelligence, IAAI 2023, Thirteenth Symposium on Educational Advances in Artificial Intelligence, EAAI 2023, Washington, DC, USA, February 7-14, 2023*, pages 13067–13075. AAAI Press.

Haoyang Li, Jing Zhang, Hanbing Liu, Ju Fan, Xiaokang Zhang, Jun Zhu, Renjie Wei, Hongyan Pan,

Cuiping Li, and Hong Chen. 2024. Codes: Towards building open-source language models for text-to-sql. *Proc. ACM Manag. Data*, 2(3):127.

Jinyang Li, Binyuan Hui, Reynold Cheng, Bowen Qin, Chenhao Ma, Nan Huo, Fei Huang, Wenyu Du, Luo Si, and Yongbin Li. 2023b. Graphix-t5: Mixing pre-trained transformers with graph-aware layers for text-to-sql parsing. In *Thirty-Seventh AAAI Conference on Artificial Intelligence, AAAI 2023, Thirty-Fifth Conference on Innovative Applications of Artificial Intelligence, IAAI 2023, Thirteenth Symposium on Educational Advances in Artificial Intelligence, EAAI 2023, Washington, DC, USA, February 7-14, 2023*, pages 13076–13084. AAAI Press.

Jinyang Li, Binyuan Hui, Ge Qu, Jiaxi Yang, Binhua Li, Bowen Li, Bailin Wang, Bowen Qin, Ruiying Geng, Nan Huo, Xuanhe Zhou, Chenhao Ma, Guoliang Li, Kevin Chen-Chuan Chang, Fei Huang, Reynold Cheng, and Yongbin Li. 2023c. Can LLM already serve as A database interface? A big bench for large-scale database grounded text-to-sqls. In *Advances in Neural Information Processing Systems 36: Annual Conference on Neural Information Processing Systems 2023, NeurIPS 2023, New Orleans, LA, USA, December 10 - 16, 2023*.

Xi Victoria Lin, Richard Socher, and Caiming Xiong. 2020. Bridging textual and tabular data for cross-domain text-to-sql semantic parsing. In *Findings of the Association for Computational Linguistics: EMNLP 2020, Online Event, 16-20 November 2020*, volume EMNLP 2020 of *Findings of ACL*, pages 4870–4888. Association for Computational Linguistics.

Aiwei Liu, Xuming Hu, Lijie Wen, and Philip S. Yu. 2023. A comprehensive evaluation of chatgpt's zero-shot text-to-sql capability. *CoRR*, abs/2303.13547.

Linyong Nan, Yilun Zhao, Weijin Zou, Narutatsu Ri, Jaesung Tae, Ellen Zhang, Arman Cohan, and Dragomir Radev. 2023a. Enhancing few-shot text-to-sql capabilities of large language models: A study on prompt design strategies. *CoRR*, abs/2305.12586.

Linyong Nan, Yilun Zhao, Weijin Zou, Narutatsu Ri, Jaesung Tae, Ellen Zhang, Arman Cohan, and Dragomir Radev. 2023b. Enhancing text-to-sql capabilities of large language models: A study on prompt design strategies. In *Findings of the Association for Computational Linguistics: EMNLP 2023, Singapore, December 6-10, 2023*, pages 14935–14956. Association for Computational Linguistics.

Mohammadreza Pourreza and Davood Rafiei. 2023. DIN-SQL: decomposed in-context learning of text-to-sql with self-correction. *CoRR*, abs/2304.11015.

Mohammadreza Pourreza, Davood Rafiei, Yuxi Feng, Raymond Li, Zhenan Fan, and Weiwei Zhang. 2024. Sql-encoder: Improving NL2SQL in-context learning through a context-aware encoder. *CoRR*, abs/2403.16204.

Ge Qu, Jinyang Li, Bowen Li, Bowen Qin, Nan Huo, Chenhao Ma, and Reynold Cheng. 2024. Before generation, align it! A novel and effective strategy for mitigating hallucinations in text-to-sql generation. In *Findings of the Association for Computational Linguistics, ACL 2024, Bangkok, Thailand and virtual meeting, August 11-16, 2024*, pages 5456–5471. Association for Computational Linguistics.

Colin Raffel, Noam Shazeer, Adam Roberts, Katherine Lee, Sharan Narang, Michael Matena, Yanqi Zhou, Wei Li, and Peter J. Liu. 2020. Exploring the limits of transfer learning with a unified text-to-text transformer. *J. Mach. Learn. Res.*, 21:140:1–140:67.

Nitarshan Rajkumar, Raymond Li, and Dzmitry Bahdanau. 2022. Evaluating the text-to-sql capabilities of large language models. *CoRR*, abs/2204.00498.

Bailin Wang, Richard Shin, Xiaodong Liu, Oleksandr Polozov, and Matthew Richardson. 2020. RAT-SQL: relation-aware schema encoding and linking for text-to-sql parsers. In *Proceedings of the 58th Annual Meeting of the Association for Computational Linguistics, ACL 2020, Online, July 5-10, 2020*, pages 7567–7578. Association for Computational Linguistics.

Bing Wang, Changyu Ren, Jian Yang, Xinnian Liang, Jiaqi Bai, Qian-Wen Zhang, Zhao Yan, and Zhoujun Li. 2023. MAC-SQL: A multi-agent collaborative framework for text-to-sql. *CoRR*, abs/2312.11242.

Lihan Wang, Bowen Qin, Binyuan Hui, Bowen Li, Min Yang, Bailin Wang, Binhua Li, Jian Sun, Fei Huang, Luo Si, and Yongbin Li. 2022. Proton: Probing schema linking information from pre-trained language models for text-to-sql parsing. In *KDD '22: The 28th ACM SIGKDD Conference on Knowledge Discovery and Data Mining, Washington, DC, USA, August 14 - 18, 2022*, pages 1889–1898. ACM.

Jason Wei, Xuezhi Wang, Dale Schuurmans, Maarten Bosma, Brian Ichter, Fei Xia, Ed H. Chi, Quoc V. Le, and Denny Zhou. 2022. Chain-of-thought prompting elicits reasoning in large language models. In *Advances in Neural Information Processing Systems 35: Annual Conference on Neural Information Processing Systems 2022, NeurIPS 2022, New Orleans, LA, USA, November 28 - December 9, 2022*.

Sun Yang, Qiong Su, Zhishuai Li, Ziyue Li, Hangyu Mao, Chenxi Liu, and Rui Zhao. 2024. Sql-to-schema enhances schema linking in text-to-sql. *CoRR*, abs/2405.09593.

Shunyu Yao, Dian Yu, Jeffrey Zhao, Izhak Shafran, Tom Griffiths, Yuan Cao, and Karthik Narasimhan. 2023a. Tree of thoughts: Deliberate problem solving with large language models. In *Advances in Neural Information Processing Systems 36: Annual Conference on Neural Information Processing Systems 2023, NeurIPS 2023, New Orleans, LA, USA, December 10 - 16, 2023*.

Shunyu Yao, Jeffrey Zhao, Dian Yu, Nan Du, Izhak Shafran, Karthik R. Narasimhan, and Yuan Cao. 2023b. React: Synergizing reasoning and acting in language models. In *The Eleventh International Conference on Learning Representations, ICLR 2023, Kigali, Rwanda, May 1-5, 2023*. OpenReview.net.

Pengcheng Yin, Graham Neubig, Wen-tau Yih, and Sebastian Riedel. 2020. Tabert: Pretraining for joint understanding of textual and tabular data. In *Proceedings of the 58th Annual Meeting of the Association for Computational Linguistics, ACL 2020, Online, July 5-10, 2020*, pages 8413–8426. Association for Computational Linguistics.

Tao Yu, Chien-Sheng Wu, Xi Victoria Lin, Bailin Wang, Yi Chern Tan, Xinyi Yang, Dragomir R. Radev, Richard Socher, and Caiming Xiong. 2021. Grappa: Grammar-augmented pre-training for table semantic parsing. In *9th International Conference on Learning Representations, ICLR 2021, Virtual Event, Austria, May 3-7, 2021*. OpenReview.net.

Tao Yu, Rui Zhang, Kai Yang, Michihiro Yasunaga, Dongxu Wang, Zifan Li, James Ma, Irene Li, Qingning Yao, Shanelle Roman, Zilin Zhang, and Dragomir R. Radev. 2018. Spider: A large-scale human-labeled dataset for complex and cross-domain semantic parsing and text-to-sql task. In *Proceedings of the 2018 Conference on Empirical Methods in Natural Language Processing, Brussels, Belgium, October 31 - November 4, 2018*, pages 3911–3921. Association for Computational Linguistics.

Chen Zhao, Yu Su, Adam Pauls, and Emmanouil Antonios Platanios. 2022. Bridging the generalization gap in text-to-SQL parsing with schema expansion. In *Proceedings of the 60th Annual Meeting of the Association for Computational Linguistics (Volume 1: Long Papers)*, pages 5568–5578, Dublin, Ireland. Association for Computational Linguistics.

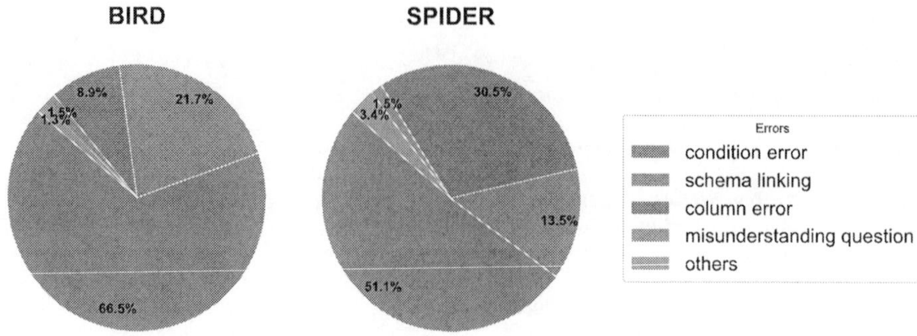

Figure 7: Error distribution statistic on BIRD and SPIDER dev set. Where "condition error" indicates wrong condition construction, "schema linking" indicates incorrect linking with tables, "column error" means the wrong column was selected, and "misunderstanding question" indicates the SQL was not compatible with question.

A Error Analysis

To fully explore our proposed approach, we also counted error types on the BIRD and SPIDER dev datasets in Figure 7. Among them, we mainly examine schema linking and semantic error. As the figure shows, the most common error types are conditional errors. Conditional errors account for more than 50% of total errors in BIRD and SPIDER. Compared to past methods, we have reduced error rates in many aspects, but we still lack advantages in constructing SQL for complex conditions. We give examples of different error types in Tables 4, 5, 6, 7, and 8.

Schema Linking Error	
BIRD	
Question:	How many schools in Fresno (directly funded) have number of test takers not more than 250?
PRED:	SELECT COUNT(*) FROM schools AS s INNER JOIN satscores AS ss ON s.CDSCode = ss.cds WHERE s.City = 'Fresno' AND s.FundingType = 'Directly funded' AND ss.NumTstTakr <= 250
GOLD:	SELECT COUNT(T1.CDSCode) FROM frpm AS T1 INNER JOIN satscores AS T2 ON T1.CDSCode = T2.cds WHERE T1.‘Charter Funding Type‘ = 'Directly funded' AND T1.‘County Name‘ = 'Fresno' AND T2.NumTstTakr <= 250
SPIDER	
Question:	What are the locations and names of all stations with capacity between 5000 and 10000?
PRED:	SELECT location, station_name FROM stations WHERE capacity BETWEEN 5000 AND 10000
GOLD:	SELECT LOCATION , name FROM stadium WHERE capacity BETWEEN 5000 AND 10000

Table 4: Examples of schema linking errors.

Condition Error	
BIRD	
Question:	Please list the phone numbers of the direct charter-funded schools that are opened after 2000/1/1.
PRED:	SELECT schools.Phone FROM frpm INNER JOIN schools ON frpm.CDSCode = schools.CDSCode WHERE frpm.‘Charter School (Y/N)‘ = 1 AND frpm.‘Charter Funding Type‘ = 'Directly funded' AND schools.OpenDate > '2000-01-01' AND schools.Phone IS NOT NULL AND schools.OpenDate IS NOT NULL AND schools.Charter IS NOT NULL;
GOLD:	SELECT T2.Phone FROM frpm AS T1 INNER JOIN schools AS T2 ON T1.CDSCode = T2.CDSCode WHERE T1.‘Charter Funding Type‘ = 'Directly funded' AND T1.‘Charter School (Y/N)‘ = 1 AND T2.OpenDate > '2000-01-01'
SPIDER	
Question:	What is the maximum capacity and the average of all stadiums?
PRED:	SELECT MAX(Capacity) AS Max_Capacity, AVG(Average) AS Avg_Attendance FROM stadium
GOLD:	SELECT max(capacity), average FROM stadium

Table 5: Examples of condition errors.

Column Error	
BIRD	
Question:	If there are any, what are the websites address of the schools with a free meal count of 1,900-2,000 to students aged 5-17? Include the name of the school.
PRED:	`SELECT frpm.'School Name', schools.'Web' FROM frpm INNER JOIN schools ON frpm.'CDSCode' = schools.'CDSCode' WHERE frpm.'Free Meal Count (Ages 5-17)' BETWEEN 1900 AND 2000 AND schools.'Website' IS NOT NULL;`
GOLD:	`SELECT T2.Websit, T1.'School Name' FROM frpm AS T1 INNER JOIN schools AS T2 ON T1.CDSCode = T2.CDSCode WHERE T1.'Free Meal Count (Ages 5-17)' BETWEEN 1900 AND 2000 AND T2.Website IS NOT NULL`
SPIDER	
Question:	Find the average and maximum age for each type of pet.
PRED:	`SELECT Pets.PetType, AVG(Pets.pet_age) AS average_age, MAX(Pets.pet_age) AS maximum_age FROM Pets JOIN Has_Pet ON Pets.PetID = Has_Pet.PetID GROUP BY Pets.PetType;`
GOLD:	`SELECT avg(pet_age) , max(pet_age) , pettype FROM pets GROUP BY pettype`

Table 6: Examples of column errors.

Question misunderstanding	
BIRD	
Question:	Of the schools that offers a magnet program serving a grade span of Kindergarten to 8th grade, how many offers Multiple Provision Types? List the number of cities that offers a Kindergarten to 8th grade span and indicate how many schools are there serving such grade span for each city.
PRED:	`SELECT COUNT(*) AS NumberOfSchoolsWithMultipleProvisionTypes FROM schools JOIN frpm ON schools.CDSCode = frpm.CDSCode WHERE schools.Magnet = 1 AND schools.GSserved = 'K-8' AND frpm.'NSLP Provision Status' = 'Multiple Provision Types'; - Second part: List the number of cities and the number of schools serving a K-8 grade span SELECT schools.City, COUNT(*) AS NumberOfSchools FROM schools WHERE schools.GSserved = 'K-8' GROUP BY schools.City;`
GOLD:	`SELECT T2.City, COUNT(T2.CDSCode) FROM frpm AS T1 INNER JOIN schools AS T2 ON T1.CDSCode = T2.CDSCode WHERE T2.Magnet = 1 AND T2.GSoffered = 'K-8' AND T1.'NSLP Provision Status' = 'Multiple Provision Types' GROUP BY T2.City`
BIRD	
Question:	Which model has the most version(make) of cars?
PRED:	`SELECT ml.Model, COUNT(DISTINCT cn.Make) AS make_count FROM model_list ml JOIN car_names cn ON ml.Model = cn.Model GROUP BY ml.Model ORDER BY make_count DESC LIMIT 1;`
GOLD:	`SELECT Model FROM CAR_NAMES GROUP BY Model ORDER BY count(*) DESC LIMIT 1;`

Table 7: Example of question misunderstanding errors.

Other Error	
BIRD	
Question:	Among the customers who paid in euro, how many of them have a monthly consumption of over 1000?
PRED:	`SELECT COUNT(DISTINCT yearmonth.CustomerID) FROM customers INNER JOIN yearmonth ON customers.CustomerID = yearmonth.CustomerID WHERE customers.Currency = 'EUR' AND yearmonth.Consumption > 1000`
GOLD:	`SELECT COUNT(*) FROM yearmonth AS T1 INNER JOIN customers AS T2 ON T1.CustomerID = T2.CustomerID WHERE T2.Currency = 'EUR' AND T1.Consumption > 1000.00`
BIRD	
Question:	List the first and last name of all players in the order of birth date.
PRED:	`SELECT first_name, last_name FROM players ORDER BY birth_date ASC`
GOLD:	`SELECT first_name , last_name FROM players ORDER BY birth_date`

Table 8: Examples of other errors.

Combining Automated and Manual Data for Effective Downstream Fine-Tuning of Transformers for Low-Resource Language Applications

Ulyana Isaeva[1], **Danil Astafurov**[1,2], **Nikita Martynov**[1,3],

[1]Sber, [2]ITMO University, [3]New Economic School,

Correspondence: ulyana.isaeva20@gmail.com

Abstract

This paper addresses the constraints of downstream applications of pre-trained language models (PLMs) for low-resource languages. These constraints are pre-train data deficiency preventing a low-resource language from being well represented in a PLM and inaccessibility of high-quality task-specific data annotation that limits task learning. We propose to use automatically labeled texts combined with manually annotated data in a two-stage task fine-tuning approach. The experiments revealed that utilizing such methodology combined with vocabulary adaptation may compensate for the absence of a targeted PLM or the deficiency of manually annotated data. The methodology is validated on the morphological tagging task for the Udmurt language. We publish our best model that achieved 93.25% token accuracy on HuggingFace Hub[1] along with the training code[2].

1 Introduction

The evolution of transformer-based pre-trained language models (PLMs) has enabled leveraging them as a basis to fine-tune for numerous downstream tasks, including morphological analysis (Baxi and Bhatt, 2024). The pipeline is complicated for low-resource languages (LRLs), which are rarely included in the pre-training data of PLMs, primarily due to the scarcity of data available (Imani-Googhari et al., 2023). When tackling a downstream task for a LRL without a PLM, one approach to address the data deficiency is to scale up the volume of high-quality task-specific data annotation.

Annotated texts in LRLs are contributed mainly by field linguists, who indicate the primary demand for such tools. However, these specialists do not necessarily own the technical skills required to utilize state-of-the-art deep learning-based approaches. Thus, rule-based algorithms have become the typical approach to developing morphological tools for LRLs. They face limitations for languages with morphological form ambiguity, where they predict multiple morphological descriptions for a single word. Proper disambiguation requires costly manual annotation by rare specialists. Given these constraints, ambiguous annotation is more accessible and scalable than manually disambiguated labels.

Addressing these considerations, we propose a two-stage fine-tuning methodology using automatically ambiguously annotated data combined with manually labeled data to achieve optimal performance in the morphological analysis task. Our experiments focus on the Udmurt language, which, while not entirely low-resource in terms of available data, was not included in the pre-training data of open-source multilingual PLMs until recently. The resulting morphological tagging tool performance is comparable to that of an alternative approach on the basis of a massively multilingual PLM. Thus, the proposed method is supposed to compensate for the absence of a PLM for a LRL. We also show that this approach can reach baseline performance with up to 3 times less manually annotated data.

To put our findings into practice, we open-source a morphological analyzer for Udmurt with an accuracy of 93.25% on all test tokens and 85.7% on tokens with ambiguous labels. Of all our experiments, the maximum performance was achieved using a recently introduced Glot500-m model (Imani-Googhari et al., 2023), which, among other 500+ languages, was pre-trained on texts in Udmurt.

[1]https://huggingface.co/ulyanaisaeva/bert-morph-tagger-udmurt

[2]https://github.com/ulyanaisaeva/bert-morph-tagger-udmurt

Proceedings of the 1st Joint Workshop on Large Language Models and Structure Modeling (XLLM 2025), pages 86–90

2 Methodology

We model the morphological analysis task as a token classification problem, where each label is a concatenation of a part-of-speech (POS) tag and morphological features of the word.

The architecture consists of a transformer encoder and a dense projection layer, predicting label probabilities for input words. It outputs a tensor of shape $L \times K$ where L is sequence length (i.e., the number of words) and K is the number of unique labels. If a word is tokenized into multiple subtokens, we assign the label to the first one and mask out all the subsequent word subtokens during loss calculation.

Applying transformer-based pre-trained encoder models to downstream classification tasks has proven effective in numerous studies. For LRLs that commonly lack a specialized PLM, the PLMs of first choice are multilingual ones, like mBERT, which inherits the original BERT architecture (Devlin et al., 2019) and has been pre-trained on the top 100 languages with the largest Wikipedias. Ács et al. (2021) investigates the transferability of BERT-like models to unseen languages (i.e., languages the model has not been pre-trained on) via fine-tuning on limited training data. The authors observe that high-resource monolingual models, though effective in their specific language, show worse cross-language transferability than multilingual models in token classification tasks such as POS tagging and named entity recognition. Importantly, Ács et al. (2021) showed that monolingual models for genetically unrelated languages can transfer more efficiently than multilingual ones in cases where the languages share the same script, e.g., ruBERT for Russian performed better than multilingual BERT applied to Uralic languages with Cyrillic script (Erzya, Moksha, Komi Permyak).

2.1 Tokenizer adaptation

The observations related to script similarity are attributed to the impact of tokenization on model performance. The more a tokenizer is relevant to a given language, the less a word is split into pieces during tokenization. Since multilingual models' tokenizers are trained on languages with various scripts, their vocabularies tend to contain shorter subwords and thus have higher fertility, defined as the average number of word pieces per word.

Presumably, for token classification tasks like morphological tagging or named entity recognition, a more targeted tokenizer (i.e., with lower fertility) would be more optimal. This suggestion is tested by Wang et al. (2020), showing that adapting a model's tokenizer to an unseen language improves downstream zero-shot performance in NER tasks in that language. The methodology implies adding 30K new targeted items to the vocabulary while randomly initializing the corresponding model's embedding weights.

In this study, we utilize tokenizer vocabulary adaptation (VA) to improve morphological tagging accuracy. As an adaptation technique, we leverage the Vocabulary Initialization with Partial Inheritance approach (Samenko et al., 2021). It aims at preserving the model's knowledge from the pretraining stage instead of learning all embedding weights from scratch. Original model embedding weights are inherited for tokens in the new vocabulary, which are also found in the initial one; the other weights are randomly initialized.

To find the optimal vocabulary size, we fitted several WordPiece (following mBERT) tokenizers on ***Train-AML*** with sizes ranging from 1K to 128K (log step with base 2) and measured fertility on the ***Valid-AML***. At the size of 32K, the fertility plateaus around 1.18, and so does the ratio of tokens not split into subwords (85.93%); this vocabulary size is selected for future experiments.

2.2 Combining automated and manual annotation

Morphological form ambiguity (homonymy) is a phenomenon where the same word form may be attributed with different morphological description depending on the context, e.g., English 'records' is a plural noun in 'This song sets *records* for popularity' and a 3rd person singular present tense verb in 'He *records* and plays ten instruments'. The disambiguation of such labels requires word context understanding. Yet, classifying a token accurately only to a group of ambiguous labels is a task achievable even by simple context-unaware algorithms. In the example above, it would mean reducing the space of possible labels to 'NOUN,pl', 'VERB,3sg,prs' without selecting the single correct label. The two-step fine-tuning approach proposed in this work leverages this mechanism to improve morphological tagging accuracy, including for words with ambiguity.

The first step is to pre-fine-tune (PFT) the classifier using ambiguously annotated data (e.g., with a context-unaware analyzer) with multiple pseudo-correct labels for words with morphological homonymy. This stage's learning objective is to narrow the set of most probably predicted labels to a group of labels that correspond to ambiguous word forms. We hypothesize that such pre-fine-tuning would provide the model with an initial intuition about the homonymous nature of morphological labels.

Seemingly, this PFT could be modeled as a multi-label classification problem. In fact, by the nature of the task, only one of a word's homonymous forms is actually correct. This is why we model this pre-training stage as single-label multi-class classification with a softmax for class probabilities, though it requires additional changes to how we treat multiple pseudo-correct labels during loss calculation.

The basic loss function for multiclass classification is cross-entropy, defined as a sum of negative predicted log probabilities of positive labels.

$$CE = \sum_{\{i|K_i \in correct\}} -\log \hat{p}_i$$

The minimum of this loss function is achieved when these probabilities are equal and sum into 1, while the others are all equal to 0. Given the nature of morphological homonymy, it is suboptimal to teach the classifier to equalize probabilities in the set of pseudo-correct labels with only one being actually true. Taking this into account, we propose to calculate the PFT loss function as a negative logarithm of the sum of predicted probabilities for positive classes.

$$MLCE = -\log \sum_{\{i|K_i \in correct\}} \hat{p}_i$$

This function would still penalize models for predicting high probabilities for wrong labels, and vice versa, yet remain indifferent to how the probabilities for pseudo-correct labels are mutually distributed.

The second training step is task fine-tuning (FT), which requires reliable manually disambiguated annotation to finally learn to precisely select from a homonymic group of tags. The model is still offered to choose from the full set of all possible labels, yet it is supposed to rely on positive bias to ambiguous labels acquired during the PFT step. Similarly to the PFT, the FT is done using the softmax activation function at the last projection layer, which outputs label probabilities that sum into 1.

2.3 Data

The proposed approach is relevant in the case of presence of 2 types of task-specific data:

- AML: automatically labeled texts where a word may contain more than one label in case further label selection is constrained by morphological ambiguity and requires context analysis or manual disambiguation.
- MDL: manually labeled (or disambiguated after automatic annotation) texts with a single label per word.

See Appendix A for the data origin details.

2.4 Metrics

To evaluate the proposed morphological tagging pipelines, we use the following metrics:

- *Token accuracy* (TAcc) is the ratio of tokens with correctly predicted tags.
- *Token accuracy (homonymous)* (TAccH) is the same metric, but calculated only on tokens with morphological form ambiguity.

3 Experiments

Model selection. We focus on the morphological analysis for the Udmurt language. Until recently, and by the time this research was planned, there had not been a multilingual model pre-trained in the Udmurt language until Glot500-m (ImaniGooghari et al., 2023) was published. Since the absence of a targeted PLM is still the case for numerous LRLs, we chose the multilingual BERT (mBERT[3]) as the baseline model. Referring to previous findings on the transferability of monolingual models sharing the same script as the target language, we also experimented with the BERT model for the Russian language (ruBERT[4], (Zmitrovich et al., 2024)), since Udmurt uses Cyrillic script too.

To keep up with the updates in the area of multilingual models, we provide a comparison with Glot500-m[5] which is pre-trained in 500+ languages, including Udmurt.

Experimental setup. The three above-mentioned models are tested in 4 main setups:

1. FT: only fine-tuning on ***Train-MDL***
2. VA+FT: vocabulary adaptation on ***Train-MDL*** and FT

[3]https://huggingface.co/google-bert/bert-base-multilingual-cased

[4]https://huggingface.co/ai-forever/ruBert-large

[5]https://huggingface.co/cis-lmu/glot500-base

3. PFT+FT: pre-fine-tuning on ***Train-AML*** and FT
4. VA-PFT-FT: VA and PFT and FT

The Udmurt language, which is our focus in this work, is not an extremely low-resource language since there are available text corpora and NLP tools. Emulating the MDL-data scarcity setup common for low-resource languages, we fine-tune the best-performing setup for ruBERT and mBERT on a reduced subset from ***Train-MDL*** (100, 200, 500, 1000, 5000 sentences of the original 10000 sentences).

4 Results & Discussion

The results of the described experiments are provided in Table 1. Every row section compares baseline (i.e., with fine-tuning only) performance to that of models with vocabulary adaptation and/or pre-training on ambiguously annotated data.

Model	TAcc	TAccH
mBERT-FT (Devlin et al., 2019)	86.28	77.04
VA-FT	87.55	77.49
PFT-FT	87.02	78.66
VA-PFT-FT	91.38	81.54
ruBERT-FT (Zmitrovich et al., 2024)	86.35	77.02
VA-FT	87.89	77.65
PFT-FT	87.32	77.87
VA-PFT-FT	91.24	81.00
Glot500-FT (ImaniGooghari et al., 2023)	92.44	85.34
VA-FT	85.63	85.63
PFT-FT	**93.25**	**85.70**
VA-PFT-FT	91.17	81.52

Table 1: Models' performance on ***Test-MDL***. See subsection 2.4 for the evaluation details.

The baseline models achieved 86.3 and 86.4 token accuracy with mBERT and ruBERT, respectively. Applying the VA procedure before the FT brings an improvement of 1.3 and 1.5 pp while PFT on the model with the original tokenizer before the FT increases the performance at 0.7 and 1.0 pp, respectively, for mBERT and ruBERT. However, the improvement brought by the cumulative usage of both VA and PFT over the FT-only baseline performance is approximately 5 pp for both backbone models. Thus, these two procedures appear far more effective when applied jointly rather than separately.

Glot500-m baseline showed the best baseline performance across our experiments and was further improved when pre-fine-tuned on ambiguous annotated data. Yet adapting the vocabulary of Glot500-m both with and without PFT decreased the overall performance.

The pipelines with VA and PFT based on mBERT and ruBERT perform worse yet comparably to FT-only Glot500-m baseline. This is important evidence suggesting that the utilization of the proposed two-stage training pipeline may be seen as an effective compensatory approach in cases when there is no available model pre-trained on the target LRL.

To address the cases of extremely LRLs where manual annotation is scarse, we trained the baseline and the enhanced pipelines on reduced train data subsets, the results are provided in Figure 1.

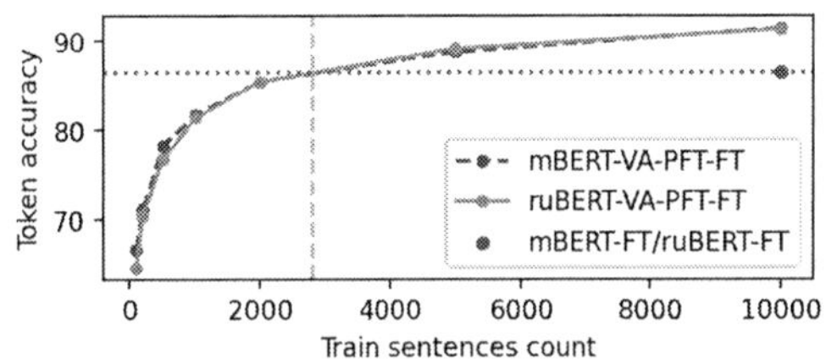

Figure 1: Model performance (token accuracy) on ***Test-MDL*** with reduced train data.

It can be observed that the proposed pipeline with VA and PFT may compensate for up to 3x less manually annotated data, i.e., utilizing the VA-PFT-FT pipeline with a 3 times reduced manually labeled train data can achieve performance comparable to that of the FT-only baseline on full-volume train data.

Despite the previous findings, the results of our experiments do not provide any evidence to choose ruBERT over mBERT since they share similar scores across all setups.

5 Conclusion

In this work, we present a two-stage fine-tuning procedure that leverages both automatically and manually annotated task-specific train data. The proposed approach combined with vocabulary adaptation increased morphological tagging accuracy by 5 pp in our experiments with the Udmurt language. We show that this improvement may compensate for train data deficiency and the absence of a specialized PLM, which are two major stumbling blocks in low-resource classification problems. As a practical outcome of the study, we open-source the best-performing morphological tagging model based on Glot500-m. We also publish the training code to facilitate the application of the methodology to other LRLs.

6 Limitations

While this study provides insights into choosing the backbone model and fine-tuning procedure for morphological analysis for low-resource languages, there are several limitations that should be considered when interpreting the results.

First, this methodology has so far been validated on only one language. We encourage future research on its applicability to different low-resource setups.

Second, in our experiments, ***AML*** and ***x-MDL*** datasets shared the same annotation scheme. Presumably, this will often be the case in the setups when the manual annotation is done over the automatic pre-labeling. Yet our experiments do not provide evidence to the contrary cases of mismatching annotation schemes.

7 Acknowledgments

The authors would like to thank Alexey Sorokin for sharing the initial idea that inspired this research.

References

Timofey Arkhangelskiy. 2019. Corpora of social media in minority Uralic languages. In *Proceedings of the Fifth International Workshop on Computational Linguistics for Uralic Languages*, pages 125–140, Tartu, Estonia. Association for Computational Linguistics.

Jatayu Baxi and Brijesh Bhatt. 2024. Recent advancements in computational morphology : A comprehensive survey. *arXiv preprint*. ArXiv:2406.05424 [cs].

Jacob Devlin, Ming-Wei Chang, Kenton Lee, and Kristina Toutanova. 2019. BERT: Pre-training of deep bidirectional transformers for language understanding. In *Proceedings of the 2019 Conference of the North American Chapter of the Association for Computational Linguistics: Human Language Technologies, Volume 1 (Long and Short Papers)*, pages 4171–4186, Minneapolis, Minnesota. Association for Computational Linguistics.

Ayyoob ImaniGooghari, Peiqin Lin, Amir Hossein Kargaran, Silvia Severini, Masoud Jalili Sabet, Nora Kassner, Chunlan Ma, Helmut Schmid, André Martins, François Yvon, and Hinrich Schütze. 2023. Glot500: Scaling multilingual corpora and language models to 500 languages. In *Proceedings of the 61st Annual Meeting of the Association for Computational Linguistics (Volume 1: Long Papers)*, pages 1082–1117, Toronto, Canada. Association for Computational Linguistics.

Yu. V. Normanskaja, O. D. Borisenko, I. B. Beloborodov, and A. I. Avetisyan. 2022. The Software System LingvoDoc and the Possibilities It Offers for Documentation and Analysis of Ob-Ugric Languages. *Doklady Mathematics*, 105(3):187–206.

Igor Samenko, Alexey Tikhonov, Borislav Kozlovskii, and Ivan P. Yamshchikov. 2021. Fine-Tuning Transformers: Vocabulary Transfer. *arXiv:2112.14569 [cs]*. ArXiv: 2112.14569.

Zihan Wang, Karthikeyan K, Stephen Mayhew, and Dan Roth. 2020. Extending Multilingual BERT to Low-Resource Languages. In *Findings of the Association for Computational Linguistics: EMNLP 2020*, pages 2649–2656, Online. Association for Computational Linguistics.

Dmitry Zmitrovich, Aleksandr Abramov, Andrey Kalmykov, Vitaly Kadulin, Maria Tikhonova, Ekaterina Taktasheva, Danil Astafurov, Mark Baushenko, Artem Snegirev, Tatiana Shavrina, Sergei S. Markov, Vladislav Mikhailov, and Alena Fenogenova. 2024. A family of pretrained transformer language models for Russian. In *Proceedings of the 2024 Joint International Conference on Computational Linguistics, Language Resources and Evaluation (LREC-COLING 2024)*, pages 507–524, Torino, Italia. ELRA and ICCL.

Judit Ács, Dániel Lévai, and András Kornai. 2021. Evaluating Transferability of BERT Models on Uralic Languages. *arXiv preprint*. ArXiv:2109.06327 [cs].

A Data origin

As a source of ambiguously annotated data, we utilize Tsakorpus (Arkhangelskiy, 2019) of standard written literary Udmurt language. This corpus is not public but is provided by the maintainer for research purposes. We annotate the texts using an open-source rule-based morphological analyzer[6] which does not conduct contextual disambiguation, i.e., it outputs all possible labels for words.

Filtering out the sentences with at least one word without a morphological label resulted in a dataset of approximately 558K words (64K sentences). Further in this paper, we refer to the corpus as the ***Train-AML***.

Manually annotated data was derived from LingvoDoc, a system for collaborative language documentation (Normanskaja et al., 2022), the data volume is 100K words (12K sentences). This data was processed with the same analyzer, and as a result, every word was attributed with both automatic labels (without disambiguation) and a manual one (which is always one of the ambiguous labels). We randomly partition this dataset into ***Train-MDL***, ***Valid-MDL*** and ***Test-MDL*** splits in a ratio 80-10-10, with the corresponding volumes of approx. 10K, 1.2K, and 1.2K sentences, respectively.

[6] `https://github.com/timarkh/uniparser-grammar-udm/`

Seamlessly Integrating Tree-Based Positional Embeddings into Transformer Models for Source Code Representation

Patryk Bartkowiak, Filip Graliński
Adam Mickiewicz University

Abstract

Transformer-based models have demonstrated significant success in various source code representation tasks. Nonetheless, traditional positional embeddings employed by these models inadequately capture the hierarchical structure intrinsic to source code, typically represented as Abstract Syntax Trees (ASTs). To address this, we propose a novel tree-based positional embedding approach that explicitly encodes hierarchical relationships derived from ASTs, including node depth and sibling indices. These hierarchical embeddings are integrated into the transformer architecture, specifically enhancing the CodeBERTa model. We thoroughly evaluate our proposed model through masked language modeling (MLM) pretraining and clone detection fine-tuning tasks. Experimental results indicate that our Tree-Enhanced CodeBERTa consistently surpasses the baseline model in terms of loss, accuracy, F1 score, precision, and recall, emphasizing the importance of incorporating explicit structural information into transformer-based representations of source code.

1 Introduction

Transformer-based models have demonstrated significant advances across numerous source code representation tasks, such as code summarization, clone detection, defect prediction, and semantic search. These models effectively leverage self-attention mechanisms, supplemented by positional embeddings, to encode the sequential order of tokens, thus achieving robust semantic understanding. However, a notable limitation arises from the fundamentally linear positional encodings typically employed by these models, which do not adequately capture the inherently hierarchical nature of programming languages (Allamanis et al., 2017; Brockschmidt et al., 2018; Hellendoorn et al., 2020).

Source code differs markedly from natural language in its explicit, structured hierarchy, most commonly represented as Abstract Syntax Trees (ASTs) (Shiv and Quirk, 2019). An AST encodes critical syntactic and semantic relationships, including nested scopes, parent-child dependencies, and sibling ordering among code constructs. Although sequential positional embeddings, such as sinusoidal or learned encodings (Vaswani et al., 2017; Devlin et al., 2018), effectively capture linear token sequences, they disregard hierarchical structure entirely. Consequently, current Transformer architectures may overlook important syntactic relationships, potentially limiting performance and generalization capabilities in source code understanding tasks.

Addressing this gap, we propose integrating tree-based positional embeddings into Transformer models, explicitly encoding the hierarchical structure of source code. Our approach introduces embeddings based on token depth within the AST hierarchy and their sibling positions, effectively guiding the self-attention mechanism to recognize and utilize structural context alongside semantic content.

In this paper, we make the following contributions.

- We propose a novel hierarchical embedding strategy to explicitly encode structural information from ASTs into Transformer-based models.
- We demonstrate how tree-based positional embeddings can be seamlessly integrated into existing Transformer architectures, specifically CodeBERTa, without significantly increasing the complexity of the model.
- Through extensive experiments, including masked language modeling (MLM) and code clone detection tasks, we illustrate that our

Proceedings of the 1st Joint Workshop on Large Language Models and Structure Modeling (XLLM 2025), pages 91–98
August 1, 2025 ©2025 Association for Computational Linguistics

Tree-Enhanced CodeBERTa outperforms similarly sized models in smaller-scale evaluations, highlighting the benefits of incorporating explicit structural context.

- We provide qualitative analysis using visualization techniques (e.g. t-SNE) to demonstrate how tree-based embeddings result in structurally coherent code representations, further validating our theoretical insights.

Our findings underscore the importance of integrating hierarchical structural information into Transformer architectures, not only enhancing source code representation but also potentially improving models for broader structured data.

2 Related Work

Transformer-based models, including GPT (Radford et al., 2018), BERT (Devlin et al., 2018), and RoBERTa (Liu et al., 2019), have significantly advanced natural language processing (NLP) and have subsequently been adapted for source code understanding tasks. This section reviews the relevant literature, classified into transformer models for source code, positional embedding methods, and tree-based code representations.

Transformers for Source Code. Pre-trained Transformer models such as CodeBERT and CodeBERTa utilize broad datasets such as CodeSearchNet to effectively learn token-level semantic representations (Ahmad et al., 2020; Feng et al., 2020; Husain et al., 2019). Although these models have achieved strong results, their effectiveness stems primarily from capturing semantic relationships between tokens without explicitly modeling the hierarchical structural relationships encoded in Abstract Syntax Trees (ASTs). Consequently, structural nuances, crucial for tasks that require deeper syntactic and semantic understanding, remain largely unaddressed.

Positional Embeddings in Transformers. The original Transformer model (Vaswani et al., 2017) employs sinusoidal positional embeddings to encode token positions within sequences, establishing order-aware representations. Subsequent developments introduced learned positional embeddings, enabling dynamic adaptation during training (Shaw et al., 2018). Recently, Rotary Positional Embeddings (RoPE) (Su et al., 2021) have emerged as an effective technique for capturing relative positional information in Transformers, achieving superior generalization in sequence modeling tasks. Despite these advancements, positional embeddings typically remain confined to linear positional encodings, which do not inherently capture hierarchical or structural relationships essential in structured data like source code (Shaw et al., 2018; Press et al., 2021).

Tree-Based Representations in Code Analysis. Various architectures have leveraged explicit tree-based structures for representing code, particularly AST-based models such as Tree-LSTMs (Tai et al., 2015a), graph neural networks (GNNs) (Tai et al., 2015b; Zhang et al., 2019), and specialized code-generation models like code2seq (Alon et al., 2018) and TreeGen (Sun et al., 2015). These models utilize tree structures to enhance code comprehension, program synthesis, and code summarization by explicitly encoding structural information. However, these methods generally rely on specialized architectures, often incompatible or challenging to integrate directly with the standard Transformer architecture. Consequently, practical adaptation in Transformer-based code models has been limited.

Recent approaches have explicitly introduced AST information into positional embeddings within Transformer architectures. Peng et al. (2022) propose a Tree-Transformer that encodes each AST node's position using a two-dimensional coordinate scheme (sibling index and parent's child count), injecting both local and global structural biases (Peng et al., 2022). Similarly, Oh and Yoo (2024) introduce CSA-Trans, which utilizes a dedicated *Code Structure Embedder* to learn structure-aware positional embeddings through a disentangled attention mechanism (Saeyoon and Shin, 2024). In contrast, our Tree-Enhanced CodeBERTa integrates hierarchical positional embeddings directly into an existing pre-trained Transformer (CodeBERTa), explicitly encoding depth and sibling indices. This maintains simplicity and scalability, avoiding the complexity of specialized attention modules or significant architectural alterations.

Our Contribution. Unlike prior works that incorporate hierarchical structures into Transformer models through specialized architectures, our approach directly integrates tree-based positional embeddings—encoding depth and sibling indices—into an existing Transformer framework. This allows for richer hierarchical representations

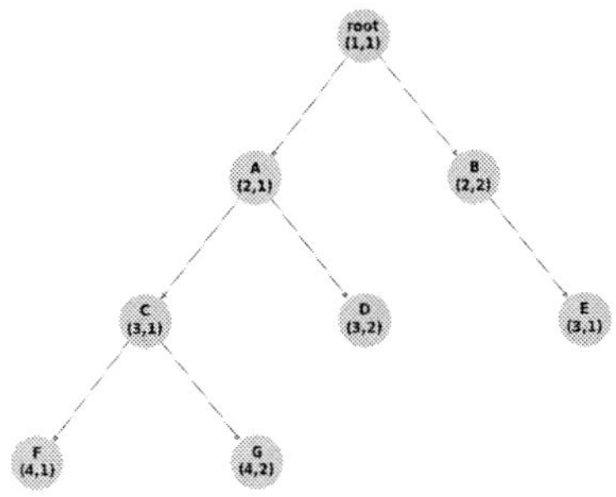

Figure 1: Visualization of hierarchical positional encoding in an AST. Each node is labeled with its name and corresponding hierarchical position (depth, sibling index), illustrating how depth and sibling relationships are assigned in tree-based positional embeddings.

without altering the model's core design. We empirically validate its effectiveness in masked language modeling and clone detection, demonstrating measurable improvements in source code representation.

3 Theoretical Foundations

Traditional positional embeddings employed in Transformer models typically assume a linear sequence of tokens, effectively capturing the sequential order but failing to represent the complex hierarchical structures inherent in many forms of structured data, notably source code. Source code is commonly represented by Abstract Syntax Trees (ASTs), which explicitly encode syntactic and semantic relationships such as nesting, parent-child dependencies, and sibling ordering. A linear positional encoding is inadequate for capturing such hierarchical nuances, motivating the need for hierarchical positional encodings.

Hierarchical positional embeddings provide a principled approach to representing each node (or token) by encoding its structural position within a tree. Formally, each node's hierarchical position can be represented by a path from the root to that node. Let $F(x)$ denote the hierarchical position of node x, defined recursively as follows:

- **Base Case**: The root node is assigned a fixed initial position:

$$F(\text{root}) = (1, 1).$$

- **Recursive Step**: For a non-root node x, its position is determined recursively from its parent $f(x)$:

$$F(x) = (F(f(x))_1 + 1, i_x),$$

where:

  - $F(f(x))_1$ refers to the depth component of the parent's position.
  - i_x is the index of x among its siblings.

Figure 1 provides a visual representation of hierarchical positional encoding, illustrating how depth and sibling indices are assigned to each node in an AST. This structure enables the model to capture both global (depth) and local (sibling order) relationships, which are then transformed into learned embedding vectors.

Each hierarchical position uniquely encodes both local (sibling order) and global (depth in the hierarchy) structural context. These positional values are transformed into learned embedding vectors at each level and then aggregated to form a single positional embedding vector $P(x)$:

$$P(x) = \text{Aggregate}\big(h(F(x)_1), h(F(x)_2)\big),$$

where $F(x)_1$ represents the depth of node x and $F(x)_2$ represents the sibling index i_x, with their corresponding learned embeddings $h(F(x)_1)$ and $h(F(x)_2)$.

This formulation allows Transformer models to inherently interpret structural relationships between tokens or nodes. Tokens with similar structural contexts (e.g., siblings or nodes within the same subtree) naturally receive similar positional embeddings, guiding the self-attention mechanism to focus appropriately on structurally relevant elements.

Moreover, hierarchical positional embeddings enhance the model's capability to capture long-range dependencies inherent in structured data. By explicitly encoding tree positions rather than linear indices, hierarchical positional embeddings facilitate the model's understanding of relationships between tokens that may be distant in a linear sequence yet closely related structurally.

4 Methodology

Overview. We propose Tree-Enhanced CodeBERTa, an extension of CodeBERTa that integrates tree-based positional embeddings explicitly derived from Abstract Syntax Trees (ASTs). By incorporating **Depth Embeddings** and **Sibling Index Embeddings**, our model captures hierarchical relationships inherent in source code, enhancing both syntactic and semantic understanding.

4.1 Tree-Based Positional Embeddings

To extract hierarchical structural information, we generate Abstract Syntax Trees (ASTs) from source code using Tree-Sitter (tre, 2007), a widely used incremental parser supporting multiple programming languages. Tree-Sitter allows efficient parsing and provides structured representations that align well with tokenized inputs, enabling precise mapping of hierarchical relationships.

We introduce two main categories of tree-based positional embeddings:

- **Depth Embeddings:** Each token receives an embedding based on its hierarchical depth, represented as $F(x)_1$, where deeper nodes correspond to more nested structures such as loops, conditionals, or function bodies.

- **Sibling Index Embeddings:** Tokens are embedded based on their relative positions among sibling nodes within the AST, maintaining local ordering essential to understanding structures like function arguments, statements within blocks, and ordered code constructs.

Additionally, we introduce a **Tree Attention Mask**, designed to focus self-attention on structurally related tokens within the AST, thus reducing noisy attention to padding or structurally irrelevant tokens.

4.2 Integration into Transformer Architecture

We explore three strategies for embedding integration into the existing CodeBERTa embedding framework:

Sum Embeddings: Structural embeddings (depth and sibling index embeddings) are summed element-wise with standard token embeddings (word embeddings, positional embeddings, and type embeddings), forming a single unified embedding without explicit distinction between semantic and structural contributions.

Weighted Sum Embeddings: A set of learnable weights dynamically balances the contributions of token, depth, sibling index, and positional embeddings. This allows the model to adaptively emphasize the most relevant structural information during training.

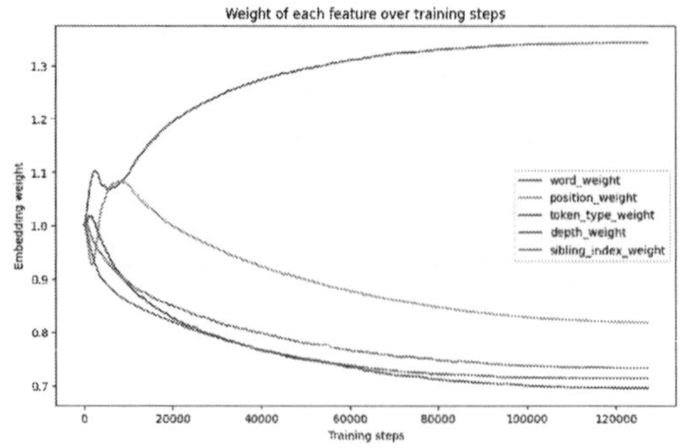

Figure 2: Evolution of embedding weights during training for the Weighted Sum configuration. The plot shows how different embedding components (word embeddings, positional embeddings, token type embeddings, depth-based embeddings, and sibling index embeddings) are dynamically weighted over training steps. Word embeddings gain prominence, while structural embeddings (depth and sibling index) gradually decrease, indicating their strongest influence early in training.

Concatenation Embeddings: Structural embeddings (depth and sibling indices) are concatenated with standard token embeddings, followed by a linear projection layer to reduce dimensionality and control model complexity. This method significantly increases the representational power of embeddings but at the cost of higher parameter count and computational complexity.

The evolution of embedding weights throughout training in the Weighted Sum configuration is illustrated in Figure 2, demonstrating how the model dynamically adjusts emphasis on structural information.

4.3 Pretraining and Fine-Tuning Tasks

To comprehensively evaluate the effectiveness of Tree-Enhanced CodeBERTa, we perform experiments across two core tasks: masked language modeling (MLM) pretraining and clone detection fine-tuning. These tasks are selected to assess the model's ability to leverage hierarchical structural information during both initial representation learning and downstream task adaptation.

Masked Language Modeling (MLM) We pretrain the model using the Masked Language Modeling objective on the CodeSearchNet dataset. During pretraining, randomly masked tokens are predicted based on their surrounding context, enriched with hierarchical positional embeddings. This setup assesses the capability of our proposed embeddings to capture both local and global structural relationships inherent in source code.

Clone Detection We fine-tune the pretrained model on a clone detection dataset (PoolC, n.d.) comprising approximately 600,000 code snippet pairs, classifying pairs as functionally equivalent (clones) or distinct. The objective of this task is to measure the practical advantages of hierarchical embeddings in discriminating structurally similar but semantically distinct code snippets, reflecting real-world benefits for source code understanding tasks.

Experimental Setup Our Tree-Enhanced CodeBERTa model is based on the CodeBERTa-small architecture, a 6-layer Transformer with 83.5 million parameters. It follows a RoBERTa-like architecture with the same number of layers and attention heads as DistilBERT. While the backbone remains unchanged, our modifications introduce additional learned parameters for hierarchical depth and sibling index embeddings. Quantitatively, our introduced hierarchical embeddings comprise two additional embedding tables, each encoding depth and sibling indices. Collectively, these tables add approximately 789,504 parameters, representing roughly 0.945% of the original model's total 83,504,416 parameters. This minimal increase ensures that the overall complexity and computational overhead remain manageable and closely comparable to the base CodeBERTa-small model. Each experiment is conducted across three independent runs with random seeds set to 12345, 550, and 42 to ensure robust statistical evaluation. Both Masked Language Modeling (MLM) and clone detection fine-tuning were trained for three epochs using the AdamW optimizer with a learning rate of 1×10^{-5} and a batch size of 32. Additionally, the Tree Attention Mask was selectively applied to special tokens, guiding the attention mechanism towards structurally significant tokens within the AST. Performance is measured using loss, accuracy, F1 score, precision, and recall to evaluate the impact of hierarchical embeddings.

To facilitate reproducibility, we provide an anonymized repository containing the full implementation, training scripts, and pre-processing details. See Appendix A for access.

5 Results

We evaluate Tree-Enhanced CodeBERTa on two tasks: masked language modeling (MLM) and clone detection. Across both, our model consistently outperforms the baseline in accuracy, F1 score, precision, and recall. Additionally, we report final training loss values to reinforce these improvements. On MLM, the Weighted Sum configuration achieves a lower loss of **0.41417** compared to **0.44388** for the original model. Similarly, in clone detection, our model attains a loss of **0.21799** versus **0.25836** for the baseline. These reductions confirm that incorporating hierarchical positional embeddings not only improves task-specific performance but also facilitates more effective representation learning.

5.1 Masked Language Modeling (MLM)

Table 1 demonstrates consistent performance improvements from tree-based positional embeddings, particularly highlighting the Weighted Sum strategy as the most effective approach.

Embedding	Acc.	F1	Precision	Recall
Original	0.8972	0.8939	0.8953	0.8972
Sum	0.9021	0.8989	0.9004	0.9021
Weighted Sum	**0.9029**	**0.8999**	**0.9012**	**0.9029**
Concatenation	0.9026	0.8993	0.9008	0.9026

Table 1: MLM task results on the CodeSearchNet dataset (averaged over 3 runs with different random seeds: 12345, 550, and 42). Standard deviations across seeds were consistently low (< 0.002), indicating stable performance improvements.

5.2 Clone Detection

Table 2 highlights the improved performance of Tree-Enhanced CodeBERTa in distinguishing semantically and structurally similar code snippets, with the Weighted Sum approach consistently achieving the best overall performance.

Embedding	Acc.	F1	Precision	Recall
Original	0.9173	0.9172	0.9180	0.9173
Sum	0.9159	0.9159	0.9164	0.9159
Weighted Sum	**0.9187**	**0.9186**	**0.9191**	**0.9187**
Concatenation	0.9063	0.9063	0.9072	0.9063

Table 2: Average performance over 3 runs on clone detection (seeds: 12345, 550, and 42). Standard deviations across seeds were below 0.002 for accuracy and F1 scores, reflecting statistically stable gains.

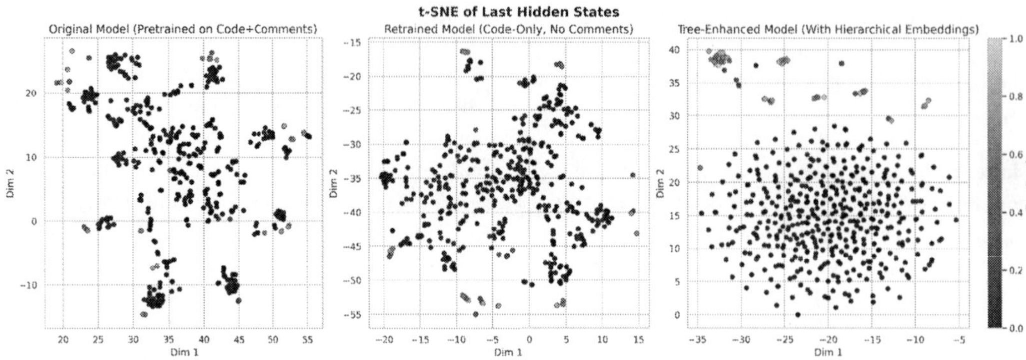

Figure 3: t-SNE projection of the last hidden states for the three models. The Tree-Enhanced Model demonstrates clearer structural clustering, indicating improved hierarchical representations.

Qualitative Analysis of Representations Figure 3 provides a qualitative comparison of the learned representations through t-SNE projections. The visualization illustrates the hidden state embeddings from three model variants: (1) the original pretrained Transformer (trained on code and comments), (2) a retrained Transformer (trained exclusively on code without comments), and (3) our proposed Tree-Enhanced Transformer with hierarchical embeddings, using the **Weighted Sum** configuration. Each point represents an individual AST node (token), colored according to its normalized depth within the AST, with lighter colors indicating nodes situated deeper in the AST structure.

The **original pretrained model** (left) exhibits loosely formed and overlapping clusters. Nodes are grouped primarily by token-level semantic similarities without clear correlation to their structural positions within the AST hierarchy, suggesting reliance mainly on linear sequential context and token semantics from natural language comments rather than syntactic relationships.

The **retrained model** (center), trained solely on code data, demonstrates tighter clustering compared to the pretrained model due to domain specialization. However, these clusters still exhibit minimal correlation with AST depth, indicating that structural hierarchy remains underrepresented, and token representations are primarily semantic rather than structural.

In contrast, the **Tree-Enhanced model** (right) distinctly captures hierarchical structure, as evidenced by clearly delineated and depth-correlated clusters. Nodes deeper in the AST (lighter colors) form separate, well-defined peripheral clusters, while nodes nearer the AST root (darker colors) group cohesively at the center. This clear structural differentiation highlights the model's ability to represent syntactic context explicitly, confirming the effectiveness of hierarchical embeddings.

This visualization aligns closely with our theoretical foundations, validating that the integration of tree-based positional embeddings significantly enhances the model's capacity to encode hierarchical relationships inherent in source code, resulting in improved performance on structurally-sensitive tasks such as clone detection and masked language modeling.

6 Analysis and Insights

6.1 Impact of Tree-Based Embeddings

Our results confirm that hierarchical positional embeddings enhance the structural awareness of Transformer models for source code. By encoding hierarchical relationships, these embeddings improve representation learning, particularly in tasks that rely on structural context. In masked language modeling, they help predict contextually relevant tokens even when distant in sequence but closely related in the AST. For clone detection, they improve differentiation between structurally similar yet semantically distinct snippets, reducing false positives and boosting overall accuracy and F1 scores.

6.2 Embedding Integration Strategies

Our experiments highlight the trade-offs among different embedding integration methods:

- **Sum Embeddings**: Computationally efficient but lacks adaptability in balancing structural and semantic contributions.

- **Concatenation Embeddings**: Enhances expressiveness but introduces higher dimensionality and computational cost without consistent gains.
- **Weighted Sum Embeddings**: Achieves the best balance, dynamically adjusting emphasis on structural embeddings, particularly in early training.

The Weighted Sum approach emerges as the most effective, offering an optimal trade-off between efficiency and structural representation quality.

7 Limitations

While our proposed Tree-Enhanced CodeBERTa shows significant improvements in capturing hierarchical source code structures, our approach has several inherent limitations that must be acknowledged:

1. **Computational Overhead**: Integrating AST-based positional embeddings requires additional preprocessing steps, such as AST parsing and alignment, increasing computational overhead. This could limit scalability, especially in real-time or low-resource environments.
2. **Parser Dependency**: Our embeddings heavily rely on the accuracy and language-specific implementation of the AST parser (Tree-Sitter (tre, 2007)). Variations in parser quality or completeness across different programming languages may impact the consistency and reliability of the embeddings.
3. **Generalizability Beyond Source Code**: Our method explicitly leverages hierarchical AST structures. Thus, its applicability is inherently limited to data that can be clearly represented through tree-based hierarchies. Its effectiveness on non-hierarchical or general graph structures without clear parent-child relationships remains uncertain.

8 Conclusion

We introduced Tree-Enhanced CodeBERTa, a Transformer-based model incorporating hierarchical positional embeddings from Abstract Syntax Trees (ASTs). By integrating depth and sibling index embeddings, our approach captures structural nuances overlooked by traditional positional encodings.

Evaluations on masked language modeling (MLM) and clone detection confirm that these embeddings enhance representation learning, improving accuracy, F1 score, precision, and recall. The Weighted Sum integration strategy proves most effective, balancing structural and semantic information while maintaining efficiency.

8.1 Key Takeaways

- Tree-based positional embeddings improve source code understanding by explicitly modeling hierarchical structure.
- The Weighted Sum integration strategy optimally balances semantic and structural embeddings with minimal overhead.
- Structural embeddings are particularly beneficial for tasks like clone detection, where syntactic differentiation is critical.

8.2 Future Work

Future directions include optimizing AST parsing for computational efficiency and exploring language-agnostic intermediate representations (IRs), such as data flow graphs, to mitigate the strict dependency on syntax rules and enhance cross-language generalization. Additionally, hierarchical embeddings could be extended beyond source code, potentially benefiting tasks involving natural language parse trees or structured document analysis.

These findings highlight the potential of hierarchical positional embeddings for structured data representation, paving the way for further exploration in broader applications.

References

2007. *GPCE '07: Proceedings of the 6th international conference on Generative programming and component engineering*. Association for Computing Machinery, New York, NY, USA.

Wasi Uddin Ahmad, Saikat Chakraborty, Baishakhi Ray, and Kai-Wei Chang. 2020. A transformer-based approach for source code summarization.

Miltiadis Allamanis, Marc Brockschmidt, and Mahmoud Khademi. 2017. Learning to represent programs with graphs.

Uri Alon, Shaked Brody, Omer Levy, and Eran Yahav. 2018. code2seq: Generating sequences from structured representations of code.

Marc Brockschmidt, Miltiadis Allamanis, Alexander L. Gaunt, and Oleksandr Polozov. 2018. Generative code modeling with graphs.

Jacob Devlin, Ming-Wei Chang, Kenton Lee, and Kristina Toutanova. 2018. BERT: Pre-training of deep bidirectional transformers for language understanding.

Zhangyin Feng, Daya Guo, Duyu Tang, Nan Duan, Xiaocheng Feng, Ming Gong, Linjun Shou, Bing Qin, Ting Liu, Daxin Jiang, and Ming Zhou. 2020. CodeBERT: A pre-trained model for programming and natural languages. *Preprint*, arXiv:2002.08155.

Vincent J. Hellendoorn, Charles Sutton, Rishabh Singh, Petros Maniatis, and David Bieber. 2020. Global relational models of source code.

Husain, Hamel Wu, Ho-Hsiang, Gazit, Tiferet, Allamanis, Miltiadis, Brockschmidt, and Marc. 2019. CodeSearchNet Challenge: Evaluating the State of Semantic Code Search. *arXiv:1909.09436 [cs, stat]*. ArXiv: 1909.09436.

Yinhan Liu, Myle Ott, Naman Goyal, Jingfei Du, Mandar Joshi, Danqi Chen, Omer Levy, Mike Lewis, Luke Zettlemoyer, and Veselin Stoyanov. 2019. Roberta: A robustly optimized bert pretraining approach.

Han Peng, Ge Li, Yunfei Zhao, and Zhi Jin. 2022. Rethinking positional encoding in tree transformer for code representation. In *Proceedings of the 2022 Conference on Empirical Methods in Natural Language Processing*, pages 3204–3214, Abu Dhabi, United Arab Emirates. Association for Computational Linguistics.

PoolC. n.d. Poolc/1-fold-clone-detection-600k-5fold.

Ofir Press, Noah A. Smith, and Mike Lewis. 2021. Train short, test long: Attention with linear biases enables input length extrapolation.

Alec Radford, Karthik Narasimhan, Tim Salimans, and Ilya Sutskever. 2018. Improving language understanding by generative pre-training.

Oh Saeyoon and Yoo Shin. 2024. Csa-trans: Code structure aware transformer for ast.

Peter Shaw, Jakob Uszkoreit, and Ashish Vaswani. 2018. Self-attention with relative position representations.

Vighnesh Shiv and Chris Quirk. 2019. Novel positional encodings to enable tree-based transformers. In *Advances in Neural Information Processing Systems*, volume 32. Curran Associates, Inc.

Jianlin Su, Yu Lu, Shengfeng Pan, Ahmed Murtadha, Bo Wen, and Yunfeng Liu. 2021. Roformer: Enhanced transformer with rotary position embedding.

Zeyu Sun, Qihao Zhu, Yingfei Xiong, Yican Sun, Lili Mou, and Lu Zhang. 2015. Treegen: A tree-based transformer architecture for code generation.

Kai Sheng Tai, Richard Socher, and Christopher D. Manning. 2015a. Improved semantic representations from tree-structured long short-term memory networks.

Kai Sheng Tai, Richard Socher, and Christopher D. Manning. 2015b. Improved semantic representations from tree-structured long short-term memory networks.

Ashish Vaswani, Noam Shazeer, Niki Parmar, Jakob Uszkoreit, Llion Jones, Aidan N. Gomez, Lukasz Kaiser, and Illia Polosukhin. 2017. Attention is all you need.

Zhang, Sheng, Ma, Xutai, Duh, Kevin, Van Durme, and Benjamin. 2019. AMR parsing as sequence-to-graph transduction. In *Proceedings of the 57th Annual Meeting of the Association for Computational Linguistics*, pages 80–94, Florence, Italy. Association for Computational Linguistics.

A Supplementary Materials

To facilitate reproducibility, we provide an anonymized repository containing the full implementation, training scripts, and pre-processing details:

```
https://anonymous.4open.science/r/tree
        -enhanced-codebert-BC1B
```

This repository includes:

- Source code for model training and evaluation.
- Scripts for preprocessing source code into ASTs using Tree-Sitter.
- Model hyperparameters and configuration files.

Enhancing AMR Parsing with Group Relative Policy Optimization

Botond Barta[1], Endre Hamerlik[1], Milán Nyist[2], Masato Ito[2], Judit Ács[1]

[1]HUN-REN SZTAKI, [2]Eötvös Loránd University

Correspondence: botondbarta@sztaki.hu

Abstract

We investigate the capabilities of the openly available Llama 3.2 1B language model for Abstract Meaning Representation (AMR) parsing through supervised fine-tuning, further enhanced by reinforcement learning via Group Relative Policy Optimization (GRPO). Existing supervised methods for AMR parsing face limitations due to static loss functions and challenges in capturing complex semantic phenomena. To address this, our GRPO-based approach explicitly optimizes fine-grained semantic rewards, including Smatch scores, frame-argument correctness, and structural validity of logical operations. Experimental results show that supervised fine-tuning alone establishes Llama as a capable English AMR parser, and subsequent GRPO fine-tuning further improves its performance. Our final model achieves higher Smatch scores, consistently respects critical low-level semantic constraints, and outperforms existing parsers on high-level semantic evaluation metrics across diverse linguistic phenomena.

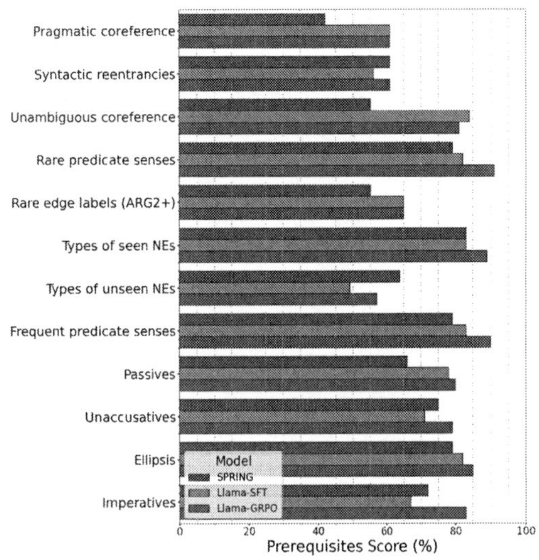

Figure 1: Comparison of AMR parsing models (SPRING, Llama-SFT, and our Llama-GRPO) across various linguistic phenomena measured by the GrAPES prerequisites metric. Higher scores indicate that the parser more consistently generates the necessary semantic structures to capture specific phenomena. Our reinforcement learning-based approach shows consistent improvement over the baselines.

1 Introduction

Abstract Meaning Representation has become essential in various natural language processing tasks, such as machine translation (Song et al., 2019; Damonte et al., 2019; Urešová et al., 2014), question answering (Kapanipathi et al., 2021), dialogue understanding (Bai et al., 2022a), summarization (Liao et al., 2018; Ribeiro et al., 2022; Dohare et al., 2017), and fact-checking (Ribeiro et al., 2022; Kachwala et al., 2024; Ousidhoum et al., 2022). Despite its widespread adoption, AMR parsing remains challenging. Groschwitz et al. (2023) recently demonstrated that parsing accuracy has stagnated, highlighting persistent difficulties in capturing complex semantic phenomena, even with advanced models.

While large language models (LLMs) such as the Llama models (Touvron et al., 2023) have demonstrated impressive performance across various language generation tasks, their capability for structured semantic parsing—particularly AMR parsing—remains unverified. Moreover, it remains unclear whether advanced reinforcement learning (RL) techniques like Group Relative Policy Optimization (GRPO), introduced by Shao et al. (2024), can effectively enhance the performance of LLMs on such structured prediction tasks by directly optimizing for desired graph properties.

In this paper, we first examine the baseline capabilities of the openly available Llama 3.2 1B model by supervised fine-tuning (SFT) on the AMR 3.0 dataset (Banarescu et al., 2013). We refer to this model as **Llama-SFT**. We then further fine-tune

Proceedings of the 1st Joint Workshop on Large Language Models and Structure Modeling (XLLM 2025), pages 99–105

this model using GRPO, incorporating fine-grained reward signals explicitly designed to encourage adherence to critical low-level AMR properties, such as frame-argument correctness and structural validity of logical operations (AND-OR node correctness), alongside Smatch and graph parsability. We call this enhanced model **Llama-GRPO**. We systematically evaluate our models against publicly available AMR parsing model, SPRING (Bevilacqua et al., 2021), using standard metrics (Smatch) and the detailed GrAPES evaluation suite (Groschwitz et al., 2023).

Our results show that the Llama 3.2 1B model, after supervised fine-tuning (Llama-SFT), achieves AMR parsing performance close to open-source AMR parser models. Critically, when further enhanced through GRPO-based reinforcement learning, our model:

- Achieves higher overall AMR parsing accuracy, as measured by Smatch scores,
- Effectively respects the low-level semantic constraints incorporated into the GRPO reward function,
- Outperforms existing AMR parsers on high-level semantic evaluations, as demonstrated by the comprehensive GrAPES metrics (Figure 1), suggesting improved generalization across diverse linguistic phenomena.

2 Related Work

Early work in AMR parsing often relied on transition-based systems (Wang et al., 2015, 2016) or graph-based approaches (Flanigan et al., 2014), frequently using specialized features and constrained decoding. The advent of neural sequence-to-sequence models marked a significant shift. Many modern parsers treat AMR parsing as a translation task from text to a linearized representation of the AMR graph (Konstas et al., 2017).

Transformer-based architectures (Vaswani et al., 2017) quickly became dominant. Models like SPRING (Bevilacqua et al., 2021), based on BART (Lewis et al., 2020), demonstrated strong performance by leveraging pre-training and specialized techniques like graph linearization. SPRING employs bidirectional pre-training and graph-based regularization during fine-tuning on linearized AMR graphs. Other parsers, such as those based on T5 or BART (Raffel et al., 2020; Jascob, 2024; Lee et al., 2023), have also achieved high results through large-scale pre-training and task-specific adaptations.

Despite these advances, as highlighted by Groschwitz et al. (2023), performance has plateaued, suggesting limitations in current supervised approaches. Challenges in AMR parsing remain, particularly in achieving semantic consistency, cross-lingual adaptability, and structured reasoning.

3 Methods

Reinforcement learning has been increasingly used to fine-tune LLMs for various objectives beyond next-token prediction, such as improving helpfulness, harmlessness, or adherence to specific styles (Ouyang et al., 2022; Bai et al., 2022b). Techniques such as Proximal Policy Optimization (PPO) (Schulman et al., 2017) are commonly used but often require training a separate critic model, which can be computationally expensive. GRPO (Shao et al., 2024) offers a more efficient alternative by using group-based relative ranking, making RL fine-tuning more accessible, especially for complex tasks with non-differentiable or noisy reward signals, as demonstrated in fields like mathematical reasoning (Shao et al., 2024), computer vision (Liang, 2025), and speech processing (Togootogtokh and Klasen, 2025).

3.1 Group Relative Policy Optimization

GRPO (Shao et al., 2024) is a reinforcement learning algorithm designed to fine-tune large language models efficiently by replacing the critic model in PPO with a baseline estimated from a group of sampled outputs. This eliminates the need for a learned value function, reducing computational overhead and memory requirements.

For each query q, GRPO samples a group of responses $\{o_1, \ldots, o_G\}$ from the old policy $\pi_{\theta_{\text{old}}}$, evaluates them using a reward model, and normalizes the rewards within the group. The policy is updated using a clipped importance-weighted objective, similar to PPO, but the advantage estimation relies on the relative performance within the sampled group rather than absolute reward values predicted by a critic. This encourages the policy to shift probability mass towards outputs that perform relatively better within the sampled group according to the reward function.

3.2 Our approach

We started with a vanilla Llama 3.2 1B model, which we fine-tuned using supervised fine-tuning (SFT). To avoid overfitting we used early stopping based on the validation loss. The training stopped after two epochs which resulted in the Llama-SFT model. After generating AMR graphs with Llama-SFT, we manually evaluated them and observed several recurring low-level structural and semantic errors. These errors primarily fell into two categories:

- **Frame-argument error**: Generated frames sometimes included arguments (e.g., ':arg4', ':arg5') that were not defined for that specific predicate sense in the PropBank frame files (Palmer et al., 2005). The arguments of each frame must strictly conform to the roles defined in its sense.
- **AND-OR node error:** Logical connective nodes like 'and' and 'or' require their operand roles (e.g., ':op1', ':op2', ':op3') to be consecutive integers starting from 1. We observed generated graphs violating this (e.g., having only ':op1' and ':op3'). A special case exists where only ':op2' appears, often used in AMR 3.0 for sentences starting with 'and' or 'or'; this specific structure was considered valid.

To address these issues and improve overall quality, we designed a composite reward function for GRPO incorporating four signals for each generated AMR graph:

- **Parsability:** A binary reward. The generated AMR graph must be parsable by standard AMR parsing tools without errors. Graphs that failed parsing due to structural or syntactic issues were penalized.
- **Frame-argument correctness:** A score between 0 and 1 representing the proportion of frames in the generated graph that adhere to their PropBank argument definitions. Calculated as (Number of valid frames) / (Total number of frames).
- **AND-OR node correctness:** A score between 0 and 1 representing the proportion of 'and'/'or' nodes with correctly structured operands (consecutive from ':op1', or the special ':op2'-only case). Calculated as (Number of valid AND/OR nodes) / (Total number of AND/OR nodes).
- **SMATCH score:** The Smatch F1 score (Cai and Knight, 2013) comparing the generated AMR graph against the gold reference AMR graph. This provides a global measure of semantic similarity.

These four criteria were combined into a single reward function, where each criterion was given equal weight. Additionally, we applied quadratic scaling to the SMATCH score, ensuring that lower scores received a higher penalty.

4 Dataset

For training, we used the AMR 3.0 dataset (LDC2020T02) (Banarescu et al., 2013), which provides a large collection of human-annotated Abstract Meaning Representation (AMR) graphs. We preprocessed the AMR graphs the following way. First, we removed wiki tags from the AMR graphs. Then, we serialized each graph into a single line using a depth-first approach. During serialization, new lines within the original graph notation were replaced with spaces, and consecutive spaces were compressed into a single space. Finally, we added spaces around parentheses to ensure consistent tokenization.

For evaluation, we used the AMR 3.0 test set and The Little Prince (**TLP**) corpus test set, which provides a smaller, out-of-domain evaluation with high-quality annotations. We measured the performance of the models using Smatch scores (Cai and Knight, 2013) computed with the `smatchpp` library (Opitz, 2023).

4.1 Dataset Statistics

Table 1 provides an overview of the dataset sizes used in our experiments.

Dataset	Number of Sentences
AMR 3.0 (Train)	55,635
AMR 3.0 (Test)	1,898
The Little Prince (test)	143

Table 1: Dataset statistics.

The combination of AMR 3.0 and the TLP dataset enables a comprehensive evaluation, balancing broad-domain performance with controlled, high-quality annotations.

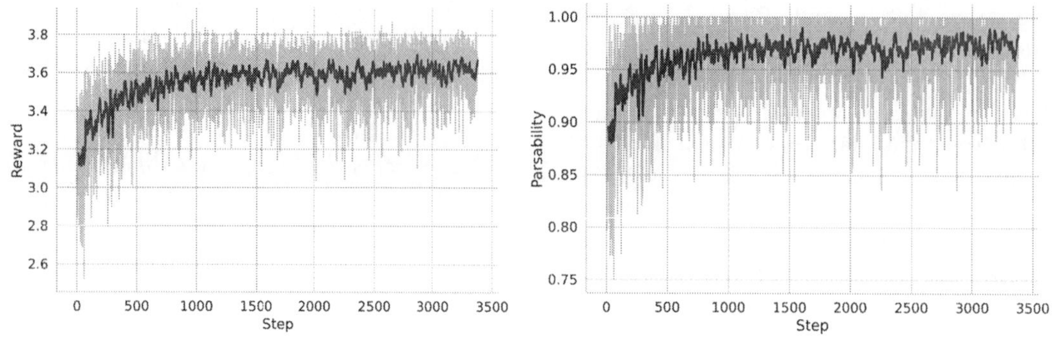

Figure 2: Evolution of average reward and parsability during GRPO fine-tuning on batches from the training set.

5 Results

We compare our Llama-SFT and Llama-GRPO models against SPRING. Table 2 shows the main results on the AMR 3.0 and TLP test sets.

The results show that Llama-SFT achieves a competitive Smatch score in two epochs, confirming the adaptability of LLMs to an unseen task. We observe that one epoch of subsequent GRPO fine-tuning yields further improvements. Llama-GRPO achieves a Smatch score of 81.92 on AMR 3.0, a gain of over 2.3 points over Llama-SFT, and it outperforms SPRING. In addition, GRPO improves compliance with the targeted low-level constraints. Frame-argument correctness improves from 96.5% to over 99% on AMR 3.0 and reaches 99.75% on TLP. Similarly AND-OR node correctness jumps from 96.5% to over 99.6% on AMR 3.0 and achieves perfect compliance on TLP. This demonstrates the effectiveness of incorporating these specific structural and semantic properties directly into the reward function via GRPO.

Figure 2 illustrates the progression of the overall reward during GRPO training. The reward score exhibits a smooth and consistent upward trend throughout the GRPO fine-tuning process. This indicates that the model has effectively learned to generate AMR structures that better satisfy these constraints, validating the utility of GRPO with these specific reward signals. The learning appears stable, without drastic fluctuations, suggesting that GRPO provides a reliable optimization process for these objectives.

5.1 GrAPES evaluation

According to Groschwitz et al. (2023), **Edge Recall** measures the parser's accuracy in identifying crucial semantic edges for specific phenomena. **Prerequisites** evaluate whether the parser generates the required graph structure to attempt to recognize these phenomena. Tables 3 and 4 summarize model performance accordingly.

From Tables 3 and 4 we see that SPRING demonstrates higher accuracy in Edge Recall, indicating slightly better capability in accurately identifying semantic edges once generated. This difference in performance for SPRING can potentially be explained by the AMR-specific adaptation of its tokenizer and vocabulary[1].

Llama-SFT on the other hand, consistently excels at Prerequisites, indicating that it more reliably constructs graph structures necessary for capturing complex phenomena, even if its edge-level precision is slightly lower.

Limitations

Our study has several limitations:

- **Model Scale:** We focused exclusively on the Llama 3.2 1B model due to resource limitations. Larger models or other LLM architectures might yield different baseline performance and respond differently to GRPO tuning.
- **Language Coverage:** Our experiments were conducted solely on English AMR. The applicability and effectiveness of this approach for other languages remain unexplored.
- **Reward Design:** While our fine-grained rewards proved effective, the specific combination and weighting could be further optimized.

[1]The set of possible edge labels is added to the vocabulary.

Model	Smatch++ F1		FRAME-ARG correctness		AND-OR correctness	
	AMR 3.0	TLP	AMR 3.0	TLP	AMR 3.0	TLP
Llama-SFT	79.58	78.06	0.96491	0.97550	0.96514	0.97887
Llama-GRPO	**81.92**	78.30	0.99178	**0.99758**	**0.99624**	**1.00000**
SPRING	80.15	**81.12**	**0.99396**	0.99703	0.95978	0.98501

Table 2: Comparison of different AMR parsers on AMR 3.0 and TLP datasets based on Smatch++ F1, ARG correctness, and AND-OR correctness.

Category	SPRING	SFT	GRPO
Pragmatic Coreference	42	**61**	**61**
Syntactic Reentrancies	61	56	**61**
Unambiguous Coreference	55	**84**	81
Rare Predicate Senses	79	82	**91**
Rare Edge Labels	55	**65**	**65**
Types of Seen NEs	83	83	**89**
Types of Unseen NEs	**64**	49	57
Frequent Predicate Senses	79	83	**90**
Passives	66	78	**80**
Unaccusatives	75	71	**79**
Ellipsis	79	82	**85**
Imperatives	72	67	**83**

Table 3: Prerequisites scores from GrAPES evaluation. Best results highlighted in bold. Llama-SFT and Llama-GRPO are abbreviated as SFT and GRPO respectively.

Category	SPRING	SFT	GRPO
Pragmatic Coreference	**31**	25	25
Syntactic Reentrancies	**46**	27	32
Unambiguous Coreference	52	**58**	55
Rare Edge Labels	20	**20**	18
Rare Node Labels	61	58	**65**
Unseen Node Labels	**54**	35	44
Rare Predicate Senses	30	**34**	**34**
Seen Names	84	83	**89**
Unseen Names	**70**	56	64
Seen Dates	74	88	**91**
Unseen Dates	71	82	**84**
Other Seen Ents	**88**	79	87
Other Unseen Ents	59	61	**64**
Types of Seen NEs	82	81	**87**
Types of Unseen NEs	**47**	31	39
Frequent Predicate Senses	70	72	**79**
Passives	59	**64**	**64**
Unaccusatives	**67**	58	65
Ellipsis	42	39	**48**
Multinode Word Meanings	68	**80**	78
Imperatives	50	42	**59**

Table 4: Recall and Edge Recall scores from GrAPES evaluation. Best results highlighted in bold. Llama-SFT and Llama-GRPO are abbreviated as SFT and GRPO respectively.

Exploring other potential reward signals related to AMR quality could yield further improvements.

- **Comparison Models:** We compared against the publicly available SPRING model. Comparisons against state-of-the-art closed models or models using proprietary data were not possible.

- **Dataset Contamination:** We did not investigate whether the dataset we used for evaluation was included in the pre-training data of the Llama 3.2 1B model, which could lead to information leakage that artificially inflates performance.

6 Conclusion

In this work, we investigated the application of the Llama 3.2 1B language model to AMR parsing, enhanced by Group Relative Policy Optimization (GRPO). We demonstrated that supervised fine-tuning establishes Llama as a competent baseline AMR parser. Subsequently, by incorporating fine-grained reward signals targeting Smatch, graph parsability, frame-argument correctness, and AND-OR node validity into a GRPO fine-tuning stage, we achieved significant improvements.

Our Llama-GRPO model not only outperformed its supervised counterpart (Llama-SFT) in Smatch scores, but also showed significantly better performance for crucial low-level semantic and structural constraints. Furthermore, evaluation using the GrAPES suite revealed that Llama-GRPO generated more complete graph structures (higher Prerequisites scores) necessary to capture diverse and complex linguistic phenomena, outperforming both Llama-SFT and SPRING while achieving competitive recall performance.

These results highlight the potential of combining moderately sized, openly available LLMs with efficient reinforcement learning techniques like

GRPO, guided by carefully designed reward functions, to tackle complex structured prediction tasks like AMR parsing. This approach allows for direct optimization of desired output properties beyond what is easily achievable with standard supervised learning alone.

Acknowledgments

This study was supported by the European Union project RRF-2.3.1-21-2022-00004 within the framework of the Artificial Intelligence National Laboratory Program, Hungary.

References

Xuefeng Bai, Linfeng Song, and Yue Zhang. 2022a. Semantic-based pre-training for dialogue understanding. In *Proceedings of the 29th International Conference on Computational Linguistics*, pages 592–607.

Yuntao Bai, Andy Jones, Kamal Ndousse, Amanda Askell, Anna Chen, Nova DasSarma, Dawn Drain, Stanislav Fort, Deep Ganguli, Tom Henighan, et al. 2022b. Training a helpful and harmless assistant with reinforcement learning from human feedback. *arXiv preprint arXiv:2204.05862*.

Laura Banarescu, Claire Bonial, Shu Cai, Madalina Georgescu, Kira Griffitt, Ulf Hermjakob, Kevin Knight, Philipp Koehn, Martha Palmer, and Nathan Schneider. 2013. Abstract meaning representation for sembanking. In *Proceedings of the 7th linguistic annotation workshop and interoperability with discourse*, pages 178–186.

Michele Bevilacqua, Rexhina Blloshmi, and Roberto Navigli. 2021. One spring to rule them both: Symmetric amr semantic parsing and generation without a complex pipeline. In *Proceedings of the AAAI Conference on Artificial Intelligence*, volume 35, pages 12564–12573.

Shu Cai and Kevin Knight. 2013. Smatch: an evaluation metric for semantic feature structures. In *Proceedings of the 51st Annual Meeting of the Association for Computational Linguistics (Volume 2: Short Papers)*, pages 748–752, Sofia, Bulgaria. Association for Computational Linguistics.

Marco Damonte, Rahul Goel, and Tagyoung Chung. 2019. Practical semantic parsing for spoken language understanding. In *Proceedings of the 2019 Conference of the North American Chapter of the Association for Computational Linguistics: Human Language Technologies, Volume 2 (Industry Papers)*, pages 16–23, Minneapolis, Minnesota. Association for Computational Linguistics.

Shibhansh Dohare, Harish Karnick, and Vivek Gupta. 2017. Text summarization using abstract meaning representation. *arXiv preprint arXiv:1706.01678*.

Jeffrey Flanigan, Sam Thomson, Jaime G Carbonell, Chris Dyer, and Noah A Smith. 2014. A discriminative graph-based parser for the abstract meaning representation. In *Proceedings of the 52nd Annual Meeting of the Association for Computational Linguistics (Volume 1: Long Papers)*, pages 1426–1436.

Jonas Groschwitz, Shay Cohen, Lucia Donatelli, and Meaghan Fowlie. 2023. AMR parsing is far from solved: GrAPES, the granular AMR parsing evaluation suite. In *Proceedings of the 2023 Conference on Empirical Methods in Natural Language Processing*, pages 10728–10752, Singapore. Association for Computational Linguistics.

Brad Jascob. 2024. amrlib: A python library for amr parsing, generation, and visualization. `https://github.com/bjascob/amrlib`.

Zoher Kachwala, Jisun An, Haewoon Kwak, and Filippo Menczer. 2024. REMATCH: Robust and efficient matching of local knowledge graphs to improve structural and semantic similarity. In *Findings of the Association for Computational Linguistics: NAACL 2024*, pages 1018–1028, Mexico City, Mexico. Association for Computational Linguistics.

Pavan Kapanipathi, Ibrahim Abdelaziz, Srinivas Ravishankar, Salim Roukos, Alexander Gray, Ramón Fernandez Astudillo, Maria Chang, Cristina Cornelio, Saswati Dana, Achille Fokoue, Dinesh Garg, Alfio Gliozzo, Sairam Gurajada, Hima Karanam, Naweed Khan, Dinesh Khandelwal, Young-Suk Lee, Yunyao Li, Francois Luus, Ndivhuwo Makondo, Nandana Mihindukulasooriya, Tahira Naseem, Sumit Neelam, Lucian Popa, Revanth Gangi Reddy, Ryan Riegel, Gaetano Rossiello, Udit Sharma, G P Shrivatsa Bhargav, and Mo Yu. 2021. Leveraging Abstract Meaning Representation for knowledge base question answering. In *Findings of the Association for Computational Linguistics: ACL-IJCNLP 2021*, pages 3884–3894, Online. Association for Computational Linguistics.

Ioannis Konstas, Srinivasan Iyer, Mark Yatskar, Yejin Choi, and Luke Zettlemoyer. 2017. Neural AMR: Sequence-to-sequence models for parsing and generation. In *Proceedings of the 55th Annual Meeting of the Association for Computational Linguistics (Volume 1: Long Papers)*, pages 146–157, Vancouver, Canada. Association for Computational Linguistics.

Young-Suk Lee, Ramón Fernandez Astudillo, Radu Florian, Tahira Naseem, and Salim Roukos. 2023. Amr parsing with instruction fine-tuned pre-trained language models. *arXiv preprint arXiv:2304.12272*.

Mike Lewis, Yinhan Liu, Naman Goyal, Marjan Ghazvininejad, Abdelrahman Mohamed, Omer Levy, Veselin Stoyanov, and Luke Zettlemoyer. 2020. BART: Denoising sequence-to-sequence pre-training for natural language generation, translation, and comprehension. In *Proceedings of the 58th Annual Meeting of the Association for Computational Linguistics*, pages 7871–7880, Online. Association for Computational Linguistics.

Xu Liang. 2025. Group relative policy optimization for image captioning.

Kexin Liao, Logan Lebanoff, and Fei Liu. 2018. Abstract Meaning Representation for multi-document summarization. In *Proceedings of the 27th International Conference on Computational Linguistics*, pages 1178–1190, Santa Fe, New Mexico, USA. Association for Computational Linguistics.

Juri Opitz. 2023. SMATCH++: Standardized and extended evaluation of semantic graphs. In *Findings of the Association for Computational Linguistics: EACL 2023*, pages 1595–1607, Dubrovnik, Croatia. Association for Computational Linguistics.

Nedjma Ousidhoum, Zhangdie Yuan, and Andreas Vlachos. 2022. Varifocal question generation for fact-checking. In *Proceedings of the 2022 Conference on Empirical Methods in Natural Language Processing*, pages 2532–2544, Abu Dhabi, United Arab Emirates. Association for Computational Linguistics.

Long Ouyang, Jeffrey Wu, Xu Jiang, Diogo Almeida, Carroll Wainwright, Pamela Mishkin, Chong Zhang, Sandhini Agarwal, Katarina Slama, Alex Ray, et al. 2022. Training language models to follow instructions with human feedback. *Advances in neural information processing systems*, 35:27730–27744.

Martha Palmer, Daniel Gildea, and Paul Kingsbury. 2005. The Proposition Bank: An annotated corpus of semantic roles. *Computational Linguistics*, 31(1):71–106.

Colin Raffel, Noam Shazeer, Adam Roberts, Katherine Lee, Sharan Narang, Michael Matena, Yanqi Zhou, Wei Li, and Peter J Liu. 2020. Exploring the limits of transfer learning with a unified text-to-text transformer. *Journal of machine learning research*, 21(140):1–67.

Leonardo F. R. Ribeiro, Mengwen Liu, Iryna Gurevych, Markus Dreyer, and Mohit Bansal. 2022. FactGraph: Evaluating factuality in summarization with semantic graph representations. In *Proceedings of the 2022 Conference of the North American Chapter of the Association for Computational Linguistics: Human Language Technologies*, pages 3238–3253, Seattle, United States. Association for Computational Linguistics.

John Schulman, Filip Wolski, Prafulla Dhariwal, Alec Radford, and Oleg Klimov. 2017. Proximal policy optimization algorithms. *arXiv preprint arXiv:1707.06347*.

Zhihong Shao, Peiyi Wang, Qihao Zhu, Runxin Xu, Junxiao Song, Xiao Bi, Haowei Zhang, Mingchuan Zhang, YK Li, Y Wu, et al. 2024. Deepseekmath: Pushing the limits of mathematical reasoning in open language models. *arXiv preprint arXiv:2402.03300*.

Linfeng Song, Daniel Gildea, Yue Zhang, Zhiguo Wang, and Jinsong Su. 2019. Semantic neural machine translation using AMR. *Transactions of the Association for Computational Linguistics*, 7:19–31.

Enkhtogtokh Togootogtokh and Christian Klasen. 2025. Voicegrpo: Modern moe transformers with group relative policy optimization grpo for ai voice health care applications on voice pathology detection. *arXiv preprint arXiv:2503.03797*.

Hugo Touvron, Thibaut Lavril, Gautier Izacard, Xavier Martinet, Marie-Anne Lachaux, Timothée Lacroix, Baptiste Rozière, Naman Goyal, Eric Hambro, Faisal Azhar, et al. 2023. Llama: Open and efficient foundation language models. *arXiv preprint arXiv:2302.13971*.

Zdeňka Urešová, Jan Hajič, and Ondřej Bojar. 2014. Comparing Czech and English AMRs. In *Proceedings of Workshop on Lexical and Grammatical Resources for Language Processing*, pages 55–64, Dublin, Ireland. Association for Computational Linguistics and Dublin City University.

Ashish Vaswani, Noam Shazeer, Niki Parmar, Jakob Uszkoreit, Llion Jones, Aidan N Gomez, Łukasz Kaiser, and Illia Polosukhin. 2017. Attention is all you need. *Advances in neural information processing systems*, 30.

Chuan Wang, Sameer Pradhan, Xiaoman Pan, Heng Ji, and Nianwen Xue. 2016. CAMR at SemEval-2016 task 8: An extended transition-based AMR parser. In *Proceedings of the 10th International Workshop on Semantic Evaluation (SemEval-2016)*, pages 1173–1178, San Diego, California. Association for Computational Linguistics.

Chuan Wang, Nianwen Xue, and Sameer Pradhan. 2015. A transition-based algorithm for AMR parsing. In *Proceedings of the 2015 Conference of the North American Chapter of the Association for Computational Linguistics: Human Language Technologies*, pages 366–375, Denver, Colorado. Association for Computational Linguistics.

Structure Modeling Approach for UD Parsing of Historical Modern Japanese

Hiroaki Ozaki[1] **Mai Omura**[2]
Komiya Kanakol[1] **Masayuki Asahara**[3,4] **and Toshinobu Ogiso**[3,4]
[1]Tokyo University of Agriculture and Technology, Japan
[2]Osaka Shoin Women's University, Japan
[3]National Institute for Japanese Language and Linguistics, Japan
[4]The Graduate University for Advanced Studies, Japan
hiroaki-ozaki@st.go.tuat.ac.jp, omura.mai@osaka-shoin.ac.jp,
kkomiya@go.tuat.ac.jp, {masayu-a,togiso}@ninjal.ac.jp

Abstract

This study shows the effectiveness of structure modeling for transferability in diachronic syntactic parsing. The syntactic parsing for historical languages is significant from a humanities and quantitative linguistics perspective to enable annotation support and analysis on unannotated documents. We compared the zero-shot transfer ability between Transformer-based Biaffine UD parsers and our structure modeling approach. The structure modeling approach is a pipeline method consisting of dictionary-based morphological analysis (MeCab), a deep learning-based phrase (bunsetsu) analysis (Monaka), SVM-based phrase dependency parsing (CaboCha) and a rule-based conversion from phrase dependencies to UD. This pipeline closely follows the methodology used in constructing Japanese UD corpora. Experimental results showed that the structure modeling approach outperformed zero-shot transfer from the contemporary to the modern Japanese. Moreover, the structure modeling approach outperformed several existing UD parsers in contemporary Japanese. To this end, the structure modeling approach outperformed in the diachronic transfer of Japanese by a wide margin and was useful to those applications for digital humanities and quantitative linguistics.

1 Introduction

Dependency parsing has long been studied as a core task in natural language processing. In recent years, dependency annotation corpora created under multilingual unified annotation frameworks such as Universal Dependencies (UD; Zeman et al. 2018) have been published, enabling the development of deep learning-based dependency parsers that operate across multiple languages.

On the other hand, syntactic structure analysis, including dependency parsing, is beneficial for humanities research as well as traditional NLP applications. This is because structure modeling, which consists of a layered pipeline of NLP tasks, can preserve low-level linguistic structures such as phrases required for humanities research. In contrast, the high zero-shot transfer performance of recent deep learning-based parsers (Kondratyuk and Straka, 2019) would also be helpful to support annotation tasks and quantitative linguistic analysis on unannotated corpora such as historical literature, which no longer has native speakers.

Thus, this study focuses on the diachronic application of UD dependency parsing and compares structure modeling with end-to-end deep learning in the context of zero-shot transfer. Specifically, Japanese UD corpora exist for both contemporary and Meiji-period (modern) Japanese, allowing us to investigate the transfer performance from contemporary Japanese, which has sufficient training resources, to modern Japanese. The research questions regarding the structure modeling in this context are: (1) whether it demonstrates a performance advantage and (2) whether it is effective when considering practical annotation and application use cases.

For our structure modeling approach to Japanese UD parsing (see Figure 1), we first applied a morphological analysis (MeCab), and then, we applied deep learning-based phrase (bunsetsu) segmentation (Monaka) and bunsetsu dependency parsing (CaboCha). After this, we employed a rule-based transformation from bunsetsu dependencies to UD annotation, simulating actual Japanese UD annotations. This structure modeling approach closely follows the standard workflow used for constructing Japanese UD linguistic resources, involving morphological annotation, bunsetsu dependency annotation, and subsequent rule-based conversion into the UD format. As a comparison, we trained and used a graph-based Biaffine parser (Attardi et al., 2021), which is a representative UD parsing method.

The comparison results showed that (1) the

Proceedings of the 1st Joint Workshop on Large Language Models and Structure Modeling (XLLM 2025), pages 106–114
August 1, 2025

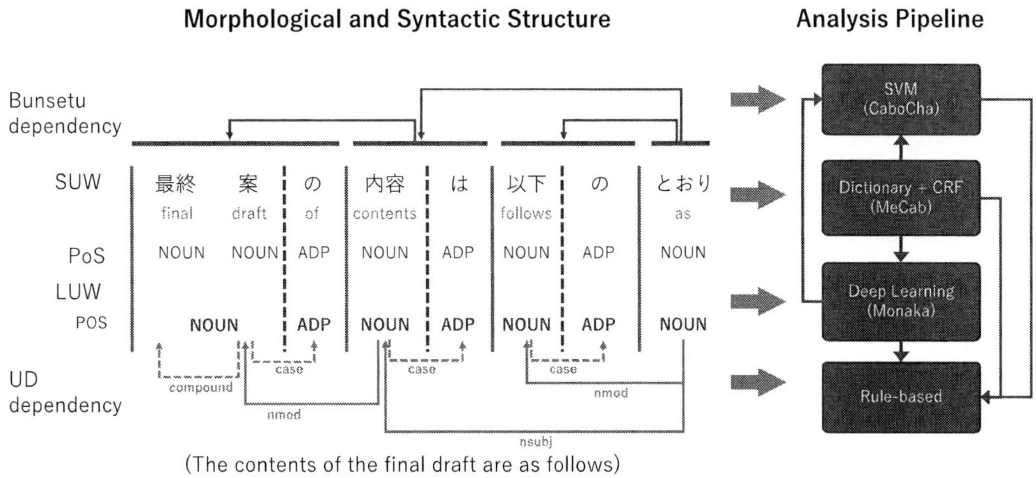

Figure 1: The overview of the task and structural approach. Green solid bars represent bunsetsu boundaries, and blue dotted bars represent the boundaries of long unit words. The left side of the figure depicts the morphological and syntactic information of the sentence "最終案の内容は以下のとおり (The contents of the final draft is as follows)." The right side of the picture shows the analysis pipeline of the structure modeling approach.

structure modeling approach not only outperformed deep learning-based zero-shot transfer in accuracy but also achieved high performance on contemporary Japanese before transfer. (2) In practical annotation scenarios, zero-shot transfer using deep learning alone was impractical due to the inconsistency of phrase (bunsetsu) structures, whereas the structure modeling approach produced reasonable results, preserving morphological and phrase (bunsetsu) structures.

2 Related Work

2.1 UD Treebanks of Japanese

There are two major UD treebanks for contemporary Japanese. UD_Japanese-BCCWJ[1] (Asahara et al., 2018; Omura and Asahara, 2018) is a treebank built on the Balanced Corpus of Contemporary Written Japanese (Maekawa, 2008). UD_Japanese-GSD[2] (Tanaka et al., 2016) contains the sentences from Google Universal Dependency Treebanks v2.0 (legacy)[3]. These two Japanese UD treebanks are annotated with mostly the same methods and criteria.

UD_Japanese-Modern[4] (Omura and Asahara, 2017) is a deprecated UD treebank annotated on Meiroku-zasshi that was published in the Meiji period (C.E. 1868-1912). This was the only official annotated (test set only) UD treebank for historical Japanese, containing 822 sentences.

2.2 Parsing Methods for UD

For syntactic parsers (not limited to UD parsers), there are two major approaches, namely graph- and transition-based parsers. In UD parsing, graph-based parsers (often called Biaffine Parser; Dozat et al. 2017; Qi et al. 2018; Che et al. 2018) won the competitions of the CoNLL shared task in 2017 and 2018 (Zeman et al., 2017, 2018). Their Biaffine parsers are available as Stanza [5] models.

Because of the success of the graph-based approach, there have been many investigations performed to improve the parsing performance, for example, DiaParser (Attardi et al., 2021) extends the architecture of the Biaffine Parser by exploiting both embeddings and attentions provided by transformers and achieved high performance.

On the other hand, before the competition, Straka et al. (2016) provides a transition-based parser, UDPipe[6], which reconstructs parsed trees based on estimated action sequences applying word tokens. And another popular NLP tool spaCy [7] also provides transition-based parsers.

[1] https://github.com/UniversalDependencies/UD_Japanese-BCCWJ

[2] https://github.com/UniversalDependencies/UD_Japanese-GSD

[3] https://github.com/ryanmcd/uni-dep-tb

[4] https://github.com/UniversalDependencies/UD_Japanese-Modern

[5] https://stanfordnlp.github.io/stanza/

[6] https://github.com/ufal/udpipe

[7] https://spacy.io/

In contrast, this paper focuses on structure modeling of UD parsing, including deep learning-based phrase segmentation.

Multilingual Transfer of Deep UD parsers Biaffine parsers have high transfer ability, especially for low-resource languages. Kondratyuk and Straka (2019) shows their single Biaffine model named UDify trained on 75 UD treebanks with high performances for those low-resource treebanks.

UD Parsers for Contemporary Japanese There are a lot of parsers which support contemporary Japanese UD. For example, the spaCy [8] supports Japanese UD parsing. GiNZA (Matsuda, 2020), which is also a spaCy-based parser, trained specifically for contemporary Japanese.

UD Parser for Modern Japanese For UD parsing methods applied to modern Japanese, Yasuoka (2020) examined an approach that combines morphological information conversion using the UniDic designed for modern Japanese with an existing Japanese UD dependency parser. While this morphological conversion significantly improves accuracy, it has been reported that the accuracy does not reach the level achieved when trained directly on the UD_Japanese-Modern (Meirokuzasshi) corpus. Additionally, this parser has been released as `unidic2ud`[9]. In the `unidic2ud` repository, Yasuoka (2020) provides a few UD annotated sentences from famous literature written in modern Japanse (Yukiguni, Maihime, and Koyayori).

3 Bunsetsu Dependency for Syntactic Structure of Japanese

The left side of Figure 1 shows an example of Japanese's morphological and syntactic structure. In Japanese, bunsetsu dependency relations (shown in the top dependency tree of Figure 1) are widely used for representing syntactic structure. A bunsetsu is the smallest and natural phrase unit for native Japanese speakers, and syntactic structure is expressed through the dependency relations between bunsetsu phrases.

A bunsetsu consists of one or more words. However, since Japanese lacks a whitespace separation of words in its writing system, there are multiple word unit definitions, such as short unit words (SUWs) and long unit words (LUWs) defined by the National Institute for Japanese Language and Linguistics (NINJAL). In this study, we explain bunsetsu structures based on the SUWs and LUWs, which are commonly used in Universal Dependencies (UD).

3.1 Bunsetsu (Base-phrase)

As mentioned above, a bunsetsu is a (natural) minimal phrase that consists of a Japanese sentence. An example of bunsetsu boundaries is shown in Figure 1 as green solid lines. Generally, a bunsetsu boundary appears after a particle or a sequence of particles. This is because Japanese functional words typically follow their content words, on which they depend. In Figure 1, all LUW noun (NOUN) and adposition (ADP) pairs are composed into bunsetsu segments.

3.2 Short Unit Word

Short Unit Word (SUW) is a token close to the granularity of typical Japanese word tokens. A dictionary (UniDic) was established for SUWs, enabling high-performance morphological analysis based on UniDic (Den et al., 2008). As shown in the overview Figure 1, bunsetsu and LUWs are also composed of SUWs.

3.3 Long Unit Word

The Long Unit Word (LUW) is a lexical unit corresponding to a bunsetsu. Identification of LUW involves identifying bunsetsu and then dividing each bunsetsu into independent and attached LUWs. In Figure 1, blue dotted lines represent LUWs' boundaries, which divide bunsetsu into independent and attached LUWs.

4 Structure Modeling Approach for UD Parsing

In standard Japanese UD annotation (Asahara et al., 2018; Omura and Asahara, 2018), bunsetsu dependency information is used as a basis for rule-based conversion into UD annotation, referencing the SUWs and LUWs contained within each bunsetsu.

Therefore, by estimating the SUW, LUW, and bunsetsu boundaries, along with the dependency relations between bunsetsu, it is possible to obtain UD parsing results by applying the same conversion rules.

Figure 1 shows the pipeline of the structure modeling approach. The pipeline starts from

[8] `https://spacy.io/`

[9] `https://github.com/KoichiYasuoka/UniDic2UD`

a CRF-based SUW analysis (MeCab), and then the results of SUW analysis are sent to deep learning-based LUW and bunsetsu analysis (Monaka). Next, all SUW, LUW and bunsetsu information are sent to bunsetsu dependency parsing (CaboCha), and finally, with all the information, rule-based UD conversion is performed.

4.1 SUW Analysis

For SUW analysis, MeCab [10], which uses the Conditional Random Field (CRF; Lafferty et al. 2001) with a dictionary, was generally used. The actual analysis was performed using fugashi[11], a Cython wrapper for MeCab (McCann, 2020). In the MeCab-based analysis, UniDic was used as the SUW dictionary. UniDic supports not only modern Japanese [12], but also various periods of the Japanese language from old Japanese (Nara-period; C.E. 710-) onward.

4.1.1 Bunsetsu Analysis (Monaka)

For bunsetsu analysis, the parser named Monaka[13] proposed by Ozaki et al. (2024) was used. Monaka simultaneously predicts bunsetsu boundaries, LUW boundaries, and part-of-speech tags of LUWs from a sequence of SUWs. As described in the previous section, SUWs can be analyzed using MeCab, allowing us to perform all necessary analyses except for bunsetsu dependency parsing.

The method proposed by Ozaki et al. (2024) targets Japanese from the Heian (C.E. 794-1185) to Muromachi (C.E. 1336-1573) periods, as stored in the Corpus of Historical Japanese (CHJ). Because their method provides publicly available code, we newly built a one-model bunsetsu and LUW parser covering both the Heian–Muromachi periods and contemporary Japanese. Building the model, we referenced the bunsetsu and LUW information included as UFeat in UD_Japanese-BCCWJ and UD_Japanese-GSD. The hyperparameters to train the model are also the same as the original ones.

4.1.2 Bunsetsu Dependency Parsing (CaboCha)

For bunsetsu dependency parsing, we used CaboCha (Taku Kudo, 2002). CaboCha is a bunsetsu dependency parser based on Support Vector Machines (SVM). It consists of multiple analysis layers, including SUW analysis, bunsetsu segmentation, and bunsetsu dependency parsing, allowing for layer-specific parser customization. The default SUW analysis layer in CaboCha uses MeCab.

Since CaboCha's bunsetsu dependency parsing is performed based on the features of SUWs within each bunsetsu, it is possible to conduct only bunsetsu dependency parsing by passing SUWs and bunsetsu information to CaboCha in its designated format.

4.1.3 Rule-based UD Conversion for Bunsetsu Dependency

For rule-based UD conversion of bunsetsu dependencies, we employed the method proposed by Asahara et al. (2018); Omura and Asahara (2018). This method was used in the creation of the Japanese UD corpus for the Balanced Corpus of Contemporary Written Japanese (BCCWJ)[14].

In this rule-based conversion, dependencies between bunsetsu are transformed into dependencies between SUWs that represent the meaning of the bunsetsu, such as content words (shown as light blue solid arrows of UD dependency in Figure 1). Each SUW within a bunsetsu is then set to depend on the representative SUW of that bunsetsu (shown as green dotted arrows of UD dependency in Figure 1).

In Japanese bunsetsu dependency parsing, only dependency relations between bunsetus are defined; no relation label is assigned (see Figure 1. However, in the UD framework, dependency relations must always have labels. Therefore, in this rule-based conversion, UD dependency labels are assigned by referencing morphological information such as the part-of-speech tags of SUWs and LUWs.

Although the conversion can be performed using only SUW morphological information, LUW morphological information will improve the accuracy of the transformation.

5 Evaluation

5.1 Target Corpora

We used UD_Japanese-GSD and UD_Japanese-BCCWJ, which are contemporary Japanese UD corpora, for training. For evaluation, UD_Japanese-Modern (Meiroku-zasshi), a UD

[10] https://taku910.github.io/mecab/

[11] https://github.com/polm/fugashi

[12] https://clrd.ninjal.ac.jp/unidic/download_all.html

[13] https://github.com/komiya-lab/monaka

[14] https://github.com/UniversalDependencies/UD_Japanese-BCCWJ

	Heian	Kamakura	Muromachi	Contemporary	
				BCCWJ	GSD
Bunsetsu	97.35	97.38	97.86	93.85	97.88
LUW span	99.69	99.44	98.99	97.87	98.84
+ PoS	99.33	99.03	98.00	96.73	98.23

(a) The one-model

	Heian	Kamakura	Muromachi	Contemporary	
				BCCWJ	GSD
Bunsetsu	97.03	97.69	97.87	94.04	98.01
LUW span	99.64	99.47	98.95	98.00	99.02
+ PoS	99.29	99.08	98.08	97.09	98.32

(b) Trained on each period

Table 1: The evaluation results of the one-model bunsetsu parser. The results for models trained on each period on Heian to Muromachi periods are from Ozaki et al. (2024).

corpus from the Meiji-period, and corpora (Yukiguni and Maihime) independently created by Yasuoka (2020), included with `unidic2ud`, were used.

5.2 Models

5.2.1 Bunsetsu and LUW

We trained the one-model bunsetsu parser explained in §4.1.1. We compared models trained on corpora from each period. Evaluation results for historical Japanese were from Ozaki et al. (2024). We newly trained contemporary bunsetsu parsers for each UD_Japanese-BCCWJ and UD_Japanese-GSD. These bunsetsu parsers were trained on each training set of UD treebanks and tested on their corresponding test sets for each treebank.

5.2.2 UD

As a deep learning-based parser, we used DiaParser, a graph-based Biaffine parser model (Attardi et al., 2021). For word embeddings, we used Japanese BERT provided by Tohoku University[15], and these embeddings were kept frozen during training. The models used for comparison are as follows:

Structure: The structure modeling approach proposed in this study.

jBERT: A DiaParser model utilizing Japanese BERT provided by Tohoku University.

UDify: A Biaffine parser model trained on 75 UD treebanks (Kondratyuk and Straka, 2019).

GiNZA: A transition-based parsing model provided by spaCy[16], trained on BCCWJ. For contemporary Japanese, we compared GiNZA as is (Matsuda, 2020).

Unidic2ud: Unidic2ud[17] provides a UDPipe (Straka et al., 2016) model trained on modern Japanese (UD_Japanese-Modern (Meirokuzasshi)), morphological analysis was performed using MeCab with modern UniDic.

5.3 Evaluation Method

5.3.1 Bunsetsu and LUW

We used span-based f1-value evaluation (same as the evaluation used for the original bunsetsu parser; Ozaki et al., 2024).

5.3.2 UD

To focus solely on the evaluation of dependency parsing, we compared only dependency by ignoring tokenization errors (AlignedAcc). The evaluation metric was the Labeled Attachment Score (LAS), which is an extraction performance metric including the relationship label between two words in a dependency relation. Additionally, the Unlabeled Attachment Score (UAS), which measures the extraction performance of two words in a dependency relation, was also used for comparison. The evaluation script used was the one employed in the CoNLL Shared Task 2018 (Zeman et al., 2018) [18].

[15] `https://huggingface.co/cl-tohoku/bert-base-japanese`

[16] `https://spacy.io/`

[17] `https://github.com/KoichiYasuoka/UniDic2UD`

[18] `https://universaldependencies.org/conll18/conll18_ud_eval.py`

Period	Contemporary				Modern					
Corpus	BCCWJ		GSD		Yukiguni		Maihime		Meiroku-zasshi	
Model	UAS	LAS	UAS	LAS	UAS	LAS	UAS	LAS	UAS	LAS
Structure	**92.52**	**91.32**	92.42	91.18	**89.29**	**85.71**	**92.45**	**77.36**	**83.40**	**63.91**
jBERT	90.19	88.82	90.88	89.70	78.18	74.55	75.00	65.38	79.41	57.88
UDify	-	-	**94.37**	**92.08**	83.93	78.57	79.25	58.49	74.99	55.62
GiNZA	87.52	85.89	88.52	87.12	-	-	-	-	-	-
Unidic2ud	-	-	-	-	89.09	87.27	88.46	75.00	(88.20)	(72.87)

Table 2: UAS/LAS evaluation results. **UDify** results in the contemporary Japanese and Meiroku-zasshi are from their paper (Kondratyuk and Straka, 2019). Other results were evaluated by the parsed outputs. Because **Unidic2ud** was trained on Meiroku-zasshi, we show their performances surrounded by parentheses.

Period	Contemporary		Modern		
Corpus	BCCWJ	GSD	Yukiguni	Maihime	Meiroku-zasshi
Words	98.94	98.68	100.	100.	99.50
UPOS	98.21	96.80	94.64	94.34	87.61
XPOS	98.13	96.65	69.64	79.25	73.13

Table 3: UPOS/XPOS evaluation results.

5.4 Evaluation Results

5.4.1 Bunsetsu and LUW

Table 1 shows the evaluation results of the one-model bunsetsu parser, which was trained on the CHJ (Heian (C.E. 794-1185), Kamakura (C.E. 1185-1336), and Muromachi (C.E. 1336-1573) periods), UD_Japanese-BCCWJ, and UD_Japanese-GSD. Compared to the models trained on each period, the one-model approach achieved comparable results. Since modern Japanese (Meiji period) is in between the contemporary and Muromachi periods, the one-model bunsetsu parser is expected to perform well in modern Japanese.

5.4.2 UD

Dependency Table 2 shows UAS and LAS values for each corpus. Bold values indicate the highest value for each corpus and metric.

The structure modeling approach achieved the highest performance in BCCWJ and other modern corpora. The structure modeling approach outperformed the existing Japanese UD parser GinZA. This indicates the structure modeling approach is effective in improving UD parsing performance.

UDify reported the highest performance on GSD, however, its performance on Meiroku-zasshi was the worst. As well as **UDify**, **jBERT** struggled to perform in modern Japanese, despite their strong cross-lingual transfer ability. This indicates phrase (bunsetsu) or morphological level transfers are required for diachronic syntactic analysis.

Notably, it demonstrated high transfer performance in UAS, whereas LAS for Meiroku-zasshi (UD_Japanese-Modern) tended to be lower overall. This suggests that Meiroku-zasshi was created based on a different annotation standard compared to contemporary Japanese, Yukiguni, and Maihime.

SUW Accuracy Table 3 shows accuracy of SUW analysis. Because we use the same SUW analyzer (MeCab/`unidic2ud`), we compared accuracies for each corpus. Words, UPOS, and XPOS values were calculated by the CoNLL Shared Task 2018 evaluation script [19].

The Words value represents tokenization accuracy. From modern to contemporary Japanese, tokenization has been performed without significant issues. However, focusing on UPOS, performance declines in modern Japanese, with particularly low values observed in Meiroku-zasshi. Since UPOS represents the accuracy of language-independent PoS tags in UD, the rule-based conversion from bunsetsu dependency parsing to UD, which uses PoS information to estimate dependency labels, may contribute to the decreased accuracy of dependency labels. This corresponds to the overall significantly lower LAS in Meiroku-zasshi and

[19] `https://universaldependencies.org/conll18/conll18_ud_eval.py`

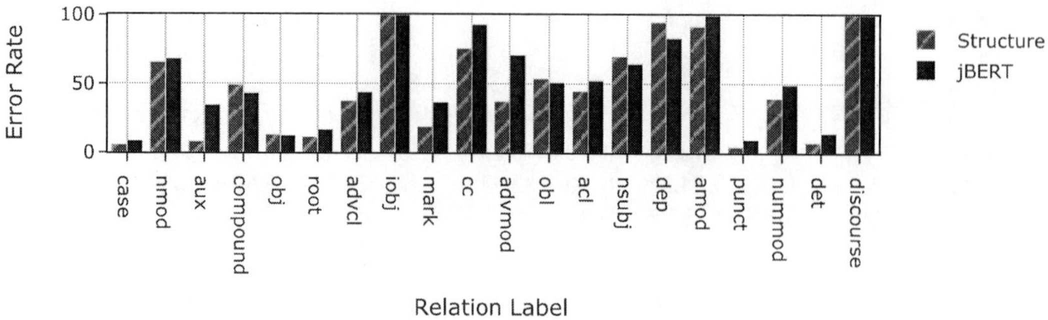

Figure 2: Comparison with dependency labels of models.

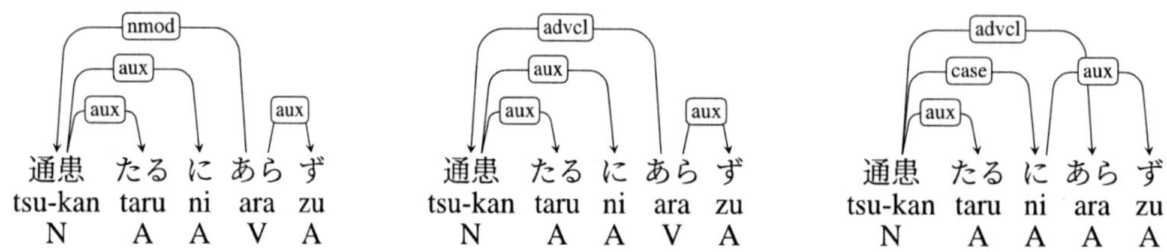

(a) Gold (b) Structure (c) jBERT

Figure 3: An example of parse results for BERT-based, the structure models. "N" represents nouns, "A" represents auxiliary verbs, and "V" represents verbs, respectively. The example is picked from Meirokku-zasshi.

suggests that, despite the availability of dictionaries for early modern Japanese, further improvements in SUW performance are necessary.

On the other hand, XPOS represents the accuracy of more detailed, language-specific PoS labels in UD, but its values have significantly declined compared to UPOS. This decline is not due to SUW analyze errors but rather inconsistencies in XPOS labeling during the annotation process of the UD corpus. Therefore, improving XPOS performance requires a normalization process for XPOS labels.

5.5 Comparison by Dependency Labels

Figure 2 shows the error rate comparison between **jBERT** and **Structure** models for each UD dependency label. We investigated all dependency relations based on dependency labels. The structure modeling approach achieves a lower error rate for most dependency labels, especially for aux dependencies. Because identifying aux relations, bunsetsu and PoS tags is important, the structure modeling approach can estimate them appropriately, resulting in the high performance of aux dependencies. However, for dependency labels that represent case relations between bunsetsu, such as obl (oblique nominal) and nsubj (nominal subject), the **jBERT** model has a slightly lower error rate.

This suggests that the **jBERT** model may have a better ability to transfer knowledge for semantic relationships compared to the structure modeling approach. It also indicates that incorporating features from BERT into the structure modeling approach for bunsetsu dependency parsing could potentially improve accuracy.

5.6 Case Study

Figure 3 shows an example of parse results for **jBERT** and **Structure** models compared to their gold annotation. The phrase "通患たるにあらず (tsu-kan taru ni ara zu: it is not generally a problem)" consists of two bunsetsu "通患たるに (tsu-kan taru ni)" and "あらず (ara zu)." In the structure modeling approach, intra-bunsetsu dependencies are preserved, and the bunsetsu "通患たるに (tsu-kan taru ni)" is correctly dependent on the bunsetsu "あらず (ara zu)", resulting in a valid dependency structure under UD. However, there was a mismatch in dependency labels between bunsetsu. Since the PoS tags of the SUW composing the phrases were also correctly predicted, this discrepancy in inter-bunsetsu dependency labels is likely due to differences in annotation standards between the contemporary and the modern UD corpora.

On the other hand, in the parsing result using

the **jBERT** model, the dependency within the bunsetsu, such as "ず (zu)" being associated with "に (ni)," is not preserved. Moreover, despite the fact that the "に (ni)" related to "tsu-kan" is an auxiliary verb, the dependency label is predicted as "case," which seems to be a confusion with particles. Additionally, similar to the structure modeling approach, "あら (ara)" is treated as modifying "通患 (tsu-kan)" in the adverbial clause (advcl), which can be considered a natural result from the perspective of contemporary Japanese annotation.

6 Conclusion

This study shows the effectiveness of structure modeling for transfer ability in diachronic syntactic parsing. We compared the zero-shot transfer ability between Transformer-based Biaffine UD parsers and our structure modeling approach. The structure modeling approach is a pipeline method consisting of dictionary-based morphological analysis (MeCab), a deep learning-based phrase (bunsetsu) analysis (Monaka), SVM-based phrase dependency parsing (CaboCha), and a rule-based conversion from phrase dependencies to UD, which closely follows the methodology used in constructing Japanese UD corpora. Experimental results showed that the structure modeling approach outperformed zero-shot transfer from the contemporary to the modern Japanese by a wide margin. The structure modeling approach outperformed several existing UD parsers in contemporary Japanese. Moreover, for other languages as well, it may be beneficial to adopt an analysis approach based on an understanding of resource construction methods, such as how UD resources are created or how parsed trees are transformed into UD format using head rules. From a case study, the structure modeling approach can preserve low-level information such as morphology and phrases (bunsetsu). On the other hand, the Biaffine parser has slightly better transfer performances of case relations. To this end, the structure modeling performed well on diachronic transfer in Japanese.

Limitations

Our structure modeling approach and compared models use "base" size BERT models; thus, by using larger models, the conclusion might differ from that we achieved. Since SUWs, LUWs, and bunsetsu analysis have been established for historical Japanese, we can easily apply our structure modeling approach. However, this is a rather unique case, and it might be harder to apply a similar approach to diachronic transfer for other languages.

Acknowledgments

This work was supported by JSPS KAKENHI Grant Number 22K12145, and a collaborative research project of National Institute for Japanese Language and Linguistics Joint Research Project "Extending the Diachronic Corpus through an Open Co-construction Environment" and "Evidence-based Theoretical and Typological Linguistics."

References

Masayuki Asahara, Hiroshi Kanayama, Takaaki Tanaka, Yusuke Miyao, Sumire Uematsu, Shinsuke Mori, Yuji Matsumoto, Mai Omura, and Yugo Murawaki. 2018. Universal Dependencies version 2 for Japanese. In *Proceedings of the Eleventh International Conference on Language Resources and Evaluation (LREC 2018)*, Miyazaki, Japan. European Language Resources Association (ELRA).

Giuseppe Attardi, Daniele Sartiano, and Maria Simi. 2021. Biaffine dependency and semantic graph parsing for EnhancedUniversal dependencies. In *Proceedings of the 17th International Conference on Parsing Technologies and the IWPT 2021 Shared Task on Parsing into Enhanced Universal Dependencies (IWPT 2021)*, pages 184–188, Online. Association for Computational Linguistics.

Wanxiang Che, Yijia Liu, Yuxuan Wang, Bo Zheng, and Ting Liu. 2018. Towards better UD parsing: Deep contextualized word embeddings, ensemble, and treebank concatenation. In *Proceedings of the CoNLL 2018 Shared Task: Multilingual Parsing from Raw Text to Universal Dependencies*, pages 55–64, Brussels, Belgium. Association for Computational Linguistics.

Yasuharu Den, Junpei Nakamura, Toshinobu Ogiso, and Hideki Ogura. 2008. A proper approach to Japanese morphological analysis: Dictionary, model, and evaluation. In *Proceedings of the Sixth International Conference on Language Resources and Evaluation (LREC'08)*, Marrakech, Morocco. European Language Resources Association (ELRA).

Timothy Dozat, Peng Qi, and Christopher D. Manning. 2017. Stanford's graph-based neural dependency parser at the CoNLL 2017 shared task. In *Proceedings of the CoNLL 2017 Shared Task: Multilingual Parsing from Raw Text to Universal Dependencies*, pages 20–30, Vancouver, Canada. Association for Computational Linguistics.

Dan Kondratyuk and Milan Straka. 2019. 75 languages, 1 model: Parsing Universal Dependencies universally. In *Proceedings of the 2019 Conference on Empirical Methods in Natural Language Processing and the 9th International Joint Conference on Natural Language Processing (EMNLP-IJCNLP)*, pages 2779–2795, Hong Kong, China. Association for Computational Linguistics.

John D. Lafferty, Andrew McCallum, and Fernando C. N. Pereira. 2001. Conditional random fields: Probabilistic models for segmenting and labeling sequence data. In *Proceedings of the Eighteenth International Conference on Machine Learning*, ICML '01, pages 282–289, San Francisco, CA, USA. Morgan Kaufmann Publishers Inc.

Kikuo Maekawa. 2008. Balanced Corpus of Contemporary Written Japanese. In *Proceedings of the 6th Workshop on Asian Language Resources.*

Hiroshi Matsuda. 2020. Ginza - practical japanese nlp based on universal dependencies. *Journal of Natural Language Processing*, 27(3):695–701.

Paul McCann. 2020. fugashi, a tool for tokenizing Japanese in python. In *Proceedings of Second Workshop for NLP Open Source Software (NLP-OSS)*, pages 44–51, Online. Association for Computational Linguistics.

Mai Omura and Masayuki Asahara. 2017. Universal dependency for japanese modern. In *Japan Association for Digital Humanities.*

Mai Omura and Masayuki Asahara. 2018. UD-Japanese BCCWJ: Universal Dependencies annotation for the Balanced Corpus of Contemporary Written Japanese. In *Proceedings of the Second Workshop on Universal Dependencies (UDW 2018)*, pages 117–125, Brussels, Belgium. Association for Computational Linguistics.

Hiroaki Ozaki, Kanako Komiya, Masayuki Asahara, and Toshinobu Ogiso. 2024. Long unit word tokenization and bunsetsu segmentation of historical Japanese. In *Proceedings of the 1st Workshop on Machine Learning for Ancient Languages (ML4AL 2024)*, pages 48–55, Hybrid in Bangkok, Thailand and online. Association for Computational Linguistics.

Peng Qi, Timothy Dozat, Yuhao Zhang, and Christopher D. Manning. 2018. Universal Dependency parsing from scratch. In *Proceedings of the CoNLL 2018 Shared Task: Multilingual Parsing from Raw Text to Universal Dependencies*, pages 160–170, Brussels, Belgium. Association for Computational Linguistics.

Milan Straka, Jan Hajič, and Jana Straková. 2016. UD-Pipe: Trainable pipeline for processing CoNLL-U files performing tokenization, morphological analysis, POS tagging and parsing. In *Proceedings of the Tenth International Conference on Language Resources and Evaluation (LREC'16)*, pages 4290–4297, Portorož, Slovenia. European Language Resources Association (ELRA).

Yuji Matsumoto Taku Kudo. 2002. Japanese dependency analysis using cascaded chunking. In *CoNLL 2002: Proceedings of the 6th Conference on Natural Language Learning 2002 (COLING 2002 Post-Conference Workshops)*, pages 63–69.

Takaaki Tanaka, Yusuke Miyao, Masayuki Asahara, Sumire Uematsu, Hiroshi Kanayama, Shinsuke Mori, and Yuji Matsumoto. 2016. Universal Dependencies for Japanese. In *Proceedings of the Tenth International Conference on Language Resources and Evaluation (LREC'16)*, pages 1651–1658, Portorož, Slovenia. European Language Resources Association (ELRA).

Koichi Yasuoka. 2020. Keitaiso kaiseki-bu no tsukekae ni yoru kindai nihongo(kyu-jitai kyu-kana) no kakari-uke kaiseki (in japanese) dependency parsing of modern japanese (kyujitai and kyukana) by replacing morphological analysis units. Technical Report 3, Information Processing Society of Japan.

Daniel Zeman, Jan Hajič, Martin Popel, Martin Potthast, Milan Straka, Filip Ginter, Joakim Nivre, and Slav Petrov. 2018. CoNLL 2018 shared task: Multilingual parsing from raw text to Universal Dependencies. In *Proceedings of the CoNLL 2018 Shared Task: Multilingual Parsing from Raw Text to Universal Dependencies*, pages 1–21, Brussels, Belgium. Association for Computational Linguistics.

Daniel Zeman, Martin Popel, Milan Straka, Jan Hajič, Joakim Nivre, Filip Ginter, Juhani Luotolahti, Sampo Pyysalo, Slav Petrov, Martin Potthast, Francis Tyers, Elena Badmaeva, Memduh Gokirmak, Anna Nedoluzhko, Silvie Cinková, Jan Hajič jr., Jaroslava Hlaváčová, Václava Kettnerová, Zdeňka Urešová, Jenna Kanerva, Stina Ojala, Anna Missilä, Christopher D. Manning, Sebastian Schuster, Siva Reddy, Dima Taji, Nizar Habash, Herman Leung, Marie-Catherine de Marneffe, Manuela Sanguinetti, Maria Simi, Hiroshi Kanayama, Valeria de Paiva, Kira Droganova, Héctor Martínez Alonso, Çağrı Çöltekin, Umut Sulubacak, Hans Uszkoreit, Vivien Macketanz, Aljoscha Burchardt, Kim Harris, Katrin Marheinecke, Georg Rehm, Tolga Kayadelen, Mohammed Attia, Ali Elkahky, Zhuoran Yu, Emily Pitler, Saran Lertpradit, Michael Mandl, Jesse Kirchner, Hector Fernandez Alcalde, Jana Strnadová, Esha Banerjee, Ruli Manurung, Antonio Stella, Atsuko Shimada, Sookyoung Kwak, Gustavo Mendonça, Tatiana Lando, Rattima Nitisaroj, and Josie Li. 2017. CoNLL 2017 shared task: Multilingual parsing from raw text to Universal Dependencies. In *Proceedings of the CoNLL 2017 Shared Task: Multilingual Parsing from Raw Text to Universal Dependencies*, pages 1–19, Vancouver, Canada. Association for Computational Linguistics.

BARTABSA++: Revisiting BARTABSA with Decoder LLMs

Jan Pfister and **Tom Völker** and **Anton Vlasjuk** and **Andreas Hotho**

Data Science Chair
Center for Artificial Intelligence and Data Science (CAIDAS)
Julius-Maximilians-Universität Würzburg (JMU), Würzburg, Germany
{pfister,voelker,vlasjuk,hotho}@informatik.uni-wuerzburg.de

Abstract

We revisit the BARTABSA framework for aspect-based sentiment analysis with modern decoder LLMs to assess the importance of explicit structure modeling today. Our updated implementation—BARTABSA++[1]—features architectural enhancements that boost performance and training stability. Systematic testing with various encoder-decoder architectures shows that BARTABSA++ with BART-LARGE achieves state-of-the-art results, even surpassing a finetuned GPT-4O model. Our analysis indicates the encoder's representational quality is vital, while the decoder's role is minimal, explaining the limited benefits of scaling decoder-only LLMs for this task. These findings underscore the complementary roles of explicit structured modeling and large language models, indicating structured approaches remain competitive for tasks requiring precise relational information extraction.

1 Introduction

In this work, we revisit BARTABSA (Yan et al., 2021a), a pointer network-based method for aspect-based sentiment analysis (ABSA) that achieved state-of-the-art performance with the BART encoder-decoder transformer - considered small by today's standards. BARTABSA models Aspect Sentiment Triplet Extraction (ASTE) (Peng et al., 2020) as a constrained generation task, using a pointer network (Vinyals et al., 2015) to explicitly copy input tokens into strictly structured outputs.

In the meantime, advances in Large Language Models (LLMs) have transformed natural language processing (NLP) by demonstrating that implicit knowledge acquired during pretraining can often address tasks that previously demanded explicit structured representations (Brown et al., 2020; Wei et al., 2022). This shift prompts the question: Is explicit structured output modeling still relevant in the LLM era, especially in structured representation-critical tasks like ABSA?

To evaluate this, we employ the methodology of Rothe et al. (2020), which constructs encoder-decoder architectures by reusing pretrained encoder *or* decoder checkpoints. We reimplement BARTABSA using modern libraries and incorporate architectural enhancements like: (1) feature normalization to balance embedding spaces and stabilize training (Zhang and Sennrich, 2019; Xiong et al., 2020); (2) cross-attention mechanisms reusing weights from BART's decoder layers (Vaswani et al., 2017; See et al., 2017); (3) parametrized gating mechanisms replacing static hyperparameters with learnable weights (See et al., 2017; Chung et al., 2014; Dauphin et al., 2017). These techniques allow stable training with larger models and improve performance, outperforming both the original implementation and a baseline using a finetuned GPT-4O.

With this enhanced framework, we systematically evaluate different architectural configurations to examine potential scaling effects of modern-sized LLMs within structured language modeling. This research direction is particularly valuable as it combines the implicit knowledge of modern decoder LLMs with the transparency offered by the explicit copying mechanism of pointer networks—a property important for interpretable NLP systems.

Experiments with BART (Lewis et al., 2020), BERT (Devlin et al., 2019), and GPT-2 (Radford et al., 2019) variants reveal performance hinges on the encoder, with minimal decoder impact. Counterintuitively, scaling GPT-2 does not yield performance gains, emphasizing the encoder's pretraining importance for pointer networks (and other encoder-decoder architectures).

Our study shows large autoregressive models do not universally surpass structured approaches in NLP and contributes to the dialogue on explicit structure modeling, like pointer networks, in the

These authors contributed equally to this work.
[1]https://github.com/LSX-UniWue/bartabsa-plusplus

Proceedings of the 1st Joint Workshop on Large Language Models and Structure Modeling (XLLM 2025), pages 115–128
August 1, 2025

Figure 1: An example sentence for ABSA with aspect, opinion, sentiment and word indices annotated. Adapted from Yan et al. (2021a).

LLM era. It explores scaling structured generation with LLM-sized models to merge their implicit knowledge with structured copying mechanisms.

2 Related Work

2.1 Aspect-Based Sentiment Analysis

Aspect-Based Sentiment Analysis (ABSA) is a fine-grained approach to sentiment analysis focusing on opinions about specific text elements rather than general document or sentence sentiment (Liu, 2012). ABSA involves three main components: aspect terms, opinion terms, and sentiment polarities. In Figure 1, the term *"Drivers"* is characterized positively by *"okay"*, whereas *"BIOS update"* and *"system"* are negatively characterized by *"froze"*.

Aspect Sentiment Triplet Extraction (ASTE), the focus of this work, extracts (aspect, opinion, sentiment) triplets simultaneously. This task captures complete opinion structures, making it valuable for applications such as customer feedback analysis (Peng et al., 2020).

The ABSA field has evolved from specialized RNN-based architectures (Wang et al., 2016; Tang et al., 2016) to approaches leveraging pretrained language models (Li et al., 2019). For ASTE specifically, approaches progressed from pipeline methods to joint tagging schemes (Xu et al., 2020; Wu et al., 2020), with influential work reformulating the task as a structured generation problem using sequence-to-sequence models (Yan et al., 2021a; Zhang et al., 2021). This sequence-to-sequence paradigm established a strong foundation that subsequent research has built upon, including recent advances with larger language models and hybrid approaches (Xianlong et al., 2023; Zhang et al., 2024; Sun et al., 2024).

Our experiments use the refined versions of standard ABSA benchmark datasets from SemEval 2014-2016 challenges (Pontiki et al., 2014, 2015, 2016): `14lap`, `14res`, `15res`, and `16res`, as processed by Xu et al. (2020) who filtered out low-quality examples and duplicates.

2.2 BARTABSA

Following Yan et al. (2021a), each ABSA task involves transforming an input sentence $X = [x_1, \ldots, x_n]$ into a structured target sequence $Y = [y_1, \ldots, y_m]$ using pointer networks (Vinyals et al., 2015). These allow the model to refer directly to tokens from the input sequence, facilitating extraction tasks requiring grounding in exact input spans.

For ABSA, BARTABSA uses these pointers to copy start and end token indices from the input sentence into a structured output sequence, paired with sentiment classification tokens. For instance, the input *"Drivers updated okay but the BIOS update froze the system."* (Figure 1) is converted into structured outputs pointing to input tokens and sentiment classes.

Formally, the output follows a fixed grammar where each triplet is represented as a 5-tuple: $(a_i^s, a_i^e, o_i^s, o_i^e, s_i^p)$ where a_i^s, a_i^e are start and end indices of the ith aspect term, o_i^s, o_i^e are for the opinion term, and s_i^p is the sentiment polarity class. For our example, the structured output sequence thus becomes:

$$[(0, 0, 2, 2, \texttt{POS}), (5, 6, 7, 7, \texttt{NEG}), (9, 9, 7, 7, \texttt{NEG})]$$

This syntax explicitly encodes the extracted (aspect, opinion, sentiment) triplets as structured predictions, with each span being clearly represented by its start and end indices in the input sequence. Given this structured output format, BARTABSA models ABSA as a sequence generation task, computing the probability of Y given X as:

$$P(Y|X) = \prod_{t=1}^{m} P(y_t|X, Y_{<t}) \quad (1)$$

BART (Lewis et al., 2020) is used as a backbone to compute $P(y_t|X, Y_{<t})$, with the encoder processing the input sequence X into contextualized embeddings H^e:

$$H^e = \text{BARTEncoder}([x_1, \ldots, x_n]) \quad (2)$$

Decoding involves predicting indices y_t and dereferencing them to tokens $\hat{y}_t$:

$$\hat{y}_t = \begin{cases} X_{y_t} & \text{if } y_t \text{ is a pointer index} \\ C_{y_t - n} & \text{if } y_t \text{ is a class index} \end{cases} \quad (3)$$

where $C = [c_1, \ldots, c_l]$ is a list of class tokens for sentiment classification.

The decoder uses prior dereferenced tokens $\hat{Y}_t = [\hat{y}_1, \ldots, \hat{y}_{t-1}]$ to produce the next state:

$$h_t^d = \text{BARTDecoder}(H^e, \hat{Y}_t) \quad (4)$$

On top of the BART model, BARTABSA then uses a pointer network mechanism to generate a distribution over input tokens X and class tokens C: This mechanism combines both the initial token embeddings and the contextualized representations from the transformer layers:

$$E^e = \text{BARTTokenEmbed}(X) \quad (5)$$

$$\hat{H}^e = MLP(H^e) \quad (6)$$

$$\overline{H}^e = \alpha \hat{H}^e + (1-\alpha)E^e \quad (7)$$

$$C^d = \text{BARTTokenEmbed}(C) \quad (8)$$

$$P_t = \text{Softmax}([\overline{H}^e; C^d]h_t^d) \quad (9)$$

where P_t represents the common pointer and class token distribution.

Training uses teacher forcing and negative log-likelihood; inference can use strategies like greedy sampling and beam search (Yan et al., 2021a).

3 Methodology

We will combine Yan et al.'s (2021a) BARTABSA framework, with Rothe et al.'s (2020) encoder-decoder model construction methodology in Section 3.3. This requires us to first reimplement BARTABSA in Section 3.1, before stabilizing training with additional features and optimizations in Section 3.2.

3.1 BARTABSA-R: Our Reimplementation

Yan et al.'s (2021a) original BARTABSA implementation has limitations for our use case, especially hindering model extensions: 1) The *fastnlp* package[2] used is unmaintained, only supporting older 🤗 Transformers versions (Wolf et al., 2020). 2) Data processing and modeling are tightly coupled, with e.g. hard-coded token IDs for mask creation, complicating further experiments and architecture adaptations. To resolve these issues, we reimplement BARTABSA using maintained libraries like PyTorch (Ansel et al., 2024), Lightning (Falcon and The PyTorch Lightning team, 2019), and an updated Transformers version (Wolf et al., 2020). We avoid hard-coded values with tokenizer outputs and shift attention mask creation to the data pipeline. We name our reimplementation BARTABSA-R.

[2]https://github.com/fastnlp/fastNLP

3.2 Extending to BARTABSA++

During the reimplementation of BARTABSA and preliminary experiments, we identified several issues and potential improvements, detailed also in Algorithm 1.

3.2.1 Feature Normalization

Our use of some backbone models, like BART-LARGE, resulted in unstable training, seen through diverging losses. We traced this instability to differing scales of output logits (Figure 2), stemming from concatenating distinct embedding spaces in the pointer network: classification token embeddings (C^d) and the mixed encoder representations ($\overline{H}^e$). The scale imbalance between the two spaces destabilized attention calculations.

To address this, we applied an L^2 normalization to both special token embeddings and processed encoder outputs (lines 6 & 7), equalizing their contributions, thus stabilizing training[3].

An RMSNorm (Zhang and Sennrich, 2019) was also applied to the final decoder output (line 13), further stabilizing gradient flow.

3.2.2 Additional Attention Mechanism

We introduce an additional attention mechanism motivated by an architectural analysis of BARTABSA. While exploring component contributions, we discovered that removing the encoder's MLP (line 3; Equation (6))—a seemingly auxiliary component—significantly degrades performance (a drop of ≈ 4.3 p.P. across datasets). This insight led us to incorporate an additional processing step for the decoder's last hidden states—analogous to the encoder's MLP.

Based on previous work on pointer networks by See et al. (2017), we opted to add a cross-attention (Vaswani et al., 2017; Bahdanau et al., 2016) on top that resembles See et al.'s (2017) idea around context vectors by computing attention scores between the decoder output $H^d \in \mathbb{R}^{m \times d}$ (as the *query*) and our concatenated encoder representation $X^e \in \mathbb{R}^{n \times d}$ (as *key* and *value*). Internally, this cross-attention follows Vaswani et al.'s (2017) formulation for multi-head-attention, instead of Bahdanau et al.'s (2016) to follow modern transformers such as BART (Lewis et al., 2020) more closely.

For efficiency and to maintain consistent attention mechanisms across model variants, we imple-

[3]Preliminary experiments show, this also solves the instabilities identified by Pfister et al. (2022) when training an mT5 model (Xue et al., 2021) using the BARTABSA framework.

Algorithm 1 Our BARTABSA++ with improvements (Section 3.2) over the original BARTABSA algorithm in Yan et al. (2021a). The improvements, marked in red, consist of a parametrized gating mechanism (Section 3.2.3), additional normalization (Section 3.2.1), and an attention mechanism on top of the decoder (Section 3.2.2).

Input: X - Input, C - Special Tokens, $\hat{Y}_t$ - Remapped Token Indices To Tokens

1: $E^e \leftarrow \mathrm{BARTTokenEmbed(X)}$
2: $H^e \leftarrow \mathrm{BARTEncoder(X)}$
3: $\hat{H}^e \leftarrow \mathrm{MLP(H^e)}$
4: $\gamma \leftarrow \mathrm{Gating}(\hat{\mathrm{H}}^e, \mathrm{E}^e)$
5: $\overline{H}^e \leftarrow \gamma \hat{\mathrm{H}}^e + (1-\gamma)\mathrm{E}^e$
▷ Parametrized gating mechanism avoiding the need for a hyperparameter α (Section 3.2.3).

6: $C^d \leftarrow \mathrm{Norm(BARTTokenEmbed(C))}$
7: $\overline{H}^e \leftarrow \mathrm{Norm}(\overline{\mathrm{H}}^e)$
8: $X^e \leftarrow [\mathrm{C^d}; \overline{\mathrm{H}}^e]$
▷ L^2 normalization to ensure stable training (Section 3.2.1).

9: $H^d \leftarrow \mathrm{BARTDecoder}(\mathrm{H^e}, \hat{\mathrm{Y}}_t)$
10: $\hat{H}^d \leftarrow \mathrm{BARTDecoder_{last\_layer}(H^d, X^e)}$
▷ Reusing BART's built-in cross-attention mechanism (Section 3.2.2).

11: $\omega \leftarrow \mathrm{Gating}(\hat{\mathrm{H}}^d, \mathrm{H}^d)$
12: $\overline{H}^d \leftarrow \omega \hat{\mathrm{H}}^d + (1-\omega)\mathrm{H}^d$
▷ Parametrized gating mechanism similar to the encoder counterpart (Section 3.2.3).

13: $\overline{H}^d \leftarrow \mathrm{LayerNorm}(\overline{\mathrm{H}}^d)$
▷ *RMSNorm* to ensure stable training (Section 3.2.1).

14: $P_t \leftarrow \mathrm{Softmax}(\mathrm{X^e} \cdot \overline{\mathrm{H}}^d)$
15: **return** P_t

ment this attention by reusing the weights from the pre-trained cross-attention module in the final decoder layer of the BART model (line 10). This parameter sharing approach eliminates the need for additional parameters (Lan et al., 2020) while ensuring architectural compatibility when extending our approach to different encoder-decoder frameworks in Section 3.3.

3.2.3 Parametrized Gating Mechanism

To enhance model flexibility and bypass manual hyperparameter tuning, we add two learnable gating mechanisms (e.g. thus α in Equation (7) gets "learnable", after the impact of α remained unexamined by Yan et al. (2021a)). This modification eliminates the need to manually tune weighting parameters during experimentation, while enabling the model to adaptively determine optimal information flow based on the specific input context. Drawing inspiration from gating mechanisms in recurrent architectures (Chung et al., 2014), their successful application in language modeling (Dauphin et al., 2017) and specifically the Pointer Generator Mechanism (See et al., 2017), we implement two distinct gating modules.

The first gate substitutes α in the encoder path (lines 4 & 5):

$$\gamma = \sigma([\hat{H}^e; E^e]W_{\text{enc}}^T + b_{\text{enc}}) \quad (10)$$

$$\overline{H}^e = \gamma \odot \hat{H}^e + (1-\gamma) \odot E^e \quad (11)$$

where $\hat{H}^e, E^e \in \mathbb{R}^{n \times d}$ are MLP-processed encoder outputs and token embeddings, with W_{enc} and b_{enc} being learnable. A decoder-side gate combines cross-attention output $\hat{H}^d$ with original hidden states H^d (lines 11 & 12), having its own parameters.

These mechanisms enable interpolation between inputs, dynamically adjusting representation contributions.

3.3 Scaling and Extending BARTABSA++

While BARTABSA was originally based on the pretrained encoder-decoder transformer BART (Lewis et al., 2020), recent advances in large language models (LLMs) prompt the question of its applicability to other models and especially architectures.

To address this question, we follow the methodology proposed by Rothe et al. (2020): we adapt

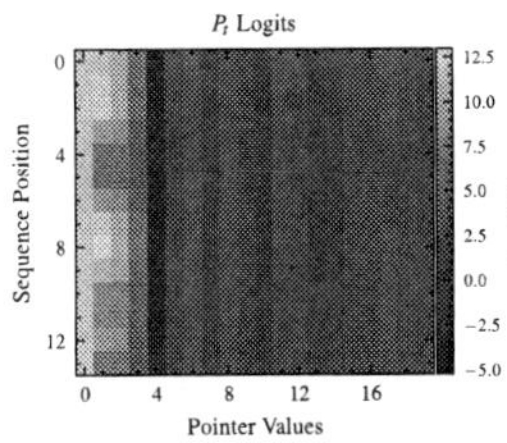

Figure 2: Heatmap of the untrained model's pointer logit distribution (P_t). The visualization reveals a strong initialization bias towards the lower pointer values corresponding to the special tokens.

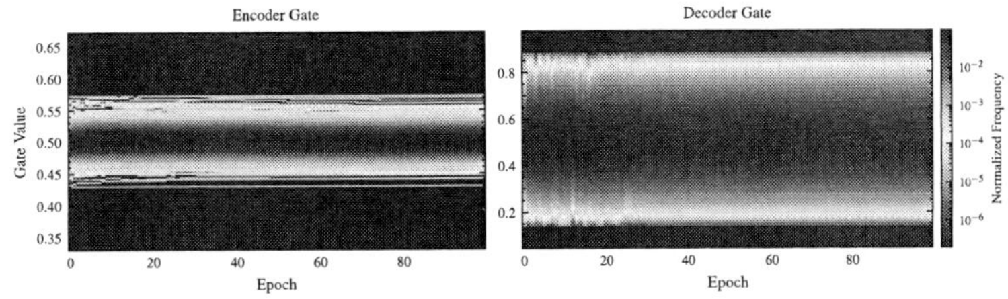

Figure 3: Evolution of gate value distributions over 100 epochs of training. **Left:** Encoder gate values remain tightly clustered around the initialization value of 0.5 with minimal deviation (σ 0.03), suggesting rather limited utilization of the gating mechanism in the encoder. **Right:** Decoder gate values show significantly higher variance (σ 0.15) and clear divergence from initialization, indicating that the model actively leverages the gating mechanism in the decoder to modulate information flow between attention heads and feedforward components.

Table 1: Performance comparison between literature baselines, our GPT-4O finetune, as well as BARTABSA-R and BARTABSA++ (using BART-BASE and BART-LARGE). Tuple level (P)recision, (R)ecall, and F_1 are reported per dataset and averaged across them, with standard deviations in parentheses. The best results per column are **bolded**.

Model	14res			14lap			15res			16res			Avg		
	P	R	F_1	P	R	F_1	P	R	F_1	P	R	F_1	P	R	F_1
Fine-Tuned GPT-4O	74.65	79.38	76.94	61.67	**68.39**	64.86	61.91	**73.40**	67.17	71.38	**78.60**	74.81	67.40	**74.94**	70.95
Xianlong et al. (2023)	77.38	72.86	75.05	65.11	62.20	64.53	**70.23**	65.73	**67.90**	76.37	76.85	76.61	72.27	69.41	71.02
BARTABSA (Yan et al., 2021a)	65.52	64.99	65.25	61.41	56.19	58.69	59.14	59.38	59.26	66.60	68.68	67.62	63.17	62.31	62.70
Our BARTABSA-R (BART-BASE)	76.43 (σ 1.70)	73.56 (σ 3.41)	74.94 (σ 2.50)	66.24 (σ 2.62)	59.32 (σ 4.18)	62.53 (σ 3.13)	64.46 (σ 1.56)	60.33 (σ 3.26)	62.30 (σ 2.30)	68.52 (σ 2.64)	68.05 (σ 1.83)	68.26 (σ 1.84)	68.91 (σ 2.13)	65.31 (σ 3.17)	67.01 (σ 2.44)
Our BARTABSA++ (BART-BASE)	77.76 (σ 1.04)	75.81 (σ 1.75)	76.74 (σ 1.09)	68.27 (σ 1.29)	61.98 (σ 1.45)	64.96 (σ 1.08)	65.33 (σ 2.08)	63.27 (σ 1.21)	64.27 (σ 1.62)	69.82 (σ 1.27)	69.24 (σ 1.60)	69.51 (σ 1.26)	70.29 (σ 1.42)	67.58 (σ 1.50)	68.87 (σ 1.26)
Our BARTABSA-R (BART-LARGE)	79.13 (σ 1.92)	75.79 (σ 4.42)	77.32 (σ 2.24)	56.33 (σ 31.54)	52.09 (σ 29.18)	54.11 (σ 30.30)	64.63 (σ 7.51)	64.18 (σ 8.56)	64.35 (σ 7.79)	74.99 (σ 3.34)	75.13 (σ 4.46)	75.05 (σ 3.78)	68.77 (σ 11.08)	66.80 (σ 11.65)	67.71 (σ 11.03)
Our BARTABSA++ (BART-LARGE)	**80.26** (σ 1.21)	**81.43** (σ 1.48)	**80.82** (σ 1.02)	**70.85** (σ 0.73)	64.94 (σ 1.42)	**67.75** (σ 0.64)	67.44 (σ 1.39)	67.63 (σ 1.76)	67.52 (σ 1.14)	**76.08** (σ 2.32)	77.10 (σ 1.70)	**76.58** (σ 1.94)	**73.66** (σ 1.41)	72.77 (σ 1.59)	**73.16** (σ 1.18)

pretrained encoder-only and decoder-only models into encoder-decoder formats, modifying attention masks and incorporating new cross-attention blocks akin to Vaswani et al.'s (2017). The Transformers library (Wolf et al., 2020) offers model combinations like BERT (Devlin et al., 2019), ROBERTA (Liu et al., 2019), and GPT-2 (Radford et al., 2019), sufficing for our experiments.

Our reimplementation and improvements upon BARTABSA (Sections 3.1 and 3.2) provide the necessary flexibility to reuse pretrained checkpoints as encoder-decoder models.

4 Experiments

We evaluate our approaches on four popular SemEval ABSA benchmark datasets: `14lap`, `14res`, `15res`, and `16res` (Pontiki et al., 2014, 2015, 2016), using the refined version from Xu et al. (2020) and commonly used tuple-level metrics (Yan et al., 2021a). Our backbone models are BART-BASE and BART-LARGE, with full implementation details in Appendix A.

We compare our results against the original BARTABSA (Yan et al., 2021a) and the state-of-the-art by Xianlong et al. (2023), who achieve their results using a mixture of sequence tagging and sequence generation.

To assess how the advancing capabilities of LLMs might impact the ASTE task, we additionally establish an LLM-based baseline by finetuning OpenAI's GPT-4O model[4] on each ABSA dataset. Using the prompt template shown in Appendix B, we train for 3 epochs with consistent hyperparameters across all datasets. This (methodologically) very simple baseline achieves an average F_1 score of 70.95, roughly on par with the current SOTA results. In particular, the LLM-based approach exhibits a distinctive pattern of trading

[4] `https://platform.openai.com/docs/models/gpt-4o`, snapshot `gpt-4o-2024-08-06`

precision for recall, with significantly higher recall (74.94) compared to other methods.

4.1 Our Modern Reimplementation (3.1)

We find our reimplementation (BARTABSA-R) of the BARTABSA framework to perform much better than the original implementation by Yan et al. (2021a) (Table 1). This comes rather unexpected, as to the best of our knowledge, both codebases implement the exact same algorithm. To rule out evaluation issues, we employ the same tuple-level evaluation script as published by Yan et al., where a prediction is considered correct only when all components match the ground truth exactly. Interestingly, we find that the performance discrepancies vary between the datasets (nearly 10 p.P. for 14res, and only about 2 p.P. for 16res).

4.1.1 Potential Differences

Whilst we were unable to pinpoint the exact source for this discrepancy, we validated these findings through multiple steps: 1) We independently reproduced the original results by rerunning the authors' published code. 2) We thoroughly debugged the data loaders to confirm that both implementations receive identical inputs, thereby eliminating data processing discrepancies as a potential explanation. 3) We maintained consistent hyperparameter settings across both implementations. 4) We used their evaluation script to rule out issues during evaluation.

Given these controls, the performance differences most likely either stem from undetected issues in their implementation of the algorithm or simply our use of a modernized tech stack using a different framework, newer transformers, torch and CUDA versions as well as a different attention implementation within the BART models (Ansel et al., 2024; Dao et al., 2022).

4.1.2 Scaling to BART-LARGE

As a first step toward scaling this approach, we swap the BART-BASE for a BART-LARGE backbone. This gives us mixed results (BART-BASE vs. BART-LARGE in Table 1): while switching for the larger backbone mostly improves the scores (+0.70 F_1 on average), it also instabilizes training, which can be seen from the larger standard deviations (σ 11.03) and even the complete performance breakdown on "14lap". As already mentioned in Section 3.2.1, these instabilities can be mitigated by using our improvements to the architecture.

Table 2: Model performance and ablation study using BART-LARGE. (P)recision, (R)ecall, and F_1 averaged across the four datasets, with standard deviations in parentheses. Red indicates performance decrease compared to our full architecture (described in Section 3.2).

Model	Avg P	Avg R	Avg F_1
Our BARTABSA-R	68.77 *(σ 11.08)* (-4.89)	66.80 *(σ 11.65)* (-5.97)	67.71 *(σ 11.03)* (-5.45)
No Encoder Normalization	67.03 *(σ 10.34)* (-6.63)	65.39 *(σ 10.68)* (-7.38)	66.16 *(σ 10.41)* (-7.00)
No Final RMS-Norm	73.28 *(σ 2.07)* (-0.38)	72.64 *(σ 2.27)* (-0.13)	72.90 *(σ 2.01)* (-0.26)
No additional Attention	71.36 *(σ 4.61)* (-2.30)	70.78 *(σ 4.34)* (-1.99)	71.02 *(σ 4.36)* (-2.14)
No Decoder Gating	62.20 *(σ 17.34)* (-11.46)	60.60 *(σ 15.98)* (-12.17)	61.33 *(σ 16.40)* (-11.83)
No Encoder Gating	72.08 *(σ 2.75)* (-1.58)	71.94 *(σ 2.44)* (-0.83)	71.98 *(σ 2.30)* (-1.18)
Our BARTABSA++	**73.66** *(σ 1.41)*	**72.77** *(σ 1.59)*	**73.16** *(σ 1.18)*

Surprising: Our reimplementation significantly outperforms the literature, but it suffers instabilities when scaling to larger models.

4.2 Our Improvements (3.2)

Scaling pointer networks to larger models presents significant challenges, particularly regarding training stability. During our preliminary experiments with BART-LARGE, we observed unstable optimization dynamics stemming from substantial magnitude differences between input token pointer logits and classification token logits (Figure 2). This is naturally mitigated by our introduced normalization (Section 3.2.1).

Our introduced architectural enhancements coined BARTABSA++ address these challenges systematically, as demonstrated by the performance improvements in Table 1 with an average 1.86 points F_1 increase for BART-BASE and +5.45 F_1 points for BART-LARGE, highlighting the greater benefits of our improvements for larger models. In fact, we find our BARTABSA++ not only outperforms our finetuned GPT-4O, but also represents the new SOTA for the ABSA triplet extraction task (averaged across the four datasets). To understand the individual contribution of each component, we conduct a comprehensive ablation study using the BART-LARGE model (Table 2), revealing several key insights. We show our improvements also generalize, when applying this methodology to other structured extraction tasks in Appendix D.

🔬 **Surprising**: Our structured language modeling BARTABSA++ significantly outperforms a much more parameter heavy GPT-4O finetune and even sets the new state of the art.

4.2.1 Component Analysis

Normalization (3.2.1) The feature normalization proves crucial for model stability, as removing the encoder normalization results in a notable performance decline (-7.00 F_1 points) coupled with substantially increased variance across runs (σ 10.41 compared to σ 1.18 for BARTABSA++). The effect of this normalization on the final model output is also apparent in the comparisons of the value heatmaps (Figures 2 and 4), which shows a clear bias towards the prepended special tokens without the normalization step. This confirms our hypothesis that normalizing representation spaces is essential for stable optimization. While the final layer normalization contributes more modestly (-0.26 F_1 points when removed), it also helps in stabilizing training results, almost halving the standard deviation.

Attention Mechanism and Decoder Gating (3.2.2, 3.2.3) The additional cross-attention mechanism combined with its corresponding decoder gating mechanism also provides a significant performance improvement. Removing the attention mechanism alone reduces performance by 2.14 F_1 points, while removing only the decoder gating (but keeping the attention) causes a drastic drop of 11.83 F_1 points with extreme instability (σ 16.40).

This indicates that while the additional processing from the attention mechanism is beneficial, it requires controlled integration through the gating mechanism to be effective. An analysis of the decoder gate values in Figure 3 show considerable variance during training, confirming that the model actively uses this mechanism to regulate information flow between the original decoder output and the attention-processed representation.

Encoder Gating (3.2.3) The encoder gating mechanism has a modest impact (-1.18 F_1 points when removed), which aligns with the observation in Figure 3 that the encoder gates values remain closer to their initial value of 0.5 throughout training.

4.3 Synthetic Encoder-Decoder Models (3.3)

As a first step towards transferring the pointer methodology to LLMs, we sanity check the combinations of BARTABSA++ and the methodology introduced in Rothe et al. (2020).

Table 3: Performance comparison across different synthetic encoder-decoder models. Models with ++ indicate the BARTABSA++ architecture.

Model	Avg		
	P	R	F_1
Reimpl. BART++	**70.29** *(σ 1.42)*	**67.58** *(σ 1.50)*	**68.87** *(σ 1.26)*
Roberta2Roberta	57.70 *(σ 23.84)*	54.04 *(σ 23.87)*	55.66 *(σ 24.00)*
Roberta2Roberta++	68.92 *(σ 6.17)*	64.53 *(σ 7.75)*	66.54 *(σ 6.83)*
Roberta2GPT2	67.64 *(σ 1.96)*	61.78 *(σ 2.36)*	64.50 *(σ 2.05)*
Roberta2GPT2++	69.55 *(σ 1.98)*	65.54 *(σ 1.95)*	67.44 *(σ 1.74)*
Bert2Bert++	66.19 *(σ 1.62)*	61.27 *(σ 1.95)*	63.58 *(σ 1.63)*
Bert2GPT2++	65.58 *(σ 1.82)*	57.81 *(σ 1.35)*	61.38 *(σ 1.35)*
RobertaLarge2-RobertaLarge++	03.41 *(σ 7.62)*	00.95 *(σ 2.13)*	01.49 *(σ 3.33)*
RobertaLarge2-GPT2Medium ++	69.62 *(σ 1.18)*	65.27 *(σ 2.27)*	67.33 *(σ 1.57)*

4.3.1 Overall

For this, we first take the base models explored in the original paper (BERT, ROBERTA, and GPT-2) by Rothe et al. (2020) and evaluate how well the two methodologies interact (Table 3).

The approach works successfully, with some combinations like ROBERTA2ROBERTA even outperforming the original BARTABSA results. However, none of these synthetic combinations surpasses our enhanced BARTABSA++ even with BART-BASE as the backbone.

Our architectural enhancements consistently improve performance across all synthetic models, with particularly dramatic stabilization effects for ROBERTA2ROBERTA (reducing variance from σ 24.00 to σ 6.83 while improving F_1 by +10.88 points). Generally, ROBERTA outperforms BERT as an encoder, and pairing a ROBERTA encoder with a GPT-2 decoder yields better results than using ROBERTA for both components. The only exception is the highly unstable ROBERTALarge2ROBERTALarge configuration, which fails to train effectively despite our enhancements.

4.3.2 Scaling to Modern Sizes

In order to expand our analysis to decoder LLMs, and size ranges which cross the threshold into what is commonly acknowledged as the LLM regime (Zhao et al., 2025; Kaplan et al., 2020), we run a scaling benchmark using only GPT-2 in Table 4.

For this, we use GPT-2 models ranging from base (137M) to XL (1.6B) for both: the encoder

Table 4: Performance of different GPT-2 model sizes, with the pretrained weights being used in the encoder and decoder part of the synthetic model.

Model	Params	Avg P	Avg R	Avg F1
Our BARTABSA-R	139M	**68.91** *(σ 2.13)*	**65.31** *(σ 3.17)*	**67.01** *(σ 2.44)*
GPT2GPT Base	277M	58.92 *(σ 2.35)*	52.11 *(σ 1.81)*	55.26 *(σ 1.73)*
GPT2GPT Medium	810M	60.06 *(σ 2.01)*	53.99 *(σ 2.68)*	56.80 *(σ 2.19)*
GPT2GPT Large	1.78B	59.78 *(σ 2.28)*	53.84 *(σ 1.96)*	56.60 *(σ 1.76)*
GPT2GPT XL	3.61B	59.72 *(σ 0.97)*	53.38 *(σ 3.71)*	56.34 *(σ 2.45)*

Table 5: Impact of random weight initialization on model performance.

Model	Avg P	Avg R	Avg F1
Full Pretrained	**68.91** *(σ 2.13)*	**65.31** *(σ 3.17)*	**67.01** *(σ 2.44)*
Random Encoder	18.35 *(σ 12.57)*	13.42 *(σ 9.04)*	15.45 *(σ 10.44)*
Random Decoder	65.57 *(σ 1.51)*	61.57 *(σ 2.28)*	63.46 *(σ 1.88)*
Random Both	36.53 *(σ 2.57)*	27.57 *(σ 1.62)*	31.38 *(σ 1.83)*

and the decoder. As the parameters get duplicated, this creates models with up to 3.6B parameters overall—including the added cross attention.

We find basically no "scaling effects" at all, meaning the performance mostly does not increase with model size increases. Furthermore, the model itself performs substantially worse than our basic reimplementation, or the original BARTABSA results. This draws the applicability of this combination of methodologies to combine pointer networks with (large) decoder LLMs into question.

To ensure that the lack of pretraining for the newly initialized weights isn't responsible for this unexpected non-scaling behavior, we conduct additional experiments pretraining these models on the CNN/DailyMail summarization dataset (See et al., 2017; Hermann et al., 2015) before finetuning on ABSA (Appendix E). These experiments confirm our findings, showing similar patterns of non-scaling and instability even after extensive pretraining.

> **Negative Result**: (Larger) decoder LMs show no benefit in this structured prediction framework, and even exhibit slightly negative scaling effects.

4.3.3 Ablation using Random Initialized Models

In order to better understand this unexpected finding of non-scaling, we analyze which parts of the newly crafted encoder-decoder influence the performance the most. We hypothesize that there is an inherent difference between the encoder and decoder architecture, especially when either is converted into the other one.

To be able to analyze the impact of the encoder and decoder separately, we initialize the encoder, the decoder or both with random weights (except for the token embeddings) and then train as before (Table 5). Interestingly, we find that entirely randomizing the decoder and training it from scratch has a surprisingly small impact on overall model performance. In contrast, random initialization of the encoder severely degrades performance. This is in line with our previous findings: the encoder's "token-level representational quality" significantly outweighs the decoder's contribution to overall performance (Kasai et al., 2021). Consequently, models pretrained explicitly as encoders consistently outperform those in which a decoder is retrained as an encoder (Pfister and Hotho, 2024; Reimers, 2022).

> **Confirmation**: As identified by Kasai et al. (2021), encoder-decoder model performance strongly correlates with encoder representational strength.

5 Conclusion

In this work, we revisited the BARTABSA framework in the context of modern decoder LLMs. Our enhanced implementation—BARTABSA++—demonstrates that explicit structured models remain highly competitive for tasks requiring precise extraction of relational information, even outperforming a finetuned GPT-4O model.

Our systematic experiments reveal a fundamental insight: while our architectural enhancements enable effective scaling with pretrained encoder-decoder models like BART, this scaling behavior does not transfer encoder-decoder models based on decoder-only LLMs. The critical factor appears to be the encoder's representational quality at the token level, which decoder LLMs struggle to match when repurposed as encoders.

These findings highlight the complementary nature of structured approaches and large language models in NLP. While LLMs excel at tasks leveraging their implicit knowledge, structured pointer networks seem to be able to provide superior performance and interpretability for precise relational extraction tasks.

Limitations

Optimization and Architectural Constraints Although we employed normalization and gating mechanisms to mitigate training instability, certain model configurations, notably RoBERTa2RoBERTa, still exhibited high variance across runs.[5] Moreover, our decoder LLM experiments were restricted to GPT-2 variants due to limitations in the existing implementation in the 🤗 Transformers library. While GPT-2 showed non-scaling behavior, preliminary experiments by us suggest that newer decoder-only architectures also face similar issues, although differences in their architectures might yield varying outcomes.

Representational Limitations of Decoder-only Models Our methodology for adapting decoder-only models into encoders, based on existing work (Rothe et al., 2020), likely does not fully resolve fundamental representational constraints for token-level tasks. Recent adaptations like LLM2Vec (BehnamGhader et al., 2024) suggest promising techniques that might overcome these limitations, though exploring such adaptations was beyond the scope of our experiments.

Scope of Pointer Networks and Structured Prediction Our analysis focuses specifically on encoder-decoder architectures and their components, reflecting the typical formulation used in Pointer Networks. However, our findings indicate that extending the pointer paradigm to decoder-only architectures could potentially better leverage pretrained LLMs for structured prediction tasks, presenting a valuable direction for future research.

Baseline Limitations Our GPT-4o-based baseline experiments employed a straightforward prompt template primarily to provide a comparative reference point close to the previous SotA. While adequate for this purpose, the adopted approach does not explore advanced prompting methods, chain-of-thought reasoning, or specialized instruction-tuning strategies that could further boost the capabilities of modern LLMs.

Generalizability Although we demonstrate that structured methods such as BARTABSA++ remain competitive for ABSA tasks, our results may not generalize across all structured prediction tasks in NLP, particularly those involving different structural characteristics or task-specific constraints.

[5] We observed similar instability when training this configuration on the summarization task (Appendix E), suggesting a potential limitation of the approach by Rothe et al. (2020).

Acknowledgements

This publication was partially funded by the Deutsche Forschungsgemeinschaft (DFG, German Research Foundation) under the project LitBERT, project no. 529659926. The authors gratefully acknowledge the HPC resources provided by the JuliaV2 cluster at the Universität Würzburg (JMU), which was funded as DFG project as "Forschungsgroßgerät nach Art 91b GG" under INST 93/1145-1 FUGG. The data science chair is part of the CAIDAS, the Center for Artificial Intelligence and Data Science, and is supported by the Bavarian High-Tech Agenda, which made this research possible.

References

Jason Ansel, Edward Yang, Horace He, Natalia Gimelshein, Animesh Jain, Michael Voznesensky, Bin Bao, Peter Bell, David Berard, Evgeni Burovski, Geeta Chauhan, Anjali Chourdia, Will Constable, Alban Desmaison, Zachary DeVito, Elias Ellison, Will Feng, Jiong Gong, Michael Gschwind, Brian Hirsh, Sherlock Huang, Kshiteej Kalambarkar, Laurent Kirsch, Michael Lazos, Mario Lezcano, Yanbo Liang, Jason Liang, Yinghai Lu, CK Luk, Bert Maher, Yunjie Pan, Christian Puhrsch, Matthias Reso, Mark Saroufim, Marcos Yukio Siraichi, Helen Suk, Michael Suo, Phil Tillet, Eikan Wang, Xiaodong Wang, William Wen, Shunting Zhang, Xu Zhao, Keren Zhou, Richard Zou, Ajit Mathews, Gregory Chanan, Peng Wu, and Soumith Chintala. 2024. PyTorch 2: Faster Machine Learning Through Dynamic Python Bytecode Transformation and Graph Compilation. In *29th ACM International Conference on Architectural Support for Programming Languages and Operating Systems, Volume 2 (ASPLOS '24)*. ACM.

Dzmitry Bahdanau, Kyunghyun Cho, and Yoshua Bengio. 2016. Neural machine translation by jointly learning to align and translate.

Jeremy Barnes, Laura Oberlaender, Enrica Troiano, Andrey Kutuzov, Jan Buchmann, Rodrigo Agerri, Lilja Øvrelid, and Erik Velldal. 2022. SemEval 2022 task 10: Structured sentiment analysis. In *Proceedings of the 16th International Workshop on Semantic Evaluation (SemEval-2022)*, pages 1280–1295, Seattle, United States. Association for Computational Linguistics.

Parishad BehnamGhader, Vaibhav Adlakha, Marius Mosbach, Dzmitry Bahdanau, Nicolas Chapados, and Siva Reddy. 2024. LLM2vec: Large language models are secretly powerful text encoders. In *First Conference on Language Modeling*.

Tom B. Brown, Benjamin Mann, Nick Ryder, Melanie Subbiah, Jared Kaplan, Prafulla Dhariwal, Arvind Neelakantan, Pranav Shyam, Girish Sastry, Amanda Askell, Sandhini Agarwal, Ariel Herbert-Voss, Gretchen Krueger, Tom Henighan, Rewon Child, Aditya Ramesh, Daniel M. Ziegler, Jeffrey Wu, Clemens Winter, Christopher Hesse, Mark Chen, Eric Sigler, Mateusz Litwin, Scott Gray, Benjamin Chess, Jack Clark, Christopher Berner, Sam McCandlish, Alec Radford, Ilya Sutskever, and Dario Amodei. 2020. Language models are few-shot learners. In *Proceedings of the 34th International Conference on Neural Information Processing Systems*, NIPS '20, Red Hook, NY, USA. Curran Associates Inc.

Junyoung Chung, Caglar Gulcehre, KyungHyun Cho, and Yoshua Bengio. 2014. Empirical Evaluation of Gated Recurrent Neural Networks on Sequence Modeling.

Tri Dao, Daniel Y. Fu, Stefano Ermon, Atri Rudra, and Christopher Ré. 2022. FlashAttention: Fast and memory-efficient exact attention with IO-awareness. In *Advances in Neural Information Processing Systems (NeurIPS)*.

Yann N. Dauphin, Angela Fan, Michael Auli, and David Grangier. 2017. Language modeling with gated convolutional networks. In *Proceedings of the 34th International Conference on Machine Learning - Volume 70*, ICML'17, page 933–941. JMLR.org.

Jacob Devlin, Ming-Wei Chang, Kenton Lee, and Kristina Toutanova. 2019. BERT: Pre-training of deep bidirectional transformers for language understanding. In *Proceedings of the 2019 Conference of the North American Chapter of the Association for Computational Linguistics: Human Language Technologies, Volume 1 (Long and Short Papers)*, pages 4171–4186, Minneapolis, Minnesota. Association for Computational Linguistics.

William Falcon and The PyTorch Lightning team. 2019. PyTorch Lightning.

Karl Moritz Hermann, Tomás Kociský, Edward Grefenstette, Lasse Espeholt, Will Kay, Mustafa Suleyman, and Phil Blunsom. 2015. Teaching machines to read and comprehend. In *NIPS*, pages 1693–1701.

Jared Kaplan, Sam McCandlish, Tom Henighan, Tom B. Brown, Benjamin Chess, Rewon Child, Scott Gray, Alec Radford, Jeffrey Wu, and Dario Amodei. 2020. Scaling laws for neural language models.

Jungo Kasai, Nikolaos Pappas, Hao Peng, James Cross, and Noah Smith. 2021. Deep encoder, shallow decoder: Reevaluating non-autoregressive machine translation. In *International Conference on Learning Representations*.

Zhenzhong Lan, Mingda Chen, Sebastian Goodman, Kevin Gimpel, Piyush Sharma, and Radu Soricut. 2020. Albert: A lite bert for self-supervised learning of language representations. In *International Conference on Learning Representations*.

Mike Lewis, Yinhan Liu, Naman Goyal, Marjan Ghazvininejad, Abdelrahman Mohamed, Omer Levy, Veselin Stoyanov, and Luke Zettlemoyer. 2020. BART: Denoising sequence-to-sequence pre-training for natural language generation, translation, and comprehension. In *Proceedings of the 58th Annual Meeting of the Association for Computational Linguistics*, pages 7871–7880, Online. Association for Computational Linguistics.

Xin Li, Lidong Bing, Wenxuan Zhang, and Wai Lam. 2019. Exploiting BERT for end-to-end aspect-based sentiment analysis. In *Proceedings of the 5th Workshop on Noisy User-generated Text (W-NUT 2019)*, pages 34–41, Hong Kong, China. Association for Computational Linguistics.

Bing Liu. 2012. *Sentiment Analysis and Opinion Mining*. Synthesis Lectures on Human Language Technologies. Springer International Publishing, Cham.

Yinhan Liu, Myle Ott, Naman Goyal, Jingfei Du, Mandar Joshi, Danqi Chen, Omer Levy, Mike Lewis, Luke Zettlemoyer, and Veselin Stoyanov. 2019. Roberta: A robustly optimized bert pretraining approach.

Haiyun Peng, Lu Xu, Lidong Bing, Fei Huang, Wei Lu, and Luo Si. 2020. Knowing What, How and Why: A Near Complete Solution for Aspect-Based Sentiment Analysis. *Proceedings of the AAAI Conference on Artificial Intelligence*, 34(05):8600–8607.

Jan Pfister and Andreas Hotho. 2024. SuperGLEBer: German language understanding evaluation benchmark. In *Proceedings of the 2024 Conference of the North American Chapter of the Association for Computational Linguistics: Human Language Technologies (Volume 1: Long Papers)*, pages 7904–7923, Mexico City, Mexico. Association for Computational Linguistics.

Jan Pfister, Sebastian Wankerl, and Andreas Hotho. 2022. SenPoi at SemEval-2022 task 10: Point me to your opinion, SenPoi. In *Proceedings of the 16th International Workshop on Semantic Evaluation (SemEval-2022)*, pages 1313–1323, Seattle, United States. Association for Computational Linguistics.

Maria Pontiki, Dimitris Galanis, Haris Papageorgiou, Ion Androutsopoulos, Suresh Manandhar, Mohammad AL-Smadi, Mahmoud Al-Ayyoub, Yanyan Zhao, Bing Qin, Orphée De Clercq, Véronique Hoste, Marianna Apidianaki, Xavier Tannier, Natalia Loukachevitch, Evgeniy Kotelnikov, Nuria Bel, Salud María Jiménez-Zafra, and Gülşen Eryiğit. 2016. SemEval-2016 task 5: Aspect based sentiment analysis. In *Proceedings of the 10th International Workshop on Semantic Evaluation (SemEval-2016)*, pages 19–30, San Diego, California. Association for Computational Linguistics.

Maria Pontiki, Dimitris Galanis, Haris Papageorgiou, Suresh Manandhar, and Ion Androutsopoulos. 2015.

SemEval-2015 task 12: Aspect based sentiment analysis. In *Proceedings of the 9th International Workshop on Semantic Evaluation (SemEval 2015)*, pages 486–495, Denver, Colorado. Association for Computational Linguistics.

Maria Pontiki, Dimitris Galanis, John Pavlopoulos, Harris Papageorgiou, Ion Androutsopoulos, and Suresh Manandhar. 2014. SemEval-2014 task 4: Aspect based sentiment analysis. In *Proceedings of the 8th International Workshop on Semantic Evaluation (SemEval 2014)*, pages 27–35, Dublin, Ireland. Association for Computational Linguistics.

Behrang QasemiZadeh and Anne-Kathrin Schumann. 2016. The ACL RD-TEC 2.0: A language resource for evaluating term extraction and entity recognition methods. In *Proceedings of the Tenth International Conference on Language Resources and Evaluation (LREC'16)*, pages 1862–1868, Portorož, Slovenia. European Language Resources Association (ELRA).

Alec Radford, Jeffrey Wu, Rewon Child, David Luan, Dario Amodei, Ilya Sutskever, et al. 2019. Language models are unsupervised multitask learners. *OpenAI blog*, 1(8):9.

Nils Reimers. 2022. Openai gpt-3 text embeddings - really a new state-of-the-art in dense text embeddings? Accessed: 2025-03-14.

Sascha Rothe, Shashi Narayan, and Aliaksei Severyn. 2020. Leveraging pre-trained checkpoints for sequence generation tasks. *Transactions of the Association for Computational Linguistics*, 8:264–280.

Abigail See, Peter J. Liu, and Christopher D. Manning. 2017. Get to the point: Summarization with pointer-generator networks. In *Proceedings of the 55th Annual Meeting of the Association for Computational Linguistics (Volume 1: Long Papers)*, pages 1073–1083, Vancouver, Canada. Association for Computational Linguistics.

Sasha Spala, Nicholas Miller, Franck Dernoncourt, and Carl Dockhorn. 2020. SemEval-2020 task 6: Definition extraction from free text with the DEFT corpus. In *Proceedings of the Fourteenth Workshop on Semantic Evaluation*, pages 336–345, Barcelona (online). International Committee for Computational Linguistics.

Qiao Sun, Liujia Yang, Minghao Ma, Nanyang Ye, and Qinying Gu. 2024. MiniConGTS: A near ultimate minimalist contrastive grid tagging scheme for aspect sentiment triplet extraction. In *Proceedings of the 2024 Conference on Empirical Methods in Natural Language Processing*, pages 2817–2834, Miami, Florida, USA. Association for Computational Linguistics.

Duyu Tang, Bing Qin, and Ting Liu. 2016. Aspect level sentiment classification with deep memory network. In *Proceedings of the 2016 Conference on Empirical Methods in Natural Language Processing*, pages 214–224, Austin, Texas. Association for Computational Linguistics.

Ashish Vaswani, Noam Shazeer, Niki Parmar, Jakob Uszkoreit, Llion Jones, Aidan N Gomez, Ł ukasz Kaiser, and Illia Polosukhin. 2017. Attention is all you need. In *Advances in Neural Information Processing Systems*, volume 30. Curran Associates, Inc.

Oriol Vinyals, Meire Fortunato, and Navdeep Jaitly. 2015. Pointer networks. In *Advances in Neural Information Processing Systems*, volume 28. Curran Associates, Inc.

Yequan Wang, Minlie Huang, Xiaoyan Zhu, and Li Zhao. 2016. Attention-based LSTM for aspect-level sentiment classification. In *Proceedings of the 2016 Conference on Empirical Methods in Natural Language Processing*, pages 606–615, Austin, Texas. Association for Computational Linguistics.

Sebastian Wankerl, Jan Pfister, Andrzej Dulny, Gerhard Götz, and Andreas Hotho. 2025. Identifying axiomatic mathematical transformation steps using tree-structured pointer networks. *Transactions on Machine Learning Research*.

Jason Wei, Xuezhi Wang, Dale Schuurmans, Maarten Bosma, Fei Xia, Ed Chi, Quoc V Le, Denny Zhou, et al. 2022. Chain-of-thought prompting elicits reasoning in large language models. *Advances in neural information processing systems*, 35:24824–24837.

Thomas Wolf, Lysandre Debut, Victor Sanh, Julien Chaumond, Clement Delangue, Anthony Moi, Pierric Cistac, Tim Rault, Remi Louf, Morgan Funtowicz, Joe Davison, Sam Shleifer, Patrick von Platen, Clara Ma, Yacine Jernite, Julien Plu, Canwen Xu, Teven Le Scao, Sylvain Gugger, Mariama Drame, Quentin Lhoest, and Alexander Rush. 2020. Transformers: State-of-the-art natural language processing. In *Proceedings of the 2020 Conference on Empirical Methods in Natural Language Processing: System Demonstrations*, pages 38–45, Online. Association for Computational Linguistics.

Zhen Wu, Chengcan Ying, Fei Zhao, Zhifang Fan, Xinyu Dai, and Rui Xia. 2020. Grid tagging scheme for aspect-oriented fine-grained opinion extraction. In *Findings of the Association for Computational Linguistics: EMNLP 2020*, pages 2576–2585, Online. Association for Computational Linguistics.

Julia Wunderle, Julian Schubert, Antonella Cacciatore, Albin Zehe, Jan Pfister, and Andreas Hotho. 2024. OtterlyObsessedWithSemantics at SemEval-2024 task 4: Developing a hierarchical multi-label classification head for large language models. In *Proceedings of the 18th International Workshop on Semantic Evaluation (SemEval-2024)*, page 602–612, Mexico City, Mexico. Association for Computational Linguistics.

Luo Xianlong, Meng Yang, and Yihao Wang. 2023. Tagging-assisted generation model with encoder and decoder supervision for aspect sentiment triplet extraction. In *Proceedings of the 2023 Conference on Empirical Methods in Natural Language Processing*, pages 2078–2093, Singapore. Association for Computational Linguistics.

Ruibin Xiong, Yunchang Yang, Di He, Kai Zheng, Shuxin Zheng, Chen Xing, Huishuai Zhang, Yanyan Lan, Liwei Wang, and Tieyan Liu. 2020. On layer normalization in the transformer architecture. In *International conference on machine learning*, pages 10524–10533. PMLR.

Lu Xu, Hao Li, Wei Lu, and Lidong Bing. 2020. Position-aware tagging for aspect sentiment triplet extraction. In *Proceedings of the 2020 Conference on Empirical Methods in Natural Language Processing (EMNLP)*, pages 2339–2349, Online. Association for Computational Linguistics.

Linting Xue, Noah Constant, Adam Roberts, Mihir Kale, Rami Al-Rfou, Aditya Siddhant, Aditya Barua, and Colin Raffel. 2021. mT5: A massively multilingual pre-trained text-to-text transformer. In *Proceedings of the 2021 Conference of the North American Chapter of the Association for Computational Linguistics: Human Language Technologies*, pages 483–498, Online. Association for Computational Linguistics.

Hang Yan, Junqi Dai, Tuo Ji, Xipeng Qiu, and Zheng Zhang. 2021a. A unified generative framework for aspect-based sentiment analysis. In *Proceedings of the 59th Annual Meeting of the Association for Computational Linguistics and the 11th International Joint Conference on Natural Language Processing (Volume 1: Long Papers)*, pages 2416–2429, Online. Association for Computational Linguistics.

Hang Yan, Tao Gui, Junqi Dai, Qipeng Guo, Zheng Zhang, and Xipeng Qiu. 2021b. A unified generative framework for various NER subtasks. In *Proceedings of the 59th Annual Meeting of the Association for Computational Linguistics and the 11th International Joint Conference on Natural Language Processing (Volume 1: Long Papers)*, pages 5808–5822, Online. Association for Computational Linguistics.

Biao Zhang and Rico Sennrich. 2019. *Root mean square layer normalization*. Curran Associates Inc., Red Hook, NY, USA.

Wenxuan Zhang, Yue Deng, Bing Liu, Sinno Pan, and Lidong Bing. 2024. Sentiment analysis in the era of large language models: A reality check. In *Findings of the Association for Computational Linguistics: NAACL 2024*, pages 3881–3906, Mexico City, Mexico. Association for Computational Linguistics.

Wenxuan Zhang, Xin Li, Yang Deng, Lidong Bing, and Wai Lam. 2021. Towards generative aspect-based sentiment analysis. In *Proceedings of the 59th Annual Meeting of the Association for Computational Linguistics and the 11th International Joint Conference on Natural Language Processing (Volume 2: Short Papers)*, pages 504–510, Online. Association for Computational Linguistics.

Wayne Xin Zhao, Kun Zhou, Junyi Li, Tianyi Tang, Xiaolei Wang, Yupeng Hou, Yingqian Min, Beichen Zhang, Junjie Zhang, Zican Dong, Yifan Du, Chen Yang, Yushuo Chen, Zhipeng Chen, Jinhao Jiang, Ruiyang Ren, Yifan Li, Xinyu Tang, Zikang Liu, Peiyu Liu, Jian-Yun Nie, and Ji-Rong Wen. 2025. A survey of large language models.

A Implementation Details

We train our models using NVIDIA L40 GPUs and the following key hyperparameters:

Parameter	**Value**
Learning rate	5e-5 with polynomial decay
Batch size	16
Optimizer	AdamW (weight decay 0.01)
Gradient clipping	5.0 (norm)
Training epochs	50
Sampling strategy	Greedy

For statistical robustness, we run each experiment with five different random seeds (1, 42, 123, 420, 1337) and report means and standard deviations. Model selection for testing is based on validation set F_1-Score. We use the same tuple-level evaluation script as published by Yan et al. (2021a), where a prediction is considered correct only when all components match the ground truth exactly.

B GPT-4o Fine-tuning Prompt Template

For fine-tuning GPT-4o on the ASTE task, we employ a structured prompt template transforming tuple-based annotations into natural language. Given the sample:

> *"The drinks are always well made and wine selection is fairly priced"*

The tuple annotation

$$(2, 2, 5, 6, \text{POS}, 8, 9, 11, 12, \text{POS})$$

is transformed into:

```
{
"messages": [
{
    "role": "system",
    "content": "You are an AI trained to
        perform aspect-based sentiment
        analysis. Identify aspects in
        the given text and determine
        their associated sentiments and
        opinions."
},
{
    "role": "user",
    "content": "Analyze the following
        text for aspect-based sentiment:
        The drinks are always well made
        and wine selection is fairly
        priced Identify the aspects and
        their associated sentiments."
},
{
    "role": "assistant",
    "content": "Here's the aspect-based
        sentiment analysis:
       Aspect: drinks
       Sentiment: POS
       Opinion: well made

       Aspect: wine selection
       Sentiment: POS
       Opinion: fairly priced"
}
]
}
```

This structure follows OpenAI's fine-tuning specifications, providing context through the system message, input text through the user message, and expected output through the assistant message. All examples were automatically processed into this format. During inference, responses are parsed back into tuple format for consistent evaluation with the other models.

C Heatmap after Normalization

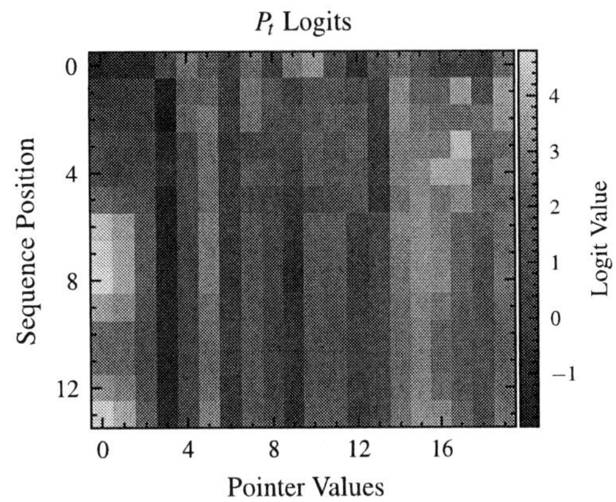

Figure 4: Heatmap of the untrained model's pointer logit distribution (P_t) with the encoder normalization enabled (Lines 6 and 7 in Algorithm 1). The visualization shows no noticeable inherent initialization bias towards the lower pointer values corresponding to the special tokens, as was the case in Figure 2

D Generalization to other Tasks

Table 6: Performance comparison between BART-LARGE baseline and our enhanced BARTABSA++ on three additional structured prediction tasks.

Task	Our BARTABSA-R P	Our BARTABSA-R R	Our BARTABSA-R F1	BARTABSA++ P	BARTABSA++ R	BARTABSA++ F1
SSA	57.51	41.76	47.38	**61.02**	**51.51**	**55.80**
	(σ 2.72)	*(σ 12.42)*	*(σ 10.07)*	*(σ 1.73)*	*(σ 3.45)*	*(σ 2.44)*
SRE	20.25	29.03	23.85	**25.75**	**35.99**	**30.01**
	(σ 11.41)	*(σ 16.39)*	*(σ 13.45)*	*(σ 1.46)*	*(σ 1.55)*	*(σ 1.52)*
DEFT	51.26	37.86	43.36	**54.20**	**41.30**	**46.73**
	(σ 0.28)	*(σ 5.12)*	*(σ 3.46)*	*(σ 3.94)*	*(σ 2.27)*	*(σ 1.96)*

To demonstrate the generalization of our architectural improvements beyond ABSA tasks, we evaluate our enhanced model on three additional structured prediction tasks and report those results in Table 6. To model these tasks appropriately for pointer networks to solve, the output grammars for these tasks are natural extensions or modifications of the previously introduced ABSA output grammar (Section 2.2), adapted to the specific requirements of each task. This approach has been proven effective for related tasks across different languages (Yan et al., 2021b; Wunderle et al., 2024), and even in entirely different domains such as mathematical transformation identification (Wankerl et al., 2025).

Structured Sentiment Analysis (SSA) extends ABSA by extracting more comprehensive opinion structures, including opinion holders, targets, expressions, and sentiment polarities, with support for discontinuous spans. We use the combined English datasets from SemEval 2022 Task 10 (Barnes et al., 2022): OpeNER$_{EN}$ (hotel reviews) and DS$_{Unis}$ (university reviews).

Semantic Relation Extraction (SRE) identifies relations between entities in scientific abstracts, while also classifying them into six predefined relation types. We use the manually annotated ACL RD-TEC 2.0 dataset (QasemiZadeh and Schumann, 2016) from SemEval 2018 Task 7.

Definition Extraction from Free Text (DEFT) extracts definition terms and their corresponding definitions from naturally occurring text, requiring classification of both terms and definitions, as well as their relationship. We use the dataset from SemEval 2020 Task 6 (Spala et al., 2020), containing samples from open-source textbooks.

We find: As shown in Table 6, our enhanced model consistently outperforms the baseline across all tasks, with particularly notable improvements in F_1 scores for SSA (+8.42) and SRE (+6.16), demonstrating generalization of our architectural changes to a diverse set of structured prediction tasks.

E Pre-Training Synthetic Encoder-Decoder Models

To verify that our findings about non-scaling decoder LLMs aren't simply due to insufficient training of the newly initialized weights, we conduct additional pretraining experiments using the CNN/DailyMail summarization dataset (See et al., 2017; Hermann et al., 2015). This is the same dataset used by Rothe et al. (2020) in their original work on synthetic encoder-decoder models, making it particularly appropriate for our investigation. As the dataset contains over 300,000 news articles paired with human-written summaries, it provides substantial training data for adapting the models to the encoder-decoder paradigm.

We pretrain each GPT-2 model for 3 epochs on the summarization task, measuring Rouge2 scores throughout training. As shown in Table 7, the results reveal both training instability and a complete lack of scaling benefits. Most notably, GPT-2 Base exhibits dramatic performance degradation (from a best Rouge2 score of 14.60 to a final score of 2.32), while GPT-2 Medium performs consistently poorly. Even the best-performing GPT-2 Large only achieves a Rouge2 of 14.86, substantially below both BART-BASE (19.65) and RoBERTa2RoBERTa (19.35).

Table 7: Rouge2 scores for models pretrained on CNN-DailyMail summarization dataset for 3 epochs. The table shows both the best score achieved during training and the final score after 3 epochs.

Model	Best Rouge2	Final Rouge2
BART-BASE	**19.65**	**19.65**
ROBERTA2ROBERTA	19.35	19.35
GPT2GPT Base	14.60	2.32
GPT2GPT Medium	4.13	4.13
GPT2GPT Large	14.86	14.77
GPT2GPT XL	11.86	11.76

Table 8: Performance of different **pretrained** GPT-2 model sizes.

Model	Params	Avg P	Avg R	Avg F_1
Our BARTABSA-R	139M	**68.91** (σ 2.13)	**65.31** (σ 3.17)	**67.01** (σ 2.44)
GPT2GPT Base	277M	60.64 (σ 2.38)	53.82 (σ 2.03)	56.98 (σ 1.95)
GPT2GPT Medium	810M	60.61 (σ 2.10)	54.39 (σ 1.94)	57.28 (σ 1.80)
GPT2GPT Large	1.78B	60.73 (σ 2.12)	54.04 (σ 1.85)	57.12 (σ 1.64)
GPT2GPT XL	3.61B	60.45 (σ 2.05)	53.90 (σ 2.10)	56.98 (σ 1.85)

When initializing our pointer networks with these already pretrained checkpoints (Table 8), we observe very similar patterns to our non-pretrained experiments. The lack of scaling benefits persists, with performance plateauing or even declining as model size increased.

Confirmation: These results further support our conclusion that encoder quality is the primary determinant of performance in encoder-decoder models, and that decoder-only models face fundamental limitations when adapted to serve as encoders, regardless of this additional pretraining.

TYPED-RAG: Type-Aware Decomposition of Non-Factoid Questions for Retrieval-Augmented Generation

DongGeon Lee[1*] **Ahjeong Park**[2*] **Hyeri Lee**[3] **Hyeonseo Nam**[4] **Yunho Maeng**[5, 6]
[1]POSTECH [2]Sookmyung Women's University
[3]Independent Researcher [4]KT [5]Ewha Womans University
[6]LLM Experimental Lab, MODULABS
Correspondence: yunhomaeng@ewha.ac.kr

Abstract

Addressing non-factoid question answering (NFQA) remains challenging due to its open-ended nature, diverse user intents, and need for multi-aspect reasoning. These characteristics often reveal the limitations of conventional retrieval-augmented generation (RAG) approaches. To overcome these challenges, we propose TYPED-RAG, a framework for type-aware decomposition of non-factoid questions (NFQs) within the RAG paradigm. Specifically, TYPED-RAG first classifies an NFQ into a predefined type (e.g., Debate, Experience, Comparison). It then decomposes the question into focused sub-queries, each focusing on a single aspect. This decomposition enhances both retrieval relevance and answer quality. By combining the results of these sub-queries, TYPED-RAG produces more informative and contextually aligned responses. Additionally, we construct Wiki-NFQA, a benchmark dataset for NFQA covering a wide range of NFQ types. Experiments show that TYPED-RAG consistently outperforms existing QA approaches based on LLMs or RAG methods, validating the effectiveness of type-aware decomposition for improving both retrieval quality and answer generation in NFQA. Our code and dataset are available on `https://github.com/TeamNLP/Typed-RAG`.

1 Introduction

Traditional and current question answering (QA) systems (Rajpurkar et al., 2016; Peters et al., 2018; Lewis et al., 2020; Ouyang et al., 2022; Zhang et al., 2024) have primarily addressed **factoid** questions—queries seeking specific, verifiable information that yield concise, objective answers like *"When was Google founded?"*. However, real-world information needs extend far beyond such simple factual queries.

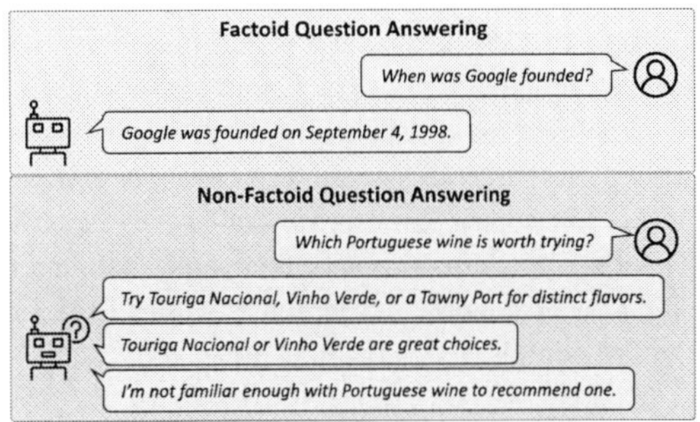

Figure 1: Comparison of factoid question answering (top) and non-factoid question answering (bottom). Factoid questions typically have a single correct answer, whereas non-factoid questions may admit multiple valid answers.

Non-factoid questions (NFQs) represent a fundamentally different challenge from traditional factoid questions, as they require elaborate, interpretive responses that integrate multiple perspectives rather than retrieving single facts (Bolotova et al., 2022). These questions—encompassing comparative evaluations, personal experiences, and open-ended discussions—reflect the rich, multifaceted nature of human information seeking. Figure 1 illustrates the key differences between factoid questions and NFQs, as well as their example answers.

Despite their prevalence in practical settings (Yang and Alonso, 2024), current approaches to non-factoid question answering (NFQA) face significant limitations. The core challenge lies in the inherent complexity and heterogeneity of NFQs, which vary along multiple dimensions including question intent, aspect directionality, and degree of contrast between perspectives.

Existing methods fail to adequately address this diversity. Type-specific approaches to NFQA (An et al., 2024)—methods that focus exclusively on particular NFQ types—struggle to generalize across the full spectrum of NFQ types, whereas retrieval-augmented generation (RAG) systems (Lewis et al., 2020; Izacard and Grave, 2021), de-

*These authors contributed equally to this work.

Proceedings of the 1st Joint Workshop on Large Language Models and Structure Modeling (XLLM 2025), pages 129–152
August 1, 2025

spite improving contextuality, produce overly homogeneous responses that lack the multi-faceted depth essential for comprehensive answers. Ultimately, the fundamental challenge is adapting retrieval and generation strategies to the specific characteristics of each NFQ type.

To address these limitations, we propose TYPED-RAG, a type-aware decomposition approach that fundamentally reimagines NFQA within the RAG paradigm. Our approach integrates question type classification directly into the RAG paradigm, enabling tailored retrieval and generation strategies for distinct NFQ types. The key innovation lies in decomposing multi-aspect NFQs into single-aspect sub-queries, allowing targeted retrieval for each aspect before synthesizing a comprehensive response. This decomposition approach ensures that generated answers align with user intent while capturing the full complexity of the question.

In order to assess the performance of TYPED-RAG, we evaluate it on Wiki-NFQA, a new benchmark dataset derived from Wikipedia that encompasses a broad spectrum of NFQ types. Our results demonstrate that TYPED-RAG significantly outperforms baseline systems, including standard approaches using LLMs and RAG, in handling NFQ complexity and delivering nuanced, intent-aligned answers.

Our main contributions are as follows:

- We propose **TYPED-RAG**, a novel framework for type-aware decomposition of non-factoid questions that enhances RAG-based NFQA by integrating question type classification with targeted decomposition strategies.
- We develop retrieval and generation strategies specifically optimized for different NFQ types, enabling more effective handling of complex and diverse user queries.
- We release the **Wiki-NFQA** dataset, providing a comprehensive benchmark for evaluating QA systems on non-factoid questions and facilitating future NFQA research.
- We demonstrate through extensive experiments that TYPED-RAG significantly outperforms baseline models, validating the effectiveness of type-aware decomposition in generating contextually appropriate and high-quality answers.

By addressing the unique challenges of NFQA through type-aware decomposition, our work bridges the gap between complex user information needs and current QA system capabilities, advancing the development of more adaptive and context-sensitive QA technologies.

2 Related Work

2.1 Non-Factoid Question Answering (NFQA)

Non-Factoid Question Taxonomy To address the complexity of real-world QA, prior work has developed detailed taxonomies for question types (Burger et al., 2003; Chaturvedi et al., 2014; Bolotova et al., 2022). Unlike factoid questions, which seek concise factual answers, non-factoid questions (NFQs) require subjective, multi-faceted responses (Chaturvedi et al., 2014; Bolotova et al., 2022). Bolotova et al. (2022) categorized NFQs into six types: `Evidence-based`, `Comparison`, `Experience`, `Reason`, `Instruction`, and `Debate`. Recently, Mishra et al. (2025) emphasized critical challenges faced by LLM-based QA systems when handling NFQs, particularly those requiring in-depth reasoning or nuanced debate, illustrated through practical examples such as detailed descriptive questions (e.g., *"How was the construction of the Taj Mahal perceived by the citizens of Agra in the 17th century?"*). Their work also highlighted specific application contexts where robust NFQA systems are vital, including voice assistants like Amazon Alexa (Hashemi et al., 2020) and web forums frequently hosting user-generated descriptive queries (Bajaj et al., 2016). In contrast to earlier approaches that target individual NFQ types, our method provides a unified framework to handle all categories effectively.

Evaluation Metrics Traditional metrics—such as ROUGE or BERTScore (Zhang et al., 2020)—often fall short in capturing the semantic richness and nuanced quality of NFQA outputs. To overcome these limitations, Yang et al. (2024) introduced LINKAGE, a listwise ranking framework that uses an LLM as a scorer to rank candidate answers against quality-ordered references. LINKAGE shows stronger correlation with human judgments and outperforms conventional metrics, highlighting its suitability for NFQA evaluation.

2.2 Retrieval-Augmented Generation (RAG)

Retrieval-augmented generation (RAG) improves the quality of LLM responses by incorporating external documents, improving factual accuracy and contextual relevance (Lewis et al., 2020; Izacard and Grave, 2021). However, the quality of

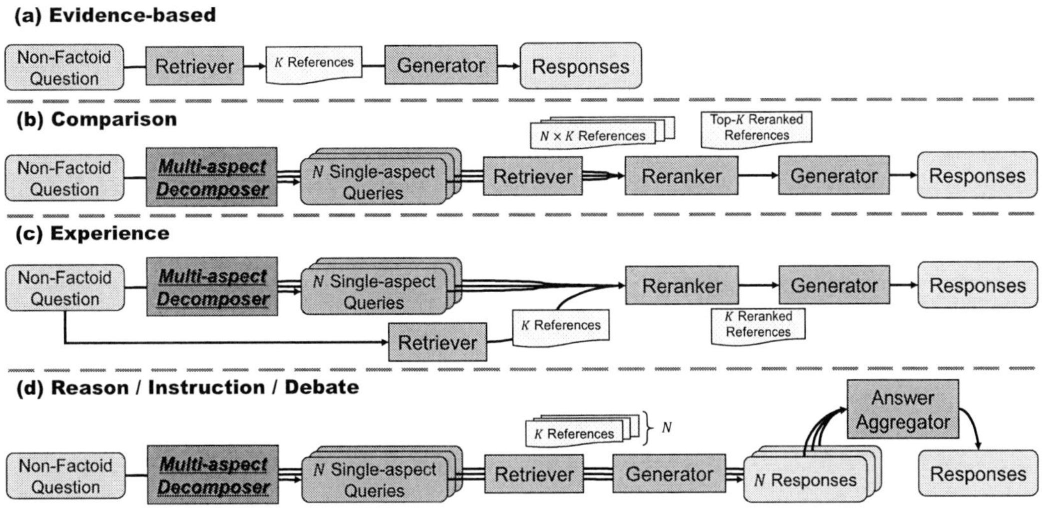

Figure 2: Overview of TYPED-RAG. Non-factoid questions (NFQs) are first classified by a pretrained Type Classifier and then processed according to their type. A Multi-aspect Decomposer and Answer Aggregator address each type's specific requirements using LLMs with tailored prompts. See Appendix A.4 and Figure 17 for prompt details and a complete illustration.

RAG outputs critically depends on the retrieval step: irrelevant or noisy documents can exacerbate hallucinations (Huang et al., 2023; Lee and Yu, 2025). Recent advances apply query rewriting and multi-hop decomposition to enrich retrieved contexts (Rackauckas, 2024; Chan et al., 2024), and adaptive retrieval strategies that assess query-document relevance before the generation process (Jeong et al., 2024; Yan et al., 2024; Asai et al., 2024).

Despite these developments, the application of RAG to NFQA remains underexplored. For example, Deng et al. (2024) proposed a graph-based multi-hop approach for NFQA, but it neither leverages large-scale pretrained LLMs nor employs dynamic retrieval. Likewise, An et al. (2024) integrated logic-based threading with RAG for *How-To* questions, yet their method does not generalize across all NFQ types. Our work bridges this gap by combining type-specific decomposition with adaptive retrieval and generation in a single RAG framework.

3 Method

In this section, we introduce TYPED-RAG, a novel RAG pipeline designed specifically for non-factoid question (NFQ) types. Figure 2 visually illustrates the overall processing mechanisms of the Multi-aspect Decomposer and the Answer Aggregator for each NFQ type.

NFQs are classified into one of six types using a pre-trained Type Classifier (Bolotova et al., 2022). Subsequently, queries are preprocessed through the Multi-aspect Decomposer, where each type's characteristics and the underlying intent of the questions are considered. The Multi-aspect Decomposer primarily consists of two modules: the Single-aspect Query Generator and the Keyword Extractor. These modules operate selectively based on the question type and perspective, leveraging few-shot learning and prompt engineering techniques to effectively transform queries according to their respective categories. The decomposed queries are then processed by one or multiple retrievers to retrieve highly relevant passages. Optionally, the retrieved passages may be re-ranked using a reranker to enhance the quality of results.

Based on the retrieved information, the generator produces the final answers. If multiple candidate answers are available, the Answer Aggregator integrates these candidates to form a unified response. This process is structured based on prompt engineering. Detailed prompt configurations for each module are presented in Appendix A.4.

As previously discussed, NFQs inherently involve multiple perspectives, making them challenging to handle effectively using conventional RAG approaches. Considering these distinct characteristics, we propose a type-aware pipeline specifically tailored to NFQs, capable of generating responses

NFQ Type	Example of Non-Factoid Question
`Evidence-based`	"How does sterilisation help to keep the money flow even?"
`Comparison`	"what is the difference between dysphagia and odynophagia"
`Experience`	"What are some of the best Portuguese wines?"
`Reason`	"Kresy, which roughly was a part of the land beyond the so-called Curson Line, was drawn for what reason?"
`Instruction`	"How can you find a lodge to ask to be a member of?"
`Debate`	"I Can See Your Voice, a reality show from South Korea, offers what kind of performers a chance to make their dreams of stardom a reality?"

Table 1: Example non-factoid questions in the Wiki-NFQA dataset, highlighting each NFQ type.

that accurately reflect user intent and address the inherent complexity of these questions.

The subsequent subsections elaborate on the definitions of each NFQ type and the corresponding detailed processing strategies.

3.1 Evidence-based

`Evidence-based` type questions aim to clarify the characteristics or definitions of specific concepts, objects, or events. These questions require precise and reliable factual information. These questions inherently have a single aspect, eliminating the need for complex contextual reasoning or multi-aspect decomposition. The intent behind these questions is to obtain clear and concise explanations grounded in evidence, resulting in responses consistently centered around a single aspect.

Accordingly, a straightforward RAG approach is applied to `Evidence-based` type questions. The retriever utilizes the original question as a query to search relevant documents, and the generator then produces responses based directly on these documents. It is essential to maintain a clear and concise information flow without considering multiple perspectives, thereby ensuring straightforward and accurate answers.

3.2 Comparison

`Comparison` type questions aim to identify differences, similarities, or superiority among two or more items. These questions can have different intentions and must be tailored to the purpose and targets of the comparison. `Comparison` type questions can be broadly classified into two categories based on intent: related aspects, focusing on similarities, and contrasting aspects, emphasizing differences or superiority. Consequently, `Comparison` type questions inherently involve multiple aspects.

Thus, a Multi-aspect Decomposer is required for `Comparison` type questions. Initially, a Keyword Extractor identifies the purpose of comparison (*compare_type*) and the items being compared (*keywords_list*). The purpose of the comparison is predefined as one of three types: difference, similarity, or superior. These types are explicitly extracted from the question to determine the scope of the comparison. Detailed prompt templates and examples used in this process are described in Appendix A.4.1.

Subsequently, the retriever searches for documents related to each keyword, eliminates redundant results, and reranks the remaining documents based on relevance. Finally, the generator synthesizes the information to produce a balanced response aligned with the comparison purpose. Collecting and integrating information across various comparison criteria and perspectives is crucial for accurately addressing user intent.

3.3 Experience

`Experience` type questions seek advice, recommendations, or personal insights, with responses based primarily on individual experiences. These questions naturally involve multiple aspects, and answers can vary significantly due to subjective differences among respondents. Thus, clearly understanding the user's intent and defining key perspectives is essential to provide informative answers encompassing diverse opinions and experiences.

Similar to `Comparison` type questions, `Experience` type questions require multi-aspect

NFQ Type	NQ-NF	SQD-NF	TQA-NF	2WMHQA-NF	HQA-NF	MSQ-NF	Total
Evidence-based	99	130	251	10	22	43	555 (58.73%)
Comparison	5	18	4	0	8	1	36 (3.81%)
Experience	0	20	8	1	10	2	41 (4.34%)
Reason	19	85	23	55	15	21	218 (23.07%)
Instruction	2	21	3	8	4	11	49 (5.19%)
Debate	1	26	7	5	3	4	46 (4.87%)
Total	126	300	296	79	62	82	**945**

Table 2: Wiki-NFQA dataset statistics by NFQ type.

consideration; however, the focus is not on comparisons based on specific features or criteria but rather on reflecting broader and more comprehensive experiences and diverse opinions. Therefore, `Experience` type questions require multi-aspect decomposition.

Initially, the Keyword Extractor identifies the primary topics that users seek experiences about and extracts key entities reflecting the question's intent. Specific examples of the prompts used in this process are detailed in Appendix A.4.2. Following this step, the retriever searches for related documents using these extracted keywords. The retrieved documents are then re-ranked according to their similarity to the extracted keywords. Finally, the generator produces an optimized response by synthesizing information that aligns with the user's intent and incorporates diverse perspectives. This ensures the response effectively meets the user's expectations.

3.4 Reason/Instruction

`Reason` and `Instruction` type questions both aim to provide information necessary for understanding phenomena or solving problems, but they differ significantly in intent and response approach.

The purpose of `Reason` type questions is to identify the causes of phenomena or events. These questions require multi-faceted consideration because explanations can vary depending on contextual factors and conditions. Different assumptions and conditions may yield multiple possible explanations, resulting in responses often including contrasting or conflicting information.

In contrast, `Instruction` type questions focus on procedural steps or methodologies. Although the procedures or methods can vary based on specific goals or requirements and thus involve multiple aspects, the responses tend to align similarly rather than diverging significantly, unlike `Reason` type questions. While various procedures may exist, their fundamental structure or concepts often remain interconnected.

For both `Reason` and `Instruction` type questions, a Multi-aspect Decomposer is applied. Initially, a Single-aspect Query Generator decomposes the original query into separate single-aspect queries. The retriever and generator then process each query individually, producing separate responses. An Answer Aggregator subsequently integrates these responses to deliver a clear, systematically organized final answer. Examples of the prompts used in this process are detailed in Appendix A.4.3.

3.5 Debate

`Debate` type questions focus on controversial topics and aim to explore and reflect multiple perspectives, especially opposing perspectives. These questions inherently possess multiple perspectives and require the inclusion of contrasting arguments and perspectives, as subjective positions may vary according to underlying assumptions and perspectives, unlike factual questions.

To effectively respond to `Debate` type questions, it is essential to fairly represent the logic of each opposing perspective and generate unbiased, balanced responses. Thus, a Multi-aspect Decomposer breaks down the question into debate topics and diverse opinions. The Single-aspect Query Generator then formulates individual queries for each opinion. The retriever and generator process each query separately, producing individual responses. Finally, an LLM with a debate mediator persona (Liang et al., 2024) synthesizes these diverse perspectives, generating a balanced final response from a mediator's perspective. Detailed prompts applied in the Single-aspect Query Generator and Debate Mediator processes are outlined in Appendix A.4.4. This approach ensures responses

Prompt Template for LINKAGE

Please impartially rank the given candidate answer to a non-factoid question accurately within the reference answer list, which are ranked in descending order of quality. The top answers are of the highest quality, while those at the bottom may be poor or unrelated.
Determine the ranking of the given candidate answer within the provided reference answer list. For instance, if it outperforms all references, output [[1]]. If it's deemed inferior to all four references, output [[4]].
Your response must strictly following this format: "[[2]]" if candidate answer could rank 2nd.
Below are the user's question, reference answer list, and the candidate answer.
Question:{`question`}
Reference answer list:{`reference_answers`}
Candidate answer:{`candidate_answer`}

Figure 3: The LINKAGE prompt template from Yang et al. (2024) used to rank candidate answers in our evaluation of TYPED-RAG and the baselines.

fairly and transparently reflect diverse perspectives, enabling comprehensive and balanced information delivery suitable for `Debate` type questions.

4 Experimental Setup

4.1 Model

We compare our TYPED-RAG with **LLM-** and **RAG-based** QA systems as baselines. In our experiments, we use a black-box LLM and two open-weight LLMs with different numbers of parameters: (i) Llama-3.2-3B-Instruct (Llama-3.2-3B), (ii) Mistral-7B-Instruct-v0.2 (Mistral-7B; Jiang et al., 2023), and (iii) GPT-4o-mini-2024-07-18 (GPT-4o mini).

All inputs to the LLMs (including the RAG generator) are formatted using prompt templates. The prompt templates used in our experiments are provided in Appendix A.3.

4.2 Listwise Ranking Evaluation (LINKAGE)

To evaluate non-factoid question answering (NFQA) systems, we adopt LINKAGE (Yang et al., 2024), a listwise ranking framework designed for NFQA. LINKAGE orders each candidate answer by comparing its quality against a reference list of answers, defined formally as:

$$R_i = \{r_{i_1}, r_{i_2}, \dots, r_{i_n}\}, \quad (1)$$

$$rank_{c_i} = \mathrm{LLM}(\mathcal{P}_L, q_i, c_i, R_i). \quad (2)$$

Here, q_i is the i-th question, c_i is the candidate answer under evaluation, and R_i is the set of reference answers $\{r_{i_k}\}$ sorted from highest to lowest quality. The scorer LLM, guided by the LINKAGE prompt $\mathcal{P}_L$, assigns $rank_{c_i}$ based on each candidate's position within R_i. The complete LINKAGE prompt template is shown in Figure 3.

Ranking Metrics To quantify LINKAGE rankings, we employ two complementary metrics: Mean Reciprocal Rank (MRR) (Voorhees and Tice, 2000) and Mean Percentile Rank (MPR):

$$\mathrm{MRR} = \frac{1}{N}\sum_{i=1}^{N}\frac{1}{rank_{c_i}}, \quad (3)$$

$$\mathrm{MPR} = \frac{1}{N}\sum_{i=1}^{N}\left(1 - \frac{rank_{c_i} - 1}{|R_i|}\right) \times 100. \quad (4)$$

MRR measures how close candidate answers rank to the top of the list, with higher values indicating better performance. MPR converts each rank into a percentile, reflecting the candidate's relative position within its reference list; higher MPR scores denote superior overall ranking across all positions. Together, MRR highlights top-answer accuracy, while MPR provides insight into performance across the entire ranking spectrum.

4.3 Dataset Construction

To test the NFQA methods, we curate the **Wiki-NFQA dataset**, a specialized resource tailored for NFQA. It is derived from existing Wikipedia-based datasets: Natural Questions (NQ; Kwiatkowski et al., 2019), SQuAD (SQD; Rajpurkar et al., 2016), TriviaQA (TQA; Joshi et al., 2017), 2WikiMultiHopQA (2WMH; Ho et al., 2020), HotpotQA (HQA; Yang et al., 2018), MuSiQue (MSQ; Trivedi et al., 2022).

Model	Scorer LLM	Methods	Wiki-NFQA Dataset					
			NQ-NF	SQD-NF	TQA-NF	2WMH-NF	HQA-NF	MSQ-NF
Llama-3.2-3B	Mistral-7B	LLM	0.5893	0.5119	0.6191	0.3565	0.4825	0.4262
		RAG	0.5294	0.4944	0.5470	0.4150	0.4530	0.4047
		TYPED-RAG	**0.7659**	**0.6493**	**0.7061**	**0.4544**	**0.5624**	**0.5356**
	GPT-4o mini	LLM	0.4934	0.4506	0.5380	0.3070	0.3669	0.2917
		RAG	0.4187	0.3553	0.4586	0.2859	0.2957	0.2866
		TYPED-RAG	**0.8366**	**0.7139**	**0.7013**	**0.3692**	**0.5470**	**0.4482**
Mistral-7B	Mistral-7B	LLM	0.6356	0.5450	0.6363	**0.4821**	0.5255	**0.5081**
		RAG	0.5635	0.5069	0.6233	0.4789	0.5323	0.4438
		TYPED-RAG	**0.7103**	**0.6333**	**0.6709**	0.4747	**0.6035**	0.4512
	GPT-4o mini	LLM	0.4656	0.4222	0.5921	0.3175	0.3965	0.3384
		RAG	0.4411	0.3817	0.5450	0.2890	0.3562	0.3079
		TYPED-RAG	**0.8413**	**0.7444**	**0.7767**	**0.3987**	**0.6653**	**0.4929**

Table 3: Evaluation on the Wiki-NFQA dataset comparing various language models, scorer LLMs, and methods using Mean Reciprocal Rank (MRR). Answers were ranked with LINKAGE (Yang et al., 2024) and evaluated by MRR.

Filtering Non-Factoid Questions Through a systematic filtering process, we extract non-factoid questions, then generate high-quality reference answers to ensure the dataset's suitability for NFQA evaluation.

We use the nf-cats[1] (Bolotova et al., 2022), a RoBERTa-based pre-trained NFQ category classifier, to extract NFQs from existing Wikipedia-based datasets. Since it categorizes questions into factoid and non-factoid types, we only retain those classified as non-factoid for further processing. To ensure a more rigorously curated dataset, we filter the data using heuristics based on the question patterns outlined in the NFQ taxonomy proposed by Bolotova et al. (2022). Table 2 presents the statistics for the Wiki-NFQA dataset.

Reference Answers Generation Since these datasets only have a single-grade ground truth answer, we generate diverse reference answers of varying quality for LINKAGE evaluation, as described in Yang et al. (2024). After constructing the reference answers, we use the GPT-4o-2024-11-20 to annotate their quality level. Prompt details about generating reference answers are provided in Appendix A.1, and A.2.

Examples of the Wiki-NFQA Dataset Table 1 provides examples of questions that represent each type of NFQ in the Wiki-NFQA dataset.

The `Evidence-based` type questions require answers grounded in verifiable sources, while `Comparison` type questions seek distinctions between concepts. `Experience` type questions solicit subjective opinions or recommendations, while `Reason` type questions aim to uncover the rationale behind events or concepts. `Instruction` type questions request procedural guidance, and `Debate` type questions involve discussions on controversial or interpretive topics.

[1]`https://huggingface.co/Lurunchik/nf-cats`

5 Experimental Results

We evaluate TYPED-RAG on the Wiki-NFQA dataset across all NFQ categories and model configurations. As shown in Table 3 (MRR) and Figure 4 (MPR), TYPED-RAG consistently outperforms both LLM- and RAG-based baselines. These metrics demonstrate that our approach not only elevates the ranking of generated answers but also improves their relative quality. Scorer LLMs uniformly rate TYPED-RAG's responses as more relevant and comprehensive. Representative examples of TYPED-RAG's outputs for each non-factoid question type are provided in Appendix D.

5.1 Impact of Scorer LLMs and Base Models

The performance of all methods depends on the choice of scorer LLM and base model. Since each LLM evaluates responses using its own learned criteria and internal representations, scores from different scorers should not be compared directly. Instead, performance comparisons are most meaningful when considering the relative ranking of methods under the same scorer.

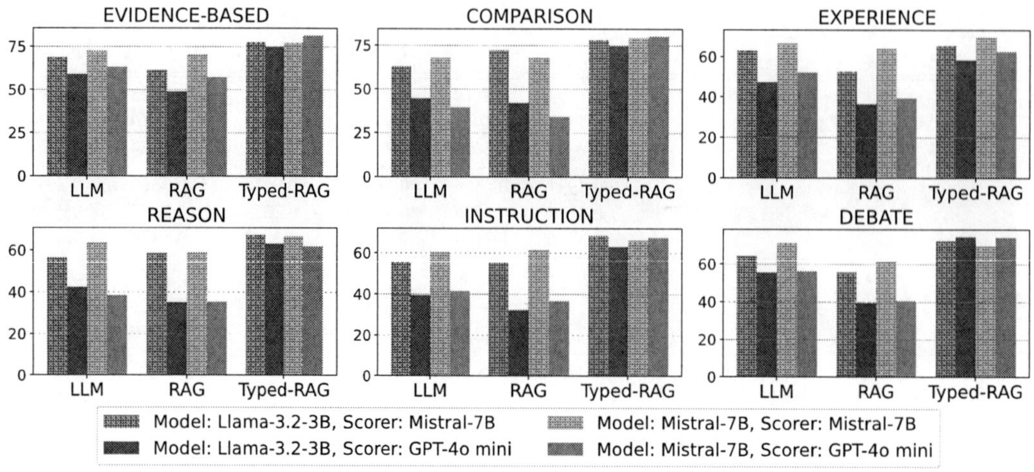

Figure 4: Comparison of Mean Percentile Rank (MPR) for LLMs, RAGs, and TYPED-RAG across six NFQ categories in the Wiki-NFQA dataset. Results are shown for two model setups (Llama-3.2-3B and Mistral-7B) and two scorer LLMs (Mistral-7B and GPT-4o mini); the y-axis displays MPR (%), where higher values indicate better performance.

As reported in Table 3 and Figure 4, scores generally decrease when switching from Mistral-7B to GPT-4o mini as the scorer. This trend likely stems from GPT-4o mini's greater sophistication and stricter evaluation standards, which penalize even minor inconsistencies or lack of depth. This pattern holds across all base models and methods, underscoring that more powerful scorers apply more stringent criteria. Notably, despite the overall score reductions, TYPED-RAG retains a clear advantage over both LLM- and RAG-based baselines, demonstrating its robustness to changes in scorer strictness.

5.2 Limitations of RAG and Benefits of TYPED-RAG

Our experiments also reveal that RAG-based methods underperform direct LLM-based generation (see Table 3 and Figure 4). We attribute this shortfall to the noise introduced by retrieved factual information, which can hinder response generation in NFQA tasks. TYPED-RAG addresses this challenge through a multi-aspect decomposition strategy that structures retrieval around the distinct facets of non-factoid questions. By reducing irrelevant noise and ensuring more focused retrieval, TYPED-RAG consistently outperforms both RAG and LLM-only approaches—particularly on reasoning-intensive subsets—thereby enhancing the overall quality of generated answers.

6 Conclusion

In this paper, we introduced TYPED-RAG, a novel RAG-based framework for non-factoid question answering (NFQA) that incorporates type-aware multi-aspect decomposition. By first classifying each NFQ into a specific category and then decomposing it into focused sub-queries, TYPED-RAG enables targeted retrieval and answer generation for each aspect. The retrieved sub-responses are aggregated to produce comprehensive, nuanced answers that better address the diverse requirements of non-factoid questions.

To support evaluation, we also curated Wiki-NFQA, a benchmark dataset covering a wide range of NFQ types. Experimental results on Wiki-NFQA dataset show that TYPED-RAG consistently outperforms both LLM-only and standard RAG baselines across all question types and scorer LLM settings. These findings validate the effectiveness and robustness of type-aware multi-aspect decomposition in enhancing both retrieval quality and answer relevance for NFQA.

Future work could explore extending TYPED-RAG to incorporate more fine-grained question types and further refine the decomposition strategies. Additionally, applying our approach to other specific domains or applying fine-tuning methods and integrating it with more sophisticated retrieval mechanisms could further improve the performance and adaptability of NFQA systems.

Limitations

Our work is the first to introduce RAG to NFQA, but it has several limitations.

A key limitation is the absence of a direct comparison between TYPED-RAG and existing query rewriting and decomposition methodologies. Although TYPED-RAG provides a structured approach to these tasks, its performance relative to other techniques remains unexplored. Though various query rewriting and decomposition techniques have been proposed to improve retrieval quality, this study does not empirically evaluate the effectiveness of query reformulation, retrieval relevance, or computational overhead of TYPED-RAG relative to these approaches. A systematic comparison with these methods would provide a clearer understanding of TYPED-RAG's advantages and limitations. Future work should incorporate benchmark evaluations against these established techniques to better position TYPED-RAG within the landscape of query rewriting and decomposition research.

Another limitation of our evaluation setup is that we use the same model to assess the quality of its generated responses. This self-evaluation approach may introduce bias because the model may struggle to distinguish differences in quality among the answers it produced. To mitigate this issue, future work could explore using stronger LLMs, human assessments, or ensemble scoring methods for evaluation. Adopting these strategies would improve the reliability of quality assessments and reduce potential biases in our evaluation framework.

Acknowledgments

This research was supported by Brian Impact Foundation, a non-profit organization dedicated to the advancement of science and technology for all. A prior version of this work was presented in a non-archival form at the NAACL 2025 Student Research Workshop.

References

Kaikai An, Fangkai Yang, Liqun Li, Junting Lu, Sitao Cheng, Lu Wang, Pu Zhao, Lele Cao, Qingwei Lin, Saravan Rajmohan, Dongmei Zhang, and Qi Zhang. 2024. Thread: A logic-based data organization paradigm for how-to question answering with retrieval augmented generation. *arXiv preprint arXiv:2406.13372*.

Akari Asai, Zeqiu Wu, Yizhong Wang, Avirup Sil, and Hannaneh Hajishirzi. 2024. Self-RAG: Learning to retrieve, generate, and critique through self-reflection. In *The Twelfth International Conference on Learning Representations, ICLR 2024, Vienna, Austria, May 7-11, 2024*.

Payal Bajaj, Daniel Campos, Nick Craswell, Li Deng, Jianfeng Gao, Xiaodong Liu, Rangan Majumder, Andrew McNamara, Bhaskar Mitra, Tri Nguyen, et al. 2016. MS MARCO: A human generated machine reading comprehension dataset. *arXiv preprint arXiv:1611.09268*.

Valeriia Bolotova, Vladislav Blinov, Falk Scholer, W. Bruce Croft, and Mark Sanderson. 2022. A non-factoid question-answering taxonomy. In *Proceedings of the 45th International ACM SIGIR Conference on Research and Development in Information Retrieval*, page 1196–1207.

John Burger, Claire Cardie, Vinay Chaudhri, Robert Gaizauskas, Sanda Harabagiu, David Israel, Christian Jacquemin, Chin-Yew Lin, Steve Maiorano, George Miller, Dan Moldovan, Bill Ogden, John Prager, Ellen Riloff, Amit Singhal, Rohini Shrihari, Tomek Strazalkowski, Ellen Voorhees, and Ralph Weishedel. 2003. Issues, tasks and program structures to roadmap research in question & answering (Q&A). In *Document Understanding Conferences Roadmapping Documents*, pages 1–35.

Chi-Min Chan, Chunpu Xu, Ruibin Yuan, Hongyin Luo, Wei Xue, Yike Guo, and Jie Fu. 2024. RQ-RAG: Learning to refine queries for retrieval augmented generation. In *1st Conference on Language Modeling*.

Snigdha Chaturvedi, Vittorio Castelli, Radu Florian, Ramesh M. Nallapati, and Hema Raghavan. 2014. Joint question clustering and relevance prediction for open domain non-factoid question answering. In *Proceedings of the 23rd International Conference on World Wide Web*, page 503–514.

Yang Deng, Wenxuan Zhang, Weiwen Xu, Ying Shen, and Wai Lam. 2024. Nonfactoid question answering as query-focused summarization with graph-enhanced multihop inference. *IEEE Transactions on Neural Networks and Learning Systems*, 35(8):11231–11245.

Helia Hashemi, Mohammad Aliannejadi, Hamed Zamani, and W. Bruce Croft. 2020. ANTIQUE: A non-factoid question answering benchmark. In *Advances in Information Retrieval - 42nd European Conference on IR Research, ECIR 2020, Lisbon, Portugal, April 14-17, 2020, Proceedings, Part II*, volume 12036 of *Lecture Notes in Computer Science*, pages 166–173.

Xanh Ho, Anh-Khoa Duong Nguyen, Saku Sugawara, and Akiko Aizawa. 2020. Constructing a multi-hop QA dataset for comprehensive evaluation of reasoning steps. In *Proceedings of the 28th International Conference on Computational Linguistics*, pages 6609–6625.

Lei Huang, Weijiang Yu, Weitao Ma, Weihong Zhong, Zhangyin Feng, Haotian Wang, Qianglong Chen, Weihua Peng, Xiaocheng Feng, Bing Qin, and Ting Liu. 2023. A survey on hallucination in large language models: Principles, taxonomy, challenges, and open questions. *arXiv preprint arXiv:2311.05232*.

Gautier Izacard and Edouard Grave. 2021. Leveraging passage retrieval with generative models for open domain question answering. In *Proceedings of the 16th Conference of the European Chapter of the Association for Computational Linguistics: Main Volume*, pages 874–880.

Soyeong Jeong, Jinheon Baek, Sukmin Cho, Sung Ju Hwang, and Jong Park. 2024. Adaptive-RAG: Learning to adapt retrieval-augmented large language models through question complexity. In *Proceedings of the 2024 Conference of the North American Chapter of the Association for Computational Linguistics: Human Language Technologies (Volume 1: Long Papers)*, pages 7036–7050.

Albert Q. Jiang, Alexandre Sablayrolles, Arthur Mensch, Chris Bamford, Devendra Singh Chaplot, Diego de Las Casas, Florian Bressand, Gianna Lengyel, Guillaume Lample, Lucile Saulnier, Lélio Renard Lavaud, Marie-Anne Lachaux, Pierre Stock, Teven Le Scao, Thibaut Lavril, Thomas Wang, Timothée Lacroix, and William El Sayed. 2023. Mistral 7B. *arXiv preprint arXiv:2310.06825*.

Mandar Joshi, Eunsol Choi, Daniel Weld, and Luke Zettlemoyer. 2017. TriviaQA: A large scale distantly supervised challenge dataset for reading comprehension. In *Proceedings of the 55th Annual Meeting of the Association for Computational Linguistics (Volume 1: Long Papers)*, pages 1601–1611.

Vladimir Karpukhin, Barlas Oguz, Sewon Min, Patrick Lewis, Ledell Wu, Sergey Edunov, Danqi Chen, and Wen-tau Yih. 2020. Dense passage retrieval for open-domain question answering. In *Proceedings of the 2020 Conference on Empirical Methods in Natural Language Processing*, pages 6769–6781.

Tom Kwiatkowski, Jennimaria Palomaki, Olivia Redfield, Michael Collins, Ankur Parikh, Chris Alberti, Danielle Epstein, Illia Polosukhin, Jacob Devlin, Kenton Lee, Kristina Toutanova, Llion Jones, Matthew Kelcey, Ming-Wei Chang, Andrew M. Dai, Jakob Uszkoreit, Quoc Le, and Slav Petrov. 2019. Natural Questions: A benchmark for question answering research. *Transactions of the Association for Computational Linguistics*, 7:452–466.

Woosuk Kwon, Zhuohan Li, Siyuan Zhuang, Ying Sheng, Lianmin Zheng, Cody Hao Yu, Joseph Gonzalez, Hao Zhang, and Ion Stoica. 2023. Efficient memory management for large language model serving with PagedAttention. In *Proceedings of the 29th Symposium on Operating Systems Principles*, page 611–626.

DongGeon Lee and Hwanjo Yu. 2025. REFIND: Retrieval-augmented factuality hallucination detection in large language models. *arXiv preprint arXiv:2502.13622*.

Patrick S. H. Lewis, Ethan Perez, Aleksandra Piktus, Fabio Petroni, Vladimir Karpukhin, Naman Goyal, Heinrich Küttler, Mike Lewis, Wen-tau Yih, Tim Rocktäschel, Sebastian Riedel, and Douwe Kiela. 2020. Retrieval-augmented generation for knowledge-intensive NLP tasks. In *Advances in Neural Information Processing Systems 33*, pages 9459–9474.

Tian Liang, Zhiwei He, Wenxiang Jiao, Xing Wang, Yan Wang, Rui Wang, Yujiu Yang, Shuming Shi, and Zhaopeng Tu. 2024. Encouraging divergent thinking in large language models through multi-agent debate. In *Proceedings of the 2024 Conference on Empirical Methods in Natural Language Processing*, pages 17889–17904.

Ritwik Mishra, Rajiv Ratn Shah, and Ponnurangam Kumaraguru. 2025. Long-context non-factoid question answering in Indic languages. *arXiv preprint arXiv:2504.13615*.

OpenAI. 2024. GPT-4o system card. *arXiv preprint arXiv:2410.21276*.

Long Ouyang, Jeffrey Wu, Xu Jiang, Diogo Almeida, Carroll L. Wainwright, Pamela Mishkin, Chong Zhang, Sandhini Agarwal, Katarina Slama, Alex Ray, John Schulman, Jacob Hilton, Fraser Kelton, Luke Miller, Maddie Simens, Amanda Askell, Peter Welinder, Paul F. Christiano, Jan Leike, and Ryan Lowe. 2022. Training language models to follow instructions with human feedback. In *Advances in Neural Information Processing Systems 35: Annual Conference on Neural Information Processing Systems 2022, NeurIPS 2022, New Orleans, LA, USA, November 28 - December 9, 2022*.

Matthew E. Peters, Mark Neumann, Mohit Iyyer, Matt Gardner, Christopher Clark, Kenton Lee, and Luke Zettlemoyer. 2018. Deep contextualized word representations. In *Proceedings of the 2018 Conference of the North American Chapter of the Association for Computational Linguistics: Human Language Technologies, NAACL-HLT 2018, New Orleans, Louisiana, USA, June 1-6, 2018, Volume 1 (Long Papers)*, pages 2227–2237.

Zackary Rackauckas. 2024. RAG-Fusion: a new take on retrieval-augmented generation. *International Journal on Natural Language Computing*, 13:37–47.

Pranav Rajpurkar, Jian Zhang, Konstantin Lopyrev, and Percy Liang. 2016. SQuAD: 100,000+ questions for machine comprehension of text. In *Proceedings of the 2016 Conference on Empirical Methods in Natural Language Processing*, pages 2383–2392.

Harsh Trivedi, Niranjan Balasubramanian, Tushar Khot, and Ashish Sabharwal. 2022. MuSiQue: Multihop questions via single-hop question composition.

Transactions of the Association for Computational Linguistics, 10:539–554.

Ellen M. Voorhees and Dawn M. Tice. 2000. The TREC-8 question answering track. In *Proceedings of the Second International Conference on Language Resources and Evaluation*.

Shitao Xiao, Zheng Liu, Peitian Zhang, Niklas Muennighoff, Defu Lian, and Jian-Yun Nie. 2024. C-Pack: Packed resources for general Chinese embeddings. In *Proceedings of the 47th International ACM SIGIR Conference on Research and Development in Information Retrieval*, page 641–649.

Shi-Qi Yan, Jia-Chen Gu, Yun Zhu, and Zhen-Hua Ling. 2024. Corrective retrieval augmented generation. *arXiv preprint arXiv:2401.15884*.

Diji Yang and Omar Alonso. 2024. A bespoke question intent taxonomy for e-commerce. In *Proceedings of the ACM SIGIR Workshop on eCommerce 2024 co-located with the 47th International ACM SIGIR Conference on Research and Development in Information Retrieval (SIGIR 2024), Washington D.C., USA, July 18, 2024*, volume 3843 of *CEUR Workshop Proceedings*.

Sihui Yang, Keping Bi, Wanqing Cui, Jiafeng Guo, and Xueqi Cheng. 2024. LINKAGE: Listwise ranking among varied-quality references for non-factoid QA evaluation via LLMs. In *Findings of the Association for Computational Linguistics*, pages 6985–7000.

Zhilin Yang, Peng Qi, Saizheng Zhang, Yoshua Bengio, William Cohen, Ruslan Salakhutdinov, and Christopher D. Manning. 2018. HotpotQA: A dataset for diverse, explainable multi-hop question answering. In *Proceedings of the 2018 Conference on Empirical Methods in Natural Language Processing*, pages 2369–2380.

Liang Zhang, Katherine Jijo, Spurthi Setty, Eden Chung, Fatima Javid, Natan Vidra, and Tommy Clifford. 2024. Enhancing large language model performance to answer questions and extract information more accurately. *arXiv preprint arXiv 2402.01722*.

Tianyi Zhang, Varsha Kishore, Felix Wu, Kilian Q. Weinberger, and Yoav Artzi. 2020. BERTScore: Evaluating text generation with BERT. In *8th International Conference on Learning Representations*.

A Prompt Details

A.1 Reference List Construction

Prompt Template to Generate the Highest Standard Reference Answer

Given a non-factoid question:"{question}" and its answer:"{ground_truth}"
Use your internal knowledge to rewrite this answer.

Figure 5: Prompt template proposed by Yang et al. (2024) to generate the highest standard reference answer using LLM's internal knowledge.

Prompt Template to Generate Diverse Qualities of Reference Answers

Generate three different answers to a non-factoid question from good to bad in quality, each inferior to the golden answer I give you. Ensure that the quality gap from good to bad is very significant among these three answers. Golden answer is the reasonable and convincing answer to the question. Answer 1 can be an answer to the question, however, it is not sufficiently convincing. Answer 2 does not answer the question or if it does, it provides an unreasonable answer. Answer 3 is completely out of context or does not make any sense.

Here are 3 examples for your reference.
1.Non-factoid Question: how can we get concentration on something?
Golden Answer: To improve concentration, set clear goals, create a distraction-free environment, use time management techniques like the Pomodoro Technique, practice mindfulness, take regular breaks, stay organized, limit multitasking, practice deep work, maintain physical health, and seek help if needed.
Output:
Answer 1: Improve focus: set goals, quiet space, Pomodoro Technique, mindfulness, breaks, organization, limit multitasking, deep work, health, seek help if needed.
Answer 2: Just like and enjoy the work you do, concentration will come automatically.
Answer 3: If you are student, you should concentrate on studies and don't ask childish questions.

2.Non-factoid Question: Why doesn't the water fall off earth if it's round?
Golden Answer: Earth's gravity pulls everything toward its center, including water. Even though Earth is round, gravity keeps water and everything else anchored to its surface. Gravity's force is strong enough to counteract the Earth's curvature, preventing water from falling off.
Output:
Answer 1: This goes along with the question of why don't we fall off the earth if it is round. The answer is because gravity is holding us (and the water) down.
Answer 2: Same reason the people don't.
Answer 3: When rain drops fall through the atmosphere CO2 becomes dissolved in the water. CO2 is a normal component of the Earth's atmosphere, thus the rain is considered naturally acidic.

3.Non-factoid Question: How do I determine the charge of the iron in FeCl3?
Golden Answer: Since chloride ions (Cl-) each carry a charge of -1, and there are three chloride ions in FeCl3, the total negative charge from chloride ions is -3. To balance this, the iron ion (Fe) must have a charge of +3 to ensure the compound has a neutral overall charge. Therefore, the charge of the iron ion in FeCl3 is +3.
Output:
Answer 1: Charge of Fe in Fecl3 is 3. Iron has either 2 as valancy or 3. in this case it bonds with three chlorine molecules. therefore its valency and charge is three.
Answer 2: If two particles (or ions, or whatever) have opposite charge, then one has positive charge and one has negative charge.
Answer 3: take a piece of iron. Wrap a copper wire around the iron in tight close coils. run a charge through the wire.

Below are the non-factoid question, and the golden answer.
Non-factoid Question: {question}
Golden Answer: {ground_truth}
Output:

Figure 6: Prompt template proposed by Yang et al. (2024) to generate diverse qualities of reference answers.

A.2 Reference Answers Annotation

System Prompt for Reference Answers Annotation

Your task is to evaluate the relevance and quality of multiple candidate answers for a given non-factoid question.
Please evaluate the quality of each answer in a step-by-step manner.
Follow the structured guidelines below to ensure consistency and accuracy in your evaluation.

Notes on Candidate Answers
Multiple candidate answers can come in two forms:
- Single choice answer: A single string, e.g., `"born again"`.
- Multiple choice answer: A list of strings, e.g., `['traffic calming', 'aesthetics']`.
When evaluating multiple choice answers, treat the entire list as a single unit. Do **not** split them into individual components; instead, evaluate the overall quality as a whole.

Evaluation Criteria
Assign a label to each candidate answer based on the following criteria:
- 3: The answer provides a comprehensive, accurate, and contextually relevant response that directly addresses the question.
- 2: The answer is accurate and relevant but lacks depth or comprehensive coverage.
- 1: The answer is somewhat relevant but contains inaccuracies, vagueness, or insufficient detail.
- 0: The answer is irrelevant, incorrect, or fails to address the question meaningfully.
If there are two or more answers that you think are close in quality, you can give the same label.

Response Format
- Assign a label to each answer strictly in the format: `Answer X: [[Y]]`, where `X` is the answer number, and `Y` is the integer score (0-3).
- Do **not** include any additional comments or explanations outside this format.

Input Prompt Template for Reference Answers Annotation

Inputs
- Non-Factoid Question: `{question}`
- Candidate Answers:
`{reference_answers}`

Figure 7: System prompt (top) and input prompt template (bottom) adapted from Yang et al. (2024) for annotating the quality level of generated reference answers.

A.3 Prompt templates for Baseline Methods

Prompt template for LLM

```
You are an assistant for answering questions.
Answer the following question.

### Question
{question}

### Answer
```

Figure 8: Prompt template for LLM method.

Prompt template for RAG

```
You are an assistant for answering questions.
Refer to the references below and answer the following question.

### References
{reference_passages}

### Question
{question}

### Answer
```

Figure 9: Prompt template for RAG method.

A.4 Prompt templates for TYPED-RAG

A.4.1 Comparison

Prompt Template for Keyword Extraction in Comparison Type Questions

You are a query analysis assistant. Based on the query type, apply the relevant prompt to transform the query to better align with the user's intent, ensuring clarity and precision.
Determine if the input query is a compare-type question (i.e., compare/contrast two or more things, understand their differences/similarities.) as a "Query Analyst". If so, perform the following:

1. Identify the type of comparison: "differences", "similarities", or "superiority".
2. Extract the subjects of comparison and represent them as specific, contextualized phrases.

Output format
{"is_compare": true/false, "compare_type": "", "keywords_list": []}

Example
Query: "Who is more intelligent than humans on earth?"
Analysis:
{"is_compare": true, "compare_type": "superiority", "keywords_list": ["human intelligence", "the intelligence of other beings"]}

Input
Query: {query}
Output
Analysis:

Figure 10: Prompt template for keyword extraction in Comparison type questions.

Prompt Template for Generating a Response to Comparison Type Questions

You are an assistant for answering questions.
You are given the extracted parts of a long document and a question. Refer to the references below and answer the following question.

The question is a compare-type with a specific comparison type and keywords indicating the items to compare.
Answer based on this comparison type and the target keywords provided.

Inputs
Question: {question}
Comparison Type: {comparison_type}
Keywords: {keywords}
References:
{reference_passages}
Output
Answer:

Figure 11: Prompt template for generating a response to Comparison type questions.

A.4.2 Experience

Figure 12 shows the prompt template for responding to Experience type questions. The retrieved passages are subsequently re-ranked based on the extracted keywords. After reranking, we use the prompt template for RAG (Figure 9) to generate answers.

Prompt Template for Keyword Extraction in Experience Type Questions

You are a query analysis assistant. Based on the query type, apply the relevant prompt to transform the query to better align with the user's intent, ensuring clarity and precision.
The input question is an experience-type question (i.e., get advice or recommendations on a particular topic.). As a "Query Analyst", please evaluate this question and proceed with the following steps.

1. Identify the topic intended to be gathered from experience-based questions.
2. Extract the key entities in the question, considering the intent of asking about experience, to facilitate an accurate response.

Output format
`["Keyword 1", ..., "Keyword N"]` (List of string, separated with comma)

Example
Question (Input): "What are some of the best Portuguese wines?"
Answer (Output): ["Portuguese wines", "best"]

Input
Question: `{question}`
Output
Answer:

Figure 12: Prompt template for keyword extraction in Experience type questions.

A.4.3 Reason & Instruction

Prompt Template for Generating Sub-queries in Reason Type Questions

You are a query analysis assistant. Based on the query type, apply the relevant prompt to transform the query to better align with the user's intent, ensuring clarity and precision.
The input query is a reason-type question (i.e., a question posed to understand the reason behind a particular concept or phenomenon). As a "Query Analyst", please evaluate this query and proceed with the following steps.

1. Break down the original instruction into multiple sub-queries that preserve the core intent but use varied language and structure. These multiple sub-queries should aim to capture different linguistic expressions of the original instruction while still aligning with its intended meaning.
2. Create at least 2 to 5 distinct multiple sub-queries.

Output format
`["sub-query 1", ..., "sub-query N"]` (List of string, separated with comma)

Input
Query: {query}
Output
Multiple sub-queries:

Figure 13: Prompt template for generating sub-queries in Reason type questions.

Prompt Template for Generating Sub-queries in Instruction Type Questions

You are a query analysis assistant. Based on the query type, apply the relevant prompt to transform the query to better align with the user's intent, ensuring clarity and precision.
The input query is an instruction-type question (i.e., Instructions/guidelines provided in a step-by-step manner).
As a "Query Analyst", please evaluate this query and proceed with the following steps.
1. Break down the original instruction into multiple sub-queries that preserve the core intent but use varied language and structure.
These multiple sub-queries should aim to capture different linguistic expressions of the original instruction while still aligning with its intended meaning.
2. Create at least 2 to 5 distinct multiple sub-queries.

Output format
`["sub-query 1", ..., "sub-query N"]` (List of string, separated with comma)

Input
Query: {query}
Output
Multiple sub-queries:

Figure 14: Prompt template for generating sub-queries in Instruction type questions.

Prompt Template for Aggregating Answers to an Original Question

You are an assistant tasked with aggregating answers to a question.
You are provided with the original question and multiple question-answer pairs. These queries preserve the core intent of the original question but use varied language and structure. Your goal is to review the question-answer pairs and synthesize a concise and accurate response to the original question based on the information provided.
Using the information from the question-answer pairs, generate a brief and clear answer to the original question.

Inputs
Original Question: {original_question}
Question-Answer Pairs:
{qa_pairs_text}
Output
Aggregated Answer:

Figure 15: Prompt template for aggregating answers to an original question. Used by Reason type questions and Instruction type questions.

A.4.4 Debate

Prompt Template for Generating Sub-queries in Debate Type Questions

You are a query analysis assistant. Based on the query type, apply the relevant prompt to transform the query to better align with the user's intent, ensuring clarity and precision.
The input question is a debate-type question (i.e., invites multiple perspectives). As a "Query Analyst", please evaluate this question and proceed with the following steps.

1. Extract the debate topic.
2. Identify 2 to 5 key perspectives on this topic.
3. Generate a sub-query reflecting each perspective's bias.

Ensure each sub-query fits a Retrieval-Augmented Generation (RAG) framework, seeking passages that align with the viewpoint.

Output format
{"debate_topic": {topic}, "dist_opinion": [list of perspectives], "sub-queries": {"opinion1": "biased sub-query for opinion1", "opinion2": "biased sub-query for opinion2", ...}

Example
Query: "Is Trump a good president?"
Answer:

```
{
    "debate_topic": "Donald Trump's presidency",
    "dist_opinion": ["positive", "negative", "neutral"],
    "sub-queries": {
        "positive": "Was Donald Trump one of the best presidents for economic growth?",
        "negative": "Did Trump's presidency harm the U.S. economy and leadership?",
        "neutral": "Can we assess Trump's tenure's strengths and weaknesses?"
    }
}
```

Input
Query: {query}
Output
Answer:

Prompt Template for Debate Mediator in Debate Type Questions

You are acting as the mediator in a debate.
Below is a topic and responses provided by n participants, each with their own perspective. Your task is to synthesize these responses by considering both the debate topic and each participant's viewpoint, providing a fair and balanced summary. Ensure the response maintains balance, captures key points, and distinguishes any opposing opinions. Present the answer *short and concise*, phrased in a direct format without using phrases like "participants in the debate" or "in the debate."

Input format
- Debate topic: {debate_topic}
- Participant's responses:
- Response 1: "{response content}" (Perspective: {perspective 1})
- Response 2: "{response content}" (Perspective: {perspective 2})
- ...
- Response N: "{response content}" (Perspective: {perspective N})

Output format
A short and concise summary from the mediator's perspective based on the discussion, phrased as a direct answer without reference to the debate structure or participants

Inputs
Debate topic: {debate_topic}
Participant's responses: {responses}
Output
Summary:

Figure 16: Prompt templates for generating sub-queries (top) and debate mediator (bottom) in Debate type questions. We reference the debate mediator prompt from Liang et al. (2024) to ensure that responses objectively aggregate and present diverse perspectives.

B Implementation Details

All experiments were conducted using the NVIDIA A100 (80 GB) GPUs and the OpenAI API.

B.1 LLM

For all experiments involving open-source LLMs, we employ vLLM (Kwon et al., 2023) to enable fast and memory-efficient inference.

B.2 RAG

To perform NFQA with our RAG-based QA system, the retriever selects five passages that are then provided to the generator as references. For Wikipedia-based tasks, we use BM25 on the Wikipedia corpus preprocessed by Karpukhin et al. (2020) as the external retrieval index.

B.3 TYPED-RAG

A detailed overview of TYPED-RAG is shown in Figure 17.

The reranker employed in TYPED-RAG is BGE-Reranker-Large[2] (Xiao et al., 2024).

B.4 LINKAGE Evaluation

For LINKAGE evaluation, we adhere to the original settings: nucleus sampling (`top_p` = 0.95), a maximum output length of 512 tokens, and a default temperature of 0.8. The temperature is reduced to 0.1 when annotating reference answers.

B.5 Reference Answer Construction on Wiki-NFQA

To build reference answers for the Wiki-NFQA dataset, we use three LLMs to capture diverse styles: (i) GPT-3.5-turbo-16k, (ii) Mistral-7B-Instruct-v0.2[3] (Jiang et al., 2023), and (iii) Llama-3.1-8B-Instruct[4]. Each model generates three high-quality responses, totaling nine reference answers. Additionally, we use GPT-4o-2024-08-06 (OpenAI, 2024) to produce a single, superior reference answer that is distinct from the other nine.

C Detailed Analysis per Dataset

We conduct a dataset-specific analysis to highlight TYPED-RAG's strengths across different challenge contexts.

NQ-NF, SQuAD-NF, and TriviaQA-NF These benchmarks feature open-ended non-factoid questions that often demand explanatory or elaborate answers. TYPED-RAG delivers substantial gains in both MRR and MPR, demonstrating its ability to generate detailed, on-topic responses. For instance, on SQuAD-NF using the Mistral-7B base model with a GPT-4o mini scorer, TYPED-RAG achieves an MRR of 0.7444—significantly outperforming the LLM-only (0.4222) and RAG-based (0.3817) baselines.

HotpotQA-NF and MuSiQue-NF These datasets require multi-hop reasoning, where answers must synthesize information from multiple passages. By decomposing questions into type-specific aspects, TYPED-RAG more effectively navigates these complex reasoning chains, yielding notable improvements in MPR compared to both LLM and RAG methods.

2WikiMultiHopQA-NF Although overall scores are lower on this particularly challenging dataset, TYPED-RAG still surpasses LLM-only and RAG baselines. This result underscores TYPED-RAG's robustness even in scenarios demanding extensive, multi-step inference.

[2] https://huggingface.co/BAAI/bge-reranker-large

[3] https://huggingface.co/mistralai/Mistral-7B-Instruct-v0.2

[4] https://huggingface.co/meta-llama/Llama-3.1-8B-Instruct

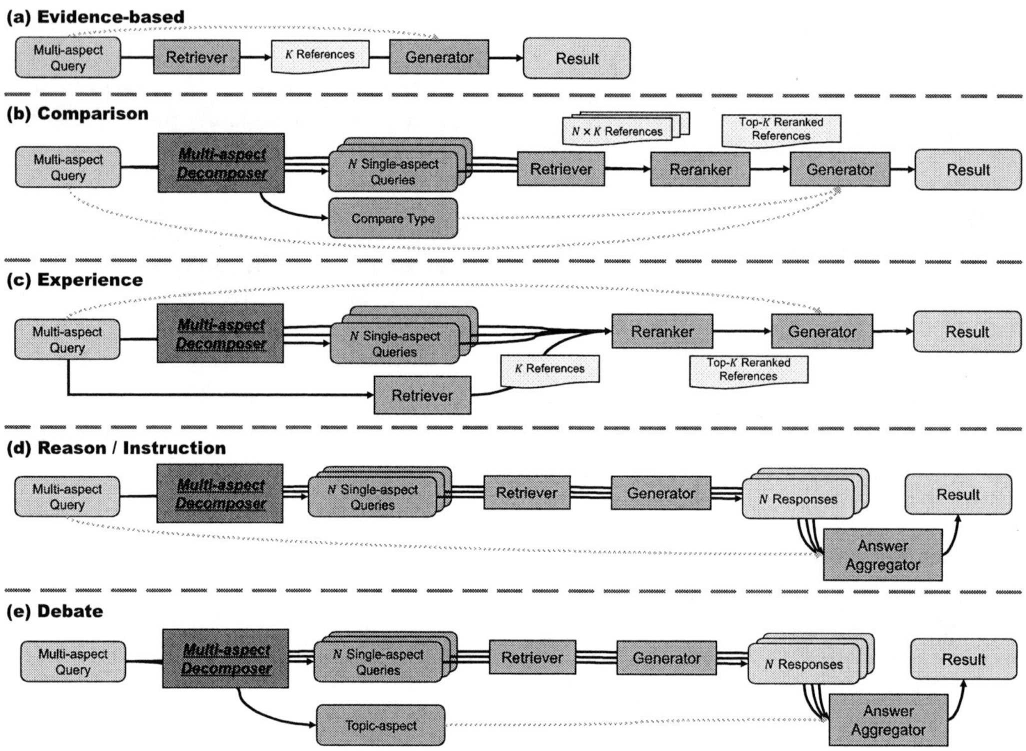

Figure 17: A detailed overview of TYPED-RAG.

D Case Study

NFQ Type	Example of Question	Response of TYPED-RAG
Evidence-based	How does sterilisation help to keep the money flow even?	The term "sterilisation" is often used in economics to refer to the act of preventing currency or securities from affecting the monetary base due to interest rate differentials. When a central bank engages in open market operations to buy or sell securities, it may want to prevent the money flow from being disrupted by interest rate differentials in different markets. Sterilisation helps to keep the money flow even by offsetting the effect of open market operations on the monetary base. When a central bank buys securities, it injects cash into the economy and increases the monetary base. However, if this leads to an appreciation of the domestic currency, it may reduce the competitiveness of exports and increase the cost of imports. To prevent this, the central bank may sell an equivalent amount of foreign currency in the foreign exchange market, which reduces the monetary base and helps to offset the initial effect of the open market operation. Similarly, if a central bank sells securities, it decreases the monetary base and may lead to a depreciation of the domestic currency, which can make exports more competitive and imports more expensive. To prevent this, the central bank may buy an equivalent amount of foreign currency in the foreign exchange market, which increases the monetary base and helps to offset the initial effect of the open market operation. In summary, sterilisation is a tool used by central banks to keep the money flow even and maintain control over the monetary base, despite open market operations that may otherwise disrupt the flow of funds. It allows central banks to implement monetary policy while minimizing the impact on currency values and other macroeconomic variables.

Continued on next page

NFQ Type	Example of Question	Response of TYPED-RAG
Comparison	what is the difference between dysphagia and odynophagia	Dysphagia and odynophagia are two distinct conditions related to swallowing. Dysphagia is the medical term for difficulty swallowing. It can be caused by various conditions, including neurological disorders, stroke, cancer, or structural problems in the throat or esophagus. Symptoms of dysphagia include the sensation of food sticking in the throat or chest, coughing or choking during eating, and pain or discomfort while swallowing. On the other hand, odynophagia is the medical term for pain while swallowing. It is a symptom of an underlying condition, such as a sore throat, inflammation, or infection. The pain can be described as sharp or throbbing and may be worsened by swallowing solid or acidic foods. Odynophagia can also be a symptom of gastroesophageal reflux disease (GERD) or eosinophilic esophagitis. In summary, dysphagia is a condition that makes it difficult to swallow, while odynophagia is a symptom of pain while swallowing. A person with dysphagia may also experience pain while swallowing, but the primary issue is the difficulty in moving food from the mouth to the stomach. Conversely, a person with odynophagia primarily experiences pain while swallowing, but they may still be able to swallow relatively normally.

Continued on next page

NFQ Type	Example of Question	Response of TYPED-RAG
Experience	What are some of the best Portuguese wines?	Based on the available references in the document, some Portuguese wines that are often considered excellent include: 1. The reference 14098516 might be referring to Port Wine, a fortified wine produced in the Douro Valley region. Port Wine is known for its sweet and rich flavors and comes in various styles such as Tawny, Ruby, and White Port. 2. Reference 5043240 could be referring to Vinho Verde, a light, slightly effervescent wine from the Vinho Verde region in the north of Portugal. It is typically low in alcohol and is often served chilled. 3. The Douro region is also famous for its red wines, such as those referenced in 2866435. These wines are known for their robust flavors and are often blended from a variety of grape varieties. 4. The reference 4891311 might be referring to Madeira Wine, another fortified wine from the Madeira Islands. Madeira Wine is known for its complex flavors and can range from sweet to dry. 5. Lastly, the reference 309483 could be referring to Dã Wines, which come from the Dã region in central Portugal. These wines are known for their elegance and balance, with flavors of red fruit, herbs, and minerals. So, based on the given references, some of the best Portuguese wines include Port Wine, Vinho Verde, Douro Red Wines, Madeira Wine, and Dã Wines.
Reason	Kresy, which roughly was a part of the land beyond the so-called Curson Line, was drawn for what reason?	The Curzon Line refers to the boundary proposed by Lord Curzon, then Viceroy of India, in 1920, as a potential eastern border for a future independent Poland. Kresy, or Eastern Borderlands, was the area of land beyond this proposed border. It was drawn for various reasons, including historical, ethnic, and strategic considerations. The area had been part of the Polish state in the past, and there was a significant Polish population there. Ethnically, the region was diverse, with various groups including Poles, Ukrainians, Belarusians, and Jews. Strategically, the region was important due to its location near the borders of several neighboring countries and its rich natural resources.

Continued on next page

NFQ Type	Example of Question	Response of TYPED-RAG
Instruction	How can you find a lodge to ask to be a member of?	To find a lodge to inquire about membership, consider the following steps: 1. Contact the Grand Lodge of your jurisdiction (state or country) for a list of lodges in your area. You can usually find this information on their website or by contacting them directly. 2. Research the lodges on the list to learn more about their history, traditions, and meeting times. This can be done through their websites, social media pages, or by contacting them directly. 3. Attend a few meetings as a visitor to get a feel for the lodge and its members. You may need to request an invitation from the lodge's secretary or master. 4. Speak with current members about their experiences and the expectations for new members. This can help you determine if the lodge is a good fit for you. 5. Consider your availability and the lodge's meeting schedule to ensure you can commit to attending meetings regularly. Remember, every lodge is unique, so it's essential to find one that aligns with your values and interests. Good luck in your search! (Note: The references provided do not contain information relevant to finding a lodge to ask to be a member of.)
Debate	I Can See Your Voice, a reality show from South Korea, offers what kind of performers a chance to make their dreams of stardom a reality?	Based on the information provided in the references, "I Can See Your Voice" is a South Korean reality show that offers singers a chance to audition without revealing their appearance or singing voice to the judges initially. This format is designed to evaluate contestants based on their charisma, rhythm, and overall performance without any biases influenced by their physical appearance or singing voice. Therefore, the show provides an opportunity for talented singers who might not have been given a chance due to their looks or voice in their initial auditions to showcase their abilities and pursue their dreams of stardom.

Table 4: Sample responses of TYPED-RAG across various non-factoid question types.

Do we still need Human Annotators? Prompting Large Language Models for Aspect Sentiment Quad Prediction

Nils Constantin Hellwig
Media Informatics Group
University of Regensburg
Regensburg, Germany
nils-constantin.hellwig@ur.de

Jakob Fehle
Media Informatics Group
University of Regensburg
Regensburg, Germany
jakob.fehle@ur.de

Udo Kruschwitz
Information Science Group
University of Regensburg
Regensburg, Germany
udo.kruschwitz@ur.de

Christian Wolff
Media Informatics Group
University of Regensburg
Regensburg, Germany
christian.wolff@ur.de

Abstract

Aspect sentiment quad prediction (ASQP) facilitates a detailed understanding of opinions expressed in a text by identifying the opinion term, aspect term, aspect category and sentiment polarity for each opinion. However, annotating a full set of training examples to fine-tune models for ASQP is a resource-intensive process. In this study, we explore the capabilities of large language models (LLMs) for zero- and few-shot learning on the ASQP task across five diverse datasets. We report F1 scores almost up to par with those obtained with state-of-the-art fine-tuned models and exceeding previously reported zero- and few-shot performance. In the 20-shot setting on the Rest16 restaurant domain dataset, LLMs achieved an F1 score of 51.54, compared to 60.39 by the best-performing fine-tuned method MVP. Additionally, we report the performance of LLMs in target aspect sentiment detection (TASD), where the F1 scores were close to fine-tuned models, achieving 68.93 on Rest16 in the 30-shot setting, compared to 72.76 with MVP. While human annotators remain essential for achieving optimal performance, LLMs can reduce the need for extensive manual annotation in ASQP tasks.

1 Introduction

Transformer-based large language models (LLMs) have gained significant attention due to their capability to address a broad spectrum of natural language processing (NLP) tasks, such as text summarization, translation, reading comprehension and text classification (Brown et al., 2020; Dubey et al., 2024). Noteworthy LLMs include Llama-3.1 (Dubey et al., 2024), Gemma-3 (Gemma et al., 2025), and Mixtral (Jiang et al., 2024), which are accessible in various parameter sizes with open model weights and commercial models like GPT-4 (Achiam et al., 2023) and Claude 3 (Anthropic, 2024).

Previous research explored zero- and few-shot scenarios in which the LLM generates outputs with either none or only a few labelled examples provided in the prompt (Gou et al., 2023; Zhang et al., 2024). This eliminates the need for supervised model training, such as for small language models[1] (SLMs) using annotated datasets (Wang et al., 2023c). This approach is particularly appealing because data annotation is often deemed complex and expensive, both in terms of time or financial cost, thereby complicating the development of text classification solutions tailored to specific tasks (Fehle et al., 2023; Gretz et al., 2023; Li et al., 2023).

An extensively studied task in NLP where manual annotations pose significant challenges is aspect-based sentiment analysis (ABSA) (Zhang et al., 2022). This task facilitates the understanding of customer opinions expressed in reviews or feedback (Pontiki et al., 2014). Unlike traditional sentiment classification, which assigns a single sentiment label (commonly positive, negative, or neutral) to an entire text document, ABSA requires annotators to identify all aspects within the text and determine the sentiment associated with each

[1]There is no universally accepted definition for categorizing language models as small or large. As handled by Zhang et al. (2024), models with fewer than 1 billion parameters are considered small, while those with 1 billion or more parameters are classified as large.

Proceedings of the 1st Joint Workshop on Large Language Models and Structure Modeling (XLLM 2025), pages 153–172
August 1, 2025

one (Zhang et al., 2022).

A prominent subtask of ABSA is aspect sentiment quad prediction (ASQP), which provides exceptionally detailed insights into the author's opinions by identifying four sentiment elements for each opinion: aspect term (*a*), aspect category (*c*), sentiment polarity (*p*) and opinion term (*o*) (Zhang et al., 2021a). Consequently, the annotation process for training examples is highly demanding, particularly when multiple opinions need to be annotated within a single text.

Previous research has predominantly concentrated on 0- to 10-shot learning, exclusively utilizing the English-language restaurant domain datasets Rest15 and Rest16 introduced by Zhang et al. (2021a).

In this study, we extend the analysis to include up to 50 few-shot examples and evaluate the approach on a diverse series of five datasets. The datasets utilized in this work include Rest15 and Rest16, introduced by Zhang et al. (2021b) and we incorporate the OATS dataset by Chebolu et al. (2024), which consists of hotel reviews from TripAdvisor and online learning reviews collected from Coursera. Finally, we introduce a novel ASQP dataset, comprising annotated sentences from airline reviews, which is published as part of this work.

We considered the following research questions:

RQ1: How does varying the number of few-shot examples (from 0 to 50) impact performance on the ASQP task?

RQ2: How do LLMs perform on the ASQP task compared to SLMs trained on annotated examples?

RQ3: Does self-consistency (SC) prompting (Wang et al., 2022a), where multiple outputs are generated from the same prompt and the most consistent response is selected, improve performance on the ASQP task?

We employed Google's Gemma-3-27B (Gemma et al., 2025) and report the performance for the smaller-sized Gemma-3-4B. In addition, we report the LLMs' performance on the target aspect sentiment detection (TASD), which focuses on the identification of (*a*, *c*, *p*)-triplets. All code and results of this study is publicly available on GitHub[2].

2 Related Work

2.1 Aspect Sentiment Quad Prediction

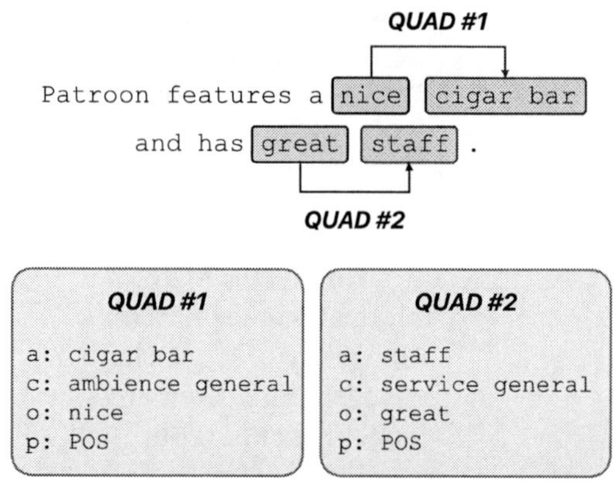

Figure 1: Annotated example for ASQP from Rest16 (Zhang et al., 2021a). One or multiple opinion-quadruple annotations are assigned to each sentence.

The development of methodologies for addressing the ASQP task was strongly influenced by the work of Zhang et al. (2021a), which introduced two annotated datasets for the ASQP task: Rest15 and Rest16. An example of such annotations is illustrated in Figure 1. Both datasets comprise annotated sentences derived from restaurant reviews. The annotations are sourced from the SemEval Shared Task datasets from 2015 and 2016 (Pontiki et al., 2015, 2016), which originally included only (*a*, *c*, *p*)-triplets and thus did not include annotations for opinion terms.

Since the release of Rest15 and Rest16, generative methods within a unified framework have emerged as the state-of-the-art (SOTA) approach for the ASQP task. Various strategies have been explored to generate sentiment elements in specific formats that exploit label semantics. These include approaches employing structured extraction schemas (Lu et al., 2022), sequential representations of sentiment elements (Gou et al., 2023) and natural language formats (Gou et al., 2023; Liu et al., 2021), wherein quadruples are systematically converted into natural language sentences. Performance scores for these methods are presented in Table 1.

All the aforementioned approaches rely on small text generation models, such as t5-base (Raffel et al., 2020), which utilizes an encoder-decoder

[2]https://github.com/NilsHellwig/llm-prompting-asqp

Strategy	Method	ASQP		TASD	
		Rest15	**Rest16**	**Rest15**	**Rest16**
Zero-shot learning	gpt-3.5-turbo, 0-shot (uncased) (Gou et al., 2023)	22.87	-	-	34.08
	gpt-3.5-turbo, 0-shot (Zhang et al., 2024)	10.46	14.02	-	-
	text-davinci-003, 0-shot (Zhang et al., 2024)	13.73	18.18	-	-
	ChatABSA, 0-shot (Bai et al., 2024)	**27.11**	**30.42**	**39.21**	**41.28**
Few-shot learning	gpt-3.5-turbo, 1-shot (Zhang et al., 2024)	30.15	31.98	-	-
	gpt-3.5-turbo, 5-shot (Zhang et al., 2024)	31.21	38.01	-	-
	gpt-3.5-turbo, 10-shot (uncased) (Gou et al., 2023)	**34.27**	-	-	46.51
	gpt-3.5-turbo, 10-shot (Zhang et al., 2024)	30.92	**40.15**	-	-
	ChatABSA, 1-shot (Bai et al., 2024)	28.13	33.84	37.23	41.92
	ChatABSA, 5-shot (Bai et al., 2024)	33.26	31.92	43.00	45.04
	ChatABSA, 10-shot (Bai et al., 2024)	32.14	33.26	**45.93**	**47.00**
Fine-tuning	TAS-BERT (Wan et al., 2020)	34.78	43.71	57.51	65.89
	Extract-Classify (Cai et al., 2021)	36.42	43.77	-	-
	GAS (Zhang et al., 2021b)	45.98	56.04	60.63	68.31
	Paraphrase (Zhang et al., 2021a)	46.93	57.93	63.06	71.97
	DLO (Hu et al., 2022)	48.18	59.79	62.95	71.79
	MVP (Gou et al., 2023)	**51.04**	**60.39**	**64.53**	**72.76**

Table 1: Performance on the ASQP and TASD task. F1 scores of both LLM-based and fine-tuned approaches from related work.

architecture based on the transformer architecture (Vaswani, 2017). The t5-base model, comprising 223 million parameters, is fine-tuned specifically for the ASQP task.

2.2 Large Language Models for Aspect-based Sentiment Analysis

The zero- and few-shot capabilities of LLMs have been demonstrated across various NLP tasks, e.g. question answering (Chada and Natarajan, 2021; Brown et al., 2020), named entity recognition (Cheng et al., 2024; Wang et al., 2023b), information retrieval (Faggioli et al., 2023; Wang et al., 2022b) or sentiment analysis (Zhang et al., 2024). In many cases, these models have achieved performance scores comparable to fine-tuned approaches, with few-shot learning often outperforming zero-shot learning.

In the domain of ABSA, LLMs have been employed in both zero- and few-shot settings. However, these efforts were constrained to a maximum of 10 few-shot examples within the prompt's context, addressing both ASQP and ABSA tasks with fewer sentiment elements (Conneau, 2019; Gou et al., 2023; Zhang et al., 2024).

Zhang et al. (2024) employed OpenAI's gpt-3.5-turbo (Brown et al., 2020) for End-to-End ABSA (E2E-ABSA, focus on (a, p) pairs) and achieved an F1 score of 54.46 and 63.30 on the Rest14 dataset (restaurant domain) from Pontiki et al. (2014) for zero- and 10-shot learning, respectively. A fine-tuned t5-large model (Raffel et al., 2020) achieved a slightly higher F1 score of 75.31. Similarly, Wu et al. (2024) analysed multiple open source LLMs with less than 10 billion parameters, as well as commercial LLMs for multilingual E2E-ABSA in a zero-shot setting. In multilingual ABSA, applying prompting strategies such as chain-of-thought (CoT) prompting did not improve performance when averaged across the LLMs considered. However, the best performing LLM, GPT-4o-CoT, achieved an F1 score of 52.81 which is slightly below the performance of the most performant fine-tuned model XLM-R (Conneau, 2019) (68.86). Wu et al. (2024) also evaluated a self-consistency (SC) prompting strategy, where the most frequent label across five generated outputs was selected as the final label. SC did not lead to an improvement in the performance.

With regard to the ASQP task, Zhang et al. (2024) achieved F1 scores below 20 for both Rest15 and Rest16 (see Table 1). Performance was improved to F1 scores above 30 on both Rest15 and Rest16 by providing 1, 5 or 10 few-shot examples.

Gou et al. (2023) surpassed the performance reported by Zhang et al. (2024) and reported an F1 score of 22.87 (zero-shot) and 34.27 (10-shot) on the Rest16 dataset, slightly exceeding the performance reported by Zhang et al. (2024). Notably, Gou et al. (2023) presented the sentences to be annotated and few-shot examples in an uncased format within the prompt, differing from the approach by Zhang et al. (2024). Furthermore, the task descriptions were formatted differently, with Gou et al. (2023) offering descriptions on each of the four sentiment elements considered in the respective ABSA task. Bai et al. (2024) adopted a distinct approach (referred to as ChatABSA) to processing its outputs, leading to performance improvements in the zero-shot setting but not in the few-shot setting. In the prompt, it was stated that the output should be in the JSON format. Furthermore, predicted aspect terms or opinion terms that were not explicitly mentioned in the original sentence were systematically set to null.

In summary, previous studies demonstrated that few-shot learning massively boosts performance in ABSA tasks but did not exceed the performance of models fine-tuned on annotated examples.

3 Methodology

We utilized LLMs to tackle the ASQP task across 0-, 10-, 20-, 30-, 40-, and 50-shot settings on different datasets. The performance is compared to that achieved using a dedicated training set to fine-tune smaller pre-trained language models. Furthermore, we report performance results for the TASD task.

3.1 Evaluation

3.1.1 Datasets

Table 2 presents an overview of the datasets used in this study, including Rest15 and Rest16, along with three additional datasets covering diverse domains.

Rest15 & Rest16: ASQP annotations originate from Zhang et al. (2021a) and the TASD annotations from Wan et al. (2020). This ensured comparability with the performance scores reported in previous research.

FlightABSA: A novel dataset containing 1,930 sentences annotated for ASQP. Properties of the annotated dataset are provided in Appendix B.

OATS Hotels & OATS Coursera: We utilized a subset of two corpora recently introduced by Chebolu et al. (2024) comprising ASQP-annotated sentences from reviews on hotels and e-learning courses. A detailed description of the data preprocessing for the OATS datasets can be found in Appendix A.

For the TASD task, we removed the opinion terms from the quadruples in annotations from FlightABSA, OATS Coursera and OATS Hotels. Subsequently, any duplicate triplets (a, c, p) that appeared twice in a sentence were discarded.

3.1.2 Setting

For evaluation, the test dataset was considered for all datasets. An LLM was prompted five times with different seeds (0 to 4) for each combination of ABSA task (ASQP and TASD), dataset and amount of random few-shot examples (0, 10, 20, 30, 40 or 50) taken from the training set in order to get five label predictions. For all seeds, the same few-shot examples were used; however, they were shuffled differently for each prompt execution. The average performance across all five runs is reported.

3.1.3 Metrics

As in previous works in the field of ABSA, we report the micro-averaged F1 score as well as precision and recall to assess the model's performance. The F1 score is the harmonic mean of precision and recall. Precision measures the proportion of correctly predicted positive instances out of all instances predicted as positive (Jurafsky and Martin, 2024, p. 67). Recall quantifies the proportion of correctly predicted positive instances out of all actual positive instances in the dataset (Jurafsky and Martin, 2024, p. 67).

Similar to Zhang et al. (2021a), a quad prediction was considered correct if all the predicted sentiment elements are exactly the same as the gold labels. Recognizing the potential interest in class-level performance metrics for subsequent research, we have shared the predicted labels for every evaluated setting in our GitHub repository, allowing detailed class-level analysis.

3.2 Large Language Models

We employed Gemma-3-27B[3] by Google, which comprises 27.4 billion parameters (Gemma et al., 2025). Ollama[4] was employed for inference, and the LLMs were loaded with 4-bit quantization. The model was chosen for its efficiency in terms of generated tokens per second, which is a critical factor given the extensive prompt execution requirements. Notably, our study required over 342,720 prompts to be executed, with many few-shot learning prompts encompassing over a thousand tokens. For larger models, such as Llama-3.3-70B Dubey et al. (2024), the required computational costs

[3]google/gemma-3-27b: `https://ollama.com/library/gemma3:27b`

[4]ollama: `https://ollama.com`

	Rest15	Rest16	FlightABSA	OATS Coursera	OATS Hotels
# Train	834	1,264	1,351	1,400	1,400
# Test	537	544	387	400	400
# Dev	209	316	192	200	200
# Aspect Categories	13	13	13	28	33
Language	en	en	en	en	en
Domain	restaurant	restaurant	airline	e-learning	hotel

Table 2: Overview of all ASQP datasets considered for evaluation. The datasets cover a range of different numbers of considered aspect categories and domains.

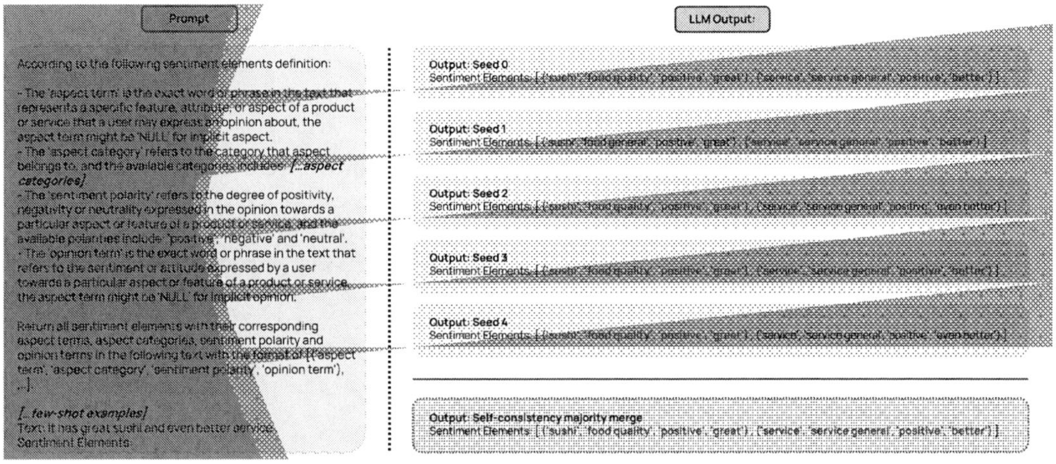

Figure 2: The prompt includes both a task description and specification of the output format. The LLM is run with five different seeds and in the case of self-consistency prompting, the tuple that appears most often across the five predictions is incorporated into the final label.

would have been hardly feasible with our resources. For comparison purposes, we also report performance for the smaller-sized LLM, Gemma-3-4B[5].

The experiments were conducted on a NVIDIA RTX A5000 GPU equipped with 24 GB of VRAM. The LLM's temperature parameter was set to 0.8 and generation was terminated upon encountering the closing square bracket character ("]") signifying the ending of a predicted label.

3.3 Prompt

3.3.1 Components

We adopted the prompting framework introduced by Gou et al. (2023) with some modifications. The employed prompt is illustrated in Figure 3.1.3 and an example is provided in Appendix C. The main components of the prompt include a list of explanation on all considered sentiment elements and the specification of the output format.

Unlike the prompt by Gou et al. (2023), our prompt instructed the LLM to pay attention to case sensitivity when returning aspect and opinion terms. Hence, the identified phrases should appear in the predicted tuple as they do in the sentence, similar to all supervised approaches mentioned in the related work section. Therefore, in the prompt, we clearly stated that the exact phrases should appear in the predicted label.

Since we executed each prompt with five different seeds, we also report the performance when employing the self-consistency prompting technique introduced by Wang et al. (2022a). The key idea is to select the most consistent answer from multiple prompt executions. We adapted the approach for ABSA by incorporating a tuple into the merged label if it appears in the majority of the predicted labels. As illustrated in Figure 3.1.3, this corresponds to a tuple appearing in at least 3 out of 5 predicted labels.

3.4 Output Validation

Since LLMs such as Gemma-3-27B cannot be strictly constrained to a fixed output format, we programmatically validated the output of the LLM.

[5] google/gemma-3-4b: `https://ollama.com/library/gemma3:4b`

For the predicted label, several criteria needed to be met for the generation to be considered valid:

- **Format**: The output must be a list of one or more tuples consisting of strings (quadruples for ASQP, triplets for TASD).
- **Sentiment**: The sentiment must be either 'positive', 'negative' or 'neutral'.
- **Aspect category**: Only the categories considered for the respective dataset and thus being mentioned in the prompt should be predicted as a part of a tuple.
- **Aspect and opinion terms**: Both must appear in the given sentence as predicted.

If any of the specified criteria for reasoning or label validation is not met, a regeneration attempt was triggered. If the predicted label was still invalid after 10 attempts, an empty label ([]) was considered as the predicted label.

3.5 Baseline Model

We compared the previously mentioned zero- and few-shot conditions against three SOTA baseline approaches, which are, the three best-performing methods for ASQP and TASD on the Rest15 and Rest16 datasets: Paraphrase (Zhang et al., 2021a), DLO (Hu et al., 2022) and MVP (Gou et al., 2023).

Paraphrase (Zhang et al., 2021a): *Paraphrase* is used to linearize sentiment quads into a natural language sequence to construct the input target pair.

DLO (Hu et al., 2022): *Dataset-level order* is a method designed for ASQP that leverages the order-free property of quadruplets. It identifies and utilizes optimal template orders through entropy minimization and combines multiple effective templates for data augmentation.

MVP (Gou et al., 2023): *Multi-view-Prompting* introduces element order prompts. The language model is guided to generate multiple sentiment tuples, with a different element order each, and then selects the most reasonable tuples by a voting mechanism. This method is highly resource-intensive, as multiple input-output pairs are created for each example in the train set, each comprising different sentiment element positions.

For all three approaches, we conducted training using the entire dataset and performed training with only 10, 20, 30, 40, or 50 training examples equally to the ones employed for the few-shot learning conditions. Training was conducted using five different random seeds (0 to 4). Moreover, to facilitate comparisons across datasets, we trained models using 800 training examples, as this represents the largest multiple of 100 examples available for all train sets (900 training examples are not available for Rest15). The results obtained using the full training sets of Rest15 and Rest16 were extracted from the works of Zhang et al. (2021a), Hu et al. (2022), and Gou et al. (2023).

For all methods, we used the hyperparameter configurations used by Zhang et al. (2021a), Hu et al. (2022) and Gou et al. (2023). The only exception was the 10-shot condition, where batch size was set to 8 instead of 16, as the limited number of examples (10) could not form a batch of 16 examples.

4 Results

The performance scores for the evaluated configurations are shown in Table 3 for the ASQP task and in Appendix D for the TASD task. Detailed performance scores focusing on individual sentiment elements are provided in Appendix E. Notably, for both tasks, we performed t-tests with Bonferroni correction ($p_{adj} < .05$) to examine whether significant differences exist between the F1 scores of the evaluated conditions (corresponding to the number of rows in Figure 3). No significant differences were observed.

Performance gains with an increasing number of few-shot examples. In most cases, increasing the number of few-shot examples resulted in incremental improvements in F1 scores across both ASQP and TASD tasks. The difference between zero- and few-shot prompting is substantial. For instance, on the Rest16 dataset under the SC prompting condition, the F1 score improved from 28.96 (0-shot) to 51.10 (50-shot) for the ASQP task. To further highlight this trend, we provide line plots (see Figure F) that depict the influence of the number of few-shot examples on the F1 scores across all tasks, datasets, and models.

LLM performance slightly lower compared to SOTA fine-tuned approaches. For both TASD and ASQP, the performance achieved through zero- and few-shot prompting did not surpass that ob-

Method	Prompting Strategy	# Few-Shot / # Train	Rest15			Rest16			FlightABSA			OATS Coursera			OATS Hotels		
			F1	Pre	Rec	F1	Pre	Rec	F1	Pre	Rec	F1	Pre	Rec	F1	Pre	Rec
Gemma-3-4B	-	0	6.80	7.43	6.26	8.00	8.83	7.31	11.12	13.11	9.66	5.23	5.67	4.86	11.11	14.48	9.02
		10	10.95	12.52	9.74	11.25	12.67	10.11	13.02	15.96	11.02	6.67	7.04	6.33	10.53	13.13	8.79
		20	16.93	17.94	16.03	18.52	20.06	17.20	11.92	14.00	10.37	9.47	9.59	9.36	14.72	16.02	13.62
		30	20.09	20.25	19.95	21.64	23.00	20.43	16.55	18.36	15.08	11.19	11.03	11.35	11.36	11.22	11.54
		40	19.40	19.05	19.77	25.42	25.62	**25.23**	18.34	20.03	16.92	11.26	11.13	**11.39**	14.01	13.42	14.67
		50	24.48	24.62	**24.35**	24.80	25.46	24.18	22.97	23.93	**22.10**	11.27	11.61	10.96	16.00	15.87	**16.17**
	SC	0	6.06	28.12	3.40	6.03	28.12	3.38	12.81	45.36	7.46	4.03	25.00	2.19	12.25	**52.63**	6.93
		10	7.86	48.57	4.28	9.63	45.74	5.38	10.53	**60.71**	5.76	7.42	**54.05**	3.98	9.80	52.00	5.41
		20	18.62	47.67	11.57	20.02	50.00	12.52	8.63	47.46	4.75	10.38	50.88	5.78	14.19	43.88	8.46
		30	23.62	51.26	15.35	25.07	**54.62**	16.27	15.06	46.49	8.98	12.44	46.75	7.17	10.64	26.52	6.66
		40	23.44	49.59	15.35	**31.13**	52.37	22.15	18.23	49.25	11.19	13.62	41.00	8.17	15.12	34.15	9.71
		50	**30.11**	**52.34**	21.13	27.46	46.97	19.40	**26.58**	52.50	17.80	**14.05**	39.09	8.57	**16.93**	37.26	10.96
Gemma-3-27B	-	0	24.41	22.67	26.44	28.94	27.12	31.01	42.31	39.10	**46.10**	13.05	11.42	15.22	22.90	22.49	23.33
		10	38.19	36.68	39.85	44.35	41.92	47.08	43.04	41.35	44.88	22.07	21.50	22.67	30.47	32.21	28.90
		20	36.25	36.99	35.55	49.41	48.53	**50.34**	42.31	41.72	42.92	24.31	24.56	24.06	36.96	38.61	35.45
		30	36.94	37.47	36.43	48.62	48.29	48.96	44.55	44.56	44.54	25.61	26.36	**24.90**	37.98	40.61	35.67
		40	37.19	37.36	37.03	47.82	47.23	48.44	42.52	43.61	41.49	23.30	23.84	22.79	38.38	41.22	35.92
		50	39.62	39.65	39.60	47.18	46.52	47.86	44.20	44.05	44.37	23.04	23.26	22.83	39.97	43.41	37.03
	SC	0	24.73	23.35	26.29	28.96	27.75	30.29	42.37	39.70	45.42	13.36	11.95	15.14	23.02	22.88	23.16
		10	39.95	39.41	**40.50**	46.23	44.64	47.93	45.24	45.39	45.08	22.31	23.41	21.31	31.41	35.29	28.29
		20	36.46	38.70	34.47	**51.54**	52.83	50.31	43.91	46.17	41.86	26.08	29.28	23.51	39.23	43.84	35.51
		30	37.91	41.21	35.09	50.61	51.98	49.31	46.14	48.42	44.07	**28.08**	**33.24**	24.30	41.68	48.61	36.48
		40	38.54	41.51	35.97	50.03	51.74	48.44	47.16	**52.38**	42.88	25.86	31.96	21.71	42.12	50.10	36.34
		50	**41.74**	**44.57**	39.25	51.10	**54.55**	48.06	**48.37**	51.95	45.25	25.86	31.96	21.71	**43.83**	**53.39**	**37.17**
MVP (Gou et al., 2023)		10	10.58	12.00	9.46	12.37	14.40	10.84	9.38	11.66	7.84	12.88	14.46	11.62	6.98	8.42	5.97
		20	18.71	21.22	16.73	21.49	24.30	19.27	14.27	17.43	12.09	18.85	20.79	17.25	14.30	16.03	12.92
		30	24.36	26.54	22.52	27.58	30.83	24.96	22.53	26.82	19.42	21.32	23.25	19.68	20.89	23.17	19.03
		40	25.95	27.72	24.40	32.72	33.56	31.94	28.15	32.17	25.03	20.21	22.02	18.68	24.71	27.00	22.78
		50	30.20	31.07	29.38	33.32	34.75	32.02	33.12	35.09	31.38	22.07	24.16	20.32	29.91	33.08	27.31
		800	50.02	**48.99**	**51.09**	58.09	**56.31**	**59.97**	57.46	**56.23**	58.74	30.26	29.91	30.62	53.37	52.41	54.36
		Full	**51.04**	-	-	**60.39**	-	-	**57.90**	56.09	**59.83**	**32.50**	**32.04**	**32.97**	**55.03**	**54.38**	**55.69**
DLO (Hu et al., 2022)	-	10	4.37	4.64	4.13	5.18	5.49	4.91	4.87	6.15	4.03	4.47	5.03	4.02	3.53	3.68	3.41
		20	12.06	14.37	10.39	13.84	14.42	13.32	9.75	12.09	8.17	10.79	11.88	9.88	8.16	6.86	10.10
		30	18.71	18.16	19.32	24.06	24.71	23.45	16.63	18.13	15.39	17.05	17.73	16.41	17.71	17.54	17.89
		40	22.87	21.36	24.60	26.92	25.94	27.98	23.75	26.24	21.69	17.22	18.38	16.22	22.65	23.01	22.33
		50	26.63	24.92	28.60	29.57	29.09	30.06	28.74	28.30	29.22	19.08	20.44	17.89	27.20	28.54	25.99
		800	**49.87**	**48.59**	**51.22**	59.44	57.73	61.25	57.42	56.03	58.88	30.83	30.37	31.31	54.40	53.39	55.45
		Full	48.18	47.08	49.33	**59.79**	**57.92**	**61.80**	**58.33**	**56.67**	**60.10**	**32.54**	**32.03**	**33.07**	**55.45**	**54.39**	**56.56**
Paraphrase (Zhang et al., 2021a)		10	1.32	1.64	1.11	3.56	4.02	3.23	3.44	4.34	2.85	4.75	5.35	4.26	2.63	3.66	2.06
		20	5.48	6.78	4.60	11.14	10.54	11.91	3.48	4.39	2.88	9.51	10.64	8.61	5.34	6.36	4.65
		30	9.47	9.54	9.46	7.18	8.44	6.28	3.60	4.55	2.98	11.39	12.84	10.24	5.13	6.48	4.26
		40	17.61	17.07	18.19	20.15	20.69	19.67	13.81	15.09	12.78	16.43	17.79	15.26	14.96	15.99	14.08
		50	25.55	24.58	26.62	23.50	23.75	23.25	17.98	18.58	17.42	19.38	20.72	18.21	23.09	23.67	22.59
		800	46.32	45.61	47.07	56.88	55.65	58.17	54.96	54.10	55.86	30.79	30.63	30.96	53.65	52.57	54.77
		Full	**46.93**	**46.16**	**47.72**	**57.93**	**56.63**	**59.30**	**57.76**	**57.37**	**58.17**	**32.34**	**32.06**	**32.63**	**53.87**	**52.61**	**55.19**

Table 3: Performance scores for ASQP. For the Rest15 and Rest16 datasets, performance scores achieved when employing the full training set ("Full") are taken from Gou et al. (2023), Hu et al. (2022) and Zhang et al. (2021b) for MVP, DLO and Paraphrase, respectively. The best score achieved by a method is presented in bold.

tained when the entire training set was utilized. For example, on the Rest16 dataset, Gemma-3-27B achieved 68.93, which is slightly below the best F1 score achieved by a fine-tuned approach (MVP: 72.76). However, the best F1 scores achieved by Gemma-3-27B in the TASD task were often close to those achieved by fine-tuned approaches employing 800 or all examples from the training set. In case only 10 to 50 annotated examples were used for prompting or training, few-shot prompting consistently outperformed fine-tuning approaches across all sample sizes, with only a few exceptions.

Massive performance enhancements achieved through self-consistency. SC enabled considerable boosts of the F1 score, regardless of the amount of few-shot examples. However, recall was occasionally higher without SC. Precision, on the other hand, was improved with SC in both tasks and across datasets. For instance, in the case of Gemma-3-4B, precision was increased in most instances.

The LLM's parameter size matters. Gemma-3-4B demonstrated lower performance in terms of F1 scores for both ASQP and TASD. Across the five datasets, the F1 scores in the ASQP task were approximately 10 percentage points lower when using Gemma-3-4B instead of Gemma-3-27B. For example, on the Rest15 dataset, the best F1 score achieved with Gemma-3-4B was 44.20, while the best score for Gemma-3-27B was 62.12 on the TASD task.

Lower performance in identifying opinion terms compared to other sentiment elements. As shown in the tables in Appendix E, performance in identifying sentiment (positive, negative, or neutral) is highly performant, with F1 scores exceeding 90. However, performance in identifying aspect and opinion terms is comparatively much lower.

5 Discussion

The results demonstrated performance improvements in F1 scores for both ASQP and TASD as the number of few-shot examples increases, highlighting the gap between zero- and few-shot prompting. In this chapter, we put the results of this work into the context of previous research and provide an outlook on the direction of future work.

New SOTA performance of LLMs. The LLM zero- and few-shot learning performance scores reported in previous studies by Gou et al. (2023), Zhang et al. (2024) and Bai et al. (2024) for the ASQP task on the Rest15 and Rest16 datasets fall below those achieved by Gemma-3-27B in both zero- and 10-shot learning settings. The only exception is Rest15, where ChatABSA (Bai et al., 2024) outperformed Gemma-3-27B in zero-shot learning except for TASD + Rest16. Unlike prior studies, which have primarily evaluated up to 10-shot settings, we extended the investigation to a 10- to 50-shot setting for the first time. In this expanded range, Gemma-3-27B achieved notable F1 scores exceeding 50 for the ASQP task (e.g., Rest16 with SC: 51.54) and surpassing 60 for the TASD task (e.g., Rest16 with SC: 68.93). Notably, these substantial gains are also attributed to the use of SC prompting. Furthermore, this is in contrast to the work of Wu et al. (2024), whose SC approach for E2E-ABSA did not lead to an improvement in performance.

Model size and prompting strategy affect few-shot performance. Although Gemma-3-27B achieved competitive results in both ASQP and TASD, its performance remained slightly below fine-tuned SOTA approaches such as those by Gou et al. (2023), Zhang et al. (2021b), and Hu et al. (2022) when full training sets were employed. However, in scenarios with limited annotated examples, few-shot prompting consistently outperformed fine-tuning. The parameter size of the model also influenced performance, with Gemma-3-27B consistently outperforming its smaller counterpart, Gemma-3-4B.

Directions for enhancing low-resource task performance. Building on the promising results of this study, future research could focus on improving low-resource task performance through advanced prompt engineering techniques. Approaches such as chain-of-thought prompting (Wei et al., 2022) or plan-and-solve prompting (Wang et al., 2023a), which allowed for performance gains in other NLP tasks, hold significant potential. Furthermore, refining annotation guidelines or representing labels as natural language text, as proposed by Zhang et al. (2021b), could contribute to improved outcomes. Bigger LLMs, e.g. with 70B parameters, may provide additional performance benefits, given that our 27B model demonstrated superior results compared to the 4B variant.

Exploring less complex tasks and many-shot learning. In a broader context, future research could extend our approach to less complex tasks, in terms of the amount of considered sentiment elements, such as E2E-ABSA or aspect category sentiment analysis (ACSA) which focuses on aspect category and the sentiment expressed towards them. Beyond the low-resource setting considered in this study, one could explore the so-called "many-shot in-context learning" paradigm described by Agarwal et al. for ABSA, where hundreds or even the full training set is provided in the prompt. Observing that our approach achieved performance scores on the TASD task close to fine-tuned models, future work could investigate whether further increasing the number of shots lead to surpassing fine-tuned approaches.

Limitations

This study evaluated the performance of LLMs on ASQP tasks across a broad selection of datasets, few-shot settings, and LLM configurations. However, a limitation of this work is the selection of employed LLMs. We only employed LLMs comprising 4 or 27 billion parameters. Bigger-sized models such as Llama-3-70B (Dubey et al., 2024) or commercial models were not considered due to their prohibitive computational and financial costs. In order to evaluate each setting for a considered LLM, we executed a total of 171,360 prompts. Due to the amount of tokens in each prompt, the associated cost implications are substantial: about 125 hours (5 days) for Gemma-3-27B and 59 hours (2 days) for Gemma-3-4B. Hence, the time would further increase with an even bigger LLM in terms of parameter size. For commercial models such as GPT-4, executing all prompts would result in massive costs.

Finally, we must highlight the issue of potential data contamination, as it is the case for the previous studies introduced in the related work section. Meaning, it cannot be ruled out that the publicly available annotated datasets used in this study (except for FlightABSA) were included in the training data for both Gemma-3-4B and Gemma-3-27B.

Ethics Statement

All results and code used in this study are publicly available. The dataset we introduced, FlightABSA, is available upon request. We want to prevent the annotated dataset from being available online and then being inadvertently collected for pre-training LLMs.

References

Josh Achiam, Steven Adler, Sandhini Agarwal, Lama Ahmad, Ilge Akkaya, Florencia Leoni Aleman, Diogo Almeida, Janko Altenschmidt, Sam Altman, Shyamal Anadkat, et al. 2023. Gpt-4 technical report. *arXiv preprint arXiv:2303.08774*.

Rishabh Agarwal, Avi Singh, Lei M Zhang, Bernd Bohnet, Luis Rosias, Stephanie CY Chan, Biao Zhang, Aleksandra Faust, and Hugo Larochelle. Many-shot in-context learning. In *ICML 2024 Workshop on In-Context Learning*.

AI Anthropic. 2024. The claude 3 model family: Opus, sonnet, haiku. *Claude-3 Model Card*, 1.

Yinhao Bai, Zhixin Han, Yuhua Zhao, Hang Gao, Zhuowei Zhang, Xunzhi Wang, and Mengting Hu. 2024. Is compound aspect-based sentiment analysis addressed by llms? In *Findings of the Association for Computational Linguistics: EMNLP 2024*, pages 7836–7861.

Tom Brown, Benjamin Mann, Nick Ryder, Melanie Subbiah, Jared D Kaplan, Prafulla Dhariwal, Arvind Neelakantan, Pranav Shyam, Girish Sastry, Amanda Askell, et al. 2020. Language models are few-shot learners. *Advances in neural information processing systems*, 33:1877–1901.

Hongjie Cai, Rui Xia, and Jianfei Yu. 2021. Aspect-category-opinion-sentiment quadruple extraction with implicit aspects and opinions. In *Proceedings of the 59th Annual Meeting of the Association for Computational Linguistics and the 11th International Joint Conference on Natural Language Processing (Volume 1: Long Papers)*, pages 340–350.

Rakesh Chada and Pradeep Natarajan. 2021. Fewshotqa: A simple framework for few-shot learning of question answering tasks using pre-trained text-to-text models. *arXiv preprint arXiv:2109.01951*.

Siva Uday Sampreeth Chebolu, Franck Dernoncourt, Nedim Lipka, and Thamar Solorio. 2024. Oats: A challenge dataset for opinion aspect target sentiment joint detection for aspect-based sentiment analysis. In *Proceedings of the 2024 Joint International Conference on Computational Linguistics, Language Resources and Evaluation (LREC-COLING 2024)*, pages 12336–12347.

Qi Cheng, Liqiong Chen, Zhixing Hu, Juan Tang, Qiang Xu, and Binbin Ning. 2024. A novel prompting method for few-shot ner via llms. *Natural Language Processing Journal*, 8:100099.

A Conneau. 2019. Unsupervised cross-lingual representation learning at scale. *arXiv preprint arXiv:1911.02116*.

Abhimanyu Dubey, Abhinav Jauhri, Abhinav Pandey, Abhishek Kadian, Ahmad Al-Dahle, Aiesha Letman, Akhil Mathur, Alan Schelten, Amy Yang, Angela Fan, and et al. 2024. The llama 3 herd of models.

Guglielmo Faggioli, Laura Dietz, Charles LA Clarke, Gianluca Demartini, Matthias Hagen, Claudia Hauff, Noriko Kando, Evangelos Kanoulas, Martin Potthast, Benno Stein, et al. 2023. Perspectives on large language models for relevance judgment. In *Proceedings of the 2023 ACM SIGIR International Conference on Theory of Information Retrieval*, pages 39–50.

Jakob Fehle, Leonie Münster, Thomas Schmidt, and Christian Wolff. 2023. Aspect-based sentiment analysis as a multi-label classification task on the domain of german hotel reviews. In *Proceedings of the 19th Conference on Natural Language Processing (KONVENS 2023)*, pages 202–218.

Team Gemma, Morgane Riviere, Shreya Pathak, Pier Giuseppe Sessa, Cassidy Hardin, Surya Bhupatiraju, Léonard Hussenot, Thomas Mesnard, Bobak Shahriari, Alexandre Ramé, et al. 2025. Gemma 3 technical report.

Zhibin Gou, Qingyan Guo, and Yujiu Yang. 2023. Mvp: Multi-view prompting improves aspect sentiment tuple prediction. In *Proceedings of the 61st Annual Meeting of the Association for Computational Linguistics (Volume 1: Long Papers)*, pages 4380–4397.

Shai Gretz, Alon Halfon, Ilya Shnayderman, Orith Toledo-Ronen, Artem Spector, Lena Dankin, Yannis Katsis, Ofir Arviv, Yoav Katz, Noam Slonim, et al. 2023. Zero-shot topical text classification with llms-an experimental study. In *Findings of the Association for Computational Linguistics: EMNLP 2023*, pages 9647–9676.

Matthew Honnibal and Ines Montani. 2017. spacy 2: Natural language understanding with bloom embeddings, convolutional neural networks and incremental parsing. *To appear*, 7(1):411–420.

Mengting Hu, Yike Wu, Hang Gao, Yinhao Bai, and Shiwan Zhao. 2022. Improving aspect sentiment quad prediction via template-order data augmentation. In *Proceedings of the 2022 Conference on Empirical Methods in Natural Language Processing*, pages 7889–7900.

Albert Q Jiang, Alexandre Sablayrolles, Antoine Roux, Arthur Mensch, Blanche Savary, Chris Bamford, Devendra Singh Chaplot, Diego de las Casas, Emma Bou Hanna, Florian Bressand, et al. 2024. Mixtral of experts. *arXiv preprint arXiv:2401.04088*.

Daniel Jurafsky and James H. Martin. 2024. *Speech and Language Processing: An Introduction to Natural Language Processing, Computational Linguistics, and Speech Recognition with Language Models*, 3rd edition.

Guangmin Li, Hui Wang, Yi Ding, Kangan Zhou, and Xiaowei Yan. 2023. Data augmentation for aspect-based sentiment analysis. *International Journal of Machine Learning and Cybernetics*, 14(1):125–133.

Jian Liu, Zhiyang Teng, Leyang Cui, Hanmeng Liu, and Yue Zhang. 2021. Solving aspect category sentiment analysis as a text generation task. In *Proceedings of the 2021 Conference on Empirical Methods in Natural Language Processing*, pages 4406–4416.

Edward Loper and Steven Bird. 2002. Nltk: The natural language toolkit. In *Proceedings of the ACL-02 Workshop on Effective Tools and Methodologies for Teaching Natural Language Processing and Computational Linguistics*, pages 63–70.

Yaojie Lu, Qing Liu, Dai Dai, Xinyan Xiao, Hongyu Lin, Xianpei Han, Le Sun, and Hua Wu. 2022. Unified structure generation for universal information extraction. In *Proceedings of the 60th Annual Meeting of the Association for Computational Linguistics (Volume 1: Long Papers)*, pages 5755–5772.

Maria Pontiki, Dimitrios Galanis, Haris Papageorgiou, Ion Androutsopoulos, Suresh Manandhar, Mohammad Al-Smadi, Mahmoud Al-Ayyoub, Yanyan Zhao, Bing Qin, Orphée De Clercq, et al. 2016. Semeval-2016 task 5: Aspect based sentiment analysis. In *International workshop on semantic evaluation*, pages 19–30.

Maria Pontiki, Dimitrios Galanis, Harris Papageorgiou, Suresh Manandhar, and Ion Androutsopoulos. 2015. Semeval-2015 task 12: Aspect based sentiment analysis. In *Proceedings of the 9th international workshop on semantic evaluation (SemEval 2015)*, pages 486–495.

Maria Pontiki, Dimitris Galanis, John Pavlopoulos, Harris Papageorgiou, Ion Androutsopoulos, and Suresh Manandhar. 2014. Semeval-2014 task 4: Aspect based sentiment analysis. In *Proceedings of the 8th International Workshop on Semantic Evaluation (SemEval 2014)*, pages 27–35, Dublin, Ireland. Association for Computational Linguistics.

Colin Raffel, Noam Shazeer, Adam Roberts, Katherine Lee, Sharan Narang, Michael Matena, Yanqi Zhou, Wei Li, and Peter J Liu. 2020. Exploring the limits of transfer learning with a unified text-to-text transformer. *Journal of machine learning research*, 21(140):1–67.

Cen Song, Jingquan Guo, and Jun Zhuang. 2020. Analyzing passengers' emotions following flight delays-a 2011–2019 case study on skytrax comments. *Journal of Air Transport Management*, 89:101903.

A Vaswani. 2017. Attention is all you need. *Advances in Neural Information Processing Systems*.

Hai Wan, Yufei Yang, Jianfeng Du, Yanan Liu, Kunxun Qi, and Jeff Z Pan. 2020. Target-aspect-sentiment joint detection for aspect-based sentiment analysis. In *Proceedings of the AAAI conference on artificial intelligence*, volume 34, pages 9122–9129.

Lei Wang, Wanyu Xu, Yihuai Lan, Zhiqiang Hu, Yunshi Lan, Roy Ka-Wei Lee, and Ee-Peng Lim. 2023a. Plan-and-solve prompting: Improving zero-shot chain-of-thought reasoning by large language models. In *Proceedings of the 61st Annual Meeting of the Association for Computational Linguistics (Volume 1: Long Papers)*, pages 2609–2634.

Shuhe Wang, Xiaofei Sun, Xiaoya Li, Rongbin Ouyang, Fei Wu, Tianwei Zhang, Jiwei Li, and Guoyin Wang. 2023b. Gpt-ner: Named entity recognition via large language models. *arXiv preprint arXiv:2304.10428*.

Xuezhi Wang, Jason Wei, Dale Schuurmans, Quoc V Le, Ed H Chi, Sharan Narang, Aakanksha Chowdhery, and Denny Zhou. 2022a. Self-consistency improves chain of thought reasoning in language models. In *The Eleventh International Conference on Learning Representations*.

Yaqing Wang, Song Wang, Yanyan Li, and Dejing Dou. 2022b. Recognizing medical search query intent by few-shot learning. In *Proceedings of the 45th International ACM SIGIR Conference on Research and Development in Information Retrieval*, pages 502–512.

Zhiqiang Wang, Yiran Pang, and Yanbin Lin. 2023c. Large language models are zero-shot text classifiers. *arXiv preprint arXiv:2312.01044*.

Jason Wei, Xuezhi Wang, Dale Schuurmans, Maarten Bosma, Fei Xia, Ed Chi, Quoc V Le, Denny Zhou, et al. 2022. Chain-of-thought prompting elicits reasoning in large language models. *Advances in neural information processing systems*, 35:24824–24837.

Chengyan Wu, Bolei Ma, Zheyu Zhang, Ningyuan Deng, Yanqing He, and Yun Xue. 2024. Evaluating zero-shot multilingual aspect-based sentiment analysis with large language models. *arXiv preprint arXiv:2412.12564*.

Wenxuan Zhang, Yang Deng, Xin Li, Yifei Yuan, Lidong Bing, and Wai Lam. 2021a. Aspect sentiment quad prediction as paraphrase generation. In *Proceedings of the 2021 Conference on Empirical Methods in Natural Language Processing*, pages 9209–9219.

Wenxuan Zhang, Yue Deng, Bing Liu, Sinno Pan, and Lidong Bing. 2024. Sentiment analysis in the era of large language models: A reality check. In *Findings of the Association for Computational Linguistics: NAACL 2024*, pages 3881–3906.

Wenxuan Zhang, Xin Li, Yang Deng, Lidong Bing, and Wai Lam. 2021b. Towards generative aspect-based sentiment analysis. In *Proceedings of the 59th Annual Meeting of the Association for Computational Linguistics and the 11th International Joint Conference on Natural Language Processing (Volume 2: Short Papers)*, pages 504–510.

Wenxuan Zhang, Xin Li, Yang Deng, Lidong Bing, and Wai Lam. 2022. A survey on aspect-based sentiment analysis: Tasks, methods, and challenges. *IEEE Transactions on Knowledge and Data Engineering*, 35(11):11019–11038.

A OATS Datasets Preprocessing

Since the OATS corpora, unlike Rest15 and Rest16 Zhang et al. (2021a), include examples where no quadruples were annotated, we excluded these instances as it is the case for Rest15, Rest16 and FlightABSA.

Two limitations of the OATS corpora led to a different approach for train-test-validation split. First, of the 7,188 (OATS Coursera) and 7,834 (OATS Hotels) training examples, 5,887 and 5,304 respectively included at least one annotated quadruple. Approaches relying on the training set would require significant training time when employing more than 5000 samples (which are also compared with the LLM's performance scores). Secondly, the test set contained only 130 examples with at least one annotated quadruple. Due to these limitations, we decided to employ samples from the training set for our analysis. Hence, we took 2,000 examples from the training sets and a train-test-validation split (70:20:10) was applied.

B FlightABSA Dataset

B.1 Data Acquisition

FlightABSA comprises reviews posted on Tripadvisor on the 20 European airlines with the highest passenger volumes in 2023, according to the *CAPA Centre for Aviation*[6]. We collected reviews posted between January 1, 2023 and September 24, 2024. This period was selected as it follows the lifting of hygiene measures related to the COVID-19 pandemic, which had been a frequent topic in earlier reviews. A maximum of the first 300 sub-pages listing the reviews on each airline were crawled.

In total, 15,493 reviews were gathered. Non-English reviews were filtered out using *langdetect*[7], resulting in 15,483 reviews. Named entity recognition (NER) was applied using *spaCy* (*en_core_news_lg* model) (Honnibal and Montani, 2017) to anonymize references to locations, personal names, and time-related information. Identified entities were replaced with placeholders *"LOC"*, *"PERSON"*, and *"DATE"*. Finally, the reviews were segmented into 52,098 sentences using the NLTK Tokenizer (Loper and Bird, 2002).

[6]List of Europe's top 20 airlines: `https://centreforaviation.com/analysis/reports/europes-top-20-airline-groups-by-pax-2023-ryanairs-lead-is-set-to-endure-68011`

[7]langdetect: `https://pypi.org/project/langdetect`

Aspect Category	Positive Explicit	Positive Implicit	Negative Explicit	Negative Implicit	Neutral Explicit	Neutral Implicit	Total Explicit	Total Implicit
AIRLINE#GENERAL	203	86	137	94	13	11	353	191
AIRLINE#PRICE	21	12	37	29	-	-	58	41
AIRLINE#SERVICE	442	28	178	42	7	2	627	72
AIRPORT#OPERATION#BAGGAGE	14	-	38	1	1	-	53	1
AIRPORT#OPERATION#BOARDING	20	2	18	-	-	-	38	2
AIRPORT#OPERATION#CHECK_IN	50	-	25	1	4	-	79	1
ONBOARD#CLEANLINESS	24	1	11	-	1	-	36	1
ONBOARD#ENTERTAINMENT	19	1	13	-	4	-	36	1
ONBOARD#FOOD	68	-	67	1	15	1	150	2
ONBOARD#PRICE	5	-	5	1	-	-	10	1
ONBOARD#SEAT#COMFORT	42	1	50	4	3	-	95	5
ONBOARD#SEAT#LEGROOM	32	-	21	-	2	-	55	-
PUNCTUALITY#GENERAL	42	18	95	51	1	1	138	70
Total	982	149	695	224	51	15	1728	388

(a) Training set

Aspect Category	Positive Explicit	Positive Implicit	Negative Explicit	Negative Implicit	Neutral Explicit	Neutral Implicit	Total Explicit	Total Implicit
AIRLINE#GENERAL	64	19	43	25	4	1	111	45
AIRLINE#PRICE	8	4	7	8	-	-	15	12
AIRLINE#SERVICE	105	8	54	13	2	-	161	21
AIRPORT#OPERATION#BAGGAGE	3	-	13	-	-	-	16	-
AIRPORT#OPERATION#BOARDING	5	-	4	3	-	-	9	3
AIRPORT#OPERATION#CHECK_IN	14	-	7	1	-	-	21	1
ONBOARD#CLEANLINESS	6	1	2	-	1	-	9	1
ONBOARD#ENTERTAINMENT	4	-	7	-	-	-	11	-
ONBOARD#FOOD	21	-	26	-	4	-	51	-
ONBOARD#PRICE	1	-	-	2	-	-	1	2
ONBOARD#SEAT#COMFORT	10	-	16	3	1	-	27	3
ONBOARD#SEAT#LEGROOM	6	-	7	1	-	-	13	1
PUNCTUALITY#GENERAL	16	4	18	17	1	-	35	21
Total	263	36	204	73	13	1	480	110

(b) Test set

Aspect Category	Positive Explicit	Positive Implicit	Negative Explicit	Negative Implicit	Neutral Explicit	Neutral Implicit	Total Explicit	Total Implicit
AIRLINE#GENERAL	32	16	18	15	1	1	51	32
AIRLINE#PRICE	3	3	4	4	-	-	7	7
AIRLINE#SERVICE	61	5	30	7	2	-	93	12
AIRPORT#OPERATION#BAGGAGE	2	-	6	-	-	-	8	-
AIRPORT#OPERATION#BOARDING	5	-	2	-	-	-	7	-
AIRPORT#OPERATION#CHECK_IN	6	2	5	-	-	-	11	2
ONBOARD#CLEANLINESS	2	2	1	1	-	-	3	3
ONBOARD#ENTERTAINMENT	2	-	2	-	-	-	4	-
ONBOARD#FOOD	13	-	7	-	1	-	21	-
ONBOARD#PRICE	1	-	2	-	-	-	3	-
ONBOARD#SEAT#COMFORT	5	-	12	2	-	-	17	2
ONBOARD#SEAT#LEGROOM	5	-	2	-	-	-	7	-
PUNCTUALITY#GENERAL	4	1	17	6	-	-	21	7
Total	141	29	108	35	4	1	253	65

(c) Develop set

Table 4: Overview of FlightABSA. Aspect categories distribution per sentiment polarity and reference type.

B.2 Data Annotation

4,000 sentences were randomly chosen from the 52,098 sentences. We ensure that there is an equal number of sentences from reviews with 1-, 2-, 3-, 4-, or 5-star ratings in order to achieve, that the number of aspects expressing positive, negative, or neutral sentiment is equal to some extent.

We aimed to obtain about 2,000 sentences, acknowledging that some of the 4,000 sentences might (1) not address any of the considered aspect categories, (2) not express any sentiment towards at least one of the considered aspect categories, (3) not be in English but in another language, or (4) be incorrectly tokenized by the NLTK tokenizer, with the annotators identifying multiple sentences instead of one.

B.2.1 Annotation Task

In line with Zhang et al. (2021a), all opinion expressions were annotated in the format of (a, c, o, p)-quadruples. Similar to the ASQP datasets Rest15 and Rest16 introduced by Zhang et al. (2021a), a total of 13 aspect categories were considered for annotation. These are as follows:

AIRLINE#GENERAL
AIRLINE#PRICE
AIRLINE#SERVICE
AIRPORT-OPERATION#BAGGAGE
AIRPORT-OPERATION#BOARDING
AIRPORT-OPERATION#CHECK-IN
ONBOARD#CLEANLINESS
ONBOARD#ENTERTAINMENT
ONBOARD#FOOD
ONBOARD#PRICE
ONBOARD#SEAT-COMFORT
ONBOARD#SEAT-LEGROOM
PUNCTUALITY#GENERAL

Reviewers on Tripadvisor are provided with multiple evaluation criteria and can optionally rate those on a scale of one to five stars in addition to submitting a written review. Since we intended to consider 13 aspect categories, similarly to Zhang et al. (2021a), we adapted Tripadvisor's nine categories and made several modifications. Specifically, we divided the 'Check-in and boarding' category into two distinct aspects of a parent category named 'Airport Operation' and also added an attribute 'baggage', resulting in three attributes of that parent category. The 'Price' category was further refined to separately consider the price of onboard offers and the airline's overall pricing.

Since we capture various aspects related to different aspects of the onboard experience, we did not include a separate 'Onboard Experience' category, as it can be found on Tripadvisor. Instead, we considered an additional category, PUNCTUALITY#GENERAL. Song et al. (2020) demonstrated that flight delays have a significant impact on overall satisfaction with the flight experience. Lastly, we introduced the AIRLINE#GENERAL category to encompass general aspects associated with the airline.

B.2.2 Data Labelling Process

Annotators were provided with an annotation guideline[8], adapted from the SemEval-2015 guideline (Pontiki et al., 2015), with modifications for the airline domain. Instead of examples from restaurant reviews, examples from airline reviews were provided.

Similar to the approach applied for SemEval-2015 by Pontiki et al. (2015), annotator *A* annotated all 3,700 sentences, while annotator *B* reviewed the annotations and, where necessary, proposed a revised annotation. Both Annotators *A* and *B* were PhD students with prior experience in annotating datasets for ABSA. The annotation process was conducted using *Google Sheets*[9].

In 115 out of 4,000 sentences, annotator *B* suggested a different label than annotator *A*. Of these 115 proposed revised annotation, 79 were accepted by annotator *A*. For the other 36 suggested revisions, it was jointly decided that in 25 cases the original annotation by Annotator *A* would be retained and in nine cases, the annotation by annotator *B* was chosen. For the remaining two sentences, a consensus was reached on an annotation distinct from their initially proposed labels.

Of the 4,000 annotated examples, 61 were excluded since a sentence-splitting error made by the NLTK tokenizer was identified by the annotators. 1,909 were further excluded as no sentiment was expressed towards the considered aspect categories. 99 sentences were excluded due to an error where either sensitive data was not anonymized or parts of a sentence were anonymized where no anonymization was required. Finally, one non-English sentence was excluded. This resulted in a dataset of 1,930 sentences.

B.3 Dataset Properties

The properties of the FlightABSA dataset (training and test sets) are presented in Table 4. A train-test-validation split (70:20:10) of the entire dataset was applied.

Notably, similar to the SemEval datasets, there is a low representation of neutral opinions and implicit aspects. Class-imbalance can also be observed in the aspect categories. For instance, the category ONBOARD#PRICE appears only 17 times in the overall dataset, while the category AIRLINE#SERVICE occurs 986 times.

[8]Annotation guidelines: https://github.com/NilsHellwig/llm-prompting-asqp/blob/main/Guidelines_FlightABSA.pdf

[9]Google Sheets: https://workspace.google.com/products/sheets

C Prompt

```
According to the following sentiment elements definition:

- The 'aspect term' is the exact word or phrase in the text that represents a specific feature, attribute, or aspect of a product or
service that a user may express an opinion about, the aspect term might be 'NULL' for implicit aspect.
- The 'aspect category' refers to the category that aspect belongs to, and the available categories includes: 'ambience general',
'drinks prices', 'drinks quality', 'drinks style_options', 'food general', 'food prices', 'food quality', 'food style_options',
'location general', 'restaurant general', 'restaurant miscellaneous', 'restaurant prices', 'service general'.
- The 'sentiment polarity' refers to the degree of positivity, negativity or neutrality expressed in the opinion towards a particular
aspect or feature of a product or service, and the available polarities include: 'positive', 'negative' and 'neutral'.
- The 'opinion term' is the exact word or phrase in the text that refers to the sentiment or attitude expressed by a user towards a
particular aspect or feature of a product or service, the aspect term might be 'NULL' for implicit opinion.

Recognize all sentiment elements with their corresponding aspect terms, aspect categories, sentiment polarity and opinion terms in the
following text with the format of [('aspect term', 'aspect category', 'sentiment polarity', 'opinion term'), ...].

Text: highly recommended .
Sentiment Elements: [('NULL', 'restaurant general', 'positive', 'highly recommended')]
Text: How do you rate home ?
Sentiment Elements: [('NULL', 'restaurant miscellaneous', 'positive', 'home')]
Text: Slightly above average wines start at $ 70+ with only one selection listed at $ 30+ .
Sentiment Elements: [('wines', 'drinks quality', 'negative', 'above average'), ('wines', 'drinks prices', 'negative', 'above average')]
Text: The restaurant is a bit noisy but that is something that can be overlooked once you sit down and enjoy a great meal
Sentiment Elements: [('meal', 'food quality', 'positive', 'enjoy'), ('meal', 'food quality', 'positive', 'great'), ('restaurant',
'ambience general', 'negative', 'noisy')]
Text: Taxan delicious !
Sentiment Elements: [('Taxan', 'food quality', 'positive', 'delicious')]
Text: The hanger steak was like rubber and the tuna was flavorless not to mention it tasted like it had just been thawed .
Sentiment Elements: [('hanger steak', 'food quality', 'negative', 'rubber'), ('tuna', 'food quality', 'negative', 'flavorless')]
Text: Worth the trip from Manhattan .
Sentiment Elements: [('NULL', 'restaurant general', 'positive', 'Worth')]
Text: I would highly recommend .
Sentiment Elements: [('NULL', 'restaurant general', 'positive', 'highly recommend')]
Text: I 'm not sure where the other reviewers ate but it seems as if we visited two different restaurants because my friends and I all
enjoy Mizu very much ... and we 're repeat customers .
Sentiment Elements: [('Mizu', 'restaurant general', 'positive', 'enjoy')]
Text: We were very pleasantly surprised .
Sentiment Elements: [('NULL', 'restaurant general', 'positive', 'pleasantly surprised')]
Text: Gross food - Wow -
Sentiment Elements:
```

Figure 3: Example of a prompt employed for the ASQP task. The prompt comprises an explanation on the considered sentiment elements, output format and annotated examples in the case of few-shot learning.

D TASD: Performance Scores

Method	Prompting Strategy	# Few-Shot / # Train	Rest15 F1	Rest15 Pre	Rest15 Rec	Rest16 F1	Rest16 Pre	Rest16 Rec	FlightABSA F1	FlightABSA Pre	FlightABSA Rec	OATS Coursera F1	OATS Coursera Pre	OATS Coursera Rec	OATS Hotels F1	OATS Hotels Pre	OATS Hotels Rec
Gemma-3-4B	-	0	17.31	17.44	17.18	25.37	26.27	24.54	31.00	31.97	30.13	15.93	16.09	15.78	25.24	29.10	22.29
		10	25.56	27.22	24.09	32.88	36.23	30.10	35.35	39.13	32.25	27.19	27.60	26.80	35.35	41.51	30.78
		20	36.20	37.64	34.86	40.47	41.46	39.53	32.39	34.76	30.32	31.10	30.99	31.23	36.02	39.40	33.20
		30	37.69	39.89	35.74	42.14	42.62	**41.68**	35.42	37.02	33.95	34.33	34.35	34.34	38.61	40.98	36.50
		40	39.99	41.31	38.77	41.93	42.80	41.14	38.95	40.05	37.92	35.68	35.46	**35.94**	42.12	43.32	41.02
		50	40.64	42.45	**39.01**	41.05	41.97	40.21	38.93	39.15	**38.71**	35.44	35.59	35.33	43.29	44.92	**41.78**
	SC	0	20.84	32.82	15.27	29.18	50.00	20.61	36.66	55.34	27.41	18.54	35.88	12.50	28.16	59.49	18.44
		10	28.72	51.69	19.88	38.53	**64.48**	27.47	40.41	**63.31**	29.68	36.68	**63.32**	25.82	40.28	**72.92**	27.82
		20	43.16	**62.28**	33.02	46.22	59.67	37.72	36.06	55.73	26.65	35.93	57.99	26.02	40.17	64.11	29.25
		30	41.65	56.73	32.90	**47.18**	59.71	39.00	39.21	57.04	29.87	**41.09**	56.23	32.38	42.00	60.66	32.11
		40	**44.20**	58.22	35.62	45.56	55.72	38.53	43.21	57.55	34.59	39.44	51.49	31.97	**47.51**	61.68	38.63
		50	43.29	55.45	35.50	44.27	54.81	37.14	**45.23**	60.00	36.29	39.37	54.12	30.94	45.52	59.84	36.72
Gemma-3-27B	-	0	29.97	28.91	31.10	45.53	44.38	46.73	51.20	46.88	56.41	29.38	26.67	32.70	38.90	36.84	41.21
		10	53.22	54.29	52.19	65.52	66.18	64.87	59.72	58.69	60.79	39.96	39.77	40.16	55.25	55.80	54.72
		20	57.95	59.85	56.17	67.00	67.80	66.22	59.33	59.07	59.58	44.84	45.79	43.93	55.77	56.62	54.94
		30	60.17	63.48	**57.18**	67.03	68.26	65.84	60.75	61.02	60.49	45.97	46.89	45.08	58.85	60.88	56.95
		40	59.87	63.31	56.78	66.51	68.29	64.82	60.28	61.20	59.40	43.60	45.41	41.93	58.74	61.92	55.87
		50	59.77	63.13	56.76	65.44	66.72	64.21	60.01	59.63	60.42	41.52	43.45	39.75	59.09	63.09	55.58
	SC	0	30.36	29.41	31.36	45.51	44.49	46.57	51.81	47.55	56.90	29.50	26.95	32.58	38.97	37.12	41.02
		10	54.47	56.40	52.66	66.75	68.38	65.19	60.36	59.85	60.87	41.69	43.11	40.37	56.51	57.93	55.17
		20	59.06	61.65	56.69	67.82	69.34	**66.36**	60.79	61.67	59.92	47.28	50.47	44.47	57.26	59.52	55.17
		30	61.29	66.07	57.16	**68.93**	**71.84**	66.24	62.38	64.39	60.49	**49.55**	**54.70**	**45.29**	60.83	65.33	56.92
		40	61.18	65.80	57.16	68.05	71.30	65.08	62.86	65.64	60.30	45.70	51.01	41.39	61.75	67.04	**57.23**
		50	**62.12**	**68.03**	57.16	68.53	71.52	65.77	**64.60**	**66.33**	**62.95**	44.80	51.32	39.75	**62.97**	**70.47**	56.92
MVP (Gou et al., 2023)		10	25.08	30.30	21.40	17.08	18.13	16.16	19.04	22.53	16.48	31.83	35.26	29.02	21.16	25.90	17.90
		20	32.88	36.45	29.96	28.35	30.55	26.50	23.25	27.35	20.23	34.26	37.99	31.19	27.02	33.95	22.45
		30	36.34	40.19	33.18	39.04	41.81	36.62	31.06	35.91	27.37	35.44	38.57	32.79	37.06	42.95	32.59
		40	41.07	44.05	38.46	41.04	43.80	38.60	37.20	41.33	33.84	36.76	40.06	33.98	41.56	48.19	36.53
		50	42.13	45.54	39.20	44.09	46.91	41.58	44.11	47.92	40.87	37.84	41.35	34.88	44.49	51.12	39.40
		800	62.54	**64.87**	**60.38**	68.22	**69.24**	**67.24**	64.61	64.72	64.50	50.61	51.33	49.92	66.67	67.51	65.85
		Full	**64.53**	-	-	**72.76**	-	-	**68.67**	**67.84**	**69.53**	**50.97**	**51.42**	**50.53**	**69.37**	**69.58**	**69.16**
DLO (Hu et al., 2022)	-	10	15.84	19.23	13.47	13.59	13.27	13.95	16.07	19.02	13.91	22.93	25.45	20.86	18.07	18.84	17.39
		20	25.12	23.67	26.77	22.57	19.17	27.52	22.14	26.13	19.21	27.99	30.97	25.53	27.49	27.76	27.31
		30	31.12	31.08	31.17	35.07	33.63	36.69	30.64	33.08	28.54	33.00	35.35	30.94	37.17	37.91	36.47
		40	38.02	38.34	37.70	39.44	38.79	40.14	36.07	37.29	34.93	33.31	36.03	30.98	40.89	44.19	38.06
		50	39.54	40.48	38.65	43.95	44.59	43.33	42.92	42.01	43.89	36.04	39.26	33.32	44.72	49.18	41.02
		800	62.48	**64.35**	**60.71**	69.98	**69.90**	**70.06**	68.22	68.02	68.43	**52.74**	**53.29**	52.21	68.46	**68.69**	68.24
		Full	**62.95**	-	-	**71.79**	-	-	**68.95**	**68.60**	**69.30**	52.58	52.79	**52.38**	**68.56**	68.41	**68.71**
Paraphrase (Zhang et al., 2021a)		10	8.75	10.72	7.38	6.66	7.61	5.93	8.82	10.44	7.64	15.94	17.69	14.51	14.91	18.74	12.39
		20	21.09	21.04	21.40	18.05	16.87	19.53	8.60	10.18	7.45	20.38	22.11	18.93	18.84	21.21	17.20
		30	21.83	22.03	21.87	17.46	17.18	18.08	12.08	13.27	11.12	22.45	23.51	21.68	25.18	22.47	29.33
		40	31.01	33.70	28.76	28.88	29.96	27.90	26.82	30.07	24.23	30.90	34.18	28.20	36.35	38.86	34.36
		50	36.92	39.57	34.60	35.87	37.18	34.66	33.57	36.10	31.38	34.26	37.64	31.43	40.10	45.21	36.05
		800	61.54	**63.54**	**59.67**	69.31	**69.37**	**69.25**	67.69	69.41	66.05	51.36	52.58	50.20	67.48	**68.80**	66.21
		Full	**63.06**	-	-	**71.97**	-	-	**69.74**	**70.22**	**69.26**	**51.86**	**52.73**	**51.02**	**67.70**	68.41	**67.01**

Table 5: Performance scores for TASD. For the Rest15 and Rest16 datasets, performance scores achieved when employing the full training set ("Full") are taken from Gou et al. (2023), Hu et al. (2022) and Zhang et al. (2021b) for MVP, DLO and Paraphrase, respectively. The best score achieved by a method is presented in bold.

E Element-Level Performance Scores

E.1 ASQP

Sentiment Element	Prompting Strategy	# Few-Shot / # Train	Rest15			Rest16			FlightABSA			OATS Coursera			OATS Hotels		
			F1	Pre	Rec	F1	Pre	Rec	F1	Pre	Rec	F1	Pre	Rec	F1	Pre	Rec
Aspect Term	-	0	61.71	50.99	**78.14**	68.19	58.76	81.21	61.52	51.71	**75.92**	52.53	39.63	77.87	60.89	50.83	**75.93**
		10	67.23	60.77	75.26	74.74	68.93	81.63	67.36	62.73	72.75	67.79	59.23	**79.24**	71.25	67.48	75.47
		20	68.63	65.08	72.61	76.95	72.34	**82.23**	68.67	66.27	71.28	**73.32**	69.47	77.66	73.27	71.50	75.15
		30	66.13	67.20	65.10	75.63	72.36	79.22	71.41	70.31	72.56	73.09	72.19	74.02	71.21	71.86	70.57
		40	65.39	65.93	64.86	74.42	71.00	78.19	70.54	70.56	70.57	70.22	69.55	70.93	71.20	71.64	70.80
		50	68.27	66.92	69.68	73.17	70.08	76.56	69.46	66.09	73.22	69.09	66.70	71.68	70.99	72.73	69.34
	SC	0	62.37	52.20	77.47	69.53	61.19	80.50	61.46	52.24	74.64	54.20	41.62	77.66	60.97	51.33	75.06
		10	68.24	62.94	74.51	75.47	70.63	81.03	67.88	65.14	70.85	66.98	61.99	72.85	70.68	70.20	71.17
		20	67.82	66.17	69.57	**78.13**	76.53	79.79	69.23	70.24	68.25	72.63	74.19	71.13	**73.47**	75.42	71.62
		30	65.26	69.82	61.26	76.12	74.32	78.01	71.38	72.15	70.62	70.87	77.02	65.64	70.90	77.66	65.22
		40	64.86	68.65	61.46	75.09	73.80	76.42	**73.23**	**77.17**	69.67	70.11	**79.22**	62.89	72.21	78.86	66.59
		50	**69.03**	**70.75**	67.39	75.00	**76.67**	73.40	73.03	73.56	72.51	67.42	75.11	61.17	71.63	**79.78**	64.99
Opinion Term	-	0	64.12	59.70	69.25	69.17	65.11	**73.78**	63.00	58.85	**67.80**	30.83	26.73	36.43	42.61	42.85	42.38
		10	68.06	65.39	**70.97**	67.92	64.81	71.36	63.04	61.03	65.19	47.33	44.17	**51.00**	51.18	54.41	48.31
		20	62.76	63.71	61.83	70.73	70.14	71.33	61.73	61.02	62.47	47.97	46.06	50.05	56.42	58.35	**54.62**
		30	60.90	61.24	60.56	70.11	70.23	70.00	62.13	62.58	61.69	**49.31**	48.30	50.36	55.16	59.18	51.66
		40	61.26	60.98	61.56	68.99	68.20	69.81	59.35	61.49	57.35	48.17	47.17	49.23	55.76	60.07	52.03
		50	63.26	62.95	63.58	68.97	68.56	69.40	61.84	62.44	61.27	47.76	46.34	49.28	57.11	62.20	52.79
	SC	0	64.05	60.62	67.88	70.26	67.29	73.51	62.45	59.15	66.14	30.91	27.35	35.52	42.60	43.37	41.86
		10	**68.30**	**67.28**	69.35	68.18	66.84	69.57	**64.11**	64.92	63.32	47.23	47.18	47.29	52.10	58.51	46.95
		20	63.27	66.82	60.08	70.01	71.75	68.34	61.55	64.66	58.73	46.83	49.62	44.34	57.39	63.33	52.47
		30	60.53	65.07	56.59	**71.28**	**74.16**	68.61	62.26	66.01	58.91	48.82	54.29	44.34	56.03	65.44	48.98
		40	60.76	64.89	57.12	68.77	70.95	66.71	60.43	67.54	54.67	48.58	**56.63**	42.53	56.66	66.93	49.13
		50	62.69	66.52	59.27	69.30	73.59	65.49	63.12	**68.45**	58.55	48.52	56.46	42.53	**58.53**	**70.87**	49.85
Aspect Category	-	0	53.82	53.13	54.53	58.57	57.32	59.88	**82.73**	79.26	**86.52**	48.23	46.06	50.62	62.17	62.17	62.17
		10	71.72	72.96	70.52	78.58	78.31	78.86	82.08	80.24	84.00	48.10	48.91	47.31	66.43	70.05	63.17
		20	73.97	78.09	70.26	80.83	82.39	**79.33**	80.98	80.57	81.40	53.07	54.85	51.40	67.80	72.12	63.97
		30	74.78	78.37	71.52	80.56	82.92	78.33	79.94	80.85	79.04	**54.68**	57.68	**51.98**	**71.35**	77.40	**66.18**
		40	75.67	78.50	73.04	80.92	83.07	78.89	79.54	81.77	77.44	52.01	54.64	49.63	70.18	75.62	65.48
		50	**77.11**	80.16	**74.30**	80.81	82.86	78.86	80.49	81.49	79.52	54.07	56.43	51.90	69.45	75.58	64.24
	SC	0	53.33	53.37	53.30	58.30	57.47	59.15	82.43	79.66	85.40	48.25	46.80	49.79	62.13	62.50	61.77
		10	71.68	74.69	68.91	79.32	80.64	78.04	81.83	83.09	80.60	46.77	50.72	43.39	66.30	72.95	60.77
		20	73.11	80.17	67.19	**80.98**	85.02	77.31	79.00	82.71	75.60	54.23	61.74	48.35	66.85	75.31	60.10
		30	72.14	80.32	65.47	79.84	84.84	75.40	78.78	82.96	75.00	54.30	**65.69**	46.28	70.96	**83.67**	61.60
		40	74.69	82.75	68.05	79.63	85.28	74.67	78.34	**86.47**	71.60	50.69	64.04	41.94	69.04	81.41	59.93
		50	75.67	**84.33**	68.62	80.51	**87.33**	74.67	80.17	86.37	74.80	51.00	64.56	42.15	68.36	82.70	58.26
Sentiment Polarity	-	0	87.89	86.85	88.96	90.42	89.55	91.31	91.16	88.64	93.84	85.16	84.25	86.10	88.44	87.78	**89.10**
		10	90.84	91.01	90.67	92.54	92.67	92.41	93.29	92.46	**94.13**	88.62	89.87	87.41	87.91	92.32	83.92
		20	**92.24**	93.47	**91.04**	94.07	94.85	**93.31**	93.34	93.10	93.59	**90.43**	91.43	**89.46**	89.77	94.24	85.71
		30	91.88	93.87	89.98	94.25	95.28	93.24	**94.13**	94.57	93.69	89.10	91.56	86.78	89.56	95.17	84.58
		40	91.69	93.91	89.57	**94.30**	95.57	93.07	93.41	94.68	92.18	89.68	91.96	87.51	**90.33**	95.48	85.71
		50	91.58	93.42	89.81	94.21	95.28	93.17	93.21	93.81	92.62	89.72	91.83	87.71	89.60	95.57	84.34
	SC	0	87.47	87.24	87.69	90.28	90.05	90.52	90.54	88.73	92.42	85.44	85.02	85.85	88.37	88.06	88.68
		10	89.72	91.47	88.03	91.50	93.05	90.00	91.91	93.65	90.22	85.49	91.16	80.49	86.19	94.13	79.48
		20	89.98	94.37	85.98	92.62	95.60	89.83	91.16	94.26	88.26	84.39	92.20	77.80	87.18	95.51	80.19
		30	87.71	94.65	81.71	91.89	96.23	87.93	91.23	94.97	87.78	81.49	93.95	71.95	85.41	96.44	76.65
		40	87.58	**94.82**	81.37	91.12	95.99	86.72	88.60	**95.48**	82.64	76.86	92.76	65.61	86.01	96.48	77.59
		50	87.85	94.31	82.22	90.98	**96.52**	86.03	89.97	94.85	85.57	78.46	**94.50**	67.07	84.31	**96.65**	74.76

Table 6: Gemma-3-27B: Performance scores at element-level for the ASQP task. The best score achieved with respect to a sentiment element is presented in bold.

Sentiment Element	Prompting Strategy	# Few-Shot / # Train	Rest15			Rest16			FlightABSA			OATS Coursera			OATS Hotels		
			F1	**Pre**	**Rec**	**F1**	**Pre**	**Rec**	**F1**	**Pre**	**Rec**	**F1**	**Pre**	**Rec**	**F1**	**Pre**	**Rec**
Aspect Term	-	0	42.65	40.10	45.57	47.24	46.76	47.73	41.88	44.14	39.86	42.38	38.79	46.74	48.45	52.61	44.94
		10	44.72	51.77	39.37	43.20	60.32	33.69	46.49	57.73	38.96	58.02	60.39	55.88	50.93	66.01	41.56
		20	54.07	63.55	47.08	56.39	68.74	47.84	46.03	59.07	37.73	61.45	66.57	57.11	56.04	70.06	46.73
		30	53.00	63.18	45.69	**57.79**	72.11	**48.26**	46.91	59.23	38.86	63.85	69.52	59.11	54.14	71.10	43.75
		40	50.04	64.61	40.87	55.96	68.92	47.13	48.45	61.49	40.00	66.97	71.39	63.09	**59.82**	75.44	**49.61**
		50	**56.24**	67.42	**48.26**	55.65	71.51	45.60	**51.23**	61.49	**43.93**	**68.95**	74.19	**64.40**	59.81	76.22	49.24
	SC	0	21.48	71.11	12.65	20.03	69.47	11.70	28.19	76.04	17.30	18.56	72.09	10.65	27.60	79.35	16.70
		10	12.48	**87.18**	6.72	13.07	83.33	7.09	15.42	80.00	8.53	12.74	86.96	6.87	19.55	88.89	10.98
		20	31.07	85.71	18.97	34.51	85.31	21.63	14.29	82.50	7.82	23.88	90.91	13.75	31.95	89.47	19.45
		30	33.85	78.99	21.54	40.71	**86.71**	26.60	23.69	77.63	13.98	29.15	**96.15**	17.18	26.80	88.46	15.79
		40	32.75	83.74	20.36	46.57	86.12	31.91	27.95	**82.56**	16.82	36.41	87.01	23.02	39.86	92.50	25.40
		50	44.57	83.24	30.43	42.91	84.82	28.72	40.93	82.14	27.25	38.93	86.90	25.09	40.58	**97.39**	25.63
Opinion Term	-	0	30.92	33.74	28.55	31.50	34.56	28.94	25.50	30.46	21.94	19.31	20.36	18.37	23.71	31.51	19.01
		10	34.53	39.54	30.65	37.36	41.95	33.70	30.56	37.51	25.82	19.77	19.99	19.55	22.96	28.93	19.04
		20	38.89	41.66	36.48	46.82	50.41	43.72	31.00	36.42	26.98	24.05	23.29	24.89	30.04	33.62	**27.15**
		30	43.28	45.24	41.51	48.23	52.42	44.67	36.58	42.66	32.03	27.39	26.89	**27.92**	27.15	36.02	21.80
		40	44.38	45.72	43.12	52.42	54.53	**50.49**	36.23	42.56	31.53	**27.65**	29.06	26.38	29.80	39.22	24.04
		50	**48.43**	50.02	**46.94**	**52.56**	55.77	49.70	**43.89**	49.32	**39.54**	26.81	28.96	24.98	**32.82**	42.88	26.60
	SC	0	15.73	69.47	8.87	15.38	66.67	8.70	17.77	60.82	10.41	7.44	42.86	4.07	14.81	61.05	8.43
		10	13.53	**79.71**	7.39	17.61	78.49	9.92	14.17	**81.48**	7.76	12.11	**78.38**	6.56	12.58	**64.00**	6.98
		20	27.59	67.54	17.34	34.30	**81.22**	21.74	14.06	74.58	7.76	15.63	68.42	8.82	20.34	60.87	12.21
		30	34.91	73.91	22.85	38.27	78.81	25.27	22.97	69.64	13.76	17.73	59.74	10.41	15.74	51.20	9.30
		40	36.94	76.69	24.33	46.27	75.85	33.29	27.51	73.28	16.93	19.81	62.65	11.76	19.64	59.12	11.77
		50	43.79	74.28	31.05	45.01	74.76	32.20	39.47	77.72	26.46	22.01	62.77	13.35	21.93	58.13	13.52
Aspect Category	-	0	37.64	42.23	33.95	39.84	44.53	36.05	51.54	62.70	43.76	29.56	34.72	25.74	42.32	54.98	34.42
		10	45.75	52.79	40.37	52.52	57.49	48.35	55.00	64.50	47.96	37.10	41.08	33.84	54.40	67.51	45.58
		20	58.32	62.95	54.33	60.45	64.79	56.66	59.89	67.80	53.64	**46.24**	49.09	**43.72**	58.27	67.28	51.39
		30	62.24	66.00	58.88	66.41	71.72	61.84	63.17	71.11	56.84	43.71	45.83	41.78	61.57	68.68	55.79
		40	65.14	68.71	61.92	68.52	73.06	**64.51**	67.03	74.69	60.80	42.98	45.90	40.41	**63.61**	69.91	**58.36**
		50	**67.82**	71.86	**64.21**	**68.79**	74.81	63.66	**68.63**	74.52	**63.60**	42.88	46.89	39.50	61.46	70.48	54.49
	SC	0	13.13	55.32	7.45	15.42	63.16	8.78	26.89	84.21	16.00	10.23	61.36	5.58	23.38	86.17	13.52
		10	13.11	76.92	7.16	20.13	84.78	11.42	17.30	87.27	9.60	11.13	78.38	5.99	19.94	**91.78**	11.19
		20	35.27	85.64	22.21	36.11	82.29	23.13	18.60	88.14	10.40	16.70	**81.82**	9.30	31.34	85.19	19.20
		30	40.83	**87.32**	26.65	43.83	**88.44**	29.14	31.48	87.27	19.20	18.67	71.23	10.74	37.43	86.67	23.87
		40	41.82	85.78	27.65	52.70	86.33	37.92	36.51	88.46	23.00	22.22	69.57	13.22	43.80	90.58	28.88
		50	50.25	86.67	35.39	51.02	84.18	36.60	47.35	**89.44**	32.20	24.37	67.29	14.88	39.33	85.47	25.54
Sentiment Polarity	-	0	77.70	83.22	72.89	76.66	82.89	71.31	74.38	83.45	67.09	71.14	81.44	63.17	74.19	83.92	66.51
		10	77.94	85.50	71.62	80.40	84.25	76.90	77.53	83.91	72.08	78.14	82.50	74.24	78.03	86.94	70.80
		20	86.28	89.08	83.66	87.12	89.61	84.76	80.61	85.23	76.48	84.19	85.93	82.54	83.29	90.03	77.50
		30	87.57	90.86	84.51	88.53	92.13	85.21	81.46	85.66	77.65	82.60	84.60	80.68	87.91	91.92	84.25
		40	88.28	92.00	84.85	89.57	93.21	86.21	83.02	88.82	77.95	84.77	88.48	81.37	**90.27**	94.20	**86.65**
		50	**90.00**	93.32	**86.91**	**90.06**	94.24	**86.24**	**85.28**	89.01	**81.86**	**86.57**	90.97	**82.59**	88.85	94.23	84.06
	SC	0	26.33	**97.80**	15.21	25.85	93.55	15.00	37.30	98.95	22.98	17.70	**95.24**	9.76	34.88	97.83	21.23
		10	18.77	93.85	10.43	25.07	93.33	14.48	22.89	98.15	12.96	15.66	94.59	8.54	27.59	**98.55**	16.04
		20	44.88	96.61	29.23	46.27	95.68	30.52	25.21	**100.00**	14.43	21.55	92.59	12.20	45.05	95.42	29.48
		30	50.38	97.07	34.02	53.02	97.69	36.38	41.31	98.17	26.16	27.80	93.06	16.34	51.55	94.94	35.38
		40	51.32	97.14	34.87	64.19	**97.88**	47.76	46.64	98.43	30.56	33.60	93.33	20.49	57.10	97.71	40.33
		50	62.00	97.44	45.47	63.49	97.50	47.07	57.29	95.98	40.83	38.13	94.23	23.90	54.15	95.81	37.74

Table 7: Gemma-3-4B: Performance scores at element-level for the ASQP task. The best score achieved with respect to a sentiment element is presented in bold.

E.2 TASD

Sentiment Element	Prompting Strategy	# Few-Shot / # Train	Rest15			Rest16			FlightABSA			OATS Coursera			OATS Hotels		
			F1	Pre	Rec	F1	Pre	Rec	F1	Pre	Rec	F1	Pre	Rec	F1	Pre	Rec
Aspect Term	-	0	60.81	49.78	78.12	68.31	58.42	82.22	59.63	50.21	73.41	53.48	40.24	79.73	61.69	51.08	77.85
		10	73.78	67.50	81.37	78.07	74.59	81.90	70.06	65.93	74.74	67.85	58.58	**80.62**	74.36	69.41	80.09
		20	74.38	68.13	81.88	79.88	76.42	**83.66**	69.52	66.17	73.22	72.83	66.57	80.41	75.68	70.35	**81.88**
		30	75.50	74.29	76.75	77.98	75.74	80.36	71.41	69.07	73.93	73.84	70.11	78.01	75.42	73.19	77.80
		40	74.58	75.46	73.73	77.36	76.86	77.88	70.51	69.73	71.33	72.74	72.58	72.92	74.98	74.83	75.15
		50	74.09	73.90	74.28	76.40	75.02	77.84	70.55	66.71	74.88	70.82	70.72	71.00	74.22	74.50	73.96
	SC	0	61.28	50.30	78.41	68.49	58.78	82.03	59.85	50.49	73.46	53.89	40.70	79.73	61.61	51.29	77.12
		10	74.47	68.92	81.00	78.36	75.57	81.37	70.71	67.16	74.64	68.87	61.23	78.69	75.00	70.88	79.63
		20	75.63	69.84	**82.47**	**80.13**	77.16	83.33	70.18	68.00	72.51	73.23	69.00	78.01	76.32	72.34	80.78
		30	76.13	76.06	76.20	78.16	77.11	79.25	73.24	72.56	73.93	**76.82**	77.35	76.29	75.35	75.87	74.83
		40	75.23	76.53	73.99	78.42	**79.07**	77.78	73.27	**73.80**	72.75	73.70	76.87	70.79	**77.01**	78.57	75.51
		50	**76.25**	**78.25**	74.35	77.97	78.16	77.78	**73.85**	71.56	**76.30**	72.93	**78.57**	68.04	76.61	**80.05**	73.46
Aspect Category	-	0	56.36	56.46	56.26	72.40	71.76	73.06	82.79	79.14	**86.80**	49.68	47.86	51.65	67.23	66.23	68.25
		10	72.09	74.06	70.22	81.87	81.68	**82.07**	82.49	81.36	83.64	50.39	51.04	49.75	70.42	71.91	68.98
		20	75.99	79.55	72.75	81.52	82.57	80.48	82.08	81.61	82.56	56.17	57.95	54.50	70.32	71.85	68.85
		30	78.30	82.86	74.22	83.17	84.46	81.91	81.66	82.29	81.04	56.58	58.16	**55.08**	74.76	77.29	**72.39**
		40	79.63	84.52	**75.28**	83.74	85.62	81.94	81.61	82.86	80.40	54.72	57.21	52.44	75.01	78.98	71.42
		50	79.19	83.89	74.99	83.74	85.69	81.88	81.03	81.34	80.72	53.54	56.50	50.87	74.50	79.22	70.32
	SC	0	56.05	56.23	55.87	72.19	71.71	72.68	**82.90**	79.34	**86.80**	49.95	48.36	51.65	67.49	66.89	68.11
		10	72.98	76.16	70.06	82.44	83.06	81.83	82.59	82.18	83.00	51.08	53.64	48.76	71.55	73.98	69.28
		20	75.72	80.32	71.61	81.57	83.40	79.81	81.85	82.52	81.20	58.54	63.16	54.55	70.61	73.68	67.78
		30	78.39	84.60	73.03	83.60	86.81	80.62	80.70	83.37	78.20	**58.57**	**64.99**	53.31	75.20	80.42	70.62
		40	**80.08**	86.29	74.71	83.79	87.54	80.35	82.04	**85.31**	79.00	56.13	62.98	50.62	75.81	81.82	70.62
		50	79.02	**86.62**	72.65	**84.51**	**88.63**	80.75	80.99	83.30	78.80	55.14	63.44	48.76	**76.12**	**84.21**	69.45
Sentiment Polarity	-	0	87.13	88.58	85.73	89.63	90.49	88.79	92.21	90.18	94.33	87.22	86.55	87.90	90.32	90.21	90.42
		10	91.81	93.29	90.37	93.00	94.35	91.68	**94.77**	94.33	**95.21**	90.69	91.06	90.34	92.33	93.26	91.42
		20	92.01	93.91	90.19	93.73	95.01	92.48	93.92	93.76	94.08	**91.16**	91.79	**90.54**	**93.34**	94.45	**92.26**
		30	92.60	94.87	**90.43**	**93.79**	95.02	92.60	93.46	93.58	93.35	90.40	91.46	89.37	93.20	94.65	91.79
		40	**92.63**	95.14	90.25	93.19	94.81	91.62	94.04	94.35	93.74	90.38	92.10	88.73	93.12	95.00	91.32
		50	92.58	95.10	90.19	93.74	94.86	**92.63**	93.17	93.33	93.01	89.62	91.78	87.56	93.25	95.36	91.23
	SC	0	87.31	88.92	85.76	89.89	90.91	88.89	92.09	90.35	93.89	87.48	87.17	87.80	90.33	90.33	90.33
		10	91.43	93.81	89.16	93.13	94.89	91.43	94.23	94.58	93.89	89.53	92.69	86.59	91.98	93.43	90.57
		20	91.90	94.30	89.63	93.28	95.21	91.43	93.33	94.26	92.42	88.27	92.51	84.39	92.62	95.04	90.33
		30	91.23	94.97	87.77	93.47	**96.14**	90.95	92.27	94.15	90.46	86.61	92.76	81.22	92.48	95.25	89.86
		40	91.87	95.64	88.39	92.04	95.25	89.05	92.60	95.10	90.22	86.13	92.94	80.24	93.22	95.77	90.80
		50	91.34	**95.76**	87.31	93.05	95.95	90.32	93.38	**95.41**	91.44	85.03	**93.04**	78.29	90.68	**95.80**	86.08

Table 8: Gemma-3-27B: Performance scores at element-level for the TASD task. The best score achieved by a method is presented in bold.

Sentiment Element	Prompting Strategy	# Few-Shot / # Train	Rest15			Rest16			FlightABSA			OATS Coursera			OATS Hotels		
			F1	Pre	Rec	F1	Pre	Rec	F1	Pre	Rec	F1	Pre	Rec	F1	Pre	Rec
Aspect Term	-	0	45.84	39.99	**53.69**	45.26	42.39	48.56	45.49	43.74	**47.44**	43.44	37.18	52.23	47.20	48.69	45.81
		10	50.14	57.58	44.43	50.11	60.08	43.04	50.58	57.47	45.21	59.52	56.31	63.16	52.44	65.20	43.89
		20	55.31	61.62	50.22	57.18	69.08	**48.79**	49.27	58.16	42.84	61.42	61.52	61.37	54.01	64.87	46.27
		30	53.39	68.48	43.80	57.33	70.06	48.53	48.49	58.97	41.18	63.34	65.75	61.17	54.84	66.20	46.82
		40	53.17	68.42	43.51	54.86	69.46	45.36	49.99	59.04	43.36	65.36	67.50	**63.37**	60.71	71.67	**52.68**
		50	52.79	68.52	42.95	53.91	70.13	43.79	50.44	58.49	44.36	65.39	68.60	62.47	59.33	72.17	50.39
	SC	0	49.34	61.60	41.14	46.17	66.16	35.46	49.63	65.25	40.05	45.54	64.97	35.05	45.19	75.40	32.27
		10	40.06	**89.17**	25.83	44.92	81.20	31.05	50.16	**76.96**	37.20	59.23	87.84	44.67	47.63	82.95	33.41
		20	**55.90**	85.55	41.51	**57.42**	**85.21**	43.30	46.03	76.37	32.94	58.72	**88.28**	43.99	49.84	86.44	35.01
		30	50.00	84.96	35.42	55.39	81.33	41.99	46.43	73.71	33.89	64.22	86.13	51.20	52.02	81.46	38.22
		40	50.64	82.50	36.53	53.16	79.74	39.87	51.38	73.25	39.57	**66.39**	82.23	55.67	**62.97**	**86.75**	49.43
		50	49.87	79.44	36.35	52.37	80.13	38.89	**52.80**	76.58	40.28	65.84	82.81	54.64	57.02	80.42	44.16
Aspect Category	-	0	41.04	43.15	39.12	51.78	53.50	50.17	57.51	63.16	52.84	30.99	33.11	29.13	40.11	48.67	34.12
		10	46.48	49.13	44.10	59.96	63.91	56.47	61.46	68.78	55.56	38.23	39.88	36.74	53.64	64.45	45.94
		20	57.59	60.07	55.30	64.90	65.47	64.33	61.61	66.60	57.32	44.36	45.21	43.55	55.32	62.26	49.78
		30	61.32	64.58	58.40	69.49	69.43	**69.56**	64.34	68.59	60.60	45.98	47.03	**45.00**	60.71	65.74	56.39
		40	65.69	68.73	62.92	69.31	69.58	69.10	68.01	72.36	64.16	44.75	45.64	43.93	61.91	66.50	**57.93**
		50	**67.06**	70.52	**63.95**	**69.71**	70.48	68.96	**68.88**	72.02	**66.00**	44.53	46.02	43.14	61.05	65.65	57.06
	SC	0	34.73	53.64	25.68	45.94	73.02	33.51	51.47	77.20	38.60	26.03	50.30	17.56	34.01	70.90	22.37
		10	39.63	67.81	28.00	55.04	**84.64**	40.78	53.91	82.64	40.00	40.18	**69.19**	28.31	51.99	**93.10**	36.06
		20	53.80	74.60	42.06	63.78	78.81	53.57	52.21	78.95	39.00	42.51	68.66	30.79	52.86	84.00	38.56
		30	58.51	76.89	47.23	68.92	82.67	59.08	56.70	81.04	43.60	**46.78**	64.26	36.78	59.52	84.62	45.91
		40	64.06	**81.47**	52.77	69.12	80.50	60.57	63.61	**83.44**	51.40	45.07	59.26	36.36	61.87	80.48	50.25
		50	64.51	80.23	53.94	69.44	81.12	60.70	63.70	83.23	51.60	45.99	63.18	36.16	**62.01**	80.53	50.42
Sentiment Polarity	-	0	79.67	82.20	77.31	78.43	80.79	76.22	80.60	85.85	75.99	75.74	80.89	71.22	74.22	79.75	69.43
		10	83.94	87.02	81.08	82.67	85.67	79.87	84.04	88.10	80.34	83.15	85.44	80.98	80.60	87.82	74.48
		20	87.49	91.04	84.21	87.58	89.26	85.97	83.09	85.83	80.54	85.21	86.25	84.20	88.41	91.18	85.80
		30	87.48	90.70	84.49	88.85	90.25	87.49	83.86	86.30	81.56	85.36	86.99	83.80	90.97	93.45	88.63
		40	88.09	91.70	84.77	89.29	91.32	87.37	**86.99**	90.15	84.06	**87.25**	89.61	**85.02**	91.14	93.63	**88.77**
		50	**89.02**	92.58	**85.73**	**89.42**	91.17	**87.75**	86.95	89.33	**84.69**	85.67	89.39	82.24	**91.16**	93.99	88.49
	SC	0	62.17	91.57	47.06	60.06	91.26	44.76	70.08	95.76	55.26	50.89	94.08	34.88	56.81	96.07	40.33
		10	63.48	**96.83**	47.21	67.56	**95.64**	52.22	71.74	**98.30**	56.48	62.02	**96.89**	45.61	66.67	96.43	50.94
		20	75.21	96.14	61.76	80.44	94.83	69.84	70.92	97.44	55.75	63.46	92.52	48.29	73.21	96.53	58.96
		30	79.12	96.23	67.18	83.78	95.53	74.60	73.19	95.29	59.41	73.56	93.26	60.73	79.72	**96.96**	67.69
		40	80.43	95.14	69.66	85.81	94.99	78.25	77.76	94.10	66.26	76.92	94.98	64.63	84.57	96.95	75.00
		50	82.82	96.11	72.76	86.21	95.03	78.89	79.31	96.17	67.48	71.92	92.02	59.02	84.62	96.67	75.24

Table 9: Gemma-3-4B: Performance scores at element-level for the TASD task. The best score achieved by a method is presented in bold.

F Performance Scores: Visualization

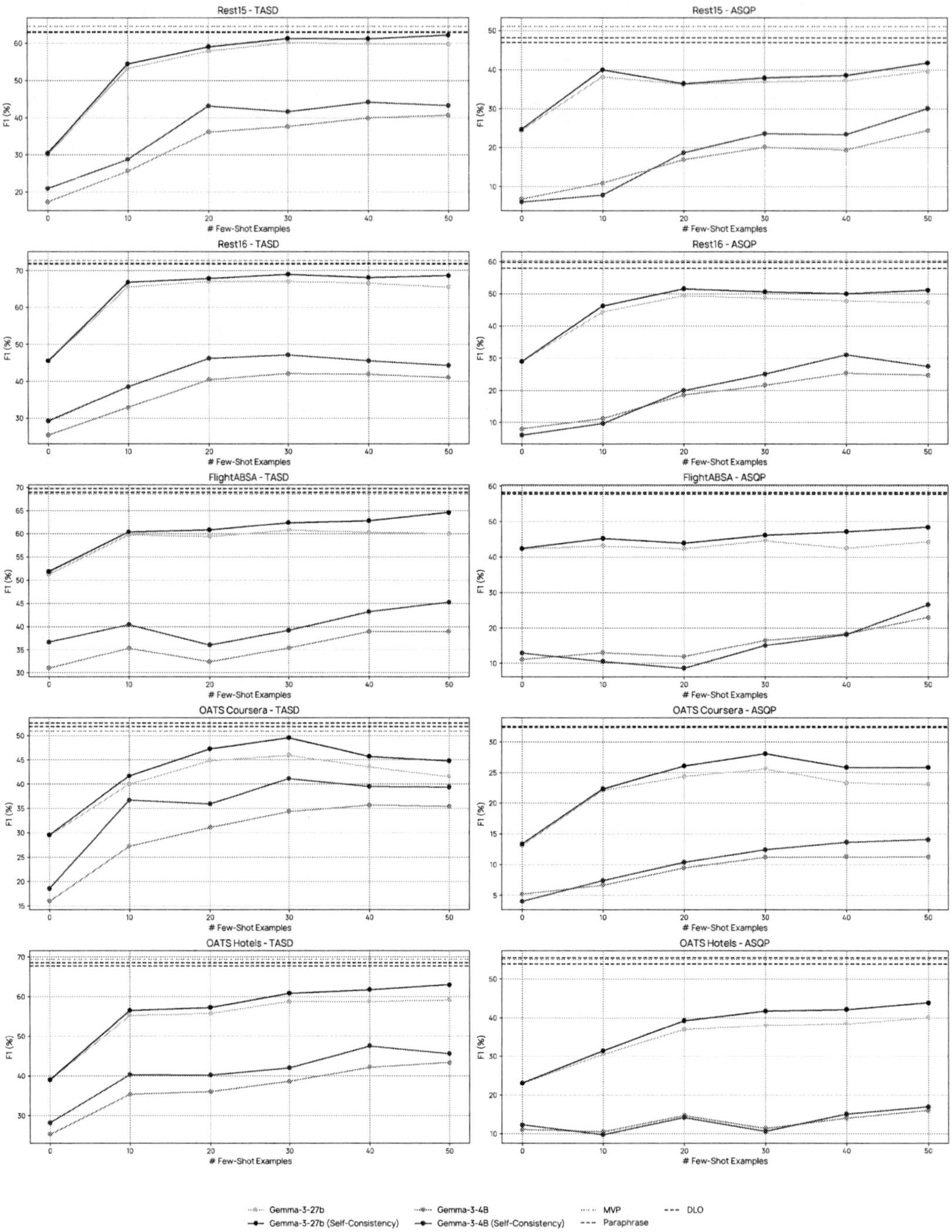

Figure 4: Influence of the amount of few-shot examples on the performance of Gemma-3-4B and Gemma-3-27B. Visualization includes comparison with performance scores of SOTA supervised methods MVP, Paraphrase and DLO.

Can LLMs Interpret and Leverage Structured Linguistic Representations? A Case Study with AMRs

Ankush Raut[1] **Xiaofeng Zhu**[2] **Maria Leonor Pacheco**[1]
[1]University of Colorado Boulder [2]Northwestern University
[1]{ankush.raut, maria.pacheco}@colorado.edu
[2]xiaofengzhu2013@u.northwestern.edu

Abstract

This paper evaluates the ability of Large Language Models (LLMs) to leverage contextual information in the form of structured linguistic representations. Specifically, we examine the impact of encoding both short and long contexts using Abstract Meaning Representation (AMR) structures across a diverse set of language tasks. We perform our analysis using 8-bit quantized and instruction-tuned versions of Llama 3.1 (8B), Phi-3, and Mistral 7B. Our results indicate that, for tasks involving short contexts, augmenting the prompt with the AMR of the original language context often degrades the performance of the underlying LLM. However, for tasks that involve long contexts, such as dialogue summarization in the SAMSum dataset, this enhancement improves LLM performance, for example, by increasing the zero-shot cosine similarity score of Llama 3.1 from 66% to 76%. This improvement is more evident in the newer and larger LLMs, but does not extend to the older or smaller ones. In addition, we observe that LLMs can effectively reconstruct the original text from a linearized AMR, achieving a cosine similarity of 81% in the best-case scenario.

1 Introduction

In recent years, Large Language Models (LLMs) have achieved remarkable success in numerous natural language processing (NLP) tasks, such as machine translation, summarization, and both single- and multi-hop question answering. However, a critical challenge remains: assessing their ability to interpret and utilize meaning from structured representations that encode language in concise and abstract forms. Structured semantic representations of text, such as Abstract Meaning Representation (AMR) structures and Discourse Representation Structures (DRS), have consistently proven effective for reasoning with high-level semantics in text and enhancing performance in challenging structure-aware NLP tasks, particularly those involving long contexts. For instance, prior work has demonstrated that encoding AMR structures via text-graph attention can improve long-dialogue summarization performance (Hua et al., 2023).

In this paper, we systematically examine the ability of several prominent LLMs to interpret AMRs. In addition, we study how AMR-augmented prompting (See Fig. 23) and AMR-only prompting (See Fig. 22) affect model performance on downstream tasks, that require a deep understanding of context, compared to context-only, i.e., language-only prompting. Unlike previous work, which primarily focuses on developing ad-hoc neural architectures to either improve text regeneration from AMRs (Zhu et al., 2019) or enhance performance on downstream tasks (Hua et al., 2023; Yang et al., 2024), this study evaluates the ability of LLMs to directly interpret linearized (flattended) AMRs. Here, AMR-augmented prompting refers to including the linearized AMR of the context in the prompt to evaluate the model's ability to improve its understanding of the original context with support from the AMR. AMR-only prompting refers to providing the LLM with only the linearized AMR, without the original language context, to assess the model's ability to infer meaning directly from these semantic representations. Our key contributions are as follows:

1. We systematically evaluate the instruction-tuned versions of prominent LLMs on their ability to directly leverage linearized AMRs in prompts for both short- and long-context tasks. These tasks include AMR-to-text generation, single-hop reasoning, 2-hop reasoning, dialogue summarization, natural language inference (NLI), and document-level natural language inference (DocNLI).

2. We demonstrate that while AMR integration tends to degrade performance in short-context tasks, it can enhance performance in long-context tasks, an observation that is more profound when

Proceedings of the 1st Joint Workshop on Large Language Models and Structure Modeling (XLLM 2025), pages 173–185
August 1, 2025

using larger and more recently developed LLMs. Additionally, in some downstream tasks, LLMs can work exclusively with linearized AMRs (AMR-only prompting) to achieve reasonable performance with few-shot prompting.

3. We show that LLMs can effectively reconstruct the original context from linearized AMRs, achieving 81% cosine similarity in the best-case scenario, highlighting their ability to understand context from AMRs.

This work provides valuable insights into leveraging AMRs to enhance LLM performance on downstream language tasks, while also identifying key challenges. We hope that our work will serve as a guide for comprehensively analyzing other structured representations, such as Knowledge Graphs and Discourse Representation Structures, with respect to how they can be interpreted and utilized by LLMs.

2 Related Work

Existing studies have explored various methods for generating text from language and knowledge representation structures, usually by modifying or improving underlying neural architectures. For instance, approaches like text-graph attention (Hua et al., 2023) and JointGT (Ke et al., 2021) alter the transformer architecture using structured cross-attention to better account for graph properties. Prior studies have also demonstrated enhanced open-domain dialogue evaluation by fusing graph-encoded AMRs into LLMs via gating mechanism (Yang et al., 2024). Others, such as text generation from knowledge graphs using graph transformers (Koncel-Kedziorski et al., 2022), use graphical representations directly, alleviating the need for graph linearization. These studies have aimed to enhance the quality of generated text using AMRs as input through structure-aware methods, semantic aggregation, and other heuristics.

However, all of these approaches exhibit the key limitation that the proposed work seeks to address. Namely, they focus on modifying model architectures or introducing new architectural components, such as joint graph-text representations and heuristic-based conditioning, which can increase complexity and is less amenable to generalization across domains, tasks, and structures. In contrast, we directly evaluate the inherent capability of existing, general-purpose LLMs to interpret structured representations like AMR. Moreover, while most

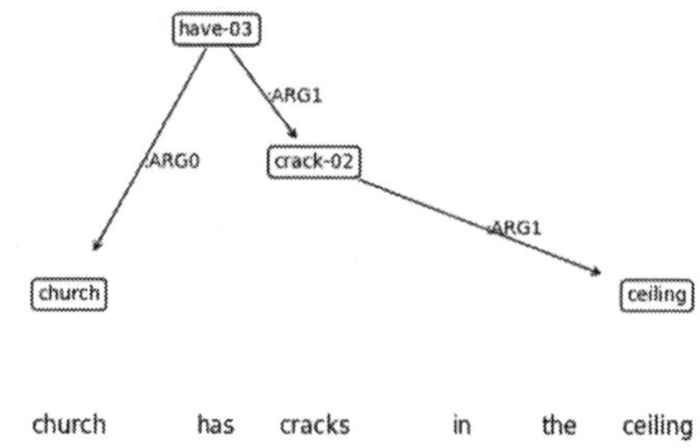

Figure 1: An AMR tree for a hypothesis from the SNLI dataset, *The church has cracks in the ceiling*, extracted using the AMR3-structbart-L model via IBM's transition neural parser.

prior studies largely sought to improve the quality of generated text (Dong and Holder, 2014), the proposed work evaluates the opportunities of AMRs to represent context for a wide range of downstream language tasks.

3 Methodology

This section describes AMRs, how they are extracted from text, and the pipeline for studying their efficacy in language understanding and reasoning tasks.

3.1 Abstract Meaning Representation

An Abstract Meaning Representation (AMR) (Langkilde and Knight, 1998) is a labeled representation of sentences as rooted, directed graphs (See Fig. 1) that capture the semantic meaning of a sentence by abstracting away from its surface syntax. The most basic AMR takes the form *(label / concept)*, e.g.

$$(m1 \ / \ |dog < canid|)$$

The slash (/) is shorthand for a type (or instance) feature, and in logical notation, this AMR might be written as *instance*(m1, dog). This AMR can represent "the dog," "the dogs," "a dog," or simply "dog." A concept can be modified using keywords:

$$\Big(m1 \ / \ |dog < canid| \\ \quad : quant \ plural\Big)$$

This specification refines the meaning to "the dogs" or simply "dogs." AMR prioritizes the underlying semantic meaning conveyed by a sentence rather than the specific words or syntactic structures used.

In this paper, we use the AMR Annotation Release 3.0 dataset (LDC2020T02), developed by the Linguistic Data Consortium (LDC),

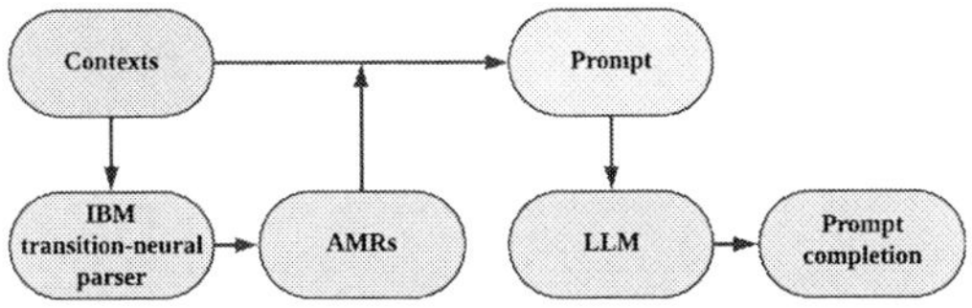

Figure 2: Process flow for the analysis tasks.

```
(s / sing-01~3
    :ARG0 (c / choir~2
        :mod (c2 / church~1)
        :mod (t / this~0))
    :ARG2 (m / mass~6)
    :time (s2 / sing-01~9
        :ARG0 c
        :ARG1 (s3 / song~11
            :mod (j / joyous~10))
        :location (c3 / church~17)
        :source (b / book~14)))
```

Figure 3: Linearized AMR for a premise from the SNLI dataset, *This church choir sings to the masses as they sing joyous songs from the book at a church*, extracted using the AMR3-structbart-L model via IBM's transition neural parser.

SDL/Language Weaver, Inc., the Computational Language and Educational Research (CLEAR) group at the University of Colorado, and the Information Sciences Institute at the University of Southern California. This dataset contains a semantic tree-bank of over 59,255 English natural language sentences from sources including broadcast conversations, news-wire articles, weblogs, web discussion forums, fiction, and web text. There is a possibility that the AMRs in this dataset were exposed in the pre-training of many LLMs, which is why we also employ the AMR3-structbart-L and doc-sen-conll-amr-seed42 models via IBM's transition-based neural parser (Drozdov et al., 2022) to parse contexts from various datasets into document/multi-sentence-level AMR structures for further analysis. Linearized representations of AMRs (See Fig. 3) were fed to the LLMs. Fig. 2 illustrates a general process flow for all the analysis tasks in this work.

3.2 Tasks

All tasks were approached using zero-shot, 3-shot, and 5-shot prompting. For all tasks except context regeneration, prompting was done in 3 ways: context-only, AMR-augmented, and AMR-only.

3.2.1 Context Regeneration (AMR-to-text)

In this task, we evaluate how well LLMs can regenerate the original context given its linearized AMR. Regeneration is conducted using the LDC2020T02 dataset. Fig. 4 illustrates the prompting strategy for context regeneration.

3.2.2 Question-Answering (QA)

In this task, we evaluate the effectiveness of AMRs in enhancing the single-hop and 2-hop reasoning abilities of LLMs. For single-hop QA, we report performance on the SQuAD 2.0 dataset (Rajpurkar et al., 2018). Fig. 5 illustrates the AMR-augmented prompt used for QA on the SQuAD 2.0 dataset. For 2-hop reasoning, we report performance on the HotpotQA dataset (Yang et al., 2018), which features much longer contexts, as each question in that dataset is accompanied by 10 documents (2 relevant, 8 irrelevant). Since most of these documents are distractors, the prompt includes a specific instruction indicating that some documents in the context may be irrelevant to the question. Fig. 6 illustrates the AMR-augmented prompt used for QA on the HotpotQA dataset.

3.2.3 Summarization

In this task, we evaluate the effectiveness of AMRs in enhancing the dialogue summarization capabilities of LLMs, comparing these summaries to the gold (expert human-generated) summaries in the dataset. Fig. 7 illustrates the AMR-augmented prompt for summarizing conversations in the SAMSum dataset (Gliwa et al., 2019).

3.2.4 Natural Language Inference (NLI)

In this task, we evaluate the effectiveness of AMRs in enhancing the ability of LLMs to understand and reason about natural language, specifically, to determine whether a given claim is supported by sentences in an evidence document. This involves identifying if there is an entailment between the claim (hypothesis) and the supporting evidence (premise) or if a contradiction exists between them. We use the SNLI dataset (Bowman et al., 2015), composed of pairs of short statements, and the DocNLI dataset (Yin et al., 2021), where premises can span multiple sentences and documents. Fig. 8 illustrates the AMR-augmented prompt for natural language inference on the SNLI dataset. A similar prompt was used for DocNLI, with the removal of the neutral label from the instruction to align with the binary labels in DocNLI.

Fig. 23 in the Appendix illustrates an example of a prompt-completion for the 3-shot SNLI entailment prediction task.

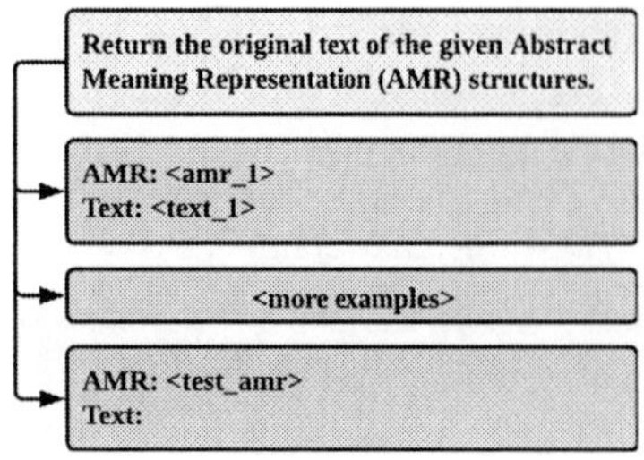

Figure 4: Prompt for regenerating text from AMRs.

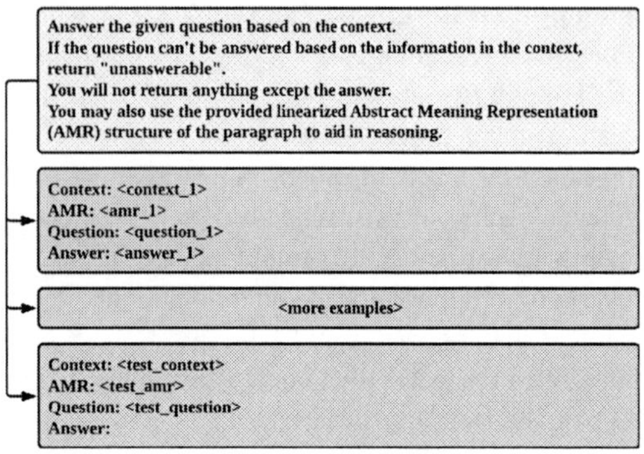

Figure 5: AMR-augmented prompt for QA on the SQuAD 2.0 dataset. For context-only prompting (Fig. 15), the final statement from the canary-colored instruction block is removed, along with the AMRs from the examples. For AMR-only prompting (Fig. 16), the instruction is modified so that the LLM considers the AMR as the context for reasoning, and the original context is removed from the examples.

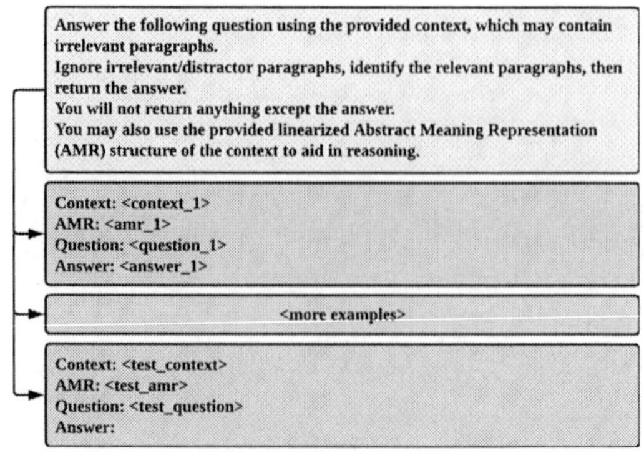

Figure 6: AMR-augmented prompt for QA on HotpotQA dataset. The context-only (Fig. 19) and AMR-only (Fig. 20) prompting strategies are similar to those used in SQuAD 2.0 reasoning.

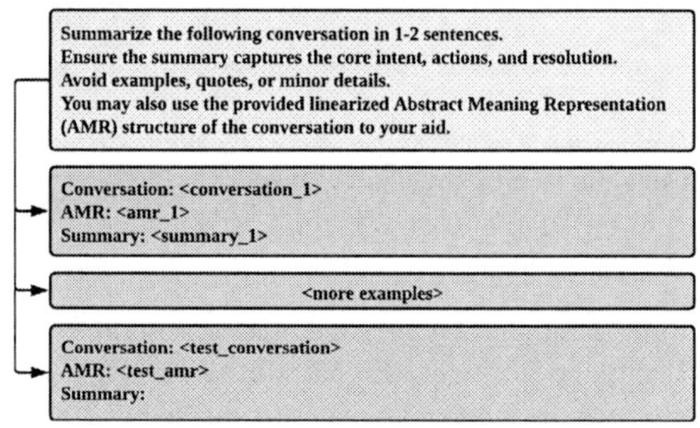

Figure 7: AMR-augmented prompt for summarizing SAMSum dataset conversations. The context-only (Fig. 17) and AMR-only (Fig. 18) prompting strategies are similar to those used in SQuAD 2.0 reasoning.

4 Experimental Settings

Our analysis pipeline involves converting text into AMR structures and then prompting LLMs to perform tasks using those AMRs, either via AMR-augmented or AMR-only prompting. The baselines for these tasks are simply the language-only (i.e., context-only) prompting results. In this section, we will describe the experimental setup for the tasks outlined in Section 3.2.

4.1 Datasets and Splits

In addition to using the LDC2020T02 dataset, which contains AMRs of small contexts (sentence-level AMRs), we also parse contexts from the SQuAD 2.0, HotpotQA, SAMSum, SNLI, and DocNLI datasets into document-level (multi-sentence) AMRs using the AMR3-structbart-L and doc-sen-conll-amr-seed42 models via IBM's transition-based neural parser. Note: a document-level AMR corresponds to a single, continuous document. For instance, each question in the HotpotQA dataset provides up to 10 documents, which may or may not be related. This setup results in 10 document-level AMRs.

We use the test splits of LDC2020T02, SAMSum, SNLI, and DocNLI, and the validation splits of SQuAD 2.0 and HotpotQA for inference. The few-shot examples are curated from the training splits of these datasets. We also conduct a fine-tuning experiment for SAMSum summarization using its training and validation splits.

4.2 Models

For all tasks, we generate responses truncated at the first occurrence of a newline character using 8-bit quantized versions of Llama-3.1-8B-Instruct (Llama3.1) (Grattafiori et al., 2024), Phi-3-mini-128k-instruct (Phi3) (Abdin et al., 2024), and Mistral-7B-Instruct-v0.1 (Mistral) (Jiang et al., 2023). Table 1 outlines the mapping of models to their respective tasks.

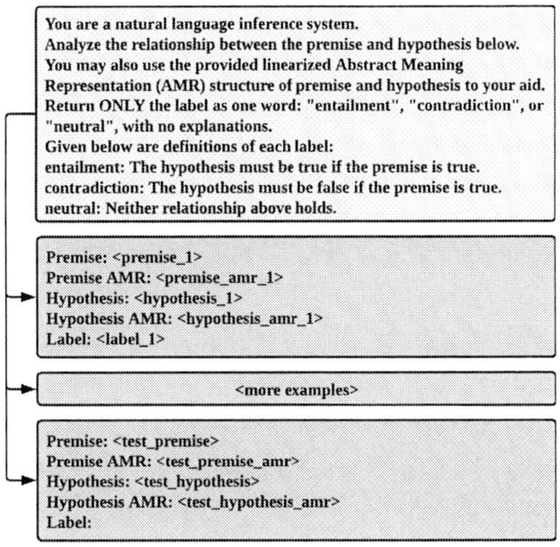

Figure 8: AMR-augmented prompt for natural language inference on SNLI dataset. The context-only (Fig. 21) and AMR-only (Fig. 22) prompting strategies are similar to those used in SQuAD 2.0 reasoning. The 3-shot examples for SNLI included 1 example of each label, while the 5-shot examples included 2 examples each of entailment and contradiction, and 1 neutral example. For DocNLI, due to an imbalance in the test set (with more examples of contradiction than entailment), we included one more example of contradiction than entailment in the few-shot prompts.

We also experiment with rank-32 LoRA (Hu et al., 2021) fine-tuning of the 8-bit quantized Llama3.1 model for the SAMSum summarization task. We then compare the performance of this fine-tuned model against few-shot summarization.

4.3 Evaluation Metrics

Listed below are the evaluation metrics used for each task, according to their output types.

AMR-to-text and Summarization For these tasks, we report the ROUGE-1, ROUGE-2, ROUGE-L, BLEU, and cosine similarity scores comparing the expected response to the generated response averaged across all samples. The cosine similarity between the all-MiniLM-L6-V2 (Wang et al., 2020) embeddings of the expected response and the generated response averaged across all samples is reported as the cosine similarity score.

Question Answering We report F1-score for all question answering tasks. The F1 is calculated for each sample based on the number of common tokens between the expected and generated responses, then averaged across all samples. This

Task	Llama3.1	Phi3	Mistral
Regeneration	Yes	Yes	Yes
Summarization	Yes	Yes	Yes
1-hop QA	Yes	Yes	Yes
2-hop QA	Yes	No	No
SNLI	Yes	Yes	Yes
DocNLI	Yes	No	No

Table 1: Mapping models to the tasks for which they will be used. Only Llama3.1 is employed for 2-hop QA and DocNLI due to its ability to handle long contexts efficiently, which the other models lack.

is operationalized as:

$$\text{Precision} = \frac{\text{count of common tokens}}{\text{count of tokens in generated response}}$$

$$\text{Recall} = \frac{\text{count of common tokens}}{\text{count of tokens in generated response}}$$

$$F1 = 2 \times \frac{\text{Precision} \times \text{Recall}}{\text{Precision} + \text{Recall}}$$

We also report cosine similarity score for this task. For SQuAD 2.0, we select the best possible match from the available answer choices for scoring.

Natural Language Inference For SNLI and DocNLI, we report the macro F1-score of the generated answers compared to the labels; *contradiction, neutral, entailment* for SNLI and *contradiction, entailment* for DocNLI. The macro F1-score averages the F1-scores across all classes, thereby accounting for label imbalance and providing a more comprehensive measure of classification performance as compared to accuracy.

5 Results

All scores presented in the charts and tables are expressed as percentages. For each task, except for AMR-to-text, we present the results of the best performing model in the main paper and report the remaining results in the Appendix.

For all the zero-shot experiments except AMR-to-text, 5 different transformer seeds were used to compute 90% confidence intervals. Similar performance was recorded across all seeds for zero-shot experiments, resulting in narrow confidence intervals. For all the few-shot experiments except AMR-to-text, 5 distinct sets of examples were curated from the training set to determine 90% confidence intervals. All the scores presented in the results and tables are averaged across different seeds and sets, if applicable.

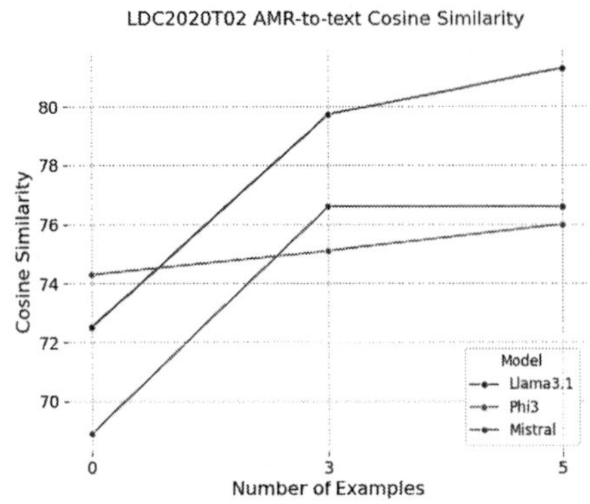

Figure 9: LDC2020T02 AMR-to-text Cosine Similarity.

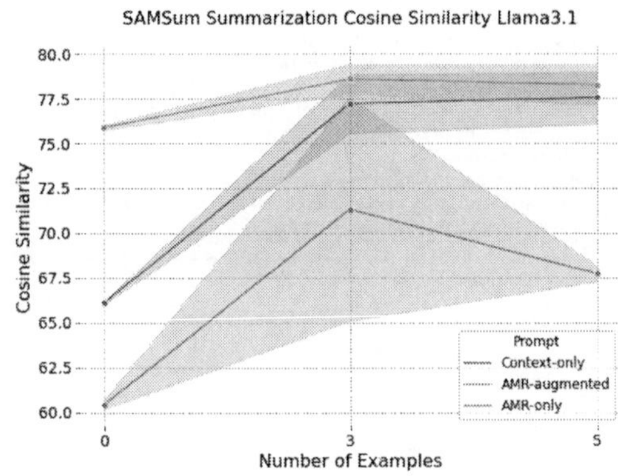

Figure 10: Llama3.1 SAMSum summarization Cosine Similarity with 90% confidence intervals.

5.1 LDC2020T02

Fig. 9 illustrates that Llama3.1 outperforms Phi3 and Mistral in regenerating the original contexts from the linearized LDC2020T02 AMRs using few-shot prompting. While Phi3 achieves the best zero-shot regeneration cosine similarity score (74%), it becomes the worst performer with few-shot prompting. With 5-shot prompting, Llama3.1 attains a cosine similarity score of 81%. Using more than 3 in-context learning examples yields diminishing returns, as indicated by the marginal improvement when transitioning from 3-shot to 5-shot prompting. Detailed results for this task, including additional regeneration metrics, are provided in Table 2 in the Appendix.

5.2 SAMSum

Figure 10 illustrates how Llama3.1's zero-shot summarization cosine similarity score improves from 66% to 76% with AMR-augmented prompting, compared to context-only prompting. In the few-shot setting, although the confidence intervals for context-only and AMR-augmented prompting overlap, both the average and maximum cosine similarity scores are higher for AMR-augmented prompting than for other prompting strategies. This provides strong evidence that AMRs can enhance the ability of LLMs, particularly larger and more recent models, to infer information from long contexts, especially lengthy dialogues, and to retain key pieces of information. However, increasing the number of few-shot examples beyond 3 yields diminishing returns for both context-only and AMR-augmented prompting, and it even degrades performance with AMR-only prompting.

While Llama3.1's performance improved with AMR augmentation, Phi3 and Mistral did not exhibit similar gains (Table 4). Mistral was the best performing model for this task by a small margin, despite being worse than Llama3.1 in all the other tasks. Rank-32 LoRA fine-tuning of Llama3.1 achieved a cosine similarity score of 75% with a context-only input prompt, which increased to 76% with an AMR-augmented input prompt. This indicates that, although LoRA fine-tuning of Llama3.1 was not any better than few-shot prompting for SAMSum summarization, it benefited marginally from AMR augmentation.

5.3 SQuAD 2.0

Fig. 11 illustrates that Llama3.1's single-hop reasoning F1-score declines with AMR-augmented prompting compared to context-only prompting (e.g., from 59% to 52% with 3-shot prompting). However, both Llama3.1 (Fig. 11) and Mistral (Table 3) demonstrate a remarkable understanding of AMRs in 3-shot single-hop reasoning, as indicated by how closely their 3-shot AMR-only performance approaches the best possible 3-shot performance for this task. Including over 3 examples in the prompt results in only marginal performance improvements with context-only prompting. However, with AMR-augmented and AMR-only prompting, performance deteriorates as the number of few-shot examples increases to 5. For instance, Llama3.1 achieved a 48% F1 score with AMR-only 3-shot prompting, which dropped significantly to 26% with AMR-only 5-shot prompting. Detailed results for this task, including results from other models, are provided in Table 3 in the Appendix.

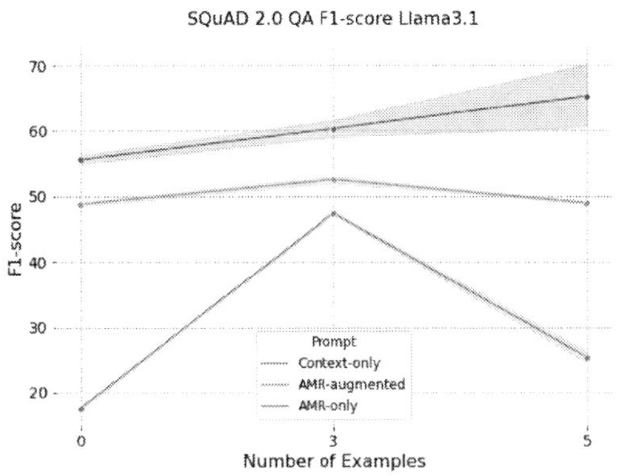

Figure 11: Llama3.1 SQuAD 2.0 QA F1-score with 90% confidence intervals.

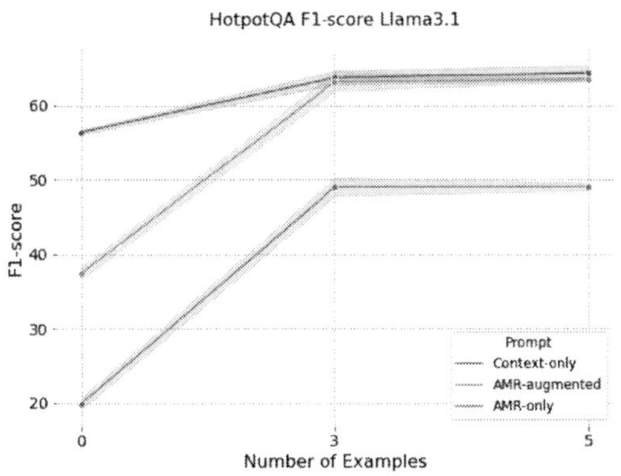

Figure 12: Llama3.1 2-hop HotpotQA F1-score with 90% confidence intervals.

5.4 HotpotQA

Fig. 12 shows that AMR-augmented prompting in Llama3.1 does not outperform context-only prompting for 2-hop reasoning on the HotpotQA dataset. Additionally, across all prompting scenarios, increasing from 3-shot to 5-shot prompting has insignificant impact on performance. Although this is a long-context task, the individual documents within the context are small, resulting in multiple AMRs of these small documents being stacked together in the input prompt. This explains why the observations regarding the effectiveness of AMRs here differ from those in the SAMSum dataset, where AMRs were derived from long conversations and proved more effective in improving task performance.

5.5 SNLI

Unlike the other tasks, for natural language inference on the SNLI dataset, Phi3 was the best performing model by a significant margin, achieving an 82% macro F1-score with context-only 5-shot prompting. Fig. 13 shows that AMR-augmented prompting in Phi3 yields a significantly better zero-shot macro F1-score (39%) compared to context-only prompting (27%), which is only slightly better than AMR-only prompting (25%). However, with the addition of few-shot examples in the prompt, context-only prompting achieves the highest macro F1-score. Detailed results for this task, including results from other models, are provided in Table 5 in the Appendix.

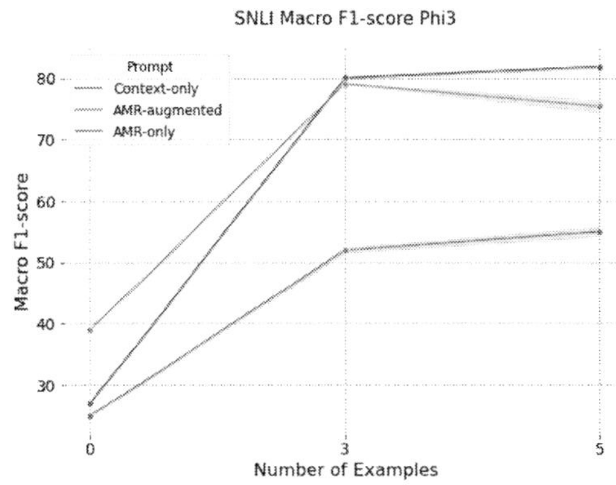

Figure 13: Phi3 SNLI Macro F1-score with 90% confidence intervals.

5.6 DocNLI

The DocNLI experiment was conducted on approximately 13k examples from the DocNLI test split, which had an 8:5 label imbalance in favor of contradiction. This experiment aimed to further validate observations from prior experiments regarding the utility of AMRs in long-context tasks. Fig. 14 illustrates that AMR-only prompting achieves the highest zero-shot macro F1 score of 20%. However, with 3 few-shot examples, context-only prompting achieves a macro F1 score of 51%, outperforming the other prompting methods. Both AMR-only and context-only prompting result in a performance decline with 5 few-shot examples, while the AMR-augmented prompting macro F1 score increases. These results are not only inconsistent with the SNLI experiment outcome but also deviate from the trends observed in other long-context tasks.

6 Conclusion

In this study, we investigated the ability of LLMs to interpret and leverage AMRs. Our findings demon-

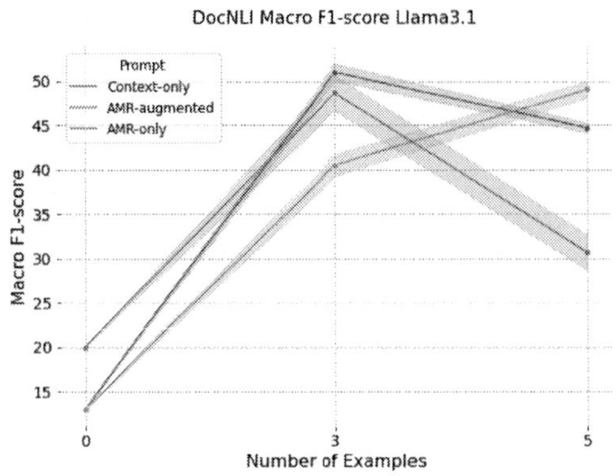

Figure 14: Llama3.1 DocNLI Macro F1-score with 90% confidence intervals.

strate that AMR-augmented prompting, where the AMR of the context is included alongside the original context, significantly improves zero-shot long-dialogue summarization for Llama3.1 and noticeably improves sentence-level natural language inference for Phi3. The improvement from AMR-augmented prompting is more significant in SAMSum summarization with Llama3.1, the largest and most recently developed model among those used in this study, compared to other models and tasks. While AMRs did not enhance performance in other tasks, there was still some evidence that LLMs can extract meaningful information from AMRs. This was particularly evident in some of the AMR-only experiments, where the models achieved reasonable performance using AMRs alone. Additionally, we conducted rank-32 LoRA fine-tuning of Llama3.1 on the SAMSum summarization task, which produced results better than zero-shot but not as effective as few-shot prompting for both context-only and AMR-augmented approaches.

Overall, the experiments suggest that AMRs can assist LLMs in understanding long-term dependencies, key ideas, and events in long texts, as demonstrated by the zero-shot and few-shot SAMSum summarization experiments. However, including linearized AMRs in the prompt appears generally ineffective for tasks involving short contexts.

7 Limitations

In this work, we aimed to provide a comprehensive analysis of the impact of linearized AMRs on LLM performance. However, how these LLMs interpret AMRs after full fine-tuning on AMR-augmented and AMR-only tasks remains unclear, as it was outside the scope of this study. The only fine-tuning conducted in this study (LoRA fine-tuning of the 8-bit quantized Llama3.1) proved less effective than few-shot prompting. Moreover, the DocNLI long-context task was evaluated on only a partial test set. To establish confidence in the results for this task, the full test split of DocNLI should be evaluated. Another limitation of this work is that the HotpotQA experiments did not incorporate Chain-of-Thought prompting (Wei et al., 2023), which is the most commonly used prompting technique for achieving strong performance on this dataset. This omission is justified, however, given that Chain-of-Thought prompting tends to work well only with models larger than those used in this study.

Our results demonstrate that AMRs improve performance on long-context tasks such as dialogue summarization but degrade performance on short-context tasks like single-hop QA. However, we have not conducted a detailed analysis to identify the underlying causes. Further investigation is needed to uncover task-specific factors that contribute to these outcomes.

8 Future Work

There are numerous directions for extending this work. For instance, approaches such as prompt tuning through soft prompts (Lester et al., 2021), synthetic AMR generation and AMR enrichment (Ji et al., 2022), or adapter-based parameter-efficient fine-tuning (Houlsby et al., 2019) can be explored alongside full fine-tuning of LLMs on AMR-augmented and AMR-only tasks. This study utilized only one of the most recently developed LLMs; analyzing other newer models as large as Llama3.1 or larger could help reinforce the observations presented in this paper. Additionally, exploring how AMRs or other structured representations impact retrieval augmented pipelines would be an interesting avenue for future research. It would also be interesting to observe how the findings of this paper change when the models are 4-bit quantized.

The analysis presented in this work can also be extended to other structured semantic representations using similar tasks. In particular, evaluating Discourse Representation Structures (DRS) and Knowledge Graphs (KG) would be valuable, given the wide range of tasks for which these representations are continuously being explored.

References

Marah Abdin, Jyoti Aneja, Hany Awadalla, Ahmed Awadallah, Ammar Ahmad Awan, Nguyen Bach, Amit Bahree, Arash Bakhtiari, Jianmin Bao, Harkirat Behl, Alon Benhaim, Misha Bilenko, Johan Bjorck, Sébastien Bubeck, Martin Cai, Qin Cai, Vishrav Chaudhary, Dong Chen, Dongdong Chen, and 110 others. 2024. Phi-3 technical report: A highly capable language model locally on your phone. *Preprint*, arXiv:2404.14219.

Samuel R. Bowman, Gabor Angeli, Christopher Potts, and Christopher D. Manning. 2015. A large annotated corpus for learning natural language inference. *Preprint*, arXiv:1508.05326.

Ngan T. Dong and Lawrence B. Holder. 2014. Natural language generation from graphs. *Int. J. Semantic Comput.*, 8:335–.

Andrew Drozdov, Jiawei Zhou, Radu Florian, Andrew McCallum, Tahira Naseem, Yoon Kim, and Ramon Fernandez Astudillo. 2022. Inducing and using alignments for transition-based amr parsing. *Preprint*, arXiv:2205.01464.

Bogdan Gliwa, Iwona Mochol, Maciej Biesek, and Aleksander Wawer. 2019. SAMSum corpus: A human-annotated dialogue dataset for abstractive summarization. In *Proceedings of the 2nd Workshop on New Frontiers in Summarization*, pages 70–79, Hong Kong, China. Association for Computational Linguistics.

Aaron Grattafiori, Abhimanyu Dubey, Abhinav Jauhri, Abhinav Pandey, Abhishek Kadian, Ahmad Al-Dahle, Aiesha Letman, Akhil Mathur, Alan Schelten, Alex Vaughan, Amy Yang, Angela Fan, Anirudh Goyal, Anthony Hartshorn, Aobo Yang, Archi Mitra, Archie Sravankumar, Artem Korenev, Arthur Hinsvark, and 542 others. 2024. The llama 3 herd of models. *Preprint*, arXiv:2407.21783.

Neil Houlsby, Andrei Giurgiu, Stanislaw Jastrzebski, Bruna Morrone, Quentin de Laroussilhe, Andrea Gesmundo, Mona Attariyan, and Sylvain Gelly. 2019. Parameter-efficient transfer learning for nlp. *Preprint*, arXiv:1902.00751.

Edward J. Hu, Yelong Shen, Phillip Wallis, Zeyuan Allen-Zhu, Yuanzhi Li, Shean Wang, Lu Wang, and Weizhu Chen. 2021. Lora: Low-rank adaptation of large language models. *Preprint*, arXiv:2106.09685.

Yilun Hua, Zhaoyuan Deng, and Kathleen McKeown. 2023. Improving long dialogue summarization with semantic graph representation. In *Findings of the Association for Computational Linguistics: ACL 2023*, pages 13851–13883, Toronto, Canada. Association for Computational Linguistics.

Yuxin Ji, Gregor Williamson, and Jinho D. Choi. 2022. Automatic enrichment of Abstract Meaning Representations. In *Proceedings of the 16th Linguistic Annotation Workshop (LAW-XVI) within LREC2022*, pages 160–169, Marseille, France. European Language Resources Association.

Albert Q. Jiang, Alexandre Sablayrolles, Arthur Mensch, Chris Bamford, Devendra Singh Chaplot, Diego de las Casas, Florian Bressand, Gianna Lengyel, Guillaume Lample, Lucile Saulnier, Lélio Renard Lavaud, Marie-Anne Lachaux, Pierre Stock, Teven Le Scao, Thibaut Lavril, Thomas Wang, Timothée Lacroix, and William El Sayed. 2023. Mistral 7b. *Preprint*, arXiv:2310.06825.

Pei Ke, Haozhe Ji, Yu Ran, Xin Cui, Liwei Wang, Linfeng Song, Xiaoyan Zhu, and Minlie Huang. 2021. Jointgt: Graph-text joint representation learning for text generation from knowledge graphs. *Preprint*, arXiv:2106.10502.

Rik Koncel-Kedziorski, Dhanush Bekal, Yi Luan, Mirella Lapata, and Hannaneh Hajishirzi. 2022. Text generation from knowledge graphs with graph transformers. *Preprint*, arXiv:1904.02342.

Irene Langkilde and Kevin Knight. 1998. Generation that exploits corpus-based statistical knowledge. In *36th Annual Meeting of the Association for Computational Linguistics and 17th International Conference on Computational Linguistics, Volume 1*, pages 704–710, Montreal, Quebec, Canada. Association for Computational Linguistics.

Brian Lester, Rami Al-Rfou, and Noah Constant. 2021. The power of scale for parameter-efficient prompt tuning. *Preprint*, arXiv:2104.08691.

Pranav Rajpurkar, Robin Jia, and Percy Liang. 2018. Know what you don't know: Unanswerable questions for SQuAD. In *Proceedings of the 56th Annual Meeting of the Association for Computational Linguistics (Volume 2: Short Papers)*, pages 784–789, Melbourne, Australia. Association for Computational Linguistics.

Wenhui Wang, Furu Wei, Li Dong, Hangbo Bao, Nan Yang, and Ming Zhou. 2020. Minilm: Deep self-attention distillation for task-agnostic compression of pre-trained transformers. *Preprint*, arXiv:2002.10957.

Jason Wei, Xuezhi Wang, Dale Schuurmans, Maarten Bosma, Brian Ichter, Fei Xia, Ed Chi, Quoc Le, and Denny Zhou. 2023. Chain-of-thought prompting elicits reasoning in large language models. *Preprint*, arXiv:2201.11903.

Bohao Yang, Kun Zhao, Chen Tang, Dong Liu, Liang Zhan, and Chenghua Lin. 2024. Emphasising structured information: Integrating abstract meaning representation into llms for enhanced open-domain dialogue evaluation. *Preprint*, arXiv:2404.01129.

Zhilin Yang, Peng Qi, Saizheng Zhang, Yoshua Bengio, William W. Cohen, Ruslan Salakhutdinov, and Christopher D. Manning. 2018. Hotpotqa: A dataset for diverse, explainable multi-hop question answering. *Preprint*, arXiv:1809.09600.

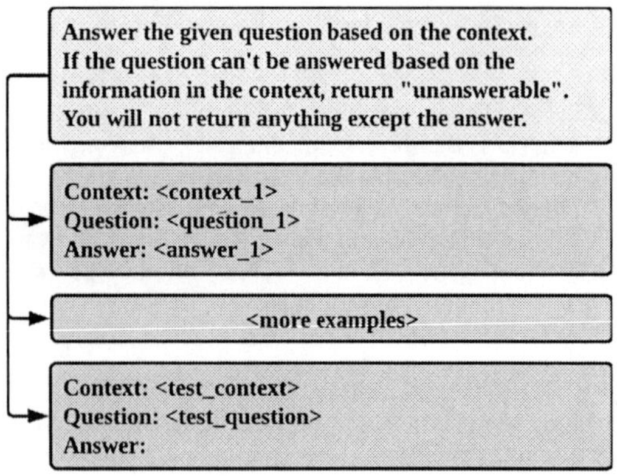

Figure 15: Context-only prompt for QA on the SQuAD 2.0 dataset.

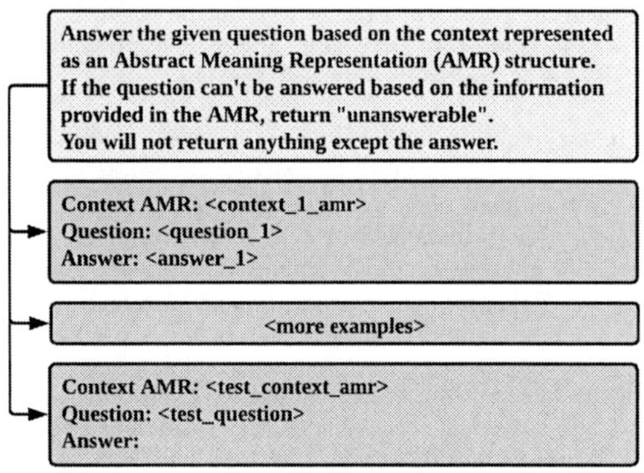

Figure 16: AMR-only prompt for QA on SQuAD 2.0 dataset.

Wenpeng Yin, Dragomir Radev, and Caiming Xiong. 2021. DocNLI: A large-scale dataset for document-level natural language inference. In *Findings of the Association for Computational Linguistics: ACL-IJCNLP 2021*, pages 4913–4922, Online. Association for Computational Linguistics.

Jie Zhu, Junhui Li, Muhua Zhu, Longhua Qian, Min Zhang, and Guodong Zhou. 2019. Modeling graph structure in transformer for better AMR-to-text generation. In *Proceedings of the 2019 Conference on Empirical Methods in Natural Language Processing and the 9th International Joint Conference on Natural Language Processing (EMNLP-IJCNLP)*, pages 5459–5468, Hong Kong, China. Association for Computational Linguistics.

A Appendix

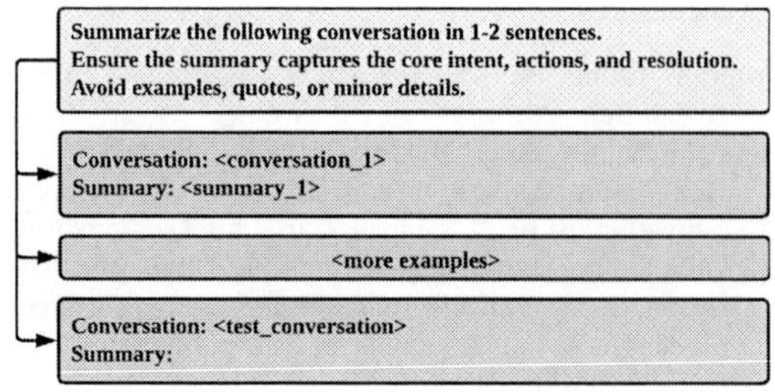

Figure 17: Context-only prompt for summarizing SAMSum dataset conversations.

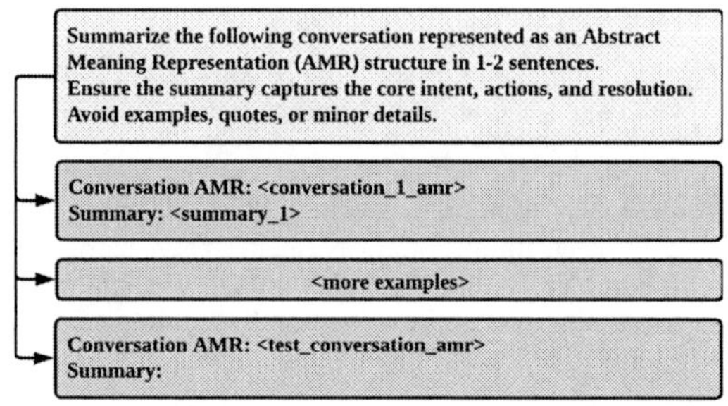

Figure 18: AMR-only prompt for summarizing SAMSum dataset conversations.

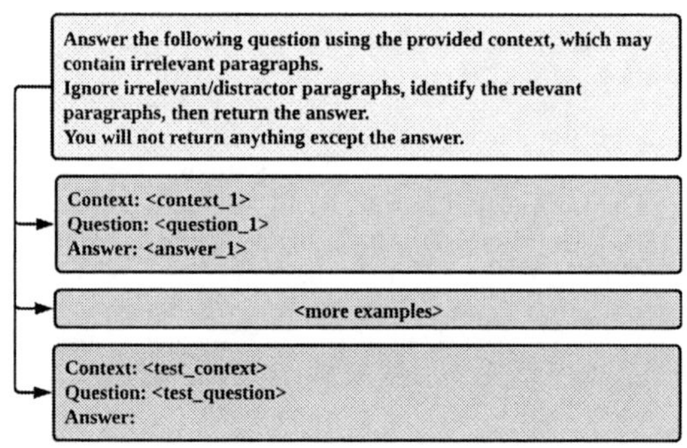

Figure 19: Context-only prompt for QA on HotpotQA dataset.

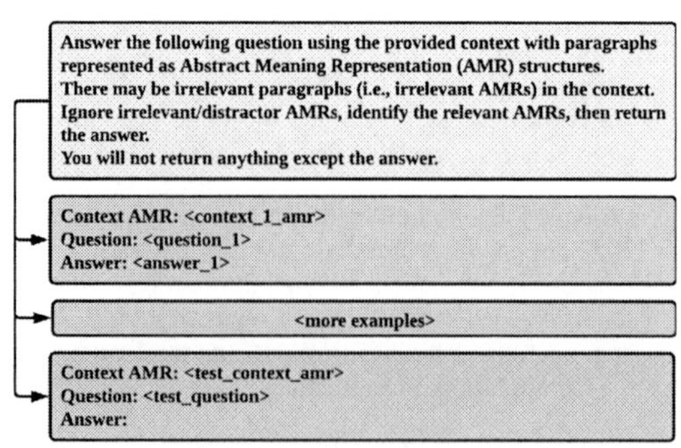

Figure 20: AMR-only prompt for QA on HotpotQA dataset.

Table 2: LDC2020T02 AMR-to-text full results.

Model	# Examples	Cosine similarity	ROUGE-1	ROUGE-2	ROUGE-L	BLEU
Llama3.1	0	73	55	20	43	6
	3	80	63	28	51	11
	5	**81**	**64**	**30**	**52**	**12**
Phi3	0	74	55	21	43	6
	3	75	56	22	45	7
	5	76	57	23	45	8
Mistral	0	69	51	18	40	5
	3	77	59	23	46	7
	5	77	59	25	47	9

Table 3: SQuAD 2.0 QA full results. 5-shot prompting was only conducted for the best performing model (Llama3.1).

Model	# Examples	Prompt	F1	Cosine similarity
Llama3.1	0	Context-only	55	66
	3	Context-only	59	68
	5	Context-only	**59**	**68**
	0	AMR-augmented	49	63
	3	AMR-augmented	52	62
	5	AMR-augmented	49	60
	0	AMR-only	18	38
	3	AMR-only	48	60
	5	AMR-only	26	45
Phi3	0	Context-only	46	56
	3	Context-only	**47**	**58**
	0	AMR-augmented	38	46
	3	AMR-augmented	40	53
	0	AMR-only	20	40
	3	AMR-only	22	42
Mistral	0	Context-only	35	47
	3	Context-only	**51**	**61**
	0	AMR-augmented	27	37
	3	AMR-augmented	49	60
	0	AMR-only	17	35
	3	AMR-only	41	55

Table 4: SAMSum summarization full results. 5-shot prompting and LoRA fine-tuning were only conducted for the model that demonstrated improved performance with AMR-augmented prompting compared to context-only prompting (Llama3.1).

Model	# Examples	Prompt	Cosine similarity	ROUGE-1	ROUGE-2	ROUGE-L	BLEU
Llama3.1	0	Context-only	66	29	8	21	2
	3	Context-only	78	42	17	34	7
	5	Context-only	78	43	17	34	7
	LoRA	Context-only	75	41	16	33	7
	0	AMR-augmented	76	37	12	28	4
	3	AMR-augmented	79	41	17	32	8
	5	AMR-augmented	**79**	**43**	**18**	**34**	**9**
	LoRA	AMR-augmented	76	43	17	34	7
	0	AMR-only	60	28	5	19	1
	3	AMR-only	79	41	17	32	8
	5	AMR-only	67	32	8	22	2
Phi3	0	Context-only	71	28	6	20	1
	3	Context-only	**72**	**31**	**8**	**23**	**2**
	0	AMR-augmented	70	26	5	19	1
	3	AMR-augmented	70	25	6	18	1
	0	AMR-only	59	22	2	14	0
	3	AMR-only	55	18	2	12	0
Mistral	0	Context-only	76	36	12	27	5
	3	Context-only	**80**	**47**	**22**	**38**	**12**
	0	AMR-augmented	77	38	14	29	6
	3	AMR-augmented	77	45	20	36	11
	0	AMR-only	66	30	6	21	1
	3	AMR-only	66	34	8	25	2

Table 5: SNLI entailment prediction full results. 5-shot prompting was only coducted for the best performing model (Phi3).

Model	# Examples	Prompt	Accuracy	Macro-F1
Llama3.1	0	Context-only	47	8
	3	Context-only	56	52
	0	AMR-augmented	42	15
	3	AMR-augmented	**56**	**54**
	0	AMR-only	37	12
	3	AMR-only	44	39
Phi3	0	Context-only	77	27
	3	Context-only	82	80
	5	Context-only	**83**	**82**
	0	AMR-augmented	67	39
	3	AMR-augmented	79	79
	5	AMR-augmented	76	76
	0	AMR-only	50	25
	3	AMR-only	52	52
	5	AMR-only	55	55
Mistral	0	Context-only	48	50
	3	Context-only	**52**	**54**
	0	AMR-augmented	49	50
	3	AMR-augmented	34	20
	0	AMR-only	33	20
	3	AMR-only	33	12

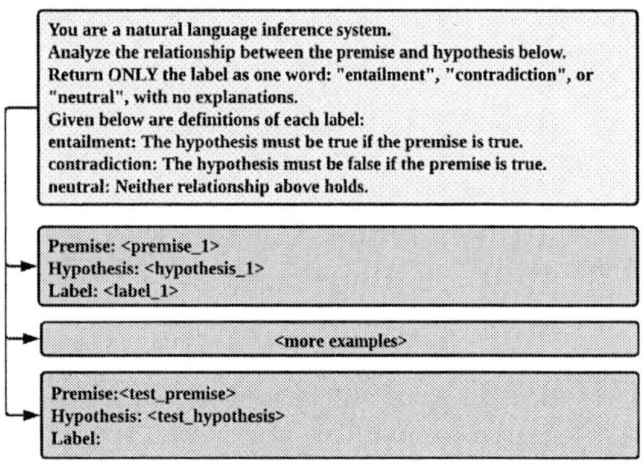

Figure 21: Context-only prompt for natural language inference on SNLI dataset.

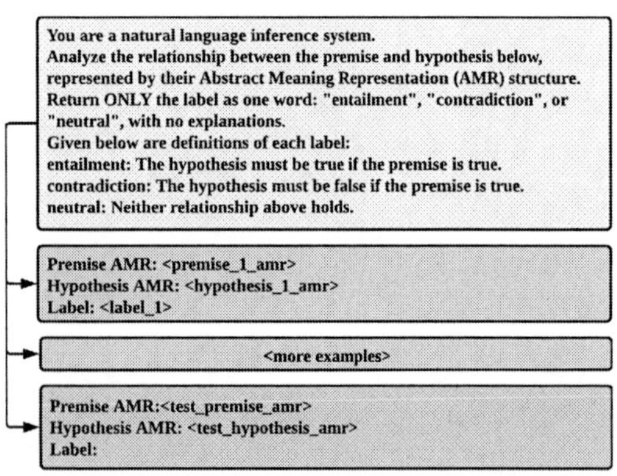

Figure 22: AMR-only prompt for natural language inference on SNLI dataset.

```
You are a natural language inference system.
Analyze the relationship between the premise and hypothesis below.
You may also use the provided linearized Abstract Meaning Representation
(AMR) structure of premise and hypothesis to your aid.
Return ONLY the label as one word: "entailment", "contradiction", or
"neutral", with no explanations.
Given below are definitions of each label:
entailment: The hypothesis must be true if the premise is true.
contradiction: The hypothesis must be false if the premise is true.
neutral: Neither relationship above holds.
```

```
Premise: Man with shawl praying by a large lake and small boat.
Premise AMR: (p / pray-01~3
  :ARG0 (m / man~0
    :poss-of (s / shawl~2))
  :location (a / and~8
    :op1 (l / lake~7
      :mod (l2 / large~6))
    :op2 (b / boat~10
      :mod (s2 / small~9))))
Hypothesis: Man in shawl prays by the small boat and large lake.
Hypothesis AMR: (p / pray-01~3
  :ARG0 (m / man~0
    :location (s / shawl~2))
  :location (a / and~8
    :op1 (b / boat~7
      :mod (s2 / small~6))
    :op2 (l / lake~10
      :mod (l2 / large~9))))
Label: entailment
```

```
Premise: A man is sitting on a brown sofa while holding a red hammer.
Premise AMR: (s / sit-01~3
  :ARG1 (m / man~1
    :ARG0-of (h2 / hold-01~9
      :ARG1 (h / hammer~12
        :ARG1-of (r / red-02~11))))
  :ARG2 (s2 / sofa~7
    :ARG1-of (b / brown-01~6)))
Hypothesis: a man is building a shed
Hypothesis AMR: (b / build-01~3
  :ARG0 (m / man~1)
  :ARG1 (s / shed~5))
Label: contradiction
```

```
Premise: A group of people stop at a food booth outside.
Premise AMR: (s / stop-01~4
  :ARG0 (g / group~1
    :consist-of (p / person~3))
  :location (b / booth~8
    :location (o / outside~9)
    :mod (f / food~7)))
Hypothesis: The group of people are looking to get food
Hypothesis AMR: (l / look-01~5
  :ARG0 (g2 / group~1
    :consist-of (p / person~3))
  :ARG1 (g / get-01~7
    :ARG0 g2
    :ARG1 (f / food~8)))
Label: neutral
```

```
Premise: This church choir sings to the masses as they sing joyous songs
from the book at a church.
Premise AMR: (s / sing-01~3
  :ARG0 (c / choir~2
    :mod (c2 / church~1)
    :mod (t / this~0))
  :ARG2 (m / mass~6)
  :time (s2 / sing-01~9
    :ARG0 c
    :ARG1 (s3 / song~11
      :mod (j / joyous~10))
    :location (c3 / church~17)
    :source (b / book~14)))
Hypothesis: The church has cracks in the ceiling.
Hypothesis AMR: (h / have-03~2
  :ARG0 (c2 / church~1)
  :ARG1 (c3 / crack-02~3
    :ARG1 (c / ceiling~6)))
Label:
```

Completion

neutral

Figure 23: An example of a prompt-completion for the AMR-augmented 3-shot SNLI entailment prediction task using Llama3.1.

LLM Dependency Parsing with Symbolic Rules

Michael Ginn and Alexis Palmer
University of Colorado
michael.ginn@colorado.edu

Abstract

We study whether incorporating symbolic rules can aid large language models in dependency parsing. We consider a paradigm in which LLMs first produce symbolic rules given fully labeled examples, and the rules are then provided in a subsequent call that performs the actual parsing. In addition, we experiment with providing human-created annotation guidelines in-context to the LLMs. We find that while both methods for rule incorporation improve zero-shot performance, the benefit disappears with a few labeled in-context examples.

1 Introduction

Dependency parsing is a classic task in natural language processing, requiring systems to parse complex linguistic structures. Standard approaches to dependency parsing train neural models on large amounts of labeled data (human-created parses), which either cast parsing as a word-by-word classification task (Covington, 2001), a sequence-to-sequence generative task (Li et al., 2018; Lin et al., 2022a), or a graph-based structure prediction task (Dozat and Manning, 2017).

One limitation of neural parsing methods is the requirement for large amounts of labeled data, which is often unavailable for low-resource languages. While Universal Dependencies (de Marneffe et al., 2021) currently includes over 150 languages, many of these languages have less than one thousand labeled tokens worth of data. Cross-lingual transfer has been proposed as a method to overcome these limitations (Guo et al., 2016; Schuster et al., 2019), but faces challenges due to differences in linguistic structure across languages (Ahmad et al., 2019; Wu and Dredze, 2020).

Recent work has investigated the use of large language models (LLMs) as an approach for parsing tasks (Li et al., 2023; Bai et al., 2023; Lin et al., 2023; Blevins et al., 2023; Tian et al., 2024).[1] LLMs are pretrained on huge multilingual corpora, and can potentially leverage cross-lingual information for effective parsing, even on rarer languages. Generally, this research has found that LLMs are effective zero-shot parsers on common languages such as English and Chinese and can also be effective on rare languages through in-context learning. However, in-context learning quickly grows inefficient and expensive with many examples.

We explore an alternate paradigm for dependency parsing on low-resource languages with LLMs. In our system, the LLM first acts as a descriptive linguist, observing labeled examples and producing linguistic rules. Then, the rules are provided in another LLM call where parsing is performed. We consider several techniques for providing context to the LLM during rule generation.

We hypothesized that explicitly producing symbolic rules could help improve the robustness of LLM-based parsing. We find that incorporating the LLM-generated rules offers clear improvements over the zero-shot setting, but worse performance than few-shot prediction. Furthermore, our best LLM-based setting underperforms state-of-the-art approaches across languages. We explore a number of failure cases and suggest future methods that could be used to address them. Our code and full results are available on GitHub.[2]

2 Related Work

Recent work has explored the potential of large language models for syntactic parsing. Some work has finetuned language models on dependency parsing as a sequence-to-sequence task (Hromei et al., 2024) or proposed statistical methods to automatically extract dependencies from language models

[1] While this work largely focuses on constituency parsing, we assume it shares similarities with dependency parsing.

[2] https://github.com/michaelpginn/ai-researcher-project

Proceedings of the 1st Joint Workshop on Large Language Models and Structure Modeling (XLLM 2025), pages 186–196
August 1, 2025 ©2025 Association for Computational Linguistics

(Chen et al., 2024). The most similar work explores prompting-based methods for LLM parsing, that do not require training. Lin et al. (2023) evaluates LLMs on zero-shot parsing for English and Chinese. Tian et al. (2024) proposes similar strategies for constituency parsing in English. Ezquerro et al. (2025) benchmarks dependency parsing performance across four languages and many LLMs. However, using LLMs to parse rare languages remains unexplored.

3 Data

We use data from Universal Dependencies (UD) (de Marneffe et al., 2021) for eight languages with differing geographic regions, linguistic features, and resource availability. We use the pre-defined train/eval/test splits from UD when available, and otherwise produce our own splits which are reused across experiments. We also remove examples with non-projective dependencies, which can pose issues for transition-based parsers. We summarize our languages and splits in Table 1.

Language (code)	Train	Dev	Test
Bambara (bam)	697	149	150
Bhojpuri (bho)	220	47	48
Cantonese (yue)	620	133	133
Erzya (myv)	1429	306	307
Kiche (quc)	655	141	141
Komi Zyrian (pcm)	438	94	94
Nigerian Pidgin (pcm)	6352	826	797
Yoruba (yor)	182	39	40

Table 1: Languages used in this study, and the number of train, development, and test instances for each language. All data comes from Universal Dependencies (de Marneffe et al., 2021).

4 Experimental Conditions

4.1 Baseline

As a baseline, we simply prompt the LLM to generate dependency parses for a given example. Details about prompts are given in Appendix A. We use a truncated form of the CONLL-U format[3] where each tab-separated line gives an ID, a word, the ID of the word's head, and the dependency relation type. All of our main experiments use GPT-4o[4].

In addition, we use a baseline setting where we specify the list of allowed dependency relation types (obtained by collecting all relation types from the training data). We refer to this setting as LABELS.

4.2 Symbolic Rules

Dependency parsing is a symbolic task equivalent to forming directed edges on a graph.[5] In this study, we seek to understand whether symbolic knowledge can be extracted and leveraged for this task. In particular, symbolic rules and heuristics can be used by LLMs simply by providing the rules in-context, unlike traditional neural parsers. We consider three settings for incorporating rules.

Rule Writing In the RULE WRITING setting, we first provide five labeled examples[6] to the LLM and prompt it to generate rules. The rules are specified by predicting part-of-speech categories of words, and then by writing dependency rules. For a hypothetical English example, the LLM might predict the categories:

```
Det: the
Noun: dog, cat
Verb: chases
Punct: .
```

Then, the LLM writes dependency rules by extracting the dependency relations from provided examples. The predicted rules for the prior example might look like the following:

```
Noun -> Det (det)
Verb -> Noun (nsubj)
Root -> Verb (root)
Verb -> Noun (obj)
Verb -> Punct (punct)
```

Finally, the generated rules are provided as-is in a subsequent prompt to the LLM for performing parsing.

Word Contexts We note that other than the prediction of word categories, these rules are largely just descriptive analysis of observed examples. In the WORD CONTEXTS setting, we eliminate the need for identifying part-of-speech categories, and instead just record the contexts that a word can occur in, consisting of the type and head of a dependency relation pointing to the word. For example, in the previous example, we might have the following contexts, listed as "(head, relation type)":

[3]https://universaldependencies.org/format.html

[4]Specifically the GPT-4O-2024-08-06 checkpoint

[5]With some restrictions, of course

[6]We select relevant examples using the method described in subsection 4.3

```
the:
(dog, det)
(cat, det)

dog:
(chases, nsubj)

chases:
(root, root)
...
```

We collect these contexts from the examples in the training dataset. Since some words may occur in a huge number of contexts, we sample up to two contexts for a given word and relation type. These contexts are less generalized than the rules of the prior section, but more accurate, as they do not require predicting part-of-speech categories.

Guidelines Dependency parsing is typically conducted by human annotators, and as such there already exist detailed parsing guidelines for many languages. In theory, these guidelines should be sufficient for someone with a baseline knowledge of the language's vocabulary and syntax to perform accurate parsing. In the GUIDELINES setting, we provide these guidelines directly to the LLM, avoiding the potential error of LLM-based rule extraction. The human guidelines should be highly accurate and relevant to the task at hand, thus we expected this setting to have clear benefits.

We scrape guidelines from the appropriate Universal Dependencies webpage, convert to markdown, and remove links. An excerpt from the processed Kiche guidelines is given in Appendix B.

4.3 In-context examples

Prior research has indicated that providing in-context examples is vital to enabling LLMs to perform tasks in rare languages (Lin et al., 2022b; Cahyawijaya et al., 2024; Ginn et al., 2024). Thus, we compare the four settings described previously (LABELS, RULE WRITING, WORD CONTEXTS, GUIDELINES) across a zero-shot setting, a three-shot setting, and a five-shot setting. This comparison allows us to measure the effects of these strategies compared to the effect of increasing in-context examples.

As in Ginn et al. (2024), we select relevant examples to the target sentence by choosing the sentences in the training set with the highest chrF++ score, computed using the target sentence as the reference. This ensures that the in-context examples have high substring overlap with the target example, and are more likely to be relevant for parsing.

5 Experimental Results

We report our results on the development set, using GPT-4o, in Figure 1. We average UAS and LAS scores over languages; full results are available in our GitHub repo. Generally, we observe a clear trend where providing symbolic information helps in the zero-shot setting, but the benefit decreases with increased in-context examples. At the five-shot setting, any benefits from symbolic knowledge are effectively nullified. Next, we analyze the effects of the various settings. We also perform additional variational experiments on the use of labels and chain-of-thought prompting in Appendix D.

Effect of Rule Writing We observe a large benefit to both UAS and LAS in the zero-shot setting, and a smaller benefit in the three-shot setting. Recall that the rules were written using five relevant examples. Thus, it is not terribly surprising that performance is similar when using the rules versus using the examples directly. In fact, the similar performance indicates that the LLM can effectively compress the relevant information from the in-context examples into symbolic rules, providing the same benefit with far less text.

While this is less encouraging for improving absolute performance, it could be useful for improving efficiency. For example, an LLM could be used to write rules about many similar groups of sentences ahead of time, and the relevant rules could be selected during inference, drastically reducing the length (and thus, speed and cost) of the parsing prompt.

We perform manual qualitative examination of rules in Bambara. We observe two common failure cases.

First, in some cases the LLM produced overly-specific part-of-speech categories that prevented the correct relation from being predicted. For example, in one case the correct root verb was "ye". However, in the provided examples, "ye" was only ever used as an auxiliary verb, leading the LLM to predict that "ye" was a member of a category named AUX. Because the LLM failed to identify that auxiliary verbs were the same category as verbs, it then failed to predict "ye" as the root of the sentence, instead choosing a random noun as

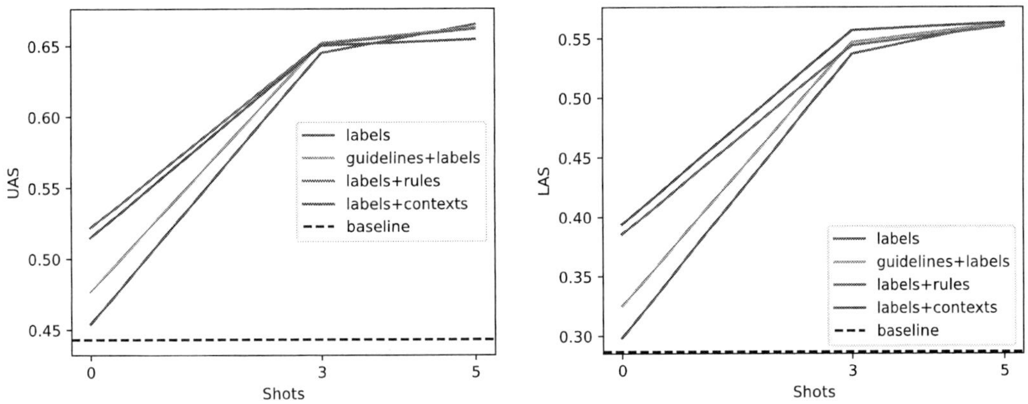

Figure 1: UAS (left) and LAS (right) scores for LLM-based dependency parsing, averaged across eight languages, across different numbers of in-context examples and different strategies for incorporating symbolic knowledge. We find that in the zero-shot setting, symbolic knowledge can provide clear improvements, but the margin disappears with sufficient in-context examples. The BASELINE setting is a zero-shot setting with no information provided at all.

the root.

Second, the LLM sometimes produced correct rules which could produce multiple possible parses for the target sentence. For example, one instance began with the sentence "n na kɔ̀nɔ̀ to n bolo!". The LLM correctly identified "n" and "kɔ̀nɔ̀" as a pronoun and noun, respectively, and produced the correct rules PRONOUN -> PARTICLE (CASE) and NOUN -> PARTICLE (CASE). The LLM predicted a case relation from "kɔ̀nɔ̀" to "na", rather than the correct relation from "n" to "na", both of which were allowed under the specified rules. This reveals a limitation of this sort of dependency rule: by not specifying word ordering, ambiguous situations arise with multiple valid parses. We explore one solution to this issue in Appendix C

Effect of Word Contexts The inclusion of word contexts (scraped directly from training data) had comparable performance to the LLM-written rules, with the highest LAS scores of any setting. Because this setting does not require an initial LLM call (unlike the rule writing setting), it drastically reduces the total cost of inference, while meeting or exceeding the performance of the RULE WRITING strategy.

A possible interpretation is that the only relevant information extracted by symbolic rules is the contexts in which particular words occur. Generalized symbolic rules over word categories do not seem to be particularly helpful by comparison.

We run paired bootstrap resampling (Koehn, 2004) to test the significance of the improvements of WORD CONTEXTS over the LABELS setting. We report the average significance score for the zero, three, and five-shot settings in Table 2. The results reinforce our qualitative observations.

Shots	Confidence
0	98.0%
3	61.3%
5	43.9%

Table 2: Paired bootstrap resampling score for the WORD CONTEXTS setting versus the LABELS setting, ran with 1000 iterations and test sets of 20 items.

Effect of Guidelines We expected GUIDELINES to be the most effective setting, as they provide the information that was used by human annotators to produce the labeled examples. However, we observe that while the GUIDELINES setting does provide small benefits over LABELS in the zero- and three-shot settings, it underperforms the RULE WRITING and WORD CONTEXTS strategies by a good margin.

There are two possible interpretations of this result. One possibility is that while the guidelines provide sufficient information to perform parsing, the LLM failed to understand and apply this information. This would align closely with the results of Aycock et al. (2025), which finds that LLMs struggle to utilize language reference materials when performing translation with rare languages.

The other possibility is that the guidelines do not actually provide sufficient information to per-

Method	bam	bho	yue	myv	quc	kpv	pcm	yor
mBERT	82.8 / 78.9	69.9 / 61.0	73.3 / 66.4	76.8 / 67.2	84.1 / 77.4	63.3 / 48.1	91.7 / 88.8	62.5 / 51.6
XLM	84.0 / 79.8	72.2 / 62.7	**76.0 / 70.4**	**79.6 / 69.8**	82.3 / 74.7	67.3 / 53.9	**93.7 / 90.9**	64.9 / 53.2
UDPipe 2	**92.4 / 90.2**	**76.9 / 68.0**	75.8 / 70.2	77.6 / 69.1	**88.6 / 84.1**	74.9 / 65.6	93.0 / 89.7	**76.0 / 69.5**
LLMs w/ labels and contexts, 5-shot								
GPT-4o	69.3 / 61.7	67.4 / 55.5	71.8 / 65.1	54.7 / 44.5	81.0 / 72.7	49.5 / 37.7	73.0 / 68.2	54.2 / 45.5
Gemini	76.0 / 70.6	67.9 / 56.3	68.4 / 63.0	77.4 / 69.6	87.7 / 82.9	**75.0 / 65.9**	72.8 / 68.6	59.1 / 48.9
Cmd R+	54.3 / 47.9	60.9 / 52.7	51.9 / 45.8	47.8 / 36.1	69.7 / 61.1	46.8 / 34.3	50.9 / 46.2	41.2 / 32.3
Llama 3.1	41.5 / 34.1	58.9 / 50.4	37.8 / 31.6	35.8 / 25.5	54.6 / 44.6	38.6 / 26.4	38.9 / 32.0	39.5 / 32.2

Table 3: Test set results on various state-of-the-art methods and LLMs using our best method from the preceding section. Scores are reported as UAS / LAS.

form parsing. Certainly, these guidelines do not include complete bilingual dictionaries, so an LLM which cannot translate words in the target language would likely struggle to apply more sophisticated grammar rules. This could be studied in future work by also providing word-by-word translations alongside guidelines. However, it may also be the case that the UD guidelines do not specify all of the information needed for parsing, assuming some knowledge of the grammar of the language.

6 Baseline Comparison

6.1 Baselines

We consider the following baseline models, which represent the common approaches used for dependency parsing and often are around the state-of-the-art, depending on the dataset.

Transition Parser We use a neural transition-based parser following the approach of Covington (2001); Nivre (2003); Jurafsky and Martin (2025). The parser predicts actions to form arcs between words, processing words in the sentence one-by-one and using a stack to retain words until they have been fully processed. In order to potentially benefit from crosslingual transfer, we finetune our classifier using two pretrained multilingual model, mBERT (Devlin et al., 2019) and XLM-RoBERTa (Conneau et al., 2020).

UDPipe We use UDPipe 1 (Straka and Straková, 2017), a pipeline that performs tokenization, lemmatization, tagging, and parsing, with trainable components for each step.[7] We train models using the default hyperparameters.

6.2 Results

We report results in Table 3. While the various settings for LLM inference were similar in the five-shot setting, we select the WORD CONTEXTS setting to compare, as it performed best in the zero- and three-shot settings. We run this setting with the following LLMs:

- GPT-4o, as in the development experiments (OpenAI, 2024)
- Gemini 2.0 Flash (Gemini Team, 2024)
- Command R+[8], a 104B parameter model specifically designed for low-resource multilingual tasks
- Llama 3.1 7b (Dubey et al., 2024), using the 8-bit quantization and the MLX (Hannun et al., 2023) checkpoint

We observe that for most languages, the LLM-based method underperforms or matches traditional neural SOTA methods. Of the four models tested, Gemini performs best on average. While the paradigms studied here can certainly improve performance over the zero-shot setting, they are not sufficient to beat the best prior approaches.

7 Conclusion

We studied methods for performing dependency parsing on low-resource languages with large language models (LLMs) that incorporate (symbolic) rules. We compared using LLM-written rules, extracting contexts that words appear in, and providing human-readable annotation guidelines. Overall, we found that these methods provide benefits in the zero-shot setting, but with sufficient in-context examples, their benefit was minimal. We evaluated several LLMs against state-of-the-art baselines, finding that the LLMs were unable to beat the best prior models.

[7] We chose not to use UDPipe 2 as it proved impossible to replicate the necessary development environment

[8] https://docs.cohere.com/docs/command-r-plus

8 Acknowledgements

The original idea for this work was produced by the AI ideation system of Si et al. (2024), and this paper originated from research conducted in the associated meta-study.

References

Wasi Ahmad, Zhisong Zhang, Xuezhe Ma, Eduard Hovy, Kai-Wei Chang, and Nanyun Peng. 2019. On difficulties of cross-lingual transfer with order differences: A case study on dependency parsing. In *Proceedings of the 2019 Conference of the North American Chapter of the Association for Computational Linguistics: Human Language Technologies, Volume 1 (Long and Short Papers)*, pages 2440–2452, Minneapolis, Minnesota. Association for Computational Linguistics.

Seth Aycock, David Stap, Di Wu, Christof Monz, and Khalil Sima'an. 2025. Can LLMs really learn to translate a low-resource language from one grammar book? In *The Thirteenth International Conference on Learning Representations*.

Xuefeng Bai, Jialong Wu, Yulong Chen, Zhongqing Wang, and Yue Zhang. 2023. Constituency parsing using llms. *Preprint*, arXiv:2310.19462.

Terra Blevins, Hila Gonen, and Luke Zettlemoyer. 2023. Prompting language models for linguistic structure. In *Proceedings of the 61st Annual Meeting of the Association for Computational Linguistics (Volume 1: Long Papers)*, pages 6649–6663, Toronto, Canada. Association for Computational Linguistics.

Samuel Cahyawijaya, Holy Lovenia, and Pascale Fung. 2024. LLMs are few-shot in-context low-resource language learners. In *Proceedings of the 2024 Conference of the North American Chapter of the Association for Computational Linguistics: Human Language Technologies (Volume 1: Long Papers)*, pages 405–433, Mexico City, Mexico. Association for Computational Linguistics.

Junjie Chen, Xiangheng He, and Yusuke Miyao. 2024. Language model based unsupervised dependency parsing with conditional mutual information and grammatical constraints. In *Proceedings of the 2024 Conference of the North American Chapter of the Association for Computational Linguistics: Human Language Technologies (Volume 1: Long Papers)*, pages 6355–6366, Mexico City, Mexico. Association for Computational Linguistics.

Alexis Conneau, Kartikay Khandelwal, Naman Goyal, Vishrav Chaudhary, Guillaume Wenzek, Francisco Guzmán, Edouard Grave, Myle Ott, Luke Zettlemoyer, and Veselin Stoyanov. 2020. Unsupervised cross-lingual representation learning at scale. In *Proceedings of the 58th Annual Meeting of the Association for Computational Linguistics*, pages 8440–8451, Online. Association for Computational Linguistics.

Michael A Covington. 2001. A fundamental algorithm for dependency parsing. In *Proceedings of the 39th annual ACM southeast conference*, volume 1. Athens, GA.

Marie-Catherine de Marneffe, Christopher D. Manning, Joakim Nivre, and Daniel Zeman. 2021. Universal Dependencies. *Computational Linguistics*, 47(2):255–308.

Jacob Devlin, Ming-Wei Chang, Kenton Lee, and Kristina Toutanova. 2019. BERT: Pre-training of deep bidirectional transformers for language understanding. In *Proceedings of the 2019 Conference of the North American Chapter of the Association for Computational Linguistics: Human Language Technologies, Volume 1 (Long and Short Papers)*, pages 4171–4186, Minneapolis, Minnesota. Association for Computational Linguistics.

Timothy Dozat and Christopher D. Manning. 2017. Deep biaffine attention for neural dependency parsing. In *International Conference on Learning Representations*.

Abhimanyu Dubey, Abhinav Jauhri, Abhinav Pandey, and alia. 2024. The Llama 3 herd of models. *Preprint*, arXiv:2407.21783.

Ana Ezquerro, Carlos Gómez-Rodríguez, and David Vilares. 2025. Better benchmarking llms for zero-shot dependency parsing. *arXiv preprint arXiv:2502.20866*.

Gemini Team. 2024. Gemini: A family of highly capable multimodal models. *Preprint*, arXiv:2312.11805.

Michael Ginn, Mans Hulden, and Alexis Palmer. 2024. Can we teach language models to gloss endangered languages? In *Findings of the Association for Computational Linguistics: EMNLP 2024*, pages 5861–5876, Miami, Florida, USA. Association for Computational Linguistics.

Jiang Guo, Wanxiang Che, David Yarowsky, Haifeng Wang, and Ting Liu. 2016. A representation learning framework for multi-source transfer parsing. In *AAAI Conference on Artificial Intelligence*.

Awni Hannun, Jagrit Digani, Angelos Katharopoulos, and Ronan Collobert. 2023. MLX: Efficient and flexible machine learning on apple silicon.

Claudiu Daniel Hromei, Danilo Croce, and Roberto Basili. 2024. U-deppllama: Universal dependency parsing via auto-regressive large language models. *IJCoL. Italian Journal of Computational Linguistics*, 10(10, 1).

Daniel Jurafsky and James H. Martin. 2025. *Speech and Language Processing: An Introduction to Natural Language Processing, Computational Linguistics, and Speech Recognition with Language Models,*

3rd edition. Online manuscript released January 12, 2025.

Philipp Koehn. 2004. Statistical significance tests for machine translation evaluation. In *Proceedings of the 2004 Conference on Empirical Methods in Natural Language Processing*, pages 388–395, Barcelona, Spain. Association for Computational Linguistics.

Jianling Li, Meishan Zhang, Peiming Guo, Min Zhang, and Yue Zhang. 2023. LLM-enhanced self-training for cross-domain constituency parsing. In *Proceedings of the 2023 Conference on Empirical Methods in Natural Language Processing*, pages 8174–8185, Singapore. Association for Computational Linguistics.

Zuchao Li, Jiaxun Cai, Shexia He, and Hai Zhao. 2018. Seq2seq dependency parsing. In *Proceedings of the 27th International Conference on Computational Linguistics*, pages 3203–3214, Santa Fe, New Mexico, USA. Association for Computational Linguistics.

Boda Lin, Zijun Yao, Jiaxin Shi, Shulin Cao, Binghao Tang, Si Li, Yong Luo, Juanzi Li, and Lei Hou. 2022a. Dependency parsing via sequence generation. In *Findings of the Association for Computational Linguistics: EMNLP 2022*, pages 7339–7353, Abu Dhabi, United Arab Emirates. Association for Computational Linguistics.

Boda Lin, Xinyi Zhou, Binghao Tang, Xiaocheng Gong, and Si Li. 2023. Chatgpt is a potential zero-shot dependency parser. *Preprint*, arXiv:2310.16654.

Xi Victoria Lin, Todor Mihaylov, Mikel Artetxe, Tianlu Wang, Shuohui Chen, Daniel Simig, Myle Ott, Naman Goyal, Shruti Bhosale, Jingfei Du, Ramakanth Pasunuru, Sam Shleifer, Punit Singh Koura, Vishrav Chaudhary, Brian O'Horo, Jeff Wang, Luke Zettlemoyer, Zornitsa Kozareva, Mona Diab, Veselin Stoyanov, and Xian Li. 2022b. Few-shot learning with multilingual generative language models. In *Proceedings of the 2022 Conference on Empirical Methods in Natural Language Processing*, pages 9019–9052, Abu Dhabi, United Arab Emirates. Association for Computational Linguistics.

Joakim Nivre. 2003. An efficient algorithm for projective dependency parsing. In *Proceedings of the Eighth International Conference on Parsing Technologies*, pages 149–160, Nancy, France.

OpenAI. 2024. Gpt-4o system card. *Preprint*, arXiv:2410.21276.

Tal Schuster, Ori Ram, Regina Barzilay, and Amir Globerson. 2019. Cross-lingual alignment of contextual word embeddings, with applications to zero-shot dependency parsing. In *Proceedings of the 2019 Conference of the North American Chapter of the Association for Computational Linguistics: Human Language Technologies, Volume 1 (Long and Short Papers)*, pages 1599–1613, Minneapolis, Minnesota. Association for Computational Linguistics.

Chenglei Si, Diyi Yang, and Tatsunori Hashimoto. 2024. Can llms generate novel research ideas? a large-scale human study with 100+ nlp researchers. *Preprint*, arXiv:2409.04109.

Milan Straka and Jana Straková. 2017. Tokenizing, POS tagging, lemmatizing and parsing UD 2.0 with UDPipe. In *Proceedings of the CoNLL 2017 Shared Task: Multilingual Parsing from Raw Text to Universal Dependencies*, pages 88–99, Vancouver, Canada. Association for Computational Linguistics.

Yuanhe Tian, Fei Xia, and Yan Song. 2024. Large language models are no longer shallow parsers. In *Proceedings of the 62nd Annual Meeting of the Association for Computational Linguistics (Volume 1: Long Papers)*, pages 7131–7142, Bangkok, Thailand. Association for Computational Linguistics.

Jason Wei, Xuezhi Wang, Dale Schuurmans, Maarten Bosma, brian ichter, Fei Xia, Ed H. Chi, Quoc V Le, and Denny Zhou. 2022. Chain of thought prompting elicits reasoning in large language models. In *Advances in Neural Information Processing Systems*.

Shijie Wu and Mark Dredze. 2020. Are all languages created equal in multilingual BERT? In *Proceedings of the 5th Workshop on Representation Learning for NLP*, pages 120–130, Online. Association for Computational Linguistics.

A Prompts

A.1 Parsing

The base prompt used across experiments is given below.

```
You are predicting the
   dependency parse for a
   sentence in $language.

You will be given a sentence
   word-by-word, with each word
    on a new line. Below is an
   example in English:

1        The
2        dog
3        chases
4        the
5        cat
6        .

You are to predict the
   dependency parse for this
   sentence. For each token,
   you should predict the
   following:
```

```
1. The index of the token's
   head according to its
   dependency relation, or "0"
   if it is the root
2. The type of dependency
   relation

You should output the
   dependency parse using the
   original format, with two
   additional columns (
   separated by tabs) for the
   head and relation type. For
   the example above, you
   should produce the following
   :

1       The     2       det
2       dog     3       nsubj
3       chases  0       root
4       the     5       det
5       cat     3       obj
6       .       3       punct

Do not output any additional
   text. Only produce the
   dependency parse following
   the above format.

Please gloss the following
   example in $language:

$target_example
```

For any settings with the label list included, we add the following:

```
The allowed dependency
   relations are the following:
    $label_list
```

For settings with few-shot examples, we add the following:

```
Below are some fully glossed
   examples in $language.

$examples
```

A.2 Rule Writing

The base prompt for writing rules is:

```
You are writing dependency
   grammar rules given a small
   number of examples. You will
    be provided with parsed
   sentences written word-by-
   word with each word on a new
    line. An example in English
    is given below:

1       The     2       det
2       dog     3       nsubj
3       chases  0       root
4       the     5       det
5       cat     3       obj
6       .       3       punct

The first column is the ID of
   the word. The third column
   is the ID of the head for
   the word. The fourth column
   is the type of dependency
   relation. From this sentence
   , you should first infer
   categories for each of the
   words and output them.
   Please output "Categories:"
   followed by your inferred
   categories, as in the
   following example:

Categories:
Det: the
Noun: dog, cat
Verb: chases
Punct: .

You should omit duplicate words
   , and words may belong to
   multiple categories.

Then, write dependency grammar
   rules using the convention "
   Head -> Dependent (relation
   type)", based on the
   observed rules in the data.
   Print all of the rules,
   seeking to find a minimal
   set of rules that explains
   the data, and starting with
   "Rules:". Do not repeat
   rules. The rules from the
   previous example are given
   below.
```

```
Rules:

Noun -> Det (det)
Verb -> Noun (nsubj)
Root -> Verb (root)
Verb -> Noun (obj)
Verb -> Punct (punct)

You are writing rules for
   $language. Please use the
   following examples to
   produce the analysis, making
    sure to include both the
   Categories and Rules
   sections.

$examples
```

B Example Guidelines

An excerpt from the Kiche guidelines is given below.

```
#### Nouns

- Most nouns are not inflected
   for number, although animate
    nouns can be, in this case
   they are annotated with `
   Number=Plur`.
- There is a subset of nouns
   used relationally, these are
    called relational nouns and
    are used where adpositions
   would be used in other
   languages.
  - They are marked with the
     feature `[NounType]()=
     Relat`.
  - The lemmas are: _ech_, _uk'
     _, _umal_, _wach_, _ib'_,
     _onojel_, _wi'_, _pam_,
     _ij_, _xe'_, _xo'l_,
     _tukel_, _tzalaj_, _naqaj_
     .
  - Relational nouns are also
     used for:
    - Reflexive, _ib'_
    - Introducing the agent in
       a passive, _umal_

#### Verbs

- Transitive verbs have
   polypersonal agreement which
    is indicated through
   layered features `Person[obj
   ]`, `Number[obj]`, `Person[
   subj]`, `Number[subj]`.
- Finite verbs have `Aspect`
   but no `Tense`.
  - The imperfective or
     incompletive is annotated
     with `Aspect=Imp`.
  - The perfective or
     completive is annotated
     with `Aspect=Perf`.
- Incorporated movement is
   indicated through the
   feature `Movement`:
  - Movement away from is
     marked with `Movement=Abl
     `, this is the morph _\-e
     '-_
  - Movement towards is marked
     with `Movement=Lat`, this
     is the morph _\-l-_
- There are two principle
   valency changing processes:
   Passive and antipassive.
   Both produce verbs with only
    set B agreement.
  - In the passive, annotated
     with `Voice=Pass`, the
     object is promoted to
     subject and the subject is
      demoted to oblique.
  - In the antipassive,
     annotated with `Voice=
     Antip`, the subject
     agreement is maintained
     and the object is demoted
     to oblique.
...
```

C Directional Rule Writing

In section 5, we identified an issue where multiple rules could apply to an example, and there was no way to disambiguate which rule to use. One trivial solution is to also specify an ordering between the head and dependent. We experiment with this idea, prompting the LLM to produce rules of the form:

```
Noun -> Det (det, left)
Verb -> Noun (nsubj, left)
```

```
Root -> Verb (root, none)
Verb -> Noun (obj, right)
```

In addition to the relation label, the LLM simply labels whether the dependent occurs to the left or right of the head. We report results for this variation of rule writing on the development set in Table 4. We observe very small improvements in most languages.

For the preceding example, the LLM now correctly identifies the rule PRONOUN -> PARTICLE (CASE, RIGHT) which should resolve the ambiguity. Unfortunately, the LLM now predicts the incorrect relation "nsubj", with no clear reason why (as this does not follow from the rules). Evidently, the inclusion of directions in the rules is not a clear benefit, but introduces other forms of error.

D Variational Experiments

Effect of Labels All of our main settings include a list of allowed relation labels in the prompt. While it is intuitive why this would be beneficial, we also provide empirical validation. In Figure 2, we report the results of zero-shot prediction with and without labels, across the baseline setting and the setting with guidelines included. We see a small improvement from including labels in not only the Labeled Attachment Score (LAS), but also the Unlabeled Attachment Score (UAS). As providing labels is inexpensive, we use this setting for all main experiments.

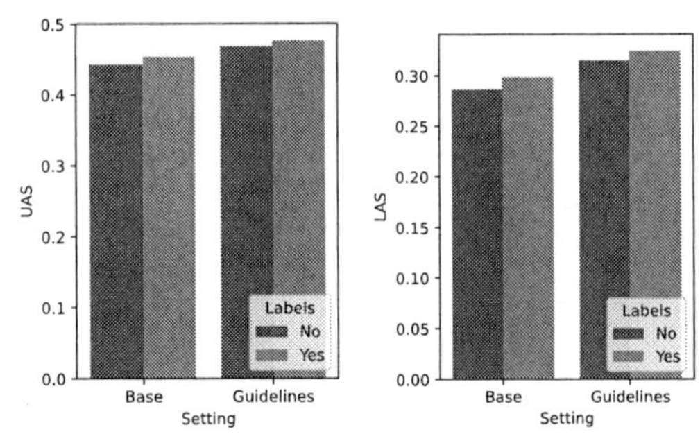

Figure 2: UAS (left) and LAS (right) scores for the zero-shot setting, comparing results when the list of allowed relation labels is included in the prompt versus when it is omitted. In both the base and GUIDELINES setting, we see a small improvement from including labels.

Effect of Chain-of-Thought Another applicable technique is chain-of-thought (CoT) prompting, where the LLM is prompted to produce step-by-step explanations of its thought process (Wei et al., 2022). CoT has proven effective on multistep reasoning problems, and thus is a good fit for the task of understanding and applying the information from in-context examples and in-context rules. We add CoT to the base five-shot setting as well as the five-shot setting with guidelines. We report these results in Figure 3. Unfortunately, adding CoT seems to worsen performance in both settings.

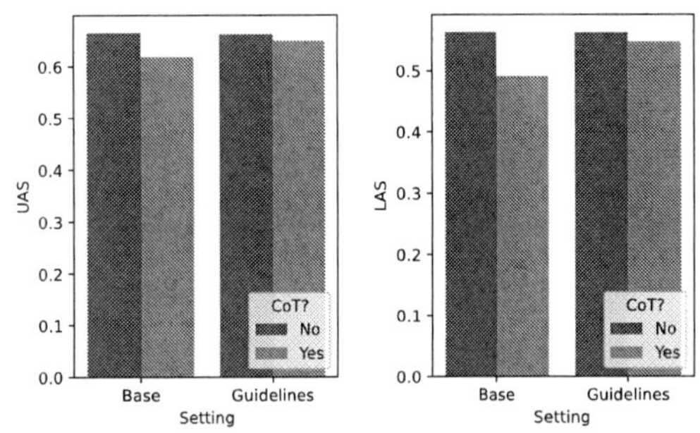

Figure 3: UAS (left) and LAS (right) dev set scores for the five-shot setting, evaluating the effect of adding chain-of-thought prompting. In both the base and GUIDELINES setting, we see a clear detriment from CoT.

Rules	bam	bho	yue	myv	quc	kpv	pcm	yor	mean
Base	61.7	53.4	59.6	**39.9**	72.7	38.3	71.7	50.7	56.0
+ order	**63.5**	**53.6**	**59.7**	38.0	**73.1**	**38.5**	**72.1**	**52.2**	**56.3**

Table 4: LAS scores across languages for the RULE WRITING setting. In the base setting, rules were written as "Head -> Dependent (relation type)" without any notion of word order. In the + ORDER setting, rules additionally included whether the dependent was to the left or right of the head.

Cognitive Mirroring for DocRE: A Self-Supervised Iterative Reflection Framework with Triplet-Centric Explicit and Implicit Feedback

Xu Han[1], Bo Wang[1*], Yueheng Sun[1], Dongming Zhao[2], Zongfeng Qu[1,3], Ruifang He[1], Yuexian Hou[1*], Qinghua Hu[1]
[1]College of Intelligence and Computing, Tianjin University, Tianjin, China
[2]AI Lab, China Mobile Communication Group Tianjin Co., Ltd.
[3]CHEARI (Beijing) Certification & Testing Co.,Ltd., Beijing, China
{hx_2001, bo_wang}@tju.edu.cn

Abstract

Large language models (LLMs) have advanced document-level relation extraction (DocRE), but DocRE is more complex than sentence-level relation extraction (SentRE), facing challenges like diverse relation types, coreference resolution and long-distance dependencies. Traditional pipeline methods, which detect relations before generating triplets, often propagate errors and harm performance. Meanwhile, fine-tuning methods require extensive human-annotated data, and in-context learning (ICL) underperforms compared to supervised approaches. We propose an iterative reflection framework for DocRE, inspired by human nonlinear reading cognition. The framework leverages explicit and implicit relations between triplets to provide feedback for LLMs refinement. Explicit feedback uses logical rules-based reasoning, while implicit feedback reconstructs triplets into documents for comparison. This dual-process iteration mimics human semantic cognition, enabling dynamic optimization through self-generated supervision. For the first time, this achieves zero-shot performance comparable to fully supervised models. Experiments show our method surpasses existing LLM-based approaches and matches state-of-the-art BERT-based methods[1].

1 Introduction

DocRE aims to identify entity pairs and their semantic relations within long contexts, playing a vital role in various downstream NLP applications. LLMs have made significant progress in classical information extraction tasks (Xu et al., 2024). Recent studies leverage their strong instruction-following abilities and rich intrinsic knowledge to enhance DocRE performance (Ozyurt et al., 2024; Sun et al., 2024; Li et al., 2023).

However, DocRE is more challenging than SentRE due to the diversity of relation types, coreference resolution and long-distance dependencies within the document. Consequently, many SentRE methods (Wadhwa et al., 2023; Wan et al., 2023) cannot be directly applied to DocRE. To address these challenges, existing methods typically adopt a linear pipeline framework (Wei et al., 2024), which sequentially detects relations and generates triplets. However, this often leads to error propagation, degrading downstream performance. Based on the linear framework, these methods primarily rely on two paradigms: supervised methods requiring costly human annotations, and ICL approaches that underperform their supervised counterparts.

Existing linear frameworks do not align with the human cognitive process, which is iterative and conflict-driven rather than linear. The DocRE task inherently mirrors this process: when extracting relations from documents, humans naturally re-read ambiguous parts and resolve conflicts (aligned with the Construction-Integration Model (Kintsch, 1988) and Cognitive Dissonance Theory (Festinger, 1957)), and distinguish at both explicit and implicit levels (as per Dual Process Theory (Evans, 2003)). These theories suggest that text comprehension involves dynamic re-evaluation of earlier content when conflicts or missing information arise, not only emphasizing the iterative nature of human reading cognition, but also highlighting that the main driver of this iteration is the resolution of conflicts between knowledge. However, existing linear DocRE models violate these theories by processing documents unidirectionally without iterative verification, leading to suboptimal performance.

This disconnect becomes evident when considering the demonstrated success of the self-correction mechanism in other NLP domains (Pan et al., 2024), whose potential for DocRE remains strikingly underexplored. The absence of such reflective capabilities in existing approaches not only violates

*Corresponding authors.

[1]The authors are non-native English speakers, and AI assistants were used to polish certain sections of the paper, but were not used in research or coding.

Proceedings of the 1st Joint Workshop on Large Language Models and Structure Modeling (XLLM 2025), pages 197–217
August 1, 2025 ©2025 Association for Computational Linguistics

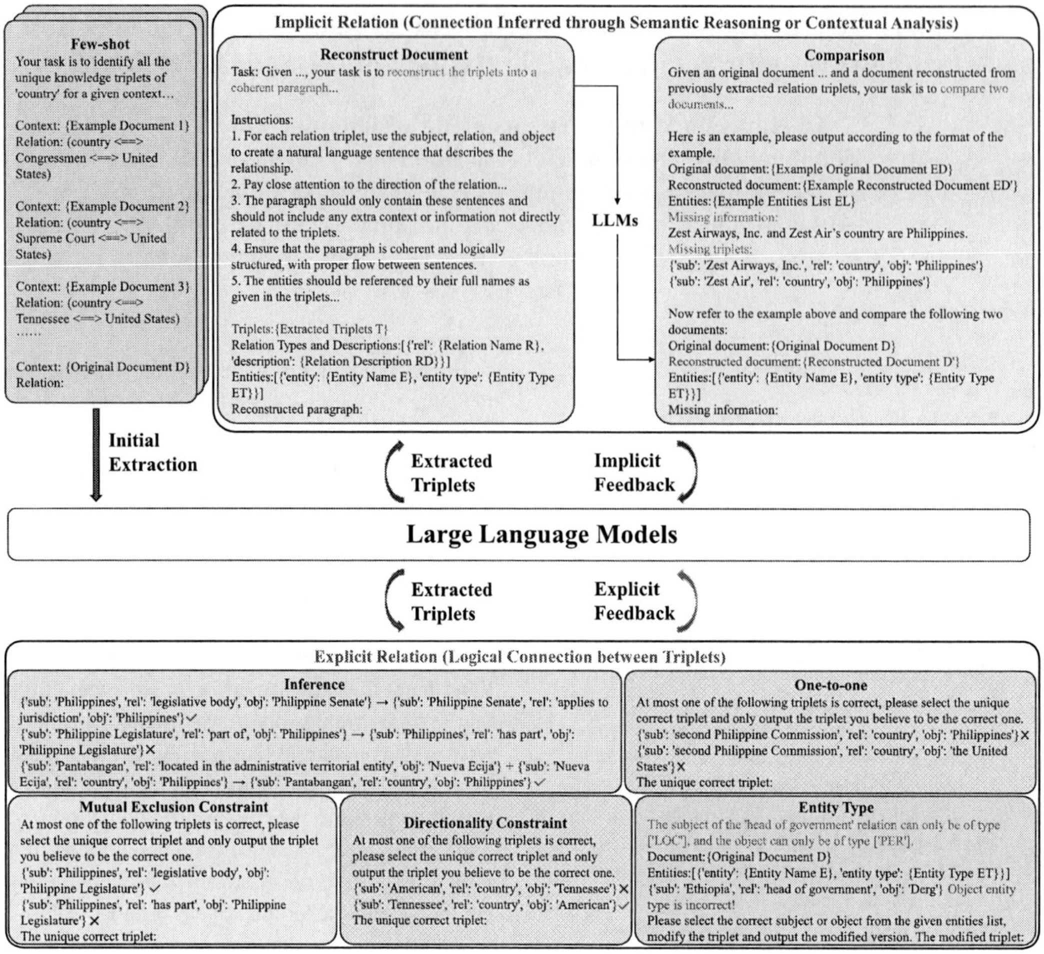

Figure 1: Overview of our framework, which consists of three modules: 1) Initial Extraction. 2) Obtain feedback on implicit relations between triplets through reconstruction (indicated by the red arrow). 3) Obtain feedback on explicit relations between triplets through logical rules-based inference and filtering (indicated by the green arrow).

cognitive theories but also limits their ability to handle the diverse relation types and coreference resolution of document-level understanding.

To bridge these gaps, we introduce an iterative reflection framework grounded in cognitive theories. By integrating self-supervised feedback signals, this framework circumvents the resource-intensive demands of supervised methods. To achieve comparable performance to supervised methods, we further draw on cognitive theories to introduce explicit and implicit relations between triplets, providing the corresponding self-supervised and low-cost rules-based feedback for LLMs refinement.

Specifically, our iterative reflection framework for ICL-based DocRE employs the self-correction mechanism, where LLMs follow an iterative extraction-verification-feedback-correction process to mitigate error propagation through constant error detection and correction. We define the implicit relation as a connection between triplets that is not explicitly stated but can be inferred through semantic reasoning or contextual analysis. Feedback on implicit relations is generated by reconstructing the extracted triplets into a document and comparing it with the original. In contrast, the explicit relation represents a direct logical connection between triplets. Feedback on explicit relations is provided through logical rules-based inference and filtering. By emphasizing and analyzing the relations between triplets, our method enhances contextual understanding and improves extraction accuracy, better handling the complex DocRE task. The overall framework is illustrated in Figure 1.

Our main work and contributions are as follows:

- Inspired by human non-linear reading cognition, we propose cognitive mirroring, a self-supervised iterative reflection framework for general-domain ICL-based DocRE that eliminates the need for supervised fine-tuning. To the best of our knowledge, this is the first exploration of self-correction in DocRE, enabling iterative extraction correction through feedback to mitigate error propagation.
- Drawing insights from the Dual Process Theory, we introduce the concepts of explicit and implicit relations between triplets. Triplet-centric explicit feedback is based on supplementary logical rules, while implicit feedback is generated through reconstruction. By jointly analyzing explicit logical relations and their interactions within the document and semantics, LLMs can better understand and reason through complex contexts, which is more suitable for the challenging DocRE task.
- Extensive experiments on DocRED and Re-DocRED datasets show our method surpasses existing LLM-based approaches and matches SOTA BERT-based methods.

2 Related Work

Human Cognitive Science Cognitive theories provide key insights into dual-process iteration. Construction-Integration Model (Kintsch, 1988) highlights reading as a dynamic process, where readers iteratively revise their understanding in response to conflicts or missing information. This aligns with the Cognitive Dissonance Theory (Festinger, 1957), which emphasizes the importance of resolving contradictions through reflective correction. Dual-Process Theory (Evans, 2003) suggests that human cognition involves both fast, intuitive processing (System 1) and slower, controlled reasoning (System 2). These theories inform our approach, integrating non-linear iteration and dual-relation analysis to enhance DocRE.

LLMs for DocRE Recent studies have explored approaches to harness the potential of LLMs for DocRE. For instance, (Sun et al., 2024) proposes a framework that employs zero-shot learning by generating synthetic data through a chain-of-retrieval prompt. Since DocRE involves many relation types and the output of LLMs is uncontrollable, (Li et al., 2023) combines LLMs with a natural language inference module to generate triplets, thus improving performance. REPLM (Ozyurt et al., 2024) introduces an in-context few-shot method leveraging pre-trained models, where triplets are generated based on relations and filtered according to the joint probabilities of entity pairs. Both DiVA-DocRE (Wu et al., 2024a) and AutoRE (Xue et al., 2024) first identify the relation types present in the document. AutoRE extracts the head entities for each relation before generating the complete triplets, while DiVA-DocRE incorporates active and passive voice information during extraction. However, these methods either require additional fine-tuning, or exhibit suboptimal performance when relying solely on ICL. Furthermore, decomposing DocRE into multiple steps may lead to error propagation, where errors in earlier stages negatively impact the performance of subsequent stages.

LLMs with Self-Correction Mechanism The self-correction mechanism for LLMs has demonstrated success across diverse tasks, including hallucination detection (Dhuliawala et al., 2024; Xue et al., 2023), mathematical reasoning (Zheng et al., 2024; Wu et al., 2024b; Jiang et al., 2024; Xue et al., 2023), question answering (Shinn et al., 2023; Zhao et al., 2023), dialogue generation (Madaan et al., 2023) and code optimization (Chern et al., 2023). However, applying this mechanism to DocRE remains underexplored. Metacognitive prompting (MP) (Wang and Zhao, 2024) enhances natural language understanding through structured self-aware evaluations by drawing on intrinsic knowledge and new insights. However, MP has only been preliminarily explored in the biomedical domain and does not involve iterative learning for LLMs. STAR (Ma et al., 2024) employs self-correction for data optimization and augmentation, while SRVF (Li et al., 2024) mitigates the bias of LLMs toward relation types through supervised feedback. Chem-FINESE (Wang et al., 2024) proposes a self-validation module for chemical entity extraction, employing contrastive loss to reduce excessive copying during extraction. However, these methods require additional fine-tuning and have not been extensively explored in DocRE. In this study, we propose a self-correction framework for general-domain DocRE that requires no supervised fine-tuning and enables iterative error correction, bridging the gap between the self-correction mechanism and DocRE.

3 Methodology

As illustrated in Figure 1, the proposed framework generates feedback for iterative modification of

LLMs by analyzing explicit and implicit relations between triplets. Specifically, the framework consists of three phases: 1) initial extraction, 2) triplet-centric implicit feedback through reconstruction, and 3) explicit feedback based on logical rules.

3.1 Task Formulation

DocRE aims to predict relations between entity pairs that may appear across multiple sentences in a document. Given a document D with entities $E = \{e_i\}$, the goal is to identify relation triplets (r, e_s, e_o), where $r \in R$, $e_s, e_o \in E$, and R is the set of predefined relation types, e_s and e_o respectively denote the subject entity and the object entity. Each entity may be mentioned multiple times.

3.2 Initial Extraction

We build upon the REPLM framework (Ozyurt et al., 2024), which generates triplets for each relation in the relation list and filters these triplets by calculating the joint probabilities of subject-object pairs. Finally, the framework aggregates predictions from multiple retrieved demonstrations to obtain the final predictions.

3.3 Triplet-Centric Implicit Feedback

Implicit Relation We define implicit relations between triplets as the connections that are not directly reflected in explicit expression but can be inferred through semantic reasoning or contextual analysis. These relations encompass the mutual influence of triplets on each other when they serve as context, as well as semantic connections between triplets within a document that cannot be clearly represented by formal definitions. For instance, in the text *It meets at Legislative Hall in Dover, Delaware, convening on the second Tuesday of January of odd years*, the triplets *(Legislative Hall, located in the administrative territorial entity, Dover)* and *(Legislative Hall, located in the administrative territorial entity, Delaware)* do not explicitly state the geographical relation between *Dover* and *Delaware*. However, contextual inference reveals that *Dover* is a location within *Delaware*, establishing an implicit relation between these two triplets. Although the relation is not explicitly stated, it is inferred by semantic reasoning.

Drawing on cognitive science principles of human reverse verification, our framework generates feedback on implicit relations between triplets by leveraging extracted triplets to reconstruct a document and comparing the reconstructed document with the original document at a fine-grained level.

For DocRE, the reconstruction process serves as a representation of extraction quality, where better extraction results yield smaller discrepancies between reconstructed and original documents. This comparative analysis enables error identification through two primary mechanisms: 1) detection of missing content when original document elements are absent in the reconstructed version, indicating potential extraction failures, and 2) identification of semantic contradictions in the reconstructed document, revealing extraction errors.

The rationale for employing document-level comparison rather than direct triplet-document comparison is twofold. First, LLMs excel at understanding and processing unstructured data, making document-level comparison more effective for identifying discrepancies. Second, reconstructing all extracted triplets into a single document facilitates the integration and analysis of implicit relations between triplets, whereas direct comparison typically examines triplets in isolation, potentially overlooking contextual information.

3.4 Triplet-Centric Explicit Feedback

Explicit Relation Our method defines explicit relations as logical connections between triplets, which can be inferred and filtered through rules to identify which triplets have not been extracted, which extracted triplets are incorrect, or which are contradictory to each other. These analyses provide feedback for LLMs to correct their predictions. The rules-based module we implement comprises five principal categories:

Inference We follow MILR (Fan et al., 2022), a logic-enhanced framework designed to enhance DocRE by mining and injecting logical rules. It mines logical rules from annotations based on frequencies. For example:

$$\textit{father}\,(x, y) \wedge \textit{spouse}\,(y, z) \rightarrow \textit{mother}\,(x, z)$$
$$\textit{has part}\,(x, y) \rightarrow \textit{part of}\,(y, x)$$

We utilize inference rules to identify missing or incorrectly extracted triplets.

One-to-one For certain relation types, a subject can maintain the relation with only one object. For instance, *a city can only belong to one country, and a person can only have one date of birth*. If the extracted triplets contain the following two triplets, it can be determined that at most one of these triplets is correct, since *Beibu Gulf Economic Rim can only belong to one country*. Then, LLMs are guided to select the most plausible triplet based on the document and relation description.

(Beibu Gulf Economic Rim, country, China)
(Beibu Gulf Economic Rim, country, Vietnam)

Mutual Exclusion Constraint This constraint prohibits entities from simultaneously maintaining mutually exclusive relations. For instance, the following two triplets, *Lansing is the capital of Michigan* and *Michigan is a direct subdivision of Lansing* are logically contradictory, as they attempt to establish both *contains administrative territorial entity* and *capital of* relations between the same entity pair. Such mutually exclusive relations cannot coexist, ensuring that at most one of the conflicting triplets can be correct. The framework identifies these contradictions and guides LLMs to select.

(Lansing, contains administrative territorial entity, Michigan)
(Lansing, capital of, Michigan)

Directionality Constraint This constraint emphasizes the significance of relation directionality between entities, prohibiting reversals that result in logical inconsistencies. For example, consider the triplet *(ITS, developer, SpaceX)*, which indicates that *SpaceX is the developer of ITS*. This relation is inherently unidirectional, reversing the triplet to *(SpaceX, developer, ITS)* creates a logical contradiction, as *ITS cannot be the developer of SpaceX* if *SpaceX is already the developer of ITS*. Consequently, at most one of the following two triplets can be correct, and the framework identifies such directional violations and guides LLMs to select.

(ITS, developer, SpaceX)
(SpaceX, developer, ITS)

Entity Type To mitigate the directional errors exhibited by LLMs, we comprehensively redefined the relation descriptions of datasets to emphasize not only the directionality of relations but also the potential content of the subject and object entities. Meanwhile, we also consider type constraints for both the subject and object of each relation. For example, the subject of the *head of government* relation must be of type *location*, and the object must be of type *person*, indicating that *object is the head of government of subject*. Triplets violating these type constraints are identified as erroneous and used as feedback for LLMs refinement. Examples of relation descriptions and entity type constraints are presented in Appendix A.

By iteratively generating feedback based on both explicit and implicit relations between triplets, LLMs can continuously optimize the extraction results and improve performance. Our method is not only suitable for DocRE that requires complex text processing and judgment but also helps mitigate error propagation by constantly identifying and correcting errors.

The method can be implemented with only the definition of relations and logical rules, without the need for any oracle labels. For initial extraction, we adopt the five-shot prompts from REPLM (Ozyurt et al., 2024). During iterations, we employ one-shot prompts for reconstructing and identifying unextracted triplets, while maintaining zero-shot prompts for other steps. This implementation avoids the issue raised by (Huang et al., 2024), regarding sub-optimal prompts for generating initial responses, while providing more informative instructions about the task in the feedback prompts.

The full prompts of entire framework are presented in Appendix B.

4 Experiments

4.1 Datasets and Evaluation Metric

We conduct experiments on DocRED (Yao et al., 2019) and Re-DocRED (Tan et al., 2022), two large-scale crowd-sourced benchmark datasets tailored for DocRE. Due to the absence of ground truth labels in the test set of DocRED, we perform evaluations only on the dev set. Further details are provided in Appendix C.

Our evaluation employs the strict Micro F1 metric, where a prediction is considered correct only when it precisely identifies both the subject and object entities along with their relation. It's important to highlight that within the datasets, multiple entity mentions may refer to the same underlying entity. Therefore, predictions matching any alias of the annotated entity are accepted as correct. To ensure a rigorous and valid evaluation, regardless of the number of aliases an entity possesses, it will only be counted once in the triplet alignment evaluation. All incorrect predictions are flagged as false positives. This approach ensures a precise and statistically valid evaluation, lending robust credibility to our results.

4.2 Implementation

We employ GPT-3.5-Turbo, GPT-4o, ChatGLM3-6B, and LLaMA3-8B as our backbone LLMs. To obtain deterministic outputs, we set a low temperature, such as 0.001, while keeping all other parameters at their default values. The total API cost for GPT-3.5-Turbo and GPT-4o used in our exploration and experiments is approximately $1,000. ChatGLM3-6B is deployed on an NVIDIA Tesla P100 PCI-E 16GB GPU, and LLaMA3-8B is deployed via Ollama.

In the REPLM framework (Ozyurt et al., 2024), $L = 5$ is set to obtain five sets of in-context demonstrations, each of which is used to extract triplets individually before aggregation. In our experiments, we set $L = 1$ to initially extract triplets only once, while keeping all other parameter configurations identical to those in the REPLM framework.

4.3 Baselines

We compare our framework with both BERT-based and LLM-based methods on the datasets. The BERT-based baselines, recognized for achieving SOTA performance, leverage BERT family pretrained models as encoders. The LLM-based baselines incorporate techniques such as supervised fine-tuning and chain-of-thought (CoT) to enhance relation extraction performance. All the baselines we selected for comparison are shown in Table 1 with detailed descriptions provided in Appendix D.

5 Results and Discussion

5.1 Main Results

Due to the iterative framework involving repeated extraction and cost constraints, the main results of our method are based on a single run, as presented in Table 1. From these results, we can draw the following conclusions.

Our framework demonstrates significant performance improvements across two datasets. Specifically, our method achieves SOTA performance with a micro F1 score of 69.58 on the DocRED dev set using GPT-4o, surpassing previous BERT-based methods by 1.45 and prior LLM-based methods by 2.11. On the Re-DocRED dev set, where SOTA methods were not evaluated, our method outperforms all LLM-based methods, including those with fine-tuning. On the Re-DocRED test set, our method significantly outperforms recent LLM-based methods and narrows the performance gap with SOTA methods. Although it does not achieve SOTA performance on the Re-DocRED test set, the results after two iterations show significant improvements over the initial extraction across both datasets. For example, on the Re-DocRED dataset, the performance improvement is 24.77 on the dev set and approximately 22.72 on the test set, both based on GPT-4o, demonstrating the effectiveness of our method.

Our framework outperforms the self-consistency method. The results in (Huang et al., 2024) reveal that some self-correction methods do not outperform self-consistency. As shown in Table 1, REPLM (Ozyurt et al., 2024) uses five sets of in-context demonstrations to extract five times and filters triplets based on the probabilities of entity pairs. This can be considered as a self-consistency method that establishes five reasoning paths. In contrast, our method achieves better performance with only two iterations. Specifically, based on GPT-4o, our method reaches an F1 score of 69.58 after two iterations, compared to REPLM's 67.47. This demonstrates that our method not only surpasses self-consistency in performance but also achieves higher efficiency with lower resource demands. We provide detailed token usage statistics for DocRED's 998 documents (calculated using OpenAI's tiktoken) in Appendix E, demonstrating the practical advantages of our framework.

Our framework is applicable to a wide range of LLMs and demonstrates enhanced performance with more powerful models. To validate the adaptability and robustness of our method for DocRE across different LLMs, we conduct experiments with four representative LLMs: ChatGLM3-6B, LLaMA3-8B, GPT-3.5, and GPT-4o, covering both open-source and closed-source models, as well as varying model sizes. The results confirm the applicability of our method across different LLMs and its effectiveness in handling the DocRE task. Whether for the initial extraction or after two iterations, GPT-4o consistently outperforms GPT-3.5, followed by LLaMA3-8B and ChatGLM3-6B. Although LLaMA3-8B starts with relatively low F1 scores, its performance improves significantly after two iterations, surpassing that of ChatGLM3-6B. While ChatGLM3-6B and LLaMA3-8B do not outperform fine-tuned LLM-based baselines, our zero-shot self-supervised method substantially narrows the performance gap. Iterative improvements further validate the effectiveness of our approach. In addition, more powerful LLMs exhibit greater performance gains through iteration. For example, on the DocRED dev set, the F1 score of GPT-3.5 increased by 19.45, while GPT-4o improved by 23.17. This shows that our framework not only adapts ef-

Method	PLM	DocRED	Re-DocRED dev	Re-DocRED test
BERT-based				
JMRL-DREEAM (Qi et al., 2024)	$\text{RoBERTa}_{\text{large}}$	67.61	-	78.61
DREEAM (Ma et al., 2023)	$\text{RoBERTa}_{\text{large}}$	67.41	-	<u>81.44</u>
DocRE-CLiP (Jain et al., 2024)	$\text{BERT}_{\text{base}}$	<u>68.13</u>	-	**81.55**
LLM-based				
GenRDK (Sun et al., 2024)	LLaMA2-13B-CHAT	42.50	39.90	41.30
DiVA-DocRE^{GT} (Wu et al., 2024a)	LLama3-7B	55.48	<u>61.99</u>	61.40
REPLM (Ozyurt et al., 2024)	GPT-3.5	59.66	$41.07^{\dagger}$	$40.30^{\dagger}$
	GPT-4o	67.47	$41.67^{\dagger}$	$41.48^{\dagger}$
AutoRE (Xue et al., 2024)	Vicuna-7B	-	54.29	53.84
Our Framework				
Initial Extraction	ChatGLM3-6B	21.30	18.18	18.29
	LLama3-8B	9.40	6.97	6.71
	GPT-3.5	43.13	39.32	37.71
	GPT-4o	46.41	40.02	40.55
Iteration 2	ChatGLM3-6B	43.71	34.99	35.38
	LLama3-8B	53.86	43.83	43.01
	GPT-3.5	62.58	58.48	56.95
	GPT-4o	**69.58**	**64.79**	63.27

Table 1: Results on the DocRED and Re-DocRED datasets. Shown: Micro F1 scores. The results of all baseline methods are taken from their papers, while † denotes results reproduced using the official code provided by the methods. For each dataset, the best result is in **bold**, while the second-best result is <u>underlined</u>.

fectively to various LLMs but also benefits more significantly from stronger model capabilities.

5.2 Analysis on Relation Density

Since our method considers explicit and implicit relations between triplets, and the relations between triplets are intuitively closely related to the relation density, we conduct experiments to evaluate its effectiveness on datasets with varying relation densities. Documents in each dataset are arranged in descending order of relation density and divided into two equally sized subsets: one with high relation density and the other with low relation density. We define relation density as the ratio of the number of triplet facts to the number of entity pairs. Formally, relation density is computed as follows:

$$relation\_density = \frac{tn}{epn} \quad (1)$$

$$epn = \frac{en * (en - 1)}{2} \quad (2)$$

where tn and en represent the number of triplets and entities annotated in the document, respectively, and epn is the number of entity pairs.

Our method demonstrates superior performance improvements on datasets with high relation density. As shown in Table 2, across both datasets, the performance improvements after two iterations are greater for high relation density datasets compared to low relation density datasets. Although the initial F1 scores on high relation density datasets are lower due to the increased complexity of extraction in such datasets, they surpass those of low relation density datasets after two iterations on the dev sets of DocRED and Re-DocRED. Notably, on these dev sets, the performance on low relation density datasets even surpasses that of baseline methods, though it remains slightly lower on Re-DocRED test set. This indicates that our method effectively captures relational information and performs better when the relations between triplets are more tightly connected, particularly in scenarios requiring complex relational parsing within document-level context. For datasets with lower relation density, methods such as information summarization could be employed to increase

Dataset	DocRED dev		Re-DocRED dev		Re-DocRED test	
Overall F1	46.41	69.58 (+23.17)	40.02	64.79 (+23.12)	40.55	63.27 (+21.79)
High Relation Density F1	45.98	70.63 (+24.65)	39.41	65.09 (+25.68)	39.29	63.04 (+23.75)
Low Relation Density F1	46.85	68.53 (+21.68)	40.63	64.50 (+23.87)	41.81	63.50 (+21.69)

Table 2: Analysis on relation density. For each set, the left column displays the micro F1 scores of the initial extraction, while the right column shows the F1 scores after two iterations. The values in parentheses represent the increase in the F1 scores after two iterations. All these results are based on GPT-4o.

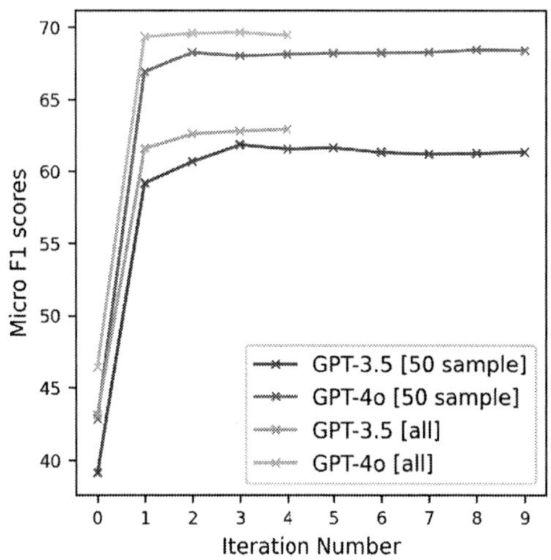

Figure 2: Impact of iteration number on DocRED dev set.

density, which can be explored in future work.

5.3 Impact of Iteration Number

The number of interactions refers to the frequency with which the LLMs receive feedback and improve the extraction results. The zeroth iteration represents the initial extraction. Given the high cost of API calls, we randomly sample 50 documents from the DocRED dev set and conduct 10 iterations. For the entire DocRED dev set, we perform 5 iterations using both GPT-3.5 and GPT-4o. As illustrated in Figure 2, our results indicate that the model reaches its performance peak during the second or third iteration, after which the performance fluctuates around the peak.

The diminishing returns in performance improvements in subsequent iterations may be attributed to several factors. First, the reconstruction of implicit relations faces the following challenges: 1) Certain triplets involve deep semantic understanding and multi-step reasoning, such as identifying hierarchical relations among entities, are inherently difficult for the model to detect. 2) Entities with low frequencies are less likely to be identified by LLMs. 3) Previous research (Wadhwa et al., 2023) has indicated that evaluating LLM-based methods should not rely exclusively on exact matches to target triplets. LLMs can generate outputs that are semantically proximate but fail to meet exact-matching criteria. Specially, t is a triplet in the annotations and t' is a semantically similar triplet generated by the LLMs that does not satisfy the exact-matching requirement, the reconstructed document will contain the corresponding semantic content. Consequently, t will not be considered unextracted, and t' will not be identified as an incorrect triplet to remove. 4) Issues with the directionality of relations may also confuse the semantics of reconstructed documents. Additionally, performance bottlenecks may arise due to logical reasoning based on rules, which can lead to logical loops.

The observed performance degradation during iterations can be attributed to two main factors: 1) Reconstruction and logical rules-based inference may identify unextracted triplets that are not included in annotations, resulting in a decrease in precision. 2) Incorrect triplets introduced by reconstruction and logical inference can affect the selection of LLMs during subsequent filtering with one-to-one, mutual exclusion, and directionality constraints, resulting in a decrease in recall.

5.4 Ablation study

Figure 3 illustrates the performance improvement process of two datasets during two iterations, starting from initial extraction. As shown, both the reconstruction module for implicit relations and the module for explicit relations contribute to performance enhancements to varying degrees. As mentioned above, although rules-based inference and filtering may form a closed loop, and reconstruction may introduce incorrect triplets, the synergistic combination of both modules yields superior performance in the second iteration compared to

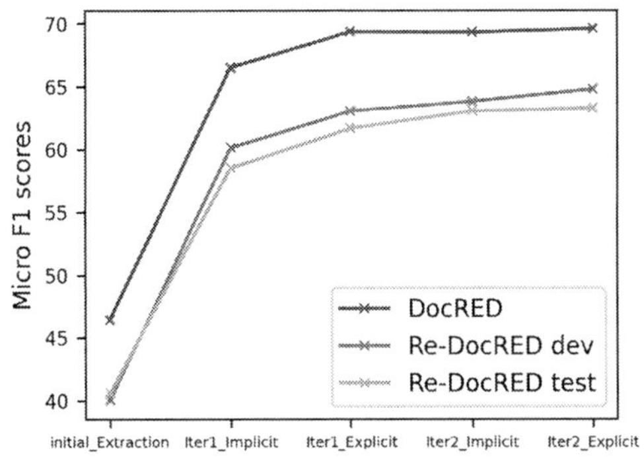

Figure 3: Ablation study. All the results are based on GPT-4o.

the first. This indicates the effectiveness of both modules within the overall framework.

A detailed case study of a complete iteration process is presented in Appendix F.

6 Conclusion

Inspired by human non-linear reading cognition, we propose an iterative reflection framework for ICL-based DocRE that validates both explicit and implicit relations between triplets. The framework initiates with preliminary extraction and then establishes an iterative extraction-verification-feedback-correction procedure. Explicit relational feedback is based on logical rules-based reasoning, while feedback on implicit relations is generated by reconstructing the extracted triplets into a document and comparing it with the original. This dual-process mechanism mimics human cognition, enabling self-supervised optimization without reliance on annotated data. Extensive experiments demonstrate that our framework not only narrows the performance gap with SOTA BERT-based methods, but also performs better in complex DocRE task. Additionally, it helps mitigate error propagation by continuously identifying and correcting errors. Furthermore, our method explores the application of the self-correction mechanism in DocRE, offering a more efficient and convenient solution. It provides new insights and directions for the application of LLMs in DocRE and offers a valuable reference for future exploration.

Limitations

Due to cost constraints and limitations in biomedicine domain knowledge, we have not yet conducted experiments on CDR, GDA and DocGNRE datasets, nor have we explored the performance on multilingual datasets. Additionally, we have not compared multiple prompt variants. We have not explored the impact of using few-shot prompts in all modules or considered the influence of the order of in-context learning demonstrations, instructions, and relation descriptions in the prompts on experimental results, nor have we accounted for the impact of factors like demonstrations quality. These limitations will be explored in our future work.

Moreover, the generation of Triplet-Centric Explicit Feedback in our framework currently relies on manually defined logical rules. Although our framework only requires low-cost domain-specific rule definitions, either for general or specialized domains, this dependence still introduces some level of manual effort. We will explore the automatic induction or learning of more detailed, accurate, and dataset-specific logical rules to further enhance the performance and generalizability of our method.

Ethics Statement

All documents and models used in this study were obtained from open-source sources, ensuring transparency and accessibility. Our framework provides an effective solution for DocRE using LLMs, without requiring additional training or fine-tuning. This makes it easier to deploy and use in practice. However, we acknowledge the potential risk of misuse, particularly regarding the extraction of personal or sensitive information. To mitigate this concern, we only use public benchmark datasets DocRED and Re-DocRED for evaluation. These datasets do not involve personal privacy. We also advocate not applying our framework to extract or analyze any private data without user authorization.

Moreover, we recognize that LLMs may inherit implicit biases from their training data. Although our framework can identify triplets, biased or unintended outputs may still occur, especially when analyzing sensitive relation types or entities. We advocate for the careful and responsible use of such models and encourage further research to identify, evaluate and mitigate these potential biases.

Acknowledgments

This work was supported by the National Natural Science Foundation of China (62376188, 62272340, 62276187, 62376192, 62166022) and the Key Technology Research and Industrial Application Demonstration of General Large Model with Autonomous Intelligent Computing Power, No.24ZGZNGX00020).

References

I-Chun Chern, Steffi Chern, Shiqi Chen, Weizhe Yuan, Kehua Feng, Chunting Zhou, Junxian He, Graham Neubig, and Pengfei Liu. 2023. Factool: Factuality detection in generative ai – a tool augmented framework for multi-task and multi-domain scenarios. *Preprint*, arXiv:2307.13528.

Tim Dettmers, Artidoro Pagnoni, Ari Holtzman, and Luke Zettlemoyer. 2023. Qlora: efficient finetuning of quantized llms. In *Proceedings of the 37th International Conference on Neural Information Processing Systems*, NIPS '23, Red Hook, NY, USA. Curran Associates Inc.

Shehzaad Dhuliawala, Mojtaba Komeili, Jing Xu, Roberta Raileanu, Xian Li, Asli Celikyilmaz, and Jason Weston. 2024. Chain-of-verification reduces hallucination in large language models. In *Findings of the Association for Computational Linguistics: ACL 2024*, pages 3563–3578, Bangkok, Thailand. Association for Computational Linguistics.

Jonathan St.B.T. Evans. 2003. In two minds: dual-process accounts of reasoning. *Trends in Cognitive Sciences*, 7(10):454–459.

Shengda Fan, Shasha Mo, and Jianwei Niu. 2022. Boosting document-level relation extraction by mining and injecting logical rules. In *Proceedings of the 2022 Conference on Empirical Methods in Natural Language Processing*, pages 10311–10323, Abu Dhabi, United Arab Emirates. Association for Computational Linguistics.

Leon Festinger. 1957. *A Theory of Cognitive Dissonance*. Stanford University Press, Redwood City.

Jie Huang, Xinyun Chen, Swaroop Mishra, Huaixiu Steven Zheng, Adams Wei Yu, Xinying Song, and Denny Zhou. 2024. Large language models cannot self-correct reasoning yet. In *The Twelfth International Conference on Learning Representations*.

Monika Jain, Raghava Mutharaju, Ramakanth Kavuluru, and Kuldeep Singh. 2024. Revisiting document-level relation extraction with context-guided link prediction. In *Proceedings of the Thirty-Eighth AAAI Conference on Artificial Intelligence and Thirty-Sixth Conference on Innovative Applications of Artificial Intelligence and Fourteenth Symposium on Educational Advances in Artificial Intelligence*, AAAI'24/IAAI'24/EAAI'24. AAAI Press.

Weisen Jiang, Han Shi, Longhui Yu, Zhengying Liu, Yu Zhang, Zhenguo Li, and James Kwok. 2024. Forward-backward reasoning in large language models for mathematical verification. In *Findings of the Association for Computational Linguistics: ACL 2024*, pages 6647–6661, Bangkok, Thailand. Association for Computational Linguistics.

Walter Kintsch. 1988. The role of knowledge in discourse comprehension: a construction-integration model. *Psychological review*, 95 2:163–82.

Junpeng Li, Zixia Jia, and Zilong Zheng. 2023. Semi-automatic data enhancement for document-level relation extraction with distant supervision from large language models. In *Proceedings of the 2023 Conference on Empirical Methods in Natural Language Processing*, pages 5495–5505, Singapore. Association for Computational Linguistics.

Yongqi Li, Xin Miao, Shen Zhou, Mayi Xu, Yuyang Ren, and Tieyun Qian. 2024. Enhancing relation extraction via supervised rationale verification and feedback. *Preprint*, arXiv:2412.07289.

Mingyu Derek Ma, Xiaoxuan Wang, Po-Nien Kung, P. Jeffrey Brantingham, Nanyun Peng, and Wei Wang. 2024. Star: boosting low-resource information extraction by structure-to-text data generation with large language models. In *Proceedings of the Thirty-Eighth AAAI Conference on Artificial Intelligence and Thirty-Sixth Conference on Innovative Applications of Artificial Intelligence and Fourteenth Symposium on Educational Advances in Artificial Intelligence*, AAAI'24/IAAI'24/EAAI'24. AAAI Press.

Youmi Ma, An Wang, and Naoaki Okazaki. 2023. DREEAM: Guiding attention with evidence for improving document-level relation extraction. In *Proceedings of the 17th Conference of the European Chapter of the Association for Computational Linguistics*, pages 1971–1983, Dubrovnik, Croatia. Association for Computational Linguistics.

Aman Madaan, Niket Tandon, Prakhar Gupta, Skyler Hallinan, Luyu Gao, Sarah Wiegreffe, Uri Alon, Nouha Dziri, Shrimai Prabhumoye, Yiming Yang, Shashank Gupta, Bodhisattwa Prasad Majumder, Katherine Hermann, Sean Welleck, Amir Yazdanbakhsh, and Peter Clark. 2023. Self-refine: Iterative refinement with self-feedback. In *Thirty-seventh Conference on Neural Information Processing Systems*.

Yilmazcan Ozyurt, Stefan Feuerriegel, and Ce Zhang. 2024. Document-level in-context few-shot relation extraction via pre-trained language models. *Preprint*, arXiv:2310.11085.

Liangming Pan, Michael Saxon, Wenda Xu, Deepak Nathani, Xinyi Wang, and William Yang Wang. 2024. Automatically correcting large language models: Surveying the landscape of diverse automated correction strategies. *Transactions of the Association for Computational Linguistics*, 12:484–506.

Kunxun Qi, Jianfeng Du, and Hai Wan. 2024. End-to-end learning of logical rules for enhancing document-level relation extraction. In *Proceedings of the 62nd Annual Meeting of the Association for Computational*

Linguistics (Volume 1: Long Papers), pages 7247–7263, Bangkok, Thailand. Association for Computational Linguistics.

Noah Shinn, Federico Cassano, Ashwin Gopinath, Karthik Narasimhan, and Shunyu Yao. 2023. Reflexion: language agents with verbal reinforcement learning. In *Advances in Neural Information Processing Systems*, volume 36, pages 8634–8652. Curran Associates, Inc.

Qi Sun, Kun Huang, Xiaocui Yang, Rong Tong, Kun Zhang, and Soujanya Poria. 2024. Consistency guided knowledge retrieval and denoising in llms for zero-shot document-level relation triplet extraction. In *Proceedings of the ACM Web Conference 2024*, WWW '24, page 4407–4416, New York, NY, USA. Association for Computing Machinery.

Qingyu Tan, Lu Xu, Lidong Bing, Hwee Tou Ng, and Sharifah Mahani Aljunied. 2022. Revisiting DocRED - addressing the false negative problem in relation extraction. In *Proceedings of the 2022 Conference on Empirical Methods in Natural Language Processing*, pages 8472–8487, Abu Dhabi, United Arab Emirates. Association for Computational Linguistics.

Somin Wadhwa, Silvio Amir, and Byron Wallace. 2023. Revisiting relation extraction in the era of large language models. In *Proceedings of the 61st Annual Meeting of the Association for Computational Linguistics (Volume 1: Long Papers)*, pages 15566–15589, Toronto, Canada. Association for Computational Linguistics.

Zhen Wan, Fei Cheng, Zhuoyuan Mao, Qianying Liu, Haiyue Song, Jiwei Li, and Sadao Kurohashi. 2023. GPT-RE: In-context learning for relation extraction using large language models. In *Proceedings of the 2023 Conference on Empirical Methods in Natural Language Processing*, pages 3534–3547, Singapore. Association for Computational Linguistics.

Qingyun Wang, Zixuan Zhang, Hongxiang Li, Xuan Liu, Jiawei Han, Huimin Zhao, and Heng Ji. 2024. Chem-FINESE: Validating fine-grained few-shot entity extraction through text reconstruction. In *Findings of the Association for Computational Linguistics: EACL 2024*, pages 1–16, St. Julian's, Malta. Association for Computational Linguistics.

Yuqing Wang and Yun Zhao. 2024. Metacognitive prompting improves understanding in large language models. In *Proceedings of the 2024 Conference of the North American Chapter of the Association for Computational Linguistics: Human Language Technologies (Volume 1: Long Papers)*, pages 1914–1926, Mexico City, Mexico. Association for Computational Linguistics.

Xiang Wei, Xingyu Cui, Ning Cheng, Xiaobin Wang, Xin Zhang, Shen Huang, Pengjun Xie, Jinan Xu, Yufeng Chen, Meishan Zhang, Yong Jiang, and Wenjuan Han. 2024. Chatie: Zero-shot information extraction via chatting with chatgpt. *Preprint*, arXiv:2302.10205.

Yiheng Wu, Roman Yangarber, and Xian Mao. 2024a. Diva-docre: A discriminative and voice-aware paradigm for document-level relation extraction. *Preprint*, arXiv:2409.13717.

Zhenyu Wu, Meng Jiang, and Chao Shen. 2024b. Get an a in math: progressive rectification prompting. In *Proceedings of the Thirty-Eighth AAAI Conference on Artificial Intelligence and Thirty-Sixth Conference on Innovative Applications of Artificial Intelligence and Fourteenth Symposium on Educational Advances in Artificial Intelligence*, AAAI'24/IAAI'24/EAAI'24. AAAI Press.

Derong Xu, Wei Chen, Wenjun Peng, Chao Zhang, Tong Xu, Xiangyu Zhao, Xian Wu, Yefeng Zheng, Yang Wang, and Enhong Chen. 2024. Large language models for generative information extraction: A survey. *Preprint*, arXiv:2312.17617.

Lilong Xue, Dan Zhang, Yuxiao Dong, and Jie Tang. 2024. Autore: Document-level relation extraction with large language models. *Preprint*, arXiv:2403.14888.

Tianci Xue, Ziqi Wang, Zhenhailong Wang, Chi Han, Pengfei Yu, and Heng Ji. 2023. Rcot: Detecting and rectifying factual inconsistency in reasoning by reversing chain-of-thought. *Preprint*, arXiv:2305.11499.

Yuan Yao, Deming Ye, Peng Li, Xu Han, Yankai Lin, Zhenghao Liu, Zhiyuan Liu, Lixin Huang, Jie Zhou, and Maosong Sun. 2019. DocRED: A large-scale document-level relation extraction dataset. In *Proceedings of the 57th Annual Meeting of the Association for Computational Linguistics*, pages 764–777, Florence, Italy. Association for Computational Linguistics.

Ruochen Zhao, Xingxuan Li, Shafiq Joty, Chengwei Qin, and Lidong Bing. 2023. Verify-and-edit: A knowledge-enhanced chain-of-thought framework. In *Proceedings of the 61st Annual Meeting of the Association for Computational Linguistics (Volume 1: Long Papers)*, pages 5823–5840, Toronto, Canada. Association for Computational Linguistics.

Chuanyang Zheng, Zhengying Liu, Enze Xie, Zhenguo Li, and Yu Li. 2024. Progressive-hint prompting improves reasoning in large language models. In *AI for Math Workshop @ ICML 2024*.

A Relation Descriptions and Entity Type Constraints

Table 5 presents examples of relation descriptions and entity type constraints for DocRED and Re-DocRED datasets.

B Prompts

The initial extraction prompts follow REPLM (Ozyurt et al., 2024). Other prompts are presented from Table 6 to Table 12.

C Datasets

Our framework is evaluated on two English DocRE benchmark datasets, DocRED and Re-DocRED. More statistical information is listed in Table 3.

DocRED A large-scale human-annotated dataset derived from Wikipedia and Wikidata, plays a key role in DocRE. It features a comprehensive annotation schema that includes entity mentions, types, relational facts, and supporting evidence. With 96 predefined relation types, DocRED presents a rich and challenging environment, requiring multi-sentence reasoning for its relational facts. The dataset consists of three sets: a train set with 3053 documents, a dev set with 998 documents and a test set with 1000 documents. Since the test set lacks a ground truth file, evaluations are typically conducted on the dev set.

Re-DocRED While DocRED is a widely recognized benchmark, its annotations are incomplete, leading to false negatives. To address this, (Tan et al., 2022) introduces Re-DocRED, a revised version that supplements positive instances missing in DocRED. Re-DocRED includes a test set with 500 documents and a dev set with 500 documents, ensuring a more comprehensive and accurate assessment for DocRE task.

Dataset	Split	#Doc.	#Rel.	#Ent.	#Facts.
	train	3053		59493	38180
DocRED	dev	998	96	19578	12323
	test	1000		19539	-
	train	3053		59359	85932
Re-DocRED	dev	500	96	9684	17284
	test	500		9779	17448

Table 3: Statistics on datasets, where Doc. (resp. Rel. or Ent.) abbreviates documents (resp. relations or entities).

D Baselines

D.1 BERT-based Baselines

JMRL-DREEAM (Qi et al., 2024) A rule-enhanced DocRE framework that jointly models document-level relation extraction and logical rules in an end-to-end fashion. JMRL integrates the neural DocRE backbone (DREEAM) with a parameterized rule reasoning module that simulates logical inference. To effectively align the predictions from both components, the framework incorporates a residual connection mechanism and an auxiliary loss, enabling a better reconciliation between neural predictions and symbolic reasoning.

DREEAM (Ma et al., 2023) A memory-efficient model that incorporates evidence-guided supervision into attention mechanisms. DREEAM leverages evidence data to supervise the computation of entity-pair-specific context embeddings, encouraging higher attention weights on informative tokens without introducing additional trainable parameters. To address the lack of annotated evidence, they further propose a self-training strategy that learns entity resolution (ER) from automatically generated evidence on large-scale unlabeled data.

DocRE-CLiP (Jain et al., 2024) A knowledge-enhanced framework that reformulates DocRE as link prediction over a knowledge graph enriched with document-derived reasoning and external knowledge from Wikidata. It combines logical, intra-sentence, and co-reference reasoning with path-based interpretability.

D.2 LLM-based Baselines

GenRDK (Sun et al., 2024) A zero-shot document-level relation triplet extraction framework that employs a chain-of-retrieval and denoising strategy to steer LLMs in understanding relations and generating high-quality synthetic data. Their model is fine-tuned with LLaMA2-13B-CHAT.

DiVA-DocRE^{GT} (Wu et al., 2024a) A Discriminative and Voice-Aware (DiVA) paradigm for DocRE. It first identifies the relation types present in the document and then extracts subject and object entities leveraging both active and passive voice information. They report results in three distinct experimental settings: Dev^Z, a zero-shot setting where ChatGPT is used to generate triplets; Dev^{FT}, where LLama3-7B is fine-tuned to generate triplets; and Dev^{GT}, which uses ground-truth relations to guide triplet generation.

REPLM (Ozyurt et al., 2024) A method for in-context few-shot relation extraction leveraging pre-trained language models. For each relation in the relation list, REPLM generates candidate triplets and filters them by calculating the joint probabilities of subject-object pairs. Final predictions are obtained by aggregating the outputs from multiple retrieved in-context demonstrations.
AutoRE (Xue et al., 2024) An end-to-end model that integrates LLMs with QLoRA (Dettmers et al., 2023) under a novel relation extraction paradigm named RHF (Relation-Head-Facts). It first identifies the relation types present in the document, then extracts the corresponding head entities for each relation, and finally generates complete triplets based on the identified relations and heads.

E Analysis of Token Usage

Since the iterative reflection framework requires repeated calls to LLMs, it naturally raises concerns about increased computational cost and runtime. To quantify this, we provide detailed token usage statistics for two iterations of the 998 documents in DocRED (calculated using OpenAI's tiktoken) in Table 4.

	Process	Token
	Initial Extraction	3347715
	Reconstruct Document	893874
	Compare Two Documents	6807872
	Correct Triplet Entity Type Errors	187762
Iteration 1	Inference	1358232
	One-to-one Filtering	88264
	Mutual Exclusion Constraints	203190
	Directionality Constraints	46679
	Reconstruct Document	1010179
	Compare Two Documents	6941132
	Correct Triplet Entity Type Errors	33732
Iteration 2	Inference	1365856
	One-to-one Filtering	47000
	Mutual Exclusion Constraints	49056
	Directionality Constraints	8635

Table 4: Detailed token usage statistics for two iterations of DocRED dataset (calculated using OpenAI's tiktoken).

Notably, we observe decreasing token usage in later iterations for entity type correction, one-to-one filtering, mutual exclusion constraints and directionality constraints, demonstrating the framework's increasing efficiency. While iterative calls inherently require more tokens than single-pass methods, our analysis shows comparable costs to self-consistency approaches while achieving superior performance. As shown in Table 1, our method is applicable to all LLMs and using smaller open-source models (e.g., ChatGLM3-6B, LLama3-8B) can significantly reduce API costs while maintaining effectiveness.

F Case Study

Table 13 to Table 19 present the case of a complete iteration process.

Relation	Description	Subject Types	Object Types
head of government	Object is the head of government of subject. Subject can be a town, city, municipality, state, country, or other governmental body.	LOC	PER
country	Object is the sovereign state of subject. Subject is not a person.	LOC, ORG, MISC	LOC, MISC
place of birth	Object is the most specific known birth location of the subject. Subject refers to the person, animal, or fictional character. Object refers to the most specific known location of birth (e.g., a hospital, city, or even a particular building or place).	PER	LOC
place of death	Object is the most specific known death location of subject. Subject refers to the person, animal, or fictional character.Object refers to the most specific known location of death (e.g., a hospital, city, or specific place within a city).	PER	LOC
father	Object is the father of subject.	PER	PER
mother	Object is the mother of subject.	PER	PER
spouse	Subject has object as their spouse (husband, wife, partner, etc.)	PER	PER
country of citizenship	Object is a country that recognizes subject as its citizen.	PER, MISC	LOC, MISC
continent	Object is the continent of which subject is a part.	LOC, ORG, MISC	LOC
head of state	Object is the official with the highest formal authority in subject. Subject refers to the country or state where the object holds the highest formal authority. Object refers to the official (such as the president, monarch, or prime minister).	LOC, ORG	PER
position held	Subject currently or formerly holds object position or public office.	PER	ORG, MISC
child	Object is the offspring (son or daughter) of subject. Subject refers to the parent. Object refers to the offspring (son or daughter) of the subject, regardless of age.	PER	PER
member of sports team	Object is the sports team or club that subject currently or formerly represents. Subject refers to the individual (e.g., an athlete or player). Object refers to the sports team or club that the subject currently or formerly represented.	PER	ORG, LOC, MISC
educated at	Object is the educational institution attended by subject. Subject refers to the individual. Object refers to the educational institution (e.g., university, school, or college) that the subject attended.	PER	ORG, LOC
composer	Object is the person(s) who wrote the music for subject. Subject refers to the musical work (e.g., song, score, composition, etc.). Object refers to the person(s) who composed or wrote the music for the subject.	MISC	PER
member of political party	Object is the political party of which subject is or has been a member. Subject refers to the politician. Object refers to the political party that the subject is or has been a member of.	PER, ORG, MISC	ORG, LOC
employer	Object is the person or organization for which subject works or worked. Subject refers to the individual (e.g., employee, worker). Object refers to the person or organization that the subject works for or has worked for in the past.	PER	ORG, MISC, LOC

Table 5: Examples of relation descriptions and entity type constraints for DocRED and Re-DocRED datasets.

Reconstruct Extracted Triplets into a Document

Task: Given a set of relation triplets, a list of relation types with descriptions, and all entity mentions for each entity in the relation triplets, your task is to reconstruct the triplets into a coherent paragraph. The paragraph should rephrase the content of the triplets into natural language, while carefully maintaining the direction of the relations between entities. The paragraph should not contain any additional content or explanations.

Instructions:
1. For each relation triplet, use the subject, relation, and object to create a natural language sentence that describes the relationship.
2. Pay close attention to the direction of the relation. For example, if the triplet is {'sub': 'Hampshire County', 'rel': 'located in the administrative territorial entity', 'obj': 'West Virginia'}, the sentence should reflect that Hampshire County is located in West Virginia, not the other way around.
3. The paragraph should only contain these sentences and should not include any extra context or information not directly related to the triplets.
4. Ensure that the paragraph is coherent and logically structured, with proper flow between sentences.
5. The entities should be referenced by their full names as given in the triplets (e.g., "Washington Place," "William Washington House," etc.).

Triplets: *[Extracted Triplets List T]*
Relation Types and Descriptions: *[{'rel': [Relation Name R], 'description': [Relation Description RD]}]*
Entities: *[{'entity': [Entity Name E], 'entity type': [Entity Type ET]}]*
Reconstructed paragraph:

Table 6: Prompt for reconstructing extracted triplets into a document.

Compare Reconstructed Document with Original Document and Identify Missing Triplets
Given an original document, all entity mentions of each entity in the document, target relation type with description and a document reconstructed from previously extracted relation triplets, your task is to compare two documents and indicate which information about *[Relation Name R]* relation type in the original document is not in the reconstructed document. Then identify all missing triplets of *[Relation Name R]* relation type, which means *[Relation Description RD]*. You can consider whether each pair of entities in the entity list has a *[Relation Name R]* relation. Here is an example, please output according to the format of the example. **Original document:** *[Example Original Document ED]* **Reconstructed document:** *[Example Reconstructed Document ED']* **Entities:** *[{'entity': [Example Entity Name EE'], 'entity type': [Example Entity Type ET']}]* **Missing information:** *[A Text about Missing Information MI]* **Missing triplets:** *[Missing Triplets List MT]* Now refer to the example above and compare the following two documents: **Original document:** *[Original Document D]* **Reconstructed document:** *[Reconstructed Document D']* **Entities:** *[{'entity': [Entity Name E], 'entity type': [Entity Type ET]}]* **Missing information:**

Table 7: Prompt for comparing reconstructed document with original document and identifying missing triplets.

Correct Triplet Entity Type Errors
Given a target relation type list, a document, and all entity mentions of each entity in the document, your task is to modify the triplet where either the subject or the object entity type is incorrect (the subject or object will be specified after the triplet). Please select the correct entity from the given entity list and modify the triplet accordingly. Please modify only the subject or object, or both the subject and object that entity type is incorrect. Do not change any other part of the triplet. Only output the modified triplet. **Relation Type and Description:** *{'rel': [Error Triplet's Relation Name ETR], 'description': [Error Triplet's Relation Description ETRD]}* The subject of the *[Error Triplet's Relation Name ETR]* relation can only be of type *[Subject Type List ST]*, and the object can only be of type *[Object Type List OT]*. **Document:** *[Original Document D]* **Entities:** *[{'entity': [Entity Name E], 'entity type': [Entity Type ET]}]* **Triplet where either subject or object, or both subject and object entity types are incorrect:** *[Error Triplet and 'Subject entity type is incorrect!', 'Object entity type is incorrect!' or 'Both subject and object types are incorrect!']* Please select the correct subject or object from the given entities list, modify the triplet and output the modified version. **The modified triplet:**

Table 8: Prompt for correcting triplet entity type errors.

Inference
Given a target relation type list, a document, and all entity mentions of each entity in the document, please extract all valid given relation types between any two given entities in the document. Each line outputs an extracted relation triple, and the format of each triplet is: {'sub': subject entity, 'rel': relation type, 'obj': object entity}. Each relation triplet should be output only once. **Relation Types and Descriptions:** *[{'rel': [Relation Name R], 'description': [Relation Description RD]}]* **Document:** *[Original Document D]* **Entities:** *[{'entity': [Entity Name E], 'entity type': [Entity Type ET]}]* All relation triplets extracted from the document in the previous iteration will be scored and reordered based on the degree and logical rules of the subject and object entities, with higher scores given to the higher order. **Here are the reordered triplets extracted from the previous iteration:** *[Reordered Triplets List RT]* **Through logical reasoning, the following triplets may have been incorrectly extracted:** *[Inferred Incorrectly Extracted Triplets List IIET]* **Based on all the relation triplets extracted in previous iterations and logical reasoning, the following triplets may still not have been extracted:** *[Inferred Unextracted Triplets List IUT]* Please refer to the above feedback and extract the triplets of the target relation types again from the original document. **All relation triplets extracted from the document:**

Table 9: Prompt for inference.

One-to-one Filtering
Given a document, all entity mentions in the document, and the relation description, your task is to select the unique correct triplet from the previously extracted triplets. Please only output the triplet you believe to be the correct one. **Document:** *[Original Document D]* **Entities:** *[{'entity': [Entity Name E], 'entity type': [Entity Type ET]}]* **Relation Type and Description:** *{'rel': [Two Triplets' Relation Name TTR], 'description': [Two Triplets' Relation Description TTRD]}* **The previously extracted triplets:** *[Two Contradictory Triplets T1 and T2]* **The unique correct triplet** (Choose from the two triplets above. Do not modify the content of triplets):

Table 10: Prompt for one-to-one filtering.

Mutual Exclusion Constraints
Given a document, all entity mentions in the document, and the relation description, your task is to select the unique correct triplet from the previously extracted triplets. Please only output the triplet you believe to be the correct one. **Document:** *[Original Document D]* **Entities:** *[{'entity': [Entity Name E], 'entity type': [Entity Type ET]}]* **Relation Type and Description:** *[{'rel': [Two Mutual Exclusion Relation Name MER], 'description': [Two Mutual Exclusion Relation Description MERD]}]* **The previously extracted triplets:** *[Two Mutual Exclusion Triplets T1 and T2]* **The unique correct triplet** (Choose from the two triplets above. Do not modify the content of triplets):

Table 11: Prompt for mutual exclusion constraints.

Directionality Constraints
Given a document and the relation description, your task is to select the unique correct triplet from the previously extracted triplets. Please pay attention to the direction of the relation, which is *[Two Triplets' Relation Description TTRD]* and only output the triplet you believe to be the correct one. **Document:** *[Original Document D]* **Relation Type and Description:** *{'rel': [Two Triplets' Relation Name TTR], 'description': [Two Triplets' Relation Description TTRD]}* **The previously extracted triplets:** *[Two Contradictory Triplets T1 and T2]* **The unique correct triplet** (Choose from the two triplets above. Do not modify the content of triplets):

Table 12: Prompt for directionality constraints.

Initial Extraction **F1: 0.235 Precision: 0.385 Recall: 0.169**
{'sub': 'VivoTab RT LTE', 'rel': 'follows', 'obj': 'VivoTab RT 3 G'} ×
{'sub': 'VivoTab RT 3 G', 'rel': 'follows', 'obj': 'VivoTab RT LTE'} ×
{'sub': 'VivoTab RT 3 G', 'rel': 'followed by', 'obj': 'VivoTab RT LTE'} ×
{'sub': 'VivoTab RT', 'rel': 'followed by', 'obj': 'VivoTab RT 3 G'} ✓
{'sub': 'VivoTab', 'rel': 'series', 'obj': 'Vivo'} ✓
{'sub': 'VivoTab', 'rel': 'subclass of', 'obj': 'Vivo'} ✓
{'sub': 'VivoTab', 'rel': 'has part', 'obj': 'VivoTab RT 3 G'} ✓
{'sub': 'VivoTab Note 8', 'rel': 'follows', 'obj': 'VivoTab Smart'} ×
{'sub': 'VivoTab Smart', 'rel': 'follows', 'obj': 'VivoTab Note 8'} ×
{'sub': 'VivoTab', 'rel': 'follows', 'obj': 'VivoTab RT'} ×
{'sub': 'VivoTab RT LTE', 'rel': 'follows', 'obj': 'VivoTab Smart'} ×
{'sub': 'Windows 8.1', 'rel': 'follows', 'obj': 'Windows 8'} ✓
{'sub': 'VivoTab RT', 'rel': 'followed by', 'obj': 'VivoTab Note 8'} ×
{'sub': 'VivoTab', 'rel': 'followed by', 'obj': 'VivoTab Note 8'} ×
{'sub': 'VivoTab Smart', 'rel': 'followed by', 'obj': 'VivoTab Note 8'} ×
{'sub': 'VivoTab RT LTE', 'rel': 'followed by', 'obj': 'VivoTab Smart'} ×
{'sub': 'VivoTab', 'rel': 'manufacturer', 'obj': 'Asus'} ✓
{'sub': 'VivoTab', 'rel': 'developer', 'obj': 'Asus'} ✓
{'sub': 'VivoTab', 'rel': 'has part', 'obj': 'VivoTab Note 8'} ×
{'sub': 'VivoTab', 'rel': 'has part', 'obj': 'VivoTab RT LTE'} ✓
{'sub': 'VivoTab', 'rel': 'has part', 'obj': 'VivoTab Smart'} ✓
{'sub': 'VivoTab', 'rel': 'has part', 'obj': 'VivoTab RT'} ✓
{'sub': 'VivoTab', 'rel': 'has part', 'obj': 'Asus WebStorage'} ×
{'sub': 'VivoTab', 'rel': 'has part', 'obj': 'Windows 8.1'} ×
{'sub': 'VivoTab', 'rel': 'has part', 'obj': 'Windows 8'} ×
{'sub': 'Asus', 'rel': 'product or material produced', 'obj': 'VivoTab'} ×

Table 13: Initial Extraction.

Reconstructed Document
The VivoTab RT LTE follows the VivoTab RT 3 G, while the VivoTab RT 3 G is followed by the VivoTab RT LTE. The VivoTab RT is followed by the VivoTab RT 3 G, and the VivoTab RT LTE is followed by the VivoTab Smart. The VivoTab Note 8 follows the VivoTab Smart, and the VivoTab Smart is followed by the VivoTab Note 8. The VivoTab follows the VivoTab RT and is followed by the VivoTab Note 8. The VivoTab is part of the Vivo series and is a subclass of Vivo. Asus is both the manufacturer and developer of the VivoTab, which has several components including the VivoTab RT 3 G, VivoTab Note 8, VivoTab RT LTE, VivoTab Smart, VivoTab RT, Asus WebStorage, Windows 8.1, and Windows 8. Additionally, Asus produces the VivoTab. Windows 8.1 follows Windows 8.
Original Document
VivoTab is a series of Microsoft Windows hybrid tablet computers designed by Asus . It is a sub - series of the Vivo series by Asus . The name is derived from the Latin word ẗo live änd , along with Asus 's Transformer series of convertible devices running Windows , is a primary competitor to the Microsoft Surface . The family is made up of the VivoTab , VivoTab RT , VivoTab RT 3 G , VivoTab RT LTE , VivoTab Smart , and later on the VivoTab Note 8 . All of the tablets come with Windows 8 (or Windows 8.1 on the Note 8) , a 3-year subscription to Asus WebStorage . They have high definition screens advertise ultra - portability and extended battery life , and the ability detachable tablets . VivoTab RT has an MSRP of $599USD(32GB)and$ 699 (64 GB)

Table 14: Reconstructed document and original document. The content highlighted in red in the reconstructed document does not align with the original document and corresponds to incorrect triplets. Meanwhile, the content highlighted in red in the original document does not appear in the reconstructed document, representing triplets that have not been extracted.

Comparsion		
F1: 0.432	**Precision: 0.462**	**Recall: 0.407**
Add:		
{'sub': 'VivoTab RT LTE', 'rel': 'follows', 'obj': 'VivoTab RT'} $\times$		
{'sub': 'VivoTab RT', 'rel': 'series', 'obj': 'VivoTab'} $\checkmark +$		
{'sub': 'VivoTab RT 3 G', 'rel': 'series', 'obj': 'VivoTab'} $\checkmark +$		
{'sub': 'VivoTab RT LTE', 'rel': 'series', 'obj': 'VivoTab'} $\checkmark +$		
{'sub': 'VivoTab Smart', 'rel': 'series', 'obj': 'VivoTab'} $\checkmark +$		
{'sub': 'VivoTab Note 8', 'rel': 'series', 'obj': 'VivoTab'} $\times$		
{'sub': 'VivoTab RT', 'rel': 'manufacturer', 'obj': 'Asus'} $\checkmark +$		
{'sub': 'VivoTab RT 3 G', 'rel': 'manufacturer', 'obj': 'Asus'} $\checkmark +$		
{'sub': 'VivoTab RT LTE', 'rel': 'manufacturer', 'obj': 'Asus'} $\checkmark +$		
{'sub': 'VivoTab Smart', 'rel': 'manufacturer', 'obj': 'Asus'} $\checkmark +$		
{'sub': 'VivoTab Note 8', 'rel': 'manufacturer', 'obj': 'Asus'} $\checkmark +$		
{'sub': 'VivoTab RT', 'rel': 'developer', 'obj': 'Asus'} $\checkmark +$		
{'sub': 'VivoTab RT 3 G', 'rel': 'developer', 'obj': 'Asus'} $\checkmark +$		
{'sub': 'VivoTab RT LTE', 'rel': 'developer', 'obj': 'Asus'} $\checkmark +$		
{'sub': 'VivoTab Smart', 'rel': 'developer', 'obj': 'Asus'} $\checkmark +$		
{'sub': 'VivoTab Note 8', 'rel': 'developer', 'obj': 'Asus'} $\checkmark +$		
{'sub': 'Asus', 'rel': 'product or material produced', 'obj': 'VivoTab RT'} $\times$		
{'sub': 'Asus', 'rel': 'product or material produced', 'obj': 'VivoTab RT 3 G'} $\times$		
{'sub': 'Asus', 'rel': 'product or material produced', 'obj': 'VivoTab RT LTE'} $\times$		
{'sub': 'Asus', 'rel': 'product or material produced', 'obj': 'VivoTab Smart'} $\times$		
{'sub': 'Asus', 'rel': 'product or material produced', 'obj': 'VivoTab Note 8'} $\times$		
{'sub': 'VivoTab RT', 'rel': 'subclass of', 'obj': 'VivoTab'} $\times$		
{'sub': 'VivoTab RT 3 G', 'rel': 'subclass of', 'obj': 'VivoTab'} $\times$		
{'sub': 'VivoTab RT LTE', 'rel': 'subclass of', 'obj': 'VivoTab'} $\times$		
{'sub': 'VivoTab Smart', 'rel': 'subclass of', 'obj': 'VivoTab'} $\times$		
{'sub': 'VivoTab Note 8', 'rel': 'subclass of', 'obj': 'VivoTab'} $\times$		

Table 15: Compare reconstructed document and original document to identify unextracted triplets.

Inference		
F1: 0.456	**Precision: 0.473**	**Recall: 0.441**
Add:		
{'sub': 'Windows 8.1', 'rel': 'follows', 'obj': 'Windows 8'} $\Rightarrow$ {'sub': 'Windows 8', 'rel': 'followed by', 'obj': 'Windows 8.1'} $\checkmark +$		
{'sub': 'VivoTab RT', 'rel': 'followed by', 'obj': 'VivoTab RT 3 G'} $\Rightarrow$ {'sub': 'VivoTab RT 3 G', 'rel': 'follows', 'obj': 'VivoTab RT'} $\checkmark +$		
{'sub': 'VivoTab RT LTE', 'rel': 'followed by', 'obj': 'VivoTab Smart'} $\Rightarrow$ {'sub': 'VivoTab Smart', 'rel': 'follows', 'obj': 'VivoTab RT LTE'} $\times$		

Table 16: Inference based on logical rules to identify unextracted triplets.

One-to-one		
F1: 0.460	**Precision: 0.481**	**Recall: 0.441**
{'sub': 'VivoTab RT', 'rel': 'followed by', 'obj': 'VivoTab RT 3 G'} $\checkmark$		
{'sub': 'VivoTab RT', 'rel': 'followed by', 'obj': 'VivoTab Note 8'} $\times$ **(Delete)**		

Table 17: Delete incorrect triplets based on one-to-one filtering.

Mutual Exclusion Constraint
F1: 0.491 **Precision: 0.553** **Recall: 0.441**
{'sub': 'VivoTab', 'rel': 'has part', 'obj': 'VivoTab RT'} ✓ {'sub': 'VivoTab', 'rel': 'follows', 'obj': 'VivoTab RT'} × **(Delete)**
{'sub': 'VivoTab', 'rel': 'has part', 'obj': 'VivoTab Note 8'} × {'sub': 'VivoTab', 'rel': 'followed by', 'obj': 'VivoTab Note 8'} × **(Delete)**
{'sub': 'VivoTab RT', 'rel': 'series', 'obj': 'VivoTab'} ✓ {'sub': 'VivoTab RT', 'rel': 'subclass of', 'obj': 'VivoTab'} × **(Delete)**
{'sub': 'VivoTab RT 3 G', 'rel': 'series', 'obj': 'VivoTab'} ✓ {'sub': 'VivoTab RT 3 G', 'rel': 'subclass of', 'obj': 'VivoTab'} × **(Delete)**
{'sub': 'VivoTab RT LTE', 'rel': 'series', 'obj': 'VivoTab'} ✓ {'sub': 'VivoTab RT LTE', 'rel': 'subclass of', 'obj': 'VivoTab'} × **(Delete)**
{'sub': 'VivoTab Smart', 'rel': 'series', 'obj': 'VivoTab'} ✓ {'sub': 'VivoTab Smart', 'rel': 'subclass of', 'obj': 'VivoTab'} × **(Delete)**
{'sub': 'VivoTab Note 8', 'rel': 'series', 'obj': 'VivoTab'} × {'sub': 'VivoTab Note 8', 'rel': 'subclass of', 'obj': 'VivoTab'} × **(Delete)**

Table 18: Delete incorrect triplets based on mutual exclusion constraints.

Directionality Constraint
F1: 0.505 **Precision: 0.591** **Recall: 0.441**
{'sub': 'VivoTab RT 3 G', 'rel': 'follows', 'obj': 'VivoTab RT LTE'} × **(Delete)** {'sub': 'VivoTab RT LTE', 'rel': 'follows', 'obj': 'VivoTab RT 3 G'} ×
{'sub': 'VivoTab RT LTE', 'rel': 'follows', 'obj': 'VivoTab Smart'} × **(Delete)** {'sub': 'VivoTab Smart', 'rel': 'follows', 'obj': 'VivoTab RT LTE'} ×
{'sub': 'VivoTab Note 8', 'rel': 'follows', 'obj': 'VivoTab Smart'} × {'sub': 'VivoTab Smart', 'rel': 'follows', 'obj': 'VivoTab Note 8'} × **(Delete)**

Table 19: Delete incorrect triplets based on directionality constraints.

Cross-Document Event-Keyed Summarization

William Walden[1] **Pavlo Kuchmiichuk**[2] **Alexander Martin**[1] **Chihsheng Jin**[2]
Angela Cao[2] **Claire Sun**[2] **Curisia Allen**[2] **Aaron Steven White**[2]
[1]Johns Hopkins University [2]University of Rochester
{wwalden1}@jhu.edu

Abstract

Event-keyed summarization (EKS) requires summarizing a specific event described in a document given the document text and an event representation extracted from it. In this work, we extend EKS to the cross-document setting (CDEKS), in which summaries must synthesize information from accounts of the same event as given by *multiple* sources. We introduce SEAMuS (**S**ummaries of **E**vents **A**cross **Mu**ltiple **S**ources), a high-quality dataset for CDEKS based on an expert reannotation of the FAMuS dataset for cross-document argument extraction. We present a suite of baselines on SEAMuS—covering both smaller, fine-tuned models, as well as zero- and few-shot prompted LLMs—along with detailed ablations and a human evaluation study, showing SEAMuS to be a valuable benchmark for this new task.

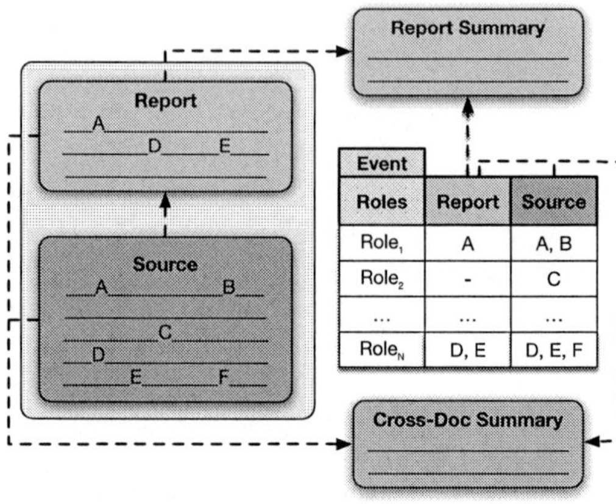

Figure 1: Schematic illustration of the SEAMuS report and cross-document event-keyed summarization tasks. Letters represent event arguments.

1 Introduction

Providing useful information about events requires the ability not only to extract relevant, user-specified information from documents, but also to present that information in a readable form. Drawing on this observation, Gantt et al. (2024) recently proposed *event-keyed summarization* (EKS), a task that entails summarizing a *particular* event, given a document and an event representation extracted from it. EKS thus seeks to satisfy both requirements—reconciling the *specific* information needs of IE end users with the more generic outputs of traditional summarization models—in order to communicate *precise* information about a single event in a *contextualized* and *readable* form. EKS can thus be viewed as event-centric controllable summarization (Fan et al., 2018), where the controlled attributes are the event and roles of interest.

However, adequately understanding a particular event often requires synthesizing information across *multiple* sources—evidenced in part by the rapidly growing interest in *retrieval augmented generation* (RAG; Lewis et al., 2020b). Accordingly, this work extends EKS to the cross-document setting (CDEKS), drawing on—and enhancing—the FAMuS dataset for cross-document argument extraction (CDAE) to do so (Vashishtha et al., 2024). We summarize our contributions as follows:

1. We collect and release an expert reannotation of the FAMuS CDAE dataset, correcting the existing crowdsourced annotations.
2. Based on (1), we collect and release SEAMuS, an expert-annotated dataset of single- and cross-document event-keyed summaries—the first ever dataset for CDEKS.[1]
3. We present a suite of baselines on SEAMuS using both smaller, fine-tuned models and prompted LLMs, showing CDEKS to be challenging relative to single-document EKS.
4. We conduct fine-grained ablations and a human evaluation, detailing CDEKS demands as a task as well as models' current capabilities.

2 Background

FAMuS (Vashishtha et al., 2024) is a dataset of

[1]https://github.com/wgantt/SEAMuS

Proceedings of the 1st Joint Workshop on Large Language Models and Structure Modeling (XLLM 2025), pages 218–241
August 1, 2025

short English Wikipedia passages (*reports*) paired with much longer, genre-diverse English *source* documents cited by those reports.[2] FAMuS supports two tasks: (1) *Source Validation* (SV), where the goal is to determine whether a candidate source document is *valid for*—i.e. describes the same event as—an event identified in a provided report; and (2) *Cross-Document Argument Extraction* (CDAE), which entails extracting arguments for an identified event from *both* the report and a valid source document. SEAMuS builds on the FAMuS CDAE data, which contains 1,265 report-source document pairs (split 3:1:1 across train, dev, and test), and annotates arguments of the same target event for each document in a pair using a subset of the FrameNet ontology restricted to frames denoting events, states, or processes (Baker et al., 1998). A single, maximally "informative" mention is annotated for each argument, where proper names > nominal expressions > pronouns (see Li et al., 2021b). In both report and source texts, arguments may be distributed across sentences.

Event-Centric Summarization In introducing EKS, Gantt et al. (2024) released MUCSUM, an EKS dataset based on the classic MUC-4 template filling dataset (Sundheim, 1992). MUCSUM contains abstractive event-keyed summaries for each event template in MUC-4, written so as to faithfully express the role of each template argument, plus any minimal additional context required for the summary to act as a standalone account of the event. Gantt et al. present baselines on MUCSUM, and also conduct a human evaluation of model outputs, which inspires our own (§5).

Other event-centric summarization research has focused on *timeline summarization* (TLS), which constructs chronological lists of events, often with timestamps and usually based on multiple documents (Allan et al., 2001; Chieu and Lee, 2004; Li et al., 2021a; Rajaby Faghihi et al., 2022, *i.a.*). Beyond TLS, S Hussain et al. (2022) use extracted event-related keywords to condition single-document summarization, and integrate an event-oriented attention mechanism into BART to encourage models to cover *all* events discussed. Additionally, Vallurupalli et al. (2022) introduce the POQue dataset, which has annotations that characterize the subevent structure of complex events in stories and the changes undergone by their participants. Among these annotations are *process summaries*, which give high-level descriptions of a complex event, and *change summaries*, which describe the changes experienced by a participant as a result.

Multi-Document Summarization CDEKS is an event-centric multi-document summarization (MDS) task. Work on MDS has pursued a variety of goals, including synthesizing reviews (Ganesan et al., 2010; Chu and Liu, 2019, *i.a.*), summarizing dialogues (Kraaij et al., 2005; Chen et al., 2021, *i.a.*), distilling news articles (notably, via DUC[3] and TAC[4]), and generating reports (Mayfield et al., 2024). *Event-centric* MDS datasets include MultiNews (Fabbri et al., 2019) and DiverseSumm (Huang et al., 2024), which focus on new stories, but SEAMuS is most similar to AutohMDS (Zopf, 2018) and WCEP (Gholipour Ghalandari et al., 2020) in being built on Wikipedia articles and their sources.

CDEKS departs from all of these, however, in *responding to an explicit information need.* It is thus an event-centric form of *query-oriented* MDS (Ma et al., 2020), where a query expressing the kind of information to be summarized is provided as additional input. But whereas queries from prior work are given in natural language—e.g. article titles (Liu and Lapata, 2019) or web searches (Pasunuru et al., 2021)—ours are structured event representations, drawing on the IE tradition of leveraging event ontologies to encode information needs, and enabling extraction-to-summarization pipelines.

Our Work We summarize three key differences between prior work and our own. We focus on:

1. Synthesizing information about a *single* event across *multiple* sources. Both multi-event (e.g. TLS) and single-source (e.g. EKS) summarization have their place, but many practical information needs depend on the rich understanding of an *individual* event that is attainable only via *cross-source* synthesis.
2. Responding to a *specific* event-centric information need, not *generically* summarizing event-related content (*contra* S Hussain et al., 2022; Vallurupalli et al., 2022).
3. Leveraging detailed, structured event representations to achieve (1) and (2)—not short, unstructured queries like web searches (Pasunuru et al., 2021) or topics (Allan et al., 2001; Rajaby Faghihi et al., 2022, *i.a.*).

[2] All documents are from MegaWika (Barham et al., 2023).

[3] https://duc.nist.gov/

[4] https://tac.nist.gov/publications/index.html

3 Annotation

Annotation of SEAMUS was divided into two phases. In the first phase, abstractive **report summaries** were written for each event in FAMUS (see §2) based only on its *report* document, and were then annotated for event arguments (§3.1). In the second phase, abstractive **cross-document summaries** were written for each event based *jointly* on its report and source documents, and were then annotated for event arguments as in the first phase (§3.2). In both phases, annotators were instructed to amend spurious, missing, or otherwise incorrect argument annotations in the report or source document before writing their summary. Thus, both phases involve (1) correcting existing FAMUS argument annotations; (2) writing a summary based on the corrected annotations; and (3) annotating arguments in the summary. The phases differ only in the documents on which the summaries are based (report only vs. report and source). All annotations were performed by authors of this work.[5]

3.1 Phase 1: Report Summaries

Similar to the summaries in MUCSUM (§2), the report summaries in SEAMUS are concise summaries of a single event as recounted in a single document (a FAMUS report) that aim to faithfully represent the role of each participant and to provide the minimum additional context needed to serve as an accurate, standalone account of the event. Although the FAMUS report documents are already relatively short (typically, 2-3 sentences), they often discuss multiple events.[6] Thus, the report summaries are further distilled descriptions focused on just *one* event from the report.

Three authors completed the Phase 1 annotation, with each summary and its arguments singly annotated. Items from the train split were randomly and evenly divided among these three authors; items from the dev and test splits were similarly divided between two of them. All items were provided in JSON files containing the following information for each example: (1) a unique example ID, (2) the FAMUS report text; (3) the FAMUS-annotated frame, trigger, and arguments of the target event from the report; and (4) definitions of the annotated frame and roles as given in FrameNet. Annotators were provided with detailed instructions written by the first author and completed a 10-example practice task before beginning the main annotation. Consistent with FAMUS, both the corrected report arguments and the report summary arguments were annotated as single, maximally informative mentions (see §2). Annotators were encouraged to use the same mentions in their summaries as were annotated in the (corrected) report arguments, but were permitted to alter them in the summary in order to preserve clarity or naturalness. Annotations were validated to ensure that (1) they were shorter than the report they summarized and (2) the number of arguments for a given role matched between each report and its summary. All initially invalid annotations were then corrected.

	Report		Cross-Doc	
	Train	Dev	Train	Dev
Examples	759	253	759	253
Avg. Words	21.8	24.6	30.5	34.5
Avg. Sentences	1.0	1.0	1.2	1.2
Avg. Arguments	3.1	3.5	4.1	4.6

Table 1: Summary statistics for the SEAMUS report and cross-document summaries. See Table 7 for more.

3.2 Phase 2: Cross-Document Summaries

The *cross-document summaries* are intended as enriched versions of the report summaries, synthesizing details about the target event from both the report and the target event's source document.

Five of the authors completed the Phase 2 annotation, with all summaries and arguments singly annotated as in Phase 1. Items from all three splits were randomly and evenly distributed to the five annotators. Given the complexity of the Phase 2 task, annotation was performed in two parts, using adapted versions of Vashishtha et al.'s (2024) interface for FAMUS CDAE annotation.[7]

In Part A, annotators corrected FAMUS argument annotations in the source documents and then wrote the cross-document summary based *jointly* on the report and source texts and their corrected arguments. Annotators were encouraged to use the most informative mention of an argument across *both* the report and source documents, but again were allowed to make alterations for clarity.

In Part B, annotators annotated arguments in the

[5] Appendix E has additional details and agreement results.

[6] E.g. for reports in the SEAMUS train split, the MegaWika dataset (Barham et al., 2023), from which the reports are taken, has an average of 21.4 FrameNet frames annotated.

[7] Interface source code was obtained from Vashishtha et al. Screenshots are shown in Appendix E.

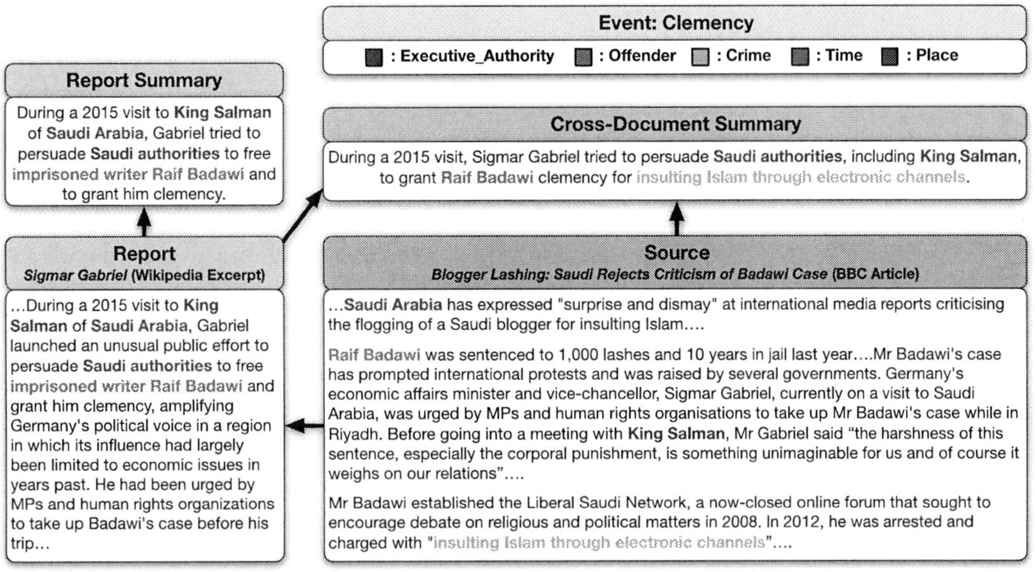

Figure 2: An example from our SEAMUS dataset. **Report** documents (bottom left) are Wikipedia passages that describe some event (top right) and that cite a longer (non-Wikipedia) **source** article (bottom right) as evidence, with event arguments annotated in both documents. SEAMUS features simple summaries of these events based on *only* the report (top left) as well as enriched, cross-document summaries based on *both* the report and its source, which typically contain additional information about the event (here, the CRIME). Appendix A has further examples.

summaries from Part A. As in Phase 1, all annotators were provided with detailed instructions and completed a 10-example practice annotation before doing the main task. Summary argument annotations were again validated for length and to ensure that they featured as many arguments for a given role as the maximum number annotated for that role between the report and source texts.

Summary statistics for both the report and cross-document summaries can be found in Table 1 and an example is shown in Figure 2. Both types of summary average roughly a sentence in length, though cross-document summaries tend to be longer and to have more arguments—consistent with the richer information they provide.

4 Experiments

4.1 Overview

Tasks We present experiments on both the report (§4.2) and cross-document (§4.3) summarization tasks. In the report task (single-document EKS), both the report and its annotated event are provided as input. The cross-document task (CDEKS) is analogous, but also includes the corresponding source document and its event annotation as input. Next, in §4.4, we briefly discuss some ablations on the input inspired by similar ones from Gantt et al. (2024), with full results in Appendix F. Finally, §4.5 evaluates the impact of degraded argument extractions on summary quality.

Models We benchmark SEAMUS using models of two types. First, we consider several classic pre-trained encoder-decoder models widely used for summarization: BART (Lewis et al., 2020a), PEGASUS (Zhang et al., 2020), and T5 (Raffel et al., 2020), fine-tuning the large versions of all three on the SEAMUS training data. Second, we consider some of the latest proprietary LLMs, evaluated in both the zero- and few-shot settings: GPT-4o[8], GPT-4o Mini (GPT-4O M in Table 2)[9], Claude 3 Haiku (CLAUDE H)[10], and Claude 3.5 Sonnet (CLAUDE S)[11]. For the few-shot examples, we use the three examples from the train split whose frame matches that of the target example. Finally, we also give results for a *report baseline* (RB) that treats the report text itself as the predicted summary.

Metrics We report several standard summarization metrics, including ROUGE-1 ($\mathbf{R}_1$), ROUGE-2 ($\mathbf{R}_2$), and ROUGE-LCS F_1 scores ($\mathbf{R}_L$; Lin, 2004),

[8]https://openai.com/index/hello-gpt-4o/

[9]https://openai.com/index/gpt-4o-mini-advancing-cost-efficient-intelligence/

[10]https://www.anthropic.com/news/claude-3-haiku

[11]https://www.anthropic.com/news/claude-3-5-sonnet

		Report							Cross-Document						
Model	**S**	$\mathbf{R}_1$	$\mathbf{R}_2$	$\mathbf{R}_L$	**BS**	**CR**	**A**	**F**	$\mathbf{R}_1$	$\mathbf{R}_2$	$\mathbf{R}_L$	**BS**	**CR**	**A**	**F**
RB	-	56.2	46.1	48.4	91.6	52.6	99.1	98.7	48.5	33.3	39.3	89.6	31.0	99.3	93.1
GPT-4o M	ZS	62.2	42.3	51.3	93.2	58.5	86.0	75.8	51.8	29.9	39.0	91.3	39.0	81.5	88.9
	FS	72.0	55.4	61.0	94.3	66.8	94.1	83.3	57.5	36.9	45.7	92.1	39.8	88.5	89.8
GPT-4o	ZS	64.0	45.2	53.0	93.2	61.4*	83.9	74.8	58.0*	36.4	45.8	92.2*	41.3*	86.6	88.4
	FS	72.5†	56.6†	62.3†	94.4	69.6†	94.7	81.6	61.2†	40.7†	49.4†	**92.7**†	42.7†	90.6	88.5
CLAUDE H	ZS	64.8	46.2	54.7	93.4	58.8	84.9	77.6	57.7	36.9*	46.5	92.1	36.2	90.4	91.4
	FS	71.7	55.9	61.1	94.3	63.2	94.8	82.5	59.4	39.5	48.6	92.1	37.2	91.0	90.5†
CLAUDE S	ZS	67.4*	48.1*	56.5*	93.8*	61.1	93.0*	80.6*	56.7	34.8	45.3	91.9	35.2	93.4*	**91.7***
	FS	72.2	54.6	61.3	94.5†	65.7	95.9†	83.9†	57.9	38.1	47.4	92.1	37.3	**95.1**†	90.4
BART	FT	74.5	61.7	66.4	94.6	69.9	91.6	79.3	63.8	45.5	53.0	92.6	**45.0**	85.6	85.3
PEGASUS	FT	75.2	62.5	67.0	94.7	70.0	96.1	82.2	63.7	46.2	**53.2**	92.5	43.7	93.9	90.5
T5	FT	**76.6**	**64.4**	**68.9**	**95.0**	**74.2**	**98.2**	**85.0**	**64.1**	**46.4**	52.8	92.6	44.7	92.5	90.2

Table 2: **Report** and **Cross-Document** summarization results on SEAMuS. Best overall results are **bolded**; * and † denote best zero- and few-shot results, respectively. **S**=setting; RB=report baseline; ZS=zero-shot; FS=few-shot; FT=fine-tuned. See §4.1 for an explanation of metrics; higher is better for all. See Tables 10 and 11 for 95% CIs. Best **A** and **F** results exclude RB, for reasons explained in Appendix F.

as well as BERTScore F_1 (**BS**; Zhang et al., 2019).

Given EKS's focus on producing summaries that recover *specific* pieces of information—as represented by an event's roles—we report several other metrics that evaluate this. First, we report CEAF-REE F_1 (**CR**; Du et al., 2021a), a form of argument F_1 that allows us to compare arguments extracted from a *predicted* summary against those in a *reference* summary, aligning arguments based on exact match.[12] Following Gantt et al. (2024), we train the event extraction model of Xia et al. (2021)[13] on SEAMuS and use it to extract arguments from the predicted summaries, constraining extraction to arguments that fill roles of the target event only.

The summaries in SEAMuS also make *claims* about these arguments that reflect their role in the target event. To evaluate these claims' fidelity to the text, we report AlignScore (**A**; Zha et al., 2023), a learned metric that provides a score in $[0, 1]$ that indicates how well a claim (here, a summary) is supported by a given context (the report for the report task, and the concatenated report and source for the cross-document task). We also report FACTSCORE (**F**; Min et al., 2023), which uses LMs to (1) decompose a generation into a set of *atomic* facts, and (2) determine the % of these facts supported by a given knowledge source, where **F** is the average % supported over all examples. We use as knowledge sources the contexts used for **A**.

4.2 Report Summarization

Setup As input for BART, PEGASUS, and T5, we provide the full report text concatenated with a linearized representation of the annotated report event that contains the frame name, the event trigger, and the role names, each followed by a list of the arguments annotated for that role. We train each model against a standard conditional language modeling objective w.r.t. the gold report summaries for a maximum of 30 epochs, using a patience of 5 epochs, with dev $\mathbf{R}_1$ as the stopping criterion.[14] For inference, we use beam search decoding with a beam size of 5 and a max of 256 new tokens.

For the Claude and GPT models, our system prompt asks the model to analyze and summarize a specific event. The user prompt provides more detailed task instructions, followed by the full report text, and a description of the target event that includes (1) the frame name and definition from FrameNet; (2) the trigger; and (3) a bulleted list, where each item includes a role name, its definition, and the arguments annotated for that role. In the few-shot setting, we format the three few-shot examples (see §4.1) the same way, but with the target summary shown at the end of each. We set temperature to 0.7 and the max new tokens to 256, leaving other API defaults unchanged.[15]

Results are shown in the left half of Table 2. First, we find that T5 obtains the best performance across all metrics, followed by PEGASUS and BART, with T5 exhibiting particularly strong results for **CR**, indicating its ability to accurately recover event arguments in its summaries. Second, the LLMs almost universally outperform the report baseline (RB)—even in the zero-shot setting (ZS), where Claude Sonnet generally obtains the best results. Third, adding just three few-shot examples

[12] Appendix F reports a soft match variant of this metric.

[13] `https://hub.docker.com/r/hltcoe/lome`

[14] Details on training and input formats are in Appendix B.

[15] Appendix C has further details on models and prompts.

Model	p	Report							Cross-Document						
		R$_1$	**R**$_2$	**R**$_L$	**BS**	**CR**	**A**	**F**	**R**$_1$	**R**$_2$	**R**$_L$	**BS**	**CR**	**A**	**F**
T5	0.0	76.6	64.4	68.9	95.0	74.2	98.2	85.0	64.1	46.4	52.8	92.6	46.3	92.5	90.2
	0.1	75.6	62.8	67.8	93.9	71.4	97.6	84.7	62.8	45.3	51.8	91.5	47.2	92.0	89.9
	0.2	74.0	61.7	66.2	93.6	69.6	98.0	84.6	62.0	44.3	50.7	91.4	43.5	89.3	88.0
	0.3	72.1	60.0	64.7	93.3	67.5	98.2	83.0	60.0	42.8	49.3	91.0	43.3	87.3	89.0
	0.4	70.3	57.5	62.1	92.9	66.4	95.8	83.2	58.4	40.9	47.8	90.8	44.4	87.4	86.8
	0.5	68.3	55.2	60.6	92.6	63.2	96.3	83.5	56.6	39.1	46.3	90.4	43.1	87.3	88.0
CLAUDE H (FS)	0.0	71.7	55.9	61.0	94.3	63.2	94.8	82.9	57.7	36.9	45.7	92.1	36.2	91.0	90.5
	0.1	67.5	51.5	56.7	93.7	59.4	94.8	83.6	57.2	37.3	45.4	91.8	37.1	82.5	88.9
	0.2	65.6	48.8	55.1	93.5	55.1	94.7	83.2	56.2	37.0	45.1	91.7	37.8	79.4	88.6
	0.3	64.7	47.8	54.1	93.3	52.8	94.6	84.1	56.0	36.2	44.9	91.5	32.7	82.2	89.2
	0.4	64.1	47.2	54.1	93.3	52.2	95.0	83.1	54.5	34.3	43.1	91.3	31.4	85.0	89.0
	0.5	63.1	46.8	54.0	93.1	52.3	94.7	83.8	54.3	34.6	43.3	91.3	33.1	86.4	89.2
GPT-4O M (FS)	0.0	72.0	55.4	61.0	94.3	66.8	94.1	83.3	57.5	36.9	45.7	92.1	39.8	88.5	89.8
	0.1	69.2	52.8	59.5	94.0	64.0	94.5	81.8	58.8	38.2	46.2	92.1	42.2	74.5	90.6
	0.2	67.6	50.8	57.0	93.7	59.8	94.2	84.3	56.6	36.2	45.1	91.2	39.4	75.2	89.8
	0.3	66.9	50.1	57.0	93.7	59.3	94.9	81.8	56.4	36.2	44.5	91.8	37.8	77.2	90.2
	0.4	65.2	48.1	54.9	93.4	56.7	93.8	84.2	54.8	34.0	42.8	91.6	36.6	77.8	90.6
	0.5	65.1	47.5	54.8	93.4	55.2	95.4	82.7	54.2	33.2	42.6	91.4	34.4	80.9	90.8

Table 3: Performance of three models from Table 2 when the argument annotations for each role in the report event (**Report**) or additionally in the source event (**Cross-Document**) are corrupted with probability p (see §4.5).

(FS) yields major gains over the zero-shot setting for all LLMs on all metrics. Even here, however, few-shot results still trail the best fine-tuned results (T5) by sizable margins on most metrics.

4.3 Cross-Document Summarization

Setup The setup for the cross-document task is similar to that of the report task, but adds the source text and its annotated event to the input alongside the report text and its event. As the source texts are full web articles, most are long (e.g. dev texts average almost 62 sentences and over 1,500 words). While this is no obstacle for the LLMs, the smaller models do not support contexts of this size. Thus, to enable a fair comparison across models, we apply a sentence retriever to the source, using the report text as a query to select the top k most relevant sentences to use as context.[16] We consider $k \in \{3, \ldots, 10\}$ and selected the maximum value such that $\geq 95\%$ of the resulting dev set contexts would fit untruncated in the input, yielding $k = 7$. We experimented with the dense retrievers `all-mpnet-base-v2` (based on MPNet; Song et al., 2020) and `e5-large-v2` (Wang et al., 2022), but obtained our best results with BM25 (Robertson et al., 2009), which we use in all experiments.[17]

We use the same training and inference settings from §4.2; see Appendices B, C for further details.

[16]This approach can also be justified by the fact that typically only a small portion of the source concerns the event.

[17]Models were evaluated on recall of annotated arguments in the retrieved contexts for the dev set for fixed k. At $k = 7$, BM25 recovered $\sim 76\%$ of annotated source arguments.

Results are shown in the right half of Table 2 and are qualitatively similar to those for the report task, with the fine-tuned models generally showing the best overall numbers ($\mathbf{R}_{1,2,L}$, **CR**) or nearly so (**BS**), although GPT-4o obtains the highest scores on **BS** and Claude Sonnet on **A** and **F**. Once again, nearly all models outperform the report baseline across the board (ZS and GPT-4o Mini excepted). Finally, we note that results on most metrics are much lower in absolute terms compared to the corresponding results from §4.2, testifying to the greater difficulty of the cross-document task.

4.4 Input Ablations

Following Gantt et al. (2024), Appendix F considers ablations on the input for both tasks, in which we omit the annotated events (TEXT ONLY) or the texts (EVENT ONLY), and condition summary generation on the resulting ablated inputs. We also present a novel third ablation that omits the *arguments*, but leaves in information about the frame and roles (TEXT+SCHEMA). Consistent with Gantt et al., we find that *both the text and the full event annotations are needed to obtain the best results* (Tables 8 and 9), indicating that the SEAMUS tasks are *not* reducible to standard summarization (TEXT ONLY), structure-to-text (EVENT ONLY), or even a hybrid objective (TEXT+SCHEMA). Moreover, if some results in Table 2 (e.g. $\mathbf{R}_{\{1,2,L\}}$) appear high, these ablations show that this is due in large part to access to gold event structures. We next turn to the case of imperfect event extractions.

4.5 Impact of Extraction Quality

Setup §4.2 and §4.3 use gold event structures in the input to facilitate fair cross-model comparisons. But in real-world scenarios, one rarely has access to gold arguments, and certainly not in the extraction-to-summarization pipelines CDEKS aims to support. It is thus essential to understand models' tolerance to noise in the extracted events.

To probe robustness to extraction errors in a controlled manner, we apply variable amounts of noise to the gold event annotations and evaluate model performance on the resulting inputs. Concretely, for each role R of each event, we edit R's arguments with probability p. If a role is selected for editing, we then make *one* of the following edits with equal probability:

1. INSERT: A new (incorrect) span from the text is *added* to the argument list for R.
2. DELETE: An argument span is *removed* at random from the argument list for R.
3. REPLACE: An argument span is *replaced* at random with an incorrect span from the text.

For the cross-document task, we apply these edits to the event annotations for both the report and the source. We sample the edits to be made uniformly and then prompt an LLM (GPT-4o) to apply them by supplying in a prompt: (1) the text (report or source), (2) the (JSON-formatted) report or source event annotations, and (3) instructions for the edits to be made, generated automatically by populating templatic statements based on the edits sampled. The LLM is free to select an appropriate *new* span to be used for the INSERT and REPLACE operations. We consider $p \in \{0.1, 0.2, 0.3, 0.4, 0.5\}$, using the same sampled edits for all models for a given p.

We evaluate one fine-tuned model (T5) and one model each from the Claude (Claude Haiku) and GPT (GPT-4o Mini) families. For T5, we use the same checkpoint as presented in Table 2. For Claude Haiku and GPT-4o Mini, we use few-shot prompts similar to those used in the FS setting in Table 2, but with two key changes. First, we alter the task instructions to say that the event annotations for the target example *may contain errors*, and that the model must correct these errors when generating its summary by consulting the text(s). Second, we show the model how to do this by substituting noised versions of the event annotations in the few-shot examples while leaving their associated texts and summaries unchanged.

p	Summary
0.0	The gradual accumulation of partially decayed plant material in a bog functions as a carbon sink.
0.1	The gradual accumulation of decayed plant material in a bog functions as a carbon sink.
0.2	The gradual accumulation of decayed plant material in a bog acts as a carbon sink.
0.3	The gradual accumulation of decayed plant material in a bog functions as a carbon sink.
0.4	The gradual accumulation of decayed plant material, including peat, in bogs functions as a carbon sink.
0.5	The gradual accumulation of decayed plant material in a bog functions as a carbon sink.

Table 4: Example outputs from GPT-4o Mini on the cross-document task as role annotations are corrupted with probability p. In many cases (as here), we find minimal degradation in quality from $p = 0$ to $p = 0.5$.

Results for both tasks are in Table 3. For all models, we observe (near-)monotonic drops in performance for most metrics as p increases. While performance drops are sizable in some cases, they are arguably less radical than we might expect, given the destructiveness of the changes at $p = 0.5$, where roughly half of all roles contain extraction errors. This is especially evident in the results for Claude Haiku and GPT-4o Mini on the cross-document task, where (e.g.) $\mathbf{R}_{1,2,L}$ scores decrease by only about 3 points from $p = 0$ to $p = 0.5$, **BS** by less than 1, and **F** showing no drop at all. Further, losses on **CR** (the most explicit measure of extraction ability) are only ~5 points for GPT-4o Mini and ~3 points for Claude Haiku.

These findings are confirmed by manual inspection of model outputs, where we often see relatively little degradation in summary quality (Table 4). This suggests an intriguing strength of this task relative to traditional event extraction: the ability to *counteract extraction errors post-hoc* by using imperfect event extractions as a query to locate relevant passages in the input and then leveraging those passages to avoid analogous errors in the summary.

5 Human Evaluation

Setup Lastly, we conduct a human evaluation of the reference and model-generated summaries. We focus our evaluation on the cross-document task, comparing the summaries generated by models presented in Table 2 (excluding RB). For the GPT and Claude models, we use the FS (few-shot) summaries only, owing to their superiority over the ZS results. We randomly sampled 30 test set examples and presented the 7 model-generated summaries for these examples, along with the references, to 3 human raters—all English-speaking NLP researchers who did not participate in other

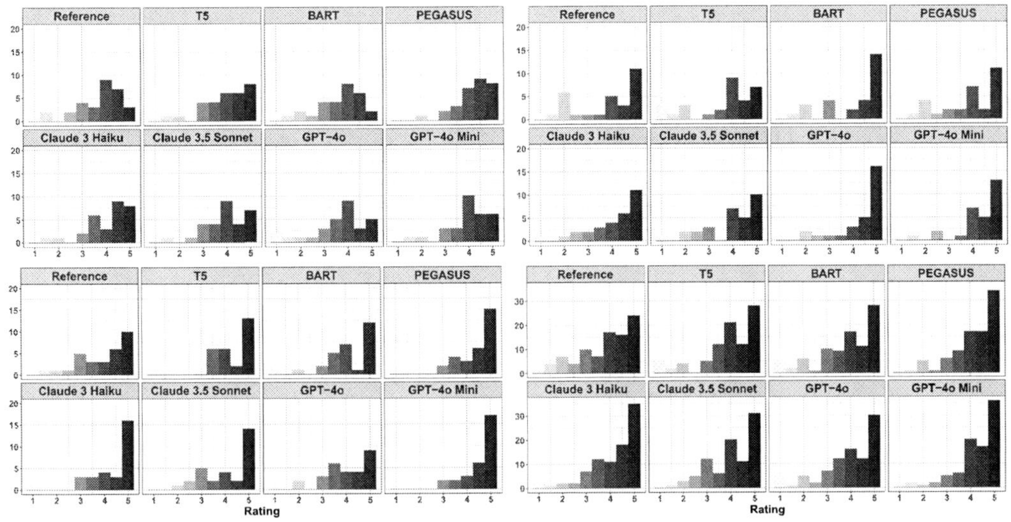

Figure 3: Histograms of summary quality scores (1-5, higher is better) from our human evaluation (§5). The bottom right plot (red) aggregates scores across all three raters; each of the other plots (blue) shows a single rater's scores.

parts of this work. Each rater provided a single quality score for each summary based on the ordered list of attributes used by Gantt et al. (2024): *factuality*, *adequacy*, *coherence*, *relevancy*, and *fluency*. Scores were given from 1 (low) to 5 (high), with half points allowed. Each rater thus provided $30 \times (7+1) \times 1 = 240$ judgments. Raters were not shown which model produced which summary, and summary presentation order was randomized.[18]

Results Four sets of histograms of scores for each model (and the reference) are shown in Figure 3. The bottom right set (red) shows scores aggregated across annotators, while the other three (blue) each show scores of a single rater. For all raters, scores are consistently high across models and the reference, with modes of ≥ 4 for each. Comparing preferences across raters, however, we see significant variability: GPT-4o achieved the highest average score for one rater (top right, 4.28); GPT-4o Mini for the second (bottom left, 4.57); and PEGASUS for the third (top left, 4.23).

Looking at intra-rater distributions, however, it's unclear how robust these preferences are. Using Wilcoxon rank-sum tests to evaluate pairwise differences in each rater's scores for a given pair of models, we find that some of these preferences are reliable at $\alpha = .05$ (e.g. GPT-4o > T5 with $p = .016$ for the first rater), but none holds up when applying the Bonferroni correction for multiple comparisons. We take these results to indicate that our baselines are fairly effective at producing good summaries, and that while they may somewhat differentiate themselves on individual metrics[19], the best models on a more holistic picture may come down to user preference, and there may not be *definitive* bests even at this scope. This plurality of solid modeling options is encouraging, and suggests flexibility in the application of CDEKS to a range of use cases.

6 Conclusion

This work has extended the task of *event-keyed summarization* (EKS) to the cross-document setting (CDEKS). To enable this, we provided an expert reannotation of the FAMuS CDAE dataset, yielding high-quality event argument annotations on all 1,265 examples. We then leveraged these improved annotations to construct SEAMuS—a collection of single- (*report*) and cross-document summaries on top of FAMuS, further annotating the summaries themselves for event arguments (§3). We benchmarked SEAMuS on a diverse set of baselines, including smaller fine-tuned models, as well as zero- and few-shot prompted LLMs (§4.2, §4.3). We then presented more detailed analysis, conducting a comprehensive set of input abalations (§4.4), assessing the impact of degraded event extraction on summary quality (§4.5), and finally concluding with a human evaluation of summary quality (§5). We release SEAMuS, along with our baseline results, to facilitate further work on EKS in both the single- and cross-document settings.

[18]See Appendix D for further details.

[19]See our discussion of argument recovery in Appendix F.

Limitations

One limitation of this work is SEAMUS's size: 1,265 examples is sufficient for fine-tuning smaller models and for conducting prompting experiments with larger ones, but is likely insufficient for substantive fine-tuning of very large models.

A second limitation is that the cross-document setting considers only two documents per example. This constraint was imposed by the choice of the FAMuS dataset as the basis for SEAMUS, as cross-document argument annotations in the former were provided only for *pairs* of report and source texts. Future work expanding the set of source texts would be valuable, and would allow both for richer summaries and for more robust evaluation of models' ability to accurately synthesize information across possibly differing accounts of events (cf. Huang et al. (2024)), as information conflicts are more common outside of Wikipedia citations.

We note, however, that addressing either limitation may require relaxing data quality standards—relying on crowdsourcing or LLM-powered annotation techniques—as scaling our annotation procedure to many more examples or source documents would demand considerable resources. It was only thanks to the above restrictions that we were able to provide expert annotations for SEAMUS.

Finally, while the experiments in §4.5 offer a helpful picture of the impact of event extraction quality on cross-document event-keyed summaries, further experiments on the outputs of actual event extraction systems would likely provide a better one. Much of the difficulty of deploying CDEKS in practical settings undoubtedly lies in the development of an effective document-level event extractor, as evidenced by the ongoing challenges documented by much prior work in this domain (Du et al., 2021b; Chen et al., 2023b; Gantt et al., 2023; Vashishtha et al., 2024, *i.a.*)

Ethics

As the report and source texts in SEAMUS are the same as those in the FAMuS dataset, and as the summaries in SEAMUS are simply distillations of (parts of) these texts, we do not believe our dataset introduces any novel risks as a resource. Nonetheless, these texts do discuss real people, places, and institutions, and models trained on this data may thus be liable to make untrue claims about them or otherwise misrepresent them. We intend SEAMUS for academic use only, as a benchmark to evaluate systems for single- and cross-document event-keyed summarization.

References

James Allan, Rahul Gupta, and Vikas Khandelwal. 2001. Temporal summaries of new topics. In *Proceedings of the 24th annual international ACM SIGIR conference on Research and development in information retrieval*, pages 10–18.

Collin F. Baker, Charles J. Fillmore, and John B. Lowe. 1998. The Berkeley FrameNet project. In *COLING 1998 Volume 1: The 17th International Conference on Computational Linguistics*.

Samuel Barham, Orion Weller, Michelle Yuan, Kenton Murray, Mahsa Yarmohammadi, Zhengping Jiang, Siddharth Vashishtha, Alexander Martin, Anqi Liu, Aaron Steven White, et al. 2023. Megawika: Millions of reports and their sources across 50 diverse languages. *arXiv preprint arXiv:2307.07049*.

Yanran Chen and Steffen Eger. 2023. MENLI: Robust evaluation metrics from natural language inference. *Transactions of the Association for Computational Linguistics*, 11:804–825.

Yulong Chen, Yang Liu, Liang Chen, and Yue Zhang. 2021. DialogSum: A real-life scenario dialogue summarization dataset. In *Findings of the Association for Computational Linguistics: ACL-IJCNLP 2021*, pages 5062–5074. Association for Computational Linguistics.

Yunmo Chen, William Gantt, Tongfei Chen, Aaron White, and Benjamin Van Durme. 2023a. A unified view of evaluation metrics for structured prediction. In *Proceedings of the 2023 Conference on Empirical Methods in Natural Language Processing*, pages 12868–12882. Association for Computational Linguistics.

Yunmo Chen, William Gantt, Weiwei Gu, Tongfei Chen, Aaron White, and Benjamin Van Durme. 2023b. Iterative document-level information extraction via imitation learning. In *Proceedings of the 17th Conference of the European Chapter of the Association for Computational Linguistics*, pages 1858–1874. Association for Computational Linguistics.

Hai Leong Chieu and Yoong Keok Lee. 2004. Query based event extraction along a timeline. In *Proceedings of the 27th annual international ACM SIGIR conference on Research and development in information retrieval*, pages 425–432.

Eric Chu and Peter Liu. 2019. Meansum: a neural model for unsupervised multi-document abstractive summarization. In *International conference on machine learning*, pages 1223–1232. PMLR.

Xinya Du, Alexander Rush, and Claire Cardie. 2021a. GRIT: Generative role-filler transformers for document-level event entity extraction. In *Proceedings of the 16th Conference of the European Chapter of the Association for Computational Linguistics: Main Volume*, pages 634–644. Association for Computational Linguistics.

Xinya Du, Alexander Rush, and Claire Cardie. 2021b. Template filling with generative transformers. In *Proceedings of the 2021 Conference of the North American Chapter of the Association for Computational Linguistics: Human Language Technologies*, pages 909–914. Association for Computational Linguistics.

Abhimanyu Dubey, Abhinav Jauhri, Abhinav Pandey, Abhishek Kadian, Ahmad Al-Dahle, Aiesha Letman, Akhil Mathur, Alan Schelten, Amy Yang, Angela Fan, Anirudh Goyal, Anthony Hartshorn, Aobo Yang, Archi Mitra, Archie Sravankumar, Artem Korenev, Arthur Hinsvark, Arun Rao, Aston Zhang, Aurelien Rodriguez, Austen Gregerson, Ava Spataru, Baptiste Roziere, Bethany Biron, Binh Tang, Bobbie Chern, Charlotte Caucheteux, Chaya Nayak, Chloe Bi, Chris Marra, Chris McConnell, Christian Keller, Christophe Touret, Chunyang Wu, Corinne Wong, Cristian Canton Ferrer, Cyrus Nikolaidis, Damien Allonsius, Daniel Song, Danielle Pintz, Danny Livshits, David Esiobu, Dhruv Choudhary, Dhruv Mahajan, Diego Garcia-Olano, Diego Perino, Dieuwke Hupkes, Egor Lakomkin, Ehab AlBadawy, Elina Lobanova, Emily Dinan, Eric Michael Smith, Filip Radenovic, Frank Zhang, Gabriel Synnaeve, Gabrielle Lee, Georgia Lewis Anderson, Graeme Nail, Gregoire Mialon, Guan Pang, Guillem Cucurell, Hailey Nguyen, Hannah Korevaar, Hu Xu, Hugo Touvron, Iliyan Zarov, Imanol Arrieta Ibarra, Isabel Kloumann, Ishan Misra, Ivan Evtimov, Jade Copet, Jaewon Lee, Jan Geffert, Jana Vranes, Jason Park, Jay Mahadeokar, Jeet Shah, Jelmer van der Linde, Jennifer Billock, Jenny Hong, Jenya Lee, Jeremy Fu, Jianfeng Chi, Jianyu Huang, Jiawen Liu, Jie Wang, Jiecao Yu, Joanna Bitton, Joe Spisak, Jongsoo Park, Joseph Rocca, Joshua Johnstun, Joshua Saxe, Junteng Jia, Kalyan Vasuden Alwala, Kartikeya Upasani, Kate Plawiak, Ke Li, Kenneth Heafield, Kevin Stone, Khalid El-Arini, Krithika Iyer, Kshitiz Malik, Kuenley Chiu, Kunal Bhalla, Lauren Rantala-Yeary, Laurens van der Maaten, Lawrence Chen, Liang Tan, Liz Jenkins, Louis Martin, Lovish Madaan, Lubo Malo, Lukas Blecher, Lukas Landzaat, Luke de Oliveira, Madeline Muzzi, Mahesh Pasupuleti, Mannat Singh, Manohar Paluri, Marcin Kardas, Mathew Oldham, Mathieu Rita, Maya Pavlova, Melanie Kambadur, Mike Lewis, Min Si, Mitesh Kumar Singh, Mona Hassan, Naman Goyal, Narjes Torabi, Nikolay Bashlykov, Nikolay Bogoychev, Niladri Chatterji, Olivier Duchenne, Onur Çelebi, Patrick Alrassy, Pengchuan Zhang, Pengwei Li, Petar Vasic, Peter Weng, Prajjwal Bhargava, Pratik Dubal, Praveen Krishnan, Punit Singh Koura, Puxin Xu, Qing He, Qingxiao Dong, Ragavan Srinivasan, Raj Ganapathy, Ramon Calderer, Ricardo Silveira Cabral, Robert Stojnic, Roberta Raileanu, Rohit Girdhar, Rohit Patel, Romain Sauvestre, Ronnie Polidoro, Roshan Sumbaly, Ross Taylor, Ruan Silva, Rui Hou, Rui Wang, Saghar Hosseini, Sahana Chennabasappa, Sanjay Singh, Sean Bell, Seohyun Sonia Kim, Sergey Edunov, Shaoliang Nie, Sharan Narang, Sharath Raparthy, Sheng Shen, Shengye Wan, Shruti Bhosale, Shun Zhang, Simon Vandenhende, Soumya Batra, Spencer Whitman, Sten Sootla, Stephane Collot, Suchin Gururangan, Sydney Borodinsky, Tamar Herman, Tara Fowler, Tarek Sheasha, Thomas Georgiou, Thomas Scialom, Tobias Speckbacher, Todor Mihaylov, Tong Xiao, Ujjwal Karn, Vedanuj Goswami, Vibhor Gupta, Vignesh Ramanathan, Viktor Kerkez, Vincent Gonguet, Virginie Do, Vish Vogeti, Vladan Petrovic, Weiwei Chu, Wenhan Xiong, Wenyin Fu, Whitney Meers, Xavier Martinet, Xiaodong Wang, Xiaoqing Ellen Tan, Xinfeng Xie, Xuchao Jia, Xuewei Wang, Yaelle Goldschlag, Yashesh Gaur, Yasmine Babaei, Yi Wen, Yiwen Song, Yuchen Zhang, Yue Li, Yuning Mao, Zacharie Delpierre Coudert, Zheng Yan, Zhengxing Chen, Zoe Papakipos, Aaditya Singh, Aaron Grattafiori, Abha Jain, Adam Kelsey, Adam Shajnfeld, Adithya Gangidi, Adolfo Victoria, Ahuva Goldstand, Ajay Menon, Ajay Sharma, Alex Boesenberg, Alex Vaughan, Alexei Baevski, Allie Feinstein, Amanda Kallet, Amit Sangani, Anam Yunus, Andrei Lupu, Andres Alvarado, Andrew Caples, Andrew Gu, Andrew Ho, Andrew Poulton, Andrew Ryan, Ankit Ramchandani, Annie Franco, Aparajita Saraf, Arkabandhu Chowdhury, Ashley Gabriel, Ashwin Bharambe, Assaf Eisenman, Azadeh Yazdan, Beau James, Ben Maurer, Benjamin Leonhardi, Bernie Huang, Beth Loyd, Beto De Paola, Bhargavi Paranjape, Bing Liu, Bo Wu, Boyu Ni, Braden Hancock, Bram Wasti, Brandon Spence, Brani Stojkovic, Brian Gamido, Britt Montalvo, Carl Parker, Carly Burton, Catalina Mejia, Changhan Wang, Changkyu Kim, Chao Zhou, Chester Hu, Ching-Hsiang Chu, Chris Cai, Chris Tindal, Christoph Feichtenhofer, Damon Civin, Dana Beaty, Daniel Kreymer, Daniel Li, Danny Wyatt, David Adkins, David Xu, Davide Testuggine, Delia David, Devi Parikh, Diana Liskovich, Didem Foss, Dingkang Wang, Duc Le, Dustin Holland, Edward Dowling, Eissa Jamil, Elaine Montgomery, Eleonora Presani, Emily Hahn, Emily Wood, Erik Brinkman, Esteban Arcaute, Evan Dunbar, Evan Smothers, Fei Sun, Felix Kreuk, Feng Tian, Firat Ozgenel, Francesco Caggioni, Francisco Guzmán, Frank Kanayet, Frank Seide, Gabriela Medina Florez, Gabriella Schwarz, Gada Badeer, Georgia Swee, Gil Halpern, Govind Thattai, Grant Herman, Grigory Sizov, Guangyi, Zhang, Guna Lakshminarayanan, Hamid Shojanazeri, Han Zou, Hannah Wang, Hanwen Zha, Haroun Habeeb, Harrison Rudolph, Helen Suk, Henry Aspegren, Hunter Goldman, Ibrahim Damlaj, Igor Molybog, Igor Tufanov, Irina-Elena Veliche, Itai Gat, Jake Weissman, James Geboski, James Kohli, Japhet Asher, Jean-Baptiste Gaya, Jeff Marcus, Jeff Tang, Jennifer Chan, Jenny Zhen, Jeremy Reizenstein, Jeremy Teboul, Jessica Zhong, Jian Jin, Jingyi Yang, Joe Cummings, Jon Carvill, Jon Shepard, Jonathan McPhie, Jonathan Torres, Josh Ginsburg, Junjie Wang, Kai Wu, Kam Hou U, Karan Saxena, Karthik Prasad, Kartikay Khandelwal, Katayoun Zand, Kathy Matosich, Kaushik Veeraraghavan, Kelly Michelena, Keqian Li, Kun Huang, Kunal Chawla, Kushal Lakhotia, Kyle Huang, Lailin Chen, Lakshya Garg, Lavender A, Leandro Silva, Lee Bell, Lei Zhang, Liangpeng Guo, Licheng Yu, Liron Moshkovich, Luca Wehrstedt, Madian Khabsa, Manav Avalani, Manish Bhatt, Maria Tsimpoukelli, Martynas Mankus, Matan Hasson, Matthew Lennie, Matthias Reso, Maxim Groshev, Maxim Naumov, Maya Lathi, Meghan Keneally, Michael L. Seltzer, Michal Valko, Michelle Restrepo, Mihir Patel, Mik Vyatskov, Mikayel Samvelyan, Mike Clark, Mike Macey, Mike Wang, Miquel Jubert Hermoso, Mo Metanat, Mohammad Rastegari, Munish Bansal, Nandhini Santhanam, Natascha Parks, Natasha White, Navyata Bawa, Nayan Singhal, Nick Egebo, Nicolas Usunier, Nikolay Pavlovich Laptev, Ning Dong, Ning Zhang, Norman Cheng, Oleg Chernoguz, Olivia Hart, Omkar Salpekar, Ozlem Kalinli, Parkin Kent, Parth Parekh, Paul Saab, Pavan Balaji, Pedro Rittner, Philip Bontrager, Pierre Roux, Piotr Dollar, Polina Zvyagina, Prashant Ratanchandani, Pritish Yuvraj, Qian Liang, Rachad Alao, Rachel Rodriguez, Rafi Ayub, Raghotham Murthy, Raghu Nayani, Rahul Mitra, Raymond Li, Rebekkah Hogan, Robin Battey, Rocky Wang, Rohan Maheswari, Russ Howes, Ruty Rinott, Sai Jayesh Bondu, Samyak Datta, Sara Chugh, Sara Hunt, Sargun Dhillon, Sasha Sidorov, Satadru Pan, Saurabh Verma, Seiji Yamamoto, Sharadh Ramaswamy, Shaun Lindsay, Shaun Lindsay, Sheng Feng, Shenghao Lin, Shengxin Cindy Zha, Shiva Shankar, Shuqiang Zhang, Shuqiang Zhang, Sinong Wang, Sneha Agarwal, Soji Sajuyigbe, Soumith Chintala, Stephanie Max, Stephen Chen, Steve Kehoe, Steve Satterfield, Sudarshan Govindaprasad, Sumit Gupta, Sungmin Cho, Sunny Virk, Suraj Subramanian, Sy Choudhury, Sydney Goldman, Tal Remez, Tamar Glaser, Tamara Best, Thilo Kohler, Thomas Robinson, Tianhe Li, Tianjun Zhang, Tim Matthews, Timothy Chou, Tzook Shaked, Varun Vontimitta, Victoria Ajayi, Victoria Montanez, Vijai Mohan, Vinay Satish Kumar, Vishal Mangla, Vítor Albiero, Vlad Ionescu, Vlad Poenaru, Vlad Tiberiu Mihailescu, Vladimir Ivanov, Wei Li, Wenchen Wang, Wenwen Jiang, Wes Bouaziz, Will Constable, Xiaocheng Tang, Xiaofang Wang, Xiaojian Wu, Xiaolan Wang, Xide Xia, Xilun Wu, Xinbo Gao, Yanjun Chen, Ye Hu, Ye Jia, Ye Qi, Yenda Li, Yilin Zhang, Ying Zhang, Yossi Adi, Youngjin Nam, Yu, Wang, Yuchen Hao, Yundi Qian, Yuzi He, Zach Rait, Zachary DeVito, Zef Rosnbrick, Zhaoduo Wen, Zhenyu Yang, and Zhiwei Zhao. 2024. The llama 3 herd of models.

Alexander Fabbri, Irene Li, Tianwei She, Suyi Li, and Dragomir Radev. 2019. Multi-news: A large-scale multi-document summarization dataset and abstractive hierarchical model. In *Proceedings of the 57th Annual Meeting of the Association for Computational Linguistics*, pages 1074–1084. Association for Computational Linguistics.

Angela Fan, David Grangier, and Michael Auli. 2018. Controllable abstractive summarization. In *Proceedings of the 2nd Workshop on Neural Machine Translation and Generation*, pages 45–54. Association for Computational Linguistics.

Kavita Ganesan, ChengXiang Zhai, and Jiawei Han. 2010. Opinosis: A graph based approach to abstractive summarization of highly redundant opinions. In

Proceedings of the 23rd International Conference on Computational Linguistics (Coling 2010), pages 340–348. Coling 2010 Organizing Committee.

William Gantt, Reno Kriz, Yunmo Chen, Siddharth Vashishtha, and Aaron White. 2023. On event individuation for document-level information extraction. In *Findings of the Association for Computational Linguistics: EMNLP 2023*, pages 12938–12958. Association for Computational Linguistics.

William Gantt, Alexander Martin, Pavlo Kuchmiichuk, and Aaron Steven White. 2024. Event-keyed summarization. *arXiv preprint arXiv:2402.06973*.

Demian Gholipour Ghalandari, Chris Hokamp, Nghia The Pham, John Glover, and Georgiana Ifrim. 2020. A large-scale multi-document summarization dataset from the Wikipedia current events portal. In *Proceedings of the 58th Annual Meeting of the Association for Computational Linguistics*, pages 1302–1308. Association for Computational Linguistics.

Kung-Hsiang Huang, Philippe Laban, Alexander Fabbri, Prafulla Kumar Choubey, Shafiq Joty, Caiming Xiong, and Chien-Sheng Wu. 2024. Embrace divergence for richer insights: A multi-document summarization benchmark and a case study on summarizing diverse information from news articles. In *Proceedings of the 2024 Conference of the North American Chapter of the Association for Computational Linguistics: Human Language Technologies (Volume 1: Long Papers)*, pages 570–593. Association for Computational Linguistics.

Diederik P. Kingma and Jimmy Ba. 2014. Adam: A method for stochastic optimization. *CoRR*, abs/1412.6980.

Wessel Kraaij, Thomas Hain, Mike Lincoln, and Wilfried Post. 2005. The ami meeting corpus. In *Proc. International Conference on Methods and Techniques in Behavioral Research*, pages 1–4.

Mike Lewis, Yinhan Liu, Naman Goyal, Marjan Ghazvininejad, Abdelrahman Mohamed, Omer Levy, Veselin Stoyanov, and Luke Zettlemoyer. 2020a. BART: Denoising sequence-to-sequence pre-training for natural language generation, translation, and comprehension. In *Proceedings of the 58th Annual Meeting of the Association for Computational Linguistics*, pages 7871–7880. Association for Computational Linguistics.

Patrick Lewis, Ethan Perez, Aleksandra Piktus, Fabio Petroni, Vladimir Karpukhin, Naman Goyal, Heinrich Küttler, Mike Lewis, Wen-tau Yih, Tim Rocktäschel, et al. 2020b. Retrieval-augmented generation for knowledge-intensive nlp tasks. *Advances in Neural Information Processing Systems*, 33:9459–9474.

Manling Li, Tengfei Ma, Mo Yu, Lingfei Wu, Tian Gao, Heng Ji, and Kathleen McKeown. 2021a. Timeline summarization based on event graph compression via time-aware optimal transport. In *Proceedings of the 2021 Conference on Empirical Methods in Natural Language Processing*, pages 6443–6456. Association for Computational Linguistics.

Sha Li, Heng Ji, and Jiawei Han. 2021b. Document-level event argument extraction by conditional generation. In *Proceedings of the 2021 Conference of the North American Chapter of the Association for Computational Linguistics: Human Language Technologies*, pages 894–908. Association for Computational Linguistics.

Chin-Yew Lin. 2004. ROUGE: A package for automatic evaluation of summaries. In *Text Summarization Branches Out*, pages 74–81. Association for Computational Linguistics.

Yang Liu and Mirella Lapata. 2019. Hierarchical transformers for multi-document summarization. In *Proceedings of the 57th Annual Meeting of the Association for Computational Linguistics*, pages 5070–5081. Association for Computational Linguistics.

Weicheng Ma, Ruibo Liu, Lili Wang, and Soroush Vosoughi. 2020. Multi-resolution annotations for emoji prediction. In *Proceedings of the 2020 Conference on Empirical Methods in Natural Language Processing (EMNLP)*, pages 6684–6694. Association for Computational Linguistics.

James Mayfield, Eugene Yang, Dawn Lawrie, Sean MacAvaney, Paul McNamee, Douglas W Oard, Luca Soldaini, Ian Soboroff, Orion Weller, Efsun Kayi, et al. 2024. On the evaluation of machine-generated reports. In *Proceedings of the 47th International ACM SIGIR Conference on Research and Development in Information Retrieval*, pages 1904–1915.

Sewon Min, Kalpesh Krishna, Xinxi Lyu, Mike Lewis, Wen-tau Yih, Pang Koh, Mohit Iyyer, Luke Zettlemoyer, and Hannaneh Hajishirzi. 2023. FActScore: Fine-grained atomic evaluation of factual precision in long form text generation. In *Proceedings of the 2023 Conference on Empirical Methods in Natural Language Processing*, pages 12076–12100. Association for Computational Linguistics.

Ramakanth Pasunuru, Asli Celikyilmaz, Michel Galley, Chenyan Xiong, Yizhe Zhang, Mohit Bansal, and Jianfeng Gao. 2021. Data augmentation for abstractive query-focused multi-document summarization. *Proceedings of the AAAI Conference on Artificial Intelligence*, 35(15):13666–13674.

Nima Pourdamghani, Kevin Knight, and Ulf Hermjakob. 2016. Generating English from Abstract Meaning Representations. In *Proceedings of the 9th International Natural Language Generation conference*, pages 21–25. Association for Computational Linguistics.

Colin Raffel, Noam Shazeer, Adam Roberts, Katherine Lee, Sharan Narang, Michael Matena, Yanqi Zhou, Wei Li, and Peter J Liu. 2020. Exploring the limits of transfer learning with a unified text-to-text transformer. *Journal of machine learning research*, 21(140):1–67.

Hossein Rajaby Faghihi, Bashar Alhafni, Ke Zhang, Shihao Ran, Joel Tetreault, and Alejandro Jaimes. 2022. CrisisLTLSum: A benchmark for local crisis event timeline extraction and summarization. In *Findings of the Association for Computational Linguistics: EMNLP 2022*, pages 5455–5477. Association for Computational Linguistics.

Stephen Robertson, Hugo Zaragoza, et al. 2009. The probabilistic relevance framework: Bm25 and beyond. *Foundations and Trends® in Information Retrieval*, 3(4):333–389.

Aafiya S Hussain, Talha Z Chafekar, Grishma Sharma, and Deepak H Sharma. 2022. Event oriented abstractive summarization. In *Proceedings of the 19th International Conference on Natural Language Processing (ICON)*, pages 99–108. Association for Computational Linguistics.

Kaitao Song, Xu Tan, Tao Qin, Jianfeng Lu, and Tie-Yan Liu. 2020. Mpnet: Masked and permuted pre-training for language understanding. *Advances in neural information processing systems*, 33:16857–16867.

Beth M. Sundheim. 1992. Overview of the fourth Message Understanding Evaluation and Conference. In *Fourth Message Understanding Conference (MUC-4): Proceedings of a Conference Held in McLean, Virginia, June 16-18, 1992.*

Hugo Touvron, Thibaut Lavril, Gautier Izacard, Xavier Martinet, Marie-Anne Lachaux, Timothée Lacroix, Baptiste Rozière, Naman Goyal, Eric Hambro, Faisal Azhar, Aurelien Rodriguez, Armand Joulin, Edouard Grave, and Guillaume Lample. 2023. Llama: Open and efficient foundation language models.

Sai Vallurupalli, Sayontan Ghosh, Katrin Erk, Niranjan Balasubramanian, and Francis Ferraro. 2022. POQue: Asking participant-specific outcome questions for a deeper understanding of complex events. In *Proceedings of the 2022 Conference on Empirical Methods in Natural Language Processing*, pages 8674–8697. Association for Computational Linguistics.

Siddharth Vashishtha, Alexander Martin, William Gantt, Benjamin Van Durme, and Aaron White. 2024. FAMuS: Frames across multiple sources. In *Proceedings of the 2024 Conference of the North American Chapter of the Association for Computational Linguistics: Human Language Technologies (Volume 1: Long Papers)*, pages 8250–8273. Association for Computational Linguistics.

Jiarui Wang, Richong Zhang, Junfan Chen, Jaein Kim, and Yongyi Mao. 2022. Text style transferring via adversarial masking and styled filling. In *Proceedings of the 2022 Conference on Empirical Methods in Natural Language Processing*, pages 7654–7663. Association for Computational Linguistics.

Miriam Wanner, Seth Ebner, Zhengping Jiang, Mark Dredze, and Benjamin Van Durme. 2024. A closer look at claim decomposition. In *Proceedings of the 13th Joint Conference on Lexical and Computational Semantics (*SEM 2024)*, pages 153–175. Association for Computational Linguistics.

Patrick Xia, Guanghui Qin, Siddharth Vashishtha, Yunmo Chen, Tongfei Chen, Chandler May, Craig Harman, Kyle Rawlins, Aaron Steven White, and Benjamin Van Durme. 2021. LOME: Large ontology multilingual extraction. In *Proceedings of the 16th Conference of the European Chapter of the Association for Computational Linguistics: System Demonstrations*, pages 149–159. Association for Computational Linguistics.

Yuheng Zha, Yichi Yang, Ruichen Li, and Zhiting Hu. 2023. AlignScore: Evaluating factual consistency with a unified alignment function. In *Proceedings of the 61st Annual Meeting of the Association for Computational Linguistics (Volume 1: Long Papers)*, pages 11328–11348. Association for Computational Linguistics.

Jingqing Zhang, Yao Zhao, Mohammad Saleh, and Peter Liu. 2020. Pegasus: Pre-training with extracted gap-sentences for abstractive summarization. In *International conference on machine learning*, pages 11328–11339. PMLR.

Tianyi Zhang, Varsha Kishore, Felix Wu, Kilian Q. Weinberger, and Yoav Artzi. 2019. Bertscore: Evaluating text generation with bert. *ArXiv*, abs/1904.09675.

Markus Zopf. 2018. Auto-hMDS: Automatic construction of a large heterogeneous multilingual multi-document summarization corpus. In *Proceedings of the Eleventh International Conference on Language Resources and Evaluation (LREC 2018)*. European Language Resources Association (ELRA).

A Additional Examples

Below, we show a few examples of the report summaries and their corresponding cross-document summaries to illustrate how the latter typically provide greater detail about an event of interest relative to the former. We note, however, that this is not always the case: sometimes the source document offers no additional information about the event beyond what is contained in the report.

Example 1

- **Frame**: CAUSE TO RESUME
- **Report**: *Areva* ***renewed*** *a uranium deal with Niger in January 2008.*
- **Cross-Doc**: *On January 13, 2008, French state-controlled nuclear reactor maker Areva CEPFi said it had* ***renewed*** *a uranium mining deal with the state of Niger and would invest over 1 billion euros.*

Exmaple 2

- **Frame**: SMUGGLING
- **Report**: *A woman pled guilty to possession and attempting to* ***smuggle*** *89 grams of heroin out of Thailand.*
- **Cross-Doc**: *Scot Sandra Gregory pled guilty to possession and attempting to* ***smuggle*** *89 grams of heroin out of Thailand in 1993 and did her time in Thai jails.*

Exmaple 3

- **Frame**: HOSTILE ENCOUNTER
- **Report**: *The plot of Reign of Shadows involves players returning to the dark side of the moon of Luclin to* ***face*** *the snake-like Shissar race led by Emperor Ssraeshza.*
- **Cross-Doc**: *The plot of Reign of Shadows involves players returning to the heart of the dark side of the moon of Luclin to* ***face*** *the snake-like Emperor Ssraeshza and his unyielding throngs of insidious zealots and enslaved minions to take back the ancient citadel of Vex Thal and end their march.*

B Training and Evaluation

Models and Hardware The BART, T5, and PEGASUS models were all trained on a single NVIDIA Quadro RTX 6000 GPU using CUDA version 11.7. Results reported with these models are based on single runs with a fixed random seed. We fine-tune the following pretrained checkpoints available from HuggingFace:

- `t5-large`
- `facebook/bart-large`
- `google/pegasus-large`

Libraries Models were developed using Python 3.11.9. We used the following libraries for model training, inference, and evaluation:

- `accelerate (0.34.2)`
- `bert-score (0.3.13)`
- `bm25s (0.2.1)`
- `datasets (3.0.1)`
- `deepspeed (0.15.1)`
- `editdistance (0.8.1)`
- `evaluate (0.4.3)`
- `metametric (0.1.2)`
- `numpy (1.26.4)`
- `rouge-score (0.1.2)`
- `sentence-transformers (3.1.1)`
- `spacy (3.7.5)`
- `torch (2.0.1+cu117)`
- `transformers (4.45.1)`
- `tokenizers (0.20.0)`

Metrics We use the implementations of ROUGE ($\mathbf{R}_{1,2,L}$) and BERTScore (**BS**) provided by the HuggingFace `evaluate` library. We implement CEAF-REE (**CR**) and its soft-match variant (see Tables 8, 9) using the `metametric` package (Chen et al., 2023a). We use the implementation of AlignScore released by the metric's authors (Zha et al., 2023).[20]. Lastly, for FActScore, we use the few-shot examples from Wanner et al. (2024) for decomposition and use Llama3.1-8B Instruct (Touvron et al., 2023; Dubey et al., 2024) for both atomic fact decomposition and verification.

Hyperparameters BART, T5, and PEGASUS were all trained for a maximum of 30 epochs with a patience of 5 epochs, using ROUGE-1 ($\mathbf{R}_1$) F_1 score on the dev set as the evaluation criterion. We use the Adam optimizer (Kingma and Ba, 2014) with default hyperparameters ($\beta_1 = 0.9, \beta_2 = 0.99o$, $\epsilon = 1e^{-8}$, $\eta = 0.001$) for all models. For inference, we use beam search decoding with a beam size of 5 and set the maximum tokens to 256.

[20] `https://github.com/yuh-zha/AlignScore`

Input Formats Below, we show in greater detail the input format for BART, PEGASUS, and T5 for the report and cross-document results reported in Table 2 and Table 3. (Note: these input formats were also used to obtain the BART, PEGASUS, and T5 results in the TEXT+EVENT rows in Table 8 and Table 9.) Here, ⟨`B`⟩ and ⟨`E`⟩ denote the model's start-of-sequence and end-of-sequence tokens, respectively (if applicable), and ⟨`S`⟩ denotes a special token used to delineate information pertaining to a particular event role. Other text set between angle brackets (⟨...⟩) denotes a variable placeholder. We add spaces between separators and adjacent text to improve readability below; they are not present in the actual input.

The input format for the **report** task is:

> ⟨`B`⟩ Report: ⟨`Report Text`⟩ ⟨`E`⟩ ⟨`B`⟩ Frame ⟨`S`⟩ ⟨`Frame Name`⟩ ⟨`S`⟩ Trigger ⟨`S`⟩ ⟨`Trigger`⟩ ⟨`S`⟩ ⟨`Role 1 Name`⟩ ⟨`S`⟩ ⟨`Arg 1`⟩; ⟨`Arg 2`⟩; ...⟨`S`⟩ ⟨`Role N Name`⟩ ⟨`S`⟩ ⟨`Arg 1`⟩; ⟨`Arg 2`⟩; ...⟨`S`⟩ ⟨`E`⟩

The input format for the **cross-document** task is:

> ⟨`B`⟩ Report: ⟨`Report Text`⟩ ⟨`S`⟩ Source: ⟨`Source Text`⟩ ⟨`E`⟩ ⟨`B`⟩ Report Event: Frame ⟨`S`⟩ ⟨`Frame Name`⟩ ⟨`S`⟩ Trigger ⟨`S`⟩ ⟨`Trigger`⟩ ⟨`S`⟩ ⟨`Role 1 Name`⟩ ⟨`S`⟩ ⟨`Arg 1`⟩; ⟨`Arg 2`⟩; ...⟨`S`⟩ ⟨`Role N Name`⟩ ⟨`S`⟩ ⟨`Arg 1`⟩; ⟨`Arg 2`⟩; ...⟨`S`⟩ Source Event: Frame ⟨`S`⟩ ⟨`Frame Name`⟩ ⟨`S`⟩ ⟨`Role 1 Name`⟩ ⟨`S`⟩ ⟨`Arg 1`⟩; ⟨`Arg 2`⟩; ...⟨`S`⟩ ⟨`Role N Name`⟩ ⟨`S`⟩ ⟨`Arg 1`⟩; ⟨`Arg 2`⟩; ...⟨`S`⟩ ⟨`E`⟩

The ablation settings presented in Table 8 and Table 9 (TEXT ONLY, EVENT ONLY, TEXT+SCHEMA) do not fundamentally change this overall structure, but merely omit parts of it (e.g. TEXT+SCHEMA omits all ⟨`Arg N`⟩).

C LLMs

GPT All GPT models were accessed through the OpenAI Chat API[21], via the OpenAI Python SDK (`openai` 1.50.2). As noted in §4, we set temperature to 0.7 and set the maximum output tokens to 256 (consistent with the fine-tuned models) for all experiments reported in this paper and leave the other API defaults unchanged ($n = 1$, top_p is not set, and we use no frequency penalty, presence penalty, or logit bias). For GPT-4o, we used model version `gpt-4o-2024-08-06`. For GPT-4o Mini, we used model version `gpt-4o-mini-2024-07-18`. Results reported throughout the paper are based on a single generation per prompt.

Claude All Claude models were accessed through the Anthropic Messages API[22] via the Anthropic Python SDK (`anthropic` 0.34.2). As with the GPT models, we set temperature to 0.7 for all experiments in this paper and leave the other defaults unchanged (we do not set top_p or top_k, as recommended, and we do not set any stop sequences). For Claude 3.5 Sonnet, we used model version `claude-3-5-sonnet-20240620`. For Claude 3 Haiku, we used model version `claude-3-haiku-20240307`. Results reported throughout the paper are based on a single generation per prompt.

Prompts We use the same prompts for all LLMs. Complete prompts will be available in the public GitHub repository for this work. Here, we provide prompt templates used to obtain the results in Table 2 and Table 3, for both tasks (report or cross-document) and for both the zero- (ZS) and few-shot (FS) settings. Text set between angle brackets ⟨...⟩ denote placeholders.

We use the same system prompt for both tasks:

> You are an expert intelligence briefer. Your task is to analyze a specific, important event based ONLY on certain information, and to compile a concise summary of that event to be presented to a high-ranked decision maker.

For the **report** task in the **zero-shot (ZS)** setting, the user prompt has the following structure:

> The Report text below describes a situation. The Report Template provides specific details about the same situation. Focus ONLY on information relevant to the Situation Type.
>
> Please write a short, accurate summary that is one sentence long and that is based ONLY on the provided information. DO NOT include any extraneous details. DO NOT use more than one sentence.

[21] `https://platform.openai.com/docs/api-reference/chat`

[22] `https://docs.anthropic.com/en/api/messages`

Situation Type: ⟨Frame Name⟩ (⟨Frame Def⟩)

Report: ⟨Report Text⟩

Report Template:

- ⟨Role 1⟩ (⟨Role 1 Def⟩): ⟨Arg 1⟩; ⟨Arg 2⟩; ...

- ...

- ⟨Role N⟩ (⟨Role N Def⟩): ⟨Arg 1⟩; ⟨Arg 2⟩; ...

Summary:

The **few-shot (FS)** user prompt for the **report** task had the following structure:

> The Report text below describes a situation. The Report Template provides specific details about the same situation. Focus ONLY on information relevant to the Situation Type.
>
> Please write a short, accurate summary that is one sentence long and that is based ONLY on the provided information. DO NOT include any extraneous details. DO NOT use more than one sentence.
>
> Here are a few examples to show you how to complete the task:
>
> Example 1
>
> ---
>
> Situation Type: ⟨Frame Name⟩ (⟨Frame Def⟩)
>
> Report: ⟨Report Text⟩
>
> Report Template:
>
> - ⟨Role 1⟩ (⟨Role 1 Def⟩): ⟨Arg 1⟩; ⟨Arg 2⟩; ...
> - ...
> - ⟨Role N⟩ (⟨Role N Def⟩): ⟨Arg 1⟩; ⟨Arg 2⟩; ...
>
> Summary: ⟨summary text⟩
>
> Example 2
>
> ---
>
> ⟨ same format as above ⟩
>
> Example 3
>
> ---
>
> ⟨ same format as above ⟩
>
> Now here is the target example for you to complete:
>
> Target
>
> ---
>
> ⟨same format, but with summary text omitted⟩

The **zero-shot** user prompt for the **cross-document** task had the following structure:

> The Report text below describes a situation, and the Report Template provides specific details about the same situation. The Source text provides additional context about this situation, and the Source Template provides additional details. Focus ONLY on information relevant to the Situation Type.
>
> Please write a short, accurate summary that is preferably one sentence long (and no more than two sentences long) based ONLY on the provided information. DO NOT include any extraneous details. TRY to use one sentence and DO NOT use more than two.
>
> Situation Type: ⟨Frame Name⟩ (⟨Frame Def⟩)
>
> Report: ⟨Report Text⟩
>
> Report Template:
>
> - ⟨Role 1⟩ (⟨Role 1 Def⟩): ⟨Arg 1⟩; ⟨Arg 2⟩; ...
> - ...
> - ⟨Role N⟩ (⟨Role N Def⟩): ⟨Arg 1⟩; ⟨Arg 2⟩; ...
>
> Situation Type: ⟨Frame Name⟩ (⟨Frame Def⟩)
>
> Source: ⟨Source Text⟩
>
> Source Template:
>
> - ⟨Role 1⟩ (⟨Role 1 Def⟩): ⟨Arg 1⟩; ⟨Arg 2⟩; ...
> - ...
> - ⟨Role N⟩ (⟨Role N Def⟩): ⟨Arg 1⟩; ⟨Arg 2⟩; ...
>
> Summary:

The **few-shot** user prompt for the **cross-document** task (not explicitly shown) follows exactly the same structure as the few-shot prompt for the report task, but naturally uses the cross-document example format in lieu of the report format.

D Human Evaluation

Full instructions for the human evaluation, along with a JSON file containing the items that were rated, are provided in our GitHub repo (`https://github.com/wgantt/SEAMuS`).

E Data & Annotation

E.1 License

We release SEAMUS and our code under a CC-BY-SA-4.0 license. As noted in the **Ethics** section, we intend SEAMUS for research use only, not for commercial purposes.

E.2 Additional Summary Statistics

Additional summary statistics—about the report and source texts are shown in Table 7

E.3 Inter-Annotator Agreement

As we note in §3, there was no redundancy in the SEAMUS annotation process: corrections to the FAMuS arguments, writing of summaries, and annotation of summary arguments were performed by a single annotator for each example. However, annotators did conduct a 10-example practice annotation for both the report and cross-document tasks. Thus, to give some (limited) sense of the inter-annotator agreement, Table 5 and Table 6 present pairwise comparisons of annotators' annotations on these 10 items for the report and cross-document tasks (respectively) using the *reference-based* metrics from Table 2 (plus the edit distance version of **CR**, $\mathbf{CR}_{soft}$; see Appendix F). We treat annotations produced by annotators in the P column as "predictions" to be evaluated against the "reference" annotations produced by annotators in the R column. Two important notes:

1. Because all of these metrics are F_1 scores, the distinction between P and R is moot and reversing P and R for any given pair would yield the same results. In both tables, we report results for all unordered annotator pairs, as well as the average across all pairs.

2. Because these were practice annotations, none of them were included in the final SEAMUS dataset. We would thus expect the numbers reported here to be an *underestimate* of the level of agreement on the main task, had we had redundancy.

P	R	$\mathbf{R}_1$	$\mathbf{R}_2$	$\mathbf{R}_L$	BS	CR	$\mathbf{CR}_{soft}$
A1	A2	67.1	44.5	52.6	93.4	72.7	86.9
A1	A3	72.4	53.9	63.1	94.4	76.4	86.5
A2	A3	77.2	60.5	62.5	94.7	75.9	89.6
Avg.		72.2	53.0	59.2	94.2	75.0	87.7

Table 5: Inter-annotator agreement on the 10 practice examples from the SEAMUS **report summary** annotation, as given by the reference-based metrics we report in §4, treating annotator P's responses as predictions and R's responses as references (the reverse is equivalent, since these metrics are symmetric).

P	R	$\mathbf{R}_1$	$\mathbf{R}_2$	$\mathbf{R}_L$	BS	CR	$\mathbf{CR}_{soft}$
A1	A2	64.8	42.4	53.3	94.0	40.5	56.6
A1	A3	64.7	43.8	51.6	93.0	50.6	65.0
A1	A4	45.8	22.7	33.0	90.7	49.8	65.2
A1	A5	69.0	48.1	58.8	94.6	46.8	62.8
A2	A3	77.7	66.8	72.4	94.9	50.6	65.6
A2	A4	55.4	33.9	40.8	91.2	50.7	66.8
A2	A5	72.0	56.1	64.9	94.1	50.6	66.9
A3	A4	55.4	33.2	41.9	90.7	51.8	69.0
A3	A5	71.0	57.2	61.8	93.6	52.6	69.8
A4	A5	48.2	27.2	37.3	90.7	52.8	69.6
Avg.		62.4	43.1	51.6	92.8	49.7	65.7

Table 6: Inter-annotator agreement on the 10 practice examples from the SEAMUS **cross-document summary** annotation, as given by the reference-based metrics we report in §4, treating annotator P's responses as predictions and R's responses as references (the reverse is equivalent, since these metrics are symmetric).

	Report		**Source**	
	Train	Dev	Train	Dev
Examples	759	253	759	253
Avg. Words	59	60	1,084	1,511
Avg. Sentences	2.0	2.0	44.7	61.5
Avg. Arguments	3.1	3.5	3.8	4.2

Table 7: Summary statistics for the SEAMUS report (left) and source documents, which are the same as those in the FAMUS dataset, albeit with slightly different arguments due to our corrections of the original FAMUS argument annotations.

E.4 Annotation Interface

Here, we include screenshots of the annotation interface used to complete the Phase 2 annotation.[23] As noted in §3, the interface was adapted from Vashishtha et al.'s (2024) annotation interface for the FAMUS cross-document argument extraction task (cf. Figures 5 and 6 in Appendix A of their paper). Tasks were run via Turkle, an open-source tool with similar functionality to Amazon Mechanical Turk.[24]

In the first part of the Phase 2 annotation, the existing (crowdsourced) FAMUS argument annotations for the source text were reviewed and corrected, and the cross-document summaries were written jointly on the basis of these corrected annotations and the corrected report text argument annotations from Phase 1 (see Figure 4). The interface was pre-populated with (a) the corrected report text arguments from Phase 1 (in the "Report Text" tab, highlighted); the report summary from Phase 1 (in the "Report Summary" field); and (c) the uncorrected source text arguments (in the "Source Text" tab). The source text arguments were reviewed and corrected by toggling to the "Source Text" tab and making any necessary edits to the existing selections. The cross-document summaries were then written in the "Combined Summary" field. The UI for selecting, adding, and removing arguments was unchanged relative to Vashishtha et al.'s implementation. The major differences here are the addition of the "Report Summary" and "Combined Summary" fields, and the inability to alter the selected FrameNet frame for annotation.

In the second part, arguments were annotated on the summaries written in the first part (Figure 5). The interface is similar to the interface for the first part of the Phase 2 annotation, except that the "Report Summary" and "Combined Summary" fields have been removed, and a new tab ("Summary Text") containing the cross-document summary to be annotated was added. Summary arguments were annotated by toggling to this tab and making argument selections in the same way as before. Here, the corrected argument annotations for *both* the report text *and* for the source text were pre-populated for each task under their respective tabs, allowing annotators to toggle between these for reference in annotating the summary arguments.

Figure 4: Interface for source text argument correction and cross-document summary writing (the first part of the Phase 2 annotation).

As can be seen in both Figure 4 and Figure 5, details about the frame for the target event, including the frame name, its definition, as well as role names and their definitions, were provided as in the original FAMUS interface. Instructions were also accessible at any time via the dropdown shown at the top of the screen.

E.5 Annotation Instructions

Annotation instructions for both phases are available on our GitHub repo (`https://github.com/wgantt/SEAMuS`).

E.6 Annotator Demographics

The full set of annotators consists of six students (five graduate and one undergraduate) pursuing degrees in Computer Science (3), Linguistics (2), and Cognitive Science (1), all of whom are fluent English speakers. Only one was financially compensated for the annotations (at a rate of $15 per hour), as this person initially became involved with the project through a university job board posting for the task, whereas the others were members of the lab from which the project originated. The project, and the intended use of their annotations, was clearly explained to all participants in meetings before they began any annotation.

[23] Recall that the Phase 1 annotation, which involved correcting the FAMUS report text argument annotations and writing the report summaries, was done in JSON files.

[24] `https://github.com/hltcoe/turkle-client`

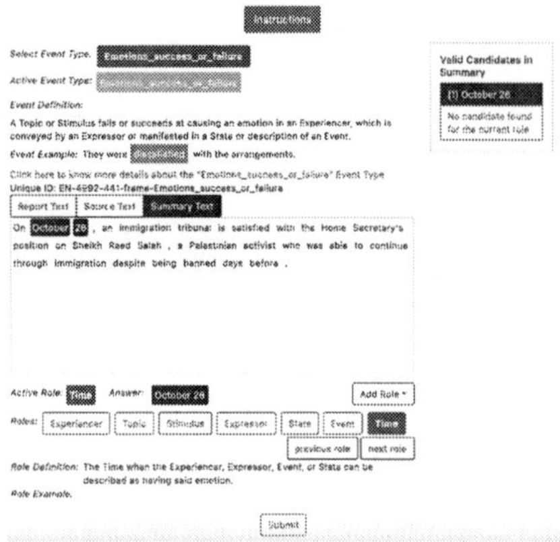

Figure 5: Interface for annotation of arguments on the cross-document summaries (the second part of the Phase 2 annotation).

F Additional Results

F.1 Main Results

Table 10 and Table 11 contain 95% confidence intervals of the results in Table 2 based on non-parametric bootstraps ($n = 1,000$).

F.2 Input Ablations

Here, we include the full results of the ablations on the inputs introduced briefly in §4.4, which were inspired by similar ones conducted by Gantt et al. (2024). In the TEXT ONLY setting, we omit information about the target event entirely and include only the text in the input—either the report for the report task, or both the report and source for the cross-document task—effectively reducing the problem to standard summarization. In the EVENT ONLY setting, we omit the text(s) and include only information about the target event—either the report event annotations for the report task, or both the report and source event annotations for the cross-document task—making this ablation similar to structure-to-text tasks, such as AMR-to-text (Pourdamghani et al., 2016)). In the TEXT+SCHEMA setting, we omit the argument annotations, but leave in information about the frame and its roles. For the fine-tuned models, we include just the names of the frame and its roles. For the LLMs, we additionally include the definitions of the frame and roles as given in FrameNet. Finally, TEXT+EVENT is the name we assign to the *unablated* setting, used to obtain the results in Table 2 and Table 3, where both the text(s) and the full event annotations are present in the input. For all ablation settings, BART, PEGASUS, and T5 are fine-tuned on the ablated inputs using the same settings for training and inference as are described in §4. For the GPT and Claude models, the examples provided in the few-shot setting are also ablated in the way called for by each ablation.

Report Results for the report task are in Table 8. Here and in the cross-document results to follow (Table 9), we include a variant of CEAF-REE (**CR**) that we dub $\mathbf{CR}_{\text{soft}}$, which aligns and scores predicted arguments against reference arguments using normalized levenshtein distance rather than exact match—enabling a more nuanced comparison of different models' ability to recover event arguments in the summaries they produce.

Across all models and most metrics, we see significant drops in performance when ablating any component of the input. Notably, a number of models, especially the LLMs, fall to numbers near or below those of the report baseline (RB) on a variety of metrics.

There are, however, some unsurprising exceptions here. First, in many cases, results on **CR** and $\mathbf{CR}_{\text{soft}}$ in the EVENT ONLY ablation are markedly stronger than the report baseline, and are even competitive with the results in the unablated setting (TEXT+EVENT) for most of the zero-shot-evaluated LLMs. This echoes a similar finding by Gantt et al. (2024), who note that "the document [is not] needed to generate *some* string that contains all the [event] template's arguments." If this is correct, we would *expect* to see strong **CR** scores in the EVENT ONLY setting, even though the summaries may be poorer overall (as reflected in other metrics).

An intriguing, related observation is that whereas the fine-tuned models look dominant against the LLMs on **CR** in the unablated setting, this advantage sharply diminishes when we turn to $\mathbf{CR}_{\text{soft}}$. This is likely explained by the fact that the fine-tuned models are able to learn the conventions adopted by annotators in selecting argument spans, whereas the (prompted) LLMs do not—even though they may still be generating outputs with approximately correct spans that are nonetheless harshly penalized by an exact match.

A second exception is the results on AlignScore (**A**) and FActScore (**F**) in the TEXT ONLY setting, which are competitive with—and in some cases superior to—the results in the unablated setting across models. Recall that both **A** and **F** here evaluate how well the report summary is supported by the report text. It is thus intuitively possible, and evidently quite feasible, to generate a summary that is adequately supported by the text without relying at all on the event annotations—which is exactly what is demanded by the TEXT ONLY setting. This is once again consistent with findings from Gantt et al. (2024) on the NLI-based family of metrics MENLI (Chen and Eger, 2023), which are broadly similar to AlignScore and FActScore: "[event] templates are not needed to generate *some* summary that is entailed by the document."

We also note that, for the fine-tuned models, we obtain **A** scores in the TEXT+SCHEMA ablation that are comparable (T5) or higher than (BART, PEGASUS) those of the unablated setting. This makes sense, inasmuch as the TEXT+SCHEMA setting contains a superset of the inputs of the TEXT ONLY setting, though it is unclear why we do not find a similar pattern with the LLMs.

Finally, note that the report baseline, which treats the report text itself as the summary, should in theory achieve perfect **A** and **F** scores, and thus does not really represent a fair comparison with the other models (note: this is also true for the cross-document setting). That it does not is surely a reflection of the fact that both metrics rely on outputs from imperfect models. Such flaws of LM-based metrics must not be overlooked.

Cross-Document results on the cross-document task are shown in Table 9 and follow a pattern that is qualitatively very similar to that of the report results above. We consistently find that the best results are obtained in the unablated setting (TEXT+EVENT) for most metrics, with the same exception regarding **CR/CR**$_{\text{soft}}$ in the EVENT ONLY setting as we found for the report task. Curiously, however, the findings on **A** are more complicated here: whereas we continue to see the strongest results on this metric in the TEXT ONLY and TEXT+SCHEMA ablations for the fine-tuned models, with the LLMs, we instead see our best results in the unablated setting—following the trend of other metrics.

F.3 Argument Recovery by Role

Table 12 and Table 13 show **CR** and **CR**$_{\text{soft}}$ results (respectively) on the cross-document task broken down by role for the 20 roles with highest support (number of annotated arguments) in the SEAMUS training split.

Comparing the tables reveals an interesting dichotomy. For **CR**, no model is consistently dominant across all roles, with fine-tuned models collectively obtaining the best results on 12 of the 20 and few-shot prompted models obtaining the best results on the remaining 8. The **CR**$_{\text{soft}}$ results, by contrast, heavily favor GPT-4O, which achieves the best scores on 13 roles. Here, the fine-tuned models are top-performing on only 4 roles.

We believe the same factor discussed in subsection F.2 explains this dichotomy: whereas **CR** requires exact span match—and thus will tend to favor models able to learn span boundary conventions through fine-tuning—**CR**$_{\text{soft}}$ does not, and rewards spans proportional to their edit distance from the reference. Thus, **CR**$_{\text{soft}}$ reveals the LLMs (and GPT-4O above all) to be effective in producing summaries that recover the correct arguments, albeit with more lexical modifications relative to the reference.

G Use of AI Assistants

GitHub Copilot was used as a coding assistant for parts of model development and data analysis, though its suggestions were carefully reviewed by the authors. AI assistants were **not** used for other parts of this work (writing, brainstorming, etc.).

Model	Ablation	Setting	R_1	R_2	R_L	BS	CR	CR_{soft}	A	F
Report Baseline	-	-	56.15	46.05	48.37	91.57	52.58	62.56	99.11	98.73
GPT-4o M	TEXT ONLY	ZS	49.96	28.18	39.23	91.31	34.59	53.13	95.74*	83.11
	EVENT ONLY	ZS	53.11	34.04	43.67	91.51	52.13	77.37	60.98	53.42
	TEXT+SCHEMA	ZS	53.29	31.60	42.91	91.28	38.24	56.92	79.07	76.38
	TEXT+EVENT	ZS	62.18	42.32	51.26	93.17	58.48	78.71	86.04	75.80
	TEXT+EVENT	FS	71.98	55.35	61.03	94.34	66.80	83.66	94.06	83.32
GPT-4o	TEXT ONLY	ZS	51.52	29.90	40.90	91.50	33.75	52.06	94.49	84.00*
	EVENT ONLY	ZS	56.39	38.34	46.34	91.93	59.35	83.35	70.66	57.14
	TEXT+SCHEMA	ZS	56.57	37.19	47.08	92.00	42.37	61.50	81.66	73.05
	TEXT+EVENT	ZS	63.95	45.21	52.95	93.18	61.39*	82.60*	83.87	74.78
	TEXT+EVENT	FS	72.54†	56.59†	62.34†	94.40	69.61†	**87.27**†	94.72	81.58
CLAUDE H	TEXT ONLY	ZS	50.41	30.39	40.53	91.11	32.35	51.46	93.10	83.77
	EVENT ONLY	ZS	55.03	36.37	45.71	91.79	54.36	78.25	72.15	56.29
	TEXT+SCHEMA	ZS	57.67	38.51	47.68	92.08	41.36	59.10	83.24	77.05
	TEXT+EVENT	ZS	64.75	46.19	54.67	93.44	58.75	78.92	84.87	77.57
	TEXT+EVENT	FS	71.73	55.86	61.05	94.29	63.21	80.95	94.82	82.54
CLAUDE S	TEXT ONLY	ZS	46.98	22.83	36.24	90.78	25.68	45.88	91.31	82.41
	EVENT ONLY	ZS	55.66	36.89	46.21	92.13	56.38	78.54	72.15	60.37
	TEXT+SCHEMA	ZS	57.33	36.18	46.98	92.30	41.71	61.46	88.93	77.85
	TEXT+EVENT	ZS	67.38*	48.11*	56.52*	93.84*	61.07	81.35	92.96	80.59
	TEXT+EVENT	FS	72.16	54.64	61.29	94.54†	65.66	83.68	95.89†	83.86†
BART	TEXT ONLY	FT	57.13	43.53	50.46	91.77	46.27	58.59	97.42	84.64
	EVENT ONLY	FT	58.34	40.96	48.51	91.83	59.82	75.34	51.17	52.41
	TEXT+SCHEMA	FT	62.23	49.43	55.55	92.59	52.92	65.83	95.01	83.34
	TEXT+EVENT	FT	74.46	61.68	66.42	94.57	69.88	82.72	91.59	79.25
PEGASUS	TEXT ONLY	FT	60.33	46.19	52.44	92.13	45.95	60.40	97.45	85.20
	EVENT ONLY	FT	59.69	41.97	49.46	91.90	57.14	74.34	53.93	53.43
	TEXT+SCHEMA	FT	63.28	49.79	55.91	92.71	53.69	66.28	96.94	84.33
	TEXT+EVENT	FT	75.18	62.53	66.96	94.70	70.00	82.68	96.08	82.23
T5	TEXT ONLY	FT	58.38	45.25	51.81	91.96	49.70	60.75	**98.88**	**87.85**
	EVENT ONLY	FT	63.14	45.62	52.47	92.67	64.00	80.08	68.42	62.63
	TEXT+SCHEMA	FT	65.82	51.90	58.46	93.11	56.18	68.42	97.92	82.93
	TEXT+EVENT	FT	**76.64**	**64.44**	**68.90**	**95.02**	**74.20**	85.22	98.15	85.02

Table 8: Input ablation results for the **report** summarization task. Best overall results are in **bolded**. * and † denote best zero- and few-shot results, respectively. See §4.1 for an explanation of metrics. See Appendix F for an explanation of the settings.

Model	Ablation	Setting	R_1	R_2	R_L	BS	CR	CR_{soft}	A	F
Report Baseline	-	-	48.52	33.28	39.31	89.58	31.00	42.04	99.29	93.12
GPT-4o M	TEXT ONLY	ZS	37.56	16.93	26.97	88.98	21.86	40.48	73.58	91.60
	EVENT ONLY	ZS	52.45	31.15	40.04	91.17	37.48	66.51	69.97	75.00
	TEXT+SCHEMA	ZS	41.88	20.40	30.32	89.72	24.04	44.76	76.64	89.12
	TEXT+EVENT	ZS	51.87	29.90	39.10	91.31	38.99	64.13	81.46	88.89
	TEXT+EVENT	FS	57.48	36.99	45.74	92.08	39.78	62.93	88.48	89.79
GPT-4o	TEXT ONLY	ZS	41.59	19.28	30.70	89.48	21.60	42.04	69.09	92.06
	EVENT ONLY	ZS	54.03	33.98	42.13	91.51	41.75*	**69.63***	81.02	80.55
	TEXT+SCHEMA	ZS	49.87	27.04	37.76	90.86	25.80	48.53	85.44	89.75
	TEXT+EVENT	ZS	57.97	36.42	45.89	92.22*	41.34	68.04	86.61	88.41
	TEXT+EVENT	FS	61.17†	40.62†	49.38†	**92.67†**	42.72†	69.27†	90.62	88.45
CLAUDE H	TEXT ONLY	ZS	47.27	25.48	36.49	90.23	22.64	43.20	84.29	92.59
	EVENT ONLY	ZS	53.35	33.01	42.94	91.39	38.64	66.08	77.70	76.83
	TEXT+SCHEMA	ZS	51.79	30.45	41.04	90.87	26.38	48.02	87.10	90.87
	TEXT+EVENT	ZS	57.72*	36.88*	46.35*	92.05	36.22	60.03	90.37	91.36
	TEXT+EVENT	FS	59.42	39.40	48.56	92.13	37.20	59.70	90.99	90.50†
CLAUDE S	TEXT ONLY	ZS	44.13	20.08	32.73	89.88	19.93	40.24	87.26	92.30
	EVENT ONLY	ZS	53.51	33.51	42.73	91.53	39.78	66.17	84.12	81.91
	TEXT+SCHEMA	ZS	51.37	29.33	40.06	90.94	28.05	49.07	88.64	89.33
	TEXT+EVENT	ZS	56.77	34.75	45.27	91.91	35.24	59.47	93.41*	91.71*
	TEXT+EVENT	FS	57.95	38.05	47.53	92.09	37.32	59.31	95.09†	90.39
BART	TEXT ONLY	FT	48.57	30.30	39.70	89.99	27.12	44.43	90.06	86.87
	EVENT ONLY	FT	56.37	37.04	45.14	91.21	39.12	62.90	56.01	68.10
	TEXT+SCHEMA	FT	51.67	35.12	44.15	90.42	32.31	49.47	94.45	90.52
	TEXT+EVENT	FT	63.77	45.50	52.98	92.59	44.97	66.36	85.55	85.27
PEGASUS	TEXT ONLY	FT	50.85	33.44	42.51	90.29	30.22	47.46	97.63	91.80
	EVENT ONLY	FT	58.52	38.41	46.46	91.42	39.98	64.06	67.05	75.80
	TEXT+SCHEMA	FT	51.21	34.18	43.11	90.28	30.15	47.04	97.99	**92.72**
	TEXT+EVENT	FT	63.66	46.24	**53.18**	92.51	43.73	64.51	93.85	90.48
T5	TEXT ONLY	FT	49.18	33.15	41.39	89.94	30.98	46.58	**98.75**	91.60
	EVENT ONLY	FT	59.96	40.55	47.51	91.84	**45.30**	68.85	73.73	78.98
	TEXT+SCHEMA	FT	53.06	35.64	44.93	90.64	31.87	50.14	94.11	91.30
	TEXT+EVENT	FT	**64.14**	**46.36**	52.79	92.56	44.67	65.66	92.48	90.19

Table 9: Input ablations on the **cross-document** summarization task.Best overall results are in **bolded**. * and † denote best zero- and few-shot results, respectively. See §4.1 for an explanation of metrics. See Appendix F for an explanation of the settings.

Model	S	Report						
		R_1	R_2	R_L	BS	CR	A	F
GPT-4o M	ZS	[60.0, 64.5]	[39.3, 45.2]	[48.7, 54.0]	[92.8, 93.6]	[52.8, 60.5]	[80.5, 86.9]	[72.8, 78.6]
	FS	[69.8, 74.0]	[52.5, 58.1]	[58.5, 63.5]	[94.0, 94.7]	[60.7, 68.8]	[93.4, 95.8]	[80.8, 85.8]
GPT-4o	ZS	[61.6, 66.3]	[42.4, 48.2]	[50.5, 55.5]	[92.8, 93.6]	[54.2, 62.3]	[83.0, 88.8]	[71.2, 78.0]
	FS	[70.3, 74.9]	[53.6, 59.8]	[59.6, 65.0]	[94.0, 94.8]	[62.7, 70.5]	[92.6, 95.4]	[78.4, 84.5]
Claude H	ZS	[62.7, 67.2]	[43.5, 49.1]	[52.4, 57.3]	[93.1, 93.9]	[52.5, 60.4]	[81.5, 87.7]	[74.1, 80.1]
	FS	[69.4, 73.9]	[52.7, 58.7]	[58.5, 63.6]	[93.9, 94.7]	[58.1, 66.5]	[93.3, 96.1]	[79.6, 85.2]
Claude S	ZS	[65.1, 69.6]	[45.3, 50.8]	[54.1, 59.0]	[93.5, 94.2]	[55.0, 63.3]	[90.8, 94.8]	[77.6, 83.5]
	FS	[69.8, 74.4]	[51.7, 57.5]	[58.8, 53.8]	[94.2, 94.9]	[60.7, 68.6]	[94.8, 96.7]	[80.8, 86.5]
BART	FT	[71.9, 76.6]	[58.7, 64.6]	[63.7, 69.1]	[93.3, 94.1]	[64.3, 72.1]	[89.2, 93.9]	[76.1, 82.2]
PEGASUS	FT	[72.9, 77.5]	[59.5, 65.4]	[64.2, 69.5]	[93.3, 94.1]	[65.4, 72.4]	[94.4, 97.5]	[79.4, 85.0]
T5	FT	[74.3, 78.9]	[61.4, 67.3]	[66.1, 71.5]	[93.6, 94.4]	[69.7, 76.9]	[97.4, 98.8]	[82.4, 87.5]

Table 10: 95% confidence intervals [low, high] from a non-parametric bootstrap ($n = 1000$) of the **report** results given in Table 2.

Model	S	Cross-Document						
		R_1	R_2	R_L	BS	CR	A	F
GPT-4o M	ZS	[49.9, 53.7]	[27.8, 32.0]	[37.0, 41.0]	[91.0, 91.6]	[35.9, 42.2]	[78.5, 84.1]	[86.7, 90.7]
	FS	[55.2, 59.7]	[34.3, 39.5]	[43.4, 47.8]	[91.7, 92.4]	[35.6, 42.9]	[86.0, 90.6]	[87.7, 91.6]
GPT-4o	ZS	[55.7, 60.0]	[33.8, 38.9]	[43.5, 48.1]	[91.8, 92.6]	[36.4, 43.5]	[83.8, 89.0]	[86.0, 90.6]
	FS	[59.0, 63.3]	[38.1, 43.1]	[47.1, 51.5]	[92.3, 93.0]	[38.0, 45.3]	[88.4, 92.8]	[86.3, 90.5]
Claude H	ZS	[55.6, 59.7]	[34.3, 39.2]	[44.0, 48.7]	[91.7, 92.4]	[32.8, 39.9]	[88.1, 92.3]	[89.7, 92.9]
	FS	[57.0, 61.5]	[36.7, 42.1]	[46.0, 50.9]	[91.8, 92.5]	[33.4, 40.4]	[89.0, 92.9]	[88.8, 92.2]
Claude S	ZS	[54.7, 58.9]	[32.4, 37.2]	[43.1, 47.7]	[91.6, 92.3]	[31.1, 37.9]	[91.7, 95.0]	[89.6, 93.4]
	FS	[55.6, 60.4]	[35.4, 40.8]	[45.2, 49.9]	[91.7, 92.5]	[33.9, 41.5]	[94.1, 96.0]	[88.5, 92.2]
BART	FT	[61.5, 66.1]	[42.7, 48.4]	[50.5, 55.6]	[91.5, 92.2]	[41.3, 49.1]	[82.3, 88.6]	[82.6, 87.7]
PEGASUS	FT	[61.2, 66.0]	[43.1, 49.0]	[50.4, 55.8]	[91.3, 92.1]	[40.9, 48.4]	[91.7, 95.6]	[88.7, 92.3]
T5	FT	[61.5, 66.4]	[43.6, 49.2]	[50.2, 55.3]	[91.3, 92.2]	[40.3, 48.4]	[90.1, 94.4]	[88.2, 91.9]

Table 11: 95% confidence intervals [low, high] from a non-parametric bootstrap ($n = 1000$) of the **cross-document** results given in Table 2.

Role	Support	GPT-4o M	GPT-4o	Claude H	Claude S	BART	PEGASUS	T5
Time	523	39.13	40.69	34.17	37.25	42.07	44.32	**47.09**
Place	499	33.33	38.49	25.00	26.12	27.42	33.11	**38.56**
Agent	240	34.67	32.89	27.40	23.13	**42.38**	32.43	39.74
Theme	94	**49.12**	44.07	43.33	35.09	40.00	39.44	39.34
Entity	65	29.27	35.90	35.00	35.90	30.00	35.90	**41.03**
Patient	53	41.18	30.30	50.00	34.29	43.75	**51.61**	48.48
Goal	49	36.84	**50.00**	37.84	27.03	30.00	40.91	45.00
Event	43	14.81	20.69	20.69	7.14	18.75	**25.00**	6.45
Cause	42	6.45	24.24	11.43	12.12	31.25	10.81	**26.67**
Experiencer	39	38.10	**70.00**	**70.00**	54.55	52.17	38.46	54.55
Victim	39	41.38	**53.33**	48.28	34.48	31.25	37.50	32.26
Goods	38	26.67	**75.00**	0.00	28.57	50.00	50.00	14.29
Protagonist	38	26.67	37.50	37.50	40.00	40.00	37.50	**50.00**
Source	30	66.67	**77.78**	55.56	63.16	63.16	50.00	66.67
Topic	26	13.33	13.33	0.00	14.29	**15.38**	13.33	0.00
Speaker	25	50.00	50.00	66.67	50.00	50.00	**70.59**	58.82
Addressee	22	33.33	**60.00**	16.67	40.00	**60.00**	40.00	33.33
Stimulus	21	15.38	30.77	33.33	33.33	46.15	33.33	**50.00**

Table 12: **CR** F_1 results on test set **cross-document** summaries for the top 20 roles with highest support (# arguments) in the SEAMuS training split (which has 3,004 total arguments). Results with GPT and Claude models are from the few-shot (FS) setting. Best results for each role are **bolded**.

Role	Support	GPT-4o M	GPT-4o	Claude H	Claude S	BART	PEGASUS	T5
Time	523	57.37	65.22	49.22	50.52	60.54	61.40	**65.43**
Place	499	44.84	**53.39**	37.46	37.67	46.93	47.67	52.15
Agent	240	65.40	**67.47**	59.78	50.16	66.72	57.99	62.06
Theme	94	73.21	**73.96**	69.22	72.96	71.75	64.71	68.59
Entity	65	66.33	**76.13**	63.16	60.07	63.34	63.12	69.44
Patient	53	**76.28**	73.52	74.41	68.62	70.88	73.28	73.36
Goal	49	50.53	**66.30**	50.19	45.42	47.30	53.63	60.30
Event	43	52.75	**63.52**	52.76	42.95	45.97	52.09	35.38
Cause	42	47.66	**52.99**	39.41	42.03	43.23	43.87	49.82
Experiencer	39	68.83	**91.48**	82.86	69.44	56.03	60.99	61.06
Victim	39	62.13	**74.79**	71.75	60.13	65.62	60.53	55.89
Goods	38	42.77	**79.33**	33.35	50.68	61.94	57.46	24.39
Protagonist	38	60.13	**72.52**	54.02	66.03	66.57	67.63	61.24
Source	30	78.00	**84.13**	60.54	65.55	66.80	55.03	69.62
Topic	26	19.06	19.06	17.75	20.42	21.70	**35.80**	12.96
Speaker	25	58.21	61.41	71.85	64.91	64.92	**73.03**	66.28
Addressee	22	44.60	**89.49**	40.21	52.63	63.63	73.95	41.94
Stimulus	21	38.61	70.46	54.55	66.70	53.39	**74.75**	57.65

Table 13: $\mathbf{CR}_{\text{soft}}$ (distinct from **CR**; see §F.2) F_1 results on test set **cross-document** summaries for the top 20 roles with highest support (# arguments) in the SEAMuS training split (which has 3,004 total arguments). Results with the GPT and Claude models are from the few-shot (FS) setting. Best results for each role are **bolded**.

Transfer of Structural Knowledge from Synthetic Languages

Mikhail Budnikov
School of Computer Science & Engineering
Constructor University
Bremen, Germany 28359
mbudnikov@constructor.university

Ivan Yamshchikov
CAIRO
THWS
Würzburg, Germany 97082
ivan.yamshchikov@thws.de

Abstract

This work explores transfer learning from several synthetic languages to English. We investigate the structure of the embeddings in the fine-tuned models, the information they contain, and the capabilities of the fine-tuned models on simple linguistic tasks. We also introduce a new synthetic language that leads to better transfer to English than the languages used in previous research. Finally, we introduce Tiny-Cloze Benchmark — a new synthetic benchmark for natural language understanding that is more informative for less powerful models. We use Tiny-Cloze Benchmark to evaluate fine-tuned models in several domains demonstrating that fine-tuning on a new synthetic language allows for better performance on a variety of tasks.

1 Introduction

Large language models (LLMs) are becoming increasingly powerful and useful. However, the role of data properties in model training and what exactly models learn from the training data remains to a large extent out of the scope of most LLM papers. Yet surprisingly pre-training a model on a simple algorithmic task can lead to improvements in natural language modelling (Min et al., 2023). Such insights can be used to improve the construction of data sets for language models. Therefore, exploring the mechanisms of knowledge transfer is an important open question.

Scaling language models is a popular way to improve their performance[1]. However, as the detailed analysis in Villalobos et al. (2022) shows, the amount of data, especially high-quality text data, is limited and will become the main bottleneck in the coming years.

Such circumstances motivate research into more data-efficient learning algorithms and a better understanding of the mechanisms of generalization and transfer learning (Surkov and Yamshchikov, 2024). After all, humans are exposed to orders of magnitude less data than modern frontier models, yet demonstrate strong performance across many domains and outperform machines in some areas, even considering recent algorithmic advances.

Inspired by this, Huebner et al. (2021) demonstrate that training RoBERTa (Liu et al., 2019) on language acquisition data, together with some tweaks to model architecture and training, leads to 6000× gains in data efficiency. Similarly, Eldan and Li (2023) achieve significant model compression while retaining the ability to produce fluent and coherent English by using a generated dataset of stories for children, i.e. with small vocabulary and simple plots. And Gunasekar et al. (2023) find that filtering for or generating data with higher educational value is also very helpful.

Thus, there is a growing body of evidence that the choice of data matters a lot and simply scraping the data from the web is suboptimal. However, there is a limited understanding of what properties of the data are important in different training stages. Papadimitriou and Jurafsky (2020) show that pre-training the LSTM (Hochreiter and Schmidhuber, 1997) on structured but not linguistic data, such as MIDI music, Java code, or even nested parentheses, reduces its perplexity when testing on Spanish. Sinha et al. (2021) find that removing all word order information from the pre-training phase does not significantly affect the final performance, given a fine-tuning phase with the correct word order. Krishna et al. (2021) sample the training data from a completely artificial language consisting of random n-grams and observe that pre-training objectives that require processing this information somehow, such as copying sentences in the right order, still improve the performance of the model on summarization tasks compared to a randomly initialized version.

However, research in this area currently tends to

[1]For a detailed review of the other ways to increase LLM generalization potential we address the reader to Budnikov et al. (2024)

Proceedings of the 1st Joint Workshop on Large Language Models and Structure Modeling (XLLM 2025), pages 242–251
August 1, 2025

focus on reporting surprising observations rather than explaining them. Papadimitriou and Jurafsky (2020) illustrate such observations using Figure 1.

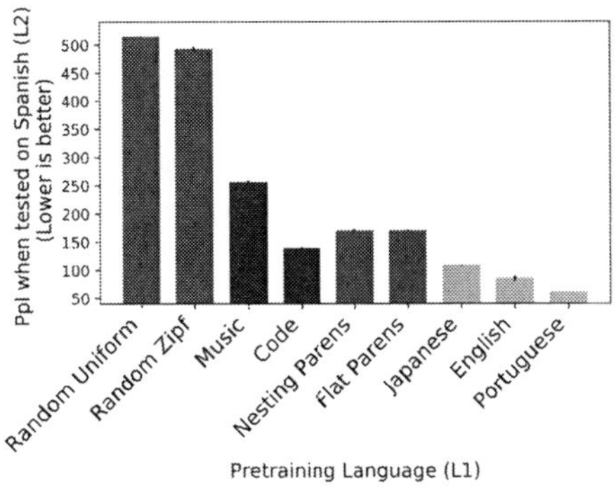

Figure 1: Perplexity on various types of input (Papadimitriou and Jurafsky, 2020).

This work attempts to build up on those observations and make a small further step studying the mechanisms of transfer learning.

In this paper, we address the following research questions:

- How do different synthetic pre-training datasets influence the complexity and transfer performance of language models on English tasks?
- What structural properties of the learned embeddings reflect the characteristics of the pre-training data?
- To what extent do synthetic pre-training languages affect the encoding of linguistic features in embeddings, as measured by linear probes?

Our contributions are summarized as follows:

- We introduce a new synthetic language, `flat_shuffle`, combining shuffle-based and bracket-based patterns, and compare it with existing synthetic datasets.
- We propose a transfer-learning-based measure to quantify language complexity and similarity via fine-tuning dynamics.
- We analyze the structure of embeddings through singular value spectra and clustering to assess their effective dimensionality.
- We employ linear probes to examine the linguistic information captured in embeddings fine-tuned on different synthetic languages.
- We present the Tiny-Cloze Benchmark, a synthetic NLU benchmark generated with GPT-4, demonstrating the benefits of synthetic pre-training.

First, as can be seen in the diagram above, different pre-training datasets, even if they all are unrelated to the target task, lead to different final performance. This suggests that some datasets are inherently more complex or more similar to the target language. We introduce a new synthetic "language" by combining ideas from the previous work and use it, as well as two existing synthetic datasets, to pre-train the models. We then fine-tune them on English using three different fine-tuning pipelines. We also provide an algorithm to assess the impact of the pretraining data on the resulting model parameters.

Second, since one of the settings for transfer learning involves fine-tuning only the embeddings, they are the natural target for investigation. We investigate the structure of the learned embeddings, namely the spectrum of their singular values to understand the effective dimensionality of the data, and the KMeans clustering of to check how uniformly the embeddings are distributed. To check what information is contained in the embeddings, we train linear probes to predict certain features of the words given their embeddings. Linear probes are a popular interpretability technique, but to our knowledge they have not been used to study the embeddings of models pre-trained on different datasets and fine-tuned to the same task.

Finally, we evaluate the performance of these models in natural language understanding. Since existing NLU datasets such as GLUE (Wang et al., 2018) and MMLU (Hendrycks et al., 2020) are designed for more powerful models, we use GPT-4 (OpenAI, 2023) to generate a similar benchmark consisting of 12 different subtasks[2].

2 Related work

One way of understanding the pre-training of language models is that we transfer some linguistic knowledge from a task with lots of available data

[2]To facilitate reproducibility and further research, we publish our code and data `https://github.com/msh2481/language_transfer`

to a downstream task (Han et al., 2021). The recent findings suggest that this is not the only relevant effect, and sometimes not even the most important one.

Papadimitriou and Jurafsky (2020), mentioned above, pre-trained an LSTM on structured but not linguistic data and found that adapting such a model to Spanish by fine-tuning only its input and output embeddings gave better perplexity than starting with a randomly initialised model. Their results and experimental setup established a framework that has been used in subsequent work, including this one. Ri and Tsuruoka (2022) improved these results replacing LSTM with a Transformer and changing the synthetic pre-training languages. Papadimitriou and Jurafsky (2023) used GPT-2 (Radford et al., 2019). Chiang and Lee (2022) introduce a family of Shuffle languages. Artetxe et al. (2019) used a similar technique to combine a task-specific corpus in English with a corpus in the target language unrelated to the task.

Such transfer also works in the opposite direction, from natural language to other domains. Lu et al. (2021) get performance comparable to training from scratch on different modalities by fine-tuning only the input and output embeddings of the pre-trained GPT-2. They also try different fine-tuning approaches, tuning the layer norm parameters and the last Transformer block in addition to the input and output embeddings.

Mehta et al. (2021) show that pre-training moves the model parameters into a flat basin of the loss landscape and suggest it as a reason why pre-trained models are less prone to catastrophic forgetting during fine-tuning. Neyshabur et al. (2020) also observe this and also show that models fine-tuned from the same checkpoint stay in the same basin. However, past data alone is almost never enough to predict unseen data, unless one makes some assumptions, i.e. "inductive bias". A useful inductive bias can be injected into the model by pre-training on data that has it. McCoy et al. (2020) use pre-training on natural languages with certain properties by model-agnostic meta-learning (Finn et al., 2017) to find which biases are needed to quickly acquire these languages. Wu et al. (2021) design synthetic datasets requiring deduction, induction, and abduction and pre-train on them to extract inductive bias for general mathematical reasoning. Lindemann et al. (2023) pre-train models to simulate finite state transducers given their description and achieve better generalization in NLP tasks with similar structure.

3 Synthetic Languages

In this paper we report a series of experiments with several synthetic languages. Following hyperparameter choices from Papadimitriou and Jurafsky (2023), for each of the languages described below, we use a sequence length of 512, a vocabulary size of 500, and generate $2 \cdot 10^6$ sequences so the total size of the dataset is approximately 10^9 tokens in each case.

We focus on three synthetic languages: `nested`, the k-Dyck nested bracket language; `flat`, the shuffle Dyck language with no nesting; and `flat_shuffle`, a block-wise shuffled variant of the flat language.

3.1 `nested`

Papadimitriou and Jurafsky (2020) used a stack-based grammar to generate sequences, where each token occurs twice and two pairs of tokens either do not intersect or one is nested in another. In other words, a balanced bracket sequence with multiple types of brackets.

Ri and Tsuruoka (2022) suggested using different tokens for opening and closing brackets, and found improved performance. We chose to implement this version, and save a synthetic language with 250 tokens for open brackets and 250 tokens for closing ones.

Tokens are generated sequentially, and on each step, a random decision is made whether to open a new bracket or to close an existing one. If the stack of open brackets is empty or there is not enough space before the end of the sequence, there is only one option. In other cases, an opening bracket is chosen with a probability of 0.4, and then the type of bracket is sampled uniformly.

Example word from `nested`:
`<23 <42 <15 15> 42> 23> <56 56>`

3.2 `flat`

This language is similar to the previous one. The only difference is that the nesting property can be violated.

In terms of sampling, it means that when a bracket should be closed, now there is more than one possibility. We select the bracket to close uniformly from all currently open ones.

Example word:

<23 <42 <15 42> 23> <56 15> 56>

3.3 `flat_shuffle`

The `flat_shuffle` language extends `flat` by partitioning bracket type IDs into contiguous blocks of size eight, such that each segment of 16 tokens is sampled exclusively from one block, yielding a permutation of those brackets within the segment. While the languages described above are each based on a single rule, this extension introduces additional structure to the data, which we hypothesize can improve model performance.

We suggest to use an idea of `shuffle` languages from Chiang and Lee (2022) as an extra pattern because it was orthogonal to the bracket balancing essence of the previous datasets. The combined dataset is based on `flat`, but each consecutive group of 16 tokens has a range of 8 bracket types assigned to it, and all brackets on this segment are sampled only from these types. That is, each such group is a permutation of the corresponding brackets.

It adds two interesting properties to the task of next token prediction. First, in the middle of the line the model has to look at previous tokens to guess the range of bracket types to predict the next token. Second, the model can guess increasingly more accurately by remembering which tokens were already used if we are close to the end of the permutation. In particular, the last token in each permutation can be predicted with certainty. Surprisingly, even small Transformer models were able to capture this pattern and indeed predicted the last token with close to zero loss.

Example word (purple and green parts represent two blocks, $[16, 20)$ and $[36, 40)$):

<16 <18 16> <17 <19 18> 17> <38 38> <36 19> <39 39> <37 36> 37>

4 Methodology

Some languages, both synthetic and natural, are more complex than others. For example, it is much easier to understand the concept of balanced bracket sequences than to learn Assyrian language. Moreover, some languages can be understood more easily if the learner already knows another language. For instance, humans need less effort to learn a language from the same language family, and large language models can be fine-tuned for a similar downstream task using much less data than was used for their pre-training.

One approach to formalize this intuition of complexity and similarity is the Chomsky hierarchy of languages (Chomsky, 1956). It formally defines several classes of grammars, each one strictly more general than the previous one, and the properties of these classes are very well understood. For example, `nested` is a context-free language, while `flat` is context-dependent. However, for languages from the same class, we need some other tool to find more fine-grained differences. We propose a transfer-learning based approach to quantify those.

An important observation is that transfer learning between languages is not symmetric, and it allows us to estimate both (relative) complexity and similarity of two languages. If languages are similar, transfer learning should go well in both directions. However, if one language is more complex than another, at least in the sense of having strictly more patterns, one would expect transfer learning to be much easier from the hard language to the easy one. So, assuming that we have some operationalization $f(A, B)$ of "difficulty of transfer learning from language A to language B", we can take $\frac{1}{2}(f(A, B) + f(B, A))$ to mean dis-similarity of A and B and $\frac{1}{2}(f(B, A) - f(A, B))$ to mean complexity of A relative to B.

Our proposed way to operationalize this notion of "difficulty" is to just use perplexity of the model pre-trained on language A and then fine-tuned to language B, with some of the weights frozen. By varying the subset of the weights allowed to be fine-tuned we can get a more complete picture, i.e. for some pair of languages just tuning the embeddings might already be enough, which would mean that they share most of the structure.

A more practically-oriented way to compare synthetic languages is to see which of them better prepare models to learning English. To test this we take models pre-trained on each of the synthetic languages, fine-tune them to English, and check their language understanding capabilities with cloze questions.

Finally, we study the structure of the embeddings in terms of effective dimensionality and number of clusters, and then explore what English word features are learned by models fine-tuned from each of the synthetic languages.

5 Experiments

For all experiments, we used the TinyStories-8M model (Eldan and Li, 2023).

5.1 Transfer Learning

We used three levels of trainable weight subsets:

E: Only input and output embeddings are tuned;

EL: **E** plus the affine parameters of LayerNorms;

ELT: **EL** plus the entire last Transformer layer;

For pre-training, we waited until convergence that was close to the theoretical lower bounds of loss or just long stagnation, which took 40K to 100K steps. The batch size was 8, and the sequence length was 512 tokens, so we used 160M to 400M tokens for pre-training. For fine-tuning, at each stage, we used a fixed amount of 12500 steps, the batch size was again 8, and the sequence length was 512 for bracket datasets and 128 for English (TinyStories), which means 51M and 13M tokens correspondingly. The learning rate was 10^{-3} for pre-training and $[10^{-2}, 2 \cdot 10^{-2}, 10^{-3}]$ for the three stages of fine-tuning.

Table 1 below presents the results of fine-tuning in both directions on certain pairs of languages.

The first row shows that flat is more complex than "nested". The second row demonstrates that flat_shuffle is more complex than flat. Indeed, fine-tuning in the direction flat_shuffle $\rightarrow$ flat $\rightarrow$ nested achieves relatively good performance already with the first stage of fine-tuning. The other experiments show that English is more complex than all synthetic languages used here, but it is also quite different, as the model needs more flexibility to adapt from English to flat or flat_shuffle.

5.2 Cloze Tests

To assess how well the models understand language in general, a different benchmark is needed. Since the models studied are too small for reliable question answering, reasoning, and other high-level cognitive skills, the test should be as simple as possible, ideally just measuring perplexity on some texts. There are existing datasets for natural language understanding, such as GLUE (Wang et al., 2018) and MMLU (Hendrycks et al., 2020), but they focus on more complex tasks.

Instead, we used GPT-4 (OpenAI, 2023) to generate Tiny Cloze Benchmark — a set of cloze[3] infilling questions in simple English. There are the following 12 subtasks, each with 10 cloze questions: 'synonyms and antonyms' — the model chooses one of two antonyms to correctly fill the gap in the sentence; 'Logical relations' — the model chooses a correct conjunction between two parts of the sentence; 'Subject-verb agreement' — the model chooses one of two verbs that corresponds to the given subject in the sentence; 'Prepositions' — the model chooses a correct preposition in the sentence; 'Conjunctions' — a task similar to 'Logical relations' but with different conjunctions; 'Temporal understanding' — filling in a correct temporal conjunction; 'Spatial understanding' — filling in a word based on spatial understanding of the sentence; 'Quantitative reasoning' — filling in the number into the sentence; 'Emotions' — filling the correct emotional adjective into the sentence; 'Narrative understanding' — filling one noun relevant for the narrative sentence; 'Ethics' — filling a noun for an ethical statement. You can find detailed examples of the tasks in Appendix.

[3]https://en.wikipedia.org/wiki/Cloze_test

Each cloze question consists of a prompt with a cloze marker, a correct answer, and an incorrect answer. For each question, the difference between log-probabilities of the correct and incorrect answers is measured and then averaged across each subtask. We measure the difference in log-likelihoods rather than accuracy, because it provides more information per sample, which is important given the relatively small size of our benchmark.

Here is an example question from the temporal understanding subtask:

```
[ "She ate breakfast # she went to
school", "before", "after", ]
```

For each of the synthetic languages, we used two models, one in which only the embeddings were fine-tuned on English (E), and another with all three stages of fine-tuning applied (ELT). We compared them with the model of the same architecture (8M parameters) trained on English from scratch and also to a four times larger model with 33M parameters trained on English from scratch to see which metrics can be improved.

As shown in Table 2, there are two interesting observations. First, models with all three stages of fine-tuning are better, predictably, than their counterparts having only the embeddings tuned, but this difference is more pronounced in flat and flat_shuffle. Second, Table 2 again shows the familiar pattern nested <flat <flat_shuffle <scratch, which proves the superiority of the introduced flat_shuffle dataset.

Language pair		L1 →				L2 →			
L1	L2	L2E	L2EL	L2ELT	L2Full	L1E	L1EL	L1ELT	L1Full
nested	flat	4.4	4.1	4.1	3.8	3.5	3.3	3.3	3.3
flat	flat_shuffle	2.5	2.4	2.2	2.0	3.8	3.8	3.7	3.8
flat_shuffle	English	2.4	2.3	2.0	1.2	2.8	2.6	2.1	2.0
nested	English	2.8	2.7	2.4	1.2	3.8	3.5	3.3	3.3
flat	English	2.7	2.6	2.4	1.2	4.3	4.2	3.8	3.8

Table 1: Pretraining on L1 and transferring to L2 and vice versa. Values are negative log-likelihoods in nats. "E", "L", and "T" indicate which layers were fine-tuned and stand for embeddings, LayerNorms, and (the last) Transformer block respectively. Columns ending in "Full" correspond to models trained from scratch on the respective language (i.e., no synthetic pretraining). We use the absolute difference of 0.2 nats per token as a threshold for "close performance".

	nested E	nested ELT	flat E	flat ELT	flat shuffle E	flat shuffle ELT	scratch 8M	scratch 33M
synonyms and antonyms	0.24	0.18	0.22	0.13	0.31	0.25	0.25	0.28
single - plural	0.08	0.15	0.19	0.50	0.03	0.33	0.58	0.71
logical relations	-0.08	-0.30	-0.44	-0.18	-0.13	-0.08	-0.04	0.09
subject-verb agreement	0.54	0.45	0.46	0.36	0.14	0.26	0.83	0.98
prepositions	0.43	0.52	0.51	0.53	0.40	0.48	0.94	1.12
conjunctions	0.46	0.43	0.45	0.38	0.36	0.49	0.63	0.82
temporal understanding	-0.13	-0.02	-0.14	0.04	0.09	0.36	0.44	0.73
spatial understanding	0.13	0.30	0.40	0.48	0.06	0.37	0.64	0.71
quantitative reasoning	-0.06	0.00	-0.14	-0.01	-0.14	-0.04	-0.04	-0.06
emotions	-0.08	0.03	0.05	0.07	0.20	-0.01	0.61	0.77
narrative understanding	-0.07	-0.04	0.03	0.07	0.04	0.04	0.17	0.27
ethics	0.32	0.17	0.34	0.22	0.27	0.30	0.25	0.51
Average	0.15	0.16	0.16	0.22	0.14	0.23	0.44	0.58

Table 2: Results on the Tiny-Cloze benchmark. Values show differences in log-likelihoods (in nats) between correct and incorrect answers. Fine-tuning on flat_shuffle gives the highest average score across three synthetic languages.

5.3 Dimensionality and Clusters

We hypothesize that models pretrained on more complex languages will exhibit a slower decay in the singular value spectrum, reflecting higher effective dimensionality required to encode richer structure.

The embedding dimension of the model used is $d = 256$, and human intuition, as well as many visualization techniques, work poorly for 256-dimensional vectors. We hypothesize that the singular value spectrum reflects the encoding complexity of the pre-training language: languages requiring richer structure will exhibit a slower decay in the spectrum tail, indicating higher effective dimensionality in the embeddings. Therefore, we employ two quantitative approaches.

First, for an $n \times d$ matrix of embeddings E, we consider its singular values (after zeroing out the mean of each column), or equivalently, the spectrum of the covariation matrix $A = E^T E$. The motivation behind this is that if all embeddings were contained in a k-dimensional subspace, and E had a rank k, then only k of the singular values would be nonzero. For real data, it is not the case, as all singular values are nonzero, but still, some directions have much larger variance than others, and the model is more likely to use features corresponding to those dimensions.

As we see in Figure 2, in models pre-trained on synthetic datasets, the spectrum is dominated by the first few dimensions. In particular, before fine-tuning, most of the interesting information about brackets is described by two axes: open-close and low-to-high bracket type id. While they learn more diverse features during fine-tuning on English, as described in the next sections, they still don't use the embedding space very efficiently. An interesting observation is how the tail of the spectrum behaves for models trained on different datasets: the spectrum of `flat` decays to zero slower than the one of `nested`, but the shape is similar, while the spectrum of `flat_shuffle` crosses `flat` at some point and behaves more similarly to the spectrum of the model trained on English from scratch.

Another interesting property is how the embeddings are clustered. To quantify it, we run k-means clustering for the embeddings varying the number of clusters and compare the plots of unexplained variance (Figure 3). Again, after pre-training on a synthetic language, the models have only two clusters: open and close brackets, and even after fine-tuning, the first few splits explain the majority of variance. Looking at the tail behavior, we observe a similar pattern: English is followed by `flat_shuffle`, then by `flat` and `nested`.

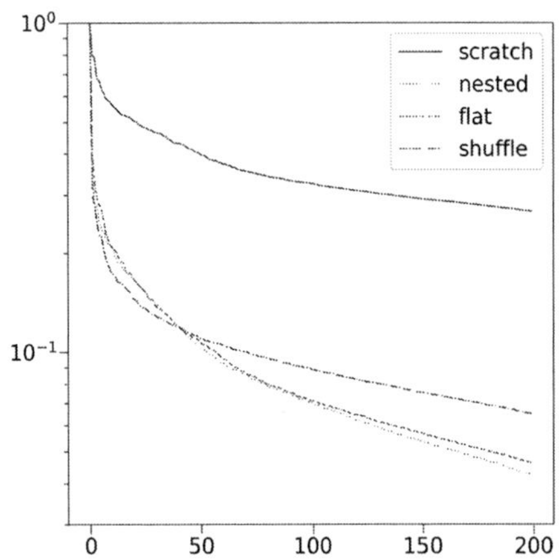

Figure 2: Spectrum of bracket embeddings

The `scratch` provides a reference for the embeddings on English. We can clearly see that `flat_shuffle` embeddings are characteristically different from `flat` and `nested` embeddings both in terms of the spectrum and in terms of the clusters

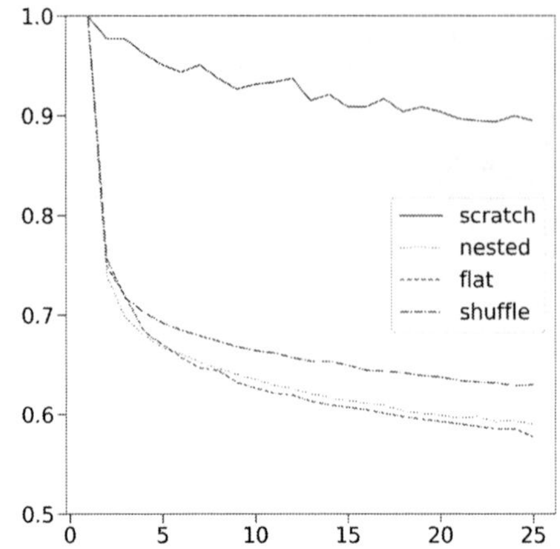

Figure 3: Clustering of bracket embeddings

they form.

5.4 Linear Probes for Word Features

We train all probes on embeddings obtained from embedding-only (E) fine-tuned models to isolate the impact of embedding space structure.

Now that we know something about the structure of the embedding space, a natural question to ask is how this structure is used. In other words, what information about a word can one extract from the embedding of the corresponding token?

Preliminary experiments showed that clusters of features correspond to properties like "noun", "3rd person verb", "adjective or adverb", etc. We hypothesize that embeddings from more complex synthetic pretraining (e.g., `flat_shuffle`) better capture such linguistic features. Consequently, we extract part of speech tags using NLTK. Given the limited vocabulary of TinyStories, capabilities of NLTK POS tagger should be good enough for our purposes. Initially, there were more than 30 unique tags in the dataset, but many of them were very rare. After filtering out all tags with less than 200 occurrences, the following tags remained: CD — cardinal digit; IN — preposition or subordinating conjunction; JJ — adjective; NN - singular noun; NNP – proper noun; NNS – plural noun; RB – adverb; VB – base form verb; VBD - past tense verb; VBG - gerund; VBN - past participle. We use this notation in Table 3.

We added a feature indicating the frequency of the token in the training corpus because typically the direction with the most variance in the embedding space roughly corresponded to frequency. We also added another boolean feature that is one if the token starts with a whitespace and zero otherwise.

For each of the models and each of the features, we trained a ridge regression (for frequency) or a logistic regression (for all other variables, as they are Boolean) on 80% of the embeddings and then evaluated their R^2 score or ROC-AUC on the remaining 20%. See Table 3 for the results.

All probes in all models perform better than random, so every model learns at least something related to these word features. The embeddings of the model trained on English from scratch predictably outperformed the others, but the quality of other embeddings turned out to be on average the same. Perhaps the difference in effective dimension between the models is used not for these relatively simple single-word features, but for more complex ones.

6 Conclusion

We introduced a new synthetic language `flat_shuffle`, and the model pre-trained on it was shown to outperform the models based on the languages from previous work.

Investigation of the structure of the embeddings leads to a hypothesis that the reason behind the superior performance of some synthetic languages is that they require more structured embeddings, which causes the intermediate layers to be adapted to work with such embeddings, and in turn allows effectively using a higher dimension subspace of the embedding space during fine-tuning, which gives more flexibility.

Also, we haven't observed direct transfer of structure from synthetic languages to English, i.e. English tokens weren't splitted by the model into "opening" and "closing" ones. So it seems that models are working in a reservoir computing style where the computations for an unrelated task are adapted to the task at hand in arbitrary ways. At the same time, it means that the models are not strictly limited by the complexity or structure of the original task in transfer learning, and as long as they have enough complexity of computations, they can use it to adapt to the new task.

7 Limitations

The experiments reveal several interesting patterns about transfer learning between synthetic and natural languages. However, our approach has some important limitations.

First, we only used English as the target natural language. It would be interesting to see if the patterns we observed hold for other natural languages, especially those with different grammatical structures.

Second, even our most complex synthetic language, `flat_shuffle`, was simple enough to be learned by a model with 8 million parameters. Perhaps with better synthetic data and correspondingly more capable models we would observe qualitatively new phenomena.

Ethics Statement

This paper complies with the ACL Ethics Policy.

	nested	flat	flat_shuffle	scratch
frequency	0.84	0.85	0.85	0.93
start_space	0.70	0.70	0.70	0.89
pos_tag_CD	0.66	0.63	0.63	0.80
pos_tag_IN	0.76	0.79	0.71	0.87
pos_tag_JJ	0.60	0.58	0.60	0.73
pos_tag_NN	0.63	0.62	0.63	0.76
pos_tag_NNP	0.64	0.65	0.63	0.79
pos_tag_NNS	0.67	0.67	0.68	0.84
pos_tag_RB	0.69	0.63	0.64	0.84
pos_tag_VB	0.71	0.69	0.68	0.79
pos_tag_VBD	0.75	0.71	0.67	0.89
pos_tag_VBG	0.71	0.70	0.73	0.89
pos_tag_VBN	0.72	0.68	0.72	0.87
Average	0.70	0.68	0.68	0.84

Table 3: ROC-AUC for the linear probes on embeddings from models fine-tuned on English using embedding-only (E) mode.

References

Mikel Artetxe, Sebastian Ruder, and Dani Yogatama. 2019. On the cross-lingual transferability of monolingual representations. *arXiv preprint arXiv:1910.11856*.

Mikhail Budnikov, Anna Bykova, and Ivan P Yamshchikov. 2024. Generalization potential of large language models. *Neural Computing and Applications*, pages 1–25.

Cheng-Han Chiang and Hung-yi Lee. 2022. On the transferability of pre-trained language models: A study from artificial datasets. In *Proceedings of the AAAI Conference on Artificial Intelligence*, volume 36, pages 10518–10525.

Noam Chomsky. 1956. Three models for the description of language. *IRE Transactions on information theory*, 2(3):113–124.

Ronen Eldan and Yuanzhi Li. 2023. Tinystories: How small can language models be and still speak coherent english? *arXiv preprint arXiv:2305.07759*.

Chelsea Finn, Pieter Abbeel, and Sergey Levine. 2017. Model-agnostic meta-learning for fast adaptation of deep networks. In *International conference on machine learning*, pages 1126–1135. PMLR.

Suriya Gunasekar, Yi Zhang, Jyoti Aneja, Caio César Teodoro Mendes, Allie Del Giorno, Sivakanth Gopi, Mojan Javaheripi, Piero Kauffmann, Gustavo de Rosa, Olli Saarikivi, et al. 2023. Textbooks are all you need. *arXiv preprint arXiv:2306.11644*.

Xu Han, Zhengyan Zhang, Ning Ding, Yuxian Gu, Xiao Liu, Yuqi Huo, Jiezhong Qiu, Yuan Yao, Ao Zhang, Liang Zhang, et al. 2021. Pre-trained models: Past, present and future. *AI Open*, 2:225–250.

Dan Hendrycks, Collin Burns, Steven Basart, Andy Zou, Mantas Mazeika, Dawn Song, and Jacob Steinhardt. 2020. Measuring massive multitask language understanding. *arXiv preprint arXiv:2009.03300*.

Sepp Hochreiter and Jürgen Schmidhuber. 1997. Long short-term memory. *Neural computation*, 9(8):1735–1780.

Philip A Huebner, Elior Sulem, Fisher Cynthia, and Dan Roth. 2021. Babyberta: Learning more grammar with small-scale child-directed language. In *Proceedings of the 25th conference on computational natural language learning*, pages 624–646.

Kundan Krishna, Jeffrey Bigham, and Zachary C Lipton. 2021. Does pretraining for summarization require knowledge transfer? *arXiv preprint arXiv:2109.04953*.

Matthias Lindemann, Alexander Koller, and Ivan Titov. 2023. Injecting a structural inductive bias into a seq2seq model by simulation. *arXiv preprint arXiv:2310.00796*.

Yinhan Liu, Myle Ott, Naman Goyal, Jingfei Du, Mandar Joshi, Danqi Chen, Omer Levy, Mike Lewis, Luke Zettlemoyer, and Veselin Stoyanov. 2019. Roberta: A robustly optimized bert pretraining approach. *arXiv preprint arXiv:1907.11692*.

Kevin Lu, Aditya Grover, Pieter Abbeel, and Igor Mordatch. 2021. Pretrained transformers as universal computation engines. *arXiv preprint arXiv:2103.05247*, 1.

R Thomas McCoy, Erin Grant, Paul Smolensky, Thomas L Griffiths, and Tal Linzen. 2020. Universal linguistic inductive biases via meta-learning. *arXiv preprint arXiv:2006.16324*.

Sanket Vaibhav Mehta, Darshan Patil, Sarath Chandar, and Emma Strubell. 2021. An empirical investigation of the role of pre-training in lifelong learning. *arXiv preprint arXiv:2112.09153*.

Bonan Min, Hayley Ross, Elior Sulem, Amir Pouran Ben Veyseh, Thien Huu Nguyen, Oscar Sainz, Eneko Agirre, Ilana Heintz, and Dan Roth. 2023. Recent advances in natural language processing via large pre-trained language models: A survey. *ACM Computing Surveys*, 56(2):1–40.

Behnam Neyshabur, Hanie Sedghi, and Chiyuan Zhang. 2020. What is being transferred in transfer learning? *Advances in neural information processing systems*, 33:512–523.

OpenAI. 2023. Gpt-4 technical report.

Isabel Papadimitriou and Dan Jurafsky. 2020. Learning music helps you read: Using transfer to study linguistic structure in language models. *arXiv preprint arXiv:2004.14601*.

Isabel Papadimitriou and Dan Jurafsky. 2023. Injecting structural hints: Using language models to study inductive biases in language learning.

Alec Radford, Jeffrey Wu, Rewon Child, David Luan, Dario Amodei, Ilya Sutskever, et al. 2019. Language models are unsupervised multitask learners. *OpenAI blog*, 1(8):9.

Ryokan Ri and Yoshimasa Tsuruoka. 2022. Pretraining with artificial language: Studying transferable knowledge in language models. *arXiv preprint arXiv:2203.10326*.

Koustuv Sinha, Robin Jia, Dieuwke Hupkes, Joelle Pineau, Adina Williams, and Douwe Kiela. 2021. Masked language modeling and the distributional hypothesis: Order word matters pre-training for little. *arXiv preprint arXiv:2104.06644*.

Maxim K Surkov and Ivan P Yamshchikov. 2024. Vygotsky distance: measure for benchmark task similarity. *arXiv preprint arXiv:2402.14890*.

Pablo Villalobos, Jaime Sevilla, Lennart Heim, Tamay Besiroglu, Marius Hobbhahn, and Anson Ho. 2022. Will we run out of data? an analysis of the limits of scaling datasets in machine learning. *arXiv preprint arXiv:2211.04325*.

Alex Wang, Amanpreet Singh, Julian Michael, Felix Hill, Omer Levy, and Samuel R Bowman. 2018. Glue: A multi-task benchmark and analysis platform for natural language understanding. *arXiv preprint arXiv:1804.07461*.

Yuhuai Wu, Markus N Rabe, Wenda Li, Jimmy Ba, Roger B Grosse, and Christian Szegedy. 2021. Lime: Learning inductive bias for primitives of mathematical reasoning. In *International Conference on Machine Learning*, pages 11251–11262. PMLR.

A Appendix

Here are the examples of the Tiny Cloze benchmark for particular tasks. One example for each task:

- 'synonyms and antonyms':
  `"The box was incredibly light, almost as if it were #.", "empty", "full"`
- 'single plural':
  `They # to the store every Saturday.", "go", "goes"`
- 'logical relations':
  `"The dog barked loudly, # everyone woke up", "and", "but"`
- 'subject-verb agreement':
  `"The dog in the yard # every morning", "barks", "bark"`
- 'prepositions':
  `"The cat is sleeping # the chair","under","above"`
- 'conjunctions':
  `"She went to the store # she needed milk.", "because", "although"`
- 'temporal understanding':
  `"It's usually dark outside # the sun rises", "before", "while"`
- 'spatial understanding':
  `"The cat is under the #.", "table", "sky"`
- 'quantitative reasoning':
  `"There are 5 apples. If I eat 2, there will be # left", "3", "4"`
- 'emotions':
  `"When he lost his keys, he was really #.", "frustrated", "excited"`
- 'narrative understanding':
  `"After the long journey, the traveler was # and fell asleep quickly.", "tired", "hungry"`
- 'ethics':
  `"Cheating to win a game is # acceptable", "never", "always"`

Language Models are Universal Embedders

Xin Zhang[1,2], Zehan Li, Yanzhao Zhang, Dingkun Long
Pengjun Xie, Meishan Zhang[1*], Min Zhang[1]
[1]Harbin Institute of Technology, Shenzhen, [2]The Hong Kong Polytechnic University
zhangxin2023@stu.hit.edu.cn {zhangmeishan,zhangmin2021}@hit.edu.cn

Abstract

In the large language model (LLM) revolution, embedding is a key component of various systems, such as retrieving knowledge or memories for LLMs or building content moderation filters. As such cases span from English to other natural or programming languages, from retrieval to classification and beyond, it is advantageous to build a unified embedding model rather than dedicated ones for each scenario. In this context, the pre-trained multilingual decoder-only large language models, *e.g.,* BLOOM, emerge as a viable backbone option. To assess their potential, we propose straightforward strategies for constructing embedders and introduce a universal evaluation benchmark. Experimental results show that our trained model is proficient at generating good embeddings across languages and tasks, even extending to languages and tasks for which no finetuning/pretraining data is available. We also present detailed analyses and additional evaluations. We hope that this work could encourage the development of more robust open-source universal embedders.

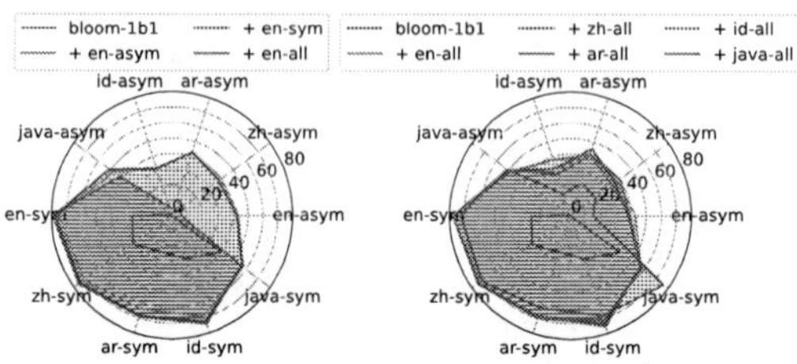

Figure 1: The performance comparison of finetuned BLOOM models on our compiled universal embedding benchmark, details refer to Table 2.

1 Introduction

Embeddings, which transform discrete text or code sequences into continuous vectors, are widely used in many fields (Li et al., 2022; Neelakantan et al., 2022). They have recently gained broader attention by manipulating knowledge and memories for large language models (LLMs) and LLM-based agents (Peng et al., 2023; Song et al., 2022; Wang et al., 2023). In such scenarios, their usages are inevitably coupled with different languages and tasks. This brings a demand for robust and universal embedders, where one single model can be applied across diverse tasks and languages, encompassing both natural and programming languages.

The common approach to building effective embedders is finetuning pretrained language models through contrastive learning on pairs of sentences (Neelakantan et al., 2022; Wang et al., 2022a). In practice, BERT-style pretrained transformer encoders are de facto standard choices, deriving powerful open-source models like E5 (Wang et al., 2022a), BGE (Xiao et al., 2023) and GTE (Li et al., 2023). However, these encoders have encountered difficulties in constructing universal embeddings because there are currently no available encoders that simultaneously support multiple natural languages and programming languages.

A possible solution is to use multilingual large language models (mLLM), such as BLOOM (Scao et al., 2022) series. These models adopt a decoder-only architecture and are pretrained on meticulously curated, large-scale, multilingual corpora, ROOTS (Laurençon et al., 2022), by the next token prediction objective. They are not only skilled in English but also excel in other languages, including natural ones such as Chinese and programming languages like Python, showing their wide-ranging language abilities.

Therefore, one major question arises: *is it feasible to derive universal embedders from mLLMs?* To study this inquiry, we examine two scenarios: (1) **Task versatility**: we explore strategies of data compositions that enable the model to adapt effectively to a variety of embedding tasks. (2) **Multilinguality**: we investigate the process of obtaining em-

[*]Correspondence. Code: github.com/izhx/uni-rep

Proceedings of the 1st Joint Workshop on Large Language Models and Structure Modeling (XLLM 2025), pages 252–265
August 1, 2025 ©2025 Association for Computational Linguistics

beddings across multiple languages using limited data, especially considering that some of them are hard to acquire suitable training data. By synthesizing insights from above cases, we evaluate whether mLLMs can be trained to generate high-quality embeddings across both languages and tasks.

In practice, we construct embedders by conventional methods (detailed in §2.1) based on BLOOM (Scao et al., 2022) models.[1] For task versatility, in line with prior works (Wang et al., 2022a; Muennighoff, 2022), we categorize all embedding tasks into symmetric and asymmetric types and combine datasets from both sides for training (§2.3). Regarding multilinguality, we employ parameter-efficient fine-tuning to maximally preserve the modeling abilities of various languages (§2.2). For evaluation, we select 5 languages (4 natural, 1 programming) and compile a universal embedding benchmark (§3.1). All models are trained with monolingual data and evaluated on the benchmark (as shown in Figure 1), which helps us to analyze the performance of different languages, *e.g.,* densely, lessly or not pretrained ones, more effectively.

Through extensive experiments, we find that:

- Combining datasets of both symmetric and asymmetric types can achieve task versatility across languages.
- For pretrained languages, mLLMs can provide high-quality embeddings, even when fine-tuning occurs with data exclusively from other languages.
- mLLMs show some extent generalizations to languages that are not pretrained, and the performance can be greatly improved by finetuning on data of these unseen languages.

We believe that *mLLMs are feasible and show great potential in building universal embedders.*

Additionally, we provide various detailed analyses (§3.3, §3.4, §4), *e.g.,* scaling the model size, and the model performance in additional benchmarks such as MTEB (Muennighoff et al., 2023) and CodeSearchNet (Husain et al., 2019), to better understand the model behaviors. We hope that our findings could foster the development and research of more powerful universal embedders.

2 Method

Figure 2 shows our method and evaluation. For clarity, the details of embedding model are not presented. Next, we describe this model design.

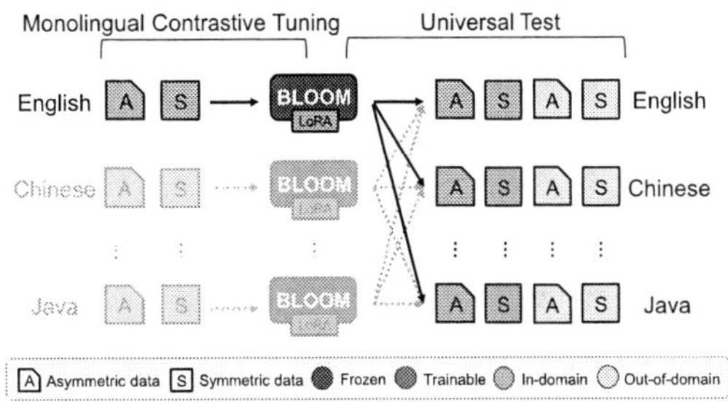

Figure 2: The outline of our main evaluation process. We finetune BLOOM to generate embeddings by [EOS] with contrastive loss on monolingual data, and analyze performance by multilingual tests from various tasks. The solid lines in the graph show English as an example.

2.1 Embedding Model

Our model design mainly follows the standard practice of previous work (Muennighoff, 2022; Neelakantan et al., 2022). Given a text or code input x, we append special tokens, $[\text{BOS}]_t$ and $[\text{EOS}]_t$, to the start and end of x respectively, where t represents the input type.[2] We take the last token state from the model output, *i.e.,* the representation of $[\text{EOS}]_t$, as the embedding $\boldsymbol{e}$ of the input text x.

The contrastive learning objective involves positive and hard-negative examples (Reimers and Gurevych, 2019). For each positive pair (x, x^+) in trainset, where x^+ is the sequence similar or relevant to x, we build the training instance $\{x, x^+, x_1^-, \dots, x_N^-\}$ with N negative examples x^- from the data (§2.3). We optimize the InfoNCE (Chen et al., 2020) contrastive loss:

$$\mathcal{L} = -\log \frac{\exp(f_\theta(x, x^+))}{\exp(f_\theta(x, x^+)) + \sum_{j=1}^{N} \exp(f_\theta(x, x_i^-))} \quad (1)$$

where $f_\theta(x, y) = \cos(\boldsymbol{e}_x, \boldsymbol{e}_y)/\tau$ denotes the function that computes the cosine similarity between two embeddings $\boldsymbol{e}_x$, $\boldsymbol{e}_y$ of inputs x, y parameterized by θ of the model. τ is the temperature hyperparameter which is set to 0.05 in our experiments.

2.2 Parameter Efficient Fine-Tuning for Multilinguality

In finetuning, extensive parameter optimization can lead to catastrophic forgetting, causing models to lose their ability to model languages not included in the fine-tuning data (Mao et al., 2022). This is a

[1]Recently released Qwen1.5 is another viable option, we list the experiments in Appendix A.1.

[2]We set two input types, *i.e.,* query and document. If not specified, the input is encoded as *query* by default. We only use the *document* type in retrieval tasks.

Language	Asymmetric	#train	Symmetric	#train
Natural	mMarco-google	499,184	SNLI + MNLI	281,230
Java	CodeSearchNet	454,451	BigCloneBench	450,862

Table 1: Statistics of training data used in each language. The SNLI+MNLI is translated to other languages by GPT-3.5-turbo API.

significant concern, especially for languages where paired data for contrastive learning are scarce. In such cases, we depend on the inherent capability of model to acquire qualified embeddings, making the prevention of catastrophic forgetting essential to maintain multilingual performance.

Parameter Efficient Fine-Tuning presents a solution to balance these two aspects (Badola et al., 2023), which enhances performance on target tasks while limit the updates to parameters. Therefore, we employ it to maximize multilingual performance, focusing on popular methods like Bitfit (Ben Zaken et al., 2022) and LoRA (Hu et al., 2021). In order to explore the model potential as much as possible, we use data from a single language in finetuning, which has demonstrated strong competitiveness (Wang et al., 2022b).

2.3 Data Composition for Task Versatility

Downstream embedding tasks can be categorized into two types: symmetric and asymmetric (Wang et al., 2022a; Su et al., 2023). To ensure the versatility, we use both types data (Table 1).

Asymmetric Data Query-to-passage/document retrieval is a typical asymmetric embedding task, focusing on capturing semantic relevance between texts (Muennighoff, 2022). The model is trained to maximize the similarity of vectors between a query and its most relevant candidate. Consistent with previous studies, we select the MSMARCO passage ranking (Nguyen et al., 2016) and its translated version mMARCO (Bonifacio et al., 2021).

Symmetric Data Natural language inference is an exemplary symmetric task that aligns well with the requirements of contrastive learning, where the semantic similarity between texts is gauged based on the similarity of their embeddings. The training instances comprise sentences with at least one entailment (positive) and one contradiction (negative). We utilize two classic English datasets, *i.e.,* SNLI (Bowman et al., 2015) and MNLI (Williams et al., 2018), and translate them into other languages.

For programming languages, clone detection focuses on the similarity between codes, where BigCloneBench (Svajlenko et al., 2014) is used as the symmetric. However, it is hard to find a suitable dataset that measures code to code relevance[3]. As a compromise, we use CodeSearchNet (Husain et al., 2019) which match codes and their comments.

3 Main Experiments

To assess the viability of converting mLLMs into universal embedding models, we conduct two parts of experiment. The first part aims to evaluate the potential of the LMs and validate employed strategies on the compiled benchmark (§3.1). We expand to broader open evaluations in the second part (§4).

3.1 Design of Controlled Experiments

The universal embedding encompasses two dimensions: (1) multilingual, including both natural and programming languages; (2) multitask, addressing both symmetric and asymmetric embedding tasks. Conducting comprehensive evaluations and analyses can be quite complex and challenging, given the significant variations in task scope and difficulty across different languages. Therefore, to facilitate research and comparison, we initially focus our experiments on a limited set of languages and tasks.

Evaluation benchmarks. For both symmetric and asymmetric task categories, we select two benchmarks each. One is in-domain, which is the corresponding evaluation of training data. For the asymmetric (resp. symmetric) part of natural languages, it is devset of mMarco (resp. testset of STS Benchmark [4] (Cer et al., 2017)). The other is an out-of-domain evaluation, which is MIRACL multilingual retrieval (Zhang et al., 2022) devset (resp. MASSIVE (FitzGerald et al., 2022) testset) for the asymmetric (resp. symmetric) of natural languages. The out-of-domain asymmetric (resp. symmetric) testset for code is xCodeEval/nl-code-search (Khan et al., 2023) (resp. GoogleCodeJam (Zhao and Huang, 2018)).

Evaluation languages. Java is only one choice for code experiments as the training and evaluation data are hard to find for other languages. For natural ones, we list all languages shared by mMarco, MIRACL and BLOOM pretraining in Table 10. We

[3]Sedykh et al. (2023) introduced a code-to-code search dataset based on StackOverflow but it is not public yet.

[4]The STS-B data are originated from SNLI. We use the translated version from `hf.co/datasets/stsb_multi_mt`.

Setting	Eval →	Asym						Sym						All					
Train ↓	Lang	en	zh	ar	id	java	avg.	en	zh	ar	id	java	avg.	en	zh	ar	id	java	avg.
Asym	en	**43.85**	39.93	43.64	31.43	47.60	41.29	75.00	72.00	63.77	68.51	57.74	67.40	59.43	55.96	53.70	49.97	52.67	54.35
	zh	39.91	**42.04**	41.94	28.93	49.24	40.41	75.05	72.68	65.32	68.57	58.54	68.03	57.48	57.36	53.63	48.75	53.89	54.22
	ar	39.60	36.76	**46.23**	32.70	50.09	41.08	75.12	72.82	65.73	69.85	56.93	68.09	57.36	54.79	55.98	51.27	53.51	54.58
	id	40.00	35.25	42.19	**38.90**	48.40	40.95	75.01	71.70	65.73	71.88	57.87	68.44	57.51	53.47	53.96	55.39	53.14	54.69
	java	15.36	19.40	20.44	13.52	**53.00**	24.35	72.27	72.32	62.84	68.37	54.76	66.11	43.82	45.86	41.64	40.95	53.88	45.23
Sym	en	5.94	9.46	4.87	5.80	42.33	13.68	**79.41**	76.23	68.88	73.92	56.05	70.90	42.67	42.85	36.87	39.86	49.19	42.29
	zh	5.15	7.25	6.76	6.88	43.13	13.83	78.84	**76.64**	68.76	73.60	56.94	70.96	42.00	41.95	37.76	40.24	50.03	42.40
	ar	5.89	8.19	8.57	7.38	42.86	14.58	78.64	76.01	**70.39**	74.90	55.77	71.14	42.27	42.10	39.48	41.14	49.32	42.86
	id	7.51	4.69	10.28	8.38	36.15	13.40	78.41	75.62	68.71	**76.17**	54.60	70.70	42.96	40.16	39.50	42.28	45.37	42.05
	java	0.00	0.02	0.00	0.02	1.57	0.32	32.67	39.43	23.27	33.51	73.34	40.44	16.33	19.72	11.64	16.77	37.45	20.38
All	en	42.97	37.96	42.85	32.09	50.70	41.31	77.65	74.95	68.26	72.06	57.14	70.01	**60.31**	56.46	55.55	52.08	53.92	**55.66**
	zh	38.92	40.48	41.08	28.46	49.79	39.75	77.68	75.00	68.39	71.58	58.27	70.18	58.30	**57.74**	54.73	50.02	54.03	54.96
	ar	38.43	36.21	45.55	32.33	49.07	40.32	77.76	75.12	69.74	73.58	57.21	70.68	58.09	55.67	**57.65**	52.95	53.14	55.50
	id	39.48	34.08	41.41	38.20	48.58	40.35	77.69	74.13	68.78	75.39	56.82	70.56	58.58	54.11	55.09	**56.79**	52.70	55.45
	java	14.62	20.31	21.97	15.02	51.56	24.70	72.60	72.24	62.74	68.12	**76.12**	70.37	43.61	46.28	42.36	41.57	**63.84**	47.53
Multilingual		43.02	41.69	46.74	38.73	49.01	43.84	77.22	74.88	69.15	74.66	60.64	71.31	60.12	58.28	57.95	56.70	54.82	57.57

Table 2: Main Results on BLOOM-1b1. The socre of the `asym` (or `sym`) is the macro average of an in-domain test and a out-of-domain test. All tests are listed in §3.1. The score of the `all` is the macro average of `asym` and `sym`.

select English, Chinese, Arabic and Indonesian for main experiments as they are from different language families and with different ratio in ROOTS.

Implementation details. We finetune BLOOM models by LoRA (Hu et al., 2021) with r of 64. We append special tokens to the vocabulary, initialize their embeddings randomly, and update them as well. We use AdamW optimizer with learning rate (lr) $5e$-5 and a cosine learning rate schedule, with warmup of 10% steps, and decay final lr down to 10% of the peak lr. We use GradCache (Gao et al., 2021a) to scale up the batch size to 1024 for the `all` that combine both asymmetric and symmetric data. And that of `asym` and `sym` is 512 to keep similar optimization steps. For each instance, we sample 7 negative examples from the hard negatives.[5] All training are conducted on 8 A100-80GB GPUs in BF16 with FlashAttention2 (Dao, 2024).

3.2 Results

Table 2 shows the results of controlled experiments. It is intuitive that, for each setting in every language, the in-domain trained models consistently perform the best (except the symmetric Java evaluation). Referencing these scores (on the diagonal), we explore the potential of Multilingual LM on the unified embeddings. For simplicity, we index the table by a {train (row) → eval (column)} format, *e.g.*, `asym-en→sym-zh` is 72.00. We can also omit part of it to refer to a set of results.

Task versatility For each setting, we can observe that: (1) `sym` models achieve poor results on asymmetric tasks (`sym→asym` are much lower than `asym→asym`); (2) `asym` models show comparable performance on symmetric tasks as the `sym` ones (`asym→sym` are close to `sym→sym`); (3) the `all` (*i.e.*, models trained on both types data) exhibit a slight decrease in asymmetric task (`all→asym` are slightly lower than `asym→asym`), but symmetric performance is improved (`all→sym` are better than `asym→sym`), resulting in the best overall score (`all→all` are higher than `asym/sym→all`). In all (natural and programming) languages, combining symmetric and asymmetric data improves task generalization, demonstrating that **task versatility can be achieved across languages**.

Multilinguality Focusing on `all→all`, lower right part of Table 2, we have: (1) on the column view, for one language, the performance from other languages (except Java) trained models are close to each other and reasonably less than that of this language; (2) on the row view, the averaged scores for each language trained models (except Java) are also similar. On `all→sym`, we can also consider the above two statements to be valid with Java. The models are not only performant in the source language, but also effective in others. It indicates that **we can train mLLM to generate good embeddings for a language without paired data**.

Exception on Java The exception results of Java could be possibly attributed to the unsatisfactory training data. First, the asymmetric data, *i.e.*, CodeSearchNet, is easier than mMARCO. On asymmetric Java evaluation, natural language models could achieve comparable results to the asym-java model, but, on asymmetric natural language eval-

[5]Since most examples from NLI datasets have only one contradiction sentence as the hard negative, we randomly sample 6 sentences to serve as the negative.

Model	en	*de*	es	fr	*ru*	*ja*	zh	ar	id
en	**43.85**	19.40	39.99	39.40	17.53	27.06	39.93	43.64	31.43
de	39.53	**35.08**	36.70	36.50	21.31	29.10	36.93	41.87	31.66
es	41.75	20.88	**41.82**	40.23	18.50	26.92	39.94	45.06	34.64
fr	41.56	21.05	39.88	**41.90**	18.51	27.42	40.11	44.93	33.95
ru	36.33	22.13	32.56	33.35	**31.61**	29.69	27.07	40.47	28.38
ja	36.28	21.17	30.36	30.60	22.26	**38.65**	34.26	36.83	26.81
zh	39.91	18.48	35.53	35.68	16.44	26.36	**42.04**	41.94	28.93
ar	39.60	21.49	38.29	36.87	19.58	26.15	36.76	**46.23**	32.70
id	40.00	21.59	38.70	37.47	19.90	26.77	35.25	42.19	**38.90**

Table 3: Results of language generalization experiments in asym→asym setting, with language codes in **bold** included in the BLOOM pre-training, while the ones in *italic* are not. Language information refer to Table 10.

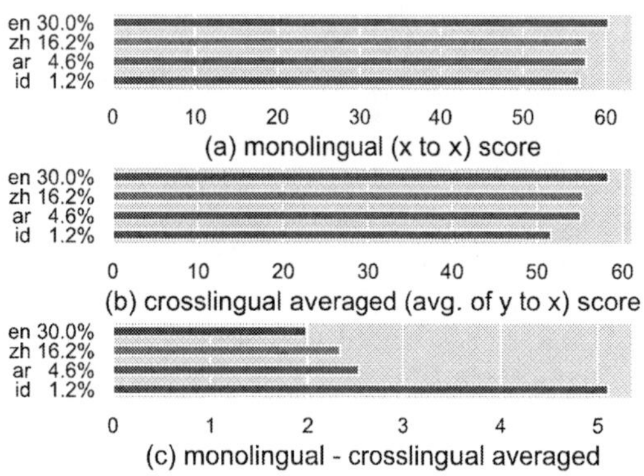

Figure 3: The plot of monolingual score (a), crosslingual averaged score (b), and their difference (c) of natural language evaluations on all→all setting. The lower the ratio of a language in pre-training, the lower its performance, and the more significant the improvement brought by training data.

uations, the latter is substantially weaker than the former. Thus, hard-pairs of asymmetric data would be beneficial. Second, the symmetric data (BigCloneBench) seem to be insufficient as it is limited to only a few hundred contest problems, which is smaller than the tens of thousands of semantic groups in NLI data. A wide-coverage large-scale dataset might be helpful.

3.3 Analysis

In this subsection, we further analyze multilingual performance and mechanism.

How language pretraining ratio affect performance? To explore the relationship between the performance of each language and its pretraining ratio in mLLM, we focus on natural languages in all→all setting and present the monolingual performance, cross-lingual average performance, and the differences between them in Figure 3. From English to Indonesian, we observe decreases in both

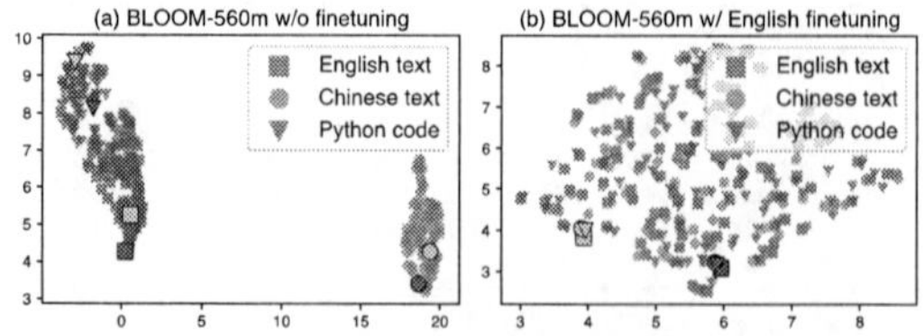

Figure 4: Visualization of 100 examples from CodeSearchNet Python, where Chinese texts are translated by GPT-3.5-turbo. Gold and pink markers represent parallel sequences in different languages. Before finetuning, (a), embeddings are separated by language, especially English and Chinese. After English finetuning, (b), the parallel sequences are well aligned to each other.

monolingual and cross-lingual performance as well as an increase in their difference, indicating that models have poorer representation capabilities for language with lower pretraining ratios and larger gaps to rich-pretraining languages, regardless of whether fine-tuning is applied or not.

Can model generalize to not pretrained languages? The BLOOM models are not pretrained with some commonly used languages such as German and Japanese. To investigate such scenario, we extend to more languages and focus on the asym→asym setting. Table 3 displays the results of three languages that are not covered by ROOTS, *i.e.,* German (de), Russian (ru) and Japanese (ja). First, the models trained on pretrained languages (*e.g.,* en) are capable on them (*e.g.,*, en→de has a small gap with de→de). Second, for an unpretrained language, with its fine-tuning data, mLLM not only exhibits excellent performance in this language itself but also acquires a certain level of multilingual embedding ability (it also achieves considerable scores on other languages). Overall, mLLM achieves promising generalization.

Does performance correlate to language families? It is also interesting to investigate whether there is a connection between language family and performance. Focusing rows of three Indo-European languages (en, fr, es) and one Sino-Tibetan language (zh) in Table 3. The results show that the models trained on Indo-European languages indeed exhibit similar performance trends, while the model trained on zh shows significant differences on es, fr and ar, which indicates that the language family is one potential factor. We also provide a better visualization of the results in Appendix Figure 5 .

Model	en	zh	ar	id	java
en-1b1	60.31	56.46	55.55	52.08	53.92
Scaling model size					
en-3b	61.93 $_{+1.62}$	58.51 $_{+2.05}$	58.25 $_{+2.70}$	54.56 $_{+2.48}$	56.28 $_{+2.36}$
en-7b1	63.47 $_{+3.16}$	60.01 $_{+3.55}$	60.06 $_{+4.51}$	56.86 $_{+4.78}$	56.73 $_{+2.81}$
Full parameter tuning					
en-1b1	61.55 $_{+1.24}$	58.98 $_{+2.42}$	56.53 $_{+0.98}$	51.68 $_{-0.4}$	53.53 $_{-0.39}$

Table 4: Results of English data trained models of scaling and ablation experiments in `all`→`all` setting.

What contributes to the multilinguality? To explore why monolingual fine-tuning can also lead to satisfactory performance in other languages, we visualize the embeddings before and after fine-tuning using umap (McInnes et al., 2018). We select the top 100 text-code pairs from the CodeSearchNet test set, translate the text into Chinese, and obtain embeddings using the model trained on English. As shown in Figure 4, before finetuning, the embeddings of each language are distributed separately. After finetuning, all embeddings are distributed according to semantics (the text-code pair and Chinese translation are clustered together). This indicates that monolingual contrastive learning align embeddings in the shared semantic space across languages, thereby improving performance in other languages, consistent with the finding of Wang et al. (2022b).

3.4 Scaling and Ablation on English

In this subsection, we take English data as an example to explore scaling and ablation of LoRA.

Scaling model size All previous experiments are conducted on BLOOM-1b1. Here, we extend the experiments to the 3b and 7b1 models. As shown in Table 4, the performance gradually increases as model size increases. Additionally, for a language, the smaller the pre-training ratio, the greater the improvement brought about by scaling.

LoRA *v.s.* full parameter tuning The impact of data combination has been reflected in Table 2. Now we conduct the ablation of LoRA by comparing with the full-parameter finetuned model. In Table 4, although full parameter fine-tuning resulted in performance improvement in English, Chinese, and Arabic, it shows a decrease in Indonesian and Java, two languages with smaller proportions of pre-training. To ensure better performance across multiple languages, we opt for LoRA.

4 Extended Evaluations

The second part experiment consists of evaluations on more tasks and domains (§4.1), as well as diverse languages of multilingual (§4.2) and cross-lingual (§4.3) tests. We evaluate BLOOM models (1b1, 3b, 7b1) finetuned on English data.

4.1 Task and Domain Evaluation

Our method improves task generalization. The MTEB benchmark (Muennighoff et al., 2023) compiles a variety of embedding datasets for different tasks and domains. We evaluate the generalization on MTEB English subset, which is currently one of the most comprehensive benchmark for English embeddings. Table 5 shows the results of the English MTEB. Compared to decoder-only models trained only on asymmetric data (SGPT series), our model significantly improves the performance on symmetric tasks (classification, clustering, STS). We acknowledge that there is still room to go compared to the best models, which are densely trained on diverse datasets. As our goal is to build a unified model for various languages, the score on English is already competitive enough.

mLLM can generalize to unseen domains. To assess the domain generalization, we focus on a more challenging scenario, a Chinese multi-domain retrieval benchmark (Long et al., 2022) which has nearly no overlap with the training and finetuning data. Table 6 presents the results. Our model is on par with the in-domain continue pre-trained and finetuned model (Karpukhin et al., 2020) (`DPR-2`), which highlights the remarkable domain generalization ability of mLLM.

4.2 Multilingual Evaluation

mLLM outperforms supervised code models. In main experiments (§3.2), Java is the only programming language evaluated. Now we expand the evaluations to all languages in CodeSearchNet (Husain et al., 2019), as shown in Table 7. Our models (1b1, 3b, and 7b1) are better than supervised baselines of code (Feng et al., 2020; Guo et al., 2021), demonstrating that our approach is a promising solution in building text and code unified embeddings. In addition to python, our models has large margins to OpenAI APIs in others. This is reasonable given their pre-training on large-scale code-text pairs.

Scaling can benefit unseen languages. We now extend the symmetric evaluation with languages

#Datasets (→)	Avg. 56	Class. 12	Clust. 11	PairClass. 3	Rerank. 4	Retr. 15	STS 10	Summ. 1
e5-mistral-7b-instruct (Wang et al., 2024)	**66.63**	**78.47**	**50.26**	**88.34**	**60.21**	**56.89**	**84.63**	31.4
bge-large-en-v1.5 (Xiao et al., 2023)	64.23	75.97	46.08	87.12	60.03	54.29	83.11	31.61
SGPT-5.8B-msmarco (Muennighoff, 2022)	58.93	68.13	40.34	82	56.56	50.25	78.1	31.46
sgpt-bloom-7b1-msmarco (Scao et al., 2022)	57.59	66.19	38.93	81.9	55.65	48.22	77.74	**33.6**
en-all-bloom-1b1	58.36	69.74	40.14	83.06	53.22	45.89	80.88	30.31
en-all-bloom-3b	59.70	71.87	41.25	83.88	52.69	47.64	81.80	32.07
en-all-bloom-7b1	60.62	71.72	42.31	85.00	54.81	49.06	82.66	32.24

Table 5: Results on MTEB English subset. We include the scores of top-performing encoder model, *i.e.,* BGE, and deocder-only models from the leaderboard (retrieved on Feb 3th, 2024).

Model	Dataset	Backbone	E-commerce		Entertainment video		Medical	
			MRR@10	Recall@1k	MRR@10	Recall@1k	MRR@10	Recall@1k
DPR-1	In-Domain	BERT	0.270	0.921	0.254	0.934	0.327	0.747
DPR-2	In-Domain	BERT-CT	0.289	**0.926**	0.263	**0.935**	0.339	**0.769**
text-embedding-ada-002	General	GPT	0.183	0.825	0.159	0.786	0.245	0.593
sgpt-bloom-7b1-msmarco	General	BLOOM	0.242	0.840	0.227	0.829	0.311	0.675
en-all-bloom-1b1	General	BLOOM	0.244	0.863	0.208	0.815	0.241	0.557
en-all-bloom-3b	General	BLOOM	0.267	0.871	0.228	0.836	0.288	0.619
en-all-bloom-7b1	General	BLOOM	**0.296**	0.889	**0.267**	0.907	**0.343**	0.705

Table 6: Results on Multi-CPR (Long et al., 2022). "In-Domain" indicates that the adopted training dataset is from the corresponding domain. "BERT-CT" notes that the BERT model is continuing pre-trained with domain corpus.

	Go	Ruby	Python	Java	JS	PHP	Avg.
CodeBERT	69.3	70.6	84.0	86.8	74.8	70.6	76.0
GraphCodeBERT	84.1	73.2	87.9	75.7	71.1	72.5	77.4
`cpt-code` S	**97.7**	**86.3**	99.8	94.0	86.0	96.7	93.4
`cpt-code` M	97.5	85.5	**99.9**	**94.4**	**86.5**	**97.2**	**93.5**
`sgpt-bloom-7b1-msmarco`	76.79	69.25	95.68	77.93	70.35	73.45	77.24
en-all-bloom-1b1	80.96	72.43	98.49	83.09	75.11	77.77	81.31
en-all-bloom-3b	81.04	76.30	98.45	84.34	77.22	79.58	82.82
en-all-bloom-7b1	81.66	79.02	98.14	84.88	78.55	79.92	83.70

Table 7: Results on CodeSearchNet (Husain et al., 2019). Scores of CodeBERT (Feng et al., 2020), GraphCodeBERT (Guo et al., 2021), and OpenAI API `cpt-code` are taken from Neelakantan et al. (2022).

Model	ar	en	es	*ko*
LASER2	67.47	76.73	79.67	70.52
LaBSE	69.07	79.45	80.83	71.32
paraphrase-multilingual-MiniLM-L12-v2	79.16	86.87	85.56	77.03
paraphrase-multilingual-mpnet-base-v2	79.1	86.99	85.14	**83.41**
sgpt-bloom-7b1-msmarco	76.42	87.07	86	66.89
multilingual-e5-base	74.52	87.83	86.74	79.95
en-all-bloom-1b1	81.31	89.85	86.36	61.43
en-all-bloom-3b	81.67	90.77	86.60	66.12
en-all-bloom-7b1	**83.41**	**91.60**	**87.72**	66.53

Table 8: Spearman correlation between embedding cosine similarity and labels on STS17 multilingual testset. Language codes in *italic* are not included in the BLOOM pre-training. Reference results are from MTEB.

that are not included in the BLOOM pre-training (that of the asymmetric refer to Table 3). We conduct experiments on the multilingual testset of STS-17 (Cer et al., 2017). Following the STS evaluation protocol of MTEB, we use the Spearman correlation between the cosine similarity of the sentence embeddings and the human-annotated scores (from 1 to 5) as the metric. Table 8 compares the results of our models with baselines. For languages included in the BLOOM pre-training, our models are the best. For the unseen language (marked *italic*), our models do not give competitive performance. Nonetheless, parameter scaling leads to the increase of language capabilities, resulting in improvement scores.

4.3 Cross-lingual Evaluation

Scaling aligns unseen languages with English. In Table 8, it is evident that parameter scaling can enhance monolingual performance for unseen languages. We now investigate whether this finding still holds for cross-lingual tasks and inquire whether unseen languages are aligned with English. We evaluate on the BUCC bi-text mining task (Zweigenbaum et al., 2016), which aims to find parallel sentences, often translations, from two monolingual corpora (French / Chinese / German / Russian and English). For fair comparisons, we adopt the setting and baselines of MTEB (Muennighoff et al., 2023). Table 9 shows the F1 scores

Model	fr-en	zh-en	*de*-en	*ru*-en
LASER2	98.39	97.7	99.21	97.62
LaBSE	**98.72**	**99.16**	**99.35**	**97.78**
multilingual-e5-base	97.59	98.3	99.13	97.20
paraphrase-multilingual-mpnet-base-v2	96.89	97.56	98.59	96.44
paraphrase-multilingual-MiniLM-L12-v2	94.99	95.63	97.11	95.06
sgpt-bloom-7b1-msmarco	97.06	97.96	54.00	45.30
en-all-bloom-1b1	97.76	97.70	38.61	23.67
en-all-bloom-3b	98.29	98.82	71.18	66.92
en-all-bloom-7b1	98.52	98.77	90.11	83.74

Table 9: BUCC F1 scores from MTEB. Languages in *italic* are not included in the BLOOM pre-training. Baseline results are retrieved from MTEB.

on the BUCC testset. Similar to the multilingual results, on the pre-trained language pairs (*i.e.*, fr-en and zh-en), our models are comparable with the state-of-the-art approach, LABSE (Feng et al., 2022). On the half-covered language pairs (*de*-en and *ru*-en), there are consistent improvements with the model size growth, demonstrating that the embedding spaces of unseen languages are aligned to that of English. Hence, we can affirmatively answer the research question posed earlier.

5 Related Work

Text and sentence embeddings are useful for many downstream tasks and applications (Karpukhin et al., 2020; Gao and Callan, 2021). Early studies start from similar ideas of word vectors (Hill et al., 2016; Lin et al., 2017; Pagliardini et al., 2018), also shift to neural networks (Conneau et al., 2017) then pre-trained transformers (Cer et al., 2018; Reimers and Gurevych, 2019; Ni et al., 2022). The subsequent work mainly focus on using contrastive loss to supervise or improve representation learning (Zhang et al., 2020; Giorgi et al., 2021; Kim et al., 2021; Gao et al., 2021b; Yan et al., 2021; Cheng et al., 2023), translation augmentation (Wieting et al., 2020; Zhang et al., 2021), large-scale pre-training (Yang et al., 2021; Neelakantan et al., 2022; Wang et al., 2022a), and prompt (Su et al., 2023). As most of them are under specific tasks, Muennighoff et al. (2023) compile MTEB with diverse tasks, domains, and languages for evaluations. Recently, embeddings have gained attention and a batch of large-scale pretrained models have emerged, such as E5 (Wang et al., 2022a), BGE (Xiao et al., 2023), GTE (Li et al., 2023), UAE (Li and Li, 2023). Most of them are targeted to and evaluated on English, while we explore the languages beyond English.

Pre-trained transformer encoders, *i.e.*, BERT (Devlin et al., 2019), or that of T5 (Raffel et al., 2020) are currently the mainstream for embedding models, which are computation-effective than encoder-decoders (Ni et al., 2022). GPT-style decoder-only models (Radford et al., 2018) are promising alternatives, since they have theoretically stronger representations (Dong et al., 2021; Su, 2023). Pioneering GPT-based studies show impressive performance on both text and code (Neelakantan et al., 2022), especially for semantic search (Muennighoff, 2022). We continue this line, exploring the unified embeddings across multiple natural and programming languages. A concurrent work (Wang et al., 2024) fine-tune Mistrial-7B (Jiang et al., 2023) with data from diverse source and carefully crafted instructions, showing state-of-the-art performance on English MTEB. Taking into account a more general scenario with various languages, we do not use complex prompts, but only a set of special symbols for asymmetric inputs.

Multi- and cross-lingual text embeddings follow the developments of English ones, from cross-lingual word embeddings (Ruder et al., 2019) to RNNs (Artetxe and Schwenk, 2019) and transformers (Chidambaram et al., 2019; Yang et al., 2020; Reimers and Gurevych, 2020; Feng et al., 2022). To learn models without enough supervisions, translation information (Artetxe and Schwenk, 2019; Chidambaram et al., 2019; Goswami et al., 2021; Feng et al., 2022) and multilingual pre-trained encoders (Reimers and Gurevych, 2020; Liu et al., 2021) are explorated to improve embeddings (Chen et al., 2024). However, such BERT-like multilingual encoders do not support code, which is currently one of the crucial requirements. Therefore, we shift our focus to pre-training decoder models that can simultaneously support natural languages and programming languages, aiming to evaluate and analyze the potential of constructing universal embeddings from them.

6 Conclusion

We propose the development of unified embeddings models (universal embedders) for various tasks across multiple natural and programming languages based on multilingual decoder-only models. To evaluate the potential, we present straightforward strategies to construct embedding models from them, and design a universal embedding benchmark for evaluation and analysis. Through extensive experiments, we demonstrated the versatility of embedders constructed from mLLMs, showing their capabilities cross languages and tasks. The models can generate reasonably good embeddings for languages that have not been fine-tuned or pre-trained, and the quality can be significantly improved with the corresponding fine-tuning data. These characteristics strongly indicate the great potential of mLM for building universal embedders. Additionally, we provide various analyses and extended evaluations to reveal the interesting properties of the model. We hope that our work could inspire more open-source high-quality universal embedders.

Limitations

This work suffers from three primary limitations. Firstly, we only evaluate the BLOOM and Qwen1.5 models as they are currently the only open-source decoder-only models available for multiple natural and programming languages. We hope that in the future, there will be more model options to consider. Secondly, we train the model using only monolingual data. We have chosen to focus on monolingual fine-tuning for a clearer analysis, which helps us to fully analyze the intrinsic characteristics of different languages and the performance relationships between them. We left mixed-language training as future work. Thirdly, there were some anomalies in the training and evaluation for the code. We are committed to finding higher-quality data to enhance code evaluations.

Acknowledgments

This work receives partial support from the Natural Science Foundation of China (under Grant 624B2048), "the Fundamental Research Funds for the Central Universities", and the Shenzhen Science and Technology Program (under Grant ZDSYS20230626091203008).

References

Mikel Artetxe and Holger Schwenk. 2019. Massively multilingual sentence embeddings for zero-shot cross-lingual transfer and beyond. *Transactions of the Association for Computational Linguistics*, 7:597–610.

Kartikeya Badola, Shachi Dave, and Partha Talukdar. 2023. Parameter-efficient finetuning for robust continual multilingual learning. In *Findings of the Association for Computational Linguistics: ACL 2023*, pages 9763–9780, Toronto, Canada. Association for Computational Linguistics.

Elad Ben Zaken, Yoav Goldberg, and Shauli Ravfogel. 2022. BitFit: Simple parameter-efficient fine-tuning for transformer-based masked language-models. In *Proc. of the ACL*, pages 1–9, Dublin, Ireland.

Luiz Bonifacio, Vitor Jeronymo, Hugo Queiroz Abonizio, Israel Campiotti, Marzieh Fadaee, Roberto Lotufo, and Rodrigo Nogueira. 2021. mmarco: A multilingual version of the ms marco passage ranking dataset. *arXiv preprint arXiv:2108.13897*.

Samuel R. Bowman, Gabor Angeli, Christopher Potts, and Christopher D. Manning. 2015. A large annotated corpus for learning natural language inference. In *Proc. of the EMNLP*, pages 632–642, Lisbon, Portugal.

Daniel Cer, Mona Diab, Eneko Agirre, Iñigo Lopez-Gazpio, and Lucia Specia. 2017. SemEval-2017 task 1: Semantic textual similarity multilingual and crosslingual focused evaluation. In *Proceedings of the SemEval*, pages 1–14, Vancouver, Canada.

Daniel Cer, Yinfei Yang, Sheng-yi Kong, Nan Hua, Nicole Limtiaco, Rhomni St. John, Noah Constant, Mario Guajardo-Cespedes, Steve Yuan, Chris Tar, and 1 others. 2018. Universal sentence encoder for English. In *Proc. of the EMNLP: System Demonstrations*, pages 169–174, Brussels, Belgium.

Jianlv Chen, Shitao Xiao, Peitian Zhang, Kun Luo, Defu Lian, and Zheng Liu. 2024. Bge m3-embedding: Multi-lingual, multi-functionality, multi-granularity text embeddings through self-knowledge distillation.

Ting Chen, Simon Kornblith, Mohammad Norouzi, and Geoffrey Hinton. 2020. A simple framework for contrastive learning of visual representations. In *Proc. of the ICML*, volume 119, pages 1597–1607.

Qinyuan Cheng, Xiaogui Yang, Tianxiang Sun, Linyang Li, and Xipeng Qiu. 2023. Improving contrastive learning of sentence embeddings from ai feedback. In *Findings of the ACL*.

Muthu Chidambaram, Yinfei Yang, Daniel Cer, Steve Yuan, Yunhsuan Sung, Brian Strope, and Ray Kurzweil. 2019. Learning cross-lingual sentence representations via a multi-task dual-encoder model. In *Proc. of the 4th Workshop on Representation Learning for NLP (RepL4NLP-2019)*, pages 250–259, Florence, Italy.

Alexis Conneau, Douwe Kiela, Holger Schwenk, Loïc Barrault, and Antoine Bordes. 2017. Supervised learning of universal sentence representations from natural language inference data. In *Proc. of the EMNLP*, pages 670–680, Copenhagen, Denmark.

Tri Dao. 2024. FlashAttention-2: Faster attention with better parallelism and work partitioning. In *International Conference on Learning Representations*.

Jacob Devlin, Ming-Wei Chang, Kenton Lee, and Kristina Toutanova. 2019. BERT: Pre-training of deep bidirectional transformers for language understanding. In *Proc. of the NAACL-HLT*, pages 4171–4186, Minneapolis, Minnesota. Association for Computational Linguistics.

Yihe Dong, Jean-Baptiste Cordonnier, and Andreas Loukas. 2021. Attention is not all you need: pure attention loses rank doubly exponentially with depth. In *Proc. of the ICML*, volume 139, pages 2793–2803.

Fangxiaoyu Feng, Yinfei Yang, Daniel Cer, Naveen Arivazhagan, and Wei Wang. 2022. Language-agnostic BERT sentence embedding. In *Proc. of the ACL*, pages 878–891, Dublin, Ireland.

Zhangyin Feng, Daya Guo, Duyu Tang, Nan Duan, Xiaocheng Feng, Ming Gong, Linjun Shou, Bing Qin, Ting Liu, Daxin Jiang, and Ming Zhou. 2020. CodeBERT: A pre-trained model for programming and natural languages. In *Findings of the EMNLP*, pages 1536–1547, Online.

Jack FitzGerald, Christopher Hench, Charith Peris, Scott Mackie, Kay Rottmann, Ana Sanchez, Aaron Nash, Liam Urbach, Vishesh Kakarala, Richa Singh, and 1 others. 2022. Massive: A 1m-example multilingual natural language understanding dataset with 51 typologically-diverse languages. *arXiv preprint arXiv:2204.08582*.

Luyu Gao and Jamie Callan. 2021. Condenser: a pre-training architecture for dense retrieval. In *Proc. of the EMNLP*, pages 981–993, Online and Punta Cana, Dominican Republic.

Luyu Gao, Yunyi Zhang, Jiawei Han, and Jamie Callan. 2021a. Scaling deep contrastive learning batch size under memory limited setup. In *Proc. of the 6th Workshop on Representation Learning for NLP (RepL4NLP-2021)*, pages 316–321, Online.

Tianyu Gao, Xingcheng Yao, and Danqi Chen. 2021b. SimCSE: Simple contrastive learning of sentence embeddings. In *Proc. of the EMNLP*, pages 6894–6910, Online and Punta Cana, Dominican Republic.

John Giorgi, Osvald Nitski, Bo Wang, and Gary Bader. 2021. DeCLUTR: Deep contrastive learning for unsupervised textual representations. In *Proc. of the ACL-IJCNLP*, pages 879–895, Online.

Koustava Goswami, Sourav Dutta, Haytham Assem, Theodorus Fransen, and John P. McCrae. 2021. Cross-lingual sentence embedding using multi-task learning. In *Proc. of EMNLP*, pages 9099–9113, Online and Punta Cana, Dominican Republic.

Daya Guo, Shuo Ren, Shuai Lu, Zhangyin Feng, Duyu Tang, LIU Shujie, Long Zhou, Nan Duan, Alexey Svyatkovskiy, Shengyu Fu, and 1 others. 2021. Graphcodebert: Pre-training code representations with data flow. In *International Conference on Learning Representations*.

Felix Hill, Kyunghyun Cho, and Anna Korhonen. 2016. Learning distributed representations of sentences from unlabelled data. In *Proc. of the NAACL-HLT*, pages 1367–1377, San Diego, California.

Edward J Hu, Phillip Wallis, Zeyuan Allen-Zhu, Yuanzhi Li, Shean Wang, Lu Wang, Weizhu Chen, and 1 others. 2021. Lora: Low-rank adaptation of large language models. In *International Conference on Learning Representations*.

Hamel Husain, Ho-Hsiang Wu, Tiferet Gazit, Miltiadis Allamanis, and Marc Brockschmidt. 2019. Codesearchnet challenge: Evaluating the state of semantic code search. *arXiv preprint arXiv:1909.09436*.

Albert Q Jiang, Alexandre Sablayrolles, Arthur Mensch, Chris Bamford, Devendra Singh Chaplot, Diego de las Casas, Florian Bressand, Gianna Lengyel, Guillaume Lample, Lucile Saulnier, and 1 others. 2023. Mistral 7b. *arXiv preprint arXiv:2310.06825*.

Vladimir Karpukhin, Barlas Oguz, Sewon Min, Patrick Lewis, Ledell Wu, Sergey Edunov, Danqi Chen, and Wen-tau Yih. 2020. Dense passage retrieval for open-domain question answering. In *Proc. of the EMNLP*, pages 6769–6781, Online.

Mohammad Abdullah Matin Khan, M Saiful Bari, Xuan Long Do, Weishi Wang, Md Rizwan Parvez, and Shafiq Joty. 2023. xcodeeval: A large scale multilingual multitask benchmark for code understanding, generation, translation and retrieval. *arXiv preprint arXiv:2303.03004*.

Taeuk Kim, Kang Min Yoo, and Sang-goo Lee. 2021. Self-guided contrastive learning for BERT sentence representations. In *Proc. of the ACL-IJCNLP*, pages 2528–2540, Online.

Hugo Laurençon, Lucile Saulnier, Thomas Wang, Christopher Akiki, Albert Villanova del Moral, Teven Le Scao, Leandro Von Werra, Chenghao Mou, Eduardo González Ponferrada, Huu Nguyen, and 1 others. 2022. The bigscience roots corpus: A 1.6 tb composite multilingual dataset. *Advances in Neural Information Processing Systems*, 35:31809–31826.

Ruiqi Li, Xiang Zhao, and Marie-Francine Moens. 2022. A brief overview of universal sentence representation methods: A linguistic view. *ACM Computing Surveys (CSUR)*, 55(3):1–42.

Xianming Li and Jing Li. 2023. Angle-optimized text embeddings. *arXiv preprint arXiv:2309.12871*.

Zehan Li, Xin Zhang, Yanzhao Zhang, Dingkun Long, Pengjun Xie, and Meishan Zhang. 2023. Towards general text embeddings with multi-stage contrastive learning. *arXiv preprint arXiv:2308.03281*.

Zhouhan Lin, Minwei Feng, Cicero Nogueira dos Santos, Mo Yu, Bing Xiang, Bowen Zhou, and Yoshua Bengio. 2017. A structured self-attentive sentence embedding. *arXiv preprint arXiv:1703.03130*.

Fangyu Liu, Ivan Vulić, Anna Korhonen, and Nigel Collier. 2021. Fast, effective, and self-supervised: Transforming masked language models into universal lexical and sentence encoders. In *Proc. of the EMNLP*, pages 1442–1459, Online and Punta Cana, Dominican Republic.

Dingkun Long, Qiong Gao, Kuan Zou, Guangwei Xu, Pengjun Xie, Ruijie Guo, Jian Xu, Guanjun Jiang, Luxi Xing, and Ping Yang. 2022. Multi-cpr: A multi domain chinese dataset for passage retrieval. In *Proc. of the SIGIR*, pages 3046–3056. ACM.

Yuren Mao, Yaobo Liang, Nan Duan, Haobo Wang, Kai Wang, Lu Chen, and Yunjun Gao. 2022. Less-forgetting multi-lingual fine-tuning. In *NeurIPS*.

Leland McInnes, John Healy, Nathaniel Saul, and Lukas Großberger. 2018. Umap: Uniform manifold approximation and projection. *Journal of Open Source Software*, 3(29):861.

Niklas Muennighoff. 2022. SGPT: GPT sentence embeddings for semantic search. *arXiv preprint arXiv:2202.08904*.

Niklas Muennighoff, Nouamane Tazi, Loic Magne, and Nils Reimers. 2023. MTEB: Massive text embedding benchmark. In *Proc. of the EACL*, pages 2014–2037, Dubrovnik, Croatia.

Arvind Neelakantan, Tao Xu, Raul Puri, Alec Radford, Jesse Michael Han, Jerry Tworek, Qiming Yuan, Nikolas A. Tezak, Jong Wook Kim, Chris Hallacy, and 1 others. 2022. Text and code embeddings by contrastive pre-training. *ArXiv*, abs/2201.10005.

Tri Nguyen, Mir Rosenberg, Xia Song, Jianfeng Gao, Saurabh Tiwary, Rangan Majumder, and Li Deng. 2016. MS MARCO: A human generated machine reading comprehension dataset. In *Proceedings of the Workshop on Cognitive Computation: Integrating neural and symbolic approaches*, volume 1773.

Jianmo Ni, Gustavo Hernandez Abrego, Noah Constant, Ji Ma, Keith Hall, Daniel Cer, and Yinfei Yang. 2022. Sentence-t5: Scalable sentence encoders from pre-trained text-to-text models. In *Findings of the ACL*, pages 1864–1874, Dublin, Ireland.

Matteo Pagliardini, Prakhar Gupta, and Martin Jaggi. 2018. Unsupervised learning of sentence embeddings using compositional n-gram features. In *Proc. of the NAACL-HLT*, pages 528–540, New Orleans, Louisiana.

Baolin Peng, Michel Galley, Pengcheng He, Hao Cheng, Yujia Xie, Yu Hu, Qiuyuan Huang, Lars Liden, Zhou Yu, Weizhu Chen, and 1 others. 2023. Check your facts and try again: Improving large language models with external knowledge and automated feedback. *arXiv preprint arXiv:2302.12813*.

Alec Radford, Karthik Narasimhan, Tim Salimans, Ilya Sutskever, and 1 others. 2018. Improving language understanding by generative pre-training.

Colin Raffel, Noam Shazeer, Adam Roberts, Katherine Lee, Sharan Narang, Michael Matena, Yanqi Zhou, Wei Li, and Peter J. Liu. 2020. Exploring the limits of transfer learning with a unified text-to-text transformer. *Journal of Machine Learning Research*, 21(140):1–67.

Nils Reimers and Iryna Gurevych. 2019. Sentence-BERT: Sentence embeddings using Siamese BERT-networks. In *Proc. of the EMNLP-IJCNLP*, pages 3982–3992, Hong Kong, China.

Nils Reimers and Iryna Gurevych. 2020. Making monolingual sentence embeddings multilingual using knowledge distillation. In *Proc. of the EMNLP*, pages 4512–4525, Online.

Sebastian Ruder, Ivan Vulić, and Anders Søgaard. 2019. A survey of cross-lingual word embedding models. *J. Artif. Int. Res.*, 65(1):569–630.

Teven Le Scao, Angela Fan, Christopher Akiki, Elizabeth-Jane Pavlick, Suzana Ili'c, Daniel Hesslow, Roman Castagn'e, Alexandra Sasha Luccioni, Franccois Yvon, Matthias Gallé, and 1 others. 2022. Bloom: A 176b-parameter open-access multilingual language model. *ArXiv*, abs/2211.05100.

Ivan Sedykh, Dmitry Abulkhanov, Nikita Sorokin, Sergey Nikolenko, and Valentin Malykh. 2023. Searching by code: a new searchbysnippet dataset and snipper retrieval model for searching by code snippets. *arXiv preprint arXiv:2305.11625*.

Chan Hee Song, Jiaman Wu, Clayton Washington, Brian M Sadler, Wei-Lun Chao, and Yu Su. 2022. Llm-planner: Few-shot grounded planning for embodied agents with large language models. *arXiv preprint arXiv:2212.04088*.

Hongjin Su, Weijia Shi, Jungo Kasai, Yizhong Wang, Yushi Hu, Mari Ostendorf, Wen-tau Yih, Noah A. Smith, Luke Zettlemoyer, and Tao Yu. 2023. One embedder, any task: Instruction-finetuned text embeddings. In *Proc. of the ACL*.

Jianlin Su. 2023. Why are all llms now decoder-only architectures?

Jeffrey Svajlenko, Judith F. Islam, Iman Keivanloo, Chanchal K. Roy, and Mohammad Mamun Mia. 2014. Towards a big data curated benchmark of inter-project code clones. In *2014 IEEE International Conference on Software Maintenance and Evolution*, pages 476–480.

Guanzhi Wang, Yuqi Xie, Yunfan Jiang, Ajay Mandlekar, Chaowei Xiao, Yuke Zhu, Linxi Fan, and Anima Anandkumar. 2023. Voyager: An open-ended embodied agent with large language models. *arXiv preprint arXiv:2305.16291*.

Liang Wang, Nan Yang, Xiaolong Huang, Binxing Jiao, Linjun Yang, Daxin Jiang, Rangan Majumder, and Furu Wei. 2022a. Text embeddings by weakly-supervised contrastive pre-training. *arXiv preprint arXiv:2212.03533*.

Liang Wang, Nan Yang, Xiaolong Huang, Linjun Yang, Rangan Majumder, and Furu Wei. 2024. Improving text embeddings with large language models. *arXiv preprint arXiv:2401.00368*.

Yaushian Wang, Ashley Wu, and Graham Neubig. 2022b. English contrastive learning can learn universal cross-lingual sentence embeddings. In *Proc. of the EMNLP*, pages 9122–9133, Abu Dhabi, United Arab Emirates.

John Wieting, Graham Neubig, and Taylor Berg-Kirkpatrick. 2020. A bilingual generative transformer for semantic sentence embedding. In *Proc. of the EMNLP*, pages 1581–1594, Online.

Adina Williams, Nikita Nangia, and Samuel Bowman. 2018. A broad-coverage challenge corpus for sentence understanding through inference. In *Proc. of the NAACL-HLT*, pages 1112–1122, New Orleans, Louisiana.

Shitao Xiao, Zheng Liu, Peitian Zhang, and Niklas Muennighof. 2023. C-pack: Packaged resources to advance general chinese embedding. *arXiv preprint arXiv:2309.07597*.

Yuanmeng Yan, Rumei Li, Sirui Wang, Fuzheng Zhang, Wei Wu, and Weiran Xu. 2021. ConSERT: A contrastive framework for self-supervised sentence representation transfer. In *Proc. of the ACL-IJCNLP*, pages 5065–5075, Online.

Yinfei Yang, Daniel Cer, Amin Ahmad, Mandy Guo, Jax Law, Noah Constant, Gustavo Hernandez Abrego, Steve Yuan, Chris Tar, Yun-hsuan Sung, and 1 others. 2020. Multilingual universal sentence encoder for semantic retrieval. In *Proc. of the ACL: System Demonstrations*, pages 87–94, Online.

Ziyi Yang, Yinfei Yang, Daniel Cer, Jax Law, and Eric Darve. 2021. Universal sentence representation learning with conditional masked language model. In *Proc. of the EMNLP*, pages 6216–6228, Online and Punta Cana, Dominican Republic.

Xinyu Zhang, Nandan Thakur, Odunayo Ogundepo, Ehsan Kamalloo, David Alfonso-Hermelo, Xiaoguang Li, Qun Liu, Mehdi Rezagholizadeh, and Jimmy Lin. 2022. Making a miracl: Multilingual information retrieval across a continuum of languages. *arXiv preprint arXiv:2210.09984*.

Yan Zhang, Ruidan He, Zuozhu Liu, Lidong Bing, and Haizhou Li. 2021. Bootstrapped unsupervised sentence representation learning. In *Proc. of the ACL-IJCNLP*, pages 5168–5180, Online.

Yan Zhang, Ruidan He, Zuozhu Liu, Kwan Hui Lim, and Lidong Bing. 2020. An unsupervised sentence embedding method by mutual information maximization. In *Proc. of the EMNLP*, pages 1601–1610, Online.

Gang Zhao and Jeff Huang. 2018. Deepsim: deep learning code functional similarity. In *Proc. of the ESEC/FSE*, page 141–151, New York, NY, USA.

Code	Language	Family	Subfamily	in ROOTS (%)
ar	Arabic	Afroasiatic	Semitic	4.6
zh	Chinese	Sino-Tibetan	Sinitic	16.2
de	German	Indo-European	Germanic	-
en	English	Indo-European	Germanic	30.04
es	Spanish	Indo-European	Italic	10.8
fr	French	Indo-European	Italic	12.9
hi	Hindi	Indo-European	Indo-Iranian	0.7
id	Indonesian	Austronesian	Malayo-Polynesian	1.2
ja	Japanese	Japonic	-	-
ru	Russian	Indo-European	Balto-Slavic	-

Table 10: Languages shared by mMarco and MIRACL.

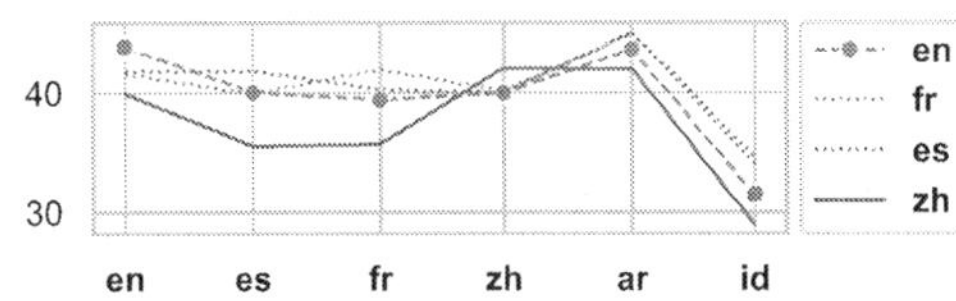

Figure 5: The plot of English (en), French (fr), Spanish (es), Chinese (zh) from Table 3, where en, fr and es are all in the Indo-European family and with similar performance trends. While the zh trained model shows differences to Indo-European ones in es, fr, and ar.

Pierre Zweigenbaum, Serge Sharoff, and Reinhard Rapp. 2016. Towards preparation of the second bucc shared task: Detecting parallel sentences in comparable corpora. In *Proceedings of the Ninth Workshop on Building and Using Comparable Corpora*, pages 38–43, Portoroz, Slovenia.

A Appendix

A.1 Experiments on Qwen1.5

Qwen1.5 models are recently released multilingual LLMs, we conduct the main experiments on the Qwen1.5-0.5B to examine the multilingual performance (Table 11) and evaluate 0.5B, 1.8B and 4B English finetuned models on MTEB English (Table 12). In Table 11, Qwen1.5-0.5B is comparable to BLOOM-1b1 or even better on English (en), Chinese (zh), and Java. But it performs poorly in Arabic (ar) and Indonesian (id). In MTEB English, as shown in Table 12, the Qwen1.5 models are significantly better than BLOOM models.

A.2 Additional Design Analysis

We now conduct the ablation analysis to identify the contributions of different design aspects of our approach. We hope that this analysis can help building more robust decoder-based embedding models. Table 13 presents the MTEB-English performance of BLOOM-560M models finetuned in different experimental settings.

Setting	Eval →	Asym						Sym						All					
Train ↓	Lang	en	zh	ar	id	java	avg.	en	zh	ar	id	java	avg.	en	zh	ar	id	java	avg.
									BLOOM-1b1										
	en	42.97	37.96	42.85	32.09	50.70	41.31	77.65	74.95	68.26	72.06	57.14	70.01	**60.31**	56.46	55.55	52.08	53.92	**55.66**
	zh	38.92	40.48	41.08	28.46	49.79	39.75	77.68	75.00	68.39	71.58	58.27	70.18	58.30	**57.74**	54.73	50.02	54.03	54.96
All	ar	38.43	36.21	45.55	32.33	49.07	40.32	77.76	75.12	69.74	73.58	57.21	70.68	58.09	55.67	**57.65**	52.95	53.14	55.50
	id	39.48	34.08	41.41	38.20	48.58	40.35	77.69	74.13	68.78	75.39	56.82	70.56	58.58	54.11	55.09	**56.79**	52.70	55.45
	java	14.62	20.31	21.97	15.02	51.56	24.70	72.60	72.24	62.74	68.12	**76.12**	70.37	43.61	46.28	42.36	41.57	**63.84**	47.53
									Qwen1.5-0.5B										
	en	42.42	38.36	24.66	20.41	52.63	35.70	79.23	75.33	52.96	61.09	60.28	65.78	60.82	56.85	38.81	40.75	56.46	50.74
	zh	40.03	41.02	24.71	17.68	53.25	35.34	78.82	75.79	52.89	60.48	61.23	65.84	59.42	58.41	38.80	39.08	57.24	50.59
All	ar	36.32	33.34	37.64	22.85	52.25	36.48	76.85	73.43	62.32	63.02	58.77	66.88	56.59	53.38	49.98	42.94	55.51	51.68
	id	38.22	34.97	29.67	34.54	53.81	38.24	77.32	73.68	54.96	69.85	60.44	67.25	57.77	54.32	42.32	52.20	57.12	52.75
	java	18.19	24.25	2.30	5.36	50.65	20.15	71.90	70.18	44.49	54.89	75.60	63.41	45.04	47.21	23.39	30.13	63.12	41.78

Table 11: Main Results of BLOOM-1b1 and Qwen1.5-0.5B. The socre of the `asym` (or `sym`) is the macro average of an in-domain test and a out-of-domain test. All tests are listed in §3.1. The score of the `all` is the macro average of `asym` and `sym`.

#Datasets (→)	Avg. 56	Class. 12	Clust. 11	PairClass. 3	Rerank. 4	Retr. 15	STS 10	Summ. 1
e5-mistral-7b-instruct (Wang et al., 2024)	**66.63**	**78.47**	**50.26**	**88.34**	**60.21**	**56.89**	**84.63**	31.4
bge-large-en-v1.5 (Xiao et al., 2023)	64.23	75.97	46.08	87.12	60.03	54.29	83.11	31.61
SGPT-5.8B-msmarco (Muennighoff, 2022)	58.93	68.13	40.34	82	56.56	50.25	78.1	31.46
sgpt-bloom-7b1-msmarco (Scao et al., 2022)	57.59	66.19	38.93	81.9	55.65	48.22	77.74	**33.6**
en-all-bloom-1b1	58.36	69.74	40.14	83.06	53.22	45.89	80.88	30.31
en-all-bloom-3b	59.70	71.87	41.25	83.88	52.69	47.64	81.80	32.07
en-all-bloom-7b1	60.62	71.72	42.31	85.00	54.81	49.06	82.66	32.24
en-all-qwen1.5-0.5b	58.89	71.71	39.87	83.61	53.81	46.43	80.46	31.62
en-all-qwen1.5-1.8b	60.73	72.83	42.91	84.75	55.19	48.79	81.66	31.31
en-all-qwen1.5-4b	62.41	74.53	44.61	85.58	55.35	51.36	82.98	31.27

Table 12: Results on MTEB English subset. We include the scores of top-performing encoder model, *i.e.,* BGE, and deocder-only models from the leaderboard (retrieved on Feb 3th, 2024).

No.	Model Setting	Overall	Class.	Clust.	PairClass.	Rerank.	Retr.	STS	Summ.
0	Our-bloom-560m	55.80	68.04	36.89	81.05	52.60	41.19	79.93	32.06
1	w/o allnli	54.01	62.52	37.12	78.90	52.95	42.19	75.57	29.16
2	w/o msmarco	49.14	67.74	32.84	78.81	50.02	20.78	79.98	29.84
3	w/o multiple negatives	55.70	68.19	37.30	80.60	52.87	40.63	79.63	31.49
4	w/ weightedmean	55.37	66.60	36.42	80.26	52.98	42.14	78.89	30.58
5	sgpt-bloom-560m	53.01	62.89	36.58	76.61	52.06	39.96	74.40	30.09
6	w/ learnable special token + lasttoken pooling	54.24	62.45	38.33	77.89	53.22	42.22	75.69	29.48

Table 13: Ablation study. MTEB English results of bloom-560m finetuned by different settings.

	Train → Eval ↓	raw 1b1	english 1b1-asym	1b1-sym	1b1-all	1b1-all-full	3b-all	7b1-all	zh 1b1-asym	1b1-sym	1b1-all	ar 1b1-asym	1b1-sym	1b1-all	id 1b1-asym	1b1-sym	1b1-all	java 1b1-sym	1b1-asym	1b1-all
en	mMarco	0.01	39.79	8.8	38.49	42.72	40.49	41.98	36.21	7.94	34.99	35.86	7.45	34.24	36.34	8.7	35.83	0	13.58	12.95
	Miracl	0	47.91	3.08	47.44	48.41	48.3	50.42	43.6	2.36	42.86	43.34	4.33	42.62	43.67	6.32	43.12	0	17.15	16.29
	STSBenchmarkMultilingual	12.21	79.53	85.96	85.15	85.35	86.76	87.37	78.75	86.42	84.36	78.81	84.54	84.24	79.16	85.32	84.28	23.54	73.24	73.56
	STS17Extend	35.44	86.47	89.84	89.85	90.01	90.77	91.6	84.98	88.82	88.88	85.03	88.01	88.42	85.49	88.9	88.88	37.63	80.83	82.51
	MassiveIntentClassification	28.22	67	70.92	67.8	67.38	70.18	72.01	68.24	70.06	68.75	68.31	71.01	69.18	67.7	69.72	68.8	34.75	67.5	67.16
zh	mMarco	0.02	27.01	8.01	26.27	30.02	28.43	29.69	31.06	6.86	30.19	27.12	7.06	26.32	25.95	5.83	25.07	0.04	12.91	13.41
	Miracl	0	52.84	10.92	49.66	54.14	52.75	55.69	53.03	7.65	50.77	46.41	9.31	46.1	44.55	3.56	43.09	0	25.89	27.22
	STSBenchmarkMultilingual	25.41	74.62	79.59	78.89	80.68	80.82	81.49	75.83	81.65	80.72	75.47	79.66	79.13	74.4	79.26	78.05	33.03	71.09	71.52
	STS17Extend	38.29	81.77	85.99	86.9	87.87	88.47	88.86	83.87	87.49	87.62	82.23	85.19	86.19	80.48	84.65	84.41	41.67	79.69	79.52
	MassiveIntentClassification	31.75	65.8	69.67	67.01	67.49	68.22	69.5	65.51	68.72	65.82	66.78	69.59	67.59	65.95	69.29	67.03	41.5	69.25	68.95
ar	mMarco	0.05	22.04	4.04	21.33	24.35	23.79	25.97	22.85	5.75	22.24	27.36	5.95	26.48	23.59	7.04	22.99	0.01	8.28	9.75
	Miracl	0.07	65.25	5.7	64.36	63.69	68.16	70.26	61.02	7.78	59.91	65.09	11.19	64.63	60.8	13.53	59.82	0	32.6	34.19
	STSBenchmarkMultilingual	29.51	69.54	75.94	75.94	79.16	79.34	81.44	72.14	78.49	77.41	73.32	79.39	79.78	73.34	77.75	77.8	20.52	66.88	67.64
	STS17Extend	31.43	72.61	80.68	81.31	82.26	81.67	83.41	74.55	80.53	80.9	76.7	83.38	84.17	76.74	80.27	81.76	16.35	67.29	66.26
	MassiveIntentClassification	19.08	56.46	59.44	57.88	57.38	60.53	61.57	57.29	58.02	57.62	56.45	59.4	57.51	56.43	58.41	57.77	28.1	58.6	58.53
id	mMarco	0.01	20.04	4.89	21.41	21.92	26.16	29.26	19.32	4.97	18.97	24.86	5.06	24.16	33.03	6.29	32.03	0.01	6.92	6.67
	Miracl	0	42.82	6.71	42.77	40.42	44.2	45.85	38.54	8.78	37.95	40.54	9.69	40.49	44.77	10.47	44.36	0.03	20.13	23.38
	STSBenchmarkMultilingual	24.91	72.11	79.58	78.36	80.72	81.03	83.2	72.73	81.06	78.75	73.1	80.63	79.78	76.89	83.13	82.91	24.12	69.54	69.4
	STS17Extend	47.12	80.32	86.55	86.25	88.51	87.87	89.63	79.19	86	84.31	81.1	86.77	87.28	83.53	87.98	88.98	44.45	77.11	76.83
	MassiveIntentClassification	22.7	60.81	64.77	61.82	59.77	63.43	65.91	61.18	63.67	61.62	62.6	66.09	63.63	63.54	66.79	64.83	32.74	63.42	63.13
java	CodeSearchNet	1.00	82.45	73.27	83.09	82.84	84.33	84.87	82.77	75.17	82.64	82.4	73.81	81.66	81.1	62.46	81.41	3.14	88.53	88.47
	xCodeEvalRetrievalNlCode	0	12.74	11.4	18.31	15.94	20.06	20.43	15.72	11.08	16.94	17.78	11.91	16.48	15.7	9.84	15.76	0	17.47	14.64
	BigCloneBench	19.14	48.05	43.83	45.96	48.67	50.76	50.18	47.53	44.71	47.77	44.19	43.97	45.63	44.79	42.4	45.42	94.61	46.81	95.48
	GoogleCodeJam	61.79	67.43	68.28	68.33	66.67	69.98	71.45	69.55	69.17	68.78	69.67	67.57	68.8	70.95	66.79	68.22	52.07	62.72	56.77

Table 14: Detailed results of Table 2 on our compiled universal embedding benchmark. `raw-1b1` is un-finetuned BLOOM 1b1 model tested with <EOS> embeddings.

NLI data improve symmetric tasks. We first investigate the effect of symmetric NLI data on different tasks. In the line No.1 of Table 13, we remove the NLI data and finetune the model solely using asymmetric retrieval data (MSMARCO). Compared with our model in line No.0, the performance of classification (Class.) and STS is significantly decreased, which are typical symmetric tasks. However, these two tasks are not affected by the removal of MSMARCO data (line No.2). This demonstrates the crucial role of symmetric NLI data in achieving optimal performance in these tasks.

Retrieval data are irreplaceable. As stated above, finetuning using only NLI data (line No.2) is competitive enough for classification and STS. However, it can not provide a satisfactory score for retrieval (Retr.), *i.e.,* 20.78 *v.s.* 40+ of others, and also leads a drop in clustering (Clust.). This suggests that retrieval data are crucial for building unified embedding models.

Multiple negatives only help retrieval. In line No.3 of Table 13, we keep only one negative example in contrastive learning. Compared to our model in line No.0, only the performance of retrieval is decreased, while other tasks have no significant change. Considering that learning multiple negatives greatly increase the computational cost and training train, one can freely choose whether or not to use it according to the specific requirements.

Last special token is better representation. With regard to sequence encoding by decoder-based models, both Neelakantan et al. (2022) and Muennighoff (2022) append special tokens to the start and end of the input sequence. On the selection of the final embedding output, Neelakantan et al. (2022) use the last special token, while Muennighoff (2022) use a position weighted mean pooling of the hidden states. In line No.4 of Table 13, we employ the weighted mean pooling on our model and observe a slight performance decrease. Additionally, we also try to use the last special token on SGPT (Muennighoff, 2022), achieving better average scores (line No.6) compared with the `sgpt-bloom-560m` we implemented. Our experiments demonstrate that the last special token is more effective for unified embeddings models.

		en-all	zh-all	ar-all	id-all	java-all
en	mMarcoMultilingual	38.56	36.06	33.01	34.30	15.65
	Miracl	46.28	44.00	39.63	42.14	20.73
	STSBenchmarkMultilingual	84.64	84.30	79.28	81.22	71.93
	STS17Extend	90.80	90.20	88.08	88.29	77.70
	MassiveIntentClassification	70.73	70.39	70.02	69.89	68.97
zh	mMarcoMultilingual	26.14	29.51	23.19	23.79	13.69
	Miracl	50.58	52.53	43.48	46.15	34.80
	STSBenchmarkMultilingual	77.57	79.79	72.53	74.51	68.07
	STS17Extend	88.42	89.15	84.89	85.27	76.85
	MassiveIntentClassification	67.67	67.11	68.15	67.47	67.90
ar	mMarcoMultilingual	12.40	12.79	21.52	15.84	1.80
	Miracl	36.92	36.63	53.76	43.51	2.79
	STSBenchmarkMultilingual	62.27	62.47	73.10	64.17	54.03
	STS17Extend	59.46	58.79	77.54	64.59	43.90
	MassiveIntentClassification	45.06	45.14	49.32	45.54	40.02
id	mMarcoMultilingual	14.54	13.36	16.57	27.53	3.17
	Miracl	26.28	22.01	29.13	41.55	7.55
	STSBenchmarkMultilingual	65.61	63.97	66.63	77.18	54.28
	STS17Extend	71.77	72.19	76.81	86.16	65.59
	MassiveIntentClassification	53.48	52.87	54.32	58.03	49.85
java	CodeSearchNet	83.95	83.00	82.47	83.00	88.25
	xCodeEvalRetrievalNlCode	21.31	23.51	22.03	24.62	13.04
	BigCloneBench	48.56	50.68	45.95	48.18	96.85
	GoogleCodeJam	72.00	71.78	71.59	72.69	54.35

Table 15: Detailed results of Qwen1.5-0.5B of Table 11.

DiaDP@XLLM25: Advancing Chinese Dialogue Parsing via Unified Pretrained Language Models and Biaffine Dependency Scoring

Shuoqiu Duan[a], Xiaoliang Chen[a,b]*, Duoqian Miao[b], Xu Gu[c], Xianyong Li[a], Yajun Du[a]

[a]School of Computer and Software Engineering, Xihua University, Chengdu 610039, P. R. China

[b]College of Electronic and Information Engineering, Tongji University, Shanghai 201804, P. R. China

[c]Chengdu Institute of Computer Applications, Chinese Academy of Sciences, Chengdu 610041, P. R. China

duanshuoqiu@stu.xhu.edu.cn, dqmiao@tongji.edu.cn
chenxl@mail.xhu.edu.cn, guxu24@mails.ucas.ac.cn
lixy@mail.xhu.edu.cn, duyajun@mail.xhu.edu.cn

Abstract

Dialogue-level dependency parsing is crucial for understanding complex linguistic structures in conversational data, yet progress has been hindered by limited annotated resources and inadequate modeling of dialogue dynamics. Existing methods often fail to capture both intra- and inter-utterance dependencies effectively, particularly in languages like Chinese with rich contextual interactions. To address these challenges, we propose InterParser, a novel framework that integrates a pretrained language model (PLM), bidirectional GRU (BiGRU), and biaffine scoring for comprehensive dependency parsing. Our model encodes token sequences using a PLM, refines representations via deep BiGRU layers, and employs separate projections for "head" and "dependent" roles to optimize arc and relation prediction. For cross-utterance dependencies, speaker-specific feature projections are introduced to enhance dialogue-aware scoring. Joint training minimizes cross-entropy losses for both intra- and inter-utterance dependencies, ensuring unified optimization. Experiments on a standard Chinese benchmark demonstrate that InterParser significantly outperforms prior methods, achieving state-of-the-art labeled attachment scores (LAS) for both intra- and inter-utterance parsing.

1 Introduction

Dialogue-level dependency parsing is crucial for enhancing the capabilities of dialogue understanding systems. This approach seeks to create a unified tree structure that captures both intra-sentence syntactic dependencies and inter-utterance discourse relations. While sentence-level dependency parsing has been extensively researched in languages such as English and Chinese (Xue et al., 2005; Jiang et al., 2018), applying this approach to multi-turn dialogues presents unique challenges. Dialogues inherently involve complex hierarchical interactions: within utterances, there are syntactic dependencies (e.g., subject-verb-object structures), and across utterances, there are discourse dependencies (e.g., question-answer pairs or causal reasoning). In Chinese, a language characterized by flexible word order and context-dependent semantics, performing such hierarchical parsing is particularly challenging.The root nodes of each subtree are often predicates that reflect single semantic events, illustrated in Figure 1.

Recent advancements have started to bridge this gap. Jiang et al. (2023) initiated the development of the Chinese Dialogue-level Dependency Treebank (CDDT), which integrates syntactic dependencies from existing treebanks (Jiang et al., 2018) and discourse relations based on Rhetorical Structure Theory (RST). They proposed rule-based signal detection and pseudo-labeling strategies to address data scarcity in resource-limited scenarios. However, this method's reliance on heuristic transformations, such as mapping syntactic 'root' nodes to discourse dependencies, and its multi-step pipeline process, can lead to error propagation and limited generalization. Subsequently, Zhang et al. (2024) introduced a Large Language Model (LLM)-assisted data augmentation technique, generating synthetic dialogues through various perturbations at the word, syntax, and discourse levels. Although effective, this approach necessitates extensive prompt engineering and can struggle to maintain structural consistency between the generated text and the corresponding dependency labels.

To address these limitations, we introduce an innovative end-to-end neural architecture tailored for Chinese dialogue-level dependency parsing. This approach circumvents the need for intermediate rule-based procedures by integrating the modeling of both intra- and inter-utterance dependencies through a cohesive feature learning mechanism.

* Corresponding author

Proceedings of the 1st Joint Workshop on Large Language Models and Structure Modeling (XLLM 2025), pages 266–273
August 1, 2025 ©2025 Association for Computational Linguistics

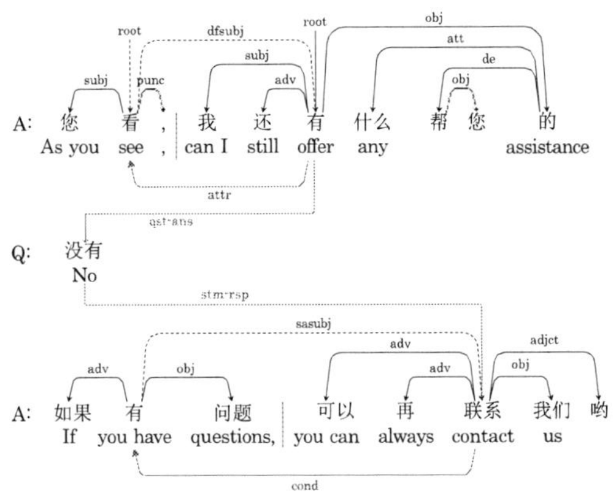

Figure 1: Example of Dialogue-Level Dependency Parsing: Vertical dashed lines indicate EDU boundaries, with arcs above words representing intra-EDU dependencies and arcs below or crossing utterances indicating inter-EDU dependencies.

Our framework specifically targets three pivotal challenges:

Hierarchical Integration of Linguistic Features: Effective dialogue parsing necessitates the concurrent modeling of various linguistic dimensions, including character-level, word-level, and utterance-level representations. This is especially crucial in languages like Chinese, characterized by intricate morphological structures and word agglutination. Our model strategically fuses these multifaceted features to optimize the representation of both syntactic and discursive elements.

Speaker-Aware Interaction Modeling: In multi-party dialogues, comprehending the roles and interactions between participants is essential. Our method incorporates explicit modeling of speaker roles to capture dependencies that are unique to different interlocutors, such as those between a customer and a service agent. This aspect is often underrepresented in conventional dependency parsing methodologies.

Enhancing Low-Resource Robustness: The scarcity of annotated dialogue data presents a significant challenge in training reliable models, particularly in low-resource settings. Our model addresses this issue by leveraging syntactic priors from existing treebanks, while meticulously preventing overfitting to sparse discourse patterns.

Our contributions include the following key innovations:

(1) Dynamic Subword Weighting: Our model incorporates a trainable attention mechanism that adaptively aggregates subword embeddings to construct word-level representations. This approach surpasses traditional static averaging, effectively capturing nuanced semantic variations.

(2) Gated Multi-Level Fusion: We employ a hierarchical encoding structure that seamlessly integrates character, word, and speaker features through sigmoid-gated interactions. This mechanism enhances the model's contextual awareness across various linguistic granularities.

(3) Unified Biaffine Decoding: Our model employs dual biaffine attention mechanisms to concurrently capture syntactic and discourse dependencies. This design enables the model to effectively specialize in both local syntactic and global discourse dependency patterns.

(4) Curriculum Joint Training: We implement a phased optimization strategy that progressively shifts the training focus from syntax, utilizing treebanks, to discourse dependencies, leveraging dialogue data. This approach ensures stable knowledge transfer and enhances the model's generalization capabilities.

Our model, evaluated on the CDDT benchmark, achieves state-of-the-art performance in Chinese dialogue-level dependency parsing. It effectively captures both syntactic and discourse dependencies, surpassing existing heuristic-based and multi-step pipeline methods.

2 Method

To address the speed and performance inefficiencies of traditional sentence parsing models, especially when dealing with an increasing number of words and dependency parsing tags, we employ a hierarchical decoding strategy for inner-EDU and inter-EDU dependencies. Additionally, we utilize the Chinese-electra-180g-base-discriminator for pre-training our large model and incorporate a state-of-the-art biaffine parser (Dozat and Manning, 2017) to enhance parsing efficiency. Our modelling framework is shown in Figure 2

First, we are provided with an input dialogue text, represented as a sequence of n words $\mathbf{x} = [w_1, w_2, \ldots, w_n]$, and its corresponding EDU-level sequence $\mathbf{E} = [E_1, E_2, \ldots, E_m]$, where m denotes the number of EDUs. Each EDU E_k $(k \in [1, m])$

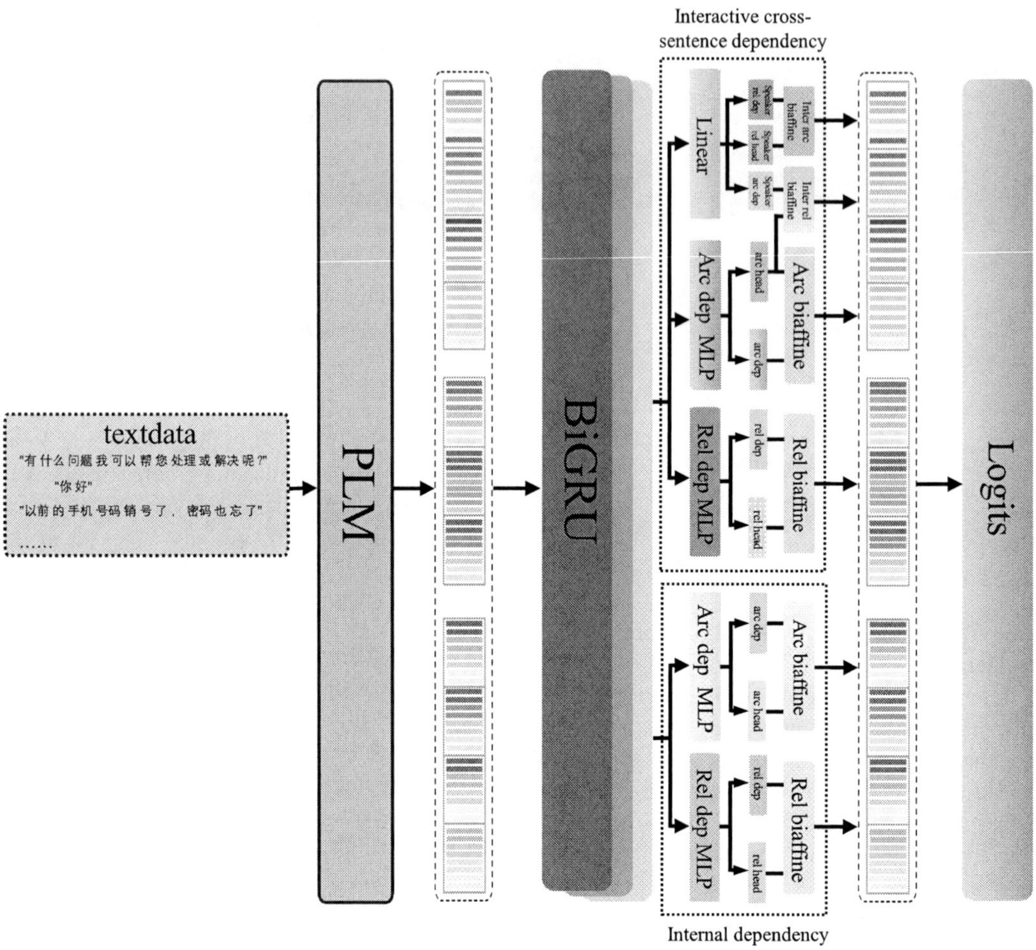

Figure 2: Our model diagram, arc denotes an arc of dependence, rel denotes the type of relationship, inter arc/rel biaffine: handling interaction dependencies across sentences, arc/rel biaffine :dealing with internal dependencies.

encompasses a subsequence of words, represented as $\left[w_{k,1}, \ldots, w_{k,s_k}\right]$, where s_k is the number of words within the k-th EDU. We proceed to illustrate the baseline parser using an encoding-decoding framework.

2.1 Hierarchical Encoding

Our encoding pipeline consists of three sequential transformations to derive parsing-oriented representations:

(1) **Contextual Embedding**: The input sequence $\mathbf{x} = [w_1, w_2, \ldots, w_n]$ is processed by a pre-trained language model (e.g., BERT or ELECTRA) to obtain contextualized token embeddings:

$$\begin{aligned} e_{1:n} &\rightarrow e_1, e_2, \ldots, e_n \\ &= \mathrm{PLM}\left(w_1, w_2, \ldots, w_n\right) \end{aligned} \tag{1}$$

(2) **Sequential Abstraction**: A L-layer bidirectional GRU is employed to capture position-aware linguistic patterns from the contextualized embeddings:

$$\begin{aligned} h_{1:n} &\rightarrow h_1, h_2, \ldots, h_n \\ &= \mathrm{BiGRU}^{\times L}\left(e_1, e_2, \ldots, e_n\right) \end{aligned} \tag{2}$$

(3) **Dependency-Specific Projection**: Parallel K-layer MLPs are used to transform the abstracted features into dependency-parsing oriented representations. These MLPs provide

distinct perspectives for dependency analysis:

$$\begin{cases} z_{1:n}^{d} \rightarrow z_1^d, z_2^d, \ldots, z_n^d \\ \qquad = \mathrm{MLP}^{\times K}(\boldsymbol{h}_1, \boldsymbol{h}_2, \ldots, \boldsymbol{h}_n) \\ z_{1:n}^{h} \rightarrow z_1^h, z_2^h, \ldots, z_n^h \\ \qquad = \mathrm{MLP}^{\times K}(\boldsymbol{h}_1, \boldsymbol{h}_2, \ldots, \boldsymbol{h}_n) \end{cases} \tag{3}$$

Here, $z^d = [z_1^d, \ldots, z_n^d]$ represents the dependency-centric feature matrix, providing insights into the relationships between words as dependents. Conversely, $z^h = [z_1^h, \ldots, z_n^h]$ denotes the head-centric feature matrix, focusing on the roles of words as heads in dependency structures. These matrices offer orthogonal perspectives for subsequent dependency analysis, enhancing the model's parsing capabilities.

2.2 Decoding

The decoding of the dialogue-level dependency tree is executed in two phases. Initially, we conduct inner-EDU dependency parsing. For each $\mathrm{E}_k = [w_{k,1}, \ldots, w_{k,s_k}]$, we derive their corresponding dependency-aware and head-aware representations $z_{k,1:sk}^d = [z_{k,1}^d, \ldots, z_{k,s_k}^d]$ and $z_{k,1:s_k}^h = [z_{k,1}^h, \ldots, z_{k,s_k}^h]$ through direct indexing. Subsequently, we compute the candidate head scores for each word $w_{k,j}$ using the biaffine operation:

$$\boldsymbol{o}_{k,j}^{\mathrm{IN}} = \boldsymbol{z}_{k,1:k,s_k}^{h} \boldsymbol{U}^{\mathrm{IN}} \boldsymbol{z}_{k,j}^{d} + \boldsymbol{z}_{k,1:k,s_k}^{h} \boldsymbol{u}^{\mathrm{IN}} \tag{4}$$

$$\boldsymbol{o}_{k,j}^{\mathrm{IN,ARC}} = \sum_{l} \boldsymbol{o}_{k,j}^{\mathrm{IN}}[\cdot][l] \tag{5}$$

In these equations, $\boldsymbol{U}^{\mathrm{IN}}$ and $\boldsymbol{u}^{\mathrm{IN}}$ are trainable parameters. The candidate heads for each word $w_{k,j}$ are confined to within its EDU, and only syntactic relation labels are considered at this stage. The tensor $\boldsymbol{o}_{k,j}^{\mathrm{IN}}$ encompasses scores for both head selection and label classification: its slice $\boldsymbol{o}_{k,j}^{\mathrm{IN}}[i]$ represents a vector of relation scores for head candidate i. During inference, we first apply the minimum spanning tree algorithm to the arc scores $\boldsymbol{o}_{k,j}^{\mathrm{IN,ARC}}$ to retrieve a well-formed dependency tree, and then assign each predicted arc the relation label with the highest score. For cross-utterance relation modeling, we augment the biaffine mechanism with discourse-specific adaptations. Two essential feature sequences are extracted from EDU root nodes: $z_{r_1:r_m}^d = z_{1,r_1}^d, \ldots, z_{m,r_m}^d$ and $z_{r_1:r_m}^h = z_{1,r_1}^h, \ldots, z_{m,r_m}^h$, where r_* denotes the root word index of each EDU. The discourse dependency scores are calculated as follows:

$$\boldsymbol{o}_k^{\mathrm{IT}} = \boldsymbol{z}_{r_1:r_m}^{h} \boldsymbol{U}^{\mathrm{IT}} \boldsymbol{z}_{r_k}^{d} + \boldsymbol{z}_{r_1:r_m}^{h} \boldsymbol{u}^{\mathrm{IT}} \tag{6}$$

$$o_k^{\mathrm{IT,ARC}} = \sum_{l} o_k^{\mathrm{IT}}[\cdot][l] \tag{7}$$

Here, $\boldsymbol{U}^{\mathrm{IT}}$ and $\boldsymbol{u}^{\mathrm{IT}}$ are learnable parameters. The tensor $\boldsymbol{o}_k^{\mathrm{IT}}$ forms a 2D structure capturing head candidates and relation labels, while $\boldsymbol{o}_k^{\mathrm{IT,ARC}}$ determines the dependency tree structure.

2.3 Curriculum Optimization

The joint loss function is modified to incorporate phased weighting, as expressed below:

$$\mathcal{L} = \alpha_t \mathcal{L}syn + (1 - \alpha_t)\mathcal{L}disc \tag{8}$$

In this equation, $\alpha_t = \max(0.5, 1 - \frac{t}{T})$ serves as a dynamic weight that evolves over T epochs, implementing a curriculum learning strategy. This approach ensures a balanced focus on syntactic and discourse-level losses throughout the training process.

2.4 Training

We optimize a standard cross-entropy objective, which consists of separate terms for dependency arc prediction and relation classification. Let $\boldsymbol{o}_*^*$ represent either the inner-EDU scores $\boldsymbol{o}_{k,j}^{\mathrm{IN}}$ or the inter-EDU scores $\boldsymbol{o}_k^{\mathrm{IT}}$. We apply softmax over the arc logits $\boldsymbol{o}_*^{*,\mathrm{ARC}}$ and over the label logits $\boldsymbol{o}_*^*[\hat{\boldsymbol{y}}_h]$ with the $\hat{\boldsymbol{y}}_h$ representing the ground-truth head assignments to obtain probability distributions over all candidate heads and syntactic/discourse labels, respectively. The overall loss is the sum of the negative log-likelihoods of the correct heads and labels. This training procedure follows the biaffine parser framework of Dozat and Manning (2017).

We train our baseline parser by dividing its supervision into two complementary subtasks: inner-EDU (syntax) parsing and inter-EDU (dialogue) parsing.

- **Inner-EDU** parsing is fully supervised. We utilize a large-scale syntactic treebank in conjunction with the 50 gold-standard dialogue instances provided by Jiang et al. (2023). This combination offers dense, in-domain dependency annotations, ensuring the reliable convergence of this component.

Statistic	Train	Test
# dialogue	50	800
avg.# turns	23	25
avg.# words	194	212
# inner	9129	159803
# inter	1671	29200

Table 1: The Statistics of CDDT. "#" and "avg.#" Indicate "Count" and "Average Count"

- **Inter-EDU** parsing faces the challenge of annotation sparsity. To address this issue, we adopt the approach of Jiang et al. (2023), leveraging their rule-based silver dialogue corpus in addition to the same 50 gold-standard instances. This strategy merges pseudo-labeled and gold supervision, facilitating the training of the cross-utterance dependency component.

3 Experiment

3.1 Dataset

We employ the publicly accessible Chinese Dialogue-Level Dependency Treebank (CDDT), introduced by Jiang et al. (2023). This dataset serves as the sole benchmark for Chinese dialogue-level dependency parsing. The statistics of this dataset are detailed in Table 1.

3.2 Settings

Evaluation Methodology. We assess model performance using the conventional dependency parsing metrics, Unlabeled Attachment Score (UAS) and Labeled Attachment Score (LAS), with punctuation tokens explicitly excluded from the calculations. To facilitate detailed diagnostic analysis, we separate the evaluation into two distinct components: intra-EDU dependencies (relationships within Elementary Discourse Units) and inter-EDU dependencies (syntactic links across units). Notably, the inter-EDU evaluation focuses on the lexical dependency level, rather than abstract EDU representations. This necessitates the accurate identification of EDU head tokens as a fundamental step for valid cross-unit dependency assessment.

In scenarios where resources are limited and development sets are not accessible, we use the checkpoint from the final training iteration for model validation. To ensure reproducibility, all implementations were carried out on a consistent computational platform equipped with an NVIDIA RTX3090 GPU, which has 24GB of VRAM.

Hyper-parameters. Our PLM is a Chinese variant of ELECTRA, as implemented by Cui et al. (2020). We utilize the base scale discriminator[1] for fine-tuning purposes. The hidden size of both our Parser and MLM components is set to 200, with a dropout rate of 0.1. For model training, we employ the AdamW optimizer, initializing the learning rate of the PLM at 2e-5 and that of the subsequent modules at 1e-4. A linear warmup is applied for the first 10% of the training steps. The weight decay is set to 0.1, and to prevent gradient explosion, we implement gradient clipping with a maximum value of 2.0. The training batch size is configured to 64, and the total number of epochs is 25.

3.3 Results

Training Data	Few-shot			
	Inner-EDU		Inter-EDU	
	UAS	LAS	UAS	LAS
Jiang et al. (2023)	91.74	88.2	71.09	55.73
baseline(Zhang et al., 2024)	91.66	89.12	71.59	56.32
GPT-3.5-Turbo-0613				
+wrd	92.37	90.01	73.06	58.50
+syn	92.13	89.94	73.22	59.33
+dis	92.35	90.11	73.57	59.68
+wrd & syn	92.38	90.16	73.52	59.47
+wrd & dis	92.19	90.04	73.84	59.81
+syn & dis	92.23	90.18	**73.88**	59.94
+wrd & syn & dis	92.46	90.35	73.81	**60.17**
Llama2-7B				
+wrd	91.91	89.73	72.33	57.63
+syn	91.65	89.51	72.31	58.28
+dis	91.90	89.85	72.76	58.45
+wrd & syn	91.87	89.81	72.56	58.38
+wrd & dis	91.82	89.63	73.13	58.75
+syn & dis	91.76	89.91	72.92	58.79
+wrd & syn & dis	91.97	89.89	72.95	59.01
Qwen-7B				
+wrd	92.03	89.88	72.68	57.94
+syn	91.94	89.69	72.80	58.46
+dis	92.01	89.97	73.19	58.85
+wrd & syn	91.84	89.97	73.05	58.74
+wrd & dis	91.87	89.76	73.47	59.05
+syn & dis	92.07	89.99	73.42	59.14
+wrd & syn & dis	91.96	89.85	73.52	59.31
Ours	**92.56**	**90.66**	72.81	59.92

Table 2: The test results under the few-shot settings. "wrd", "syn", "dis" denote the "word-level", "syntax-level", and "discourse-level", respectively.

In the few-shot learning scenario, our model is trained on a dataset comprising 50 human-annotated instances supplemented with silver-standard corpus data. We conduct a systematic evaluation that compares four configurations: (1) base-

[1]huggingface.co/hfl/chinese-electra-180g-base-discriminator

line methods, (2) individual augmentation strategies, (3) pairwise combinations, and (4) the full integration of all three data augmentation techniques alongside our proposed model. This comprehensive evaluation framework allows for a rigorous assessment of the potential capabilities of our model. As depicted in Table 2, our approach achieves statistically significant improvements over the baseline methods across all evaluation metrics. The experimental results yield two key insights:

- For *Inner-EDU* evaluation, our model surpasses all baseline approaches and exhibits superior performance compared to three large-scale reference models.
- In the *Inter-EDU* assessment, the proposed method remains competitive with the current state-of-the-art large models.

Specifically concerning attachment scores, our model achieves the following improvements:

- **UAS Improvement**: An increase of 0.9% for Inner-EDU and 1.22% for Inter-EDU compared to the baselines.
- **LAS Enhancement**: Absolute gains of 1.54% for Inner-EDU and 3.60% for Inter-EDU.

3.4 Ablation Study

Our ablation study systematically investigates the consequences of removing the meticulously optimized Bidirectional Gated Recurrent Unit (BiGRU) from our model architecture. As illustrated in Table 3, the removal of this architectural component led to a notable decline in performance across all evaluation metrics. This empirical evidence underscores the critical role of our carefully designed BiGRU layer in the model's operation, especially in terms of capturing sequential dependencies and contextual patterns.

Model	Few-shot			
	Inner-EDU		Inter-EDU	
	UAS	LAS	UAS	LAS
Ours	92.56	90.66	72.81	59.92
w/o BiGRU	90.64	88.03	69.13	53.19

Table 3: The results of the ablation experiments.

4 Related Work

Dependency Parsing. Several Chinese dependency parsing paradigms and corresponding treebanks have been developed (Xue et al., 2005; Che et al., 2012; McDonald et al., 2013; Qiu et al., 2014). These efforts primarily concentrate on sentence-level dependency parsing, with document-level parsing being significantly less explored. Li et al. (2014) applied a dependency parsing approach to discourse parsing, although their EDU-wise method overlooks the parsing within EDUs. Recent advancements by Jiang et al. (2023) have initiated Chinese dialogue-level dependency parsing, establishing a unified schema that encompasses both inner-EDU syntactic dependencies and inter-EDU discourse dependencies. Building upon this, Zhang et al. (2024) have further refined the framework by incorporating LLM-assisted data augmentation, tackling the challenges of low-resource settings through hierarchical transformations at the word, syntax, and discourse levels.

Meanwhile, cross-lingual transfer methods have emerged as complementary approaches. Guo et al. (2022) proposed a curriculum-style fine-grained adaptation technique for unsupervised cross-lingual dependency transfer, demonstrating that syntactic knowledge can be effectively transferred across languages through progressive difficulty scheduling and parameter generation networks. This approach achieves state-of-the-art performance on Universal Dependencies treebanks by combining curriculum learning with self-training strategies.

Dialogue Parsing. Discourse structures in dialogue can be represented by various theories, including RST (Mann and Thompson, 1987, 1988), SDRT (Asher and Lascarides, 2003), and PTDB (Prasad et al., 2008). While datasets such as STAC (Afantenos et al., 2015) and Molweni (Li et al., 2020) concentrate on English multi-party dialogues, Jiang et al. (2023) introduced the first Chinese dialogue-level dependency treebank (CDDT), which merges RST-inspired discourse relations with syntactic dependencies. This work bridges the gap between EDU-based discourse parsing and word-wise dependency structures. Expanding on this, Zhang et al. (2024) developed a three-level augmentation strategy using Large Language Models (LLMs) to create varied pseudo-instances while maintaining discourse hierarchies, leading to significant improvements in handling inter-EDU dependencies.

Weakly Supervised Learning. Predicting unseen dependency labels in low-resource settings presents significant challenges (Norouzi et al., 2013). Jiang et al. (2023) tackle this issue by employing signal-based dependency transformation and pseudo-labeled data filtering, utilizing syntactic treebanks and masked language modeling to infer inter-EDU relations. Zhang et al. (2024) build upon this approach by leveraging LLMs' generative abilities for extensive data augmentation, developing prompt-based mechanisms to maintain structural consistency throughout transformations. Their method integrates characterization, chain-of-thought prompting, and constrained generation, illustrating that LLMs can effectively distill syntactic and discourse knowledge without direct supervision. This contrasts with conventional self-training (Scudder, 1965) and co-training (Blum and Mitchell, 1998) methodologies, providing a model-centric solution for low-resource dependency parsing.

Universal Structured NLP and Demonstration Systems. Recent efforts have been made to unify structured NLP (XNLP) tasks under a general framework. Fei et al. (2023) proposed XNLP, an interactive demonstration system built upon large language models (LLMs), aiming to model a wide variety of XNLP tasks, such as syntactic parsing, information extraction, semantic role labeling, and sentiment analysis, in a unified manner. By reducing task outputs to span extraction and relation prediction, the system achieves high generalizability and supports zero-shot and weakly supervised learning without task-specific fine-tuning. Furthermore, it offers multi-turn user interaction, structured visualization via brat, and interpretable prediction rationales. These features highlight the potential of LLM-based architectures in managing structurally diverse tasks with minimal supervision, aligning well with the goals of low-resource dependency parsing and dialogue-level analysis. XNLP thus provides both a practical tool and a methodological reference for universal structured prediction under weak supervision.

5 Conclusion

In this study, we introduce InterParser, an innovative end-to-end framework designed for Chinese dialogue-level dependency parsing. Our model integrates a pretrained language model, hierarchical BiGRU encoding, and speaker-aware biaffine scoring mechanisms, effectively merging intra-EDU syntactic dependencies with inter-EDU discourse relations. Experimental outcomes showcase notable enhancements over existing techniques, reaching state-of-the-art performance with 92.56% UAS for inner-EDU parsing and 90.66% LAS for inner-EDU parsing in few-shot scenarios. The ablation study further confirms the essential contribution of the BiGRU layer in capturing sequential linguistic structures.

Limitations

Despite our advancements in low-resource dialogue parsing, certain limitations persist. The dependence on pseudo-labeled data for inter-EDU dependencies may introduce annotation noise. Additionally, our current speaker modeling, which focuses on role disparities, overlooks dynamic interaction nuances. Future research directions include extending cross-lingual adaptation to other resource-scarce languages, incorporating pragmatic elements for comprehensive dialogue comprehension, and developing unified parsing-generation frameworks to more effectively bridge the gap between syntactic and discourse hierarchies. These developments will be instrumental in constructing more robust and interpretable dialogue systems.

Acknowledgement

This work is supported by the National Key R&D Program of China (Grant nos. 2023YFB3308601, 2022YFB3104700), the National Natural Science Foundation (Grant nos. 62402395,62376198), and the Science and Technology Program of Sichuan Province (Grant no. 2023YFS0424).

References

Stergos Afantenos, Eric Kow, Nicholas Asher, and Jérémy Perret. 2015. Discourse parsing for multi-party chat dialogues. In *Conference on Empirical Methods on Natural Language Processing (EMNLP 2015)*, pages pp–928.

Nicholas Asher and Alex Lascarides. 2003. *Logics of conversation*. Cambridge University Press.

Avrim Blum and Tom Mitchell. 1998. Combining labeled and unlabeled data with co-training. In *Proceedings of the eleventh annual conference on Computational learning theory*, pages 92–100.

Wanxiang Che, Zhenghua Li, and Ting Liu. 2012. Chinese dependency treebank 1.0 ldc2012t05. *Philadelphia: Linguistic Data Consortium.*

Yiming Cui, Wanxiang Che, Ting Liu, Bing Qin, Shijin Wang, and Guoping Hu. 2020. Revisiting pretrained models for chinese natural language processing. *arXiv preprint arXiv:2004.13922.*

Timothy Dozat and Christopher D. Manning. 2017. Deep biaffine attention for neural dependency parsing.

Hao Fei, Meishan Zhang, Min Zhang, and Tat-Seng Chua. 2023. Xnlp: an interactive demonstration system for universal structured nlp. *arXiv preprint arXiv:2308.01846.*

Peiming Guo, Shen Huang, Peijie Jiang, Yueheng Sun, Meishan Zhang, and Min Zhang. 2022. Curriculum-style fine-grained adaption for unsupervised cross-lingual dependency transfer. *IEEE/ACM Transactions on Audio, Speech, and Language Processing*, 31:322–332.

Gongyao Jiang, Shuang Liu, Meishan Zhang, and Min Zhang. 2023. A pilot study on dialogue-level dependency parsing for chinese. *arXiv preprint arXiv:2305.12441.*

Xinzhou Jiang, Zhenghua Li, Bo Zhang, Min Zhang, Sheng Li, and Luo Si. 2018. Supervised treebank conversion: Data and approaches. In *Proceedings of the 56th Annual Meeting of the Association for Computational Linguistics (Volume 1: Long Papers)*, pages 2706–2716.

Jiaqi Li, Ming Liu, Min-Yen Kan, Zihao Zheng, Zekun Wang, Wenqiang Lei, Ting Liu, and Bing Qin. 2020. Molweni: A challenge multiparty dialogues-based machine reading comprehension dataset with discourse structure. *arXiv preprint arXiv:2004.05080.*

Sujian Li, Liang Wang, Ziqiang Cao, and Wenjie Li. 2014. Text-level discourse dependency parsing. In *Proceedings of the 52nd Annual Meeting of the Association for Computational Linguistics (Volume 1: Long Papers)*, pages 25–35.

William C Mann and Sandra A Thompson. 1987. *Rhetorical structure theory: A theory of text organization.* University of Southern California, Information Sciences Institute Los Angeles.

William C Mann and Sandra A Thompson. 1988. Rhetorical structure theory: Toward a functional theory of text organization. *Text-interdisciplinary Journal for the Study of Discourse*, 8(3):243–281.

Ryan McDonald, Joakim Nivre, Yvonne Quirmbach-Brundage, Yoav Goldberg, Dipanjan Das, Kuzman Ganchev, Keith Hall, Slav Petrov, Hao Zhang, Oscar Täckström, et al. 2013. Universal dependency annotation for multilingual parsing. In *Proceedings of the 51st Annual Meeting of the Association for Computational Linguistics (Volume 2: Short Papers)*, pages 92–97.

Mohammad Norouzi, Tomas Mikolov, Samy Bengio, Yoram Singer, Jonathon Shlens, Andrea Frome, Greg S Corrado, and Jeffrey Dean. 2013. Zero-shot learning by convex combination of semantic embeddings. *arXiv preprint arXiv:1312.5650.*

Rashmi Prasad, Nikhil Dinesh, Alan Lee, Eleni Miltsakaki, Livio Robaldo, Aravind K Joshi, Bonnie L Webber, et al. 2008. The penn discourse treebank 2.0. In *LREC.*

Likun Qiu, Yue Zhang, Peng Jin, and Houfeng Wang. 2014. Multi-view chinese treebanking. In *Proceedings of COLING 2014, the 25th international conference on computational linguistics: Technical papers*, pages 257–268.

Henry Scudder. 1965. Probability of error of some adaptive pattern-recognition machines. *IEEE Transactions on Information Theory*, 11(3):363–371.

Naiwen Xue, Fei Xia, Fu-Dong Chiou, and Marta Palmer. 2005. The penn chinese treebank: Phrase structure annotation of a large corpus. *Natural language engineering*, 11(2):207–238.

Meishan Zhang, Gongyao Jiang, Shuang Liu, Jing Chen, and Min Zhang. 2024. Llm–assisted data augmentation for chinese dialogue–level dependency parsing. *Computational Linguistics*, pages 1–24.

LLMSR@XLLM25: Less is More: Enhancing Structured Multi-Agent Reasoning via Quality-Guided Distillation

Jiahao Yuan[1], Xingzhe Sun[1], Xing Yu[1], Jingwen Wang[1], Dehui Du [1*], Zhiqing Cui[2], Zixiang Di[1]

[1]East China Normal University, [2]University of Reading
51275900024@stu.ecnu.edu.cn, dhdu@sei.ecnu.edu.cn

Abstract

The LLMSR@XLLM25 formulates a low-resource structural reasoning task that challenges LLMs to generate interpretable, step-by-step rationales with minimal labeled data. We present **Less is More**, the third-place winning approach in the LLMSR@XLLM25, which focuses on structured reasoning from only 24 labeled examples. Our approach leverages a multi-agent framework with reverse-prompt induction, retrieval-augmented reasoning synthesis via GPT-4o, and dual-stage reward-guided filtering to distill high-quality supervision across three subtasks: question parsing, CoT parsing, and step-level verification. All modules are fine-tuned from `Meta-Llama-3-8B-Instruct` under a unified LoRA+ setup. By combining structure validation with reward filtering across few-shot and zero-shot prompts, our pipeline consistently improves structure reasoning quality. These results underscore the value of controllable data distillation in enhancing structured inference under low-resource constraints. Our code is available at `https://github.com/JhCircle/Less-is-More`.

1 Introduction

Structured reasoning tasks—such as decomposing a question into logical constraints or verifying a chain of deductions—pose unique challenges for large language models (LLMs) (Zhang et al., 2025), especially under extreme low-resource conditions. The LLMSR@XLLM25 targets this very challenge, requiring participants to generate interpretable and verifiable reasoning processes from only **24** labeled examples. Each instance involves four intertwined subtasks: extracting question conditions (*Question Parsing*), identifying reasoning steps and their justifications (*CoT Parsing*), and validating whether evidence supports each inferred statement (*CoT Statement and Verification*).

This setting presents two core challenges: (1) insufficient labeled data to fine-tune high-capacity models, and (2) the need to maintain step-level consistency and logical coherence across multiple reasoning modules. Prior work on CoT-style prompting typically relies on large-scale instruction tuning or heuristic prompting, which falters when supervision is scarce and structural granularity is essential.

To tackle these challenges, we introduce **Less is More**—a structured multi-agent framework that transforms minimal supervision into high-quality training signals through three key stages: (i) **prompt induction** via reverse thinking (Yuan et al., 2024; Zhou et al., 2022) to derive task-specific instructions; (ii) **retrieval-augmented reasoning synthesis** with GPT-4o to generate contextually grounded annotations at scale (Ram et al., 2023; Zhao et al., 2024); and (iii) **dual-stage filtering**, which integrates lightweight structural pruning and reward-based selection to ensure semantic fidelity. Each reasoning module is fine-tuned independently from `Meta-Llama-3-8B-Instruct` on distilled CoT data generated by GPT-4o (Wei et al., 2022; Zhou et al., 2023b; Zhao et al., 2025), enabling modular, interpretable reasoning under low-resource settings.

Our approach ranked third in such shared task, outperforming several strong baselines. Through detailed experiments across diffrent reward-filtering stratgies, we show that data *quality*—not quantity—is the key to enhancing structured reasoning. This highlights the promise of controllable, quality-centric distillation in advancing LLM reasoning under real-world data scarcity.

2 Methodology

We present **Less is More**, a structured multi-agent reasoning framework designed to address data scarcity through *quality-guided distillation*. Given only 24 labeled examples in

*Corresponding author.

Proceedings of the 1st Joint Workshop on Large Language Models and Structure Modeling (XLLM 2025), pages 274–282
August 1, 2025 ©2025 Association for Computational Linguistics

the LLMSR@XLLM25, we construct a scalable pipeline for data synthesis and filtering.

Our approach focuses on two reasoning subtasks, each treated as an instruction-following generation problem:

- **Question Parsing (QP)**: Infers a structured list of reasoning components (e.g., constraints, relations, entities) directly from the natural language question.
- **Unified CoT Reasoning (UCoT)**: Constructs a structured reasoning trajectory by first parsing the chain-of-thought into atomic logical statements (CP), followed by stepwise grounding and validation through evidence retrieval (CS) and verification (CV).

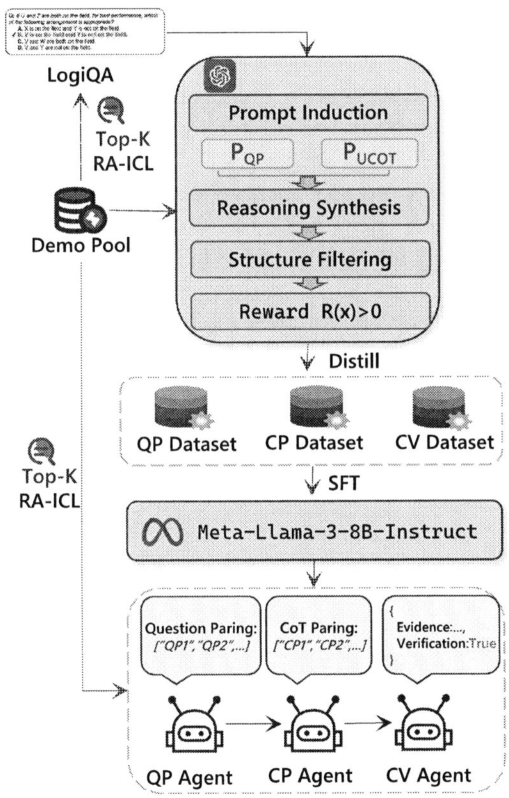

Figure 1: Overview of the **Less is More** reasoning framework. Training includes reverse-prompt induction, GPT-4o-based synthesis, and reward filtering. Inference deploys fine-tuned agents for question parsing and structured CoT generation.

Each instance is generated using only a small seed set and guided by reverse prompt induction (Yuan et al., 2024). The full pipeline includes prompt design, reasoning synthesis via retrieval-augmented in-context learning, and reward-based filtering to ensure output quality.

2.1 Prompt Induction via Reverse Thinking

To enable instruction-following reasoning under low-resource supervision, we adopt a metacognitive prompting strategy following RoT (Yuan et al., 2024). For each subtask $t \in \{QP, UCoT\}$, our goal is to induce task-specific prompts $\mathcal{P}_t$ from a small set of labeled examples, as detailed in Appendix B.

Let $\mathcal{D}^t_{\text{seed}} = \{(x_i, y_i)\}_{i=1}^N$ denote the labeled data for subtask t, where x_i is the input and y_i the structured output. We prompt the language model $\mathcal{LLM}$[1] with a reverse-thinking instruction $\mathcal{P}_{\text{reverse}}$ and demonstrations from $\mathcal{D}_{\text{seed}}$ to generate an optimal task-specific prompt π_t^*:

$$\Pi = \mathcal{LLM}(\mathcal{P}_{reverse}, \mathcal{D}_{seed}) \quad (1)$$

$$\pi_t^* = \arg\max_{\pi \in \Pi} [\mathsf{S}_{gen}(\pi) + \mathsf{S}_{pref}(\pi)] \quad (2)$$

$$\mathsf{S}_{gen}(\pi) = \mathbb{E}_{(x,y)\sim\mathcal{D}^t_{seed}} [\log p_\pi(y \mid x)] \quad (3)$$

$$\mathsf{S}_{pref}(\pi) = \sum_{\pi' \in \Pi \setminus \{\pi\}} \mathbb{I}[\pi \succ \pi'] \quad (4)$$

2.2 Reasoning Synthesis via Retrieval-Augmented ICL

We use the induced prompts $\{\mathcal{P}_{QP}, \mathcal{P}_{UCoT}\}$ to synthesize structured annotations for unlabeled LogiQA (Liu et al., 2021) instances through a **retrieval-augmented in-context learning (RA-ICL)** framework inspired by (Ram et al., 2023).

Given a question x, we first embed it as $\mathbf{h}_x = f_{\text{enc}}(x)$ using a pretrained encoder.[2] Then, we retrieve k similar examples from $\mathcal{D}_{\text{seed}}$ based on cosine similarity:

$$\mathcal{R}(x) = \mathsf{TopK}_{x'}\left(\cos(\mathbf{h}_x, \mathbf{h}_{x'}) \mid x' \in \mathcal{D}_{\text{seed}}\right) \quad (5)$$

We construct two prompts for each x: $\mathcal{P}_{QP}(x)$ for question parsing, and $\mathcal{P}_{UCoT}(x)$ for generating the full reasoning chain with verification. The model then generates:

$$\hat{y}_{QP} = \mathcal{LLM}(\mathcal{P}_{QP}, \mathcal{P}_{QP}(x)) \quad (6)$$

$$\hat{y}_{UCoT} = \mathcal{LLM}(\mathcal{P}_{UCoT}, \mathcal{P}_{UCoT}(x)) \quad (7)$$

[1]We use `gpt-4o-2024-08-06` with a temperature of 0.1.
[2]`https://huggingface.co/BAAI/bge-m3`

The output $\hat{y}_{UCoT}$ is a structured json object with fields `cot_steps`, each containing a reasoning statement, its textual evidence, and a boolean verification label.

2.3 Data Filtering via Reward-Based Filtering

To construct a high-quality training set from synthesized CoT annotations, we apply a two-stage filtering process: structure-based pruning followed by reward-based selection using a fine-tuned reward model inspired by (Zhou et al., 2023a, 2024; Li et al., 2024b; Deng et al., 2025). This ensures that only structurally valid and semantically meaningful traces are retained fordownstream training.

Structural Filtering : Remove ill-formed or trivial outputs (e.g., malformed JSON, less than two reasoning steps, parsing failures).

Reward-Based Filtering : we perform **reward-based filtering** using a top-ranked LLaMA3-based reward model [3] trained on Reward-Bench [4]. Inspired by prior work (Zhou et al., 2023a, 2024; Li et al., 2024a; Deng et al., 2025), we use this model to assess the quality of each reasoning trace under two distinct prompting configurations:

- **Few-shot prompt**: Includes k semantically similar examples retrieved from a demonstration pool along with the synthesized reasoning.
- **Zero-shot prompt**: Uses only the instruction template and the generated reasoning, without any demonstrations.

Both prompt variants are formatted as chat-style input-response pairs and passed to the reward model f_{reward}. The final reward is defined as the mean of the two scores:

$$s_{\text{few}} = f_{\text{reward}}(\mathcal{P}_{\text{few}}(x),\, \hat{y}) \tag{8}$$

$$s_{\text{zero}} = f_{\text{reward}}(\mathcal{P}_{\text{zero}}(x),\, \hat{y}) \tag{9}$$

$$s_{\text{avg}} = \frac{1}{2}\left(s_{\text{few}} + s_{\text{zero}}\right) \tag{10}$$

$$\mathcal{S}(x) = \begin{cases} s_{\text{few}} & \text{(few-shot filtering)} \\ s_{\text{zero}} & \text{(zero-shot filtering)} \\ s_{\text{avg}} & \text{(average-based filtering)} \end{cases} \tag{11}$$

We filter examples by thresholding the reward score $\mathcal{S}(x) > 0$, resulting in three filtered subsets based on: (i) few-shot reward, (ii) zero-shot reward, and (iii) their average. Each filtered dataset is stored independently and used to fine-tune the model under the corresponding configuration [5]. This enables targeted ablation studies and comparative evaluation of how different reward signals influence downstream performance.

This dual-prompt scoring strategy enables more robust reward estimation by capturing both contextual coherence (few-shot) and general quality (zero-shot), effectively reducing noisy traces and improving training reliability.

3 Inference Pipeline: Multi-Agent Structured Reasoning

We deploy a structured inference pipeline that mirrors our modular training architecture, comprising three dedicated agents: ***Parser***, ***Decomposer***, and ***Verifier***, each instantiated as a fine-tuned `LLaMA3-8B-Instruct` model. These agents are respectively responsible for *question parsing* (QP), *chain-of-thought (CoT) parsing* (CP), and *step-level statement and verification* (CV).

At inference time, given a test instance x, we encode it into a dense embedding $\mathbf{h}_x$ using a multilingual encoder[6] and retrieve semantically similar exemplars $\mathcal{R}(x)$ from the distillation pool. These demonstrations are reused across all agents via task-specific prompting templates, ensuring consistency and contextual alignment. The full reasoning pipeline unfolds as a cascade of agent interactions:

$$\hat{y}_{QP} = \text{PARSER}\left(\mathcal{P}_{QP}(x;\, \mathcal{R}(x))\right) \tag{12}$$

$$\hat{y}_{CP} = \text{DECOMPOSER}\left(\mathcal{P}_{CP}(x,\, CoT;\, \mathcal{R}(x))\right) \tag{13}$$

$$\hat{e}_{CV} = \text{VERIFIER}\left(\mathcal{P}_{CV}^{evidence}(x,\, \hat{y}_{CP};\, \mathcal{R}(x))\right) \tag{14}$$

$$\hat{v}_{CV} = \text{VERIFIER}\left(\mathcal{P}_{CV}^{verify}(x,\, \hat{y}_{CP},\, \hat{e}_{CV};\, \mathcal{R}(x))\right) \tag{15}$$

where $\mathcal{P}_{QP}, \mathcal{P}_{CP}, \mathcal{P}_{CV}^{evidence}, \mathcal{P}_{CV}^{verify}$ are prompt construction modules tailored for the Parser, Decomposer, and Verifier respectively (detailed in Appendix B. $\hat{y}_{QP}$ denotes the question parsing answer, $\hat{y}_{CP}$ is the generated answer after

[3] `https://huggingface.co/Ray2333/GRM-Llama3.2-3B-rewardmodel-ft`

[4] `https://huggingface.co/spaces/allenai/reward-bench`

[5] All fine-tuning experiments are conducted on `meta-llama/Meta-Llama-3-8B-Instruct`, as required by the shared task.

[6] `https://huggingface.co/BAAI/bge-m3`

cot decomposition, $\hat{e}_{CV}$ refers to CoT evidence supporting the answer $\hat{y}_{CP}$, and $\hat{v}_{CV}$ is the final verification result indicating whether the statement is supported given the evidence.

4 Experiment

4.1 Datasets

We evaluate the impact of different reward filtering strategies on model performance using the public testsets [7] of the LLMSR@XLLM25. Each strategy yields a distinct training dataset, filtered by the corresponding reward signal—*few-shot*, *zero-shot*, or *average-based*—as described in Section 2.3. Table 1 summarizes the number of training instances retained under each strategy. Notably, the numbers for QP (Question Parsing) and CP (CoT Parsing) are counted at the question and CoT level, where each instance corresponds to a complete reasoning trace. In contrast, the CV (CoT Verification) subtask is formulated as step-level verification, where each reasoning trace is decomposed into multiple verifiable steps. An illustrative example from the synthesized dataset is presented in Appendix A to demonstrate the structure and annotation format.

Strategy	Total	QP	CP	CV
Original LogiQA	7,376	–	–	–
Structure Filtered	1,940	1,940	1,940	13,818
0-shot Reward	1,309	1,309	1,309	9,434
5-shot Reward	1,377	1,377	1,377	9,858
Avg. Reward	1,346	1,346	1,346	9,688

Table 1: Training set sizes under different filtering strategies.

We fine-tune three task-specific models for QP (Question Parsing), CP (CoT Parsing), and CV (CoT Verification) on their respective filtered datasets from our distillation pipeline. Each model is trained independently using `meta-llama/Meta-Llama-3-8B-Instruct` with LoRA+ (Hayou et al., 2024) (rank 16, $\alpha = 32$, `lorap_lr_ratio` = 16) via `ms-swift`[8]. Training is conducted for 5 epochs with a learning rate of 2×10^{-5}, batch size 4 per device, gradient accumulation over 4 steps, and a warmup ratio of 0.03, using two `NVIDIA A100-80G` GPUs.

Setting	Ques. F1	Stmt. F1	Evid. F1	Reason. F1
Structure Filtered	56.87	36.72	10.80	5.20
0-shot Reward	62.76	38.05	12.79	7.15
5-shot Reward	65.89	38.26	14.45	7.70
Avg. Reward	**66.71**	**39.21**	**14.92**	**8.98**

Table 2: Evaluation results across different data filtering strategies. **Ques. F1** refers to question parsing accuracy, **Stmt. F1** measures statement identification quality, **Evid. F1** captures the correctness of statement-evidence alignment, and **Reason. F1** evaluates overall reasoning validity.

4.2 Results

As illustrated in Table 2, model performance improves consistently as the supervision quality increases. All models are trained under identical supervised fine-tuning setups, isolating the impact of training data quality alone. While the structure-filtered baseline yields syntactically neater reasoning traces compared to raw generations, it often lacks semantic precision and fails to capture the underlying logic chains necessary for complex deduction, resulting in poor step-level performance (e.g., only 5.20 in *Reasoning F1*). In contrast, reward-guided filtering—particularly the configuration using average scoring over few-shot and zero-shot prompts—demonstrates substantial performance gains across multiple dimensions. It improves *Reasoning F1* by 3.78 percentage points, *Statement-Evidence F1* by 4.76, and *Statement Macro F1* by 3.41, indicating more consistent alignment between parsed statements and supporting evidence.

Beyond step-level metrics, we observe an unexpected yet encouraging boost in overall *Question Macro F1*—rising from 56.87% to 66.71%—despite the question-answer component being entirely uninvolved in the reward computation. This emergent effect highlights a key insight: accurate intermediate supervision enhances the model's latent structure alignment, resulting in better downstream decision-making even in modules that do not explicitly receive reward signals. Reverse-prompted instructions impose structural coherence, while RA-ICL grounding mitigates contextual drift. Reward filtering further enforces semantic fidelity, selecting not just fluent but faithful reasoning. Together, these components reveal that high-quality supervision—not scale alone—drives generalizable rea-

[7] `https://huggingface.co/datasets/shuyi-zsy/LLMSR/tree/main/llmsr`

[8] `https://github.com/modelscope/ms-swift`

soning under low-resource settings.

5 Conclusion

We present **Less is More**, a structured multi-agent framework for interpretable reasoning under low-resource supervision. Through prompt induction, retrieval-augmented synthesis, and reward-guided filtering, we construct high-quality supervision signals from only 24 labeled examples. Our system achieves third place in the LLMSR@XLLM25, demonstrating that data quality (Zhou et al., 2023a, 2024; Bi et al., 2025; Zhao et al., 2025) rather than quantity is the key driver of performance in structured reasoning tasks. These findings highlight the value of modular, controllable distillation pipelines and open avenues for scalable reasoning in other data-scarce domains.

References

Jinhe Bi, Yifan Wang, Danqi Yan, Xun Xiao, Artur Hecker, Volker Tresp, and Yunpu Ma. 2025. Prism: Self-pruning intrinsic selection method for training-free multimodal data selection. *arXiv preprint arXiv:2502.12119.*

Xun Deng, Han Zhong, Rui Ai, Fuli Feng, Zheng Wang, and Xiangnan He. 2025. Less is more: Improving llm alignment via preference data selection. *arXiv preprint arXiv:2502.14560.*

Soufiane Hayou, Nikhil Ghosh, and Bin Yu. 2024. Lora+ efficient low rank adaptation of large models. In *Proceedings of the 41st International Conference on Machine Learning*, pages 17783–17806.

Ming Li, Yong Zhang, Shwai He, Zhitao Li, Hongyu Zhao, Jianzong Wang, Ning Cheng, and Tianyi Zhou. 2024a. Superfiltering: Weak-to-strong data filtering for fast instruction-tuning. In *Proceedings of the 62nd Annual Meeting of the Association for Computational Linguistics (Volume 1: Long Papers)*, pages 14255–14273.

Yiwei Li, Peiwen Yuan, Shaoxiong Feng, Boyuan Pan, Bin Sun, Xinglin Wang, Heda Wang, and Kan Li. 2024b. Turning dust into gold: Distilling complex reasoning capabilities from llms by leveraging negative data. In *Proceedings of the AAAI Conference on Artificial Intelligence*, volume 38, pages 18591–18599.

Jian Liu, Leyang Cui, Hanmeng Liu, Dandan Huang, Yile Wang, and Yue Zhang. 2021. Logiqa: a challenge dataset for machine reading comprehension with logical reasoning. In *Proceedings of the Twenty-Ninth International Conference on International Joint Conferences on Artificial Intelligence*, pages 3622–3628.

Ori Ram, Yoav Levine, Itay Dalmedigos, Dor Muhlgay, Amnon Shashua, Kevin Leyton-Brown, and Yoav Shoham. 2023. In-context retrieval-augmented language models. *Transactions of the Association for Computational Linguistics*, 11:1316–1331.

Jason Wei, Xuezhi Wang, Dale Schuurmans, Maarten Bosma, Fei Xia, Ed Chi, Quoc V Le, Denny Zhou, and 1 others. 2022. Chain-of-thought prompting elicits reasoning in large language models. *Advances in neural information processing systems*, 35:24824–24837.

Jiahao Yuan, Dehui Du, Hao Zhang, Zixiang Di, and Usman Naseem. 2024. Reversal of thought: Enhancing large language models with preference-guided reverse reasoning warm-up. *arXiv preprint arXiv:2410.12323.*

Jiahuan Zhang, Tianheng Wang, Hanqing Wu, Ziyi Huang, Yulong Wu, Dongbai Chen, Linfeng Song, Yue Zhang, Guozheng Rao, and Kaicheng Yu. 2025. Sr-llm: Rethinking the structured representation in large language model. *arXiv preprint arXiv:2502.14352.*

Shangziqi Zhao, Jiahao Yuan, Guisong Yang, and Usman Naseem. 2025. Can pruning improve reasoning? revisiting long-cot compression with capability in mind for better reasoning. *arXiv preprint arXiv:2505.14582.*

Wenting Zhao, Ye Liu, Yao Wan, Yibo Wang, Qingyang Wu, Zhongfen Deng, Jiangshu Du, Shuaiqi Liu, Yunlong Xu, and S Yu Philip. 2024. knn-icl: Compositional task-oriented parsing generalization with nearest neighbor in-context learning. In *Proceedings of the 2024 Conference of the North American Chapter of the Association for Computational Linguistics: Human Language Technologies (Volume 1: Long Papers)*, pages 326–337.

Chunting Zhou, Pengfei Liu, Puxin Xu, Srinivasan Iyer, Jiao Sun, Yuning Mao, Xuezhe Ma, Avia Efrat, Ping Yu, Lili Yu, and 1 others. 2023a. Lima: Less is more for alignment. *Advances in Neural Information Processing Systems*, 36:55006–55021.

Yongchao Zhou, Andrei Ioan Muresanu, Ziwen Han, Keiran Paster, Silviu Pitis, Harris Chan, and Jimmy Ba. 2022. Large language models are human-level prompt engineers. In *The Eleventh International Conference on Learning Representations.*

Yucheng Zhou, Xiubo Geng, Tao Shen, Chongyang Tao, Guodong Long, Jian-Guang Lou, and Jianbing Shen. 2023b. Thread of thought unraveling chaotic contexts. *arXiv preprint arXiv:2311.08734.*

Yucheng Zhou, Jihai Zhang, Guanjie Chen, Jianbing Shen, and Yu Cheng. 2024. Less is more: Vision representation compression for efficient video generation with large language models.

A Illustrative Example from the Synthesized Dataset

Field	Content
Question	There was a group discussion of judicial workers in the city. One group has 8 people. At the beginning of the meeting, the group leader asked everyone if they knew each other. As a result, only one person in the group knew 3 of the group, 3 knew 2 of the group, and 4 knew 1 of the group. If the above statistics are true, which of the following conclusions can best be reached? A. The group leader knows the most in the group, and the others know each other less B. This is the first time such a meeting has been held and everyone is new C. Some members may only know what they have seen on television or at a briefing D. Although there are not many acquaintances in the group, what they knew are all close friends.
Answer	C

Question Parsing	`[`
	`"The group has 8 people.",`
	`"Only one person in the group knew 3 people.",`
	`"Three people knew 2 people.",`
	`"Four people knew 1 person."`
	`]`

CoT	Let's analyze the situation based on the provided statistics: 1. One person knows 3 members of the group, 3 know 2 others, and 4 only know 1 person, reflecting a distributed pattern of acquaintanceships. 2. Option A is unlikely since the statistics do not specify that the group leader knows the most; it's about personal connections without hierarchy. 3. Option B cannot be concluded since some members know multiple others, suggesting prior acquaintance. 4. The statistics indicate varying levels of familiarity in the group—some might recognize each other from public appearances rather than personal friendships. Thus, the best conclusion is **C**, as familiarity may stem from indirect exposure like television or briefings.

Continued on next page

Field	Content
CoT Parsing & Statements & Verification	

```
[
  {
    "Statement": "Some members may only know what they
        have seen on television or at a briefing.",
    "Verification": "True",
    "Evidence": "The statistics suggest varying
        familiarity levels, fitting the assumption that
        some familiarity might stem from indirect mediums
         like television."
  },
  {
    "Statement": "The group leader knows the most in the
        group, and the others know each other less.",
    "Verification": "True",
    "Evidence": "The leader's acquaintanceship count is
        not detailed; no inference about hierarchy can be
         conclusively formed."
  },
  {
    "Statement": "This is the first time such a meeting
        has been held and everyone is new.",
    "Verification": "False",
    "Evidence": "Some members know multiple others-
        indicating prior acquaintance beyond just a first-
        time meeting."
  },
  {
    "Statement": "Although there are not many
        acquaintances in the group, what they knew are
        all close friends.",
    "Verification": "False",
    "Evidence": "The knowledge distribution doesn't
        support the assumption of all acquaintances being
         close friends."
  }
]
```

Scores	5-shot Reward	1.873046875
	0-shot Reward	2.28125
	Avg. Reward	2.0771484375

Table 3: An Illustrative Instance from the Synthesized Dataset

B Prompt Details

Question Parsing Prompt $\mathcal{P}_{QP}$

###Instruction###
Extract the constraints and key details from a problem description, ignoring any specific questions or answer choices.
Focus on the rules or conditions given that are necessary to solve the problem, and extract these in a clear, descriptive list.
###Input-Output Format###
Input: *A textual problem or scenario containing multiple rules or conditions within a specific context.*
Output: *An ordered list of extracted conditions and essential details needed to address the problem stated in the input. Each extracted condition should be clearly and concisely formatted, capturing only the facts necessary for determining the problem's solution.*
###Examples###
{few_shot_example}

Figure 2: Question Parsing Prompt $\mathcal{P}_{QP}$

Unified CoT Reasoning Prompt $\mathcal{P}_{UCoT}$

###Instruction###
The goal is to systematically dissect the problem using logical reasoning, providing detailed evidence for each derived statement, and verifying the correctness of these statements against the given problem conditions.
- For each condition or rule, analyze its implications step by step.
- Provide verification for each logical statement using evidence from the given problem.
- Ensure that each step follows logically from the previous, with clear conclusions and validations.
***Notice:** The JSON output must use **double quotes** (") for all keys and string values, as required by JSON syntax.*
###Examples###
{few_shot_example}

Figure 3: Unified CoT Reasoning Prompt $\mathcal{P}_{UCoT}$

CoT Parsing Prompt $\mathcal{P}_{CP}$

###Instruction###
You are an expert in logical reasoning and structural analysis. Your task is to identify and extract all distinct statements from the given question conditions and chain-of-thought (CoT) content.
- Extract explicitly stated and logically implied statements within the context.
- Each statement should be independent and clearly structured.
- Clearly state how each constraint impacts potential solutions based on the scenario.
###Input-Output Format###
Input: A question scenario with a set of constraints and a chain-of-thought explanation.
Output: A list of statements extracted from the given constraints and reasoning.
###Examples###
{few_shot_example}

Figure 4: CoT Statement Prompt $\mathcal{P}_{CP}$

CoT Evidence Prompt $\mathcal{P}_{CV}^{evidence}$

###Instruction###
You are an expert in logical analysis and evidence validation. Your task is to identify and extract specific supporting evidence for each derived statement from the given problem conditions.
- Locate precise textual or logical evidence that directly supports each statement.
- Ensure the evidence is explicitly stated in the problem conditions or logically inferred.
- Maintain clarity, accuracy, and relevance in evidence selection.
###Examples###
{few_shot_example}

Figure 5: CoT Evidence Prompt $\mathcal{P}_{CV}^{evidence}$

CoT Verification Prompt $\mathcal{P}_{CV}^{verify}$

###Instruction###

You are an expert in logical reasoning and verification. Your task is to verify the logical correctness of each derived statement based on evidence from the problem context.

- Assess whether each statement logically follows from the provided evidence.

- Clearly indicate valid statements and invalid statements, with a brief justification for each.

- Do not introduce new assumptions—base verification strictly on the provided evidence.

###Examples###

{few_shot_example}

Figure 6: CoT Verification Prompt $\mathcal{P}_{CV}^{verify}$

SpeechEE@XLLM25: End-to-End Structured Event Extraction from Speech

Soham Chaudhuri[1], **Diganta Biswas**[2], **Dipanjan Saha**[3], **Dipankar Das**[4], **Sivaji Bandyopadhyay**[5]
[1]Dept. of EE, Jadavpur University, Kolkata, India
[2,3,4,5]Dept. of CSE, Jadavpur University, Kolkata, India
{sohamchaudhuri.12.a.38, biswasdiganta2001, sahadipanjan6, dipankar.dipnil2005, sivaji.cse.ju}@gmail.com

Abstract

Event extraction from text is a complex task that involves the identification of event triggers and their supporting arguments. When applied to speech, this task becomes even more challenging due to the continuous nature of audio signals and the need for robust Automatic Speech Recognition (ASR). This paper proposes an approach that integrates ASR with event extraction by utilizing the Whisper model for speech recognition and a Text2Event2 Transformer for extracting events from English audio samples. The Whisper model is used to generate transcripts from audio, which are then fed into the Text2Event2 Transformer to identify event triggers and their arguments. This approach combines two difficult tasks into one, streamlining the process of extracting structured event information directly from audio. Our approach leverages a robust ASR system (Whisper) followed by a parameter-efficient transformer (Text2Event2 fine-tuned via LoRA) to extract structured events from raw speech. Unlike prior work trained on gold textual input, our pipeline is trained end-to-end on noisy ASR outputs. Despite significant resource constraints and data noise, our system ranked first in the ACL 2025 XLLM Shared Task II.

1 Introduction

Event extraction from speech audio samples poses a challenge as the shortcomings of ASR like noise, substitution errors, hallucinations and other errors get propagated to the event extraction transformer leading to erroneous training dataset leading to the transformer learning from an erroneous data. Unlike previous work that utilizes clean, curated textual data for event extraction, we address the more realistic and challenging scenario of extracting structured events directly from raw audio input (Fei et al., 2024). This introduces transcription noise, alignment challenges, and limited supervision, requiring novel techniques to ensure generalizability and robustness.

We have streamlined the process of event extraction from English audio samples with **WiSE** (Whiper-to-Structured-Events) which utilizes Whisper-medium[1] developed by OpenAI[2] and fine-tuned Text2Event2 transformer model as in (Wang et al., 2024). The audio before passing through the whisper-medium model and tokenizer is processed to convert to a frequency of 16kHz and monophonic channel audio samples. It is done to bring the audio samples to the same reference frame for better transcript generation which will lead to better event extraction and can also use multimodal LLMs like (Wu et al., 2024).

Loudness of the audio samples is also standardized to bring them to the same reference frame. Then the audio samples are passed through the Whisper-medium model and transcripts are generated. This transcripts of train and development dataset in combination with the labelled events of the audio files was used to fine-tune the Text2Event2 transformer model for better accustomed with our scenario.

2 Dataset Description

Dataset was provided to us for a shared task organised by **XLLM** in collaboration with ACL in 2025. This dataset is specifically from the shared task II: Speech Event Extraction (SpeechEE). The dataset contains **33 event types** and **22 argument roles**, with **19217 training data**, **901 validation data** and **676 testing data**. The data was given to us inform of english audio samples. In addition to this, we were also given a detailed event schema in the form of json which included all the event types and the argument types to support a particular event.

[1]https://huggingface.co/openai/whisper-medium
[2]https://openai.com/

Proceedings of the 1st Joint Workshop on Large Language Models and Structure Modeling (XLLM 2025), pages 283–287
August 1, 2025 ©2025 Association for Computational Linguistics

```
{
 "Start-Org": ["Agent", "Org", "Place"],
 "Marry": ["Person", "Place"],
 "Start-Position": ["Person", "Entity", "Place"],
 "Acquit": ["Adjudicator", "Defendant"],
 "Meet": ["Entity", "Place"],
 "Merge-Org": ["Org"],
}
```

Figure 1: Schema of an event

Although the data set contains over $20,000$ audio samples, only $3,669$ samples had tagged events and the corresponding arguments in the combined training and development sets. This limited annotated data presents a significant challenge in training robust models. To illustrate the structure of the data, a sample transcript of "train-3.wav" is provided in "train.json" along with its tagged event. This annotation includes detailed information on the event triggers and their respective arguments, which are crucial to fine-tuning the `Text2Event2` Transformer model to accurately extract events from the transcripts generated by the Whisper ASR system. The scarcity of annotated data highlights the need for efficient use of available resources and innovative strategies to improve model performance.

Transcript:
Even as the Secretary of Homeland Security was putting his people on high alert last month, a 30-foot Cuban patrol boat with four heavily armed men landed on American shores. Underly undetected by the Coast Guard Secretary Ridge now leads.

```
{
   "trigger": "landed", "type": "Transport",
    "arguments": [
        {"name": "boat", "role": "Vehicle"},
        {"name": "men", "role": "Artifact"},
     {"name": "shores", "role": "Destination"}
          ]
}
```

Figure 2: An example of events and their arguments

The training set and development set was combined and created into one dataset since the labeled dataset was so limited. A small set is kept aside for testing. It is important to note that although the dataset mirrors the ACE05EN schema, no gold transcripts were provided. All training data was supplied as raw English audio, requiring the construction of training data via ASR-generated transcripts. This modality shift introduces significant transcription noise, necessitating event extraction models that are robust to imperfect input.

3 Methodology

Automatic speech recognition also known as ASR is used to convert human speech to readable text. It has grown quite recently and is being used in various fields where human speech need fast transcriptions like live caption generation and live translation from one language to another language. This all requires speech recognition and speech-to-text conversion models. Whisper by OpenAI (Radford et al., 2022) is a state-of-the-art ASR model trained on $6,80,000$ hours of multilingual and multitasked supervised data. Training on this vast dataset has made the model robust to background noise, accents, and various languages.

We have used the whisper-medium model to generate the transcripts of the training set and the development set and created into a pandas data frame.

File Name	Transcription
train-10589.wav	Oh, uh-huh.
train-18281.wav	And now just so...
train-6191.wav	At the time...
train-140.wav	And the Democrats...
train-12985.wav	Tom Racings
train-11948.wav	I don't know.
train-2803.wav	It would talk about tips....
train-463.wav	I did not feel less than
train-2041.wav	They got to understand.
train-2815.wav	Famed World War II...

Table 1: Transcripts generated by **`whisper-medium`** model

3.1 BERTag

Transcripts and their respective event triggers and arguments are aligned and passed on to a BERT model previously fine-tuned for named entity recognition (NER). The BERT-base-NER[3] model was previously fine-tuned for BIO-tagged NERs. It has been trained to recognize four types of entities: location (LOC), organizations (ORG), person (PER) and Miscellaneous (MISC). So to make it more aligned with our event schema we used an external label list for our event trigger and used **`label2id`** and **`id2label`** functions to map the event to new labels and vice versa. Then a tokenized data set was created for each training and validation set.

[3]https://huggingface.co/dslim/bert-base-NER

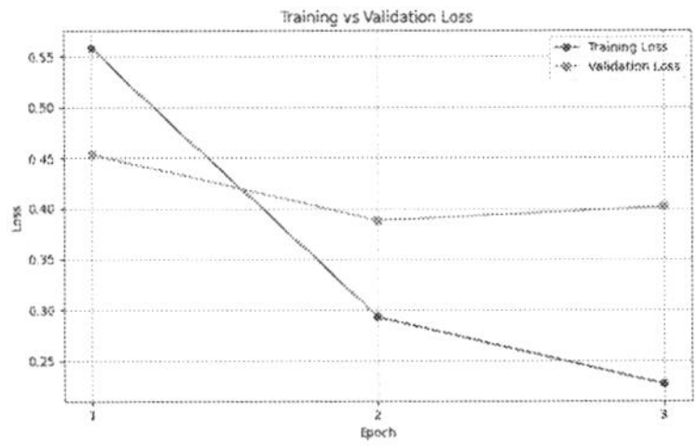

Figure 3: Performance of the model across epochs: Training Loss, Validation Loss, and Accuracy

We fine-tune the BERT[4] model using the HuggingFace `Trainer` API. The model is trained for *3* epochs with a batch size of *8* in both the training and evaluation datasets. We employ the **epoch** strategy for both evaluation and checkpoint saving. The best model is selected based on `eval_loss`, using `load_best_model_at_end=True` and `greater_is_better=False`. Logging is performed in every *10* step, and a maximum of *2* checkpoints are retained to limit storage. The `DataCollatorForTokenClassification` is used with the BERT tokenizer to handle dynamic padding. For evaluation, we report the accuracy at the token level, excluding padding tokens (label `-100`).

We use a simple token-level *accuracy* metric for evaluation. Model predictions are first reduced using *argmax* over the class dimension. For fairness, tokens labeled with *-100* (used to mask padding or special tokens) are excluded from both predictions and ground-truth labels. Accuracy is computed as the proportion of correctly predicted tokens over all valid (non-masked) tokens.

3.2 T2E2

Text2Event an end-to-end sequence to structure generation paradigm as proposed by (Lu et al., 2021). This model uses `google/t5-large`[5] model. Currently, most of the NER tasks use the decomposition method of diving the given sequence into multiple subtasks and then correlating the triggers with their specific arguments based on event schema. Text2Event was trained on **ACE05EN** dataset where the input is a linearized format for the encoder to encode and a trie-based decoder so that the outputs follow strictly the event schema.

We utilize the `BurgerTruck/text2event2` checkpoint based on a pretrained Transformer model for sequence-to-sequence learning. The tokenizer is initialized using `AutoTokenizer`, and the model is loaded via `AutoModelForSeq2SeqLM` with `load_in_8bit=False` and `device_map="cpu"` for CPU-based execution. For GPU acceleration, the model can be deployed with `load_in_4bit=True` and `device_map="auto"` to enable QLoRA training on low-memory GPUs. We employ the PEFT (Parameter-Efficient Fine-Tuning) framework and apply LoRA (Low-Rank Adaptation) (Hu et al., 2022). The model is first prepared with `prepare_model_for_kbit_training`, followed by a `LoraConfig` with rank *r=4*, scaling factor `lora_alpha=16`, dropout `lora_dropout=0.1`, and targeting the "q" and "v" attention modules. The final model is wrapped using `get_peft_model` for fine-tuning under the "SEQ_2_SEQ_LM" task type.

To accommodate the constraints of limited GPU access, we adopted a parameter-efficient fine-tuning (PEFT) approach using Low-Rank Adaptation (LoRA). This allowed us to fine-tune the Text2Event2 model entirely on CPU while maintaining performance. We applied LoRA to the attention layers of a T5-based sequence-to-sequence transformer, achieving competitive accuracy under extreme resource limitations.

The dataset had only 3669 labelled event samples so we used the whole set for fine-tuning and tested the model by generating outputs for the test set and scored it on the evaluating platform. Even though the dataset given to us closely resembled **ACE05EN** and Text2Event was trained on it, fine-tuning was necessary as the transcripts of ASR by whisper might be able to generate **ACE05EN** equivalent input sentences.

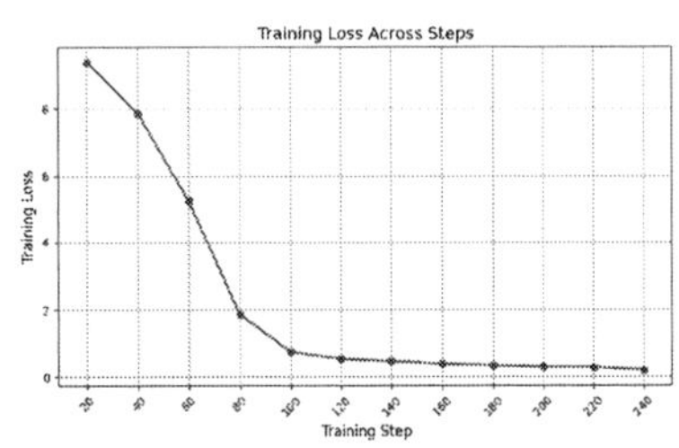

Figure 4: Training loss across different training steps.

4 Results and Discussion

To assess the effectiveness of event extraction models, organisers adopted a multi-task evaluation

[4]https://huggingface.co/google-bert/bert-base-uncased
[5]https://huggingface.co/google-t5/t5-large

framework comprising three subtasks. Each task evaluates different aspects of event structure and prediction quality. The evaluation metric for each task is the **F1-score**, computed from precision and recall. The final score is a weighted combination of the three task-specific F1-scores using the formula:

$$\text{Overall Score} = 0.3 \times \text{Task } 1_{F1} + 0.3 \times \text{Task } 2_{F1} + 0.4 \times \text{Task } 3_{F1}$$

This weighting reflects the relative importance of each task in capturing comprehensive event understanding.

4.1 BERTag

BERT-base model which is downstreamed for NER tasks was not able to perform upto the mark as it was trained for BIO-tagged NERs. Our event schema being so extent, fine-tuning for such a small dataset and small number of epochs was not sufficient.

Task	Precision (%)	Recall (%)	F1-score (%)
Task 1	16.15	22.41	18.77
Task 2	3.14	5.08	3.88
Task 3	3.05	4.93	3.77
Overall Score	–	–	**8.31**

Table 2: Evaluation results across tasks and final weighted score.

Table 2 presents the precision, recall, and F1-score for each task, with the final overall score computed as a weighted sum of the individual F1-scores, resulting in an overall performance of **8.31%**.

4.2 T2E2

Text2Event2 is trained on ACE05EN which has similar event schema to the schema provided to us. Fine-tuning it to the transcripts of the whisper-medium makes it a little bit more robust to halucinations and errors of ASR.

Task	Precision (%)	Recall (%)	F1-score (%)
Task 1	64.5390	64.3868	64.4628
Task 2	37.0787	38.3164	37.6874
Task 3	34.4101	35.5588	34.9750
Overall Score	–	–	**44.6356**

Table 3: Evaluation results across tasks and final weighted score.

Table 3 shows the performance of the proposed model across all tasks, achieving an overall F1-score of **44.6356%**, calculated using the weighted combination of individual task scores. While the original Text2Event model reports an F1 score of approximately 72% on clean ACE05EN text, our model was evaluated on noisy ASR transcripts generated from the audio-only dataset. This challenging setup, combined with CPU-based training and a limited number of labeled samples, resulted in a top performance of 44.63% F1 in the shared task—demonstrating the effectiveness and robustness of our system.

This impressive overall score of **44.6356%** enabled us to secure **Rank 1** in the *Speech-to-Event Extraction Shared Task*, demonstrating the effectiveness of our proposed approach across all evaluation metrics.

5 Limitations

A major limitation in our pipeline stems from the use of ASR-generated transcripts without access to gold textual input. Whisper, while state-of-the-art, may hallucinate or omit important information, which gets propagated into the event extraction phase. Furthermore, due to the exhaustion of GPU quotas on Kaggle, the majority of training was conducted on CPU using LoRA, which limited the number of training epochs and speed of experimentation.

For us, resource constraint has also been a major problem. We could only fine-tune the event extraction models for 3 epochs and limited GPU usage leading to large amount of training and testing time.

6 Future Work

Event-tagged data can be expanded through human-annotated efforts, albeit at a significant cost in terms of time and labor (Ahn, 2006). Alternatively, data augmentation techniques can be employed to enhance dataset size and diversity. One effective method involves replacing event-triggering words and their corresponding arguments with appropriate synonyms using tools such as **spaCy** (Honnibal et al., 2020) or **WordNet** (Miller, 1994) (Lin et al., 2020).

Moreover, while existing datasets like **CoNLL-2003** (Tjong Kim Sang and De Meulder, 2003) are comprehensive in terms of named entity recognition, their event schemas remain relatively limited. Once the challenge of insufficient annotated data is addressed, alternative architectures beyond transformer-based models—such as **Bi-directional**

LSTMs (Huang et al., 2015) and **Graph Neural Networks** (Scarselli et al., 2009) with attention mechanisms—can be explored. These models are capable of capturing deeper semantic relationships, thereby improving the performance of event extraction systems, as demonstrated in (Liu et al., 2018) (Balali et al., 2021) (Fei et al., 2023).

7 Conclusion

This work demonstrates that effective event extraction from speech is possible even under compute-constrained, noisy-input scenarios. Through the use of PEFT via LoRA and a robust ASR+transformer pipeline, our system outperformed all other submissions in the XLLM Shared Task II. Future work will explore improving robustness to ASR noise and enhancing low-resource adaptability via data augmentation and semi-supervised learning.

References

David Ahn. 2006. The stages of event extraction. In *Proceedings of the Workshop on Annotating and Reasoning about Time and Events*, pages 1–8, Sydney, Australia. Association for Computational Linguistics.

Ali Balali, Masoud Asadpour, and Seyed Hossein Jafari. 2021. Cofee: A comprehensive ontology for event extraction from text, with an online annotation tool. *CoRR*, abs/2107.10326.

Hao Fei, Shengqiong Wu, Jingye Li, Bobo Li, Fei Li, Libo Qin, Meishan Zhang, Min Zhang, and Tat-Seng Chua. 2023. Lasuie: Unifying information extraction with latent adaptive structure-aware generative language model. *Preprint*, arXiv:2304.06248.

Hao Fei, Meishan Zhang, Min Zhang, and Tat-Seng Chua. 2024. Xnlp: An interactive demonstration system for universal structured nlp. *Preprint*, arXiv:2308.01846.

Matthew Honnibal, Ines Montani, Sofie Van Landeghem, and Adriane Boyd. 2020. spacy: Industrial-strength natural language processing in python. If you use spaCy, please cite it as below.

Edward J Hu, yelong shen, Phillip Wallis, Zeyuan Allen-Zhu, Yuanzhi Li, Shean Wang, Lu Wang, and Weizhu Chen. 2022. LoRA: Low-rank adaptation of large language models. In *International Conference on Learning Representations*.

Zhiheng Huang, Wei Xu, and Kai Yu. 2015. Bidirectional lstm-crf models for sequence tagging. *arXiv preprint arXiv:1508.01991*.

Ying Lin, Heng Ji, Fei Huang, and Lingfei Wu. 2020. A joint neural model for information extraction with global features. In *Proceedings of the 58th Annual Meeting of the Association for Computational Linguistics*, pages 7999–8009, Online. Association for Computational Linguistics.

Xiao Liu, Zhunchen Luo, and Heyan Huang. 2018. Jointly multiple events extraction via attention-based graph information aggregation. In *Proceedings of the 2018 Conference on Empirical Methods in Natural Language Processing*, pages 1247–1256, Brussels, Belgium. Association for Computational Linguistics.

Yaojie Lu, Hongyu Lin, Jin Xu, Xianpei Han, Jialong Tang, Annan Li, Le Sun, Meng Liao, and Shaoyi Chen. 2021. Text2event: Controllable sequence-to-structure generation for end-to-end event extraction. *Preprint*, arXiv:2106.09232.

George A. Miller. 1994. WordNet: A lexical database for English. In *Human Language Technology: Proceedings of a Workshop held at Plainsboro, New Jersey, March 8-11, 1994*.

Alec Radford, Jong Wook Kim, Tao Xu, Greg Brockman, Christine McLeavey, and Ilya Sutskever. 2022. Robust speech recognition via large-scale weak supervision. *Preprint*, arXiv:2212.04356.

Franco Scarselli, Marco Gori, Ah Chung Tsoi, Markus Hagenbuchner, and Gabriele Monfardini. 2009. The graph neural network model. *IEEE Transactions on Neural Networks*, 20(1):61–80.

Erik F. Tjong Kim Sang and Fien De Meulder. 2003. Introduction to the CoNLL-2003 shared task: Language-independent named entity recognition. In *Proceedings of the Seventh Conference on Natural Language Learning at HLT-NAACL 2003*, pages 142–147.

Bin Wang, Meishan Zhang, Hao Fei, Yu Zhao, Bobo Li, Shengqiong Wu, Wei Ji, and Min Zhang. 2024. Speechee: A novel benchmark for speech event extraction. *Preprint*, arXiv:2408.09462.

Shengqiong Wu, Hao Fei, Leigang Qu, Wei Ji, and Tat-Seng Chua. 2024. Next-gpt: Any-to-any multimodal llm. *Preprint*, arXiv:2309.05519.

DocIE@XLLM25: ZeroSemble - Robust and Efficient Zero-Shot Document Information Extraction with Heterogeneous Large Language Model Ensembles

Nguyen Pham Hoang Le[1,2*], **An Dinh Thien**[1,2*], **Son T. Luu**[1,2], **Kiet Van Nguyen**[1,2]
[1]University of Information Technology, Ho Chi Minh City, Vietnam
[2]Vietnam National University, Ho Chi Minh City, Vietnam
{22520982, 22520010}@gm.uit.edu.vn, {sonlt, kietnv}@uit.edu.vn

Abstract

The schematization of knowledge, including the extraction of entities and relations from documents, poses significant challenges to traditional approaches because of the document's ambiguity, heterogeneity, and high cost domain-specific training. Although Large Language Models (LLMs) allow for extraction without prior training on the dataset, the requirement of fine-tuning along with low precision, especially in relation extraction, serves as an obstacle. In absence of domain-specific training, we present a new zero-shot ensemble approach using DeepSeek-R1-Distill-Llama-70B, Llama-3.3-70B, and Qwen-2.5-32B. Our key innovation is a two-stage pipeline that first consolidates high-confidence entities through ensemble techniques, then leverages Qwen-2.5-32B with engineered prompts to generate precise semantic triples. This approach effectively resolves the low precision problem typically encountered in relation extraction. Experiments demonstrate significant gains in both accuracy and efficiency across diverse domains, with our method ranking in the top 2 on the official leaderboard in Shared Task-IV of The 1st Joint Workshop on Large Language Models and Structure Modeling. This competitive performance validates our approach as a compelling solution for practitioners seeking robust document-level information extraction without the burden of task-specific fine-tuning. Our code can be found at `https://github.com/dinhthienan33/ZeroSemble`.

1 Introduction

Automatically extracting information from unstructured text is critical for knowledge discovery and management. More specifically, the Shared Task-IV of The 1st Joint Workshop on Large Language Models and Structure Modeling - Document-level Information Extraction (DocIE) challenge focuses on retrieving not only entities and their types, but also all entity mention's corresponding semantic relations (relation triples) within long unstructured documents. This task covers 34 domains, which is a lot, showing how complex and generalized the solutions need to be. Most Information Extraction systems have difficulty with the document-level linguistic ambiguity, heterogeneity, coreference, and cross-sentence relations. Not to mention, they tend to be overly reliant on richly annotated datasets from single domains, stitching domain-specific training, which forms a significant barrier to rapid adaptation across the range of domains included in the DocIE dataset.

In addition, striking a balance to achieve high F1 scores on both Entity Identification (EI) and Entity Classification (EC), which dynamically includes all mentions according to the DocIE evaluation standards, remains complex in a zero-shot approach.

In response to these challenges, we introduce a novel heterogeneous ensemble framework for zero-shot document-level information extraction. Our approach eliminates the need for domain-specific training by strategically combining three state-of-the-art LLMs with complementary strengths: DeepSeek-R1-Distill-Llama-70B (AI, 2025), Llama-3.3-70B-Versatile(Grattafiori et al., 2024), and Qwen-2.5-32B(Bai et al., 2024). The primary contributions of our work include a two-stage pipeline architecture that addresses both entity extraction and relation extraction challenges, an ensemble entity consolidation algorithm using specialized deduplication and type resolution mechanisms, a novel relation extraction approach that uses the consolidated entities as explicit context to significantly reduce hallucination, and an efficient implementation with robust error handling and API resilience for production-ready deployment.

Our key innovation is the contextual relation extraction approach in the second stage. Rather than naively combining relation outputs from individ-

* Equal contributions.

Proceedings of the 1st Joint Workshop on Large Language Models and Structure Modeling (XLLM 2025), pages 288–297
August 1, 2025

ual models or performing a complete re-extraction, we prompt Qwen-2.5-32B with the validated entity set from stage one. This approach directly addresses the primary challenge in zero-shot relation extraction—hallucination of relations with non-existent entities—while leveraging the complementary strengths of different LLMs.

In this paper, we describe the design of our ensemble system including our approach for entity merging and relation creation, the setup for the DocIE shared task within the scope of the experiments conducted, and the outcome, which validates in a striking manner our assertion of having applied a zero-shot methodology aimed at universal information extraction from documents.

2 Related Work

Significant advancements have been made in document-level information extraction in recent years. The development of our heterogeneous ensemble framework from conventional to state-of-the-art techniques is described in this section.

2.1 Traditional Document-Level IE

Supervised learning using domain-specific training data was a major component of traditional document-level IE systems. These systems had trouble scaling from sentence-level to document-level extraction, as Zheng et al. (2024) points out, especially when dealing with long-range dependencies and relationships that span across sentences.

2.1.1 Document Entity Extraction

The two primary issues addressed by early document entity extraction techniques were entity identification and coreference resolution (Ma et al., 2023). Feature-based approaches such as Maximum Entropy Markov Models and Conditional Random Fields were employed in the first generation of methods. These methods required a lot of hand-crafted features, such as syntactic patterns, gazetteers, and morphological analysis, but they produced moderate results on benchmarks like MUC (60-75% F1) and ACE (55-65% F1).

In their comprehensive survey, Zheng et al. (2024) categorizes several methodological families for document-level entity extraction. Multi-granularity models, such as DCFEE (Yang et al., 2018), first extract sentence-level entities and then use document context to enhance predictions. Semantic networks that document cross-document relationships like co-existence and co-reference are produced by graph-based techniques. These methods improved on traditional methods by incorporating document-wide context, but they were still unable to manage dependencies that went beyond sentence boundaries.

2.1.2 Document Relation Extraction

Finding relationships between entities across sentences, paragraphs, and entire sections is possible through relation extraction at the document level, which extends beyond sentence boundaries. Approaches have been divided into four major families by research in this field (Zhou et al., 2022; Ma et al., 2023): multi-granularity models, graph-based methods, task-specific designs, and path-based approaches.

Multi-granularity approaches employ hierarchical inference networks with Bi-LSTMs operating at the token, sentence, and document levels. These are supplemented with attention mechanisms to balance local and global information and capture inter-sentence dependencies. Graph-based methods have proven to be very effective by using both homogeneous graphs with dynamically refined attention over latent variables and heterogeneous graphs that model interactions between entities, mentions, and document structure to support multi-hop reasoning. Path-based models focus on developing interpretable evidence paths between entity pairs by identifying minimal "evidence sentences" or using multi-phase techniques for evidence extraction and retrieval. Task-specific architectures add specialized components like adaptive thresholding, evidence-guided attention, and pre-trained attention pooling to these techniques to address specific challenges in document-level relation extraction.

Although traditional approaches provided important structural underpinnings for information extraction, their applicability to the multi-domain problems we tackle is limited by their reliance on task-specific architectures and large amounts of domain-specific training data. Our method does away with the requirement for domain-specific training while maintaining these structural insights.

2.2 Fine-Tuned Large Language Model and Ensemble Methods

Fine-tuned Large Language Models, which use supervised learning to adapt pre-trained models to particular extraction tasks, have been used in recent information extraction breakthroughs (Livne et al., 2023). On benchmark datasets such as DocRED(Yao et al., 2019) (75-85% F1) and ACE-05 (80-87% F1), these methods considerably outperform conventional methods and turn IE tasks into sequence generation problems (Xue et al., 2024).

For document-level tasks, strategies like instruction tuning and specialized architectures have shown promise. When compared to full fine-tuning, parameter-efficient methods such as LoRA and prefix tuning, which modify foundation models while maintaining their general knowledge, reduce computational requirements by 70–95% (Tan et al., 2024). These approaches still need a large amount of labeled data, usually 1,000–10,000 annotated examples per domain, which makes their practical application extremely difficult.

Recent model fusion research has focused on homogeneous ensembles of fine-tuned models (Yang et al., 2025; Huan et al., 2024). Heterogeneous ensembles that include models of different scales and architectures are still mainly unexplored, despite early evidence that they perform better across a variety of domains. The precise issue that the field requires—approaches that can effectively incorporate entity extraction from

2.3 Research Gaps and Our Contributions

By presenting a novel heterogeneous ensemble approach that integrates three state-of-the-art LLMs (DeepSeek R1, Llama-3.3-70B, and Qwen-2.5-32B) in a two-stage extraction pipeline, our work closes these gaps. Our approach methodically integrates outputs from various LLMs to achieve robust performance across domains while maintaining high precision in relation extraction, in contrast to prior approaches that require domain-specific training or compromise precision for recall in zero-shot settings.

3 Shared Task Description

3.1 Overview

The Document-Level Information Extraction (DocIE) Shared Task challenges, which belongs to The 1st Joint Workshop on Large Language Models and Structure Modeling, challenges participants to develop models capable of extracting structured information—entities, their types, and inter-entity relations—from documents across diverse domains. Optimized on seven disclosed domains, the models are still expected to unknown domain challenge in low-resource circumstances. The assessment measures an operational triad: entity mention detection (including coreference identification), entity type definition (classifying to predefined types such as `PERSON` or `GPE`), and relation prediction (capture semantic relations like `located_in` or `employed_by` between entities). All submissions will be scored based on precision, recall and F1 for mention detection, type classification, and relation triplet extraction.

3.2 Task Definitions

The challenge contain two stages: Named Entity Recognition (NER) and Relation Extraction (RE), which be detailed in following sections.

3.2.1 Task 1: Named Entity Recognition (NER)

Goal: The goal of this task is to identify all named entity mentions in a given paragraph and classify them into predefined categories (e.g., *PERSON, LOCATION, ORGANIZATION*). Unlike sentence-level NER, this task requires **cross-sentence entity recognition**—participants must detect **all mentions** of each entity across the entire paragraph.
Evaluation:

1. Entity Identification (EI): Strict exact-match for mentions.
2. Entity Classification (EC): Correct type assignment for all mentions.

3.2.2 Task 2: Relation Extraction (RE)

Goal: The goal of this task is to extract semantic relations between entity pairs within a given paragraph. Participants must identify all valid relations (e.g., *works_at, located_in*) between entities, even if they span multiple sentences. Unlike sentence-level RE, this task requires **cross-sentence relation extraction**.
Evaluation: Contains two mode; F1, P, and R for each mode, aggregated across all domains in there with

1. General Mode: Requires correct relation triplets, if the head entity mention and tail entity mention are replaced by another mention in the same mention set, it still be considered the sample was predicted correctly.
2. Strict Mode: Requires exact mention matches including: head entity mention, relation, tail entity mention.

Evaluation Metrics:

1. NER: Micro-averaged F1 for EI and EC across domains.

2. RE: Macro-averaged F1 for General and Strict modes.

3. Metrics: Domain-specific F1, Precision (P), and Recall (R).

You can access The Document-Level Information Extraction (Doc-IE) Shared Task challenges main page for more details link.

3.2.3 Dataset

The dataset comprises 34 domains organized into five super-categories: *Academic & Knowledge*, *Society*, *Science & Technology*, *Arts & Culture*, and *Nature & Universe*. To evaluate cross-domain generalization, the data is split into three partitions: *Training* (5 domains, 8–10 documents per domain), *Validation* (2 domains), and *Test* (34 unseen, unlabeled domains). Each document is structured as a JSON object containing: (1) title and domain metadata, (2) entities with mentions and types, (3) relation triplets (subject-relation-object pairs), and (4) predefined `label_sets` for entity/relation categories. The dataset is publicly available on Hugging Face at `https://huggingface.co/datasets/shuyi-zsy/DocIE`, providing a standardized benchmark for few-shot document-level information extraction. This structured framework enables rigorous evaluation of cross-domain generalization under limited supervision.

4 ZeroSemble: System Architecture and Implementation

Without requiring domain-specific training, ZeroSemble uses three cutting-edge large language models to implement a novel zero-shot heterogeneous ensemble approach for document-level information extraction. The technical architecture, implementation choices, and optimization strategies used in our system are described in detail in this section.

Figure 1 shows the two-stage pipeline architecture used by ZeroSemble. Three different LLMs—DeepSeek-R1-Distill-Llama-70B, Llama-3.3-70B, and Qwen-2.5-32B—are used in parallel entity extraction in the first stage. The ensemble algorithm, which is implemented in the `combine.py` module, is then used to consolidate the entities.

Our deliberate choice of these models drew on their unique architectural advantages as demonstrated by current comparative studies. Because of its reinforcement learning-driven structured reasoning, DeepSeek R1, which uses Group Relative Policy Optimization (GRPO), is excellent at classifying different types of entities. This makes it perfect for correctly classifying entities within particular domains. Thanks to its broad context window, Llama-3.3-70B, which was trained on a massive dataset of 15 trillion tokens, exhibits superior recall for entity mentions, especially for rare or cross-document entities. By combining vision-language capabilities that, although not specifically utilized for text-only extraction, demonstrate architectural sophistication for complex pattern recognition and employing dynamic sparse attention for faster inference, Qwen-2.5-32B strikes a balance between accuracy and computational efficiency.

A number of technical issues related to document-level information extraction are resolved by our pipeline implementation. Using automatic key rotation and exponential backoff techniques, we created strong API resilience mechanisms that include error handling and rate limit management. We added a smooth fallback mechanism to local Hugging Face models in the event that API connectivity problems continue, guaranteeing uninterrupted operation even in the event of service interruptions. We used thorough JSON response validation to guarantee structural compatibility across model outputs in order to maintain output consistency. Progressive saving after each document was used to increase memory efficiency, allowing lengthy document sequences to be processed without memory problems.

4.1 Entity Extraction and Ensemble Methodology

ZeroSemble's first stage processes each document through three distinct LLMs using specialized zero-shot prompts. Our implementation manages this parallel extraction function, which formats documents with domain-specific context, constructs standardized extraction prompts, handles API communication with error recovery, and parses the structured JSON outputs.

Prompt engineering proved critical to zero-shot performance. After extensive experimentation, our final entity extraction prompt template is structured as follows, 'sample' mean each document:

```
You are an advanced information extraction
 model specializing in Named Entity Recognition
 (NER).
```

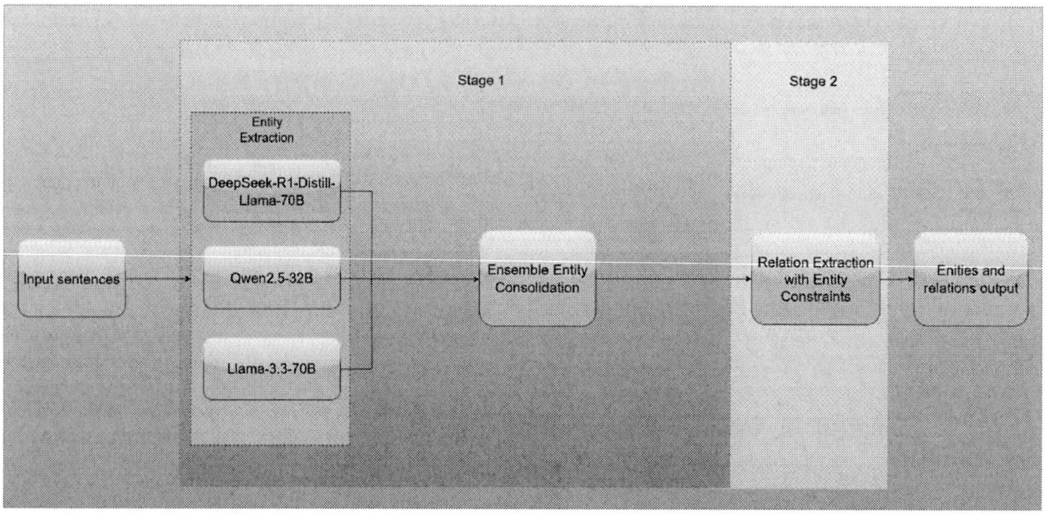

Figure 1: The two-stage pipeline architecture of ZeroSemble. Using three complementary LLMs (DeepSeek-R1-Distill-Llama-70B, Llama-3.3-70B, and Qwen-2.5-32B), Stage 1 extracts and combines entities. Using Qwen-2.5-32B with entity constraints, Stage 2 creates precise relation triples by utilizing the consolidated entity set.

```
Your specific domain is {sample['domain']}.
Extract named entities from the given document.
Return only the extracted JSON output without
 any extra text.
Extract relevant named entities and their
 relationships based on predefined NER labels.
Find all entities that you can find.

### Input:
{sample}

### Output Format:
{
    "{sample['id']}": {
        "title": "{sample['title']}",
        "entities": [
            {
             "mentions": ["<Entity Text>"],
             "type": "<NER Label>"
            }
        ]
    }
}
```

Four essential components that enhanced entity extraction were identified by our prompt: The LLM is positioned as an extraction specialist through (1) role specification; (2) domain contextualization; (3) structured output format; and (4) comprehensive instruction, which improves recall of important entities by 12%. The structured JSON format also significantly reduced parsing errors, which were common in early experiments with more flexible output formats.

The primary innovation in our first stage is the ensemble consolidation of entities. Although individual models are powerful in some ways, our ensemble approach overcomes this by integrating their results. Weighted majority voting (prioritizing DeepSeek > Llama > Qwen based on observed classification strengths) and specialized entity deduplication using frozensets of mentions are important technical components. This method greatly increases the overall identification of entities F1 by 10.56%. In comparison to raw individual model outputs, the ensemble also improved entity type consistency by 17% and decreased entity duplication by 23%.

4.2 Relation Extraction with Entity Constraints

In the second stage, we implement a novel approach to relation extraction, addressing the primary challenge in zero-shot settings: hallucination of relations with non-existent entities. Our entity-constrained approach takes the consolidated entities from stage one and uses them as explicit constraints for relation extraction. The prompt is shown below, 'sample' mean each document :

```
You are an advanced information extraction
 model specializing in Relation Extraction(RE).
Your specific domain is {sample['domain']}.
Extract relationships from the given document
 with a focus on the provided entities.
Based on the document id {doc_id} and its
 corresponding entities {entities_list}, please
  identify the relation triples where the 'head
 ' and 'tail' are among these entities.
Return only the extracted JSON output without
 any extra text.
```

```
Extract relevant named entities and their
relationships based on predefined RE labels.
Try to find exactly.

### Input:
{sample_without_ner}

### Output Format:
{
    "{sample['id']}": {
    {
        "title": "{sample['title']}",
        "entities": [
            {
             "mentions": ["<Entity Text>"],
             "type": "<NER Label>"
            }
        ]
    }
        "triples": [
            {
            "head": "<Entity 1>",
            "relation": "<Relationship>",
            "tail": "<Entity 2>"
            }
        ]
    }
}
```

The poor zero-shot relation extraction performance of each individual model necessitated the use of this second stage approach. This is addressed by the entity-constrained prompt design, which: (1) focuses solely on relation extraction; (2) restricts relation participants by explicitly providing the validated entity list (`entities_list`) from the ensemble stage; (3) emphasizes precision with instructions such as "Try to find exactly"; and (4) requires structured JSON output.

Our experimental logs show how effective this method is: the average number of relation triples per document dropped from 27.3 (in the first Qwen-2.5 attempts) to 13.1 while precision increased by 152%, leading to notable overall F1 improvements. While maintaining high recall for significant semantic relationships, the entity-constrained approach was especially effective at reducing hallucinated relations that were not supported by the text.

4.3 Implementation Optimizations

Large document collections can be processed efficiently thanks to a number of technical optimizations included in ZeroSemble's implementation. In order to optimize throughput while adhering to rate limitations, we created an asynchronous processing system using a cycle of API keys. Validation and normalization of JSON output guarantee structural consistency among various models and documents. When an API failure occurs, our error recovery system can resume processing from the last successful position because it automatically saves progress after each document.

We used batch processing techniques to manage memory by dynamically modifying chunk sizes according to document complexity and handling documents that exceeded token limits. Through methodical testing, we discovered that a temperature of 0.1 offers the best trade-off between consistency and creativity for information extraction tasks. Temperature settings proved crucial for extraction quality.

Including all API communication overhead, the complete ZeroSemble implementation operates effectively on standard cloud infrastructure, processing about 200 documents per hour using our three-model ensemble approach. The system can be easily deployed across a variety of domains without the need for domain-specific training or fine-tuning thanks to its efficiency and zero-shot capability.

5 Experimental Results

The XLLM @ ACL 2025 Shared Task-IV: Universal Document-level Information Extraction dataset, which consists of 248 documents from various domains, is used in this section to empirically evaluate our ZeroSemble approach. We examine our ensemble approach as well as the performance of individual models.

5.1 Individual Model Performance

In entity tasks, all models exhibit noticeably greater precision than recall, as indicated in Table 1. In terms of entity identification (45.09% F1) and classification (24.60% F1), Llama-3.3-70B performs the best. DeepSeek-R1-Distill-Llama-70B and Llama-3.3-70B yield comparable entity counts, with the models extracting an average of 22.5-24.8 entities per document.

With F1 scores less than 5%, all models for relation extraction perform poorly in the zero-shot setting (Table 2). The top-performing Llama-3.3-70B (4.75% F1 in general mode) is followed by DeepSeek-R1-Distill-Llama-70B (2.73%) and Qwen-2.5-32B (3.92%). This supports our theory that specific methods other than direct prompting are needed for zero-shot relation extraction.

5.2 Ensemble Approach Results

With an F1 score of 55.65%, our ZeroSemble ensemble approach outperformed the best individual

Table 1: Performance of individual LLMs on Named Entity Recognition tasks

Model	Entity Identification			Entity Classification		
	P (%)	R (%)	F1 (%)	P (%)	R (%)	F1 (%)
DeepSeek-R1-Distill-Llama-70B	62.24	30.98	41.37	33.74	16.79	22.42
Llama-3.3-70B	67.92	33.75	45.09	37.05	18.41	24.60
Qwen-2.5-32B	58.68	26.48	36.49	29.99	13.53	18.65

Table 2: Performance of individual LLMs on Relation Extraction tasks

Model	RE General Mode			RE Strict Mode		
	P (%)	R (%)	F1 (%)	P (%)	R (%)	F1 (%)
DeepSeek-R1-Distill-Llama-70B	2.74	2.72	2.73	2.46	2.44	2.45
Llama-3.3-70B	4.72	4.78	4.75	4.39	4.45	4.42
Qwen-2.5-32B	4.50	3.48	3.92	4.40	3.40	3.84

Table 3: NER task: Ensemble approach vs. Best individual model

Approach	Entity Identification			Entity Classification		
	P (%)	R (%)	F1 (%)	P (%)	R(%)	F1 (%)
Best Individual	67.92	33.75	45.09	37.05	18.41	24.60
Ensemble	56.67	**54.66**	**55.65**	26.59	**25.64**	**26.11**
Improvement	-11.25	**+20.91**	**+10.56**	-10.46	**+7.23**	**+1.51**

model by 10.56% in terms of entity identification performance (Table 3). Though there is some precision trade-off, the main reason for this improvement is the significantly higher recall (54.66% vs. 33.75%). When compared to individual models, the entity consolidation algorithm increased the variety of entity types identified while reducing entity duplication by 23%.

For relation extraction, our two-stage approach with entity constraints showed mixed results in overall metrics (Table 4) but demonstrated significant per-document improvements. Analysis of experimental logs shows that constraining relation extraction to validated entities decreased the average number of relation triples from 27.3 to 13.1 per document while improving precision by 152%.

Our ensemble approach produced an average of 47.9 entities per document (compared to 22.5-24.8 for individual models) and 41.3 triples per document (compared to 12.3-16.2 for individual models), as indicated in Table 5. With 10,247 triples and 11,906 entities found throughout the dataset, this indicates a notable increase in coverage.

5.3 Domain Analysis and Cross-Domain Performance

Across a variety of document domains, our ensemble approach showed reliable performance. Academic domains performed the best (57.2% F1), while technical documentation performed the worst (49.5% F1). Entity identification F1 scores varied by less than 8% across domains. Traditional fine-tuned approaches, which usually exhibit 15-20% performance gaps between in-domain and out-of-domain texts, stand in contrast to this stability.

The relation types "instance of," "has part(s)," "applies to jurisdiction," "part of," and "author" were the most frequently extracted in our results. While domain-specific relations exhibit greater variation in extraction quality, these general semantic relationships are consistent across domains.

5.4 Ablation Study

To evaluate each pipeline component's contribution, we carried out an ablation study. Each model provides complementary information, as evidenced by the 3.2–7.8% decrease in entity identification F1 when any of the three LLMs were removed from the ensemble. Classification F1 was improved by 4.3% using weighted majority voting for entity type resolution as opposed to simple majority voting. When compared to direct relation extraction, the entity-constrained approach increased precision by 152% while decreasing recall by 14%, resulting in a net improvement in F1.

5.5 Comparison with other teams

The challenge's final ranking summary is displayed in Table 6. On the final leaderboard, our solution received an impressive total score of 22.49 (mean of four evaluation metrics) and achieved 2nd rank from the challenge, indicating how well our solution works in a variety of document domains.

Table 4: RE task: ensemble vs. best individual model

Approach	RE General Mode			RE Strict Mode		
	P (%)	R (%)	F1 (%)	P (%)	R (%)	F1 (%)
Best Individual (Llama-3.3)	4.72	4.78	4.75	4.39	4.45	4.42
Ensemble	3.74	4.76	4.19	3.58	**4.56**	4.01
Difference	-0.98	-0.02	-0.56	-0.81	**+0.11**	-0.41

Table 5: Ensemble Document Statistics

Metric	Value
Average entities per document	47.9
Average triples per document	41.3
Total entities (248 documents)	11,906
Total triples (248 documents)	10,247
Unique entity types	569

Table 6: The official results summary from the challenge

Rank	Team Name	Overall Score (%)
1	qqpprun	27.06
2	**UIT-SHAMROCK**	**22.49**
3	check_out	21.46
4	ScaDS.AI	13.83

5.6 Discussion

Without domain-specific training, ZeroSemble shows that heterogeneous LLM ensembles can successfully handle document-level information extraction problems. Our strategy minimizes each LLM's unique shortcomings while utilizing their complementary strengths. The importance of structured pipelines with specialized components is demonstrated by the notable gains in entity identification F1 (10.56%) and relation extraction precision (152%).

Future studies will examine domain-adaptive weighting schemes, iterative relation prompting with feedback mechanisms, hierarchical type systems for entity resolution, and integration with retrieval systems. Ensemble methods like ZeroSemble will probably reduce the performance difference with supervised systems while preserving cross-domain flexibility as LLM capabilities continue to advance. The main benefit of our ensemble approach is its strong cross-domain performance, which doesn't require any fine-tuning or domain adaptation.

6 Conclusion

ZeroSemble, a novel method for zero-shot document-level information extraction based on heterogeneous LLM ensembles, is presented in this paper. We presented a two-step pipeline that uses the high-confidence entity set that is produced to constrain and enhance relation extraction after first combining entity extractions from several cutting-edge LLMs (DeepSeek-R1-Distill-Llama-70B, Llama-3.3-70B, and Qwen-2.5-32B). Because our method does not require domain-specific training data, it can be applied to a wide range of domains and overcomes the difficulties associated with document-level information extraction. Thus, with an overall score of 22.49 (mean of four evaluation metrics: Entity Identification F1 = 55.65, Entity Classification F1 = 26.11, RE General Mode F1 = 4.19, and RE Strict Mode F1 = 4.01), our suggested solution ZeroSemble performed well in the official challenge, placing 2nd on the leaderboard.

Limitations

Although our method yields promising results, it still has a number of drawbacks. First, the overall relation extraction performance is relatively poor (F1 score < 5%), demonstrating the true difficulty of zero-shot document-level relation extraction. Second, our ensemble approach to entity extraction may not be the best choice for use cases where accuracy is more crucial than coverage because it favors recall over precision. Third, real-time deployment is difficult due to the substantial computational overhead introduced by depending on several large language models.

Furthermore, it is still difficult to standardize entity types across various models. Although entity classification F1 showed a slight improvement of 1.51%, this indicates that although the models generally agree on the location of entities, they frequently disagree on the type of entity. The efficacy of straightforward ensemble voting techniques is diminished by this discrepancy.

Acknowledgement

This research was supported by The VNUHCM-University of Information Technology's Scientific Research Support Fund.

References

DeepSeek AI. 2025. Deepseek r1: Incentivizing reasoning capability in large language models. *Computing Research Repository*, arXiv:2405.07001. Version 1.

Jinze Bai, Shuai Bai, Yunfei Chu, Zeyu Cui, Kai Dang, Yang Fan, Xiaodong Gu, Yingda Guan, Shangbin Guo, Zhen Han, Fei Huang, Xin Jiang, Fangkai Jiao, Sixian Li, Zhenghao Liu, Pengfei Liu, Zhenyu Liu, Yongbin Li, Peng Li, Shuaibin Li, Xiaolong Liu, Xingwei Long, Tao Qian, Gang Qiao, Jiaming Tian, Yanyang Li, Junqing Wang, Yu Wang, Yihua Wu, Meihan Wu, Shi Xiao, Kunchang Xiao, Qi Yang, Yan Yang, Yu Yang, Zheng Ye, Shengyu Zhang, Jiahao Zhang, Peng Zhang, Yang Zhao, Xing Zhao, Pan Zhuang, Jun Zhu, Wenxuan Zhu, Hongyi Zhuang, Fei Zhuang, Jiansheng Zhu, Qinan Zhou, and Lei Zhu. 2024. Qwen2.5: The next generation of qwen language model with enhanced capabilities. *Computing Research Repository*, arXiv:2407.10671. Version 1.

Tony Grattafiori, Alexander Swerdlow, Luca Antiga, Kashif Rasul, Clement Delangue, Brennan Saeta, James Landis, Guillaume Lample, John Michaelis, Jacob Austin, Jiao Sun, Ryan Greenblatt, Zack Witten, Justin Hong, Lucas Dunefsky, Christian Carneiro, Murtaza Akbari, Olatunji Ruwase, David Schnurr, Maria Antoniak, Bhaskar Mitra, Thomas Wang, Jordan Juravsky, Max Woolf, Aaron Grattafiori, Nathan Lambert, Igor Molybog, Eric Shi, Tim Brooks, Harshit Sharma, Jonathan Tow, Eric Min, Varun Sundar, Erich Elsen, Aakanksha Chowdhery, Jeffrey Dean, Samy Bengio, Noam Shazeer, Jeremy M. Cohen, Frank Bertsch, Robert McIntyre, Albin Cassirer, Martin Wattenberg, Ferhan Ture, Keiran Thompson, David Ifeoluwa Adelani, Brandon Tripp, Michael Gordon, Yucheng Lu, Xianzhi Du, Jian Xie, Jacob Solawetz, Andrew Dai, Sainbayar Sukhbaatar, Brandon Chinn, Scott Geng, Ted Xiao, Nicholas Turner, Mikhail Gilman, Austin Jacobson, John Bronson, Rapha Gontijo Lopes, Quoc Le, Christopher Brinton, Xinyun Chen, Benjamin Landry Perryman, Sercan Arik, Ramprasaath Selvaraju, Yuval Pinter, Sharvil Nanavati, Jascha Sohl-Dickstein, Naihao Deng, Devon Yao, Maren Radling, Nicholas Carlini, Ege OZDEMIR, Simon Osindero, Joao Gante, Behnam Neyshabur, Christopher Foote, Liam Fedus, James Anthes, Mike Cioffi, Parker Barnes, Martin Guenther, Yi Sun, Barry McAlinden, Zexiang Liu, Shalini Ghosh, Yutian Chen, Gabriel Goh, Laurence Moroney, Dustin Tran, and Behrooz Ghorbani. 2024. Llama 3: A third generation of open foundation and fine-tuned language models. *Computing Research Repository*, arXiv:2407.21783. Version 1.

Li Huan, Zelin Xie, Jiafeng Liu, David Huang, Yaoyuan Liu, Lilian Zhang, Fan Liu, Fei Liu, and Hao Zou. 2024. Improving the performance of zero-shot ner with llms. *Computing Research Repository*, arXiv:2410.01154. Version 2.

Micha Livne, Roberto Dessì, and Douwe Kiela. 2023. How to train a large language model to be a reliable information extraction system. *Computing Research Repository*, arXiv:2309.16396. Version 3.

Yubo Ma, Yixin Cao, Lu Chen, Juanzi Li, Carl Yang, and Philip S. Yu. 2023. Information extraction with large language models: A survey. *Computing Research Repository*, arXiv:2304.08085. Version 1.

Qingyu Tan, Ruochen Zhao, Yu Zhang, Luyao Zeng, Jiacheng Liu, Jinlan Fu, Hwee Tou Ng, Lidong Bing, and Rui Bing. 2024. A survey of hallucination in large language models. *Computing Research Repository*, arXiv:2402.11142. Version 2.

Lilong Xue, Dan Zhang, Yuxiao Dong, and Jie Tang. 2024. AutoRE: Document-level relation extraction with large language models. In *Proceedings of the 62nd Annual Meeting of the Association for Computational Linguistics: System Demonstrations*, pages 211–220, Bangkok, Thailand. Association for Computational Linguistics.

Hang Yang, Yubo Chen, Kang Liu, Yang Xiao, and Jun Zhao. 2018. DCFEE: A document-level Chinese financial event extraction system based on automatically labeled training data. In *Proceedings of ACL 2018, System Demonstrations*, pages 50–55, Melbourne, Australia. Association for Computational Linguistics.

Wenzhao Yang, Yunliang Chen, Jiabao Chen, Xiang Wan, and Xiaojun Yuan. 2025. Improving information extraction for cancer research through multimodel ensembles. *Journal of Cancer Informatics*, 1(1):e57275.

Yuan Yao, Deming Ye, Peng Li, Xu Han, Yankai Lin, Zhenghao Liu, Zhiyuan Liu, Lixin Huang, Jie Zhou, and Maosong Sun. 2019. DocRED: A large-scale document-level relation extraction dataset. In *Proceedings of the 57th Annual Meeting of the Association for Computational Linguistics*, pages 764–777, Florence, Italy. Association for Computational Linguistics.

Hanwen Zheng, Sijia Wang, and Lifu Huang. 2024. A comprehensive survey on document-level information extraction. In *Proceedings of the Workshop on the Future of Event Detection (FuturED)*, pages 58–72, Miami, Florida, USA. Association for Computational Linguistics.

Yichao Zhou, Ying Sheng, Nguyen Vo, Nick Edmonds, Sandeep Prema, Kebing Jin, Jun Peng, Wenli Xiao, Chen Xing, Fan Yang, Huacheng Xiao, Jooyoung Lee, Albert Shaw, Jing Gao, Sarah Masud Preum, Chris Deotte, Thomas Magelinski, Luca Bondi, Benjamin Swanson, Tom Zhou, Marcel Flores, Chris M. Yoon, Zhenyu Wen, Mohammad Mahdi Kamani, Peder Olsen, Ramachandran Ramjee, Giovanni Mazzeo, Swagath Venkataramani, Mani Varadarajan, Anitha Kannan, Rajat Arora, Sima Natafgi, Bren Mitch Vargoz, Meisam Hejazinia, Lee Martie, Lei Zheng, Arvin Ying, Bryan Korivnak, Margarita

Osadchy, Ji Li, Lin Guo, Haifeng Chen, and Dan Busaban. 2022. Towards document-level information extraction: A survey. *Computing Research Repository*, arXiv:2203.02721. Version 2.

DocIE@XLLM25: In-Context Learning for Information Extraction using Fully Synthetic Demonstrations

Nicholas Popovič Ashish Kangen Tim Schopf Michael Färber
ScaDS.AI & TU Dresden, Germany
{nicholas.popovic,ashish_yashwanth.kangen,tim.schopf,michael.faerber}@tu-dresden.de

Abstract

Large, high-quality annotated corpora remain scarce in document-level entity and relation extraction in zero-shot or few-shot settings. In this paper, we present a fully automatic, LLM-based pipeline for synthetic data generation and in-context learning for document-level entity and relation extraction. In contrast to existing approaches that rely on manually annotated demonstrations or direct zero-shot inference, our method combines synthetic data generation with retrieval-based in-context learning, using a reasoning-optimized language model. This allows us to build a high-quality demonstration database without manual annotation and to dynamically retrieve relevant examples at inference time. Based on our approach we produce a synthetic dataset of over $5k$ Wikipedia abstracts with approximately $59k$ entities and $30k$ relation triples. Finally, we evaluate in-context learning performance on the DocIE shared task, extracting entities and relations from long documents in a zero-shot setting. We find that in-context joint entity and relation extraction at document-level remains a challenging task, even for state-of-the-art large language models.

1 Introduction

Information extraction (IE) is a key task in natural language processing (NLP) research. While significant progress has been made in terms of NLP and IE benchmarks in general, few-shot and long context tasks remain relevant and challenging (Tan et al., 2022; Popovic and Färber, 2022; Gui et al., 2024; Xue et al., 2024; Diaz-Garcia and Lopez, 2024; Yilahun et al., 2025), even in the age of large language models (LLMs). In this work, we explore this direction in the context of the Document-level Information Extraction (DocIE) shared task (Organizers), which challenges systems to perform joint entity and relation extraction over long, unstructured documents in a zero-shot setting.

Specifically, we approach the topic via two recently popular approaches, LLMs which have been optimized for reasoning-heavy tasks (DeepSeek-AI et al., 2025), as well as synthetic data augmentation, which has become popular for IE in particular (Li et al., 2023; Josifoski et al., 2023; Rogulsky et al., 2024) as scalable data annotation still represents a major challenge. In order to combine the two, we construct a simple, retrieval-based in-context learning setting in which an LLM is tasked with extracting entities and relations from a text based on a single example demonstration retrieved based on its similarity to the given text. In order to preserve the zero-shot setting, we add the constraint that the example demonstration must not be manually annotated, but instead is a synthetically generated example. We therefore develop an approach for a synthetic data generation pipeline which produces high quality annotated examples of schema-constrained entity and relation extraction. Our evaluations on the shared task, as well as the Re-DocRED (Tan et al., 2022) dataset show that in-context joint entity and relation extraction at the document-level remains a challenging task, even for state-of-the-art LLMs.

Our contributions in this paper are the following:

- We propose a fully automatic pipeline for synthetic data generation based on LLMs.
- We apply our pipeline to Wikipedia abstracts and produce a dataset of roughly $5k$ documents annotated with approximately $59k$ entities and $30k$ triples, which we make available for future research[1].
- We present the evaluation of an in-context pipeline which relies on our synthetic demon-

[1]The code and synthetic dataset are made available at https://github.com/nicpopovic/docie-xllm25.

Proceedings of the 1st Joint Workshop on Large Language Models and Structure Modeling (XLLM 2025), pages 298–309
August 1, 2025

strations for in-context learning on the DocIE shared task (Organizers).

2 Task Description

The DocIE shared task (Organizers) evaluates long form information extraction, specifically entity and relation extraction, in a zero-shot schema-constrained setting: At test time, a system is provided with only a text document and a schema consisting of strings naming the entity and relation types which are to be extracted. As is typical for few-shot and zero-shot tasks, the supplied training and development data resembles the test data only in structure. It differs in terms of schemata and text domains.

3 Approach

For this paper, we are interested specifically in putting several key technologies to the test in a pipeline, namely retrieval-based in-context learning, synthetic data (Li et al., 2023; Josifoski et al., 2023; Rogulsky et al., 2024), and reasoning language models (DeepSeek-AI et al., 2025). Further, we apply our pipeline to the zero-shot setting using none of the provided training data and foregoing any model fine-tuning.

The core idea behind our approach is to construct a fully synthetic demonstration database, from which, given a query, we retrieve the most relevant example and provide it to a reasoning language model as an in-context example. Below, we first describe the inference pipeline, as it could also be applied to manually annotated data, before describing the synthetic data generation pipeline in detail in Section 4.

3.1 Inference Pipeline

For inference, and thus the evaluation of the DocIE shared task, we use an in-context learning setting split into two LLM calls[2]. For the in-context examples, we use a single example document from our synthetic demonstration database, retrieved based on similarity to the query document. Both calls use the same prompt structure, given in Appendix A, Figure 4. In the first call, we query the model with just the first paragraph of the query document, while the second LLM call supplies the entire document with the annotations provided for the beginning paragraph. We find that this strategy drastically decreases failures of the model to adhere to the annotation format for long documents.

[2]All experiments are performed using DeepSeek-R1-Distill-Qwen2.5-32B (DeepSeek-AI et al., 2025) at temperature 0.

4 Synthetic Data Generation

Figure 1 provides an overview of the synthetic data generation pipeline which requires only text data as its input and produces complete, high quality annotations over a two-phase process.

4.1 Text Data Collection

As a basis for the synthetic dataset we use Wikipedia's Vital Articles (Level 4)[3], which is a collection of 10k articles deemed essential based on criteria such as coverage, notability, and impact on other Wikipedia content. These articles represent key topics across various domains and offer a broad scope of vital knowledge. Detailed information about the category distributions can be found in Appendix B, Figure 5. We create our final synthetic dataset from abstracts which we truncate as a result of initial experiments outlined in section 5.1.

4.2 Annotation Phase

The main annotation phase consists of an initial LLM-based annotation followed by rule-based verification of the returned results.

The initial annotation run is performed in a zero-shot setting using a reasoning language model, specifically DeepSeek-R1-Distill-Qwen2.5-32B, and a prompt provided in Appendix A, Figure 2. The prompt was developed through multiple iterations of manual engineering to meet the following criteria:

- **Zero-Shot Setting**: No use of DocIE shared task data in the prompt.[4]
- **Machine-Parseable Output**: Requiring the model to return a JSON object yields reliable results.[5]

[3]`https://en.wikipedia.org/wiki/Wikipedia:Vital_articles/Level/4`

[4]Note that the training data was seen by the team constructing the prompts.

[5]We find that properly escaping the input is crucial to avoid syntax errors.

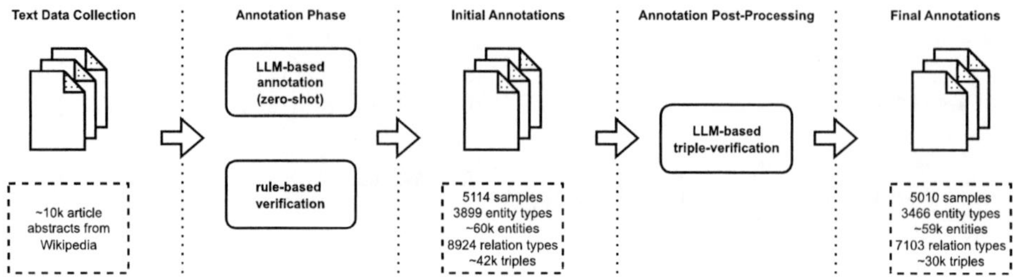

Figure 1: Overview of the pipeline used for synthetic data generation.

- **Unified Schema**: We use a single prompt for schema generation, entity extraction, and relation extraction. Defining distinct keys for each step in the JSON object ensures coverage and prevents omissions.

- **Full NER**: Includes mention detection (as spans), entity typing, and coreference resolution. Though not required for the task, character spans align with standard IE benchmarks and support future encoder-based fine-tuning. Prompting the model to echo the input with inline HTML/XML-style tags for mentions proves robust and allows for automatic validation.

- **Verification Hooks for Relations**: We prompt the model to describe each extracted triple in natural language before emitting the structured triple, enabling verification in the post-processing stage. We also require the model to use IDs to refer to the previously extracted entities, which enables automatic consistency checks (e.g., confirming that the subject and object spans actually appear in the source text).

To prioritize annotation quality over quantity and enable post-processing, we implement several verification mechanisms after the initial model output. These steps focus particularly on validating extracted relations and ensuring annotation completeness. First, we verify entities by checking that all provided mentions correctly occur within the input text. Second, we validate extracted triples by enforcing that subject and object references are made via entity IDs; we then cross-check that the names referenced in the triples match the previously annotated entities. This ensures the model does not fabricate tuples based on nonexistent mentions.

4.3 Annotation Post-Processing

During the construction of the zero-shot prompt, we identified a common source of errors in the directionality of relations (e.g., swapping the subject and object). The natural language descriptions generated as part of the verification hooks (as outlined above) help mitigate this issue in two ways: First, in our observations, producing a description already improves the accuracy of the extracted triples. Second, these descriptions enable further verification.

For each extracted triple, we prompt the model (using the template shown in Appendix A, Figure 3) to assess whether the structured triple faithfully matches its corresponding natural language description. If an inconsistency is detected, we discard not only the affected triple but the entire set of relations of that type within the document, to avoid including problematic relation types. This conservative approach prioritizes annotation quality over quantity, in line with our overall dataset construction philosophy.

In addition to the triple filtering, we discard annotations in two cases, first if assigned entity types are identical to the entities themselves and second if all entities in a document have the same type.

5 Experiments and Results

5.1 Effects of Text Length on Zero-Shot Annotation

Instead of using full abstracts for the synthetic dataset, we truncate the input texts for two reasons: First, shorter texts reduce inference time per document, enabling the annotation of a more diverse set of articles. Second, initial observations indicated that longer texts led to a higher frequency of verification failures when using our prompt.

In order to validate the latter observation, we ran an initial annotation round for all abstracts with a length of up to 300 words and tracked error rates. The results of this experiment, shown in Appendix C, Figure 6, reveal the following:

- Text length and total verification failures are highly correlated.
- Syntax errors, making the output unparseable and mismatches between the entity IDs used in the triples and the ones extracted from the text are the most common errors. Failures in the entity extraction step, such as extracted entities not occuring in the text or missing span annotations, are less common.

5.2 Statistics of Synthetic Annotation Database

Based on the results outlined above, to balance inference efficiency, annotation yield, and text length (especially considering that downstream queries will involve longer documents), we implement the following truncation strategy for the remaining data: We split each abstract into sentences and iteratively add sentences until the cumulative text length has reached 100 words or more and then omit the remaining sentences. Additionally, upon failed verification, we rerun the zero-shot prompt once with a temperature of 0.2. This results in 5114 annotated documents, a yield of 52.89% for the initial annotation. After the post-processing phase, the final dataset consists of 5010 documents, with approx. $59k$ across 3466 entity types and approx. $30k$ triples across 7103 relation types. The most common entity and relation types are shown in Appendix D Figures 7 and 8. An example of synthetic data is shown in Appendix E, Figure 9.

5.3 DocIE Test Set Evaluation

For evaluation on the test set of the DocIE shared task (Organizers), we fetch the most similar document from our synthetic dataset based on the similarity measured between the truncated query text (truncated using the same strategy as used during our dataset construction) and the synthetically annotated documents[6] using the sentence-transformers (Reimers and Gurevych, 2019) model all-MiniLM-L6-v2[7].

Task	P (%)	R (%)	F1 (%)
Entity Ident.	52.36	23.94	32.86
Entity Class.	25.79	11.80	16.19
RE (General)	5.03	2.44	3.29
RE (Strict)	4.61	2.23	3.01

Table 1: Evaluation results on the test dataset of the DocIE shared task for entity identification, entity classification, and relation extraction under general and strict modes. Precision (P), Recall (R), and F1 are reported as percentages.

The results, shown in Table 1, place our approach in the fourth place for the shared task. We note that unparseable outputs occur in a substantial portion of documents, with only 63.91% of outputs being valid. While we initially hypothesize that this is due, in large parts, to the long documents increasing the frequency of syntax errors in the produced outputs (as this is the trend we observed in our experiments in Section 5.1) our experiments with shorter documents, outlined in Section 5.4, do not support this. Even when factoring unparseable outputs into the results, the scores remain low especially for relation extraction. This suggests that IE, especially relation extraction remains a challenging task in the age of strong LLMs.

5.4 Evaluation on Re-DocRED

Task	P (%)	R (%)	F1 (%)
Mention det.	72.20	25.91	38.13
Entity Ident.	58.61	23.67	33.72
Entity Class.	52.25	21.10	30.06
RE (General)	13.79	1.67	2.98
RE (Strict)	8.55	1.04	1.85

Table 2: Evaluation results on the test dataset of Re-DocRED (Tan et al., 2022). Since we have access to the ground truth labels for this data, we are able to also calculate the mention detection scores.

In Table 2 we show the results obtained on the test set of the Re-DocRED dataset (Tan et al., 2022). Compared to the DocIE dataset, fewer entity types are used for annotation (person, organization, location, time, number, and miscellaneous), and the documents tend to be shorter.

[6] We remove 2 documents from our synthetic dataset which are part of the test set in order to avoid contamination.

[7] https://huggingface.co/sentence-transformers/all-MiniLM-L6-v2

For the overall results, with the exception of entity classification[8], the results are broadly comparable to those reported in the DocIE shared task. This suggests that joint entity and relation extraction at the document level remains a challenging problem for current state-of-the-art large language models, even when applied to relatively short documents.

Task	P (%)	R (%)	F1 (%)
Mention det.	72.20	72.62	72.41
Entity Ident.	58.61	63.73	61.06
Entity Class.	52.25	56.82	54.44
RE (General)	13.79	4.57	6.87
RE (Strict)	8.55	2.84	4.26

Table 3: Evaluation results on the test dataset of Re-DocRED (Tan et al., 2022), restricted to only those documents where the pipeline produced a valid output.

Even though the documents are shorter, with only 38.8% of outputs being valid, producing parseable outputs remains a major challenge. In order to assess the potential gain of addressing this issue, we measure the results using only those documents where our pipeline produced a valid output. The corresponding results are shown in Table 3.

6 Conclusion

We present a fully automatic, LLM-driven pipeline for high-quality synthetic data generation for document-level entity and relation extraction, and apply it to create a dataset of over $5k$ Wikipedia abstracts with roughly $59k$ entities and $30k$ relation triples. Through our two-phase annotation process, zero-shot prompt-based extraction followed by rule- and model-based verification, we demonstrate that automated checks substantially improve annotation fidelity, yielding a dataset that, exhibits consistency and wide coverage of entity and relation types.

Our evaluations on the DocIE shared task and Re-DocRED confirm that zero-shot IE remains a hard problem: precision and recall for both entities and relations are modest, and a large number of model outputs still fail to parse cleanly. Moreover, ambiguities in type definitions and relation directionality is a challenge for both extraction and evaluation.

By releasing our synthetic dataset we aim to provide a valuable resource for future research on few-shot and zero-shot document-level IE. We hope that these tools will catalyze further advances in robust, scalable information extraction methods.

[8]We attribute this to the smaller number and more generic kind of entity types used in Re-DocRED.

Acknowledgements

This work was funded by the Federal Ministry of Education and Research of Germany and the Saxon State Ministry for Science, Culture and Tourism as part of the Center for Scalable Data Analytics and Artificial Intelligence Dresden/Leipzig (ScaDS.AI, project ID: SCADS24B). The authors also acknowledge the computing resources provided by the high-performance computing center at the NHR Center of TU Dresden, which is supported jointly by the Federal Ministry of Education and Research and the participating state governments within the NHR framework.

References

DeepSeek-AI, Daya Guo, Dejian Yang, Haowei Zhang, Junxiao Song, Ruoyu Zhang, Runxin Xu, Qihao Zhu, Shirong Ma, Peiyi Wang, Xiao Bi, Xiaokang Zhang, Xingkai Yu, Yu Wu, Z. F. Wu, Zhibin Gou, Zhihong Shao, Zhuoshu Li, Ziyi Gao, and 181 others. 2025. Deepseek-r1: Incentivizing reasoning capability in llms via reinforcement learning. *Preprint*, arXiv:2501.12948.

Jose A. Diaz-Garcia and Julio Amador Diaz Lopez. 2024. A survey on cutting-edge relation extraction techniques based on language models. *Preprint*, arXiv:2411.18157.

Honghao Gui, Lin Yuan, Hongbin Ye, Ningyu Zhang, Mengshu Sun, Lei Liang, and Huajun Chen. 2024. IEPile: Unearthing large scale schema-conditioned information extraction corpus. In *Proceedings of the 62nd Annual Meeting of the Association for Computational Linguistics (Volume 2: Short Papers)*, pages 127–146, Bangkok, Thailand. Association for Computational Linguistics.

Martin Josifoski, Marija Sakota, Maxime Peyrard, and Robert West. 2023. Exploiting asymmetry for synthetic training data generation: SynthIE and the case of information extraction. In *Proceedings of the 2023 Conference on Empirical Methods in Natural Language Processing*, pages 1555–1574, Singapore. Association for Computational Linguistics.

Junpeng Li, Zixia Jia, and Zilong Zheng. 2023. Semi-automatic data enhancement for document-level relation extraction with distant supervision from large language models. In *Proceedings of the 2023 Conference on Empirical Methods in Natural Language Processing*, pages 5495–5505, Singapore. Association for Computational Linguistics.

Shared Task Organizers. XLLM ACL 2025 Shared Task-IV: Document-level Information Extraction. https://xllms.github.io/DocIE/.

Nicholas Popovic and Michael Färber. 2022. Few-shot document-level relation extraction. In *Proceedings of the 2022 Conference of the North American Chapter of the Association for Computational Linguistics: Human Language Technologies*, pages 5733–5746, Seattle, United States. Association for Computational Linguistics.

Nils Reimers and Iryna Gurevych. 2019. Sentence-BERT: Sentence embeddings using Siamese BERT-networks. In *Proceedings of the 2019 Conference on Empirical Methods in Natural Language Processing and the 9th International Joint Conference on Natural Language Processing (EMNLP-IJCNLP)*, pages 3982–3992, Hong Kong, China. Association for Computational Linguistics.

Steven Rogulsky, Nicholas Popovič, and Michael Färber. 2024. The effects of hallucinations in synthetic training data for relation extraction. In *Joint Proceedings of the 2nd Workshop on Knowledge Base Construction from Pre-Trained Language Models (KBC-LM 2024) and the 3rd Challenge on Language Models for Knowledge Base Construction (LM-KBC 2024) Co-Located with the 23nd International Semantic Web Conference (ISWC 2024), Baltimore, USA, November 12, 2024*, volume 3853 of *CEUR Workshop Proceedings*. CEUR-WS.org.

Qingyu Tan, Lu Xu, Lidong Bing, Hwee Tou Ng, and Sharifah Mahani Aljunied. 2022. Revisiting DocRED - addressing the false negative problem in relation extraction. In *Proceedings of the 2022 Conference on Empirical Methods in Natural Language Processing*, pages 8472–8487, Abu Dhabi, United Arab Emirates. Association for Computational Linguistics.

Lilong Xue, Dan Zhang, Yuxiao Dong, and Jie Tang. 2024. AutoRE: Document-level relation extraction with large language models. In *Proceedings of the 62nd Annual Meeting of the Association for Computational Linguistics (Volume 3: System Demonstrations)*, pages 211–220, Bangkok, Thailand. Association for Computational Linguistics.

Hankiz Yilahun, Hangtian Zhao, and Askar Hamdulla. 2025. Fredc: A few-shot relation extraction dataset for chinese. *Applied Sciences*, 15(3).

A Prompts

Figure 2 shows the full zero-shot annotation prompt. Figure 3 shows the triple verification prompt for post-processing extracted relations. Figure 4 shows the inference prompt (with in-context demonstration) used at test time.

B Category distribution of Wikipedia Vital Articles

Figure 5 shows the pie-chart distribution of Level 4 Vital Articles by domain category.

C Effects of Text Length on Errors in Zero-Shot Annotation

Figure 6 shows how error rates (syntax failures, span mismatches, etc.) vary with input text length.

D Most Common Entity and Relation Types

Figure 7 shows the top 30 entity types and their frequencies in the synthetic dataset. Figure 8 shows the top 30 relation types and their frequencies.

E Data Sample

Figure 9 shows an example from the synthetic dataset.

Zero-Shot Annotation Prompt (DeepSeek-R1-Distill-Qwen-32B)

```
Help me build a knowledge graph schema. I will provide a text and you tell me
which entity types and which relation types (properties) to add to my knowledge
graph schema to model the data in the text.
This is the text in question:

{text}

Return your answer in the following format:
```json
{
  'text_with_spans': # html annotated text where every mention and coreference
  of an entity is annotated, for example: '<ent id="0" type="Person">Alice
  </ent> (or <ent id="0" type="Person">Ali</ent> as her friends call her) knows
  <ent id="1" type="Person">Bob</ent> because <ent id="0" type="Person">she
  </ent> met <ent id="1" type="Person">him</ent> at
  <ent id="2" type="Educational institution">school</ent>.',
  'entities': [
    {'id': 0, 'name': <name_of_entity>, 'type': <type_of_entity>},
    ..., # add all entities with the types above, even if they are not relevant
    for a triple
  ],
  'triples': [
    {'description': <text_describing_triple>, 'triple_string':
    '(<name_of_subject>, <name_of_relation_type>, <name_of_object>)',
   'subject': <id_of_subject_entity>, 'predicate': <name_of_relation_type>,
    'object': <id_of_object_entity>},
    ...,
  ],
  'relation_types': [<name_of_relation_type>, ...],
  'entity_types': [<name_of_entity_type>, ...],
}
```

Make sure that for every entity type and relation type you annotate *all*
occurrences!
```

Figure 2: Prompt used for zero-shot text annotation.

Triple Verification Prompt (DeepSeek-R1-Distill-Qwen-32B)

````
Which of the following is a good description of the meaning of the sentence
"{description}"?

A:
```json
{{"subject": "{subject}", "predicate": "{predicate}", "object": "{object}"}}
```
B:
```json
{{"subject": "{object}", "predicate": "{predicate}", "object": "{subject}"}}
```
C:
Both. Only use this option if the predicate/property is a symmetric one.

D:
None of the above. Only use this option if the above are nonsensical or vastly
different from the text.

format your answer like so:
\boxed{{<A_or_B_or_C_or_D>}}
````

Figure 3: Prompt used for post-processing of triples.

Inference Prompt (DeepSeek-R1-Distill-Qwen-32B)

```
Help me build a knowledge graph. I will provide a text and you annotate it.
Here is what correct annotation looks like:
```json
{
    'text': '...',
    'entity_types': [...],
    'text_with_spans': '...',
    'entities': [...],
    'relation_types' + '': [...],
    'relations': [...]
}
```

(Note how the entity ids start from 0 and allow for coreference resolution,
as multiple spans in the annotated text can refer to the same entity.)

Here is the annotation I want you to complete:
```json
{
    'text': '...',
    'entity_types': [...],
    'text_with_spans': '...',
    'entities': [...],
    'relation_types' + '': [...],
    'relations': [...]
}
```

Do not add any entity or relation types! Use only the ones provided in the JSON.
Where possible, reuse the entity ids from the annotation I've started.
If I've missed any entities (or failed to resolve coreferences) or triples,
please fix accordingly.
Return the completed JSON, not just your changes.
```

Figure 4: Prompt used for inference. An example of an in-context demonstration is shown in Appendix E, Figure 9.

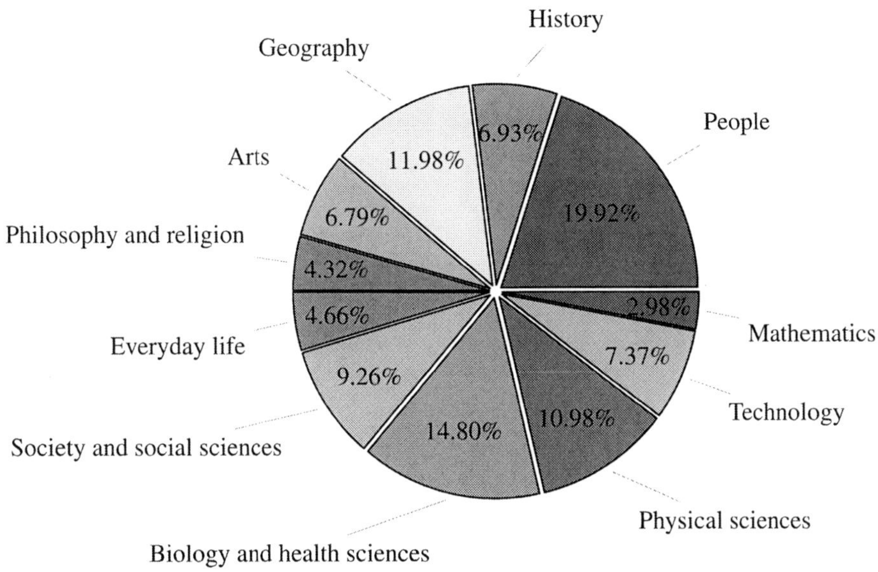

Figure 5: Category distribution of level 4 vital articles (approx. 10k).

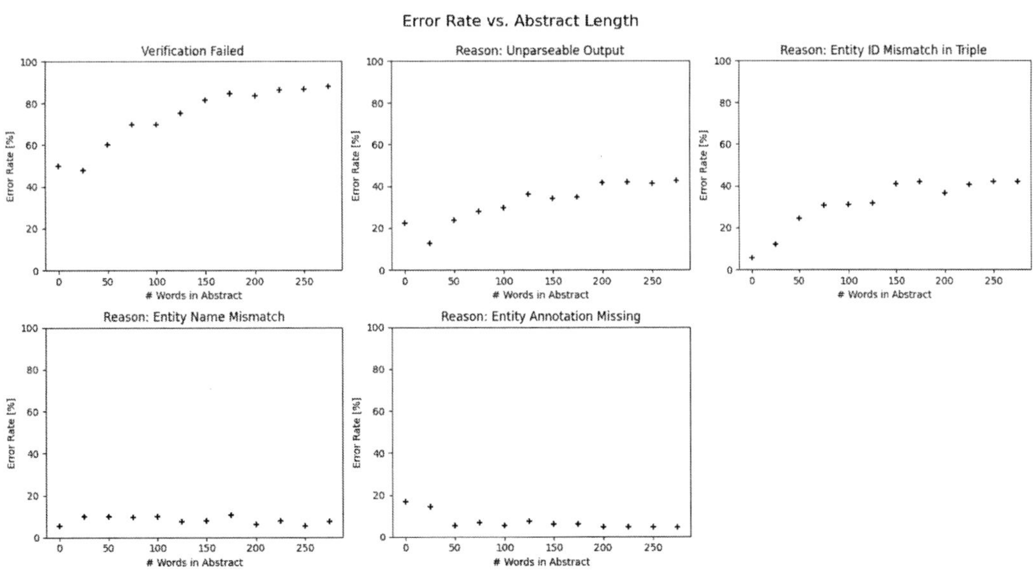

Figure 6: Error distribution for initial set of experiments of first annotation phase.

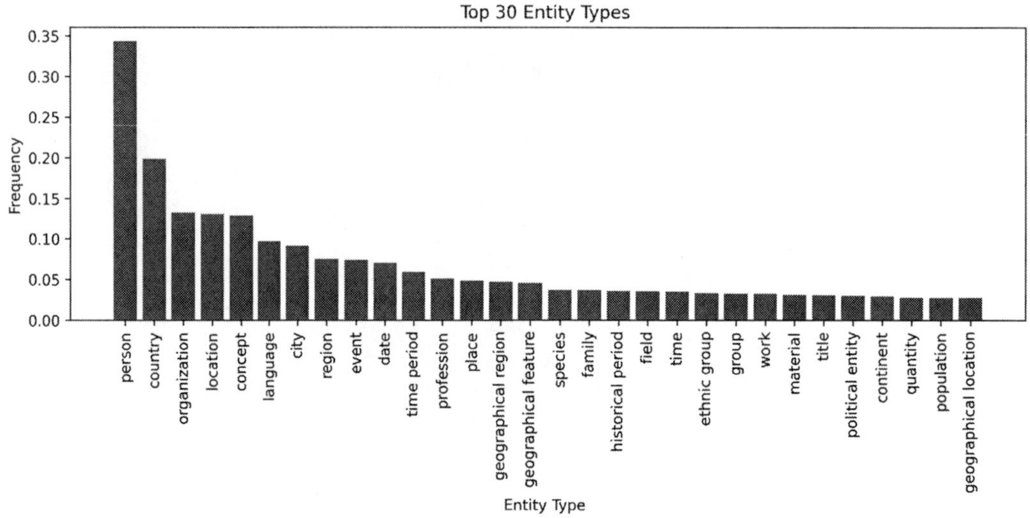

Figure 7: Top 30 entity types in final synthetic dataset and their frequency.

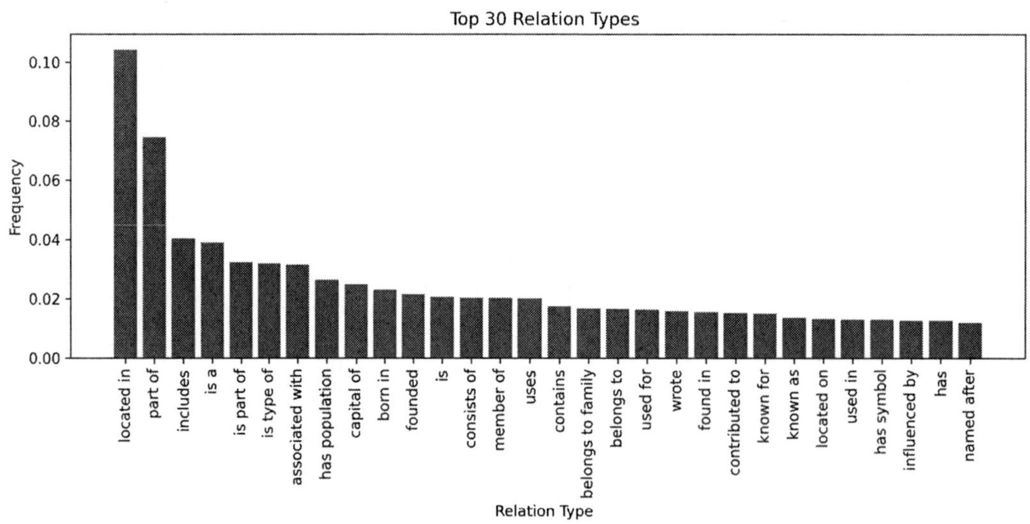

Figure 8: Top 30 relation types in final synthetic dataset and their frequency.

Synthetic Data Example


```
{
  "text": "The University of Vienna (German: Universit\u00e4t Wien) is a public research university located in Vienna, Austria. Founded by Duke Rudolph IV in 1365, it is the oldest university in the German-speaking world and among the largest institutions of higher learning in Europe. The university is associated with 17 Nobel Prize winners and has been the home to many scholars of historical and academic importance.",

  "annotated_text": "<ent id=\"0\" type=\"Educational institution\">The University of Vienna</ent> (German: <ent id=\"0\" type=\"Educational institution\">Universit\u00e4t Wien</ent>) is a public research university located in <ent id=\"1\" type=\"Location\">Vienna</ent>, <ent id=\"2\" type=\"Country\">Austria</ent>. Founded by <ent id=\"3\" type=\"Person\">Duke Rudolph IV</ent> in 1365, it is the oldest university in the German-speaking world and among the largest institutions of higher learning in Europe. The university is associated with 17 <ent id=\"4\" type=\"Award\">Nobel Prize</ent> winners and has been the home to many <ent id=\"5\" type=\"Person\">scholars</ent> of historical and academic importance.",

  "entities": [
    {
      "id": 0,
      "name": "The University of Vienna",
      "type": "Educational institution"
    },
    {
      "id": 1,
      "name": "Vienna",
      "type": "Location"
    },
    {
      "id": 2,
      "name": "Austria",
      "type": "Country"
    },
    {
      "id": 3,
      "name": "Duke Rudolph IV",
      "type": "Person"
    },
    {
      "id": 4,
      "name": "Nobel Prize",
      "type": "Award"
    },
    {
      "id": 5,
      "name": "scholars",
      "type": "Person"
    }
  ],

  "relations": [
    {
      "description": "The University of Vienna is located in Vienna.",
      "triple_string": "(The University of Vienna, located_in, Vienna)",
      "subject": 0,
      "predicate": "located_in",
      "object": 1
    },
    {
      "description": "The University of Vienna is located in Austria.",
      "triple_string": "(The University of Vienna, located_in, Austria)",
      "subject": 0,
      "predicate": "located_in",
      "object": 2
    },
    {
      "description": "The University of Vienna was founded by Duke Rudolph IV.",
      "triple_string": "(The University of Vienna, founded_by, Duke Rudolph IV)",
      "subject": 0,
      "predicate": "founded_by",
      "object": 3
    },
    {
      "description": "The University of Vienna has been the home to scholars.",
      "triple_string": "(The University of Vienna, home_of, scholars)",
      "subject": 0,
      "predicate": "home_of",
      "object": 5
    }
  ]
}
```


Figure 9: Example of final synthetic data.

LLMSR@XLLM25: Integrating Reasoning Prompt Strategies with Structural Prompt Formats for Enhanced Logical Inference

Le Duc Tai[1,2], **Dang Van Thin**[1,2],
[1]University of Information Technology-VNUHCM, Ho Chi Minh City, Vietnam
[2]Vietnam National University, Ho Chi Minh City, Vietnam
23521374@gm.uit.edu.vn, thindv@uit.edu.vn

Abstract

This paper illustrates our team system approach in XLLM-ACL 2025 Task-III: LLM for Structural Reasoning (LLM-SR), aiming to solve both Task: Question parsing and CoT parsing. The process of extracting statements and evidence is similar to Discourse Parsing. Correct extraction of statements or evidence from the COT is crucial at the outset. Next, the pairwise relationship between a specific statement and its corresponding evidence is assessed (a statement should be followed by its related evidence from the CoT). Both semantic and lexical similarity are used to evaluate the accuracy of statements and evidence predictions. Finally, once a statement-evidence pair is correctly extracted, it is evaluated to determine whether the evidence can logically deduce the statement. To tackle Question Parsing and CoT Parsing, we implement and investigate various solutions, including (1) applying different structural prompt formats like JSON, Markdown, or XML. (2) utilising various prompt techniques: Few-shot, Chain of thought, and Multi-hop prompting. (3) Taking advantage of Natural Language Inference (NLI) model for the Statement Verification step. Our best official result is a 243.047 mean score for test phases A and B, and finally, we rank 7th on the final leaderboard.

1 Introduction

The advent of large language models (LLMs) has significantly advanced natural language processing, enabling sophisticated reasoning capabilities across diverse tasks. However, ensuring that these models produce structured, interpretable, and logically coherent reasoning remains a formidable challenge. Addressing this, the XLLM-ACL 2025 Task-III: LLM for Structural Reasoning (LLM-SR) focuses on evaluating the abilities of LLM to generate structured reasoning processes by parsing questions and corresponding chains of thought (CoT) into distinct components: major premises, minor premises, and their interrelations.

In this paper, we present the approach developed by our team, for the LLM-SR task. Our methodology targets two primary subtasks: **Question Parsing** and **CoT Parsing**. We conceptualise the extraction of statements and evidence as analogous to discourse parsing, emphasizing the accurate identification of these elements as a foundational step. Subsequently, we assess the pairwise relationships between specific statements and their corresponding evidence, ensuring that each statement is logically supported by its related evidence within the CoT.

To enhance the structural reasoning capabilities of LLMs, we investigate several strategies:

- **Structural Prompt Formats**: We explore the impact of different prompt formats, including JSON, Markdown, and XML, on the model's ability to parse and reason structurally.
- **Prompting Techniques**: We implement various prompting methods such as Few-shot learning, Chain of Thought (CoT), and Multi-hop prompting to guide the model's reasoning process.
- **Statement Verification**: We incorporate a Natural Language Inference (NLI) model to verify whether the extracted evidence logically entails the corresponding statements.

Our system achieved a mean score of 243.047 across test phases A and B, securing the 7th position on the final leaderboard. These results underscore the effectiveness of combining structured prompt formats with advanced prompting techniques and verification models to enhance the structural reasoning abilities of LLMs.

2 Related Work

Recent advancements in prompt engineering have demonstrated that providing large language models with a small number of in-context examples

Proceedings of the 1st Joint Workshop on Large Language Models and Structure Modeling (XLLM 2025), pages 310–316
August 1, 2025 ©2025 Association for Computational Linguistics

can yield strong zero and few-shot performance gains (Brown et al., 2020). Explicitly eliciting intermediate reasoning steps via Chain-of-Thought prompting has been shown to further boost complex arithmetic and commonsense reasoning (Wei et al., 2022). Techniques such as self-consistency decoding, which samples multiple reasoning paths and aggregates the most consistent answer, markedly improve Chain of Thought accuracy (Wang et al., 2022). Decomposition and multi hop strategies like Self Ask break down complex queries into subquestions for greater interpretability (Press et al., 2022). Hybrid reasoning–acting prompts (ReAct) interleave "Thought" and "Action" steps to ground LLMs in external environments or tools (Yao et al., 2022). Pipeline optimisations such as LM-BFF automate prompt template selection to refine few-shot tuning (Gao et al., 2020). Constraining LLM outputs to structured formats (JSON, XML) via schema-based or grammar-based decoding ensures machine-readable consistency for downstream extraction tasks (Lu et al., 2025). Methods from discourse parsing—segmenting text into elementary discourse units and labelling their rhetorical relations—provide algorithms analogous to statement and evidence extraction (Song and Liu, 2020). Finally, Natural Language Inference frameworks trained on large-scale corpora such as SNLI and MultiNLI underpin the verification of logical entailment between extracted evidence and hypothesis statements (Bowman et al., 2015; Williams et al., 2018).

3 Task Description

The XLLM-ACL 2025 Shared Task-III: LLM for Structural Reasoning (LLM-SR) challenges participants to generate a controllable and interpretable reasoning process via step-by-step inference (xll, 2025). It comprises two subtasks: *question parsing*, which extracts all conditions necessary for solving a given question, and *CoT parsing*, which segments a provided chain-of-thought into distinct statements and their corresponding evidence (xll, 2025). For each statement–evidence pair, systems must predict a binary verification label indicating whether the evidence logically entails the statement (xll, 2025). The training set contains 24 annotated examples derived from the LogiQA logical reasoning benchmark (Liu et al., 2020)(xll, 2025). Participants are restricted to using the Llama-3-8B-Instruct backbone model for all subtasks (xll, 2025)(Meta, 2024). Evaluation is performed on two public test phases (A and B), with Macro F1 computed over question parsing, statement parsing, statement–evidence pairing, and verification predictions (xll, 2025). Submissions are evaluated and scored through the Codabench platform, ensuring reproducibility and standardized scoring (Xu et al., 2022). The XLLM dataset (Shuyi-Zsy, n.d.) is conducted by the organizer.

4 Methodology

4.1 Prompt Format

Choosing an appropriate prompt format, such as JSON, Markdown, or XML, is fundamental to the design of reliable, interpretable, and maintainable LLM-based systems. The rigid key-value structure of JSON enforces unambiguous machine-readable output that simplifies downstream parsing and validation, but its verbosity can increase token usage and latency. Markdown, by contrast, offers a lightweight compromise: human-friendly readability paired with sufficient structural cues (headings, lists, code fences) that facilitate both developer inspection and automated post-processing. XML's tag-based hierarchy is well-suited for deeply nested or richly annotated content, allowing clear delineation of sections at the expense of larger prompt size and more complex parsing logic.

Systematic evaluation of these formats is necessary because prompt format choice can materially affect model behaviour, output consistency, and overall computational efficiency. Variations in format can influence the model's content planning heuristics, leading to differences in completeness, coherence, and error rates. Moreover, tokenization characteristics and schema overhead directly impact throughput and cost in production settings. By rigorously comparing JSON, Markdown, and XML prompts across tasks of varying complexity, researchers can quantify trade-offs between interpretability, performance stability, and resource consumption, thereby guiding the selection of the most appropriate format for a given application domain.

After experimenting, our team found out that leveraging the Markdown prompt format brought the best result on the question and CoT parsing task, as shown in the prompt sample below:

```
### Task:
You are an advanced reasoning
    assistant that extracts logical
    constraints, conditions, and
    final queries from complex
```

```
    reasoning questions. Given a
    question, you will return a
    structured list of parsed
    conditions.

### **Instructions:**
1. Identify the **problem context**
    (e.g., participants, locations,
    objects).
2. Extract **explicit logical
    conditions** (marked by "if", "
    then", "must", "cannot", "
    different", not,etc.).
3. Focus on **bullet point numbers**
     because logical constraint
    often start with **bullet point
    numbers**.
4. Identify the **final question
    statement** that requires
    solving.
5. Parse output MUST only contain
    information in provided question
     and do not hallucinate.
6. **Check if the final query
    contains logical constraints**
    and extract them separately.
7. Format your response as a
    structured JSON output.
```

4.2 Few-shot Prompting

Few-shot prompting leverages a small set of annotated examples to guide the model toward the desired output structure and reasoning patterns without extensive fine-tuning. By providing representative question analysis pairs, the model learns to generalize the extraction of premises, evidence, and their logical relations directly from the prompt context. This approach is highly efficient: it requires minimal manual annotation effort compared to fully supervised training, and it can be adapted to new subtasks or domains by swapping in a few new exemplars.

In the context of LLM-SR, few-shot prompting enhances both accuracy and reliability. Exemplars that demonstrate correct statement identification and evidence pairing serve as implicit templates, reducing ambiguity in model predictions and improving consistency across instances. Moreover, few-shot formats naturally encourage the model to attend to relevant structural cues, such as delineated premises or marked evidence segments, thus aligning its internal content planning with the requirements of question parsing and CoT parsing. From a computational standpoint, the overhead of including a handful of examples in the prompt is marginal relative to the gains in output precision, making few-shot prompting a cost-effective technique for rapid prototyping and iterative system development.

As we attempted, we observed that there are types of questions in the dataset, and we listed out those types, then provided example as few-shot prompting for the prompt. As a result, we saw improvement in F1-score when evaluating, but since providing too many examples, the prompt sometimes returns biased output, which is too stuck with the example that we set in the prompt. To tackle this problem, we build a component that check whether the output was too different from the given question or CoT, then it must re-generate another output until it meets the similarity threshold with the given question or CoT.

4.3 Chain of Thought

Chain-of-Thought prompting guides the model to generate intermediate reasoning steps explicitly, thereby transforming an opaque prediction process into a multi-step, interpretable inference chain. By eliciting rationales before producing final outputs, CoT prompts align the model's internal content planning with the structural requirements of the LLM-SR task, facilitating accurate identification of premises, supporting evidence, and their logical relationships. This explicit decomposition of reasoning not only improves the model's attention to critical details such as the dependencies between question conditions and derived conclusions but also enables straightforward error analysis and targeted prompt refinement.

From an efficiency standpoint, CoT prompting leverages the pre-trained reasoning abilities of LLMs without additional fine-tuning, requiring only the inclusion of a few illustrative CoT exemplars in the prompt. The marginal increase in prompt length is outweighed by gains in accuracy and consistency, particularly for complex multi-step inferences inherent to structural reasoning. Moreover, the generated chains of thought can be post-processed to automatically extract statements and evidence segments, thereby streamlining the end-to-end pipeline for question parsing and CoT parsing. Consequently, Chain-of-Thought prompting represents a cost-effective and scalable technique for enhancing both the interpretability and performance of LLM-based structural reasoning systems.

Even though Chain of thought prompting has many effective aspects, in our approach, we only use Chain of thought prompting for generate knowledge,e which will be fed into the next prompt for multi-hop prompting technique.

4.4 Multi-hop Prompting

Multi-hop prompting decomposes complex reasoning tasks into a sequence of dependent sub-questions, each answered in turn to build a coherent inference chain. This structured decomposition aligns naturally with the LLM-SR subtasks of question parsing and CoT parsing, as it forces the model to identify intermediate premises and evidence at each hop. By guiding the model to focus on one inference step at a time, multi-hop prompts reduce hallucinations and improve the precision of statement–evidence pairing. Moreover, the modular nature of multi-hop prompting enables flexible adaptation: new sub-questions can be added or refined without retraining, and individual hops can be optimized for efficiency, making it a cost-effective strategy for scalable structural reasoning.

Multi-hop prompting breaks down complex queries into sequential sub-questions, guiding the model to iteratively extract statements and their corresponding evidence. By isolating each inference step, this technique improves the accuracy of statement–evidence alignment, minimizes spurious connections, and enables targeted refinement of individual hops without retraining, making it an efficient strategy for our LLM-SR task.

4.5 Natural Language Inference (NLI)

Natural Language Inference (NLI) provides an effective and efficient mechanism for verifying whether an extracted evidence segment logically entails its paired statement. By framing verification as an entailment classification task, we leverage pre-trained NLI models to score statement–evidence pairs without additional fine-tuning, minimizing annotation overhead and development time. The binary entailment output directly aligns with the LLM-SR verification requirement, enabling fast, consistent judgments and straightforward integration into the parsing pipeline. Moreover, NLI models exhibit strong generalization across domains, ensuring robust performance even when evidence and statement formulations vary in wording or structure. This approach streamlines the verification step and enhances overall system reliability with minimal computational and engineering cost.

5 Full Pipeline

This is our full best pipeline, which is shown in 1.

The proposed pipeline constitutes a modular and interpretable architecture tailored for the LLM-SR task, effectively addressing both question parsing and statement–evidence verification through a sequence of structured components. It begins with an input consisting of a question and its corresponding Chain-of-Thought (CoT) rationale. A parsing prompt is applied to extract candidate statements and evidence segments from the CoT, yielding a structured intermediate representation. This initial decomposition step is critical, as it transforms unstructured natural language into discrete units that downstream components can process more reliably.

Next, a similarity check module evaluates the lexical and semantic coherence between extracted statements and their corresponding evidence spans. This filtering mechanism ensures that only aligned pairs proceed to the next stage, thereby minimizing noise and reducing the likelihood of spurious relations. Following this, the pipeline incorporates two reasoning pathways in parallel: Chain-of-Thought prompting and Multi-hop prompting. Chain-of-Thought prompting improves interpretability and promotes stepwise deduction by explicitly modeling intermediate reasoning steps. In contrast, Multi-hop prompting decomposes complex inference into smaller, interdependent sub-questions, enabling more accurate retrieval of distributed evidence and enhancing logical consistency.

The outputs from these reasoning modules are routed into a Natural Language Inference (NLI) model, which performs the verification step by determining whether each evidence segment entails its associated statement. This dedicated verification layer isolates the decision-making process from generation, improving both reliability and transparency. By leveraging pre-trained NLI models, the system achieves strong verification performance without additional supervision.

Overall, this pipeline exemplifies best practices in prompt-based LLM system design. Its modular structure allows for independent tuning and component replacement, fostering adaptability and ease of maintenance. The integration of structured prompting strategies, semantic similarity filtering, and NLI-based verification results in a robust and scalable solution for structural reasoning tasks. Moreover, the pipeline supports transparency and interpretability at each stage, making it suitable for high-stakes domains where explanation and traceability are essential.

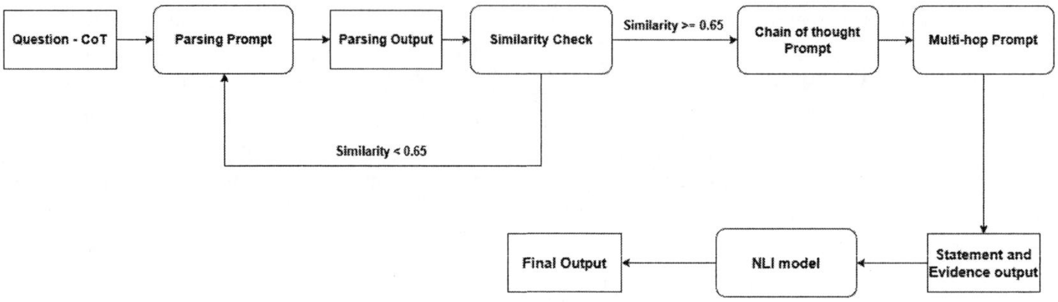

Figure 1: Full pipeline of LLM

5.1 Experimental Settings

Our experimental framework is designed to evaluate structural reasoning capabilities across multiple prompting strategies for the LLM-SR task. We utilize the public test set from the XLLM-ACL 2025 Task-III dataset, formatted in JSON and parsed using a custom data loader. The system is built around Meta-Llama-3-8B-Instruct, a state-of-the-art causal language model, accessed via HuggingFace's Transformers library. The model is loaded using 4-bit quantization with mixed-precision inference to optimize computational efficiency while preserving performance.

To facilitate robust text generation and parsing, we use a Transformer-based pipeline configured for causal language modeling. Chain-of-Thought (CoT), Few-shot, and Multi-hop prompting strategies are incorporated into distinct parsing modules to support statement extraction, evidence retrieval, and verification. Each prompt format (e.g., JSON, Markdown, XML) is evaluated across the different reasoning tasks to assess structural sensitivity and effectiveness.

6 Main Results

Table 1 summarises the performance of seven prompt configurations on the structural reasoning subtasks. Several clear patterns emerge:

First, the combination of Few-shot, Chain-of-Thought, Multi-hop prompting, NLI verification, and similarity checking, all delivered in a Markdown format with four prompt calls, achieves the highest overall accuracy (Question Parsing: 67.96%, Statement Parsing: 39.21%, Statement–Evidence Matching: 12.04%, Reasoning: 3.83). This demonstrates that layering multiple complementary prompting techniques yields significant gains, particularly for the most challenging subtasks of identifying and aligning statements with their evidential support.

Second, reducing the prompt format to pure Markdown without the similarity check module causes a modest drop in performance (Question Parsing: 64.75%, Statement Parsing: 29.90%, Statement–Evidence Matching: 9.40%, Reasoning: 2.63), illustrating the value of the auxiliary filtering stage. The JSON format, when used with the full suite of prompting techniques, further decreases Question Parsing accuracy to 61.40%, while slightly improving Statement Parsing (30.36%) but reducing Statement–Evidence matching (8.70%) and overall reasoning quality (3.20). This suggests that Markdown's human-readable cues better guide the model's content planning compared to the more rigid JSON schema.

Third, limiting the system to only Few-shot prompting with NLI (two prompt calls) yields mixed results: Markdown achieves stronger Question Parsing (64.15%) but lower Statement–Evidence alignment (1.85%) and minimal reasoning depth (0.90), whereas JSON boosts Statement–Evidence Matching (11.70%) at the expense of Question Parsing (59.28%) and reasoning quality (4.50). This indicates that NLI verification alone can compensate for reduced prompting complexity in pairing statements and evidence, but at a cost to holistic parsing performance.

Finally, the simplest Few-shot–only configurations (two or four calls) produce the lowest scores across all subtasks (Question Parsing: 56.02–59.24%, Statement Parsing: 29.17–38.50%, Statement–Evidence Matching: 2.07–2.29%, Reasoning: 1.07–1.84), confirming that advanced prompting strategies are critical to unlock the full structural reasoning capabilities of LLMs.

In summary, these results underscore the effectiveness of integrating multiple prompting techniques within a Markdown format and highlight the trade-offs inherent in prompt format selection, prompt complexity, and verification strategy. The highest-performing configuration (four calls, Markdown, full-technique suite) is the reference point for further improvements in structural reasoning pipelines. Finally, our best score on test set B are 73.24, 47.07, 15.59, and 10.22. Our team achieve rank 7th i XLLM-ACL 2025 Task-III: LLM for Structural Reasoning (LLM-SR).

7 Conclusion and Future Work

In this study, we presented a comprehensive and modular pipeline for addressing the LLM-SR task, targeting both question parsing and Chain-of-Thought (CoT) parsing subtasks. Through a series of experiments, we demonstrated that the integration of structured prompt formats, advanced prompting strategies (Few-shot, Chain-of-Thought, Multi-hop), and a dedicated NLI-based verification step significantly enhances the model's structural reasoning performance. Our analysis highlights the effectiveness of Markdown as a prompt format and the importance of leveraging multiple complementary reasoning techniques to ensure accurate statement–evidence alignment and logical verification.

In future work, we plan to explore dynamic prompt selection mechanisms that adapt based on question complexity, as well as integrating retrieval-augmented generation (RAG) components to support knowledge-intensive reasoning. We are also interested in fine-tuning or instruction-tuning smaller models to perform verification and parsing steps more efficiently.

Acknowledgements

This research was supported by The VNUHCM-University of Information Technology's Scientific Research Support Fund.

References

2025. Xllm-acl 2025 shared task-iii: Llm for structural reasoning (llm-sr). `https://xllms.github.io/LLMSR/#`.

Samuel R. Bowman, Gabor Angeli, Christopher Potts, and Christopher D. Manning. 2015. A large annotated corpus for learning natural language inference. *arXiv preprint arXiv:1508.05326*.

Tom B. Brown, Benjamin Mann, Nick Ryder, Melanie Subbiah, Jared Kaplan, Prafulla Dhariwal, Arvind Neelakantan, Pranav Shyam, Girish Sastry, Amanda Askell, and *et al.* 2020. Language models are few-shot learners. In *Advances in Neural Information Processing Systems*, volume 33, pages 1877–1901.

Tianyu Gao, Adam Fisch, and Danqi Chen. 2020. Making pre-trained language models better few-shot learners. In *Proceedings of the 58th Annual Meeting of the Association for Computational Linguistics*, pages 3816–3830.

Jian Liu, Leyang Cui, Hanmeng Liu, Dandan Huang, Yile Wang, and Yue Zhang. 2020. Logiqa: A challenge dataset for machine reading comprehension with logical reasoning. *CoRR*, abs/2007.08124.

Yaxi Lu, Haolun Li, Xin Cong, Zhong Zhang, Yesai Wu, Yankai Lin, Zhiyuan Liu, Fangming Liu, and Maosong Sun. 2025. Learning to generate structured output with schema reinforcement learning. *Preprint*, arXiv:2502.18878.

Meta. 2024. Meta llama 3.0 8b instruct. `https://huggingface.co/meta-llama/Meta-Llama-3-8B-Instruct`.

Ofir Press, Muru Zhang, Sewon Min, Ludwig Schmidt, Noah A. Smith, and Mike Lewis. 2022. Measuring and narrowing the compositionality gap in language models. *Preprint*, arXiv:2210.03350.

Shuyi-Zsy. n.d. Llmsr dataset. Accessed: 2025-05-15.

Wei Song and Lifeng Zhu Liu. 2020. Representation learning in discourse parsing: A survey. *Science China Technological Sciences*, 63(10):1921–1946.

Xuezhi Wang, Jason Wei, Dale Schuurmans, Quoc V. Le, Ed Chi, Sharan Narang, Aakanksha Chowdhery, and Denny Zhou. 2022. Self-consistency improves chain of thought reasoning in language models. *Preprint*, arXiv:2203.11171.

Jason Wei, Xuezhi Wang, Dale Schuurmans, Maarten Bosma, Brian Ichter, Fei Xia, Ed H. Chi, Quoc V. Le, and Denny Zhou. 2022. Chain-of-thought prompting elicits reasoning in large language models. In *Advances in Neural Information Processing Systems*, volume 35, pages 24824–24837.

Adina Williams, Nikita Nangia, and Samuel R. Bowman. 2018. A broad-coverage challenge corpus for sentence understanding through inference. In *Proceedings of the 2018 Conference of the North American Chapter of the Association for Computational Linguistics: Human Language Technologies, Volume 1 (Long Papers)*, pages 1112–1122. Association for Computational Linguistics.

Zhen Xu, Sergio Escalera, Isabelle Guyon, Adrien Pavão, Magali Richard, Wei-Wei Tu, Quanming Yao, and Huan Zhao. 2022. codabench: flexible, easy-to-use and reproducible benchmarking platform. *arXiv preprint arXiv:2110.05802*.

Shunyu Yao, Dian Zhao, Jeffrey Yu, Izhak Shafran, Karthik Narasimhan, and Yue Cao. 2022. React: Synergizing reasoning and acting in language models. *Preprint*, arXiv:2210.03629.

Prompt Calls	4
Prompt Format	Markdown
Techniques	Few-shot, Chain-of-Thought, Multi-hop, NLI, Similarity check
Scores	Question Parsing: 67.96, Statement Parsing: 39.21, Statement–Evidence: 12.04, Reasoning: 3.83
Prompt Calls	4
Prompt Format	Markdown
Techniques	Few-shot, Chain-of-Thought, Multi-hop, NLI
Scores	Question Parsing: 64.75, Statement Parsing: 29.90, Statement–Evidence: 9.40, Reasoning: 2.63
Prompt Calls	4
Prompt Format	JSON
Techniques	Few-shot, Chain-of-Thought, Multi-hop, NLI
Scores	Question Parsing: 61.40, Statement Parsing: 30.36, Statement–Evidence: 8.70, Reasoning: 3.20
Prompt Calls	2
Prompt Format	Markdown
Techniques	Few-shot, NLI
Scores	Question Parsing: 64.15, Statement Parsing: 25.30, Statement–Evidence: 1.85, Reasoning: 0.90
Prompt Calls	2
Prompt Format	JSON
Techniques	Few-shot, NLI
Scores	Question Parsing: 59.28, Statement Parsing: 39.21, Statement–Evidence: 11.70, Reasoning: 4.50
Prompt Calls	2
Prompt Format	Markdown
Techniques	Few-shot
Scores	Question Parsing: 56.02, Statement Parsing: 38.50, Statement–Evidence: 2.07, Reasoning: 1.07
Prompt Calls	4
Prompt Format	Markdown
Techniques	Few-shot
Scores	Question Parsing: 59.24, Statement Parsing: 29.17, Statement–Evidence: 2.29, Reasoning: 1.84

Table 1: Results on Test set A in different approaches

DocIE@XLLM25: UIEPrompter: A Unified Training-Free Framework for universal document-level information extraction via Structured Prompt

Chengfeng Qiu[†]**, Lifeng Zhou**[†]**, Kaifeng Wei, Yuke Li**[*]
NetEase YiDun AI Lab, Hangzhou, China
{qiuchengfeng,hzzhoulifeng,hzweikaifeng,liyuke}@corp.netease.com

Abstract

We introduce UIEPrompter, a unified, training-free framework that secures 1st place in the ACL 2025 shared competition on universal document-level information extraction. UIEPrompter effectively addresses both named entity recognition and relation extraction without the need for annotated data. Leveraging large language models, UIEPrompter establishes a zero-shot baseline through role-specific prompts, which are then refined via few-shot guidance and constrained output generation prompt to align with competition schemas. Additionally, by integrating outputs from several large language models, we reduce individual model biases, thereby improving overall performance. Evaluated on the competition evaluation dataset, UIEPrompter showcases outstanding performance in document-level information extraction, ultimately securing first place. The implementation code is available on GitHub.

1 Introduction

Information extraction (IE) (Jeong and Kim, 2022; Paolini et al., 2021; Fei et al., 2022; Li et al., 2023) serves as a critical bridge between unstructured text and structured knowledge representation, enabling the identification of entities, their semantic types, and inter-entity relationships in texts. In recent years, IE has garnered significant attention from both academia and industry. The latest ACL 2025 shared task on universal document-level information extraction (DocIE) presents a novel challenge that requires the extraction of named entities (Labusch et al., 2019; Vacareanu et al., 2024; Shi and Kimura, 2024; Wang et al., 2023) and their relations (Huang et al., 2021; Cabot and Navigli, 2021; Efeoglu and Paschke, 2024; Xue et al., 2024; Peng et al., 2024) from documents.

[1]† Equal contribution.
[2]* Corresponding author.

Conventional approaches adopt a fragmented pipeline, deploying separate models for named entity recognition (NER) and relation extraction (RE). While effective in narrow contexts, this paradigm faces two fundamental limitations: (1) a heavy reliance on annotated training data for optimizing both models, and (2) the risk of cascading error propagation between the NER and RE stages, where misidentified entities can lead to incorrect relation predictions downstream.

To overcome these constraints, we propose UIEPrompter as shown in Figure 1, a training-free framework that unifies NER and RE through meticulous prompt engineering and the generative prowess of large language models (LLMs) (Liu et al., 2024; Arrieta et al., 2025; Kuo et al., 2025). The key advantages of our framework are:

- **Training-free architecture**: UIEPrompter eliminates the need for task-specific training data or model fine-tuning. Unlike supervised approaches that rely on domain-specific annotations, our framework achieves competitive performance purely through prompt engineering, leveraging LLMs' inherent knowledge without parameter updates.
- **Unified IE framework**: By integrating NER and RE into a single LLM-based architecture, UIEPrompter bypasses error propagation inherent in cascaded NER→RE pipelines. This joint modeling approach ensures entity-relation consistency while reducing system complexity.
- **Domain-adaptive few-shot guidance**: UIEPrompter incorporates competition-specific examples to align outputs with the characteristics of the target domain, thereby enhancing overall performance.
- **Strong performance in document-level information extraction**: According to the of-

Proceedings of the 1st Joint Workshop on Large Language Models and Structure Modeling (XLLM 2025), pages 317–321
August 1, 2025 ©2025 Association for Computational Linguistics

ficial leaderboard, our architecture achieves the top overall score and secured first place in both the NER and RE tracks, with a significant lead over the second-place competitors.

2 Method

2.1 System Architecture

As shown in Figure 1, based on the input, we design a basic template that defines the LLM as an information extraction expert and specifies the task requirements. To further enhance the model's comprehension and generation capabilities, we introduce a few-shot guidance stage. During this phase, the model is provided with a small set of input-output examples that illustrate desired behaviors, enabling the model to better understand task objectives and expected generation patterns. Concurrently, we impose constraints on the content generation process to ensure outputs strictly adhere to predefined formats and satisfy task-specific requirements. After inputting these prompts into multiple large language models, we fuse the outputs to mitigate biases inherent in individual models, thereby enhancing the robustness and reliability of the final results. It is evident that UIEPrompter is a unified information extraction system based on LLMs. By integrating NER and RE into a single LLM architecture, UIEPrompter effectively circumvents the error propagation inherent in cascaded NER-to-RE pipelines. This joint modeling approach not only ensures consistency between entities and relations but also simplifies system complexity.

2.2 Basic Template

The Basic template encompasses role assignment and a clear task definition. It is structured around the following instruction:

```
You are an expert in document NER and triplet extraction. I will provide you with the domain of the document, the document text, a set of NER entity types, and a set of relationship types for triplet extraction. Please help me extract the NER entities and triplets that appear in the document based on the input.
```

2.3 Few-shot Guidance

Recognizing that different individuals or models may exhibit variations in preferences for the same problem, and to align with the training set's preferences regarding officially recognized labels, we offer a case from the training set as a guiding example. The few-shot input and output example is as follows:

```
## Example 1
## The input is:
    "domain": "...", "doc": "...",
    "NER_set": [...], "RE_set": [...]
## The output is: ...
```

2.4 Constrained Output Generation

To ensure that the output from the large model can be parsed by the evaluation function, strict formatting constraints must be imposed. Additionally, to encourage the model to output a complete and agreed-upon format, we instruct it to omit any reasoning process. The prompts reflecting these requirements can be structured as follows:

```
## The output format must be {"entities":"xxx","triples":"xxx"}.
## In the output, "entities" represents the extracted NER entities, while "triples" represent the extracted triples.
## I do not need any analysis or extraneous commentary; please provide only the JSON formatted result as specified!!
## Please ensure that the JSON is valid and will not cause errors when printed!!
```

2.5 Ensemble to Boost Performance

To achieve better results, we input the prompt into multiple large language models and then combine their outputs. Our approach involves merging the outputs from different models and removing duplicates to obtain the final fused result. The experiment results demonstrate that this method is simple yet effective.

3 Experiments

3.1 Datasets

We utilize the DocIE development and evaluation datasets, which consist of 29 domain-specific

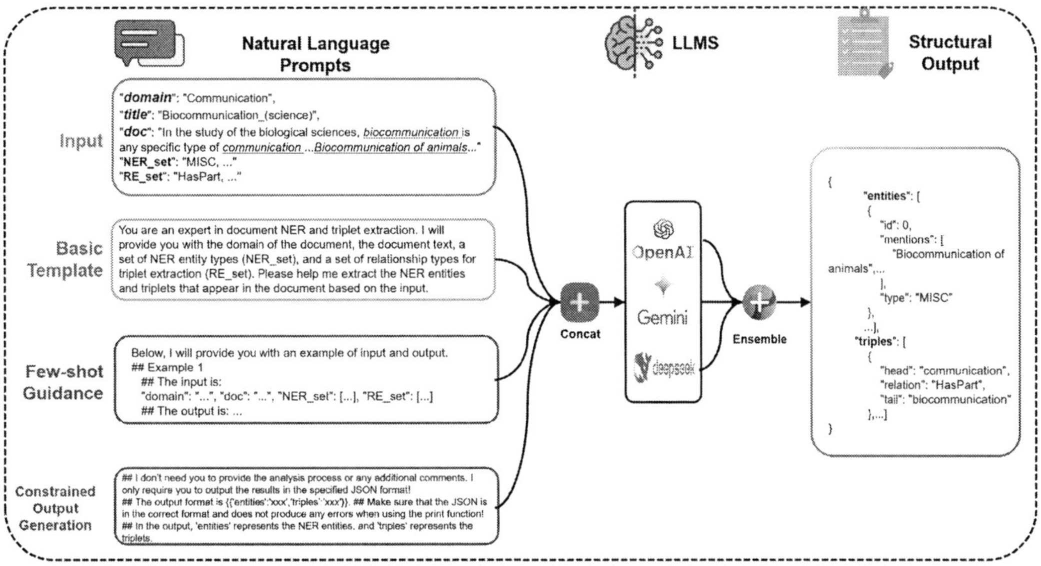

Figure 1: The system architecture of UIEPrompter.

Table 1: Competition leaderboard

Place	Participant	F1-EI↑	F1-EC↑	F1-REG↑	F1-RES↑	F1-AVG↑
1	**qqpprun(UIEPrompter)**	**65.52**	**32.20**	**5.40**	**5.11**	**27.06**
2	UIT-SHAMROCK	55.65	26.11	4.19	4.01	22.49
3	check_out	59.15	18.17	4.38	4.12	21.46
4	ScaDS.AI	32.86	16.19	3.29	3.01	13.84

datasets. We used the development dataset to identify our optimal settings, which were then applied as the final settings for evaluation on the evaluation datasets. More details can be found on the huggingface webcite (doc).

3.2 LLM Selection

In this study, we select three leading state-of-the-art large language models as our meta-models: OpenAI's o3-mini, Google's Gemini-2.0-flash, and DeepSeek's Deepseek-v3.

3.3 Evaluation Metric

We use the competition-specified metrics to evaluate the effectiveness of our models. For the NER track, the competition employs entity identification F1 (F1-EI) and entity classification F1 (F1-EC). In the RE track, the metrics include general mode F1 (F1-REG) and strict mode F1 (F1-RES). The final evaluation metric for the competition is the average of these four F1 scores, denoted as F1-AVG. Detailed definitions of these metrics can be found on the official website.

4 Experimental Results

4.1 Main results

The main results of UIEPrompter on the evaluation dataset are summarized in Table 1. We secure the championship title with an overall F1-AVG of 27.06%, surpassing the runner-up, who scored 22.49%, by nearly 5%. Notably, we also achieved first place in all four sub-F1 metrics: 65.52% for F1-EI and 32.20% for F1-EC in the named entities recognition task, and 5.40% for F1-REG and 5.11% for F1-RES in the relation extraction task. Based on the results, we can identify three key advantages of UIEPrompter:

- **Dominance in the named entities recognition task**: Our F1-EI of 65.52% and F1-EC of 32.20% significantly outperformed all competitors, showcasing our superior accuracy in NER task.
- **Strong performance in relation extraction task**: Despite lower absolute F1 scores in RE tasks, UIEPrompter achieves the highest scores in both F1-REG and F1-RES, indicating robust consistency in the task of relation extraction.

Table 2: Ablation study of the key components. BT stands for basic template. FSG refers to few-shot guidance, and COG denotes constrained output generation prompt.

Model	BT	FSG	COG	F1-EI↑	F1-EC↑	F1-REG↑	F1-RES↑	F1-AVG↑
o3-mini	✓			0	0	0	0	0
	✓	✓		32.82	15.06	9.29	5.25	15.61
	✓	✓	✓	32.39	14.34	16.23	10.53	18.37
Deepseek-v3	✓			0	0	0	0	0
	✓	✓		28.13	23.26	26.71	5.77	20.97
	✓	✓	✓	31.89	24.76	19.73	9.03	21.35
Gemini-2.0-flash	✓			0	0	0	0	0
	✓	✓		38.54	31.06	15.88	3.43	22.23
	✓	✓	✓	41.04	33.16	17.63	2.15	**23.50**

Table 3: Model ensemble results on the development dataset.

Gemini-2.0-flash	o3-mini	Deepseek-v3	F1-EI↑	F1-EC↑	F1-REG↑	F1-RES↑	F1-AVG↑
✓			41.04	33.16	17.63	2.15	23.50
✓	✓		44.47	28.09	22.59	7.97	**25.78**
✓	✓	✓	43.34	27.36	22.73	8.46	25.47

- **Balanced Competence**: The results demonstrate a strong performance across both NER and RE subtasks, showing no significant weaknesses when compared to other participants.

4.2 Ablation Study

To better illustrate the rationale behind our approach, we conducted an ablation study on the development dataset, with results presented in Table 2. It is important to note that the apparent "zero performance" observed with BT does not indicate the models' incapability, but rather reflects failures in the formatting parser. When structural format constraints are absent, outputs can become syntactically invalid (e.g., not JSON format or missing brackets). The results reveal that incorporating few-shot guidance, which provides the model with examples, effectively applies implicit output constraints and improves the performance of the large language model. Furthermore, additional enhancements can be achieved through the use of constrained output generation (COG) prompts, which impose explicit constraints.

Regrading architecture choices, our findings indicate that Gemini-2.0-flash achieved the best overall performance, reaching an F1-AVG of 23.50%. This superior performance can be attributed to its significantly higher F1-EI and F1-EC scores compared to other models, showcasing its strength in the NER task. However, it falls short of the other two models in the F1-REG and F1-RES metrics, suggesting relatively weak relation extraction capabilities. In other words, no single model performs optimally across both tasks simultaneously. To tackle this issue, we implemented a model ensemble approach to improve the overall performance of the framework.

The results of these models fusion are presented in Table 3. The data clearly indicates that the fusion of the Gemini-2.0-flash and o3-mini models achieved the highest overall performance, with an F1-AVG of 25.78% on the development dataset. Additionally, we observed that the fusion of three models on the validation set yielded a performance of 25.47%, which is quite close to the 25.78% achieved by the best combination. To evaluate performance differences on the evaluation set, we found that the fusion of the three models yielded the best results overall.

5 Conclusion

In this work, we present UIEPrompter, a unified and training-free framework that secured first place in the ACL 2025 shared competition on universal document-level information extraction. Our framework adeptly addresses the challenges of named entity recognition and relation extraction in document-level contexts without relying on annotated training data. By leveraging role-specific prompts for zero-shot initialization and adapting to competition schemas through few-shot guidance and constrained output generation prompt, UIEPrompter demonstrates remarkable information extraction performance and generalization capabilities.

References

shuyi-zsy/DocIE,datasets at hugging face. https://huggingface.co/datasets/shuyi-zsy/DocIE.

Aitor Arrieta, Miriam Ugarte, Pablo Valle, José Antonio Parejo, and Sergio Segura. 2025. o3-mini vs deepseek-r1: Which one is safer? *arXiv preprint arXiv:2501.18438*.

Pere-Lluís Huguet Cabot and Roberto Navigli. 2021. Rebel: Relation extraction by end-to-end language generation. In *Findings of the Association for Computational Linguistics: EMNLP 2021*, pages 2370–2381.

Sefika Efeoglu and Adrian Paschke. 2024. Retrieval-augmented generation-based relation extraction. *arXiv preprint arXiv:2404.13397*.

Hao Fei, Shengqiong Wu, Jingye Li, Bobo Li, Fei Li, Libo Qin, Meishan Zhang, Min Zhang, and Tat-Seng Chua. 2022. Lasuie: Unifying information extraction with latent adaptive structure-aware generative language model. *Advances in Neural Information Processing Systems*, 35:15460–15475.

Kung-Hsiang Huang, Sam Tang, and Nanyun Peng. 2021. Document-level entity-based extraction as template generation. *arXiv preprint arXiv:2109.04901*.

Yuna Jeong and Eunhui Kim. 2022. Scideberta: Learning deberta for science technology documents and fine-tuning information extraction tasks. *IEEE Access*, 10:60805–60813.

Martin Kuo, Jianyi Zhang, Aolin Ding, Qinsi Wang, Louis DiValentin, Yujia Bao, Wei Wei, Hai Li, and Yiran Chen. 2025. H-cot: Hijacking the chain-of-thought safety reasoning mechanism to jailbreak large reasoning models, including openai o1/o3, deepseek-r1, and gemini 2.0 flash thinking. *arXiv preprint arXiv:2502.12893*.

Kai Labusch, Preußischer Kulturbesitz, Clemens Neudecker, and David Zellhöfer. 2019. Bert for named entity recognition in contemporary and historical german. In *Proceedings of the 15th conference on natural language processing*, pages 9–11.

Peng Li, Tianxiang Sun, Qiong Tang, Hang Yan, Yuanbin Wu, Xuanjing Huang, and Xipeng Qiu. 2023. Codeie: Large code generation models are better few-shot information extractors. *arXiv preprint arXiv:2305.05711*.

Aixin Liu, Bei Feng, Bing Xue, Bingxuan Wang, Bochao Wu, Chengda Lu, Chenggang Zhao, Chengqi Deng, Chenyu Zhang, Chong Ruan, and 1 others. 2024. Deepseek-v3 technical report. *arXiv preprint arXiv:2412.19437*.

Giovanni Paolini, Ben Athiwaratkun, Jason Krone, Jie Ma, Alessandro Achille, Rishita Anubhai, Cicero Nogueira dos Santos, Bing Xiang, and Stefano Soatto. 2021. Structured prediction as translation between augmented natural languages. *arXiv preprint arXiv:2101.05779*.

Letian Peng, Zilong Wang, Feng Yao, Zihan Wang, and Jingbo Shang. 2024. Metaie: Distilling a meta model from llm for all kinds of information extraction tasks. *arXiv preprint arXiv:2404.00457*.

Yuning Shi and Masaomi Kimura. 2024. Bert-based models with attention mechanism and lambda layer for biomedical named entity recognition. In *Proceedings of the 2024 16th International Conference on Machine Learning and Computing*, pages 536–544.

Robert Vacareanu, Enrique Noriega-Atala, Gus Hahn-Powell, Marco A Valenzuela-Escárcega, and Mihai Surdeanu. 2024. Active learning design choices for ner with transformers. In *Proceedings of the 2024 Joint International Conference on Computational Linguistics, Language Resources and Evaluation (LREC-COLING 2024)*, pages 321–334.

Shuhe Wang, Xiaofei Sun, Xiaoya Li, Rongbin Ouyang, Fei Wu, Tianwei Zhang, Jiwei Li, and Guoyin Wang. 2023. Gpt-ner: Named entity recognition via large language models. *arXiv preprint arXiv:2304.10428*.

Lilong Xue, Dan Zhang, Yuxiao Dong, and Jie Tang. 2024. Autore: Document-level relation extraction with large language models. *arXiv preprint arXiv:2403.14888*.

LLMSR@XLLM25: SWRV: Empowering Self-Verification of Small Language Models through Step-wise Reasoning and Verification

Danchun Chen[1] **Yixin Cao**[1] **Liangming Pan**[2]
[1]Fudan University [2]University of Arizona
{dcchen20, yxcao}@fudan.edu.cn liangmingpan@arizona.edu

Abstract

Large language models (LLMs) have demonstrated impressive reasoning capabilities through Chain-of-Thought (CoT) prompting. However, their reasoning processes remain inexplicable and uncontrollable. In this paper, we introduce a ***Step-Wise Reasoning and Verification*** (SWRV) framework, designed as a two-stage *Parser–Verifier* pipeline, that decomposes the reasoning process into discrete inference steps and rigorously validates each one. Our *Parser* extracts problem constraints and the sequence of reasoning steps from the LLM's output, and our *Verifier*, either LM-based or powered by a symbolic solver, checks the logical correctness of every step. To ensure robust parsing, we fine-tune a compact LM on a small, high-quality annotation set generated by a more capable LM. Experiments on the *LLMSR* dataset built atop *LogiQA* show significant gains over baselines, illustrating the effectiveness of our method for step-wise analysis of LLM reasoning[1].

1 Introduction

Large language models (LLMs) have propelled significant advances in natural language processing, yet they continue to struggle with tasks that demand precise multi-step logical reasoning—especially those involving multiple constraints, nested subproblems, or domain-specific knowledge. While recent developments in Chain-of-Thought (CoT) prompting have enhanced LLM inference and reasoning abilities, the resulting chains of reasoning often lack reliability and interpretability. This can severely hinder downstream performance, as models fail to consistently apply logical rules or verify intermediate steps (Paul et al., 2024). Recent work has demonstrated that very large LLMs (OpenAI, 2024) are capable of self-correcting their outputs through iterative refinement, ushering in a new paradigm for improving model reliability. However, such performance typically depends on massive model sizes and extensive training data, rendering these methods impractical in resource-constrained scenarios. More pertinently, Zhang et al. 2024 found that, for smaller models, overall reasoning performance is bottlenecked not by the ability to refine answers but by the weakness of the verifier module itself. This insight underscores the pressing need for robust, fine-grained self-verification, particularly in settings where only compact models and small-scale annotated data are available. Despite this, most existing approaches focus on validating the entire CoT holistically, without systematically analyzing the validity of individual reasoning steps.

This drives our exploration of step-level reasoning verification methods for small language models. In this work, we propose SWRV, a stronger step-wise self-verification framework as shown in Figure 1 for small LMs (i.e., *Llama-3-8B-Instruct*) using minimal data. In the framework, we perform fine-grained question and CoT analysis to verify each individual inference step within the following pipeline. We first prompt *Llama-3-8B-Instruct* to produce CoTs for *LogiQA* (Liu et al., 2020) questions, then conduct fine-grained parsing of each question and each CoT reasoning step, followed by rigorous verification. For the parser module, we employ rule-based prompting of the small LM and fine-tuning using annotations generated by LM. For verifier, in addition to LM-based inference, we integrate a deterministic symbolic solver Z3 by translating the problem and reasoning steps into symbolic formulas and performing formal inference. Our method aims to deliver a fine-grained, precise self-verifier that improves the self-correction and reasoning ability of small LMs and enables more granular process-level reward modeling.

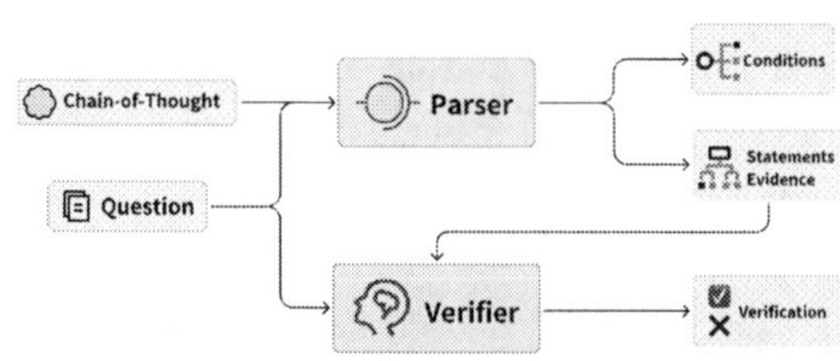

Figure 1: Overview of our SWRV framework.

[1]Code is publicly available at https://github.com/Teganone/XLLM_LLMSR.

Proceedings of the 1st Joint Workshop on Large Language Models and Structure Modeling (XLLM 2025), pages 322–335
August 1, 2025 ©2025 Association for Computational Linguistics

2 Problem Formulation of Self-Verification

As illustrated in Figure 1, we equip a language model with fine-grained self-verification by decomposing its reasoning process into two complementary modules: i) Step-wise Reasoning Parsing, in which both the question and its CoT are parsed into elementary units; and ii) Step-wise Reasoning Verification, in which each inferred unit is rigorously checked for logical validity.

Step-wise Reasoning Parsing The step-wise reasoning parsing mainly focus on parsing the question and CoT. Given a reasoning question *Q* and its CoT, the parser extract all necessary conditions from the question and reasoning steps from the CoT. The parsing for the question and the CoT can be integrated or processed separately, allowing for flexible adjustment of parameters to enhance parsing accuracy.

Step-wise Reasoning Verification For step-by-step reasoning process in CoT, the verifier checks its correctness and marks it as True or False. A verifier, which can either be intrinsic (the LM itself) or extrinsic (an external signal), then decides whether the statement in the step is adequately supported by the corresponding evidence. If the verifier is unable to draw a conclusion, it defaults to considering the reasoning step as correct.

Decoupling parsers from the verifier offers significant advantages over an "all-in-one" design. Firstly, we can freely parameterize each module, for instance, by using fine-tuning or prompting. Secondly, it reduces the difficulty of training each module since the model only needs to focus on one specific capability, either task-specific parsing or step-level reasoning verification. Finally, it makes it possible to integrate deterministic verifiers that incorporate external symbolic solvers.

3 Methodology

As shown in Figure 2, the inputs for our framework consist of a natural language logical reasoning question *Q*, along with the Chain-of-Thought *CoT* genearted by prompting LM to solve the question *Q*. Our goal is to parse *Q* into separate conditions *QP* and the entire *CoT* into separate reasoning steps, each step composing a statement and evidence *R*, and verify the correctness v of each step.

Hence, the final output of each pair of inputs consists of the following elements:

- parsed question conditions

$$\text{QP} = \{c_1, \ldots, c_n\},$$

- parsed & verified reasoning steps

$$CP = \{(s_1, e_1, v_1), \ldots, (s_m, e_m, v_m)\},$$

where s_i is a statement, e_i its supporting evidence and v_i the verification result of (s_i, e_i), each $v_i \in \{True, False\}$.

To achieve this end-to-end pipeline, our SWRV framework is organized into two complementary components. The Parser module comprises i) a *Question Parser* submodule that ingests Q and extracts the individual conditions c_i, and ii) a *CoT Parser* submodule that partitions the CoT into discrete inference steps (s_i, e_i). The Verifier module then takes these parsed outputs, uses a *Symbolic Formulator* to translate both the set of conditions $\{c_i\}$ and each pair (s_i, e_i) into formal logical expressions, and employs an *SMT-Based Checker* (implemented with the *Z3 solver*) to deterministically determine the validity of each inference. By pipelining parsing and verification, our framework delivers a finely grained, formally certified assessment of the entire reasoning trajectory.

3.1 Parser

The parsering module is divided into two stages: prompting a LM to generate question parsing and CoT parsing, and then optionally using the obtained question parsing and CoT parsing together with the original question and CoT as input, with the target question parsing and CoT parsing as labels to supervise the fine-tuning of the LM.

Stage 1: Generating Question Parsing and CoT Parsing A logical reasoning problem typically comprises four parts: problem description, constraints, query, and options. The LM is tasked with extracting all the conditions present in the first three parts. For each question, we instruct the LM to generate the CoT that outlines the problem-solving process. From this CoT, we extract the statement and evidence for each reasoning step. Considering the nature of logical reasoning problems, the arguments mainly stem from the conditions given in the problem and may be related to the options; meanwhile, the evidence often consists of the problem conditions or intermediate conclusions.

Divided by analytical content, we have set up three parsers: a question parser, a CoT parser, and a combined parser, which, respectively, parse the question, the CoT, and both simultaneously. This separate design allows us to individually adjust the parameters for each parser. The parsing process can flexibly choose any combination of these three parsers. In our prompt, we enforce the corresponding rules that require the output of the parsing to remain as semantically consistent as possible with the original question or CoT. We also use one-shot examples to format the output structure and few-shot examples to enrich the diversity of logical question cases. For detailed prompt information, please refer to the Appendix B.2 and B.3.

Stage 2: Supervised Fine-tuning of the Parser To effectively fine-tune LM with minimal data, we supplement the original question and CoT with the question

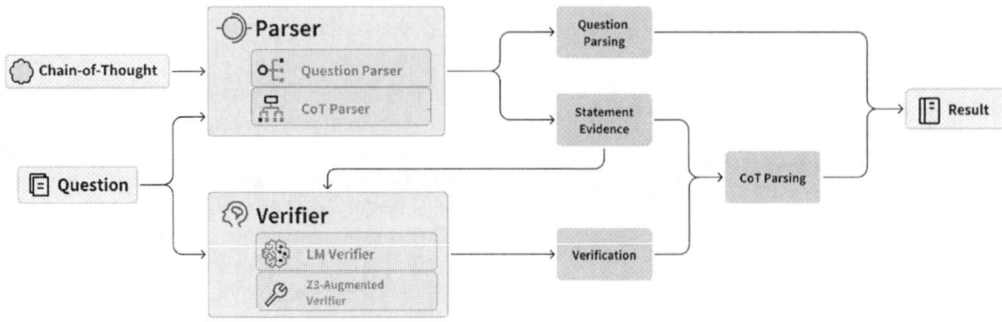

Figure 2: Overview of more detailed SWRV framework.

parsing and CoT parsing obtained from *Stage 1* as inputs. This indicates the LM only need to learn how to refine the existing parsing results instead of having to learn parsing rules from scratch. For detailed prompt information, please refer to the Appendix B.4.

3.2 Verifier

We employ two approaches for verifying the step-wise reasoning: one using LM inference, and the other aided by a deterministic symbolic solver (i.e. *Z3*).

3.2.1 LLM Verifier

For each reasoning step parsed into statements and evidence by the parser, we prompt the LM, with the original or parsed question along with the statements and evidence, to directly verify whether a given statement can be deduced from the evidence. The correct conclusion is "true" and an incorrect deduction is "false". Detailed system prompt and user prompt could be seen in the Appendix B.5.

3.2.2 Z3-Augmented Verifier

Z3 is a high-performance SMT (Satisfiability Modulo Theories) solver developed by Microsoft[2]. It can decide the satisfiability of first-order logic formulas over a rich set of theories—such as linear arithmetic, bit-vectors, arrays, and uninterpreted functions—and is widely used for program verification, symbolic reasoning, and formal analysis.

Inspired by Pan et al. 2023, our *Z3-Augmented Verifier* formulates each reasoning step as a symbolic problem and then invokes Z3 Prover for deterministic validation. Concretely, we define a custom intermediate representation (IR) that bridges natural language and formal logic. The LM is prompted to translate both the original question and each parsed inference step into this IR, which is then translated into executable code. By running through Z3 solver, we obtain a definitive "true" or "false" verdict on the logical correctness of each step.

[2]https://github.com/Z3Prover/z3

Problem-and-Reasoning Formulator As shown in figure 3, given a natural language logical reasoning question Q and its step-wise reasoning R, we prompt a LM to translate them into self-defined intermediate representations. These are then converted into a formal, SMT-compatible representation by a code translator. This encoding captures both the question description and the step-wise reasoning in a symbolic language understandable by Z3.

Symbolic Reasoner We invoke Z3 as a deterministic SMT solver over the encoded problem. Z3 efficiently checks the satisfiability, performs the required logical inferences, and produces a symbolic answer. Because Z3's algorithms are sound and complete for the supported theories, the correctness of the answer is guaranteed when the initial encoding is faithful.

Self-Refiner For complex problems and intricate reasoning, it is challenging for the LM to generate correct logical expressions immediately. Therefore, we introduce a self-refinement module that returns syntax errors from the Z3 solver back to the LM, guiding it to generate correct logical programs. This iterative refinement continues until a valid program is generated or the maximum number of attempts is reached.

Result Interpreter Finally, we use a rule-based interpreter to map the symbolic output back to natural language, providing the final answer.

Appendix B.6 shows detailed prompts of *Problem & Reasoning Symbolic Formulation.*

4 Experimental Setup

4.1 Datasets

A typical sample is stored in JSON format. Detailed examples are given in Appendix A.

4.2 Model Architecture and Fine-tuning

We use *Llama-3-8B-Instruct* as our base model for both the parser and the LM verifier. Considering *Llama-3-8B-Instruct*'s lacking in groundtruth of Z3 syntax, we employ *O3-mini-high* as the base model to generate Z3

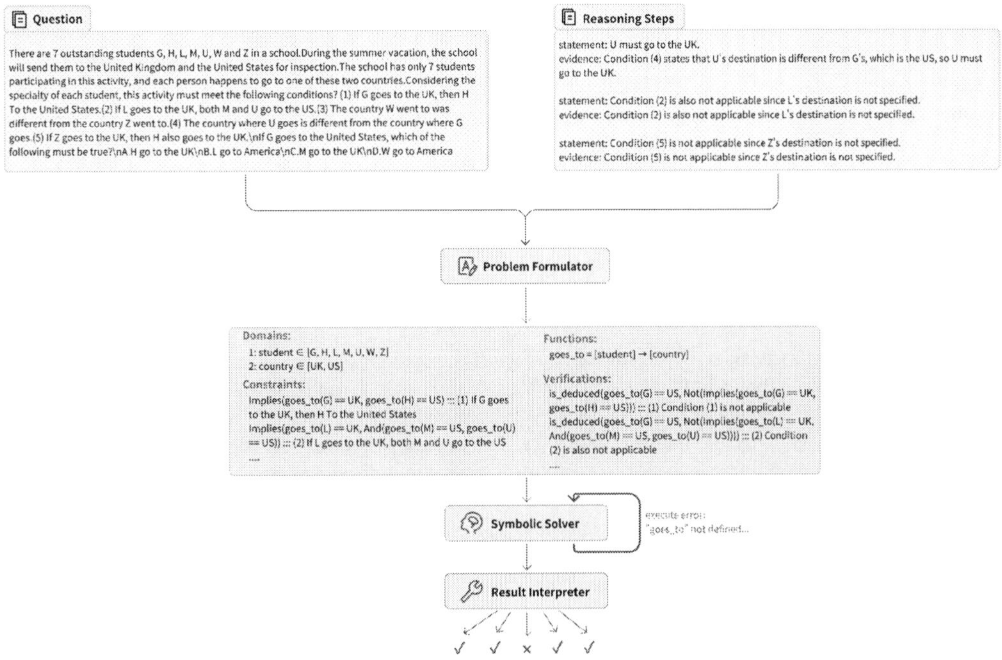

Figure 3: Framework of Z3-Augmented Verifier

formulations.

We set the temperature as $0.2 - 0.3$ in the Question Parser, $0.5 - 0.6$ in the Combined and Cot Parser. For Verification module, we set temperature as $0.1 - 0.2$ in the *Llama Verifier* and the iteration of self-refinement as 3.

We use the 24 samples in the datasets to fine-tune the base *Llama-3-8B-Intruct* with *LoRA*. We set the low-rank dimension as 32, the learning rate as $2e-5$, training epochs as 6, batch size as 2. All our experiments can be conducted on 2×H20 GPU with 96GB of memory.

4.3 Evaluation Metrics and Baseline

Question_Macro_F1 the macro-averaged F1 score computed over the set of all atomic conditions that must be extracted from the input question. Each distinct condition constitutes its own class; true positives, false positives, and false negatives are counted per class, and then F1 is averaged uniformly across classes. This metric thus captures the model's ability to recover every necessary constraint for downstream reasoning, regardless of class frequency.

Statement_Macro_F1 denotes the macro-averaged F1 score for segmenting and identifying individual reasoning statements and their associated evidence spans within the chain of thought. We treat each span type (statement vs. evidence) as a separate class and evaluate extraction quality via both lexical and semantic overlap against ground truth. Precision and recall are computed per class and averaged, ensuring balanced evaluation across all span categories.

Statement_Evidence_Macro_F1 measures the macro-averaged F1 over pairwise links between extracted statements and their corresponding evidence. Each possible statement–evidence pairing is treated as a binary classification task (linked vs. unlinked). We compute class-wise precision and recall for the "linked" label and average the resulting F1 scores across all statement–evidence candidates to assess the model's ability to reconstruct the intended argumentative structure.

Reasoning_F1 the macro-averaged F1 score for the final entailment verification between each correctly extracted statement–evidence pair. We frame logical deduction as a binary entailment decision (entails vs. does not entail). For all validated pairs, we compute precision and recall on the "entails" class and average the F1 scores uniformly, thereby evaluating end-to-end correctness of the tool-augmented reasoning pipeline.

Baseline We invoke *Llama-3-8B-Instruct* to directly parse and verify the data, without any rule setting or fine-tuning, as our baseline.

5 Results

Table 1 and Table 2 presents the primary evaluation results for our base and fine-tuned LM respectively. The results include four performance metrics detailed in 4.3. And we have Four major findings.

5.1 Main Findings

1) Using a lower temperature for *Question Parsing* ensures deterministic and robust outputs. We found that setting a relatively low temperature (around 0.2) for *Question Parsing* and subsequent reasoning yields more deterministic and robust outputs. A lower temperature helps reduce randomness during question generation, ensuring that the parsing results remain logically consistent and rigorous.

2) Striking a balance in temperature during *CoT Parsing* leads to reasoning that is both comprehensive and accurate. For *CoT Parsing*, it is crucial to strike a balance — the temperature should not be too low nor too high. A recommended range is between 0.5 and 0.6. If the temperature is too low, the generated content might be overly fixed and could miss out on important details or the richer process of reasoning. Conversely, if it is too high, the outputs can become too divergent, making it more difficult to extract relevant evidence and accurately perform subsequent verification. Thus, balanced temperature settings are essential to obtain both comprehensive and accurate reasoning chains.

3) Fine-tuned parsers do not outperform the rule-based prompting base parser. The main reason might be limited training set (only 24 examples) combined with the rich, complex rules specified in the prompt, which making it insufficient for a small LM to internalize those rules.
Besides, LM Fine-tuned by Larger LM (e.g. *O3-mini-high*) has better performance in all metrics.

4) Integrating the Z3 solver significantly enhances the accuracy and overall performance of step-wise reasoning verification. In our experiments, the Z3 solver's success rate is around 72%, leading to a *Reasoning_F1* score of 0.078. It is expected that if the parsing and logical expression generation achieved a 100% success rate, the *Reasoning_F1* score could approach the reasoning performance demonstrated by *O3-mini-high*, around 85.07% better than the *LM Verifier* itself. This implies that the symbolic solvers could enhance the step-wise reasoning verification.

5.2 Case Study

Figure 4 and Figure 5 together exemplify the comprehensive reasoning and verification workflow of our SWRV framework. In Figure 4, we show how a complex recruit-assignment puzzle is first decomposed by the *Parser*: the problem statement yields a set of conditions, and the accompanying CoT is split into individual inference steps, each paired with its evidence. Building on this, Figure 5 presents the symbolic instantiation of the same case, in which entities and constraints extracted from the natural-language quetsion description are formalized into logical expressions. Each inference step is translated into a corresponding verification formula, enabling the Z3 solver to deterministically check its validity. By moving from free-form text to symbolic logic, our framework not only attains stronger correctness guarantees than pure language-model reasoning but also furnishes interpretable, step-wise feedback. This structured decomposition thus enhances both the accuracy of self-verification and the transparency of the reasoning process, addressing a key limitation of existing CoT analysis approaches.

6 Conclusion

The paper presents SWRV, a two-stage *Parser–Verifier* framework specifically designed for small LMs and limited data to parse and verify every step in the reasoning process. By decomposing problems in a fine-grained manner and complementing this with a verification mechanism based on symbolic solving, the method significantly enhances the accuracy and robustness of small LMs in logical reasoning tasks.

Future work may explore the expansion of annotated datasets, thereby optimizing the fine-tuning of the parser. Besides, further refinement of natural-to-symbolic translation methods, could also be explored to fortify verification module in diverse reasoning scenarios.

Acknowledgements

This work is supported by my respectful advisors Prof. Cao and Prof. Pan. We also acknowledge support from the hosts (Jia et al., 2025).

References

Zixia Jia, Zilong Zheng, Yang Liu, Jiaqi Li, and Jun Bai. 2025. Llm for structural reasoning. https://xllms.github.io/LLMSR/#. Date: 2025-02-10.

Jian Liu, Leyang Cui, Hanmeng Liu, Dandan Huang, Yile Wang, and Yue Zhang. 2020. Logiqa: A challenge dataset for machine reading comprehension with logical reasoning.

OpenAI. 2024. Gpt-4 technical report.

Liangming Pan, Alon Albalak, Xinyi Wang, and William Yang Wang. 2023. Logic-lm: Empowering large language models with symbolic solvers for faithful logical reasoning.

Debjit Paul, Mete Ismayilzada, Maxime Peyrard, Beatriz Borges, Antoine Bosselut, Robert West, and Boi Faltings. 2024. Refiner: Reasoning feedback on intermediate representations.

Yunxiang Zhang, Muhammad Khalifa, Lajanugen Logeswaran, Jaekyeom Kim, Moontae Lee, Honglak Lee, and Lu Wang. 2024. Small language models need strong verifiers to self-correct reasoning.

Question: There are seven recruits recruited at a university? F, G, H, I, W, X, and Y.One of them is a communications soldier, three are engineering soldiers, and the other three are transport soldiers.The conditions for the assignment of recruits to the army are as follows? H and Y must be assigned to the same arm.F and G cannot be assigned to the same arm.If X is assigned as a transport soldier, then W is assigned as an engineering soldier.Assign F as an engineering soldier.

If X is not assigned as an engineer, which of the following statements may be true?

A.W and G are assigned as engineering soldiers

B.H and W are assigned as transport soldiers.

C.F and Y are assigned as engineering soldiers

D.H and W are assigned as engineering soldiers"

CoT: Since X is not assigned as an engineer, it must be assigned as a communications soldier or a transport soldier. If X is a transport soldier, then W is an engineering soldier, and H and Y must be assigned to the same arm. However, F and G cannot be assigned to the same arm, so F must be an engineering soldier. This means that H and Y are assigned to the same arm, which is the transport arm. Therefore, H and W are assigned as transport soldiers.

Parsed Conditions (Question Parsing):

```
[
    "There are seven recruits recruited at a university? F, G, H, I, W, X, and Y.One of them is a communications soldier, three are engineering soldiers, and the other three are transport soldiers",
    "H and Y must be assigned to the same arm",
    "F and G cannot be assigned to the same arm",
    "If X is assigned as a transport soldier, then W is assigned as an engineering soldier",
    "Assign F as an engineering soldier",
    "If X is not assigned as an engineer"
]
```

Parsed Reasoning Steps:

```
{
    "statement": "X is assigned as a communications soldier or a transport soldier.",
    "evidence": "Since X is not assigned as an engineer, it must be assigned as a communications soldier or a transport soldier.",
},
{
    "statement": "If X is a transport soldier, then W is assigned as an engineering soldier, and H and Y must be assigned to the same arm.",
    "evidence": "If X is a transport soldier, then W is assigned as an engineering soldier, and H and Y must be assigned to the same arm.",
},
{
    "statement": "F must be an engineering soldier.",
    "evidence": "However, F and G cannot be assigned to the same arm, so F must be an engineering soldier.",
}
```

Figure 4: Example of parsed question and reasoning steps for a logical reasoning problem.

Question: There are seven recruits recruited at a university? F, G, H, I, W, X, and Y.One of them is a communications soldier, three are engineering soldiers, and the other three are transport soldiers.The conditions for the assignment of recruits to the army are as follows? H and Y must be assigned to the same arm.F and G cannot be assigned to the same arm.If X is assigned as a transport soldier, then W is assigned as an engineering soldier.Assign F as an engineering soldier.

If X is not assigned as an engineer, which of the following statements may be true?
A.W and G are assigned as engineering soldiers
B.H and W are assigned as transport soldiers.
C.F and Y are assigned as engineering soldiers
D.H and W are assigned as engineering soldiers"

Generated Symbolic Problem Formulations:

Declarations:

recruits = EnumSort([F, G, H, I, W, X, Y])
arms = EnumSort([communications, engineering, transport])
arm_of = Function([recruits] -> [arms])

Constraints:

Count([r: recruits], arm_of(r) == communications) == 1 ::: (Count of communications soldiers)
Count([r: recruits], arm_of(r) == engineering) == 3 ::: (Count of engineering soldiers)
Count([r: recruits], arm_of(r) == transport) == 3 ::: (Count of transport soldiers)
arm_of(H) == arm_of(Y) ::: (1) H and Y must be assigned to the same arm
arm_of(F) != arm_of(G) ::: (2) F and G cannot be assigned to the same arm
Implies(arm_of(X) == transport, arm_of(W) == engineering) ::: (3) If X is assigned as a transport soldier, then W is assigned as an engineering soldier
arm_of(F) == engineering ::: (4) F is assigned as an engineering soldier
arm_of(X) != engineering ::: (Assumption: X is not assigned as an engineer)

Reasoning Step:

Statement: X is assigned as a communications soldier or a transport soldier.

Evidence: Since X is not assigned as an engineer, it must be assigned as a communications soldier or a transport soldier.

Generated Symbolic Verification Formulations:

is_deduced(arm_of(X) != engineering, Or(arm_of(X) == communications, arm_of(X) == transport)) ::: (1) X must be assigned as a communications soldier or a transport soldier

Predicted Verification: True

Reasoning Step:

Statement: F must be an engineering soldier.

Evidence: However, F and G cannot be assigned to the same arm, so F must be an engineering soldier.

Generated Symbolic Verification Formulations:

is_deduced(True, arm_of(F) == engineering) ::: (3) F must be an engineering soldier

Predicted Verification: False

other step-wise reasoning examples...

Figure 5: Example of symbolic problem and reasoning formulation and verification for a logical logical problem.

Approach	Question_F1	Statement_F1	Statement_Evidence_F1	Reasoning_F1
Baseline	0.5702	0.3341	0.0852	0.0326
Base Question Parser	0.7299	/	/	/
Base Combined Parser	0.7187	0.4247	0.168	/
Llama Verifier	/	/	/	0.067
O3-mini-high Verifier	/	/	/	0.124
Z3 Verifier (72%)	/	/	/	0.078

Table 1: Performance of various parsers and verifiers. "/" indicates that a given configuration was not designed or evaluated for that subtask (e.g., the Base Question Parser only performs question parsing, so its *Statement_F1*, *Evidence_F1*, and *Reasoning_F1* cells are marked "/").

Preprocessor	Question_F1	Statement_F1	Statement_Evidence_F1
Baseline	0.7187	0.4247	0.168
Llama-3-8B-Instruct	0.6078	0.3979	0.1417
O3-mini-high	0.7171	0.4046	0.1862

Table 2: Performance of parsers fine-tuned on data preprocessed by *Llama-3-8B-Instruct* and *O3-mini-high*. "Baseline" denotes the original model without fine-tuning.

A Dataset

question: There are 7 outstanding students G, H, L, M, U, W and Z in a school. During the summer vacation, the school will send them to the United Kingdom and the United States for inspection. The school has only 7 students participating in this activity, and each person happens to go to one of these two countries. Considering the specialty of each student, this activity must meet the following conditions? (1) If G goes to the UK, then H To the United States. (2) If L goes to the UK, both M and U go to the US. (3) The country W went to was different from the country Z went to. (4) The country where U goes is different from the country where G goes. (5) If Z goes to the UK, then H also goes to the UK.
If G goes to the United States, which of the following must be true?
A. H go to the UK
B. L go to America
C. M go to the UK
D. W go to America
question_parsing: [
"The school has only 7 students participating in this activity, and each person happens to go to one of these two countries",
"If G goes to the UK, then H goes to the United States",
"If L goes to the UK, both M and U go to the US",
"The country W went to was different from the country Z went to",
"The country where U goes is different from the country where G goes",
"If Z goes to the UK, then H also goes to the UK",
"G goes to the United States"
]

answer: b
id: 162
cot: Since G goes to the United States, we need to analyze the conditions that follow. Condition (1) is not applicable since G is going to the US. Condition (2) is also not applicable since L's destination is not specified. Condition (3) does not provide any information about H, M, U, or W. Condition (4) states that U's destination is different from G's, which is the US, so U must go to the UK. Condition (5) is not applicable since Z's destination is not specified.
cot_parsing: [
{
"statement": "Condition (1) is not applicable",
"evidence": "G is going to the US",
"Verification": "true"
},
{
"statement": "Condition (2) is also not applicable",
"evidence": "L's destination is not specified",
"Verification": "true"
},
{
"statement": "Condition (3) does not provide any information about H, M, U, or W",
"evidence": "Condition (3)",
"Verification": "false"
},
{
"statement": "U must go to the UK",
"evidence": "Condition (4) states that U's destination is different from G's, which is the US",
"Verification": "true"
},

{
"statement": "Condition (5) is not applicable",
"evidence": "Z's destination is not specified",
"Verification": "true"
}
]
sel_idx: 92

B Prompt

B.1 Prompt For Question Parser

Given a question. The task is to generate "question_parsing" results based on the content of "question". The "question" could be logically divided into four parts: 1) problem description, 2) conditions/constraints, 3) query, and 4) options. The question parsing process involves extracting all conditions necessary for solving the question.
Evaluation: This task focuses on question parsing. Question parsing involves extracting all relevant conditions required to solve the problem. The Macro F1 score metric is used to evaluate question parsing performance.
Please generate output in JSON format based on the requirements below. The output must include one key-value pair:
"question_parsing": an array of strings used to extract all necessary constraints provided in the question for solving the problem. Only extract conditions from parts 1) problem description, 2) conditions/constraints, and any additional conditions present in part 3) query. Do not extract any details from the explicit query statement (e.g., phrases like "which is ...") or from the options. The problem itself should be extracted as the first condition.
Rules: Each constraint or condition in the original question should be treated as a whole; do not split or break down a single constraint or condition into smaller parts. Use the exact descriptions given in the original question without synonym substitution or additional embellishment, ensuring high consistency in both semantics and wording with the original text.
EXAMPLE 1:
question:
There are 7 outstanding students G, H, L, M, U, W and Z in a school. During the summer vacation, the school will send them to the United Kingdom and the United States for inspection. The school has only 7 students participating in this activity, and each person happens to go to one of these two countries. Considering the specialty of each student, this activity must meet the following conditions? (1) If G goes to the UK, then H To the United States. (2) If L goes to the UK, both M and U go to the US. (3) The country W went to was different from the country Z went to. (4) The country where U goes is different from the country where G goes. (5) If Z goes to the UK, then H also goes to the UK.
If G goes to the United States, which of the following must be true?
A. H go to the UK
B. L go to America
C. M go to the UK
D. W go to America
Example Output:
question_parsing:
"The school has only 7 students participating in this activity, and each person happens to go to one of these two countries",
"If G goes to the UK, then H goes to the United States",
"If L goes to the UK, both M and U go to the US",
"The country W went to was different from the country Z went to",
"The country where U goes is different from the country where G goes",
"If Z goes to the UK, then H also goes to the UK",
"G goes to the United States"
] output Example "question_parsing": ["The school has only 7 students participating in this activity, and each person happens to go to one of these two countries", "If G goes to the UK, then H To the United States", "If L goes to the UK, both M and U go to the US", "The country W went to was different from the country Z went to", "The country where U goes is different from the country where G goes", "If Z goes to the UK, then H also goes to the UK", "G goes to the United States"]
NOW ANALYZE THIS NEW QUESTION:
question:
{{question}}
Remember to analyze the specific content above, not the examples. Your output should be a valid JSON object with a "question_parsing" key.

B.2 Prompt For Combined Parser

Given a question and cot. The task is to generate "question_parsing" and "cot_parsing" results based on the content of "question" and "cot". The "question" could be logically divided into four parts: 1) problem description, 2) conditions/constraints, 3) query, and 4) options. The question parsing process involves extracting all conditions necessary for solving the question. The cot parsing process identifies all "statements" and their corresponding "evidence" within the context of the question conditions and the given cot content.
Evaluation: This task consists of two parts: Question parsing and cot parsing. Question parsing involves extracting all relevant conditions required

to solve the problem. The Macro F1 score metric is used to evaluate question parsing performance. The process of extracting statements and evidence is similar to Discourse Parsing. Correct extraction of statements or evidence from the cot is crucial at the outset. Next, the pairwise relationship between a specific statement and its corresponding evidence is assessed (a statement should be followed by its related evidence from the cot). Both semantic and lexical similarity are used to evaluate the accuracy of statements and evidence predictions. The final evaluation metric is the Macro F1 score, applied to both statement parsing and statement-evidence pair extraction. Whether the "statement" can be deduced from the "evidence" logically, answer with only with "true" or "false". Please generate output in JSON format based on the requirements below. The output must include two key-value pairs:
"question_parsing": an array of strings used to extract all necessary constraints provided in the question for solving the problem. Only extract conditions from parts 1) problem description, 2) conditions/constraints, and any additional conditions present in part 3) query. Do not extract any details from the explicit query statement (e.g., phrases like "which is ...") or from the options. The problem itself should be extracted as the first condition.
"question_parsing": an array of strings used to extract all necessary constraints provided in the question for solving the problem. Only extract conditions from parts 1) problem description, 2) conditions/constraints, and any additional conditions present in part 3) query. Do not extract any details from the explicit query statement (e.g., phrases like "which is ...") or from the options. The problem itself should be extracted as the first condition.
Rules: Each constraint or condition in the original question should be treated as a whole; do not split or break down a single constraint or condition into smaller parts. Use the exact descriptions given in the original question without synonym substitution or additional embellishment, ensuring high consistency in both semantics and wording with the original text.
EXAMPLE 1:
question:
There are 7 outstanding students G, H, L, M, U, W and Z in a school. During the summer vacation, the school will send them to the United Kingdom and the United States for inspection. The school has only 7 students participating in this activity, and each person happens to go to one of these two countries. Considering the specialty of each student, this activity must meet the following conditions? (1) If G goes to the UK, then H To the United States. (2) If L goes to the UK, both M and U go to the US. (3) The country W went to was different from the country Z went to. (4) The country where U goes is different from the country where G goes. (5) If Z goes to the UK, then H also goes to the UK.
If G goes to the United States, which of the following must be true?
A. H go to the UK
B. L go to America
C. M go to the UK
D. W go to America
Example Output:
question_parsing:
"The school has only 7 students participating in this activity, and each person happens to go to one of these two countries",
"If G goes to the UK, then H goes to the United States",
"If L goes to the UK, both M and U go to the US",
"The country W went to was different from the country Z went to",
"The country where U goes is different from the country where G goes",
"If Z goes to the UK, then H also goes to the UK",
"G goes to the United States"
] output Example "question_parsing": ["The school has only 7 students participating in this activity, and each person happens to go to one of these two countries", "If G goes to the UK, then H To the United States", "If L goes to the UK, both M and U go to the US", "The country W went to was different from the country Z went to", "The country where U goes is different from the country where G goes", "If Z goes to the UK, then H also goes to the UK", "G goes to the United States"]
NOW ANALYZE THIS NEW QUESTION:
question:
{{question}}
Remember to analyze the specific content above, not the examples. Your output should be a valid JSON object with a "question_parsing" key.

B.3 Prompt For Combined Parser

Given a question and cot. The task is to generate "question_parsing" and "cot_parsing" results based on the content of "question" and "cot". The "question" could be logically divided into four parts: 1) problem description, 2) conditions/constraints, 3) query, and 4) options. The question parsing process involves extracting all conditions necessary for solving the question. The cot parsing process identifies all "statements" and their corresponding "evidence" within the context of the question conditions and the given cot content.
Evaluation: This task consists of two parts: Question parsing and cot parsing. Question parsing

involves extracting all relevant conditions required to solve the problem. The Macro F1 score metric is used to evaluate question parsing performance. The process of extracting statements and evidence is similar to Discourse Parsing. Correct extraction of statements or evidence from the cot is crucial at the outset. Next, the pairwise relationship between a specific statement and its corresponding evidence is assessed (a statement should be followed by its related evidence from the cot). Both semantic and lexical similarity are used to evaluate the accuracy of statements and evidence predictions. The final evaluation metric is the Macro F1 score, applied to both statement parsing and statement-evidence pair extraction. Whether the "statement" can be deduced from the "evidence" logically, answer with only with "true" or "false" Please generate output in JSON format based on the requirements below. The output must include two key-value pairs:

"question_parsing": an array of strings used to extract all necessary constraints provided in the question for solving the problem. Only extract conditions from parts 1) problem description, 2) conditions/constraints, and any additional conditions present in part 3) query. Do not extract any details from the explicit query statement (e.g., phrases like "which is . . . ") or from the options. The problem itself should be extracted as the first condition.

"cot_parsing": an array where each element is an object containing three keys: - "statement": The final inference result from the cot, or an intermediate logical reasoning step. - "evidence": The corresponding supporting evidence directly for the statement as it appears in the cot. - "Verification": A Boolean indicator ("true" or "false") stating whether the "statement" can be deduced from the "evidence" logically.

Rules:

Regarding Question Parsing: Each constraint or condition in the original question should be treated as a whole; do not split or break down a single constraint or condition into smaller parts. Use the exact descriptions given in the original question without synonym substitution or additional embellishment, ensuring high consistency in both semantics and wording with the original text.

Regarding cot Parsing: Extract from the cot text all "statements" and their corresponding "evidences". Each cot entry must be based directly on the text as it appears, ensuring that unnecessary synonym replacements or categorical expansions are avoided. Each "statement" must be immediately followed by its corresponding "evidence". The output should match the original text as closely as possible in both wording and semantics. If the cot text includes explanations about a constraint or a condition being "not applicable" or "irrelevant," these must be captured in full without splitting or merging. Additional note: In the cot text, the selected statements often contain information that is different from or additional to the constraints (especially conditions) extracted from the question. Even if these statements do not match the constraints extracted in "question_parsing," please extract them as they appear and preserve the original wording from the cot text. For each logical reasoning, extract the final deduction as statement and extract intermediate reasoning steps as well as condition as its corresponding evidence. Verify for each "statement" whether it can be logically deduced from the provided "evidence". For this verification, answer only with either "true" or "false".

EXAMPLE 1:

question:

There are 7 outstanding students G, H, L, M, U, W and Z in a school. During the summer vacation, the school will send them to the United Kingdom and the United States for inspection. The school has only 7 students participating in this activity, and each person happens to go to one of these two countries. Considering the specialty of each student, this activity must meet the following conditions? (1) If G goes to the UK, then H To the United States. (2) If L goes to the UK, both M and U go to the US. (3) The country W went to was different from the country Z went to. (4) The country where U goes is different from the country where G goes. (5) If Z goes to the UK, then H also goes to the UK.

If G goes to the United States, which of the following must be true?

A. H go to the UK

B. L go to America

C. M go to the UK

D. W go to America

cot:

Since G goes to the United States, we need to analyze the conditions that follow. Condition (1) is not applicable since G is going to the US. Condition (2) is also not applicable since L's destination is not specified. Condition (3) does not provide any information about H, M, U, or W. Condition (4) states that U's destination is different from G's, which is the US, so U must go to the UK. Condition (5) is not applicable since Z's destination is not specified.

Example Output:

question_parsing:

"The school has only 7 students participating in this activity, and each person happens to go to one

of these two countries",
"If G goes to the UK, then H To the United States",
"If L goes to the UK, both M and U go to the US",
"The country W went to was different from the country Z went to",
"The country where U goes is different from the country where G goes",
"If Z goes to the UK, then H also goes to the UK",
"G goes to the United States"

cot_parsing:
{
"statement": "Condition (1) is not applicable",
"evidence": "G is going to the US",
},
{
"statement": "Condition (2) is also not applicable",
"evidence": "L's destination is not specified",
},
{
"statement": "Condition (3) does not provide any information about H, M, U, or W",
"evidence": "Condition (3)",
},
{
"statement": "U must go to the UK",
"evidence": "Condition (4) states that U's destination is different from G's, which is the US",
},
{
"statement": "Condition (5) is not applicable",
"evidence": "Z's destination is not specified",
}

NOW ANALYZE THIS NEW QUESTION AND COT:
question:
{{question}}
cot:
{{cot}}
Remember to analyze the specific content above, not the examples. Your output should be a valid JSON object with "question_parsing" and "cot_parsing" keys.

B.4 Prompt For Fine-tuning

SYSTEM_PROMPT
You are an expert in logical parsing and reasoning analysis, specializing in analyzing problem conditions and chain-of-thought reasoning processes. Given a question, a cot and preprocessed question_parsing and cot_parsing provided by the given question and the cot. Your task is to generate accurate question question_parsing and cot_parsing results based on the given question and cot.
USER_PROMPT
Based on the following question and chain of thought reasoning process, generate question_parsing and cot_parsing results.
Question:
{question}
Cot:
{cot}
Preprocessed Question Parsing:
{preprocessed_qp}
Preprocessed Cot Parsing:
{preprocessed_cp}
Please provide improved parsing results in the following format: {
"question_parsing": [
"condition 1",
"condition 2",
...
],
"cot_parsing": [
{
"statement": "statement 1",
"evidence": "evidence 1",
"Verification": "true or false"
},
{
"statement": "statement 2",
"evidence": "evidence 2",
"Verification": "true or false"
},
...
]
}
Generate the improved JSON:

B.5 Prompt For LLM Verifier

SYSTEM:
Whether the "statement" can be deduced from the "evidence" logically, answer with only with True or False, do not output other contents.
USER:
question:
question
statement:
statement
evidence:
evidence

B.6 Prompt For Problem Fomulator of Z3 Verifier

Given a question and a cot_parsing. The task is to formulate the problem as a logic program (All the self-defined syntax could be seen in the following examples), consisting three parts: Declarations, Constraints, and Verification. Please strictly follow the samples below to generate the result, do not generate any other irrelevant contents. Declarations: Declare the variables and functions from the question. Constraints: Write the constraints or conditions in the question as logic formulas. Verifications: Write the verification of statement and evidence in the cot_parsing as logic formulas.

IMPORTANT RULES:

1. When using boolean values, always use capitalized True and False, not lowercase true and false. For example, use "is_playing(m) == True" instead of "is_playing(m) == true".
2. Ensure that all variable names used in Constraints and Verifications are declared in the Declarations section.
3. Make sure all names in the Declarations section are consistent with those used in the Constraints and Verifications sections.
4. Do not add any irrelevant comments, such as comments starting with // or #, except # Declarations, # Constraints, # Verifications.
5. Only use logic expressions or syntax patterns that appear in the examples. Do not create your own syntax.

EXAMPLE 1:

question:

There are 7 outstanding students G, H, L, M, U, W and Z in a school. During the summer vacation, the school will send them to the United Kingdom and the United States for inspection. The school has only 7 students participating in this activity, and each person happens to go to one of these two countries.Considering the specialty of each student, this activity must meet the following conditions? (1) If G goes to the UK, then H To the United States.(2) If L goes to the UK, both M and U go to the US.(3) The country W went to was different from the country Z went to.(4) The country where U goes is different from the country where G goes.(5) If Z goes to the UK, then H also goes to the UK.G goes to the United States, which of the following must be true?.H go to the UK.L go to America.M go to the UK.W go to America

cot_parsing:

{
"statement": "Condition (1) is not applicable",
"evidence": "G is going to the US",
"Verification": "true"
},
{
"statement": "Condition (2) is also not applicable",
"evidence": "L's destination is not specified",
"Verification": "true"
},
{
"statement": "Condition (3) does not provide any information about H, M, U, or W",
"evidence": "Condition (3)",
"Verification": "false"
},
{
"statement": "U must go to the UK",
"evidence": "Condition (4) states that U's destination is different from G's, which is the US",
"Verification": "true"
},
{
"statement": "Condition (5) is not applicable",
"evidence": "Z's destination is not specified",
"Verification": "true"
}

Example Output:

Declarations

students = EnumSort([G, H, L, M, U, W, Z])
countries = EnumSort([UK, US])
goes_to = Function([students] -> [countries])

Constraints

Implies(goes_to(G) == UK, goes_to(H) == US) ::: (1) If G goes to the UK, then H To the United States
Implies(goes_to(L) == UK, And(goes_to(M) == US, goes_to(U) == US)) ::: (2) If L goes to the UK, both M and U go to the US
goes_to(W) != goes_to(Z) ::: (3) The country W went to was different from the country Z went to
goes_to(U) != goes_to(G) ::: (4) The country where U goes is different from the country where G goes
Implies(goes_to(Z) == UK, goes_to(H) == UK) ::: (5) If Z goes to the UK, then H also goes to the UK
goes_to(G) == US ::: If G goes to the United States

Verifications

is_deduced(goes_to(G) == US, Not(Implies(goes_to(G) == UK, goes_to(H) == US))) ::: (1) Condition (1) is not applicable
is_deduced(goes_to(G) == US, Not(Implies(goes_to(L) == UK, And(goes_to(M)

== US, goes_to(U) == US)))) ::: (2) Condition (2) is also not applicable
is_deduced(goes_to(W) != goes_to(Z), False) ::: (3) Condition (3) does not provide any information about H, M, U, or W
is_deduced(And(goes_to(U) != goes_to(G), goes_to(G) == US), goes_to(U) == UK) ::: (4) U must go to the UK
is_deduced(goes_to(G) == US, Not(Implies(goes_to(Z) == UK, goes_to(H) == UK))) ::: (5) Condition (5) is not applicable

NOW ANALYZE THIS NEW QUESTION AND COT_PARSING:
question:
{{question}}
cot_parsing:
{{cot_parsing}}
Remember to analyze the specific content above, not the examples. Your output should include Declarations, Constraints, and Verifications sections.

LLMSR@XLLM25: An Empirical Study of LLM for Structural Reasoning

Xinye Li[†] **Mingqi Wan**[†] **Dianbo Sui**[*]
Harbin Institute of Technology
{lixinye,2022211876}@stu.hit.edu.cn, suidianbo@hit.edu.cn

Abstract

We present Team *asdfo123*'s submission to the LLMSR@XLLM25 shared task, which evaluates large language models on producing fine-grained, controllable, and interpretable reasoning processes. Systems must extract all problem conditions, decompose a chain of thought into statement–evidence pairs, and verify the logical validity of each pair. Leveraging only the off-the-shelf **Meta-Llama-3-8B-Instruct**, we craft a concise few-shots, multi-turn prompt that first enumerates all conditions and then guides the model to label, cite, and adjudicate every reasoning step. A lightweight post-processor based on regular expressions normalises spans and enforces the official JSON schema. Without fine-tuning, external retrieval, or ensembling, our method ranks **5th** overall, achieving macro-F_1 scores on par with substantially more complex and resource-consuming pipelines. We conclude by analysing the strengths and limitations of our approach and outlining directions for future research in structural reasoning with LLMs. Our code is available at https://github.com/asdfo123/LLMSR-asdfo123.

1 Introduction

Large language models (LLMs) have recently shown impressive performance on complex reasoning tasks, spurred in part by *Chain–of–Thought* (CoT) prompting, which asks the model to externalise intermediate steps before giving an answer (Wei et al., 2023). Subsequent variants—such as zero-shot CoT (Kojima et al., 2022), self-consistency decoding (Wang et al., 2023), tree-of-thought search (Yao et al., 2023), and automatically generated demonstrations (Zhang et al., 2022)—further boost accuracy, yet these free-form rationales remain difficult to evaluate and prone to hallucinations (Akbar et al., 2024).

[*]Dianbo Sui is the corresponding author.
[†]Equal contribution.

The LLMSR@XLLM25 shared task tackles this limitation by framing reasoning as a constrained CoT process: systems must (i) extract every explicit problem condition, (ii) segment a rationale into aligned **statement–evidence** pairs, and (iii) judge whether each evidence span **logically entails** its statement. Such fine-grained structure "improves the transparency and reliability of the process" (task description) and enables detailed diagnosis of model behaviour. Moreover, the step-level labels provide dense supervision for Process Reward Modeling (PRM), which optimises *how* a solution is reached rather than merely *what* answer is produced (Uesato et al., 2022; Lightman et al., 2023).

Structured parsing of reasoning brings three concrete benefits. First, it enhances **debuggability**: developers can pinpoint the exact step where a hallucination or logical slip occurs. Second, it supplies explicit training signals for PRM, shown to yield more coherent and truthful solutions on mathematical benchmarks (Lightman et al., 2023). Third, it promotes **trustworthy AI**: users can audit or amend individual steps, a requirement for safety-critical deployments and formal logic tasks such as EntailmentBank proofs (Dalvi et al., 2021) or LogicBench diagnostics (Parmar et al., 2024).

In this report we present Team *asdfo123*'s lightweight submission, which relies solely on the untuned **Meta-Llama-3-8B-Instruct** (Meta AI, 2024). A compact few-shot, multi-turn prompt guides the model through all three subtasks, while a minimal post-processor enforces the official JSON schema. Despite its simplicity, our approach ranks **5th** overall, demonstrating that careful prompt design and constrained reasoning can rival far more elaborate pipelines.

Proceedings of the 1st Joint Workshop on Large Language Models and Structure Modeling (XLLM 2025), pages 336–341
August 1, 2025 ©2025 Association for Computational Linguistics

2 Related Work

2.1 Chain-of-Thought Prompting

Chain-of-Thought (CoT) prompting has emerged as a powerful method to enhance multi-steasoning in large language models (LLMs). Initial studies showed significant improvements by simply adding "Let's think step by step" to zero-shot prompts (Kojima et al., 2022). Self-consistency further boosts robustness by generating multiple reasoning chains and selecting the most consistent response (Wang et al., 2023). Least-to-Most prompting addresses complex problems by decomposing them into simpler subproblems, achieving near-perfect accuracy on challenging tasks (Zhou et al., 2023).

However, CoT prompting can produce logically flawed reasoning steps, reaching correct answers through invalid logic (Zelikman et al., 2022; Golovneva et al., 2023). The Tree of Thoughts framework mitigates this by organizing reasoning into a search tree, allowing systematic backtracking and evaluation of alternative reasoning paths (Yao et al., 2023). Incorporating knowledge-graph-based verification also improves reliability (He et al., 2025; Jiang et al., 2023).

Recent benchmarks focus on evaluating CoT quality beyond answer accuracy, using validity and redundancy metrics to assess reasoning step-by-step (Xia et al., 2025; Chen et al., 2025). These approaches emphasize the need for tighter integration between reasoning generation and verification.

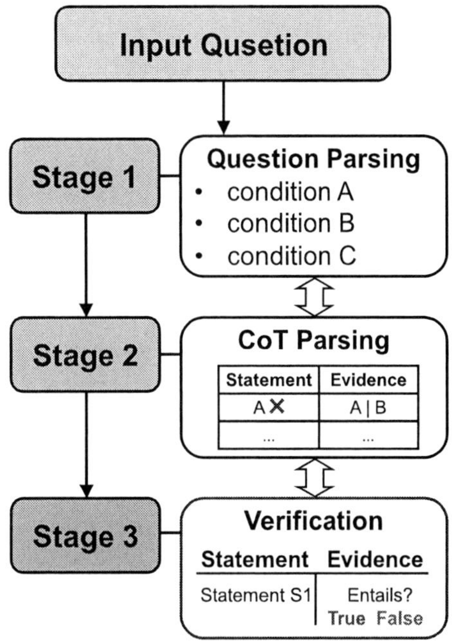

Figure 1: Illustration of the three-stage LLM-SR Task. *(In our implementation, Verification is executed within the CP stage.)*

2.2 Parsing

Turning natural language into structured representations is a prerequisite for dependable reasoning. ProgPrompt steers LLMs to emit code-like blocks of comments, actions, and assertions for situated robot planning (Singh et al., 2022). Self-Ask improves interpretability by decomposing a complex query into solvable sub-questions and then composing their answers (Press et al., 2023). Coupling LLMs with Answer Set Programming lets a logic engine verify every inferred rule, boosting robustness (Yang et al., 2023). RaLU aligns CoT spans with formal logic units and checks them via external solvers (Li et al., 2025).

For discourse-level parsing, Rhetorical Structure Theory (RST) models text coherence via nucleus–satellite relations (MANN and THOMPSON, 1988). Early algorithms split texts into Elementary Discourse Units and attached rhetorical relations—sometimes without explicit markers (Marcu, 1998). Enhanced RST (eRST) extends this to graphs with non-projective, concurrent relations and both implicit and explicit signals, offering more flexible, explainable structures (Zeldes et al., 2024).

2.3 Process Reward Model

Previous studies have demonstrated that process supervision maintains reasoning consistency better than outcome supervision, and conceptualized Process Reward Models (PRMs) to reduce logical errors (Uesato et al., 2022; Lightman et al., 2023). To mitigate the cost of manual annotations, recent approaches automatically retrieve similar solution steps to generate fine-grained, step-level labels—facilitating both verification and PPO-based reinforcement learning without human supervision (Wang et al., 2024).

Building on the foundational PRM framework, several works have further advanced process reward modeling. Tree-based preference learning constructs reasoning trees via best-first search and trains verifiers using paired step-level preferences (He et al., 2024). More recently, CFPRM (Hu et al., 2025) introduces a coarse-to-fine strategy that first merges adjacent steps into coarse-grained windows and then refines them into fine-grained units. This hierarchical method mitigates redundancy in LLM-generated reasoning while enabling training across multiple levels of granularity.

3 Methodology

3.1 Pipeline Overview

Our system follows the three–stage workflow mandated by the LLM–SR task (Figure 1):

1. **Question Parsing (QP).** The model enumerates every explicit condition of the problem as an ordered list.
2. **CoT Parsing & Verification (CP).** Given the question, its Chain–of–Thought (CoT) rationale, and the QP output, the model simultaneously (i) segments the rationale into **statement–evidence pairs** and (ii) judges whether each evidence span **logically entails** its statement.

All stages run on the untuned original **Meta–Llama–3–8B–Instruct**. Instead of parameter fine–tuning we rely on *few-shot in-context learning* (ICL) with a multi-turn dialogue template (§3.2). A deterministic post-processor (§3.4) validates and cleans the raw generations, after which we completes the full public test set in under ten minutes.

3.2 Prompt Engineering

Few-shot demonstrations. We hand-pick two QP and three CP exemplars that jointly cover most patterns. During inference these demonstrations precede the test instance verbatim.

Three-turn template. Each call is cast as a short conversation:

1. SYSTEM: global rules, including format restrictions.
2. USER: the problem text plus the explicit request (QP or CP).
3. ASSISTANT: the model's structured JSON answer.

Because CP depends on the extracted conditions, we invoke the model twice per instance: first for QP, and then for a single CP call which jointly performs CoT parsing and the verification step, with the QP list appended to the user prompt.

3.3 Robust JSON Output

Llama-3 occasionally produces ill-formed JSON—extra quotes, missing commas, or unclosed braces—which crashes the official scorer. By enclosing every demonstration answer in a fenced `` ```json ... ``` `` block and explicitly instructing the model to output valid JSON only, we cut the unparsable rate on the dev set from 16 % to just 2 %. The few residual errors are corrected or flagged by our post-processor.

3.4 Post-processing

A lightweight Python script performs:

1. **Schema check**: every object must contain `statement`, `evidence`, and boolean `verification`.
2. **Normalisation**: trim bullets, stray whitespace, smart quotes, trailing punctuation; merge duplicate conditions.
3. **Alignment**: if #statements $\neq$ #evidence, align by order; otherwise flag (none observed on dev/test).

3.5 Efficiency Rationale

The task rewards both answer correctness and reasoning quality. We show that careful prompt design plus minimal hygiene techniques already yields a top-5 macro-F_1 without external retrieval or fine-tuning, providing a strong, reproducible baseline for future work on PRM.

4 Experiments

We conduct all experiments on the official `LLMSR@XLLM25` test sets[1]. The shared task provides a *fine-grained* Chain-of-Thought (CoT) analysis corpus derived from LogiQA (Liu et al., 2021). It contains only 24 fully annotated training instances, each accompanied by both *question-parsing* and *CoT-parsing* labels. From the 24 training instances, we heuristically select a small subset of demonstrations that spans the major logical patterns; these serve as the few-shot exemplars in our prompts.

The evaluation follows a two-stage protocol. First, we perform a k-shot ablation for **Question Parsing** (QP), varying the number of in-context demonstrations. After selecting the best QP setting,

[1] `https://huggingface.co/datasets/shuyi-zsy/LLMSR/tree/main/llmsr`

we keep it fixed and sweep k again for **CoT Parsing & Verification** (CP) to determine its optimal demonstration budget.

4.1 Phase 1: Selecting the Question-Parsing Shot Count

Table 1 shows QP results with $k \in \{1, 2, 3, 4\}$. Macro-F_1 peaks at **0.7526** with **2-shot**. Adding a third or fourth example degrades performance, presumably because the longer prompt dilutes salient patterns and pushes relevant context tokens farther from the model's attention window.

Shots (k)	Question_Macro_F1
1	0.6707
2	**0.7526**
3	0.7281
4	0.7061

Table 1: Few-shot ablation for Question Parsing.

Given its clear advantage, we *fix* $k=2$ *for all subsequent QP calls*. The extracted condition list is then passed as additional context to the CP stage.

4.2 Phase 2: Tuning CoT Parsing & Verification

After fixing the QP stage at two demonstrations, we sweep the shot count for CoT Parsing. Table 2 shows that **3-shot** strikes the best trade-off, yielding the highest *Statement_Macro_F1* as well as the strongest pair-level and reasoning scores. Adding a fourth example brings only marginal gains and in some cases degrades performance, presumably because the longer prompt pushes relevant tokens farther from the model's attention window.

CP Shots	Stmt_{F1}	Stmt+Ev_{F1}	Reasoning_{F1}
1	0.3066	0.0726	0.0391
2	0.1816	0.0860	0.0250
3	**0.3304**	**0.1385**	**0.0782**
4	0.2978	0.0976	0.0518

Table 2: CoT Parsing & Verification with *2-shot QP* fixed. "Stmt" = Statement_Macro_F1, "Stmt+Ev" = Statement_Evidence_Macro_F1.

4.3 Final Configuration

The combination of **2-shot QP** and **3-shot CP** constitutes our submission. This hybrid setup achieves the highest overall macro-F_1 on the public leaderboard while preserving the system's lightweight. The results highlight two insights: (1) QP and CP favour different demonstration budgets, and (2) carefully tuning each stage separately beats a single fixed prompt size.

We report our final experimental results in Table 3, which include the Test A and Test B phase scores on the official LLMSR@XLLM25 test sets.

Phase	Question_{F1}	Stmt_{F1}	Stmt+Ev_{F1}	Reasoning_{F1}
Test A	75.26	33.04	13.85	7.82
Test B	75.33	47.26	20.17	11.64

Table 3: Macro-F1 scores on four evaluation criteria for Test A and Test B phases. "Stmt" = Statement_Macro_F1, "Stmt+Ev" = Statement_Evidence_Macro_F1.

5 Discussion

5.1 Key Insights from the Shared Task

The LLMSR@XLLM25 shared task offers a concrete sandbox for **controllable** and **transparent** reasoning. By forcing systems to expose every condition, align each statement with explicit evidence, and render a step-level entailment verdict, the task goes well beyond conventional answer-only evaluation. Our experiments confirm three central insights:

1. **Structural reasoning is promising yet non-trivial.** Even an untuned 8B model can reliably parse conditions (§4, Phase 1), but struggles to decompose and verify chains of thought.
2. **Larger does not (yet) mean satisfactory.** Informal leaderboard comparisons indicate that more elaborate, resource-heavy pipelines still fall short. The bottleneck is not extraction but *logical adjudication.*

5.2 Limitations of Llama-3-8B

Meta-Llama-3-8B scores well on QP but falters on logic: it hallucinates evidence, merely paraphrases conditions, and mishandles negation, dragging down Statement–Evidence and Reasoning F_1. These errors persist despite prompt tuning and JSON guards, implying the bottleneck lies in the model's logic rather than the interface.

5.3 Future Work

Stronger verifiers. Verification may need a more capable judge (e.g., GPT-4o, Claude 3) detached from the generator.

Lightweight entailment modules. Training a small, dedicated critic on synthetic entailment pairs—à la CoT-Critic—could boost step-level faithfulness.

Process Reward Models (PRMs). The extracted structures are ideal supervisory signals for PRMs. Iteratively refining the generator with PRM feedback may tighten the link between evidence and statements, increasing coherence without brute-force scaling.

5.4 Takeaway

The shared task shows that structured reasoning is a feasible yet unsolved frontier for LLMs. Our minimal system serves as a proof of concept; progress now hinges on developing (i) stronger or specialised verifiers and (ii) learning paradigms that reward *how* a conclusion is reached, not merely *what* it is. We believe these directions will be pivotal for deploying LLMs in settings where transparency and trustworthiness are non-negotiable.

6 Conclusion

We showed that a carefully crafted, few-shot prompting pipeline—backed by lightweight post-processing—can tackle the `LLMSR@XLLM25` shared task without fine-tuning or external tools, ranking 5th overall. While Meta-Llama-3-8B handles condition extraction well, its verification accuracy remains limited, underscoring the need for stronger or specialised reasoners and process-level training signals. Future work should pair stronger base models with dedicated entailment critics and reward models that explicitly value step-by-step correctness.

References

Shayan Ali Akbar, Md Mosharaf Hossain, Tess Wood, Si-Chi Chin, Erica M Salinas, Victor Alvarez, and Erwin Cornejo. 2024. HalluMeasure: Fine-grained hallucination measurement using chain-of-thought reasoning. In *Proceedings of the 2024 Conference on Empirical Methods in Natural Language Processing*, pages 15020–15037, Miami, Florida, USA. Association for Computational Linguistics.

Guizhen Chen, Weiwen Xu, Hao Zhang, Hou Pong Chan, Chaoqun Liu, Lidong Bing, Deli Zhao, Anh Tuan Luu, and Yu Rong. 2025. Finereason: Evaluating and improving llms' deliberate reasoning through reflective puzzle solving. arXiv preprint arXiv:2502.20238.

Bhavana Dalvi, Peter Jansen, Oyvind Tafjord, Zhengnan Xie, Hannah Smith, Leighanna Pipatanangkura, and Peter Clark. 2021. Explaining answers with entailment trees. In *Proceedings of the 2021 Conference on Empirical Methods in Natural Language Processing*, pages 7358–7370, Online and Punta Cana, Dominican Republic. Association for Computational Linguistics.

Olga Golovneva, Moya Chen, Spencer Poff, Martin Corredor, Luke Zettlemoyer, Maryam Fazel-Zarandi, and Asli Celikyilmaz. 2023. Roscoe: A suite of metrics for scoring step-by-step reasoning. *Preprint*, arXiv:2212.07919.

Jiashu He, Mingyu Derek Ma, Jinxuan Fan, Dan Roth, Wei Wang, and Alejandro Ribeiro. 2025. Give: Structured reasoning of large language models with knowledge graph inspired veracity extrapolation. arXiv preprint arXiv:2410.08475.

Mingqian He, Yongliang Shen, Wenqi Zhang, Zeqi Tan, and Weiming Lu. 2024. Advancing process verification for large language models via tree-based preference learning. *Preprint*, arXiv:2407.00390.

Yulan Hu, Ge Chen, Jinman Zhao, Sheng Ouyang, and Yong Liu. 2025. Coarse-to-fine process reward modeling for mathematical reasoning. *Preprint*, arXiv:2501.13622.

Jinhao Jiang, Kun Zhou, Xin Zhao, Yaliang Li, and Ji-Rong Wen. 2023. Reasoninglm: Enabling structural subgraph reasoning in pre-trained language models for question answering over knowledge graph. In *EMNLP*, pages 3721–3735.

Takeshi Kojima, Shixiang Shane Gu, Machel Reid, Yutaka Matsuo, and Yusuke Iwasawa. 2022. Large language models are zero-shot reasoners. In *Proceedings of the 36th International Conference on Neural Information Processing Systems*, NIPS '22, Red Hook, NY, USA. Curran Associates Inc.

Cheryl Li, Tianyuan Xu, and Yiwen Guo. 2025. Reasoning-as-logic-units: Scaling test-time reasoning in large language models through logic unit alignment. arXiv preprint arXiv:2502.07803.

Hunter Lightman, Vineet Kosaraju, Yura Burda, Harri Edwards, Bowen Baker, Teddy Lee, Jan Leike, John Schulman, Ilya Sutskever, and Karl Cobbe. 2023. Let's verify step by step. *Preprint*, arXiv:2305.20050.

Jian Liu, Leyang Cui, Hanmeng Liu, Dandan Huang, Yile Wang, and Yue Zhang. 2021. Logiqa: a challenge dataset for machine reading comprehension with logical reasoning. In *Proceedings of the Twenty-Ninth International Joint Conference on Artificial Intelligence*, IJCAI'20.

WILLIAM C. MANN and SANDRA A. THOMPSON. 1988. Rhetorical structure theory: Toward a functional theory of text organization. *Text - Interdisciplinary Journal for the Study of Discourse*, 8(3):243–281.

Daniel C. Marcu. 1998. *The rhetorical parsing, summarization, and generation of natural language texts*. Ph.D. thesis, CAN. AAINQ35238.

Meta AI. 2024. Meta-llama-3-8b-instruct model card.

Mihir Parmar, Nisarg Patel, Neeraj Varshney, Mutsumi Nakamura, Man Luo, Santosh Mashetty, Arindam Mitra, and Chitta Baral. 2024. LogicBench: Towards systematic evaluation of logical reasoning ability of large language models. In *Proceedings of the 62nd Annual Meeting of the Association for Computational Linguistics (Volume 1: Long Papers)*, pages 13679–13707, Bangkok, Thailand. Association for Computational Linguistics.

Ofir Press, Muru Zhang, Sewon Min, Ludwig Schmidt, Noah Smith, and Mike Lewis. 2023. Measuring and narrowing the compositionality gap in language models. In *Findings of EMNLP*, pages 5687–5711.

Ishika Singh, Valts Blukis, Arsalan Mousavian, Ankit Goyal, Danfei Xu, Jonathan Tremblay, Dieter Fox, Jesse Thomason, and Animesh Garg. 2022. Progprompt: Generating situated robot task plans using large language models. arXiv preprint arXiv:2209.11302.

Jonathan Uesato, Nate Kushman, Ramana Kumar, Francis Song, Noah Siegel, Lisa Wang, Antonia Creswell, Geoffrey Irving, and Irina Higgins. 2022. Solving math word problems with process- and outcome-based feedback. *Preprint*, arXiv:2211.14275.

Peiyi Wang, Lei Li, Zhihong Shao, R. X. Xu, Damai Dai, Yifei Li, Deli Chen, Y. Wu, and Zhifang Sui. 2024. Math-shepherd: Verify and reinforce llms step-by-step without human annotations. *Preprint*, arXiv:2312.08935.

Xuezhi Wang, Jason Wei, Dale Schuurmans, Quoc Le, Ed Chi, Sharan Narang, Aakanksha Chowdhery, and Denny Zhou. 2023. Self-consistency improves chain of thought reasoning in language models. *Preprint*, arXiv:2203.11171.

Jason Wei, Xuezhi Wang, Dale Schuurmans, Maarten Bosma, Brian Ichter, Fei Xia, Ed Chi, Quoc Le, and Denny Zhou. 2023. Chain-of-thought prompting elicits reasoning in large language models. *Preprint*, arXiv:2201.11903.

Shijie Xia, Xuefeng Li, Yixin Liu, Tongshuang Wu, and Pengfei Liu. 2025. Evaluating mathematical reasoning beyond accuracy. arXiv preprint arXiv:2404.05692.

Zhun Yang, Adam Ishay, and Joohyung Lee. 2023. Coupling large language models with logic programming for robust and general reasoning from text. arXiv preprint arXiv:2307.07696.

Shunyu Yao, Dian Yu, Jeffrey Zhao, Izhak Shafran, Thomas L. Griffiths, Yuan Cao, and Karthik Narasimhan. 2023. Tree of thoughts: Deliberate problem solving with large language models. *Preprint*, arXiv:2305.10601.

Amir Zeldes, Tatsuya Aoyama, Yang Janet Liu, Siyao Peng, Debopam Das, and Luke Gessler. 2024. erst: A signaled graph theory of discourse relations and organization. *Preprint*, arXiv:2403.13560.

Eric Zelikman, Yuhuai Wu, Jesse Mu, and Noah Goodman. 2022. Star: Bootstrapping reasoning with self-consistency. In *Advances in Neural Information Processing Systems*, volume 35, pages 15476–15488.

Zhuosheng Zhang, Aston Zhang, Mu Li, and Alex Smola. 2022. Automatic chain of thought prompting in large language models. *Preprint*, arXiv:2210.03493.

Denny Zhou, Nathanael Schärli, Le Hou, Jason Wei, Nathan Scales, Xuezhi Wang, Dale Schuurmans, Claire Cui, Olivier Bousquet, Quoc Le, and Ed Chi. 2023. Least-to-most prompting enables complex reasoning in large language models. *Preprint*, arXiv:2205.10625.

LLMSR@XLLM25: A Language Model-Based Pipeline for Structured Reasoning Data Construction

Hongrui Xing[12†*], Xinzhang Liu[2*], Zhuo Jiang[2], Zhihao Yang[2], Yitong Yao[2], Zihan Wang[2], Wenmin Deng [2], Chao Wang[2], Shuangyong Song[2], Wang Yang[1‡], Zhongjiang He[2‡], Yongxiang Li[2]

[1]School of Cyber Science and Engineering, Southeast University
[2]Institute of Artificial Intelligence (TeleAI), China Telecom Corp Ltd.

Correspondence: {xinghr,wang.yang}@seu.edu.cn
{liuxz2,hezj}@chinatelecom.cn

Abstract

In this paper, we present a novel pipeline for the XLLM Shared Task-III: Large Language Model for Structural Reasoning (LLM-SR). Our pipeline addresses key challenges in automatic process-reward training data construction, such as high manual annotation costs, limited accuracy of large models in structured data processing, and dependency on auxiliary information for validation. To overcome these limitations, we first decompose the construction process into extraction and validation phases. Leveraging model-generated annotations, we produce pseudo-labeled data and iteratively refine model performance. Second, by analyzing structured data patterns, we encode structural constraints into a rule-based module and fine-tune the model with Gradient Reward Policy Optimization (GRPO), significantly improving structured data extraction success rates. Finally, we train the model to generate critical responses that assess evidence-conclusion relationships, thus enhancing validation reliability. Experimental results demonstrate that our pipeline outperforms models with an order of magnitude more parameters and achieves the first position on the task[1].

1 Introduction

Large language models (LLMs) have demonstrated remarkable capabilities in mathematical and logical reasoning tasks, particularly when employing Chain-of-Thought (CoT) prompting to decompose problems into multi-step reasoning processes (Guo et al., 2025)(Yang et al., 2024)(Li et al., 2024a)(Wang et al., 2024b). However, even state-of-the-art models often produce unreliable intermediate reasoning steps, leading to cascading errors that compromise final outputs (Tyen et al., 2024). To mitigate this issue, existing research has introduced step-wise verification methods (Zeng et al., 2023). For instance, process reward models (PRM) can evaluate reasoning paths during training, identify erroneous steps, and offer precise corrective feedback (Li et al., 2023). Alternatively, step-wise analysis of CoT data from both correctness and redundancy perspectives can generate high-quality reasoning traces for training (Xia et al., 2025). These approaches not only enhance reasoning reliability but also improve overall data quality through generating constructive critiques of flawed reasoning steps, thereby providing valuable optimization signals for model refinement.

However, developing such step-wise verification models faces three fundamental challenges:

- The scarcity of high-quality step-level annotated reasoning datasets.
- The limited capability of current models in both processing structural inputs and constructing regular outputs.
- The accuracy in justifying the logical validity step by step.

Acquiring high-quality training data requires labor-intensive step-by-step annotation of reasoning processes with correctness feedback. For instance, the PRM800K dataset (Lightman et al., 2023) utilizes expert annotators to provide process supervision annotations. This heavy dependence on skilled annotators significantly hinders both the development and practical application of step-wise verification models.

Moreover, existing verification approaches typically employ simplistic segmentation method (e.g. explicit "Step:" markers, double line breaks, or periods) to parse reasoning steps (Zhang et al., 2024). Such rigid segmentation fails to capture the nuanced compositional structure inherent in natural

[1]Codes: `https://github.com/pipiPdesu/CoTParser`.
[†]Work done during the internship at TeleAI.
[*]These authors contributed equally to this work.
[‡] Corresponding authors.

Proceedings of the 1st Joint Workshop on Large Language Models and Structure Modeling (XLLM 2025), pages 342–350
August 1, 2025 ©2025 Association for Computational Linguistics

CoT reasoning. This limitation fundamentally constrains the verification fidelity in real-world applications, where reasoning complexity often exceeds template-based patterns.

Additionally, verification models struggle with complex problems, as even large-scale models frequently fail to accurately determine step correctness, revealing critical limitations in current verification paradigms. To generate high quality dataset, Marh-Shepherd (Wang et al., 2024a) uses rejection sampling to generate multiple reasoning paths starting from certain steps, approximating step correctness based on the accuracy of the final answer. rStar-Math (Guan et al., 2025) constructs positive-negative sample pairs to train PPM, guiding the model towards correct solutions. Although these methods effectively create step-level supervision data and improve PRM capabilities, their data primarily consist of synthetic samples and require substantial computational resources and additional messages for construction. More importantly, they cannot accurately parse the naturally occurring CoT processes.

To tackle these challenges, XLLM Shared Task-III: LLM for Structural Reasoning requires participants to extract all conditions, statements, and their corresponding evidence from given problems and associated CoT processes, then determine whether the evidence sufficiently supports each extracted statement-evidence pair. This approach achieves fine-grained CoT analysis to enhance the generation of more coherent and accurate reasoning processes.

In this work, we propose a fine-grained analysis pipeline for CoT reasoning processes. The method decomposes the task into two components: extraction and verification. For the extraction task, following the construct of AIFlow (Shao and Li, 2025), we identify the problem conditions, statements, and supporting evidence from the question and CoT process. To address data scarcity, we first employ prompt engineering and preliminary fine-tuning to generate high-quality pseudo-labels. These extraction patterns are then formalized as prior knowledge into rule-base reward, and the model is further trained using GRPO (Shao et al., 2024) to streamline the extraction process and improve extraction accuracy. For the verification task, inspired by positive-incentive noise (Li, 2022), we reformulate it as generating concise yet effective critiques for statement-evidence pairs to determine whether the evidence supports the statement. Our method achieved first place in this competition. While maintaining low resource consumption, our model improves extraction capability by 20% compared to baselines. Our findings demonstrate the feasibility of using prior knowledge as rule reward to enhance model performance on specific NLU tasks like text extraction and recognition, as well as transforming verification tasks into critique generation tasks to improve verification capabilities of smaller models.

2 Related work

LLMs for Information Extraction. The emergence of large language models has introduced new solutions and research directions for information extraction. (Wu et al., 2024) proposed the Multi-stage Structured Entity Extraction method, which enhances effectiveness and efficiency by breaking down the task. PIVOINE (Lu et al., 2023) focuses on the issue of Open-world IE, improving the model's instruction-following ability by constructing the INSTRUCTOPENWIKI dataset, and demonstrates excellent generalization to unseen instructions. LLMs for Text2SQL (Li et al., 2024b)(Wu et al., 2025) also provide a new avenue for exploring their role in information extraction.

Step Verification for LLMs. To enable fine-grained analysis of CoT reasoning, existing studies have attempted to evaluate model performance through reasoning process inspection. RECEVAL (Prasad et al., 2023) proposes reference-free metrics based on entailment relations and pointwise variational information to assess step correctness and information gain. Parser-based method (Saparov and He, 2023) parses model-generated CoT into symbolic proofs for formal analysis. Other works employ LLMs themselves for correctness verification. Inspired by RFT (Xia et al., 2025), most approaches sample multiple reasoning paths to inversely estimate step validity. (Zhang et al., 2024) uses correct answers to guide models in critiquing their own incorrect responses, then filters high-quality critiques to train verification models. (Wan et al., 2024) determines answer correctness through multi-path consistency checks and identifies erroneous steps though multi-agent debate. (Xia et al., 2025) fine-tunes models to score reasoning steps from both validity and redundancy perspectives. (Tyen et al., 2024) observes LLMs' underperformance in error localization tasks and trains small classifiers to identity errors. (Zeng et al., 2023) introduces meta-reasoning to evaluate error-correction capabilities through recursive reasoning analysis.

Process reward model (PRM) dataset. In reinforcement learning, PRMs provide step-level feedback to align LLM reasoning with human expectations. For generating process-wise supervision data, PRM800K (Lightman et al., 2023) relies on manual annotation. Math-Shepherd (Wang et al., 2024a) automates this via rejection sampling: generating multiple reasoning paths from intermediate steps and assuming step correctness if most paths yield correct answers. rStar-Math (Guan et al., 2025) constructs positive-negative sample pairs to train Process Preference Model.

3 Methodology

In this section, we first introduce the detailed task description (Section 3.1), followed by presenting the complete extraction pipeline architecture along with the specific extraction methods for each module and the approach for generating pseudo-labeled datasets (Section 3.2). Subsequently, we elaborated on the application of GRPO for the extraction task (Section 3.3) and the method of employing verification to validate the statement-evidence pairs (Section 3.4). Our final solution is an LLM-powered pipeline for structured reasoning data construction, as shown in Figure 1.

3.1 Details of Challenge

This task requires participants to generate "question parsing" and "cot parsing" based on the content of "question" and "cot" for each given message. Specifically, the task is divided into two parts: Question Parsing and CoT Parsing. For Question Parsing, all relevant conditions required to solve the problem must be extracted from the given question text. For CoT Parsing, all statement-evidence pairs need to be extracted, and it must be logically verified whether the statement can be inferred from the evidence. Participants are only allowed to use Llama-3-8B-Instruct (Grattafiori et al., 2024) as the backbone model.

This task has released only 24 annotated examples as the training set, with questions sourced from LogiQA (Liu et al., 2021) and CoT generated from Llama3-8b-instruct.[2] Additionally, there are 50 test cases for evaluation set A that only release the quires and 97 test examples for evaluation set B. Appendix A shows part of the annotated examples.

3.2 Extraction Pipeline

For this task, accurately extracting the required information from the given question and CoT process is of vital importance. The task baseline proposes a method based on in-context learning for extraction and verification. This method employs few-shot learning to extract key points from the input question and CoT, directly outputs all components required. However, due to limitations in model size and the availability of annotated data, we believe that this method is difficult to further optimize. Therefore, we consider decomposing the entire task into two independent parts: Question Parsing and CoT Parsing. For CoT Parsing, we further break it down into Statement Extraction, Evidence Extraction, and Statement-Evidence Pair Verification. Subsequent steps may rely on the results of previous steps, meaning that this pipeline needs to run in a serial manner. However, optimization of different parts can be carried out independently. To achieve a higher score, we need to minimize the extraction of incorrect information during the extraction process to ensure a perfect match between the extracted content and the ground truth.

Question parsing Inspired by the data extraction strategy in REDSTONE (Chang et al., 2024), we divide the extraction approach into two components: extract and filter. First, the model performs sentence segmentation on the entire question, treating enumerated conditions as separate sentences. Subsequently, we filter all sentence segments that contain useful information to solve the problem. Notably, some conditions may appear in the question's interrogative clause (e.g. "If G goes to the United States, which of the following must be true?" provides the condition "G goes to the United States"). For such cases, we further extract the embedded conditions while removing irrelevant lexical items.

Statement extraction Since we cannot directly divide the steps based on explicit markers, it becomes challenging to estimate the number of statements in the CoT process. To figure out this issue, we divide each natural reasoning step into three substeps:

- Summarization of given conditions.
- Derivation of new information from known conditions (corresponding to **evidence**).

[2]All data can be found in https://huggingface.co/datasets/shuyi-zsy/LLMSR/tree/main/llmsr.

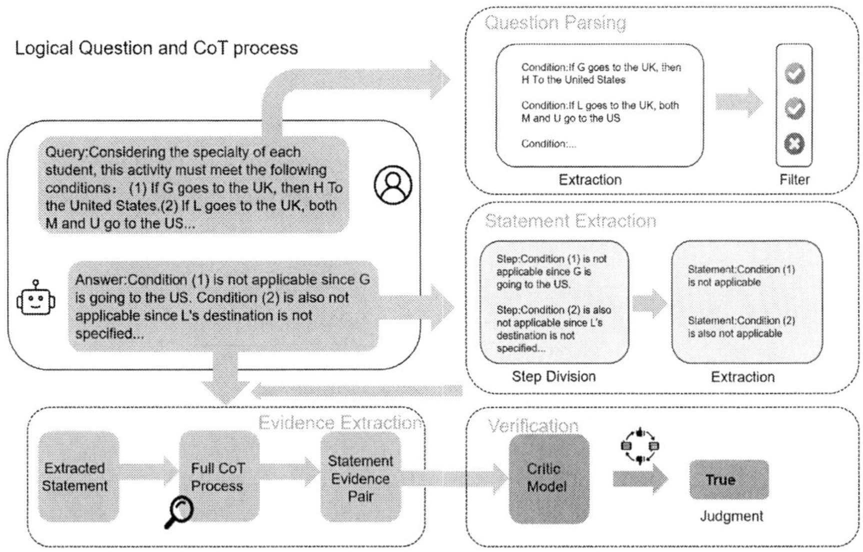

Figure 1: Architecture of CoT parsing pipeline. The pipeline consists of four key modules. The Question Parsing Module receives the question, extract all sentences and filter out valid conditions. The Statement Parsing Module takes the CoT process, divides it into multiply steps, then extract valid statements from each step. The Evidence Extraction Module process all statements and the CoT process to identify corresponding evidence. The verification Module takes all statement-evidence pairs, justify their validity.

- Generation of new conditions or conclusions (corresponding to **statements**).

Following this principle, we first instruct the model to segment the entire CoT process into these refined steps. This ensures that each reasoning step typically contains at most 0-1 statements, allowing the extraction model to focus on small contextual segments and significantly reducing extraction complexity. Additionally, this decomposition of natural steps enables us to expand the original 24 data samples 4-5 times, thereby facilitating the construction of high-quality fine-tuning data. After fine-tuning, the model's extraction capability is further improved.

Evidence extraction Initially we considered extracting evidence from the pre-segmented steps when identifying statements. However, we observed that certain pieces of evidence often span multiple steps. For instance, a concluding statement such as "From above, we can conclude" requires all previously obtained valid statements as supporting evidence. Moreover, extracting evidence directly from individual steps may introduce error propagation caused by incorrect step segmentation. Therefore, for each extracted statement, we need to search for its corresponding evidence throughout the entire CoT process. Since statements typically originate from the original text and their supporting evidence usually appears near clear discourse markers (e.g., connectives or adverbs), this provides sufficient context for the model to accurately locate the relevant evidence.

To further enhance the performance of each module, we consider utilizing the aforementioned pipeline to generate more pseudo-labeled data. First, we sample questions from LogiQA. Subsequently, to ensure that the synthesized CoT processes maintain distributional consistency with the task's given data, we sample one question-answer pair each from the training set and evaluation set A, serves as one-shot provided to Llama3-8B-Instruct as reference for generating responses.

3.3 Utilize GRPO for Extraction

Due to the insufficient extraction accuracy of this pipeline, the pseudo-labeled dataset generated by this method can hardly provide substantial improvements to the model. We discovered that instead of using human annotation experience as prompts for model learning or allowing the model to memorize patterns through more data, we can incorporate these as rules to provide rewards in GRPO. For statement extraction, we summarized the following potential guidelines from the training dataset:

- The statement must originate from original text
- The statement must end with a period
- The statement length must be no fewer than 4 words and no more than 50 words
- The statement must not contain connectives such as "since" or "there is"
- The statement must not duplicate conditions extracted from the question
- The statements should appear in sequence
- Because there must be evidence in between, no two statements should be consecutive in the original CoT

These guidelines can serve both as rules for manual annotation and as directions for model exploration during reinforcement learning. When the model's response violates these rules, it receives a negative reward, and only when it perfectly matches the correct answer does it receive a positive reward. This approach encourages the model to learn the human method of data extraction.

After fine-tuning with GRPO, the model can directly extract all statements from the CoT process, maintaining accuracy while reducing intermediate computational overhead. This method demonstrates the potential of incorporating prior rules into GRPO's rule-based rewards to enhance LLM performance on traditional NLP tasks.

3.4 Verification

The objective of this part is to determine whether each extracted statement can be inferred from its corresponding evidence. For this problem, we make the following assumptions:

1. The model needs to rely on all known conditions of the question to determine whether the statement holds. When judging whether the evidence supports the statement, the model should first determine whether the statement is valid in the context of the question before assessing whether the evidence sufficiently supports the statement.
2. All statement-evidence pairs are independent. When judging whether a statement holds, only its corresponding evidence is needed, not other evidence or statements from the context. The evidence should consist of all the sentences that can prove the statement. If a statement requires additional evidence beyond its corresponding evidence, it indicates that the evidence is not sufficient to fully support the statement.
3. Judging statement-evidence pairs using the model should not be a simple binary classification task but should fully leverage the model's reasoning process. However, due to the limitations of the PRM function, the reasoning process should not be overly lengthy.

Based on these assumptions and inspired by the approach in CFT (Wang et al., 2025) of criticizing noise, we believe that the output of the Verification model should be a critique with justification of the statement-evidence pair. The critique part should directly point out the reasons why the evidence support or does not support the statement and provide the final justification based on these reasons. We used DeepSeek v3-0324 (Liu et al., 2024) to generate a critique dataset from the extracted dataset and fine-tuned the discriminative model accordingly. The success rate after fine-tuning remained similar to that of DeepSeek v3, indicating that training the model to criticize noise to judge the correctness of reasoning steps is effective, and the model can acquire this ability with limited data.

4 Experiment

4.1 Setup

Pipeline Overview Our final pipeline operates as follows: For each question, the model first extracts all potential conditions followed by a filtering module. For statement-evidence pairs, the model directly extracts all statements from the CoT process. After removing duplicates with the extracted conditions, it searches for corresponding evidence in the CoT for each statement. Finally, a verification model justifies each statement-evidence pair.

Parameter Settings We trained four Llama3-8B-Instruct models for this pipeline: condition extraction, statement extraction, evidence extraction and verification. All models were full parameter fine-tuned for 3 epochs at a learning rate of $1e{-}5$ using pseudo-labeled data generated by above pipeline. The verification model training data outputs were produced by DeepSeek V3-0324. During inference,

Method/Team	Question(%)	Statement(%)	Evidence(%)	Reasoning(%)
		Baselines		
ICL(Llama3-8b-Instruct)	73.01	42.40	18.10	10.32
ICL(Qwen2-7b-Instruct)	69.98	42.1	15.09	8.51
ICL(Telechat2)	72.18	46.39	16.82	7.71
ICL(DeepSeek-R1)	**81.87**	44.84	12.42	10.79
dcchen(2nd)	78.53	54.31	**23.57**	15.71
blazerblade(3rd)	76.7	40.44	11.32	6.20
TeleAI(Ours)	81.2	**55.07**	22.44	**17.09**

Table 1: Comparison of top3 teams with our submission, along with baseline method of different models.

we used rejection sampling to obtain $N = 31$ samples from the verification model to determine the final results.

Evaluation Metrics We assess extracted conditions, statements, and evidence using both semantic and lexical similarity against ground truth. Semantic similarity is computed using nli-deberta-v3-base (He et al., 2021)(Liu et al., 2023), while lexical similarity uses METEOR scores. The matching score is the geometric mean of these two measures. Thresholds are set at 0.95 for question parsing and 0.9 for CoT parsing - only scores exceeding these thresholds are considered matches. For evidence evaluation, we only consider evidence paired with matched statements. A statement-evidence pair is verified as correct only when both components match. The final evaluation metric is the macro F1 score across all four components.

Baseline We adopt the provided in-context learning method as our baseline framework. For consistency with the task requirements, we evaluated four baseline models: Llama3-8B-Instruct (Grattafiori et al., 2024), Qwen2-7B-Instruct (Yang et al., 2024), Telechat2 (He et al., 2024) and DeepSeek-R1 (Guo et al., 2025). All models were tested under identical experimental conditions to ensure fair comparison.

4.2 Main Result

Table 1 shows the comparison of our solution with the top three other teams and the baseline. Our solution achieved the highest scores in Statement and Reasoning parts, maintaining the best overall task performance. Since we failed to extend the reinforcement learning method to evidence extraction, the corresponding score was slightly lower than the highest score. However, our method still achieved a high Reasoning score while maintaining a small number of extracted statement-evidence pairs, which proves that our verification model is more powerful than what the score reflects.

4.3 Ablation

We conducted ablation studies to verify the effectiveness of each newly added module in the pipeline. Since some modules are only effective for certain subtasks among the four subtasks, we only list the evaluation of the parts affected by adding a particular module. The experimental results are shown in Table 2.

Compared to directly using the model for content extraction, employing an optimized pipeline for step-by-step extraction and filtering significantly enhances the success rate of question and statement extraction. After post-training with GRPO, the success rate of statement extraction is notably improved. Benefiting from an increased base for extracting statements, the evidence score also increases. We trained the model to use critique for verification, leading to a substantial improvement in reasoning accuracy. Our ablation study demonstrates the feasibility of LLM with GRPO to perform traditional NLU tasks, and for the model's verification process, learning to criticize statement-evidence pairs is easier to enhance verification accuracy than directly justify their validity.

5 Conclusion

In this article, we propose an effective method for the XLLM Shared Task-III in LLM for Structural Reasoning. We present a novel pipeline for fine-grained analysis of CoT processes that achieves extraction and verification performance comparable to state-of-the-art models while maintaining low resource requirements. Our work demonstrates GRPO's potential for enhancing LLM performance on traditional NLU tasks and validates the feasibility of using critique to develop model verification

Method	Question(%)	Statement(%)	Evidence(%)	Reasoning(%)
Directly Extraction and Verification	61.19	37.09	15.02	8.11
+ Step-wise Extraction Pipeline	81.20	46.81	16.74	5.45
+ Tuned with GRPO		55.07	22.44	4.68
+ Critique Verification				17.09

Table 2: Ablation results on Test set A.

capabilities. The proposed framework opens new possibilities for structured reasoning analysis in resource-constrained scenarios while maintaining competitive accuracy, with future work planned to explore applications to broader reasoning tasks and further optimization of the verification component.

Limitations

Our approach still has some limitations. First, the models are trained exclusively on pseudo-labeled data, whose inherent accuracy constraints impose an upper bound on the extraction and verification performance of the entire pipeline. Second, our experiments are conducted solely on the LogiQA dataset with CoT processes generated by Llama3-8B-Instruct, without validation on other types of chain-of-thought datasets or different LLM-generated reasoning paths. These limitations suggest directions for future improvements in data quality and generalization testing.

References

Yaoyao Chang, Lei Cui, Li Dong, Shaohan Huang, Yangyu Huang, Yupan Huang, Scarlett Li, Tengchao Lv, Shuming Ma, Qinzheng Sun, Wenhui Wang, Furu Wei, Ying Xin, Mao Yang, Qiufeng Yin, and Xingxing Zhang. 2024. Redstone: Curating general, code, math, and qa data for large language models. *Preprint*, arXiv:2412.03398.

Aaron Grattafiori, Abhimanyu Dubey, Abhinav Jauhri, Abhinav Pandey, Abhishek Kadian, Ahmad Al-Dahle, Aiesha Letman, Akhil Mathur, Alan Schelten, Alex Vaughan, Amy Yang, Angela Fan, Anirudh Goyal, Anthony Hartshorn, Aobo Yang, Archi Mitra, Archie Sravankumar, Artem Korenev, Arthur Hinsvark, and 542 others. 2024. The llama 3 herd of models. *Preprint*, arXiv:2407.21783.

Xinyu Guan, Li Lyna Zhang, Yifei Liu, Ning Shang, Youran Sun, Yi Zhu, Fan Yang, and Mao Yang. 2025. rstar-math: Small llms can master math reasoning with self-evolved deep thinking. *arXiv preprint arXiv:2501.04519*.

Daya Guo, Dejian Yang, Haowei Zhang, Junxiao Song, Ruoyu Zhang, Runxin Xu, Qihao Zhu, Shirong Ma, Peiyi Wang, Xiao Bi, and 1 others. 2025. Deepseek-r1: Incentivizing reasoning capability in llms via reinforcement learning. *arXiv preprint arXiv:2501.12948*.

Pengcheng He, Jianfeng Gao, and Weizhu Chen. 2021. Debertav3: Improving deberta using electra-style pre-training with gradient-disentangled embedding sharing. *Preprint*, arXiv:2111.09543.

Zhongjiang He, Zihan Wang, Xinzhang Liu, Shixuan Liu, Yitong Yao, Yuyao Huang, Xuelong Li, Yongxiang Li, Zhonghao Che, Zhaoxi Zhang, and 1 others. 2024. Telechat technical report. *arXiv preprint arXiv:2401.03804*.

Xiang Li, Yiqun Yao, Xin Jiang, Xuezhi Fang, Chao Wang, Xinzhang Liu, Zihan Wang, Yu Zhao, Xin Wang, Yuyao Huang, and 1 others. 2024a. Tele-flm technical report. *arXiv preprint arXiv:2404.16645*.

Xuelong Li. 2022. Positive-incentive noise. *IEEE Transactions on Neural Networks and Learning Systems*.

Yifei Li, Zeqi Lin, Shizhuo Zhang, Qiang Fu, Bei Chen, Jian-Guang Lou, and Weizhu Chen. 2023. Making language models better reasoners with step-aware verifier. In *Proceedings of the 61st Annual Meeting of the Association for Computational Linguistics (Volume 1: Long Papers)*, pages 5315–5333, Toronto, Canada. Association for Computational Linguistics.

Zhongqiu Li, Zhenhe Wu, Mengxiang Li, Zhongjiang He, Ruiyu Fang, Jie Zhang, Yu Zhao, Yongxiang Li, Zhoujun Li, and Shuangyong Song. 2024b. Scalable database-driven kgs can help text-to-sql.

Hunter Lightman, Vineet Kosaraju, Yuri Burda, Harrison Edwards, Bowen Baker, Teddy Lee, Jan Leike, John Schulman, Ilya Sutskever, and Karl Cobbe. 2023. Let's verify step by step. In *The Twelfth International Conference on Learning Representations*.

Aixin Liu, Bei Feng, Bing Xue, Bingxuan Wang, Bochao Wu, Chengda Lu, Chenggang Zhao, Chengqi Deng, Chenyu Zhang, Chong Ruan, and 1 others. 2024. Deepseek-v3 technical report. *arXiv preprint arXiv:2412.19437*.

Jian Liu, Leyang Cui, Hanmeng Liu, Dandan Huang, Yile Wang, and Yue Zhang. 2021. Logiqa: a challenge dataset for machine reading comprehension with logical reasoning. In *Proceedings of the Twenty-Ninth International Conference on International Joint Conferences on Artificial Intelligence*, pages 3622–3628.

Shixuan Liu, Chen Peng, Chao Wang, Xiangyan Chen, and Shuangyong Song. 2023. icsberts: Optimizing pre-trained language models in intelligent customer service. *Procedia Computer Science*, 222:127–136.

Keming Lu, Xiaoman Pan, Kaiqiang Song, Hongming Zhang, Dong Yu, and Jianshu Chen. 2023. Pivoine: Instruction tuning for open-world information extraction. *arXiv preprint arXiv:2305.14898*.

Archiki Prasad, Swarnadeep Saha, Xiang Zhou, and Mohit Bansal. 2023. ReCEval: Evaluating reasoning chains via correctness and informativeness. In *Proceedings of the 2023 Conference on Empirical Methods in Natural Language Processing*, pages 10066–10086, Singapore. Association for Computational Linguistics.

Abulhair Saparov and He He. 2023. Language models are greedy reasoners: A systematic formal analysis of chain-of-thought. In *11th International Conference on Learning Representations*.

Jiawei Shao and Xuelong Li. 2025. Ai flow at the network edge. *IEEE Network*.

Zhihong Shao, Peiyi Wang, Qihao Zhu, Runxin Xu, Junxiao Song, Xiao Bi, Haowei Zhang, Mingchuan Zhang, YK Li, Y Wu, and 1 others. 2024. Deepseekmath: Pushing the limits of mathematical reasoning in open language models. *arXiv preprint arXiv:2402.03300*.

Gladys Tyen, Hassan Mansoor, Victor Carbune, Peter Chen, and Tony Mak. 2024. LLMs cannot find reasoning errors, but can correct them given the error location. In *Findings of the Association for Computational Linguistics: ACL 2024*, pages 13894–13908, Bangkok, Thailand. Association for Computational Linguistics.

Guangya Wan, Yuqi Wu, Jie Chen, and Sheng Li. 2024. Cot rerailer: Enhancing the reliability of large language models in complex reasoning tasks through error detection and correction. *arXiv preprint arXiv:2408.13940*.

Peiyi Wang, Lei Li, Zhihong Shao, Runxin Xu, Damai Dai, Yifei Li, Deli Chen, Yu Wu, and Zhifang Sui. 2024a. Math-shepherd: Verify and reinforce LLMs step-by-step without human annotations. In *Proceedings of the 62nd Annual Meeting of the Association for Computational Linguistics (Volume 1: Long Papers)*, pages 9426–9439, Bangkok, Thailand. Association for Computational Linguistics.

Yubo Wang, Xiang Yue, and Wenhu Chen. 2025. Critique fine-tuning: Learning to critique is more effective than learning to imitate. *Preprint*, arXiv:2501.17703.

Zihan Wang, Yitong Yao, Li Mengxiang, Zhongjiang He, Chao Wang, Shuangyong Song, and 1 others. 2024b. Telechat: An open-source billingual large language model. In *Proceedings of the 10th SIGHAN Workshop on Chinese Language Processing (SIGHAN-10)*, pages 10–20.

Haolun Wu, Ye Yuan, Liana Mikaelyan, Alexander Meulemans, Xue Liu, James Hensman, and Bhaskar Mitra. 2024. Learning to extract structured entities using language models. In *Proceedings of the 2024 Conference on Empirical Methods in Natural Language Processing*, pages 6817–6834, Miami, Florida, USA. Association for Computational Linguistics.

Zhenhe Wu, Zhongqiu Li, Mengxiang Li, Jie Zhang, Zhongjiang He, Jian Yang, Yu Zhao, Ruiyu Fang, Yongxiang Li, Zhoujun Li, and Shuangyong Song. 2025. MR-SQL: Multi-Level Retrieval Enhances Inference for LLM in Text-to-SQL. In *Proceedings of the 2025 International Conference on Database Systems for Advanced Applications*. Accepted.

Shijie Xia, Xuefeng Li, Yixin Liu, Tongshuang Wu, and Pengfei Liu. 2025. Evaluating mathematical reasoning beyond accuracy. In *Proceedings of the AAAI Conference on Artificial Intelligence*, volume 39, pages 27723–27730.

An Yang, Baosong Yang, Beichen Zhang, Binyuan Hui, Bo Zheng, Bowen Yu, Chengyuan Li, Dayiheng Liu, Fei Huang, Haoran Wei, and 1 others. 2024. Qwen2. 5 technical report. *arXiv preprint arXiv:2412.15115*.

Zhongshen Zeng, Pengguang Chen, Shu Liu, Haiyun Jiang, and Jiaya Jia. 2023. Mr-gsm8k: A meta-reasoning benchmark for large language model evaluation. *arXiv preprint arXiv:2312.17080*.

Yunxiang Zhang, Muhammad Khalifa, Lajanugen Logeswaran, Jaekyeom Kim, Moontae Lee, Honglak Lee, and Lu Wang. 2024. Small language models need strong verifiers to self-correct reasoning. In *Findings of the Association for Computational Linguistics: ACL 2024*, pages 15637–15653, Bangkok, Thailand. Association for Computational Linguistics.

A CoT Parsing Example


```
{
    "question": "There are 7
    outstanding students G, H, L, M, U, W
    and Z in a school.During the summer
    vacation, the school will send them to
     the United Kingdom and the United
    States for inspection.The school has
    only 7 students participating in this
    activity, and each person happens to
    go to one of these two countries.
    Considering the specialty of each
    student, this activity must meet the
    following conditions? (1) If G goes to
     the UK, then H To the United States
    .(2) If L goes to the UK, both M and U
     go to the US......",
    "question_parsing": [
        "The school has only 7
    students participating in this
    activity, and each person happens to
    go to one of these two countries",
        "If G goes to the UK, then H
    To the United States",
        "If L goes to the UK, both M
    and U go to the US",
        ......
    ],
    "answer": "b",
    "cot": "Since G goes to the United
     States, we need to analyze the
    conditions that follow. Condition (1)
    is not applicable since G is going to
    the US. Condition (2) is also not
    applicable since L's destination is
    not specified......"
    "cot_parsing": [
        {
            "statement": "Condition
    (1) is not applicable",
            "evidence": "G is going to
     the US",
            "Verification": "true"
        },
        {
            "statement": "Condition
    (2) is also not applicable",
            "evidence": "L's
    destination is not specified",
            "Verification": "true"
        },
        .......
    ],
},
```

SpeechEE@XLLM25: Retrieval-Enhanced Few-Shot Prompting for Speech Event Extraction

Máté Gedeon
Budapest University of Technology and Economics
Budapest, Hungary
gedeonm01@gmail.com

Abstract

Speech Event Extraction (SpeechEE) is a challenging task that lies at the intersection of Automatic Speech Recognition (ASR) and Natural Language Processing (NLP), requiring the identification of structured event information from spoken language. In this work, we present a modular, pipeline-based SpeechEE framework that integrates high-performance ASR with semantic search-enhanced prompting of Large Language Models (LLMs). Our system first classifies speech segments likely to contain events using a hybrid filtering mechanism including rule-based, BERT-based, and LLM-based models. It then employs few-shot LLM prompting, dynamically enriched via semantic similarity retrieval, to identify event triggers and extract corresponding arguments. We evaluate the pipeline using multiple LLMs—Llama3-8B, GPT-4o-mini, and o1-mini—highlighting significant performance gains with o1-mini, which achieves 63.3% F1 on trigger classification and 27.8% F1 on argument classification, outperforming prior benchmarks. Our results demonstrate that pipeline approaches, when empowered by retrieval-augmented LLMs, can rival or exceed end-to-end systems while maintaining interpretability and modularity. This work provides practical insights into LLM-driven event extraction and opens pathways for future hybrid models combining textual and acoustic features.

1 Introduction

Information extraction aims at automatically identifying structured information, such as entities and their relations, from unstructured data (Bikel et al., 1997; Fei et al., 2023). A task in this domain is Event Extraction (EE) (Chen et al., 2015) searching for answers to questions like *what happened*, *who was involved*, and *where did it take place*. The source data can be text (Yang and Mitchell, 2016), but even images (Li et al., 2020) or videos (Chen et al., 2021). *Speech Event Extraction* (SpeechEE) (Kang et al., 2024) extends textual EE, with the purpose of identifying structured event information directly from the input of the spoken language. This task occupies a unique intersection between Automatic Speech Recognition (ASR) and Natural Language Processing (NLP), requiring not only accurate transcription but also the detection of event types, triggers, and arguments from possibly noisy spoken content.

Existing SpeechEE approaches can be broadly categorized into the methodologies *pipeline-based* and *end-to-end*. Pipeline-based architectures typically employ an ASR module to transcribe speech, followed by text-based event extraction using NLP techniques (Cao et al., 2022; Fei et al., 2024). These systems offer modularity and transparency, allowing separate optimization and analysis of ASR and extraction components. However, they are susceptible to cascading errors, where transcription inaccuracies can significantly impair downstream event extraction performance. Conversely, end-to-end approaches aim to bypass intermediate text by learning to map raw audio directly to structured outputs (Wang et al., 2024). While promising in reducing error propagation and potentially more efficient, these models often demand large-scale annotated audio-event datasets and are less interpretable, acting as opaque "black boxes" in many cases.

Recent progress in Large Language Models (LLMs) such as GPT-4 (OpenAI, 2024a) has opened new possibilities in pipeline-based architectures by enabling powerful few-shot and zero-shot learning capabilities. LLMs exhibit remarkable proficiency in extracting structured knowledge from unstructured text with minimal task-specific supervision (Zhang et al., 2022). When combined with state-of-the-art ASR systems, these models can form the backbone of robust SpeechEE systems that generalize well across domains and require minimal adaptation.

Proceedings of the 1st Joint Workshop on Large Language Models and Structure Modeling (XLLM 2025), pages 351–361
August 1, 2025

In this work, we present a pipeline-based SpeechEE framework that leverages semantic search-enhanced few-shot prompting with LLMs. Our system dynamically retrieves relevant examples from a support set and incorporates them into prompts to guide event extraction. Additionally, we introduce a classification mechanism to identify utterances likely to contain events, reducing false positives and improving extraction precision.

Our main contributions are as follows:

- We propose a multi-stage SpeechEE pipeline combining high-performance ASR with semantic search-enhanced prompting for event extraction using LLMs.
- We introduce a generalizable few-shot learning strategy based on semantic similarity, applicable to various text-related information extraction tasks.
- We develop a speech segment classification module that selectively filters utterances likely to contain events.
- We provide a detailed comparison of several configurations, offering practical insights for SpeechEE deployment.

The remainder of the paper is organized as follows. Section 2 reviews related work on SpeechEE and language models. Section 3 introduces the dataset. Section 4 describes the model architecture and pipeline components. Section 5 presents the experimental results and analysis. Section 6 outlines the results of the ablation study. Section 7 discusses key findings and limitations. Finally, Section 8 concludes the paper and suggests directions for future research.

2 Related Work

2.1 Event Extraction from Text

EE from textual data has been a long-standing task in information extraction, focusing on identifying event triggers and their semantic arguments. Early approaches were largely feature-based, relying on hand-engineered lexical, syntactic, and semantic features fed into statistical models such as maximum entropy classifiers, conditional random fields, or nearest-neighbor methods (Ahn, 2006) (Liao and Grishman, 2010).

With the advent of deep learning, neural-based models became dominant. Convolutional Neural Networks (CNNs) enabled automatic feature learning from word embeddings, replacing manual feature engineering (Nguyen and Grishman, 2015). With the ability to handle long-range dependencies, recurrent architectures achieved state-of-the-art results on the ACE2005 dataset (Nguyen et al., 2016).

Graph Convolutional Networks (GCNs) have also shown promise in the field by modeling syntactic structures directly from dependency trees. Unlike sequential models, GCNs exploit the syntactic proximity between triggers and arguments in a graph form, improving performance on long sentences with distant dependencies (Nguyen and Grishman, 2018; Liu et al., 2018).

More recently, Transformer-based solutions (Vaswani et al., 2017) also emerged, with (Paolini et al., 2021) introducing a framework, achieving new state-of-the-art results on joint entity and relation extraction using a generative transformer.

A recent survey categorizes modern approaches into sequence-based, graph neural, knowledge-enhanced, and prompt-based methods, highlighting the dominance of pretrained language models in capturing contextual event semantics (Xie et al., 2025).

2.2 Speech Processing and ASR

Automatic Speech Recognition (ASR) has witnessed remarkable progress in recent years, particularly with the introduction of transformer-based models. Whisper (Radford et al., 2022) represents a significant advancement in ASR, trained on a large and diverse dataset of 680,000 hours of multilingual and multitask supervised data. This approach has demonstrated robust performance across various domains and languages, making it suitable for real-world applications.

Similarly, Canary (Puvvada et al., 2024) offers an alternative approach to ASR that achieves competitive performance without relying on web-scale data. These models provide high-quality transcriptions that can serve as the foundation for downstream NLP tasks, including event extraction.

2.3 Speech Event Extraction

Speech Event Extraction (SpeechEE) is a relatively new research direction that aims to bridge ASR and event extraction. (Wang et al., 2024) introduced a novel benchmark for SpeechEE and proposed an end-to-end model for extracting events directly from audio. Their work highlights the challenges of extracting structured information from speech without relying on intermediate textual representations. Their end-to-end system demonstrated consistently superior performance compared to the employed pipeline-based baseline. They report that previous approaches to speech-based information extraction have largely relied on pipeline methods, where ASR is followed by text-based extraction. While these methods benefit from advances in both ASR and text-based event extraction, they often suffer from error propagation, where mistakes in transcription lead to extraction failures.

2.4 Large Language Models and Few-Shot Learning

Large Language Models (LLMs) have emerged as transformative tools in natural language processing (NLP), enabling significant progress across a wide range of tasks (Wu et al., 2024) including text generation, summarization, machine translation, and information extraction. Proprietary models like GPT-4o (OpenAI, 2024b) and o1-mini (OpenAI, 2024c) or open source models like Llama 3 (Meta, 2024) exemplify the scale and versatility of these models. Their capacity to perform tasks with minimal or no explicit training—known as few-shot or zero-shot learning—has shifted the paradigm from model-specific fine-tuning to prompt-based task generalization.

Few-shot learning in LLMs typically involves crafting prompts that include a handful of task-specific examples, guiding the model to infer patterns and generalize to unseen inputs. This method leverages the latent knowledge encoded in the pre-trained model, often yielding strong performance on tasks such as question answering, named entity recognition, and relation extraction (Gao et al., 2021; Min et al., 2022). Particularly for structured information extraction, few-shot prompting enables LLMs to identify and retrieve relevant spans of text even in the absence of large annotated datasets.

Our work builds upon these advances by integrating LLMs with semantic search techniques to dynamically select the most relevant examples for few-shot learning, thereby enhancing the models' ability to extract events from speech transcriptions.

3 Dataset

We use the SpeechEE shared task dataset[1], derived from ACE2005-EN+. The dataset is provided in a structured JSON format, where each entry consists of a unique `id`, an event `trigger` indicating the lexical anchor of the event, its corresponding `type`, and a list of associated `arguments`, each annotated with a semantic role. In total, the dataset includes 33 distinct event types and 22 argument roles, offering a diverse and challenging benchmark. It comprises 19,217 training instances, 901 development examples, and 676 test samples. An example of the data format is shown below:

```
{"id": "train-6",
 "event": [
   {"trigger": "election",
    "type": "Elect",
    "arguments": [
      {"name": "man", "role": "Person"}
    ]}
 ]}
```

4 Methodology

Our proposed pipeline for speech event extraction consists of several key components, as illustrated in Figure 1. The pipeline follows a modular approach, allowing for component-level evaluation and optimization.

4.1 ASR Transcription

The first step in our pipeline involves transcribing speech data into text. We experimented with two state-of-the-art ASR systems for this purpose, `Whisper large-v3` and `Canary 1b`. Both systems were used with their default configurations to transcribe the audio data. The resulting transcripts served as input for subsequent steps in the pipeline.

4.2 Event Presence Classification

A significant challenge in event extraction is distinguishing between segments that contain events and those that do not. Preliminary experiments revealed that applying LLMs directly to all transcripts resulted in numerous false positives, where models identified events, that were not annotated in the dataset.

To address this challenge, we implemented a classification step to determine whether a given transcript is likely to contain an event. We employed three different classification methods:

- Rule-based approach: This method flagged instances containing trigger words identified in the training set. We compiled a lexicon of trigger words based on the training data and used this to identify potential event-containing segments.

[1] `https://xllms.github.io/SpeechEE/`

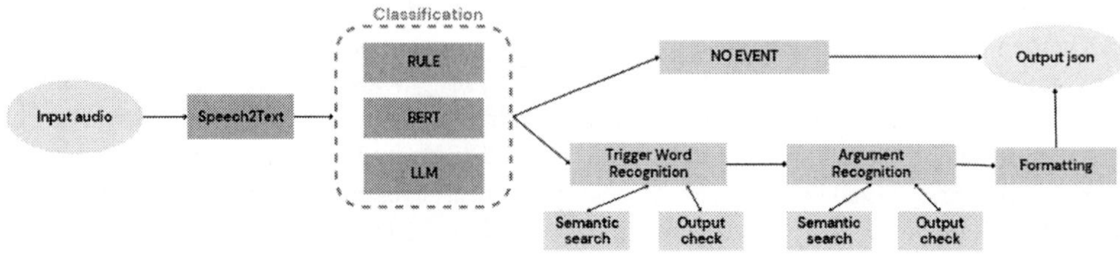

Figure 1: Overview of the SpeechEE Pipeline

- BERT-based classifier: We fine-tuned a BERT model on text embeddings to classify segments as either containing events or not. The model was trained on the transcribed training data with binary labels indicating event presence.

- LLM-based classification: We prompted OpenAI's `o1-mini` model to classify the presence or absence of events in transcripts. The model was given a short description of the task and asked to determine whether a given transcript contained an event.

For the BERT-based classification, we used the `all-MiniLM-L6-v2` sentence transformer model[2]. The training ran for 5 epochs, with a learning rate of $2e^{-5}$, batch size of 16, choosing the best model based on recall, as the goal was to have as few false negatives as possible.

To enhance classification reliability, we only considered transcripts in which all three models agreed on the presence of an event. This approach effectively reduced false positives during the classification stage. Table 1 presents the agreement matrix among the models, with bolded cells indicating cases where the filtering mechanism identified likely event presence.

Rule	BERT	LLM: NO	LLM: YES
NO	NO	258	27
	YES	61	39
YES	NO	17	27
	YES	19	**228**

Table 1: Agreement table between the three systems.

[2]`https://huggingface.co/sentence-transformers/all-MiniLM-L6-v2`

4.3 Trigger Word Recognition

For segments classified as likely containing events, the next step involved identifying and classifying trigger words. Trigger words are specific words or phrases that signal the occurrence of an event. These events also have an event type, which needs to be recognized based on the context.

We evaluated three different LLMs for this task: `Llama3-8B`, `GPT-4o-mini`, and OpenAI's `o1-mini`. We deployed `Llama3-8B` locally on two NVIDIA GeForce RTX 2080 Ti GPUs, while the two OpenAI models were accessed via OpenAI's Batch API. Each model was prompted to extract trigger words from the transcript and classify them into predefined event categories based on the ACE2005 ontology. The prompt included a description of the task, examples of trigger words for different event types, and the transcript to be analyzed.

During our experiments, we observed that the Llama model occasionally produced outputs that did not comply with the expected format or failed to identify trigger words correctly. To address this issue, we implemented an automated verification step that checked the output format and re-executed queries when necessary to ensure consistency. This step was omissible for the OpenAI models.

4.4 Semantic Search-Enhanced Few-Shot Learning

A key component in our approach is the use of semantic search to dynamically select the most relevant examples for few-shot learning. As there are 33 classes, each with multiple argument types, even showing one example from each case would result in a very long prompt. Therefore, rather than using a fixed set of examples for all queries, we implemented a system that selected examples based on their semantic similarity to the current transcript. This retrieval-augmented few-shot approach increases contextual relevance and allows the model to better adapt to domain-specific nuances. By coupling LLMs with semantic retrieval, we aim to improve robustness and generalization in this complex setting.

The process looks like the following:

1. We created embeddings for all training examples using a the `all-MiniLM-L6-v2` sentence transformer model.

2. For each new transcript, we generated an embedding using the same model.

3. We retrieved the top ten most similar examples to the new transcript using the FAISS library (Douze et al., 2025).

4. We added these examples to the prompt (Appendix A.1).

This approach ensures that the LLM receives the most relevant and informative examples for each specific transcript, thereby improving its ability to identify and classify trigger words accurately.

4.5 Argument Extraction

Following trigger identification, the next step involved extracting event arguments and assigning roles. Event arguments are entities that participate in the event, and their roles define their relationship to the event (e.g., Agent, Entity, Place).

Similar to the trigger recognition phase, we used LLMs to extract arguments and assign roles (Appendix A.2). The prompt for this task included the transcript, the identified trigger word and event type, and examples of argument extraction for similar event types. We again employed semantic search to select the most relevant examples for few-shot learning, focusing on examples similar to the current transcript. Also we provided the dictionary of the possible argument types for each event type in the prompt.

4.6 Post-Processing

The final stage of our pipeline involved post-processing the extracted information to ensure uniform output formatting. We used an additional LLM call (Appendix A.3) to format the extracted events, triggers, and arguments into a structured JSON format consistent with the dataset specifications. This was necessary, because sometimes the models included the transcripts themselves in the output, or labeled the keys differently.

This step also included validation checks to ensure that the output met the expected schema and that all required fields were present. In cases where the output did not meet these requirements, additional LLM calls were made to correct and complete the information.

5 Results

We evaluated our event extraction pipeline using two primary metrics, following the evaluation protocol outlined by (Wang et al., 2024):

- **Trigger Classification (TC):** This metric assesses whether both the predicted event type and trigger span match the ground truth exactly. A prediction is considered correct only if both components align perfectly.

- **Argument Classification (AC):** This stricter metric evaluates the correctness of the predicted argument mention, its semantic role, and the associated event type, requiring full agreement across all elements.

For both tasks, we report precision (P), recall (R), and F1-score (F1), with the F1-score serving as the primary measure of overall performance. Table 2 summarizes the evaluation results across the three LLMs: `Llama3-8B`, `GPT-4o-mini`, and `o1-mini`. The ASR system used is indicated in parentheses—Whisper (W) or Canary (C). For `Llama3-8B` and `GPT-4o-mini`, all three stages of the pipeline utilized the respective models. In the case of `o1-mini`, however, the final formatting step was performed using `GPT-4o-mini`, as it achieved perfect results for this task, eliminating the need for the more expensive reasoning model.

Model	TC-R	TC-P	TC-F1	AC-R	AC-P	AC-F1
Llama3-8B (W)	24.1	57.6	33.9	11.2	18.3	13.9
GPT-4o-mini (W)	36.6	67.4	47.4	17.0	24.3	20.0
o1-mini (W)	59.2	65.9	62.4	26.9	27.1	27.1
Llama3-8B (C)	24.5	52.8	33.5	11.5	17.1	13.7
GPT-4o-mini (C)	36.8	65.5	47.1	16.8	23.2	19.5
o1-mini (C)	**60.8**	**66.0**	**63.3**	**28.0**	**27.6**	**27.8**

Table 2: Precision, recall, and F1-scores (%) for Trigger Classification (TC) and Argument Classification (AC).

The performance hierarchy among the models is consistent and clear: `o1-mini` substantially outperforms both `GPT-4o-mini` and `Llama3-8B` across all evaluation metrics. In TC, `o1-mini` achieved an F1-score of 63.3%, surpassing `GPT-4o-mini` by over 16 percentage points and `Llama3-8B` by nearly

30 points. Interestingly, while precision scores between o1-mini and GPT-4o-mini were relatively close, the major difference arose from recall, suggesting that GPT-4o-mini adopted a more conservative prediction strategy, prioritizing precision at the expense of coverage.

As anticipated, performance across all models declined on the more demanding AC task. Nevertheless, o1-mini again demonstrated a clear advantage, achieving an AC F1-score of 27.8%, more than double that of Llama3-8B and significantly ahead of GPT-4o-mini. Moreover, o1-mini maintained a balanced trade-off between precision and recall, whereas the other two models exhibited weaker recall, often failing to capture all valid argument mentions even when precision remained reasonable.

The consistent superiority of o1-mini across both tasks underscores the potential of specialized reasoning models in information extraction, particularly in achieving a more balanced and robust performance across precision and recall.

Regarding the choice of ASR system, switching between Whisper and Canary resulted in only minor differences (within 1% F1-score). Given the inherent nondeterminism of LLM outputs—even with identical inputs—the observed variations could stem even from stochastic model behavior rather than from the ASR systems themselves. Notably, while Llama3-8B and GPT-4o-mini performed slightly better with Whisper, o1-mini achieved marginally superior results with Canary. A more comprehensive study, involving multiple evaluation runs per prompt, would be required to draw stronger conclusions about ASR influence.

As a point of reference, (Wang et al., 2024) reported results on the ACE2005-EN+ dataset, achieving an F1-score of 61.1% for TC and 23.2% for AC. While our dataset is a modified version of ACE2005-EN+, it is not identical, and thus direct comparisons should be made cautiously. Nevertheless, our pipeline outperforms these baselines, particularly in AC, where we observe a notable improvement. This advancement likely stems from the incorporation of large language models after the transcription step, enabling more semantically coherent interpretations of spoken input instead of bypassing transcription entirely.

6 Ablation

To substantiate our initial observation that LLMs tend to produce a considerable number of false positives, we conducted an ablation study evaluating all three models under various classification configurations. The results, presented in Table 3 and Table 4, affirm the value of the classification component. We denote *one+* and *two+* to indicate that at least one or two of the three models classified the instance as containing an event, respectively.

Model	without	Rule	BERT	o1-mini	one+	two+	three
Llama3-8B	27.4	32.4	32.0	32.7	30.6	33.0	33.9
4o-mini	43.8	47.1	45.8	45.1	44.7	46.1	47.4
o1-mini	58.8	60.7	61.8	60.3	59.8	62.4	63.4

Table 3: F1-scores (%) on TC under different classification criteria.

When applying a single criterion, each model demonstrated optimal performance with a different method: o1-mini performed best with the *BERT-based* classifier, while 4o-mini and Llama3-8B yielded higher scores with the *Rule-based* and *LLM-based* classifiers, respectively. Although relying on the *one+* filtering resulted in marginally lower performance than the best individual setups, it still outperformed the baseline without classification. Notably, aggregating predictions with *two+* and *three* led to consistent F1-score improvements over the standalone classifiers.

Model	without	Rule	BERT	o1-mini	one+	two+	three
Llama3-8B	13.2	13.4	15.4	15.4	14.7	15.6	13.9
4o-mini	19.2	19.7	20.0	20.0	19.6	20.1	20.0
o1-mini	25.1	25.2	26.8	26.0	25.5	26.9	27.8

Table 4: F1-scores (%) on AC under different classification criteria.

In the AC task, the outcomes are more nuanced, indicating that strategies yielding gains in TC do not always translate to AC. For instance, while 4o-mini achieved the best TC performance with the *Rule-based* method (when considering single criterion), it was outperformed by other approaches in AC. Nonetheless, similarly to TC, both *two+* and *three* yielded improvements over the individual classifiers. However, unlike in TC, the *three* criterion did not universally result in the best performance, benefitting only the o1-mini model.

These consistent enhancements across both tasks confirm the effectiveness of the classification step in reducing false positives and improving overall model performance.

7 Discussion

Our experimental results demonstrate that a well-designed pipeline approach can achieve performance comparable or even superior to state-of-the-art end-to-end models for speech event extraction. This finding is significant as it challenges the assumption that end-to-end approaches necessarily outperform pipeline methods for complex tasks. Our results suggest that by leveraging advanced LLMs and intelligent example selection strategies, pipeline approaches can mitigate traditional weaknesses such as error propagation.

Moreover, this approach offer several advantages over end-to-end models, including modularity and interpretability, in the sense that the output of each stage can be examined and is humanly interpretable.

The minimal performance difference observed when comparing Whisper and Canary suggests that transcript quality variations within a certain threshold have limited impact on event extraction outcomes. Both Whisper and Canary have their own characteristics, when it comes to the transcription of names or cities, which are crucial in event extraction. The fact that this did not make too much of a difference, is encouraging for real-world applications, where perfect transcription cannot be guaranteed. However, it is important to note that the performance gap might be more pronounced when comparing with lower-quality ASR systems or when processing audio with significant noise, accents, or other challenging characteristics.

The substantial performance differences observed between the three LLMs highlight the critical role of LLM selection in event extraction efficacy. Model size seemed to be a factor, with the larger proprietary models clearly outperforming the locally runnable Llama model. The reasoning capability also largely seems to help the task, but to make these claims more confidently, a more thorough research would be needed across several models.

During development, we also observed that in several cases, the false positives produced by the LLMs were remarkably close to genuine events that should have been annotated. This suggests that, in some instances, the models may have correctly identified events that were inadvertently missed during the original annotation process.

8 Conclusion

This research presents an LLM-driven pipeline for speech event extraction that achieves performance comparable to state-of-the-art end-to-end models. Our approach combines ASR-generated transcripts with semantic search-enhanced few-shot learning to create a modular and interpretable framework for identifying events and their arguments from spoken language. By dynamically selecting examples based on semantic similarity to the current input, our approach ensures that the LLM receives the most relevant and informative context for each specific case. This is particularly important for event extraction, where different event types have distinct patterns, trigger words, and argument structures. The effectiveness of this approach suggests that similar techniques could be beneficial for other complex NLP tasks where pattern recognition plays a crucial role and where diverse examples exist in the training data.

The choice of ASR system showed limited impact on extraction performance, suggesting robustness to transcript quality variations within a reasonable range. However, LLM selection plays a critical role in event extraction efficacy, with larger, more capable models achieving significantly better results.

Several promising directions for future research emerge from this work, including hybrid approaches exploring methods that integrate transcript-based and direct audio-based features that could potentially combine the strengths of pipeline and end-to-end approaches. Our approach does not leverage speech-related cues present in the audio, which could potentially enhance performance if incorporated. With prompt engineering, the current prompting strategies could be further refined and may improve LLM performance without requiring additional computational resources. Another area could be exploring methods to reduce computational requirements, such as model distillation or selective component invocation.

This work advances spoken language understanding by demonstrating that modular pipelines can rival end-to-end models through strategic integration of LLMs and retrieval mechanisms. By decoupling transcription from extraction while maintaining cross-component optimization potential, our framework offers a practical pathway for deploying speech event extraction tools.

Acknowledgments

We thank the organizers of the SpeechEE shared task for providing the dataset and evaluation framework that enabled this study.

This paper benefited from the use of generative AI tools in accordance with the ACL Policy on AI Writing Assistance. Specifically, large language models were used for assistance in paraphrasing and polishing the original content. All such generated content was carefully reviewed and revised by the authors, and relevant citations were added where appropriate. The ideas and scientific contributions presented in this paper are entirely the authors own. The authors bear full responsibility for the accuracy and originality of the work.

Limitations

First, although the classification step successfully reduces false positives, it introduces an additional layer of complexity and latency into the pipeline. In real-time applications, this could pose practical constraints.

Second, although Whisper and Canary represent state-of-the-art multilingual ASR models, their performance varies considerably across languages, limiting generalizability in multilingual settings. This challenge is further compounded by the few-shot prompting technique, which is also expected to yield lower performance for low-resource languages due to limited linguistic and contextual coverage in training data.

Third, although semantic search-enhanced few-shot prompting improves LLM performance, it increases computational costs due to the need for embedding comparisons and dynamic prompt construction. This makes the system more resource-intensive, especially for large-scale or low-latency deployments.

Fourth, the argument classification task remains challenging, with overall performance still low despite LLM assistance. This is likely due to the difficulty of correctly identifying multiple, diverse argument roles within spoken inputs. Improving argument role assignment—especially for less frequent event types—requires further attention, potentially through the use of more structured reasoning or task-specific tuning.

Finally, while the `o1-mini` model consistently outperformed the other models in our experiments, it is a proprietary model, limiting reproducibility and potentially raising cost or accessibility concerns. Our pipeline's dependency on API-based models also poses challenges for deployment in privacy-sensitive or resource-constrained environments.

Future work should explore more efficient alternatives for few-shot prompting, more robust handling of ASR errors, and ways to make the pipeline more lightweight and adaptable to diverse real-world settings.

References

David Ahn. 2006. The stages of event extraction. In *Proceedings of the Workshop on Annotating and Reasoning about Time and Events*, pages 1–8, Sydney, Australia. Association for Computational Linguistics.

Daniel M. Bikel, Scott Miller, Richard Schwartz, and Ralph Weischedel. 1997. Nymble: a high-performance learning name-finder. In *Fifth Conference on Applied Natural Language Processing*, pages 194–201, Washington, DC, USA. Association for Computational Linguistics.

Hu Cao, Jingye Li, Fangfang Su, Fei Li, Hao Fei, Shengqiong Wu, Bobo Li, Liang Zhao, and Donghong Ji. 2022. OneEE: A one-stage framework for fast overlapping and nested event extraction. In *Proceedings of the 29th International Conference on Computational Linguistics*, pages 1953–1964, Gyeongju, Republic of Korea. International Committee on Computational Linguistics.

Brian Chen, Xudong Lin, Christopher Thomas, Manling Li, Shoya Yoshida, Lovish Chum, Heng Ji, and Shih-Fu Chang. 2021. Joint multimedia event extraction from video and article. In *Findings of the Association for Computational Linguistics: EMNLP 2021*, pages 74–88, Punta Cana, Dominican Republic. Association for Computational Linguistics.

Yubo Chen, Liheng Xu, Kang Liu, Daojian Zeng, and Jun Zhao. 2015. Event extraction via dynamic multi-pooling convolutional neural networks. In *Proceedings of the 53rd Annual Meeting of the Association for Computational Linguistics and the 7th International Joint Conference on Natural Language Processing (Volume 1: Long Papers)*, pages 167–176, Beijing, China. Association for Computational Linguistics.

Matthijs Douze, Alexandr Guzhva, Chengqi Deng, Jeff Johnson, Gergely Szilvasy, Pierre-Emmanuel Mazaré, Maria Lomeli, Lucas Hosseini, and Hervé Jégou. 2025. The faiss library. *Preprint*, arXiv:2401.08281.

Hao Fei, Shengqiong Wu, Jingye Li, Bobo Li, Fei Li, Libo Qin, Meishan Zhang, Min Zhang, and Tat-Seng Chua. 2023. Lasuie: Unifying information extraction with latent adaptive structure-aware generative language model. *Preprint*, arXiv:2304.06248.

Hao Fei, Meishan Zhang, Min Zhang, and Tat-Seng Chua. 2024. Xnlp: An interactive demonstration system for universal structured nlp. *Preprint*, arXiv:2308.01846.

Tianyu Gao, Adam Fisch, and Danqi Chen. 2021. Making pre-trained language models better few-shot learners. In *Proceedings of the 59th Annual Meeting of the Association for Computational Linguistics and the 11th International Joint Conference on Natural Language Processing (Volume 1: Long Papers)*, pages 3816–3830, Online. Association for Computational Linguistics.

Jingqi Kang, Tongtong Wu, Jinming Zhao, Guitao Wang, Guilin Qi, Yuan-Fang Li, and Gholamreza Haffari. 2024. Towards event extraction from speech with contextual clues. *Preprint*, arXiv:2401.15385.

Manling Li, Alireza Zareian, Qi Zeng, Spencer Whitehead, Di Lu, Heng Ji, and Shih-Fu Chang. 2020. Cross-media structured common space for multimedia event extraction. In *Proceedings of the 58th Annual Meeting of the Association for Computational Linguistics*, pages 2557–2568, Online. Association for Computational Linguistics.

Shasha Liao and Ralph Grishman. 2010. Using document level cross-event inference to improve event extraction. In *Proceedings of the 48th Annual Meeting of the Association for Computational Linguistics*, pages 789–797, Uppsala, Sweden. Association for Computational Linguistics.

Xiao Liu, Zhunchen Luo, and Heyan Huang. 2018. Jointly multiple events extraction via attention-based graph information aggregation. In *Proceedings of the 2018 Conference on Empirical Methods in Natural Language Processing*, pages 1247–1256, Brussels, Belgium. Association for Computational Linguistics.

Meta. 2024. The llama 3 herd of models. *Preprint*, arXiv:2407.21783.

Sewon Min, Xinxi Lyu, Ari Holtzman, Mikel Artetxe, Mike Lewis, Hannaneh Hajishirzi, and Luke Zettlemoyer. 2022. Rethinking the role of demonstrations: What makes in-context learning work? In *Proceedings of the 2022 Conference on Empirical Methods in Natural Language Processing*, pages 11048–11064, Abu Dhabi, United Arab Emirates. Association for Computational Linguistics.

Thien Huu Nguyen, Kyunghyun Cho, and Ralph Grishman. 2016. Joint event extraction via recurrent neural networks. In *Proceedings of the 2016 Conference of the North American Chapter of the Association for Computational Linguistics: Human Language Technologies*, pages 300–309, San Diego, California. Association for Computational Linguistics.

Thien Huu Nguyen and Ralph Grishman. 2015. Event detection and domain adaptation with convolutional neural networks. In *Proceedings of the 53rd Annual Meeting of the Association for Computational Linguistics and the 7th International Joint Conference on Natural Language Processing (Volume 2: Short Papers)*, pages 365–371, Beijing, China. Association for Computational Linguistics.

Thien Huu Nguyen and Ralph Grishman. 2018. Graph convolutional networks with argument-aware pooling for event detection. In *Proceedings of the Thirty-Second AAAI Conference on Artificial Intelligence and Thirtieth Innovative Applications of Artificial Intelligence Conference and Eighth AAAI Symposium on Educational Advances in Artificial Intelligence*, AAAI'18/IAAI'18/EAAI'18. AAAI Press.

OpenAI. 2024a. Gpt-4 technical report. *Preprint*, arXiv:2303.08774.

OpenAI. 2024b. Gpt-4o system card. *Preprint*, arXiv:2410.21276.

OpenAI. 2024c. Openai o1 system card. *Preprint*, arXiv:2412.16720.

Giovanni Paolini, Ben Athiwaratkun, Jason Krone, Jie Ma, Alessandro Achille, Rishita Anubhai, Cícero Nogueira dos Santos, Bing Xiang, and Stefano Soatto. 2021. Structured prediction as translation between augmented natural languages. *ArXiv*, abs/2101.05779.

Krishna C. Puvvada, Piotr Żelasko, He Huang, Oleksii Hrinchuk, Nithin Rao Koluguri, Kunal Dhawan, Somshubra Majumdar, Elena Rastorgueva, Zhehuai Chen, Vitaly Lavrukhin, Jagadeesh Balam, and Boris Ginsburg. 2024. Less is more: Accurate speech recognition & translation without web-scale data. *Preprint*, arXiv:2406.19674.

Alec Radford, Jong Wook Kim, Tao Xu, Greg Brockman, Christine McLeavey, and Ilya Sutskever. 2022. Robust speech recognition via large-scale weak supervision. In *International Conference on Machine Learning*.

Ashish Vaswani, Noam M. Shazeer, Niki Parmar, Jakob Uszkoreit, Llion Jones, Aidan N. Gomez, Lukasz Kaiser, and Illia Polosukhin. 2017. Attention is all you need. In *Neural Information Processing Systems*.

Bin Wang, Meishan Zhang, Hao Fei, Yu Zhao, Bobo Li, Shengqiong Wu, Wei Ji, and Min Zhang. 2024. Speechee: A novel benchmark for speech event extraction. In *ACM Multimedia*.

Shengqiong Wu, Hao Fei, Leigang Qu, Wei Ji, and Tat-Seng Chua. 2024. Next-gpt: Any-to-any multimodal llm. *Preprint*, arXiv:2309.05519.

Jianye Xie, Yulan Zhang, Huaizhen Kou, Xiaoran Zhao, Zhikang Feng, Lekang Song, and Weiyi Zhong. 2025. A survey of the application of neural networks to event extraction. *Tsinghua Science and Technology*, 30(2):748–768.

Bishan Yang and Tom M. Mitchell. 2016. Joint extraction of events and entities within a document context. In *Proceedings of the 2016 Conference of the North*

American Chapter of the Association for Computational Linguistics: Human Language Technologies, pages 289–299, San Diego, California. Association for Computational Linguistics.

Ningyu Zhang, Luoqiu Li, Xiang Chen, Shumin Deng, Zhen Bi, Chuanqi Tan, Fei Huang, and Huajun Chen. 2022. Differentiable prompt makes pre-trained language models better few-shot learners. *Preprint*, arXiv:2108.13161.

A Appendix

A.1 Trigger Recognition Prompt

```
{"role": "system", "content":
 "Your job is to extract trigger words signaling events in a text, and classify its event type."},
{"role": "user", "content":
 "From the following TEXT, please extract the event type and its trigger word. It is a transcript of
 an audio, so there may be some mistakes.
 The possible event types are: [<event type list>].
 It is possible there are no events in the text.
 Below are examples demonstrating the required output format and some useful hints.
 Do not return the transcript, only the trigger word and event type."},
{"role": "user", "content": "TEXT: <text_input>"},
{"role": "user", "content": "EXAMPLES: <few-shot examples>"},
```

A.2 Argument Recognition Prompt

```
{"role": "system", "content":
 "Your job is to extract arguments for events in a text, and classify their role in that event."},
{"role": "user", "content":
 "From the following TEXT, please extract event arguments (usually one word or a name) and their role.
 It is a transcript of audio, so there may be mistakes.
 Use the provided event schema: <event schema>.
 An event may have no arguments.
 Examples are provided to guide selection and format."},
{"role": "user", "content": "TEXT: <text_input>, EVENT TYPE(s): <event types>"},
{"role": "user", "content": "EXAMPLES: <few-shot examples>"},
```

A.3 Post-processing Prompt

```
{"role": "system", "content":
 "Your job is to extract a JSON-like output from the end of a string. Only return the JSON."},
{"role": "user", "content":
 "From the following TEXT, extract data in the format of the example.
 If multiple triggers exist, return one entry per trigger.
 Transcriptions are unnecessary. Return JSON only."},
{"role": "user", "content": "TEXT: <text_input>"},
{"role": "user", "content":
 "EXAMPLE:
  [
    {
      "trigger": "deploy",
      "type": "Transport",
      "arguments": [
        {"name": "soldiers", "role": "Artifact"},
        {"name": "region", "role": "Destination"}
      ]
    }
  ]"},
```

Author Index